Java™ Web Services

Robert Brunner, Frank Cohen, Francisco Curbera, Darren Govoni, Steven Haines, Matthias Kloppmann, Benoît Marchal, K. Scott Morrison, Arthur Ryman, Joseph Weber, Mark Wutka

SAMS
201 West 103rd Street, Indianapolis, Indiana 46290

Unleashed

Java™ Web Services Unleashed

International Standard Book Number: 0-672-32363-x

Library of Congress Catalog Card Number: 2001097776

Printed in the United States of America

First Printing: April, 2002

04 03 02 01 4 3 2 1

Trademarks

All terms mentioned in this book that are known to be trademarks or service marks have been appropriately capitalized. Sams Publishing cannot attest to the accuracy of this information. Use of a term in this book should not be regarded as affecting the validity of any trademark or service mark.

IBM, DB2, and WebSphere are trademarks or registered trademarks of IBM Corporation in the United States, other countries, or both.

Java and all Java-based trademarks and logos are trademarks or registered trademarks of Sun Microsystems, Inc. in the United States, other countries, or both.

Microsoft is a trademark or registered trademark of Microsoft Corporation in the United States, other countries, or both.

Other company, product, and service names may be trademarks or service marks of others.

Warning and Disclaimer

Every effort has been made to make this book as complete and as accurate as possible, but no warranty or fitness is implied. The information provided is on an "as is" basis. The authors and the publisher shall have neither liability nor responsibility to any person or entity with respect to any loss or damages arising from the information contained in this book.

Associate Publisher
Michael Stephens

Acquisitions Editor
Todd Green

Development Editor
Tiffany Taylor

Managing Editor
Charlotte Clapp

Project Editor
Andy Beaster

Copy Editor
Margo Catts

Indexer
Chris Barrick

Proofreader
Andrea Dugan

Technical Editors
Earl Bingham
Chuck Canvaness
Harold Finz
Grant Holland

Team Coordinator
Lynne Williams

Interior Designer
Gary Adair

Cover Designer
Aren Howell

Page Layout
Ayanna Lacey

Contents at a Glance

Contents

Part IV Completing Web Services 451

17 Handling Security in Web Services 453

18 Web Services and Flows (WSFL) 477

About the Authors

Robert J. Brunner is an author and member of the research staff at the California Institute of Technology, where his research focuses on knowledge discovery in large, distributed datasets. He also was an instructor at the Center for Advanced Computing Technology at the California State Polytechnic University in Pomona, where he taught and developed applications using both Java and XML. He's currently a member of the Java Data-Mining Expert Group, and is also writing *Enterprise Java Database Programming* (ISBN:0-201-76734-1) for Addison-Wesley.

Frank Cohen is a software entrepreneur who has contributed to the worldwide success of personal computers since 1975. He began by writing operating systems for microcomputers, helping establish video games as an industry, helping establish the Norton Utilities franchise, leading Apple's efforts into middleware and Internet technologies, and most recently serving as principal architect for the Sun Community Server, Inclusion.net, and TuneUp.com. Frank maintains the open-source Load project and is CEO for PushToTest, a scalability and performance testing solutions company. You can reach Frank at `fcohen@pushtotest.com`.

Francisco Curbera holds a Ph.D. in Computer Science from Columbia University, and is currently a Research Staff Member at IBM's T.J. Watson Research Center. He has worked for several years on the use of markup languages for application development and composition of software components, including the definition of the Bean Markup Language (BML), and the design of algorithms for managing XML documents. More recently, he has been involved in the definition and implementation of several Web services specifications. He is one of the authors of the Web Services Description Language (WSDL) and of the Web Services Flow Language (WSFL).

Darren Govoni is a Distinguished Engineer at Cacheon, Inc. in San Francisco, where he is responsible for product architecture and technology roadmapping. Darren is an active writer and speaker on Java technologies, P2P systems, Web services, and adaptive computing. In 1999, Darren founded Metadapt Design Systems with an emphasis on design metaphors for complex adaptive systems. His research forms the basis for Cacheon technology and products. Previously, he contributed to *JXTA: Java P2P Programming* (ISBN: 0-672-32366-4). He can be reached at `dgovoni@metadapt.com`.

Steven Haines is currently the technical Product Manager for all J2EE products at Quest Software and part of the architectural team that defines the technical and strategic direction of future products; he previously worked as the architect on a various range of J2EE products from large-scale B2B e-commerce applications to tight high-volume Web-driven applications. He has taught Java at Learning Tree University, with topics ranging from beginning Java through advanced courses, including JSP/Servlet-based Web development and Enterprise JavaBeans. In addition to publishing *Java 2 From Scratch* (Que, ISBN: 0-7897-2173-2) in late 1999, he writes an Enterprise Java column on InformIT.com.

Matthias Kloppmann is a Senior Software Engineer with IBM Software Group's lab in Böblingen, Germany. He holds an M.S. in Computer Science and Electrical Engineering from the University of Stuttgart. Matthias has many years of experience with building workflow systems, both in C++ and, more recently, in Java. He has participated in the creation of WSFL, the Web Services Flow Language, and the design of the XML and Web services extensions for MQSeries Workflow. Currently, Matthias is working as a workflow architect on WebSphere, IBM's J2EE application server.

Benoît Marchal is a writer and consultant. He has been working with Java since 1996 at Pineapplesoft. In 1997, he co-founded the XML/EDI Group, a think-tank that promotes the use of XML for e-commerce. He is a columnist for Gamelan and developerWorks. He also wrote the two editions of *XML by Example* (Que, 2nd edition ISBN: 0-7897-2504-5) and *Applied XML Solutions* (Sams, ISBN: 0-672-32054-1). More details on these topics are at `http://www.marchal.com`.

K. Scott Morrison is the Director of Architecture and Technology for Infowave Software. He is currently leading a number of teams confronting the challenges in opening corporate data stores to an ever-increasing variety of wireless devices. He is a frequent and very popular speaker on topics in XML, Java, and wireless system architectures. Prior to his joining Infowave, Scott was the Senior Architect in the e-business division at IBM's Pacific Development Centre. While at IBM, his focus was on building high-volume, high-transaction rate Web systems for travel and transportation, as well as designing and auditing Internet security architectures for government and financial sector clients.

Scott began his career by spending eight years involved in medical imaging research at the University of British Columbia. Here, he worked on Positron Emission Tomography (PET) brain scanner design, produced educational CDROMs about Alzheimer's disease for physicians, and conducted original research into neurodegenerative disorders. He has been published extensively in leading journals in medicine and in physics. He has also been a consultant on a number of feature film and television productions. Scott's current research interests lie in enterprise XML messaging architectures, Java/XML integration, and development frameworks for wireless systems.

Arthur Ryman is a Senior Technical Staff Member at the IBM Canada Laboratory, where he has worked as a software developer since 1982. He is currently the architect for Web Services tools in WebSphere Studio Application Developer. Prior to that, he was the solution architect for VisualAge for Java, specializing in tools for developing servlets and JavaServer Pages. Arthur is a member of the IBM Academy of Technology, an Adjunct Professor of Computer Science at York University, Toronto, and a Sun Certified Java Programmer.

Joseph Weber is a frequent contributor to a variety of magazines and other resources. *Java Web Services Unleashed* marks Mr. Weber's 10th book. Joe has provided Senior Leadership in software definition, research, development, and implementation for Fortune 200 and large government organizations. He has been working with Java since its early alpha stages and has helped advise a number of Fortune 500 companies on the goals of Java. Mr. Weber has served on advisory committees for and taught classes at universities in the Midwest. Previously, Joe co-wrote Que's *Special Edition Using Java* (1.3 edition ISBN: 0-7897-2468-5).

Mark Wutka has been programming since the Carter administration and considers programming a relaxing pastime. He managed to get a computer science degree while designing and developing networking software at Delta Air Lines. Although he has been known to delve into areas of system and application architecture, he isn't happy unless he's writing code—usually in Java. As a consultant for Wutka Consulting, Mark enjoys solving interesting technical problems and helping his coworkers explore new technologies. He has taught classes, written articles and books, and given lectures. His first book, *Hacking Java*, outsold Stephen King at the local technical bookstore. He's also known for having a warped sense of humor.

Most recently, Mark wrote *Special Edition Using Java Server Pages and Servlets* (ISBN: 0-7897-2441-3) and *Special Edition Using Java 2 Enterprise Edition* (ISBN: 0-7897-2503-7) He plays a mean game of Scrabble, a lousy game of chess, and is the bane of every greenskeeper east of Atlanta. He can be reached via e-mail at `mark@wutka.com`. You can also visit his company Web site at `http://www.wutka.com`.

Tell Us What You Think!

As the reader of this book, *you* are our most important critic and commentator. We value your opinion and want to know what we're doing right, what we could do better, what areas you'd like to see us publish in, and any other words of wisdom you're willing to pass our way.

As an Associate Publisher for Sams, I welcome your comments. You can fax, e-mail, or write me directly to let me know what you did or didn't like about this book—as well as what we can do to make our books stronger.

Please note that I cannot help you with technical problems related to the topic of this book, and that due to the high volume of mail I receive, I might not be able to reply to every message.

When you write, please be sure to include this book's title and author as well as your name and phone or fax number. I will carefully review your comments and share them with the author and editors who worked on the book.

Fax: 317-581-4770

E-mail: feedback@samspublishing.com

Mail: Michael Stephens, Associate Publisher
Sams Publishing
201 West 103rd Street
Indianapolis, IN 46290 USA

Introduction

Welcome to the book

Welcome to the Web services revolution—a revolution that is going to change the way that businesses interact, and ultimately the way that people think about building applications. In your hands you hold information that is going to guide you along some very exciting paths.

Is this Book for You?

This book takes you through a whole host of concepts, techniques, APIs, and even a little academia to help you use Java to build Web services. You will learn about the standard Web services stack of XML, UDDI, WSDL, and SOAP. You'll experience the depth of the Java XML package, otherwise known as the JAX Pack. Finally, you're going to see some real working examples of Web services in action.

This book has been designed to teach you a lot of things by guiding you right to the advanced information and providing hard-hitting examples. Before you continue, though, you should understand that this book makes some assumptions about you, the reader.

This book does not try to teach you Java. Although you do not have to necessarily be an expert in the language, this book will only help you learn those portions of the Java API that are directly related to the Web services infrastructure.

This book does not try to teach you XML. This book skips past a lot of XML techniques and jumps right into more advanced XML concepts. There is a brief overview of XML schema, but in general you are also expected to have at least some grasp of the concepts of DTDs and schema.

How This Book Is Organized

This book is organized into five parts. Each part covers a large chunk of information about how the Web services environment is organized.

Part I, "Introduction to Web Services" introduces you to how businesses will need to change to fully take advantage of Web services. It introduces you to the direction Web services are going, and the tools a Web service developer will need, as well as the steps to becoming a Web services provider. Then the introductory section takes you through the development of a simple Web service.

Part II, "Basic Web Services Concepts," walks you through all the language-independent functions of Web services. This part shows you the details of the most common Web service communication protocol—SOAP. It takes you through the UDDI (universal description, discovery, and integration) process, including how to find any service that's being offered or to list your own Web service for others to find it. Then you will learn how to use the standard Web Service Description Language (WSDL) to define or read a description for any Web service.

Part III, "The JAX Pack," discusses all of the Java XML APIs. It starts with JAXP, which is the standard XML parsing API. It then shifts gears and takes you through JAXB, a binding API that enables you to serialize even the most complicated Java objects into XML. JAXR is your passport to UDDI, and JAXM is a messaging API that enables Java developers to communicate to SOAP and other wire formats. This part of the book concludes with coverage of JAX-RPC, which is a key API for performing RPC communication with XML.

Part IV, "Completing Web Services," is designed to complete the entire picture of Enterprise-class Web services. Chapter 17 covers security issues relating to Web services, and Chapters 18 and 19 discuss two of the more recent additions to Web services: the Web Services Flow Language (WSFL) and the invocation language.

Part V, "Implementing Web Services," is designed to allow you to experience some full life-cycle Web service development. These chapters are intended to be the icing on the cake and you'll want to savor every bit. The first example takes you through building a standard Web service with JSP technology. The second exposes an EJB system to the world of Web services. The book finishes up with a chapter teaching testing issues specific to Web services and two chapters that expose you to tools available to make your life easier.

Conventions Used in This Book

This book uses various stylistic and typographic conventions to make it easier to use.

Note

When you see a note in this book, it indicates additional information that may help you avoid problems or that should be considered in using the described features.

Tip

Tip paragraphs suggest easier or alternative methods of executing a procedure. Tips can help you see that little extra concept or idea than can make your life much easier.

Caution

Cautions warn you of hazardous procedures (for example, activities that delete files).

Downloading Example Code Files

You can download the source code for examples presented in this book from `http://www.samspublishing.com`. When you reach that page, enter this book's ISBN number (067232363X) in the search box to access information about the book and to obtain a Source Code link.

Introduction to Web Services

PART I

IN THIS PART

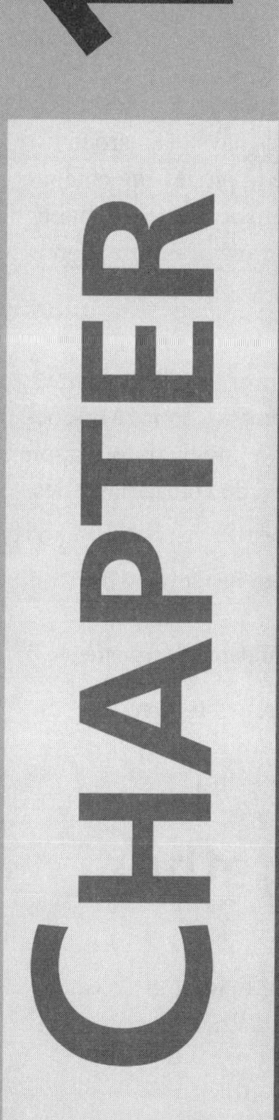

What Are Web Services?

By Joe Weber and Darren Govoni

In This Chapter

If you've picked up this book you are probably already aware of all the turmoil going on in the Web environment. Many things are changing about the Web. These changes are bringing about exciting opportunities. People are able to communicate at a faster and faster pace. Concepts such as P2P (Point to Point) are evolving faster than ever and the Web is becoming an ever-increasing part of everyday computing life.

This book will introduce you to one of the most exciting sets of technologies designed to calm the turbulent waters. Web services are designed to create defined boundaries between applications across the Internet and to allow partners, aggregators, and vendors to quickly and easily interact.

B2B Means A2A

Probably the fastest growing area of development continues to be around the concept of business-to-business (B2B) communication. B2B computing systems have been around for decades. Teller machines talk to banks, cash registers talk to credit processing companies, inventory flow systems procure new product from vendors, logistics systems obtain tracking information from shippers, and so on. B2B means that the flow of information is from application to application.

On the Web a person enters data.... Whoa. That doesn't seem right. Why does the Internet mean that people need to get involved? Well, it doesn't. Clever designers figured out a long time ago that they could write programs to read the contents of an HTML document or user interface and use a technique called screen scraping to find the information they needed for their applications. Others utilized FTP to upload and download data files. Still more used proprietary protocols to wire together custom applications.

The problem with all those clever developers was that they needed to be clever. They needed to modify the application anytime something changed, and if they wanted to share data between one another they all needed to talk about the standard for transfer.

Developers of EDI applications figured out that standard transfer protocols were a necessity. Web services bring all the functionality of EDI to the Web. As some have put it, Web services are the HTML for applications.

Bringing All the Pieces Together

The concept of Web services is simple. It's not unlike a football scenario.

Web services brings all the players together onto a common playing field. It gives each of the players access to a directory of the other players. Then it defines a common set of symbols by which to define plays.

When a coach wants to field a team he simply needs to open up the directory. He can find a group of players with the skills and abilities he needs. Finally, he can send them a playbook to get ready for the game.

In Web services lingo, XML (eXtensible Markup Language) serves as the common set of symbols and the language by which all communication takes place. That directory can be any number of things, but UDDI (Universal Description, Discovery, and Integration) provides one such standard. WSDL (the Web Services Description Language) enables the coach to assemble all the plays, and SOAP (the Simple Object Access Protocol)—or some other transport—lets the coach send the plays to the players.

Ideology Wars Without Just One Winner

For years now developers have fought a war over who had the best programming language. "I want to develop everything in Java!" many would shout. Others, feeling the pressure of the giant, turned and developed Microsoft Visual Basic applications. Still more worked in C/C++, Smalltalk, and Cobol. The wars raged on and each language claimed a company or separate divisions within one.

But a serious problem emerges when two departments in a company start to look like they have erected the Berlin wall: Innovation and productivity get strained. As one department continues to lob mythical bombs in the direction of the others sometimes there is a victory—which means rewriting the old systems, or painfully integrating with them. Worse, when one company acquires another, the victor can be forced to sift through legions of disparate systems to try to get them to interact.

Compound that scenario with the fact that COBOL is still the number one programming language in the world, and not even enterprising Java developers knew how to crack every nut.

Interoperability for Everyone

Web services can bring peace to this situation. Like Java's platform neutrality, Web services promises language neutrality. XML is XML to a Java developer, and—surprise, surprise—XML is also just XML to a Microsoft .NET developer writing Visual Basic. So now a VB developer and a Java developer can both talk to the corporate EDI server written in PL/I, and neither gets hurt.

Web services will allow organizations to think about software in a truly modularized form. Although CORBA (Common Object Request Broker Architecture) and other similar initiatives tried to bring distributed architectures about, the efforts involved in any such endeavor stifled the evolution.

Perhaps one of the most important rules of any network is Metcalf's law, which states that the value of the network is the square of the devices connected to it. This means that for every person able to talk freely on a network the network's value grows exponentially. The value of Web services is that they let everybody participate in the network as neutral players.

Changing Businesses Everywhere

The most significant change brought about by Web services will not be for developers. The biggest change is going to be in how businesses interact and think about software development. Just as procurement systems made virtually every type of manufacturing a commodity, so to will Web services bring application services toward the commodity realm (*toward*, but not *to*).

Web services can enable businesses to interact and offer services that were heretofore extremely expensive to develop. Consider this example: A bed-and-breakfast can now easily offer guests the capability to automatically purchase airline tickets and rent a car. Now the B&B's clients can have a full-service experience from a mom-and-pop shop. Best of all, the B&B can talk to three different travel agencies without the nightmare of three different wires. Because all three travel agencies have the same Web service definition, the only thing the B&B programmer needs to do is arrange contracts with all three.

In addition, one of the most significant changes today is that businesses "get it." The CEO understands that the Internet enables people to talk together and communicate in ways that are faster than ever before. They understand they need to be connected directly to their suppliers, their partners, and their logistics vendors. They understand that if their clients can't connect them, their clients will go to somebody else.

Software development in general is on its way to being developed in new ways. If Web services become truly pervasive, much software development will become orchestration of services. Each Web service will provide some large or small function the business needs and the majority of IT developers will be able to simply orchestrate how these services communicate.

But fear not, developers, this doesn't mean you will be out of a job. This means that business will be able to actually bring down the barriers to entry, and increase their capabilities. It means that as a developer you will have greater opportunities to do the really exciting things, and will not have to spend all that time reproducing the same thing time and time again.

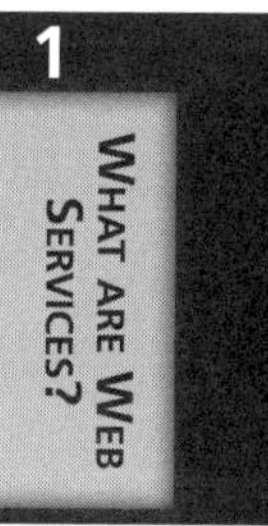

What Are Web Services?

So now that you've read the rhetoric, the more basic question probably comes to your mind: What in the world are Web services?

The answer is both incredibly simple and fairly complicated at the same time. It's complicated because if you ask 12 experts on the subject to define Web services you are bound to get 12 different responses. If you ask 50 you'll probably get 49 different responses. The answer is not necessarily so complicated that all 50 experts couldn't agree, but the answer is changing. The good news is that it's changing because Web services are so dynamic they can reach into dozens of areas of a business.

A Simple Definition

In seeking a simple definition of what Web services are, the easiest thing is to simply break down the two words inherent in the question.

So why *Web*? The answer is really twofold. The first answer is related to marketing. The term was coined in the midst of the Web boom. Everybody wanted to be a Web or .com company, so it seemed logical to express the new technology in terms of the Web. The second answer is technology-related. James Gosling put it simply: "They layer across HTTP." Most services that will be offered will, in fact, be offered across HTTP. The reason is not really that HTTP is the best transport option (far from it), but rather that HTTP is a known commodity and it's something that organizations feel comfortable offering willy-nilly across their firewalls (somewhat naively). This combines to mean that Web services capabilities can be delivered into almost every enterprise today, and there's no need to bridge additional IT issues.

Why *services*? The term *services* is directly akin to the S in the term ASP, or Application Service Provider. An ASP offers up product not directly as an installation, but rather as a service (typically over the Web). Web services follow a similar paradigm. A service is simply offered to developers and non-browser-based applications, instead of being limited to the traditional HTTP environment.

Combining both terms leads to a simple definition that Web services are a solution for providing application-to-application communication over the Internet.

The Bigger Picture

The bigger picture involves a much more complicated answer. Web services are the combination of several standard sets of technology. The most important by far is XML. The reason for this is that XML is not language-dependant. As was mentioned earlier, XML is XML to a Java developer and it's still XML to C/C++, Visual Basic, or Cobol programmers. Better still, with just a little bit of patience, that same XML can be read by a person. So Web services enable individuals programming in all of these different languages to input data into a system and get it back out in a neutral fashion.

This is very similar to the capability to post data over HTTP. The difference is the richness, layering capabilities, portability, and readability inherent in an XML structure. In addition, with XML schema the data can be validated on both ends of the communication wire.

With XML, and XML-based technologies such as SOAP and UDDI, the entire wire format is vendor-, platform- and language-neutral. Quite simply, it leverages XML human- and machine-level neutrality just as Java extended the byte code neutrality.

The Reach of Web Services

So how does this all fit together? The answer can be best explained by an example. Consider a simple weather system.

Jane Doe has a business around providing accurate weather data and weather prediction for any locale. Jane has been selling this historically by allowing people to come to her Web site and (using a password) gain access to the data.

As a smart entrepreneur, Jane has come to realize that she can gain significant new revenue by partnering with other vendors. So, for instance, she wants to sell a top-tier seed producer her services. The seed producer will in turn sell the information as an add-on product to the farmers.

To do this type of data transfer in the past, the seed producer would have to do one of two things. They could write some custom code to go out and read Jane's Web site, post in whatever data was necessary for each individual farmer's locale, read back the resulting HTML, and scrape out the information they wanted to package for the farmer. Or Jane's IT group and the IT group at the seed producer would sit down and work out some proprietary transfer.

What Web services and XML provide is a very straightforward way to make this easier, starting from the way in which the seed company discovers that Jane even exists in the first place. In this case, the seed company can go to a UDDI server, inquire about weather information providers and find Jane. From the UDDI server they can obtain a fairly simple document that describes the XML that Jane will expect from them (for the farmer's location). In that same document they will see the data that Jane will send back. This document is written in a standard XML schema called WSDL.

From this point, the seed company can use simple tools to generate Java skeleton classes based on the WSDL document. The classes will contain simple methods such as `setLocale()` and `getTemperature()`, which can be easily called from a JSP page, servlet, or other business logic. The seed company can then integrate the business intelligence nearly automatically.

Web services simply extends across the reach of applications across the network, bringing portability normally associated with heavyweight RPC (Remote Procedure Call) mechanisms such as CORBA and EDI to the masses.

The Impact of Web Service Technologies

This section takes a close look at the core technologies involved in the basic Web services platform and why they are important to businesses. It also considers the effects these technologies will have on the way businesses operate or assess Web services as a strategic platform.

XML (extensible Markup Language)

XML is at the root of Web services for some key reasons. First, it provides a common syntactical way of expressing structured data in the form of human-readable documents. Second, the structure that it provides is easily navigated by third party applications, which is to say, applications that did not generate the XML. This separation is key to the success of XML as an application-neutral data exchange. And third, XML namespaces enable applications to share semantic elements contained within a particular document. All this is necessary to bridge system implementations in a common, yet neutral manner.

Because XML provides a way to convey information via structured data, it will be vital for businesses to understand the structure of the information they generate and process. This will involve creating *schemas* that represent a complete list of terms, relations, and entities involved in the aspects of the business. Schemas are templates that describe properly formatted XML documents and are used to generate and process correctly formatted information specific to the business.

This has taken place already in the relational database world. To benefit from using a relational model, it is necessary to make decisions about what data is important to your business and what relationships exist between the data elements. As soon as an appropriate data model exists, it's possible to mine useful correlations out of it to optimize your business processes and knowledge. This is what *data mining* seeks to accomplish.

Another similar event occurred with the major shift to object-oriented languages. As a result, businesses could define their system applications in terms of real-world entities and relationships that better mapped to the programming language facilities used to create the system. This created a tighter correspondence between real-world business actions and objects and programming language representations of them. The real-world model and the programming model were moving closer together. This made developing applications for a particular domain much easier to manage because application objects looked and behaved in concordance with their real-world counterparts.

These two technological shifts, relational and object-oriented, marked a change in the way businesses thought about themselves and their software systems. Today, these shifts are seen as marked improvements in efficiency and productivity. Similarly, we are in the age of XML, and metadata and businesses are called to re-think how they define and structure themselves in concordance with the technologies and services they interact with and deliver.

WSDL (Web Services Definition Language)

WSDL provides the template through which Web services are described and subsequently published. It is the WSDL representation of a Web service that is discovered and used in the binding process via a directory.

The transition to Web services will require that existing business objects and functions be precisely described with WSDL documents and published in online registries.

> **Note**
>
> Some cases might not require or even warrant publishing services into a registry for ad hoc access. Rather, service binding information is embedded directly in applications that would seek to use it.

Software tools are currently available that automatically generate WSDL documents from a given service object, such as an Enterprise JavaBean (in the J2EE world) or a COM object (in the Windows world). Listing 1.1 appears on the W3C WSDL Web site and provides a simple example of a Web service descriptor for stock quotes.

LISTING 1.1 Example Web Service Descriptor

```
<?xml version="1.0"?>
<definitions name="StockQuote"
```

LISTING 1.1 continued

```
targetNamespace="http://example.com/stockquote.wsdl"
          xmlns:tns="http://example.com/stockquote.wsdl"
          xmlns:xsd1="http://example.com/stockquote.xsd"
          xmlns:soap="http://schemas.xmlsoap.org/wsdl/soap/"
          xmlns="http://schemas.xmlsoap.org/wsdl/">

    <types>
       <schema targetNamespace="http://example.com/stockquote.xsd"
              xmlns="http://www.w3.org/2000/10/XMLSchema">
           <element name="TradePriceRequest">
              <complexType>
                  <all>
                      <element name="tickerSymbol" type="string"/>
                  </all>
              </complexType>
           </element>
           <element name="TradePrice">
              <complexType>
                  <all>
                      <element name="price" type="float"/>
                  </all>
              </complexType>
           </element>
       </schema>
    </types>

    <message name="GetLastTradePriceInput">
        <part name="body" element="xsd1:TradePriceRequest"/>
    </message>

    <message name="GetLastTradePriceOutput">
        <part name="body" element="xsd1:TradePrice"/>
    </message>

    <portType name="StockQuotePortType">
        <operation name="GetLastTradePrice">
           <input message="tns:GetLastTradePriceInput"/>
           <output message="tns:GetLastTradePriceOutput"/>
        </operation>
    </portType>

    <binding name="StockQuoteSoapBinding" type="tns:StockQuotePortType">
        <soap:binding style="document" transport=
                  "http://schemas.xmlsoap.org/soap/http"/>
        <operation name="GetLastTradePrice">
           <soap:operation soapAction=
                  "http://example.com/GetLastTradePrice"/>
           <input>
               <soap:body use="literal"/>
```

LISTING 1.1 continued

```
        </input>
        <output>
            <soap:body use="literal"/>
        </output>
    </operation>
</binding>

<service name="StockQuoteService">
    <documentation>My first service</documentation>
    <port name="StockQuotePort" binding="tns:StockQuoteSoapBinding">
       <soap:address location="http://example.com/stockquote"/>
    </port>
</service>

</definitions>
```

This example and others, including the complete specification, can be found at `http://www.w3.org/TR/wsdl`.

UDDI (Universal Description Discovery and Integration)

As you know already, WSDL documents become entries in a UDDI registry where they can be searched, found, and bound to. UDDI acts as the yellow pages for Web services, and it is designed to be universal in the sense that you can describe and publish any kind of Web service hosted by any kind of implementation.

Comparing the UDDI model to the telephone directory Yellow Pages should come as no surprise. The paradigm translates perfectly, but rather than humans (customers) looking up other humans (merchants), you now have applications (requestors) looking up other applications (providers). This all contributes toward business automation. As businesses identify their core operation assets and embody them as exposed services, they can scale their operations better. Using Web services allows the service implementation details to be altered without any disruption to the procedure for dynamically binding to it. Scalability is thus improved when disruptions due to implementation details are minimized or eliminated.

UDDI is a keystone directory facility that enables published services to be grouped together. However, there will be many UDDI directories, just as there is no single universal set of yellow pages. It might even be that UDDI repositories will cluster geographically like real yellow pages, but this need not be a restriction. More likely, you will find UDDIs that host constituents that are naturally interested in one another. So, for specific niches, verticals, or service chains, some directories will provide access to all members of intersecting value so that they can find each other more readily. For example, a general contractor that builds commercial office space might tie its information system to service directories that host vendors providing services tailored to commercial construction and not, say, residential construction. Many different services can be conveniently offered in one place in the context of commercial construction for easy discovery and automation.

Note

For more information on UDDI—the specification, best practices, and industry forums surrounding it—please visit `http://www.uddi.org`.

SOAP (Simple Object Access Protocol)

SOAP has quickly become an important aspect of Web services. It is the protocol of choice for Web service vendors to use to transport messages between Web service entities. SOAP is an XML-based transport protocol and rides atop lower-level transport protocols such as HTTP, which, in turn, rides atop a true transport protocol such as TCP/IP. SOAP messages can, in fact, be delivered by a variety of different ways including SMTP (Simple Mail Transport Protocol). It is stateless, and therefore the sender and receiver need not maintain a stateful session to communicate. All the necessary state is in the message.

Technically speaking, SOAP is low-enough level that businesses need not address it directly. Web service software often masks the transport protocol and message format from application developers. Therefore, it (that is, learning SOAP) is not particularly a skill to be invested in directly—unless your business is to build Web service products, application servers, or middleware technologies.

Note

SOAP has been assimilated into the W3C under the title "XML Protocol." For more information on it, including usage scenarios, visit `http://www.w3c.org/2000/xp/`.

ebXML (Electronic Business XML)

ebXML is a business interchange specification with the spirit and intent of EDI but with the benefits of XML and SOAP. ebXML is sanctioned by UN/CEFACT (United Nations Centre for Trade Facilitation and Electronic Business) as well as OASIS (Organization for the Advancement of Structured Information Standards) and is technically mature with complete specifications for architecture, business processes, and implementation technologies.

ebXML is designed to enable new e-marketspaces. It is perceived by many to be an evolution of the EDI movement, because it not only embodies all the major tenets of EDI, but it also provides the extensibility, flexibility, and schema capability of the XML world.

With ebXML, businesses will be able to find trading partners, establish dynamic supply chains, and optimize their business operations. ebXML is an exciting and complex set of specifications based around simple business modeling ideas. It provides a common trading and exchange platform via which companies around the world can define, discover, and deliver dynamic goods and services. Figure 1.1 is extracted from the ebXML business process architecture and identifies the major steps involved in an ebXML conversation.

The process shown in Figure 1.1 is not unlike that involving pure Web services, but it is a bit more complex. A company specifies metadata describing the endpoint service they require. Published services are eligible candidates for a requestor to discover. The platform enables the requestor to dynamically specify the criteria required for a match. For example, suppose your system were searching for a goods supplier, but also needed to ensure that the goods could be delivered within 24 hours. You need a mechanism via which you can unambiguously specify such things in a way that both the service provider and requestor understand. This allows a degree of precision when systems are automatically searching for and binding to services on-demand. In ebXML, this results in a *binding agreement* that is generated to indicate that both systems agree to each other's requirements and constraints before transacting. The process is not much different from in real life, where humans review and sign contracts before they exchange goods.

The core technologies of Web services make much of this process possible for ebXML, which augments them to include business process schemas, namespaces, and rules of engagement.

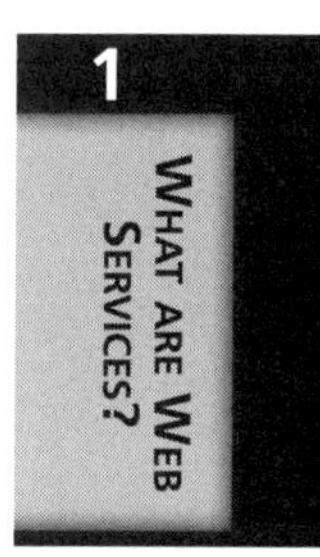

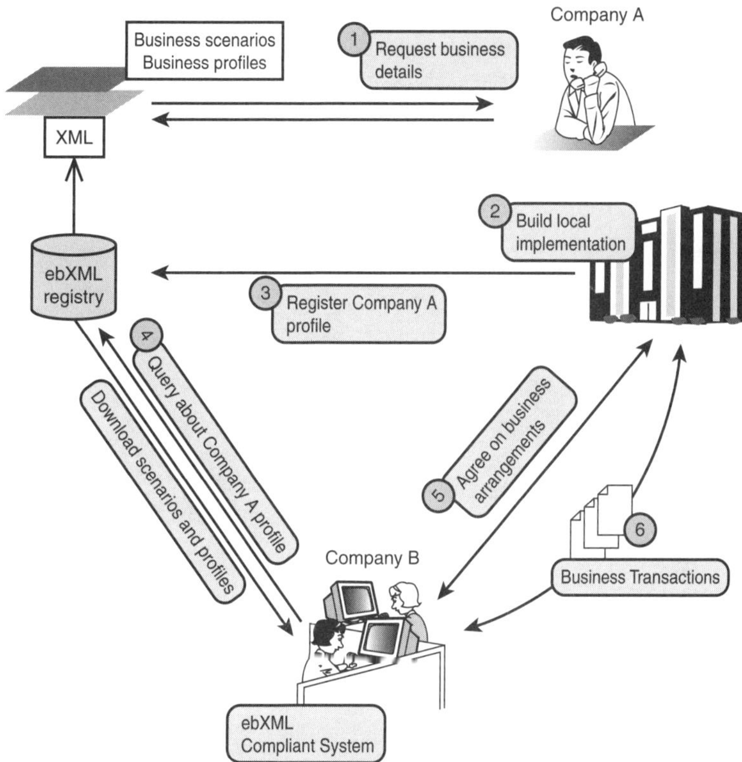

FIGURE 1.1
ebXML business process architecture.

> **Note**
>
> See `http://www.ebxml.org` for presentations, white papers, technical documents, and the like.

Summary

In this chapter, you were introduced to Web services. With a birds-eye view of what Web services are and how they're useful, you should have a good understanding of the intent behind them. Foremost is the capability to glue systems together in ad hoc ways using a single, common, and neutral discovery and invocation stack, which is the Web services platform. As you learned earlier, this platform comprises primarily components (SOAP, XML, UDDI, WSDL) that come together to provide a business service as what has been called a *Web service*. The key differentiator is the platform neutrality provided as these technologies work together.

In the next chapter, you will be introduced to the various aspects of Web services (for example, business, technical, and so on) in more detail. You will also receive overviews of new paradigms and business models that will impact the way we perceive networked commerce.

CHAPTER 2

The Internet and Web Services: Changing Business

By Darren Govoni

In This Chapter

This chapter explores how the Web services movement has and will likely impact the way businesses operate across the Internet. It is certain that the Internet has paved the way for exciting new business models. Both a breeding ground of innovation and a graveyard of lost hopes, the Internet rewards only the most prudent and well-thought-through endeavors.

Web services have been touted over the past year as a major new trend in Internet computing. Most large companies have recognized Web services as an interesting, if not important strategic direction for them in the future. IBM, Sun, and Microsoft are already delivering platforms and tools based on Web services.

When technology inflections occur, it often sparks opportunities for existing businesses as well as new revenue models and products. This chapter dives deeper into the possibilities Web services offers and examines many of the issues regarding it. Foremost, the platform is designed to enable smoother interchange between and within business applications. However, many of the premises behind Web services have been around for some time.

A New Old Thing

The basic idea behind Web services is not particularly new. In fact, it's old. One of the important aspects of Web services is its ability to act as a common language and messaging platform across disparate systems. However, this vision was quite like that of days prior.

The OMG's IIOP (Internet Inter-Orb Protocol) was supposed to be the Internet standard for system-to-system interchange—much as CORBA was to be the broker for large-scale applications. These specifications had the backing of many companies and grew to be quite large and complex. As it turned out, CORBA did not quite become the ubiquitous platform OMG had hoped. One perceived reason for this was that it grew too large and complex for vendors to economically implement. Another issue surrounded IIOP and its extensibility and true interoperability across platforms, which proved difficult to establish across some products. Additionally, IIOP lacked the self-describing and namespace features brought forth with XML. This made XML an attractive basis for messaging protocols—and a good number of industrial systems are based on inter-system messaging, such as banks, airline reservation systems, and stock trading platforms.

Note

Although weaknesses in IIOP turned attention toward XML as a protocol language to address Web services, IIOP is still an active protocol in distributed computing platforms such as CORBA and J2EE/Enterprise JavaBeans (RMI/IIOP).

Message-based commerce has been going for some time and EDI (Electronic Data Interchange) still dominates it. Unknown to most of us, EDI transactions are initiated on our behalf when we engage in various activities such as transferring funds, receiving direct deposit payments, or buying merchandise.

Note

EDI is governed by a consortia standards body, the Accredited Standards Committee X12, and is further bolstered by the international standards body UN/EDIFACT (United Nations Directories For Electronic Data Interchange for Administration, Commerce, and Transport). Visit `http://www.unece.org/trade/untdid/welcome.htm` for more details.

One of the problems with traditional batch-oriented EDI messages is that they lack the extensibility, self-describing data, and networked namespace type-model that XML provides. Because of the tight governance of EDI message elements and semantics, this is not a looming problem for past EDI adopters; however, in the fast-paced e-commerce Internet, where companies need to adapt quickly, those processes are too lengthy and rigid. Chapter 3 will introduce other aspects of EDI and how it relates to Web services.

The capability XML offers you to control and define your own namespace semantics as well as refer to broadly scoped schemas is what makes XML compelling as an interchange language between companies. EDI is addressing this with its semantic elements as part of the interactive EDI movement, but even that lacks the true extensibility of XML.

One reason why namespaces and semantics are important is that businesses do not typically share a common vocabulary of terms (or data elements). Similarly-named terms can have different meanings to different businesses in a conversation. It is essential, therefore, that data messages provide some way of ascertaining meaning somewhere in the context of the transaction (say, in the message itself). The message receiver needs a uniform way of extracting the vital components of the message. XML provides the basic syntax and structure behind such a common interchange language. Ascertaining in what *namespace* a term originates enables a message recipient to determine whether the intended meaning is pertinent or not. The namespace associated with elements of the document is published within the document itself, and the recipient can cross-reference it against known or valid namespaces, thus allowing it to accept or reject elements or entire messages.

Metamodeling Your Business

For any given business, a set of processes define the critical functions and data the business uses. In addition, there are objects, both real and virtual, that play roles in these processes. Then there is the information that participates in the workflows of the business. That information is becoming more structured as well as plentiful. Because there is so much data, it is useful to describe it in such a way that you can retrieve it more efficiently and subsequently exchange it with foreign processes.

The *metadata* that describes your data can also describe the processes and objects involved in your operations. The relations between metadata form metamodels as sets of metadata define aspects between entities of your business. Such entities can be real or modeled as application objects. The metamodel is not typically affected by variations at the implementation model level.

Therefore, when you think about Web services you're also talking about self-describing business processes and data for which models will emerge. Each Web service contains metadata about the service and about its input requirements—which is to say the parameters and types necessary to invoke the service.

When coupling takes place between two business services it is because their metamodels "snap" together effectively (that is, the corresponding inputs and output types, namespaces and information models relate). The underlying systems, processes, objects, and information are therefore de-coupled from one another. Metamodeling your business will assist you in identifying and exposing your company's critical processes for Web service usage independent of their actual implementation or application-specific models.

The Technical Appeal of Web Services

We've already touched on why the core technologies of the Web services platform are appealing individually, but what about the whole package? What are the overarching reasons why this platform exists? Why it is important from a technical perspective?

One Glue to Bind Them All

Companies have been addressing the issue of integrating disparate systems—both within their networks and between other networks—for some time. It became clear that various ways of doing this came into being and each way provided its own set of protocols. This led to further fragmentation among systems and applications downstream. With the advent of XML-based interoperability and messaging, the notion of a single service-offering platform became more attractive and possible. It is much more economical for solution providers and companies to solve such service provisioning and publishing problems once and then simply forget about it.

The real ROI (return on investment) comes from the active use and integration of services exposed via the Web services platform. The logical need in this case is for one glue to bind them all. This need is especially important in large companies where systems must ultimately communicate, and, of course, last.

Coupling Versus De-Coupling

With a single glue platform, the appeal of universal interconnectivity between disparate systems is now very appealing. In other words, the manner in which two systems interact is separate from how that actually happens—the *how* is constant and the *what* can vary according to system needs. The *what* has to do with the exchange of data and functionality (that is, what actually takes place). The *how* is, of course, the Web services platform.

The fundamental issue here is a categorical problem within and between all systems, and that is one of *coupling* and *de-coupling*. On one side, your goal is to bring together disparate systems that would not otherwise be capable of interacting. This is the coupling side. Conversely, you want systems to have a degree of loose separation such that they are not rigid and affected by internal change. For systems to join into ad hoc unions, they must be de-coupled and abstracted from implementation details that might affect high-level interoperability. One key requires that they share a common way of expressing functional operations semantically. These mutual contracts will ride atop the binding mechanisms of Web services. Exchange contracts for doing general, ad hoc business using Web services is already underway—ebXML is one such mechanism.

At a business level, this is very exciting. It will afford much more fluid commerce and value/supply chaining even down to the individual transaction level. This could mean that depending on the characteristics of a given transaction, the entities involved could vary optimally. For example, suppose you are a general contractor and have a variety of lumber suppliers you order from regularly. It might be the case that one supplier offers a much reduced rate for bulk orders, even more so than the other suppliers. You would like to encode this knowledge in your automation system so that orders that exceed the specified amount go to the correct supplier and all other orders are directed elsewhere—all to minimize your costs.

From a technical perspective, the coupling/de-coupling issue is of great value and is addressed directly by Web services. Merchants will publish Web service entries in UDDI registries and therefore service requestors might not have *a priori* knowledge about some merchant with which they might benefit from doing business. The coupling occurs just in time as the Web service platform performs the discovery and service binding and will be directed to do so by your application-level business logic and schemas. For this reason, it has also been referred to as *just-in-time integration.*

Defining with Metadata

Metadata will becomean ever more important concept within companies, even more so than today. The Web services platform facilitates the verbose description of service entities as part of their publication in UDDI repositories. This mechanism will help service requestors differentiate between services. The more time spent honing this process at runtime, the less efficiently the system operates—so metadata is a vital facet of this new service-based ecology.

The need for rich metadata will have positive, yet long-term effects on business. It will force businesses to truly understand the meta-qualitative descriptions of their data and systems. Categorizing their processes and information was, for a long time, not necessary because the systems that were built were closed and rigid. Because business aspects can now be exposed for commerce, it is necessary to describe them in such a way that they can be found and bound easily. Just as content is scanned and indexed, now entire businesses will be sought for their qualities that define exactly what they do, what they can and can't do, and possibly how they do it. That increase in automation and precision will benefit the flow of business.

This trend is already emerging as similar businesses try to define common schemas—or language templates—so that they can transact. This process must start now, to make the transition to full automation possible when the technology is ready, and it is almost there.

However, there are some challenges to overcome in this process. One involves defining the languages via which commerce can proceed in a way that is consistent across parties. So, for example, if I come across a service attribute called "light", is it an adjective as in *light*-weight or a noun as in visible *light*? These kinds of ambiguities are problematic when appropriate namespaces are not used. And even with the use of namespaces, the trouble of multiple, yet semantically similar namespaces might still exist. Unfortunately, this is a political process and must have a critical mass of industry support to take hold. The "Vertical Ontologies" section, later in this chapter, explores this topic further.

The key point to understand here is that metadata is almost as valuable as the underlying data itself, and some might even say it's more valuable. For businesses, they must undergo complex BPM (Business Process Modeling) to identify all the objects, relationships, and their attributes, and generate sufficient metadata that reflects the business models.

Security Facades

Another technical appeal of the Web services platform involves security. One problem plaguing the free and useful interchange of corporate information is the plethora of various security regimes, logins, and authentication methods. Coupling disparate security systems is by no means straightforward and is among the hardest problems to successfully resolve.

However, because the Web services platform seeks homogeneity within the *how* aspect of transacting, it must deal with security. Current Web-based security measures can be applied to Web services at the access level, but client authentication methods are problematic as you also want to permit ad hoc use of your services, but certainly not ad hoc abuse.

In the meantime, the Web services platform (by its nature) provides a veiling mechanism to hide security and implementation details of your real corporate network by simply façading it (see Figure 2.1). To this extent, you can embed, prune, and fashion policies for exposure on the Web without compromising the nature of the policies used internally. Access to sensitive data is governed by what you choose to expose as a Web service. For example, should you choose to embody only a certain set of internal functions as Web services, it should be impossible to breach the Web services layer to gain further access to your business functions or discover their security details—much like it probably is already.

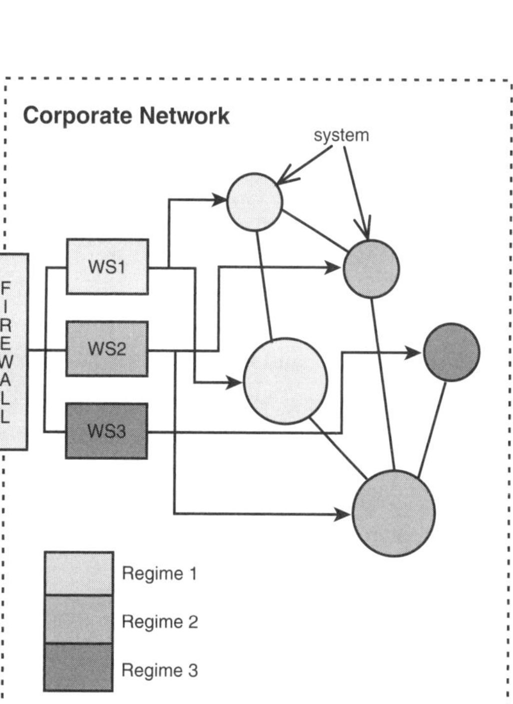

FIGURE 2.1
Security veiling with Web services.

Business Roles

The essential design of Web services involves cooperation between various business roles as depicted in Figure 2.2. These roles reflect the duties that must be fulfilled to complete the publishing, discovery, and binding of Web services. Three primary roles are involved in a common Web service conversation as reflected in the fundamental architecture. They are the *service requestor*, *service provider*, and the *service broker*. The following sections take a deeper look into these roles and the coming effects and issues related to them.

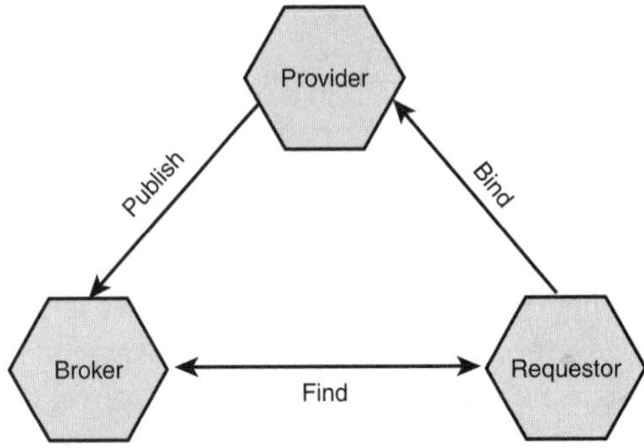

FIGURE 2.2
The Web services triumvirate.

Service Requestor

In the Web services triad, the requestor is simply that; the one who requests a particular service. In reality, though, requesting is more than simply requesting; it involves specifying important characteristics about the desired service so the service can effectively be found in a UDDI registry. To help this process, it is useful for both service requestors and providers to adopt some generally known or available dictionary of terms. Such terms are used in the metadata characteristics that define the entities being represented in a Web services directory.

Because we are only dealing with *descriptors* of services, there need to be enough meaningful terms to associate with the service at various levels. For example, maybe you request only services that are implemented transactionally to ensure backend data integrity. Banks, for example, require this. On another level, you might choose only services that specify that their parent companies are members of a particular organization or interest body—or that the service itself contains caveats and classifications that are relevant to your domain.

The requestor must be concerned about these issues and have that information before finding and using interesting services. It is beyond the scope of the Web service platform and technologies exactly how requestors obtain such knowledge and whether it has to be provided manually or can be obtained by other means.

In all likelihood, particular vertical domains will identify these uniformities to ensure more seamless operations within their market as a whole.

Service Broker

The service broker is responsible for pairing up requestors and providers. For this to happen, a service provider (one who provides the implementation of the service) must publish a descriptor of the service to the brokers registry via UDDI. As mentioned earlier, the service descriptor is a WSDL document that contains relevant characteristics and metadata about the service that's useful for search, retrieval and of course, binding.

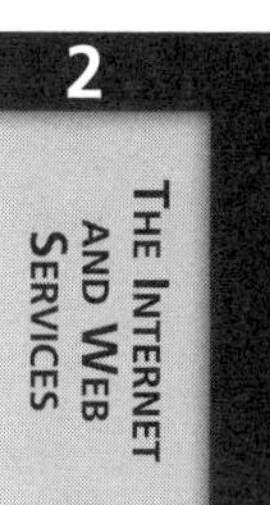

The broker provides the registry and interface via which requests can be made. It then returns an enumeration of matches based on a query. After that is completed, the broker is finished and not involved in further communications between requestor and provider. That is, it has completed the brokering process when the requestor binds to the service provider directly and accesses the service. The broker is then no longer needed.

So, what does this mean to business? It means that most businesses wanting to leverage or use Web services will need to decide which brokers to use and how many if that is the case. Why is this necessary? Because there is no single central registry or broker through which everyone can connect. Rather, there will be various brokers, possibly servicing specific interests and/or vertical markets. This trend toward registry fragmentation still carries with it the dilemma of knowing precisely which registries will house the services in which you are most interested.

As an analogy, consider Web search engines. There are many search engines, and some people use a variety of different ones to obtain different results. This is not the most desirable situation, especially if you're looking for services to exercise an important business transaction. How will this be solved? At this point, it is unclear. Possibly, there is an opportunity for service brokerage companies to fill in the gaps and provide consolidated access to various provider networks transparently.

Service Provider

The service provider is responsible for publishing and implementing the service. This process involves mapping the details of the service implementation onto an appropriate descriptor in the form of a WSDL document. That document is then published in a service brokers UDDI registry where it is parsed and indexed for effective search and retrieval. The information the provider publishes provides the requestor with the data it needs to create a binding to the service at runtime. Subsequently, the requestor issues operations against the service and moves data back and forth from the service at will.

The service implementation can take any form, and the Web services specification does not dictate exactly how services are implemented. Rather, it specifies a set of protocols via which a consistent platform can be built.

Service providers will become important as enterprises seek to couple their business activities together to create more streamlined supply chains, partner networks, and high-speed commerce systems. Many businesses already reveal their systems over the Internet, but in the form of Web applications that are driven by browser-based environments. As such, a human is needed to interact with these backend systems to glean useful information. Moving such systems towards Web services will allow for backend-to-backend connectivity between companies, and this will permit streamlined operations and information exchange. Service providers are required for this to happen.

Security Issues and Concerns

One of the TBDs ("to be done"s) for Web service involves completing a security model that can protect Web service providers from malicious use, attack or theft. We already have ways using encryption via standards such as SSL (secure sockets layer), but one trouble involves understanding *who* the requestor is and what access privileges it has been or will be granted.

There is somewhat of a paradox lurking here. The idea behind Web services, on the one hand, is to allow the requestor and provider to de-couple. Discovery happens via a third party: the broker. If certain discoveries are to be allowed or disallowed, the broker must have some knowledge of this, but often the broker will be a separate entity from the provider entirely. The security concerns push the broker and provider closer together, which is not entirely desirable.

The other concern is how to manage access control via ACLs (access control lists) as a provider, in such a way that requestors who need your service can use it in a timely manner. If it requires you to approve every request, then, of course, the usefulness of just-in-time binding is diminished.

The good news is that these issues are being worked on and for now, current Web security measures can control access to Web services. Also, most companies are using them within their corporate networks only at the moment, and most corporate networks are protected by firewalls.

Effects on Business Models

There are two ways of assessing the impact of Web services on business models. One involves how Web services impacts existing business models and the other, how it will affect forthcoming business models. Existing business are already affected by Web services as major players investigate the applicability of the technology, both as an internal process improvement technology and as an external revenue-generating or collaboration technology. Early opinions hold that Web services will gestate within corporate networks as a common integrating platform tying different systems together—legacy systems such as SAP, PeopleSoft, Oracle, and other CRM/ERP-type systems would tie into corporate portals. One hope is that with this new integration paradigm, applications can be combined and offered in efficient ways far more readily, and that should lead to overall business improvement.

For large companies, a plague often results from frequent mergers and acquisitions, which creates a landscape of disparate non-communicating systems. Inevitably, these companies seek to aggregate their data and systems into streamlined variations that can be offered as new or tailored products and services in a speedy fashion. Before Web services, such a process involved a medley of point solutions for each system. Clearly, the cost and management of a variety of solutions competes with that of a variety of problems. Web services thus provide a *lingua franca*, so to speak, for this sort of objective.

Given this observation, how are business models affected by the benefit of Web services in this context? Businesses are finding that they can indeed offer new value-added services to their customers when they're capable of exchanging information and processing between systems in a well-known and publicly understood way. As such, the very understanding of what products and services a business can provide expands. Business models then become much more malleable in the face of malleable technology—and this is generally a good thing for business.

Any time there is a major inflection point in technology, a mosaic of opportunity arises for new businesses and business models. For example, telephones brought about all sorts of new ways to conduct business, some directly related, others indirectly related. The point is that a world that includes Web services offers many interesting choices for new business models. Some will involve the facilitation of automation directly between businesses, allowing them to be completely de-coupled from supply chain providers and logistics. Others might be related to simple B2C transactions, and yet others will seek to turn existing human-centric services into system-centric ones.

In years past, B2B exchanges were all the rage. The anticipated revenue opportunities of cooperating business exchange hubs were impressive at the time and the *potential* certainly outweighed the *practical* in that aspect. The notion of business-to-business was not new then and is not new now. It is indeed, however, inevitable. Businesses will find the most optimal ways to engage in commerce or risk extinction. Because of these forces, technologies that truly succeed at B2B will prevail. Web services provides another hopeful chance at catalyzing that market. The challenge for businesses is to find ways to seamlessly leverage one another. In today's economy, competition reigns supreme, but in tomorrow's, it may very well be cooperation that reigns supreme.

The Business Case

As with any new technology, the goal is to quickly identify the business opportunities. Web services have a variety of opportunities, both internal and external to business operations. Internally, Web services serves as an ideal integration technology that can expedite the coupling of applications and systems together. By bearing the upfront cost of converting existing application services to Web services, cost savings can be reaped in future combinations, deployments, and integration projects, as well as external monetization of such services. If delivering applications and/or e-services is core to your business model, it will become strategic to maneuver quickly and offer specialized applications to fickle customers and their needs.

Wherein Lies the ROI?

Where can you expect to find return on investment with the adoption of Web services technologies? A compelling case was made earlier on why the underlying technologies are an improvement over prior approaches. We further expanded on the general appeal of the Web services platform as a whole and even presented some of the impacts to business this exciting movement will present. A solid cost-benefit analysis might reveal some of the following ROI elements. A few observations provide clues as to where the initial returns might be found.

- A unified service architecture can lower the cost of future integration projects.
- A unified service architecture can facilitate new products and services more quickly.
- Exposing internal services can lead to monetizing functional aspects of the business.
- Exposing internal services can lead to automatic commerce, which can raise the ceiling on transaction volume.
- Automatic supply-side management can streamline complex business networks.

These are just a few ways of looking at the Web service landscape. For each, there is a cost involved and that is the cost of turning existing assets and functions into Web services. The perception, then, is that these services can be offered more readily to customers or trading partners alike. This requires that such a demand already exist, and for most large companies this is true. Many resources that exist within large companies are not commonly made available so that other parts of the company can uniformly discover and take advantage of them. Making this possible should impact ongoing efforts to streamline systems and react to changing business needs. ROI exists in many facets of this process; compressing time is certainly one key portion of it.

Doesn't This Sound a Bit Like B2B?

The quick uprising of B2B was mirrored equally by its quick demise, but did it really die, or just lose its media appeal? B2B companies sought to provide an exchange haven for supply-side integration. That is, coupling suppliers with consumers. In complex supply chain management, the act of search, discovery, integration, and management was laborious and human-driven. B2B exchange hubs sought to automate this process by providing a common platform via which entities can register, be discovered, and couple into commerce-related transactions. So this sounds very similar to aspects of Web services and ebXML. Why did B2B lose favor as a lucrative marketspace? There are many opinions on why this happened, so let's take a closer look.

B2B exchanges made their money by tolling transactions and selling their software directly to businesses wanting to participate in collaborative commerce. A similar problem existed when the telephone was introduced. In the early days of the telephone, people were skeptical about paying for it because no one had them, so they couldn't call anyone. Likewise, a B2B exchange is useful only after a critical mass is achieved and enough participants exist to provide a comfortable level of choice and automation. If only one supplier of a particular good exists in the exchange, companies lose the ability to choose and micro-monopolies might emerge. Not a favorable condition, indeed.

Therefore, until those critical masses appeared, the B2B users—which is to say, the companies—bore a cost. That cost was necessary to keep the B2B exchanges operating and came well in advance of profits bound to that cost. If the cost is not offset by some gain, it will not return on the investment. If a technology does not show a positive outlook, potential, or trend, especially in economically tough times, it will be momentarily abandoned. This is one take on the evolution of B2B. Businesses will indeed continue to seek ways to automate their operations, but only if the costs are overshadowed by the return. For this to happen, a middle-man company like a B2B exchange may not be needed.

Companies will soon have the capability to direct their own inter-business discovery and coupling in ways more automated and expansive than even the B2B exchanges did. Removing the middle-man might be the missing ingredient needed for companies to endure the necessary growth period before complex and profitable business Webs emerge. However, this remains to be seen. The hope is that the recurring costs of owning or providing Web services are less than those involved in exchange hub membership. However, in both cases, the need must exist and drive businesses to adopt coupling technologies like Web services, which are non-proprietary, open, and accepted.

Business Directions and Perspectives

This chapter has discussed the rationale behind Web services from a technical and business perspective and has even presented some thoughts on where the ROI might exist for companies adopting Web services as a corporate technical solution. In the future, some companies will see a real business opportunity by the new Web services landscape. This translates into new kinds of businesses as well as new ways to address old problems.

Service Chain Integration

As indicated, Web services will provide a valuable unifying platform to re-deliver services and provide new streamlined applications. However, beyond the internal uses of Web services lie the external opportunities. The idea of provisioning information as a subscription or service is entirely not new. We are all familiar with various forms of information subscription, in both hard and soft mediums.

So called "data marts" deliver information streams and databases as a service over the internet. Often, the information is delivered or retrieved as static content, and is often aged by the time it reaches a human. Specialized data marts aggregate related data across different databases and offer specialized information to vertical markets such as finance, health care, or textiles.

Aggregation and provisioning is often an important contribution to data-sensitive markets. The world of Web services now deals with the sharing and publishing of *active processes* between organizations. "Active processes" refers to the business's functional aspects or behavior. This seems a natural evolution—one from the *static* to the *active*.

The idea of *service aggregation* refers to the method of combining existing services into new services. Composite services should be easier to both access and discover. The value-add the service aggregator provides is in the provisioning of specialized services. Because the complex effort involved has already been completed, it is more attractive.

Most of us are already familiar with supply chains, which represent a network comprised of providers and consumers of goods. For example, when you buy a cheeseburger, there are many companies (and their products) involved in the ultimate assembly of cheeseburgers, which must occur economically. In the realm of Web services and service integration, we refer to this same concept as *service chain integration*. The idea is the same, except instead of buns, cheese and meat patties moving down the chain, it is service interactions (and specifically Web service interactions).

Figure 2.3 represents a model showing various providers coupled together into service chains. Across the same set of providers (and subsets of them) there can be a variety of different service chains offering different aggregate services. These service chains are indicated by a different number to convey overlapping interactions between provider networks.

Some service providers aggregate services offered by other providers and therefore appear to offer many services, which are actually invoked across the service chain and not by the sole service provider. Requestors will typically be unaware of this complexity and that is a service to them.

FIGURE 2.3
Service chain integration.

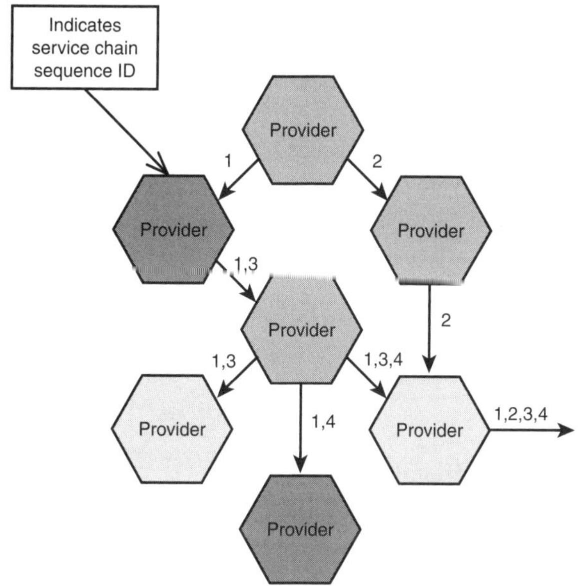

The Web services platform will now allow business processes to be linked together in ad hoc ways. In the external world, businesses use a variety of means to find each other and do business cooperatively. So, consider this for a moment: If you were running a small wordworking shop that specializes in doghouses and were in search of lumber suppliers, you might start by looking through the Yellow Pages. You are likely to also phone one or more of the suppliers you found and discuss aspects of their goods and services such as cost, type, delivery methods, and so on. When you found one that agreed with your requirements you might initiate a process exchange. For each doghouse specially ordered, you might fill out a specific document requesting the necessary lumber cut for the new doghouse. Maybe you phone the order in to expedite it. Upon delivery, you typically get receipts and sign further documents.

These processes, however common, are not terribly automated. If this could be streamlined to occur on demand and the time intervals could be minimized, more transactions can be processed and hence more revenue generated. However, the cost per transaction must be low and the system maintenance costs must not overbear the additional revenue generated.

The WSP—Web Service Provider

By now, we have all encountered acronyms such as ISP (Internet Service Provider) and ASP (Application Service Provider). WSPs, or Web Service Providers, might soon emerge as well. WSPs are companies whose service offerings are Web services. No different than data-marts or other broadcasting information services, WSPs can envelope access to disparate information sources and processes and deliver them to customers for immediate application integration. This type of service is also not new; it adds value by bringing together resources and offering them bundled together to more accurately meet customer needs. In this case, customer needs require that such information and business processes be in the form of Web services. Such customers might quickly utilize these services in various ad hoc ways—ways not of particular interest to the WSP. As such, the WSP has the potential to reach many consumers.

Just as we see the mass consumption of information and content for countless vertical markets, interest groups, and communities, eventually such offerings can be leveraged between systems where their ultimate fashion and destination are known only to the consumers along the way.

A Simple WSP Scenario

Consider a WSP that provides financial information on particular sectors within a vertical market. The vertical market is agriculture and the sectors include things such as corn, wheat, and farming equipment. A WSP might find that there is a strong demand for up-to-date information on the volumes of corn and wheat moved between farms and distribution silos. Furthermore, it might provide numbers on the amount consumed for particular regions over that same period of time. This particular WSP also tracks data about farming equipment, which is a different industry than corn or wheat farming, but somewhat related. All the data is connected to the different systems involved in the moving of products and is quite near real time.

These three distinct areas of interest can be gathered by a backend system and accessed through a single service that might exist to assist market researchers interested in the correlations between them.

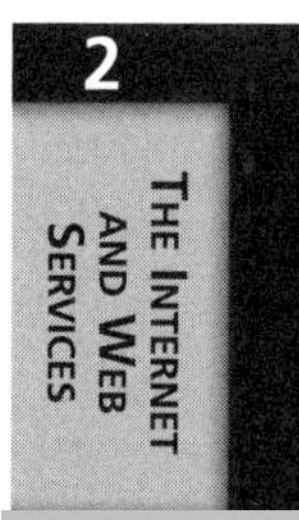

The WSP will likely maintain backend access to a variety of different information sources across sectors, but the advantage is that access to such information and processes can be combined or fashioned to groups or even individual customers according to their desires.

Listing 2.1 shows how such a WSP might expose a set of Web services regarding our scenario.

LISTING 2.1 A complex WSDL descriptor for the WSP scenario.

```
<?xml version="1.0"?>
<definitions name="GetCornWheatTractorFutures"

targetNamespace="http://someagriculture.com/futures.wsdl"
          xmlns:tns="http://someagriculture.com/futures.wsdl"
          xmlns:xsd1="http://someagriculture.com/futures.xsd"
          xmlns:soap="http://schemas.xmlsoap.org/wsdl/soap/"
          xmlns="http://schemas.xmlsoap.org/wsdl/">

    <types>
       <schema targetNamespace="http://someagriculture.com/futures.xsd"
              xmlns="http://www.w3.org/2000/10/XMLSchema">
           <element name="GetCornDataInterval">
              <complexType>
                  <all>
                      <element name="interval" type="string"/>
                  </all>
              </complexType>
           </element>
           <element name="GetCornDataResponse">
              <complexType>
                  <all>
                      <element name="response" type="string"/>
                  </all>
              </complexType>
           </element>
           <element name="GetWheatDataInterval">
              <complexType>
                  <all>
                      <element name=" interval " type="string"/>
                  </all>
              </complexType>
           </element>
           <element name="GetWheatDataResponse">
              <complexType>
                  <all>
                      <element name="response" type="string"/>
                  </all>
              </complexType>
```

LISTING 2.1 continued

```
          </element>
          <element name="GetTractorsDataInterval">
             <complexType>
                 <all>
                     <element name="interval" type="string"/>
                 </all>
             </complexType>
          </element>
          <element name="GetTractorsDataResponse">
             <complexType>
                 <all>
                     <element name="response" type="string"/>
                 </all>
             </complexType>
          </element>
      </schema>
   </types>

   <message name="GetCornDataRequest">
       <part name="body" element="xsd1:GetCornDataInterval"/>
   </message>
   <message name="GetCornDataResponse">
       <part name="body" element="xsd1:GetCornDataResponse"/>
   </message>

   <message name="GetWheatDataRequest">
       <part name="body" element="xsd1:GetWheatDataInterval"/>
   </message>
   <message name="GetWheatDataResponse">
       <part name="body" element="xsd1:GetWheatDataResponse"/>
   </message>

   <message name="GetTractorDataRequest">
       <part name="body" element="xsd1:GetTractorDataInterval"/>
   </message>
   <message name="GetTractorDataResponse">
       <part name="body" element="xsd1:GetTractorDataResponse"/>
   </message>

   <portType name="GetFuturesActivityPortType">
       <operation name="GetCornActivityData">
          <input message="tns:GetCornDataRequest"/>
          <output message="tns:GetCornDataResponse"/>
       </operation>
       <operation name="GetWheatActivityData">
          <input message="tns:GetWheatDataRequest"/>
          <output message="tns:GetWheatDataResponse"/>
       </operation>
       <operation name="GetTractorActivityData">
          <input message="tns:GetTractorDataRequest"/>
```

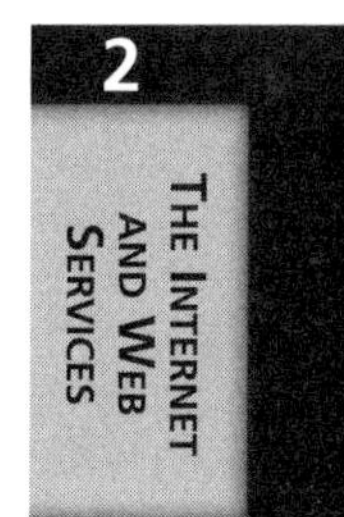

LISTING 2.1 continued

```
        <output message="tns:GetTractorDataResponse"/>
     </operation>
  </portType>

  <binding name="GetFuturesActivitySoapBinding" type="tns:
                                  GetFuturesActivityPortType">
     <soap:binding style="document" transport="http://schemas.xmlsoap.org/
                                  soap/http"/>
     <operation name="GetCornActivityData">
        <soap:operation soapAction="http://someagriculture.com/
                                  GetCornActivityData "/>
        <input>
            <soap:body use="literal"/>
        </input>
        <output>
            <soap:body use="literal"/>
        </output>
     </operation>
     <operation name= "GetWheatActivityData">
        <soap:operation soapAction="http://someagriculture.com/
                                  GetWheatActivityData "/>
        <input>
            <soap:body use="literal"/>
        </input>
        <output>
            <soap:body use="literal"/>
        </output>
     </operation>
     <operation name="GetTractorActivityData">
        <soap:operation soapAction="http://someagriculture.com/
                                  GetTractorActivityData "/>
        <input>
            <soap:body use="literal"/>
        </input>
        <output>
            <soap:body use="literal"/>
        </output>
     </operation>
  </binding>

  <service name="GetFuturesActivityService">
     <documentation>Service for gathering data on corn, wheat
                                  and tractors</documentation>
     <port name="GetFuturesActivityPort" binding=
                                  "tns:GetFuturesActivitySoapBinding">
        <soap:address location="http://someagriculture.com/getfutures"/>
     </port>
  </service>

</definitions>
```

As you can see in the service descriptor, access to corn, wheat, and tractor data is provided by service messages where the request requires an interval—presumably some date range of interest—and the response is a data document of some particular format. For these purposes, this simply illustrates what the service specifies and how it appears in WSDL, which hides the precise implementation details from a would-be requestor.

So why would such a service be useful? Markets produce vast quantities of data and market researchers understand them based on trends in the data, and they often seek complex correlations between different sets of data. Compiling these correlations as well as gathering the data is a difficult and lengthy chore and part of why such results are published quarterly and seldom sooner. If researchers can access WSP services and have those services tailored to provide them with specific streams of data on demand, then building systems to automate the consumption and analysis of this data might be possible. Web services is just one way to approach this, but a way that accommodates a variety of front-end applications from any consumer system.

Vertical Ontologies

An ontology is essentially a taxonomy with relationships. Figure 2.4 is an entity-relation (ER) diagram that presents a simple model for a bird.

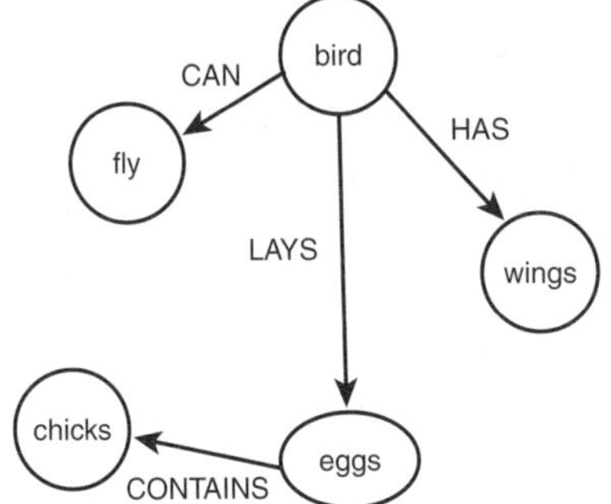

FIGURE 2.4
A simple ontology.

The entities (birds, wings, fly) are bound together by relations (HAS, CAN, LAYS). Semantic networks are generated by interconnected ontologies and serve to provide knowledge in response to queries such as `* HAS wings`, which can be interpreted to mean, "Match any entity that bears the relation `HAS` to the entity `wings`."

Web services are described by sets of metadata that can form the basis for ontological classification of business services. This is useful when you need to provide complex inferencing mechanics across service taxonomies for a particular domain or possibly across domains. For example, the classical syllogism comes to mind:

1. All mammals have hair.
2. A dog has hair.
3. Therefore, a dog is a mammal.

Aristotle claimed that all knowledge was *discovered* from simple logical constructions like this, with the new knowledge being line 3 and premises 1 (minor) and 2 (major) existing prior to it.

Part of the automation hopes of Web services involves a classification scheme that enables the discovery of appropriate services through a variety of means—possibly through direct searching or inferencing mechanisms.

Vertical ontologies are collections of entities and relationships with precise meaning to a group of related requestors and providers in a particular vertical market. Why is this important? As was explained earlier, the requestor bears the responsibility of knowing how to express the request for a particular service. Therefore, the requestor must request precisely, so that a service match is not ambiguous and its accuracy can be determined.

There will exist an inertial force seeking to align the ontologies of requestors and providers such that they become mutually beneficial and enabling. As this trend propagates within particular market segments and verticals, a distillation should occur over time. Competing ontologies do not serve the best interest of the groups involved, because the real goal is to conduct commerce and not to produce complex language schemas.

Therefore, expect to see industries respond in much the same way as they are currently with regards to XML schemas and XML-based message interchange. Much of today's existing DTD and XML schema-based languages will likely be used as a basis for Web service markup and metadata, which, in turn, will be a basis for ontological classification of terms, processes, and business entities.

This is an evolutionary process and one that will likely never be finished. As such, a market's understanding of itself and how it operates to the benefit of the industry as a whole will be in constant motion. Much as corporations seek representation within a standards body for their own strategic needs, expect to see vertically aligned interest groups and standards bodies arise with the goal of defining and governing effective e-commerce ontologies to be used globally. This process has already begun.

Summary

Although the new age of Web services promises to offer a wealth of new business opportunities and Internet application solutions, there are many ancillary issues that need to be resolved first. These include organizing trading Webs that define the language terms (into taxonomies and ontologies) needed to interoperate with other business services. Tools and technologies to facilitate Web service adoption are already on the market, and businesses are evaluating the cost-benefits of the platform. This year, we should begin to see real Web services at play within organizations, with external Web services to follow afterwards.

As this process evolves, the attraction of Web services will grow as well. Similar to the early days of the telephone where early sales were impeded by the dilemma of no one else having phones, so too must Web services overcome the early-adopters paradox. However, the telephone soon became ubiquitous and it is quite possible that Web services will, too.

The next chapter discusses the process involved in becoming a Web services provider.

CHAPTER 3

Becoming a Web Services Provider

by Benoît Marchal

IN THIS CHAPTER

This chapter addresses an aspect of Web services that is still evolving rapidly. Admittedly, the technologies surrounding Web services are not standing still. Far from it! They are being actively developed and they evolve almost daily. Still, the technical road is well mapped out.

In other words, we have a reasonably clear picture of what to expect on that front. For example, there is no doubt that XML and SOAP are the two cornerstones of Web services. However, the vision is less clear for the business model supporting Web services, and this chapter is partly about the said business model.

You see, the problem is that the technology is so new that the industry that benefits from it is still in its infancy. We lack proven examples of working business models.

The business model behind Web services is not a secondary issue, though. In fact, it is my strong belief that developers (that's you) will play a very important role in shaping that market.

Although, as I've just explained, this chapter is more tentative than the technical ones, I hope you will find food for thought as you read it. Read it, criticize it, but, most importantly, do not ignore the issues it covers.

Searching for Practical Examples

Developers have a very important role to play in the adoption of new technologies. Not only do we support the technology, but we also have to educate our organizations in how to best benefit from new developments. The business models supporting Web services are still being written as you read, and you have an important role to play in writing those business models.

Lacking a reliable crystal ball to predict the future, I will turn to past experience to help me shed some light on the future of Web service providers. I know of two markets that are close to what Web services may turn into: EDI (supported by Value-Added Networks) and ISPs (Internet Service Providers). The discussion of ISPs focuses on hosting providers, sometimes also referred to as ASPs (Application Service Providers).

A Look Down Memory Lane: EDI

If you are reading this book, I can safely assume you are familiar with ISPs and Web hosting, but you might not be so familiar with the EDI market. In Chapter 2, "The Internet and Web Services: Changing Business," you were introduced to EDI and how it compares and contrasts to XML as a messaging system. Let me take a moment to further describe the EDI market to you and to explain why it's relevant to Web providers.

EDI stands for *Electronic Data Interchange*. It was originally introduced more than 20 years ago, and it aimed to provide an early form of e-commerce. The exact meaning of e-commerce is lost in hype.

When thinking of e-commerce, most people think of Amazon.com or other online shops. There are more popular and older forms of e-commerce, however. Online shops cater primarily for the business-to-consumer (B2C) side of e-commerce.

The other side is business-to-business (B2B) e-commerce, or the buying, selling, and other commercial transactions that take place between businesses. B2B commerce is less well known than the consumer-oriented side, mainly because it is less visible, more abstract: We shop in various stores (online and offline) every day, but few of us really care where the stores are buying their goods.

Stores (businesses) buying goods from their suppliers (other businesses) is B2B commerce. And the surprise is that it accounts for a very large volume of activity, because behind the supplier there is another supplier, and another, and another.

Let's take an example. You have bought *Java Web Services Unleashed* at a bookstore. The bookstore bought the same book from a distributor. The distributor bought it from Sams. Sams had the book manufactured by a printer. To manufacture the book, the printer bought paper and ink. You get the idea.

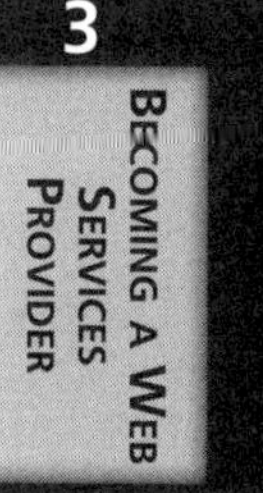

So, for a single, consumer-orientated transaction (you buying the book), there have been several business-to-business transactions. This multiplying effect means that B2B commerce—and consequently, B2B e-commerce—is destined to outnumber consumer activity by a wide margin.

Electronic Data Interchange Concepts

Probably the oldest form of e-commerce is EDI, which is solely concerned with B2B e-commerce. The idea behind EDI is very simple: To do business, companies have to exchange enormous amounts of paperwork. Let's replace the paperwork with electronic files.

For example, if my company decides to buy goods from yours, we'll issue a purchase order. We also expect the goods to come with an invoice. To pay the invoice, we might cut a check.

Do we write these documents with a pen and paper? Unlikely—most companies use some sort of accounting software (anything from QuickBooks to SAP) that tracks orders, invoices, and payments.

Take the following test: Go to the mail department and watch as the clerks shift through the morning mail. You will find that most documents are printed by a computer (and incidentally, you'll understand why Intuit makes so much money selling checkbooks), most of them by the sender's ERP (Enterprise Resource Planning). Follow the paper trail and you'll find the same documents are being routed to…your own ERP!

So the process is to print commercial documents, send them by postal mail and key them in at the receiving end. The paperwork and all the manual processing it requires is a small annoyance for small corporations like mine, but it's a major cost for larger organizations.

More than 20 years ago, some companies realized they could simplify things by building a more direct link between the two accounting software systems. Instead of spitting out a paper purchase order, my computer produces a file. I can e-mail you the file and you can feed it straight into your accounting package. No paper or postal mail is involved, and it's better than regular e-mail because the commercial documents are automatically imported.

Some of the benefits of EDI include:

- Electronic documents take less time to exchange and process.
- Typing and re-typing the same document is a major cause of errors (for example, it's easy to type 10,000 instead of 100,000). Electronic documents eliminate the retyping and associated errors.
- Processing electronic documents requires less human resources.

How big is EDI? According to Forrester Research, B2B e-commerce (comprising EDI and Internet transactions) is valued at $671 billion in 1998. Why don't we hear more about it? One of the reasons may be that most transactions take place on private networks, not the Internet. In fact, Internet transactions represented only $92 billion.

Most transactions taking place on private networks are not based on XML. Instead they use the EDI specific-formats, such as UN/EDIFACT and ANSI X12.

EDI and Web Services Compared

Do you see the similarities between EDI and Web services? Beyond the obvious technical differences (private networks as opposed to the Internet, obscure file formats as opposed to XML), both intend to automate and improve the flow of information between corporations.

Lacking a better frame of reference, Web service providers can learn a lot from more than 20 years of EDI experience. You'll read about some of these issues in a moment, but I also want to highlight two features that distinguish EDI from Web services:

- EDI is capital-intensive.
- EDI focuses on cost savings.

Setting up an EDI infrastructure is pricey, which partly explains why it is not more popular. EDI really was designed for large corporations doing business frequently. It lacks the agility of e-commerce on the Internet. In contrast, Web-based solutions, such as Web services, are more affordable and can be deployed more quickly.

EDI focuses exclusively on cost savings; its aim is to reduce the amount of paperwork so that business can be done more efficiently. However, reducing costs is only one half of its impact. It also enables new ways of doing business. For example, because an electronic order is sent and processed in minutes instead of days for its paper counterpart, it is possible to keep less inventory and re-order more frequently. This in turn frees financial resources.

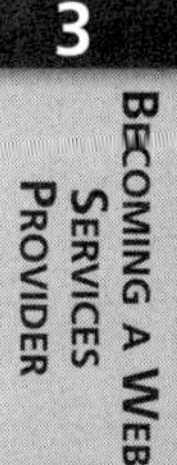

Keep these differences in mind as you review the EDI experience. Despite the differences, there are two important lessons to learn from EDI:

- It is crucial to document the application and, more specifically, its APIs properly. Documentation is important in any software project, but it is even more important when the project involves the IT departments of two or more companies.

  This is a very important topic but, fortunately, one that is well addressed by Web services standards. Turn to Chapter 11, "WSDL," for coverage of this all-important topic.
- The more partners that can join the exchange—in other words, the larger the community surrounding a Web service—the more valuable it becomes. In practice, it means that Web services should be cheap to implement and cheap to deploy. Although that may not be the case yet, past Internet experiences show that we can expect a lowering of the entry costs.

Web Service Availability

Over the last few years, I participated in several projects that helped me sharpen my vision of what Web services should look like in the future. Here's the vision: the transparent Web services economy.

The Internet and Transparent Markets

One of the fundamental laws of a capitalist economy is that a transparent market—one where every player has access to all product and pricing information—is the ideal market. The transparent market will, over time, converge towards the best pricing for the best products with the best level of services.

That's the economic theory, at least. In practice, it is very difficult to create transparent markets. The stock market and, possibly, eBay are the best approximations we know of. Yet the theory is useful in guiding our actions. For example, the antitrust laws are derived directly from this theory.

When it comes to the Internet, you can read this law in many interesting ways—particularly if you are a proponent of open software and open standards. This section applies these principles to Web services. Web services are a fertile soil for the development of a transparent market and ultimately more e-commerce solutions.

Technically speaking, Web services are based on open standards (HTML, HTTP, SMTP). Open standards enable anybody, no matter what computer he or she uses, to join and participate in the online economy.

Conversely, other forms of e-commerce have not achieved widespread adoption because they failed to build a transparent market. EDI (Electronic Data Interchange) is a prime example: It is a good idea and one that works. However, it never captured a significant market share because it is a relatively closed club with such high membership dues that few businesses can afford to join.

For Small Business, Too

The involvement of all businesses, no matter how big or small, is crucial to the development of a transparent market. Small businesses, although they seldom make the front page of magazines, are the bread and butter of the U.S. and European economies. They provide the dynamism that the market needs as they develop new products, challenge established players and strive to grow or, more simply, are content to exploit a useful niche.

However, for small businesses to participate in any market, the price must be right; small businesses have small means. Fortunately, on the Internet, the price is right. Internet access is so cheap no business can afford not to have it.

Furthermore, Web sites rent for low monthly fees and good editors can turn anybody into a passable Webmaster. Even building a fully-fledged online shop is cheap: Most ISPs offer shopping carts at reasonable rates. And for those who prefer to join an established mall, there's Amazon's zShops and similar offerings from Yahoo! and Lycos.

The Transparent Web Service Economy

Yet, so far, the Internet is geared towards B2C e-commerce, as opposed to B2B e-commerce. This is mostly because the standards it supports are geared toward end users. A Web site is intended for human consumption. It works well with a consumer that does his own shopping manually. It does not work so well with B2B e-commerce because a Web site can't interface with ERP packages and the other software used within the organization.

What is required to build a successful business market online? Again, the most successful market is a transparent market. Experience has shown that the technical equivalent of a transparent market is open standards. On the Internet, for B2B e-commerce, open standards mean XML and Web services.

This leads me to what I call the Web service economy, which is simply a B2B online market. To be successful, such a market must be transparent or, technically, built on XML and other Web standards. In the Web service economy, any business—small/big, Windows/Macintosh/Linux/PalmOS/AS400—can participate at a reasonable cost.

We're not there yet. The closest things today are XML marketplaces such as Ariba or mySAP. However, they are closed technically and expensive to join. With the advent of Web service standards and their availability in software development tools, you should expect that, in the next 2-4 years, closed solutions will gradually be replaced by Web services.

The same transformation happened in the consumer arena. Until 1996-1997, if you had asked any Web designer to build an online shop, he or she would have turned to his or her programmer's editor and written one for you. Few businesses could afford it. In 1997, the same person could have sold you a packaged product. Not a custom-made shop, but a standard product that lacked few features when compared to Amazon.com. It was not exactly cheap, yet (most of those products cost between $3,500 and $10,000), but it was already cheaper than a custom-built solution. Furthermore, the products were more powerful and better tested than custom-built solutions.

Today most ISPs offer shopping carts for $50-$200 per month. HTML editors, such as NetObjects, enable you to edit and manage your shop from your desktop. Many proprietary solutions, such as ActiveX, have come and gone. The winners have succeeded because they were built on transparent solutions.

Finding Web Services Applications

Web service providers will look for Web services applications proactively. In doing so, it is essential that they look not only at how to automate existing solutions but also at how to take advantage of the nature of Web services to rethink the business model.

When ISPs launched, they sold their services as cheaper alternatives to familiar products. Web sites were sold as cheaper and more widely distributed marketing brochures. Likewise, e-mail was marketed a cheaper and faster replacement to postal mail.

There's some truth in there, but it misses interesting points. For example, Web sites can do more than marketing brochures. Web sites are also effective solutions to distribute up-to-the-minute information on products, such as their availability.

E-mail does more than traditional postal mail, too. Because it is both cheaper and faster, it enables more interactive communications with customers.

Looking for Opportunities

When looking for Web services opportunities, it is essential that you realize that they can do more than just automate existing procedures. Web services can deliver new forms of doing business.

When I was studying computer science, our teachers told us that unless we worked for a software editor or a hardware manufacturer, we would work in a cost center. At the time I didn't know what a cost center was, but here's how it was explained to me: The accounting department is a typical cost center. It costs money to pay the accountant and his or her secretary's salaries, but they contribute nothing to the bottom line. The law—not to mention good business sense—requires a company to account for its revenues and expenses, so it needs an accountant, but the accountant does not generate value. An accountant works only to support the other, moneymaking departments. A cost center is an expense that is accepted as part of the cost of doing business, but that does not contribute to total income.

As a young computer scientist, I was facing a life as a cost of doing business. Indeed, it makes good business sense to install software and automate as much of the administrative tasks as possible, but it does not contribute to the company's earnings. Computers can also dramatically lower the expenses, but reducing the costs in other departments is not, by itself, a revenue-making activity.

This line of reasoning, common at the time, has led to the widespread belief that IT departments exist solely to serve the other departments. I meet many computer scientists who adopt this point of view. They use words like "the business comes first" where "the business" stands for "the money-making departments."

That is true, but only up to a certain point. More specifically, that was a very sensible attitude 10 years ago when IT was mostly used to process information more efficiently. Today, with the advent of the Internet, IT is a new opportunity in its own right and, as developers, we have to help our users recognize this.

For an information-driven company, computer systems are like factories in the industrial age: the flesh and blood of the business. In the Industrial Age, businessmen would invest in good factories. Although building factories was expensive—a very serious cost indeed—a factory was also the foundation of the business.

We need to view IT in the same light. Computer systems are the flesh and blood of tomorrow's powerhouses. The dotcom failures are a keen reminder that creating cool technology is not enough to demonstrate good business sense, and that turning a profit remains a business priority. However, it makes sense to treat IT, and Web services in particular, as opportunities to grow the business.

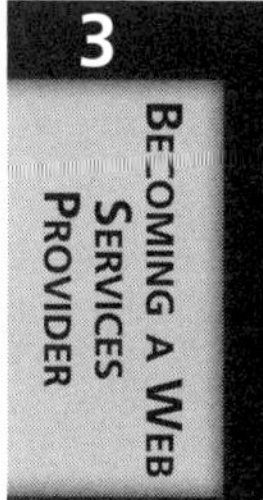

Want proof? I lack the space for a detailed explanation, but look at distributors and supermarkets. To turn a profit they need more than good stores (the Industrial Age investment); they need to manage the logistics efficiently. This, in turn, requires computer systems (the Information Age investment).

Why It Matters

For an example, look at ordering and inventory management. Typically a manufacturer learns about the sales of its products through the orders from its resellers.

Suppose your company produces office chairs and you launch a new model of chair. How do you find how well the new chair sells? You can infer it is doing well if you receive frequent re-orders from your resellers. You might suppose it is not doing so well if your orders are low.

That's indirect information. It's useful, but not as useful as the direct sales information collected by your resellers. For example, reseller sales might be disappointing, but more detailed information would reveal that the chair is doing extremely well in certain markets. Re-ordering by resellers also always lags behind actual sales, which does not help with planning production efficiently. For example, you might refrain from producing new chairs because the initial sales have been low and risk running out of stock when sales finally pick up.

Web services offer opportunities to manage sales reports more efficiently. For example, a Web service could give you instant access to the sales information at the resellers' point. Instead of learning about the sales with a delay from a few weeks to several months, you could follow sales almost in real time and better adapt chair production.

Different Web Service Providers

If you look at the markets for ISPs and EDI, you'll find that different types of services are being provided. It is likely that similar roles will also evolve to support Web services:

- Tool vendors, whose companies offer tools that enable the other parties to work. For example, HTML editors provide tools that help Web site developers in their businesses. With EDI, the tool vendors offer so-called "EDI translators."

  With Web services, the vendors are different and their products are more sophisticated (application servers), but the need to offer products remains.
- Developers, in the broadest sense of the term. These are the companies (and sometimes individuals) that build the Web sites or design the EDI interface. They may be part of the IT division or they may be subcontractors.

  Similarly, you should expect a lively development industry will develop for Web services.
- Host providers and Value-Added Networks (VANs). (The latter is popular in the EDI industry.) They are responsible for running and maintaining the Web site or the EDI network.

  Given the complexity of Web services, you should expect that companies will specialize in offering those services.

  Note that hosting comes in different sizes and flavors, from hosts that serve the largest publishers (for example, Akamai, `http://www.akamai.com`) to hosts that serve the SoHo markets (for example, Pair Networks, `http://www.pair.com`). (SoHo stands for Small Office/Home Office businesses.)

Web Services for Smaller Businesses

I cannot stress enough the importance of providing services for small businesses. So far, the Web service industry has concentrated on the largest players. For example, application servers cost several thousands of dollars—way out of reach to the smallest organizations.

Yet the Web has grown in popularity because it was accessible to every company, no matter its size. For Web services to develop, they will have to be similarly accessible.

Again, it is interesting to compare this with the evolution of EDI. EDI started as a solution for large organizations: Banks, car manufacturers, and utilities were among the early adopters. Only those companies could afford to build and run an EDI system. However, one of the things they learned quickly is that to do commerce you need at least two parties: the buyer and the supplier. Likewise, to do commerce electronically, you need at least two parties that can interact electronically. The technology has to support this and, frankly, EDI has never been very successful in that respect.

It is interesting to notice that this lack of success with small enterprises happens despite the fact that a large subsegment of the EDI industry focuses on enabling the smallest organizations to participate in the process. (However, its primary motive is to find partners for the largest corporations.)

A capability to reach out to the broadest base of partners, and therefore to provide affordable services, has been a key differentiating factor between various EDI providers. It has also been a key element in the success or failure of EDI projects.

There are no reasons to believe things will be different with Web services. If you are looking for a profitable segment in which to specialize, you might consider enabling Web services for the small and medium-sized organizations.

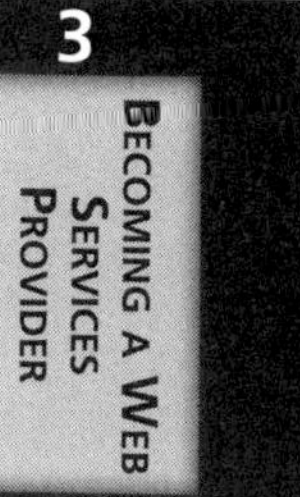

Preparing for the Future

With the enthusiastic adoption of Web services standards, products, and protocols, there's little doubt that Web services will be an integral part of our online future.

For Consultants and Developers

If you're a consultant or a developer, you're doing the right thing by reading this book. Soon your customers or your users will ask you to integrate Web service aspects in their Web sites, so you have to learn and get ready right now.

As you plan your strategy, keep these issues in mind:

- Transparent markets always win, so it pays to encourage your customers and users to stick to the standards. If you develop your Web services in Java, you have the guarantee that they will remain open and available to the largest user base possible.
- Be prepared to adopt tools and packaged products as they become available. For early projects, you may have to use crude tools to develop the applications. However, expect that packaged solutions will become available over time, and be ready to adopt them when they offer a competitive advantage (that is, they lower the cost).

- Your customers and users may need help to identify the best solutions to deploy services. You will need to use your experience as a trained developer to point to them where savings may occur.

Small Businesses

Most small businesses are well advised to continue deploying the Internet and wait before joining the Web service revolution. This is still a time for pioneers, and it is expensive to be a pioneer.

Large Corporations

Large corporations should plan their move toward Web services right now. The market is maturing quickly; standards are available and development tools are better and more usable every day. Now is the time to stake your claim.

As you plan your solution, remember the economic laws. The transparent market wins. You should resist vendors who try to lock you into their proprietary solutions. You may benefit in the short term, but it will hurt your medium- to long-term developments.

Also keep in mind that revamping existing business processes as Web services may not offer the most economic advantages. It is more advantageous to look for issues that are improperly addressed by the current technology and take advantage of the new integration facilities that Web services offer to build a better solution.

The earlier discussion on using Web services for real-time inventory is a good example of this line of thought. In this example, the company looks for innovative services (in this case, offering real-time access to previously unavailable data) instead of simply automating the existing processes (such as the ordering process).

Software Vendors

Software vendors that sell to business users should also look at integrating Web services. The demand will come and it will come soon. Again, it pays to remember that proprietary solutions will hurt you in the long run, so stick to open ones.

An interesting benefit of Web services for software vendors is that it enables them to offer services to their customers, as well as to software, which may mean new revenues.

For example, suppose you sell software to chemical laboratories. Your software helps them track analysis results. You could enhance the software with a Web service solution that, for example, would let laboratory customers check on the progress of their tests. Your software already collects the data, and it is a simple issue to distribute it through a new mechanism.

What should you include in the next product upgrade? You might want to consider adding a Web server to your software. The Web server would let the laboratories publish the information your application is collecting (as the preceding paragraph explained) as a Web service. You could also start selling a tracking application to customers of the laboratories. The tracking application would use the Web service to interact with the laboratory and report the results of their test batches. So far, Web services mean you have sold upgrades to your flagship product and, maybe, a new lighter application to the customers of the laboratories, but you could do better.

Laboratories are probably not really interested in managing the Web services. They would most likely be happy to let another party (that may be you or a third party) operate the Web service. This is particularly true if you recall that a Web service may require stringent security measures that the laboratory may not know how to implement properly.

Offering this hosting option (either directly or through partner hosts) creates yet another source of revenue for you. Better still, the revenue is a recurring one: every month you will be paid to manage the service.

ISPs and ASPs

If you currently sell hosting, Web services is a chance to offer more services to your customers. Initially, you will need to offer access to an application server, such as Tomcat (`http://jakarta.apache.org`), WebLogic (`http://www.bea.com`), JBoss (`http://www.jboss.org`) or WebSphere (`http://www.ibm.com`). Over time, expect to offer packaged Web service applications, such as the laboratory solution introduced in the previous subsections.

Summary

Web services offer new opportunities to Web developers such as yourself. As you work on enabling Web services in your organization, it is essential you keep two issues in mind:

- You can deploy Web services to automate existing processes, but it will be more advantageous to look for new opportunities that Web services enable.
- Proprietary, closed systems do not mix well with Web services. In this brave new world of open access to information, the most benefits are derived from open systems.

The next chapter begins the discussion of how to build Web services.

CHAPTER 4

Building Web Services with Java

By Robert Brunner

IN THIS CHAPTER

In Chapters 2 and 3, "The Internet and Web Services: Changing Business" and "Becoming a Web Services Provider," you should have gained a better appreciation of just what Web services are all about and why they are so popular. But now you might just be wondering why you would want to use Java to build Web services. After all, other options do exist; you could use Perl, Python, or Microsoft .NET.

The simple answer is that Java provides the perfect complement to XML: one provides a portable data format, the other a portable language format. With Java you have a wide range of Enterprise APIs (Application Programming Interfaces) that enable you to easily connect to databases, interact with messaging services, or connect to legacy systems.

The Java approach is to provide the developer with maximum power and flexibility. You can select the best virtual machine that satisfies your needs, the best JDBC driver implementation, the best J2EE server, the best Web server, or even the best hardware and operating system. If you later change your mind, you can easily modify your application, often without any code changes.

This chapter looks in more detail at some of the Java building blocks that can be used to build Web services.

Web Services Architecture

Before jumping into the specific Java tools that you can use to build Web services, you need to examine the different types of Web service architectures that you might utilize. This chapter explores two categories. You use the first category of architecture to build new applications that are exposed, at least in part, via a Web service. The other option involves exposing existing applications via a Web service.

By all accounts, business-to-business communications will be one of the dominant application areas for the deployment of Web services. This should be especially true early on in the growth of Web services, because it is easier to make two applications communicate successfully than it is to do the same with a server and a myriad of clients. As an example, a company might want to join an online market. Part of the entrance requirement might be to implement a Web service that provides a product listing. This sort of application would follow a server-to-server communication path, as shown in Figure 4.1.

FIGURE 4.1
A server-to-server communication example for a Web service architecture. In this model, the Web service is a new application.

A particular business might want to extend this application to enable individuals to connect to the product listing Web service directly. In this case, the client server architecture provides business-to-consumer communication. In this model, unlike a HTML application, the server isn't able to control how the service appears to the client. Instead, the service would need to follow an industry-standard approach that enables a client to "shop" at different online markets, as demonstrated in Figure 4.2.

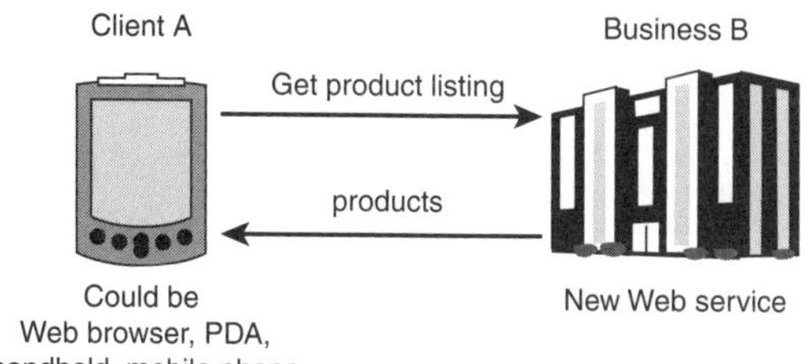

FIGURE 4.2
A client-to-server communication example for a Web service architecture. In this model, the Web service is a new application, but the client can now change services by utilizing industry standards.

If a business doesn't want to follow the two-tier model laid out in the previous example, the other option is to employ a middle tier, which sits between the new Web service—for example, the product listing service—and the client. Although this introduces extra complexity, it does enable the Web service to be customized for different types of clients. For example, a wireless client might want to utilize WML, whereas a high-bandwidth client might prefer a Swing application, as demonstrated in Figure 4.3.

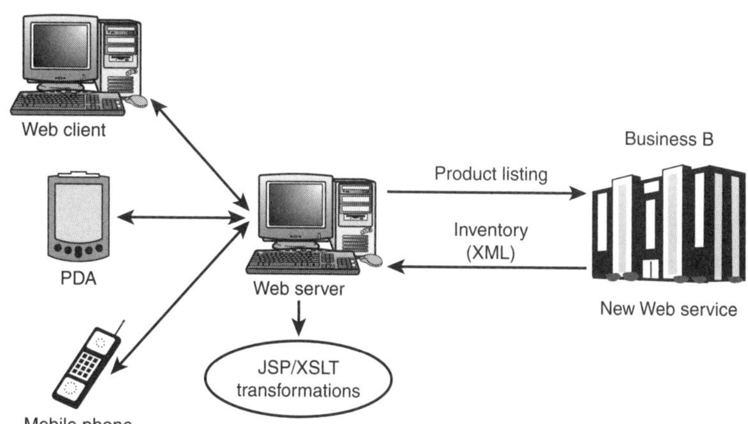

FIGURE 4.3
A client-to-server communication example that utilizes a middle tier to customize the Web service to the client's needs and capabilities.

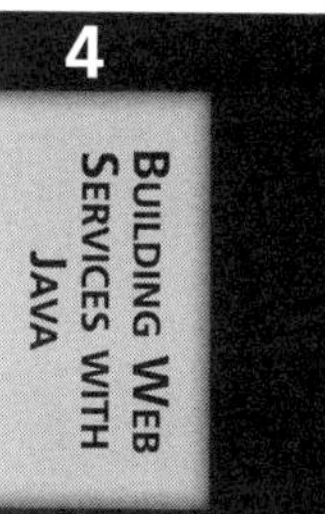

At the other end of the spectrum are the vast quantities of existing services that are written in everything from COBOL to C to C++ and even Java. Businesses will not want to, and may not be able to, abandon these legacy applications. Instead, they will want to wrap them in a Web service blanket that enables them to be exposed to a myriad of new clients. This model applies in all three of the previous cases as well, as shown in Figure 4.4.

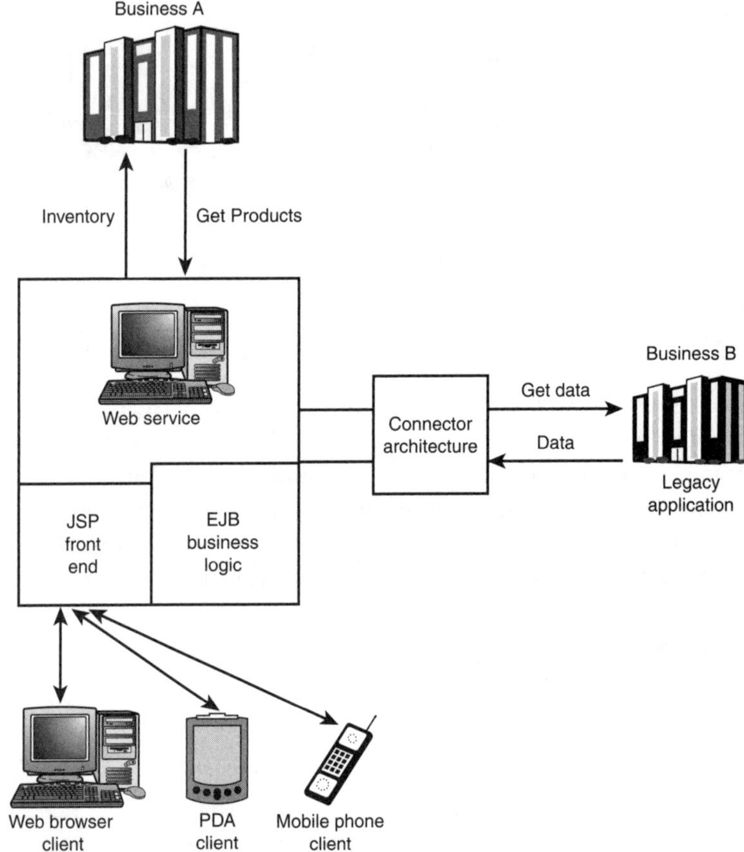

FIGURE 4.4
Existing legacy applications can be wrapped into Web services, allowing corporations to leverage existing services as they migrate to an online communication model.

No matter which the fundamental architecture is employed to build your Web service, however, Java is the perfect language to use. From the wide support for Enterprise requirements to the rich interactive user interfaces, Java has something for everyone. With the widespread adoption of Java among the software community, and the competition between vendors to satisfy the needs of the developer, you couldn't ask for a better solution.

Java Building Blocks

The one constant in developing Web service applications is the requirement for a server application that either implements, wraps, or exposes the desired service. Java provides an excellent framework for building server applications, as evidenced by the JigSaw, Jetty, and Tomcat servers, all Java, all free.

Downloading and Installing Tomcat

To demonstrate using Java to build Web services, we will use the Tomcat server, which provides the reference implementation for the servlet and JSP specifications. Tomcat is developed by Jakarta, a project of the Apache Software Foundation. The main page for the Jakarta project (`http://jakarta.apache.org`) contains information on a variety of popular open source Java tools, including Tomcat, Junit, and Ant.

The Tomcat server is the official reference implementation for the JSP and Servlet specifications. This is important for two reasons. First, there are multiple versions of Tomcat, applicable to different specifications, so you need to be careful when downloading to ensure that you get the correct version. Second, if a Web application works on Tomcat, it must work on any other server that is compliant with the specification (otherwise the other server wouldn't be compliant).

The Tomcat developers have assembled on the Web site a large amount of well written information that describes the server, its installation, as well as instructions for developing and deploying applications that use Tomcat. In this book, we use version 4 of Tomcat.

To simplify installation, you'll probably want to download a binary version of the Tomcat server. If you click on the Binaries link under Download on the Tomcat home page, you are taken to the main Jakarta binary download page, shown in Figure 4.5. From here you need to scroll down until you find the latest release build of the version 4 Tomcat server. Because Tomcat is an open source project, you have access to any version of the server, including development milestones as well as nightly builds. Unless you are very adventurous, you should stick to only the release builds.

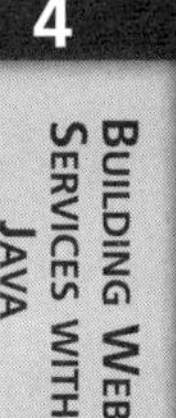

Following this link takes you to the Tomcat release build download page, shown in Figure 4.6. This Web site allows you to access the source package for the Tomcat server, RPM packages to install Tomcat on a Linux system, as well as binary packages. The rest of the Web page contains useful information regarding the Tomcat package.

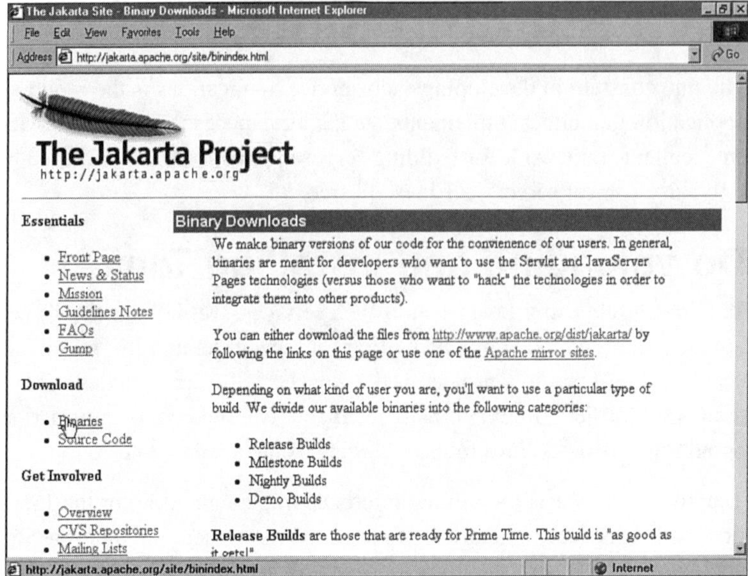

FIGURE 4.5
The primary Jakarta download Web site.

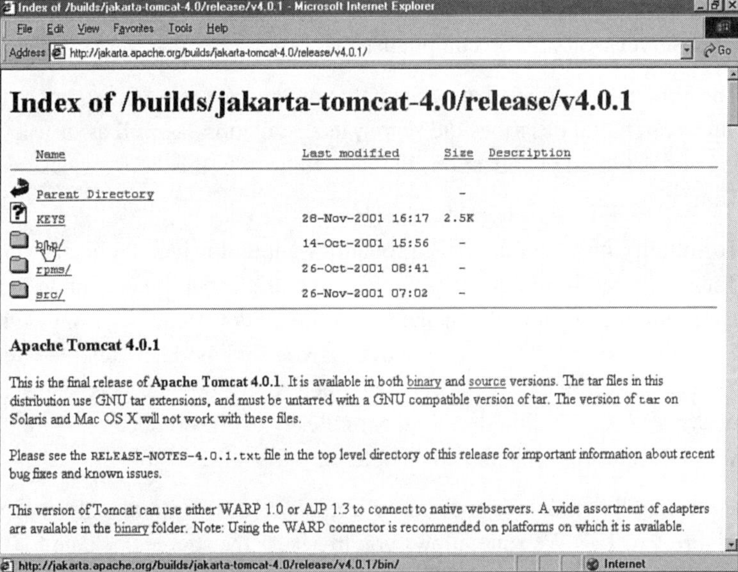

FIGURE 4.6
The primary Tomcat download Web site.

If you are working on Linux, follow the RPMS link and download and install the server appropriately. To actually access the software for Windows, however, you should click on the BIN folder, which takes you to the binary download directory shown in Figure 4.7.

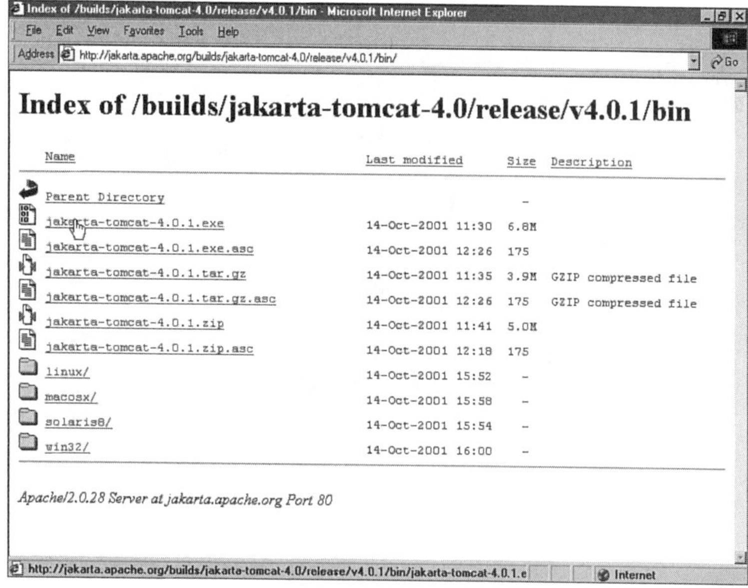

FIGURE 4.7
The Tomcat binary package download Web site.

From here, you can download either a Windows executable that eases installation, or a Zip package containing the Tomcat server. If you already have Java installed, the executable approach is the easiest, because it installs everything and adds Start and Stop icons to your desktop. Alternatively, you can download the Zip file and install the server by unzipping the package into an appropriate directory. If you follow this approach, you will end up with a Tomcat directory hierarchy, as shown in Figure 4.8.

Becoming Familiar with Tomcat

At this point, you have successfully installed the Tomcat server. Before you jump into the next section, however, a brief overview of working with Tomcat is in order. First, the start and stop scripts (either shell script or batch files) are in the `bin` subdirectory. Configuration information, which you won't need to worry about, is located in the `conf` directory. To simplify deployment, you drop new Web applications into the `webapps` folder, and include a customized deployment descriptor, called `web.xml`. Finally, before JSP pages can be served to a client, they need to be compiled, which the Tomcat server does for you automatically. The intermediate files are generated in the `work` directory.

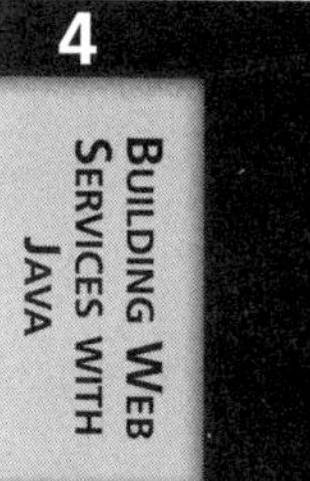

To start the Tomcat server, you need to run the startup script, located in the `bin` directory. After the server is running, open a Web browser and surf to `http://localhost:8080/`. If you see the welcome screen shown in Figure 4.9, you are in business. Otherwise, retrace your steps, and make sure you have an appropriate JDK installed on your system.

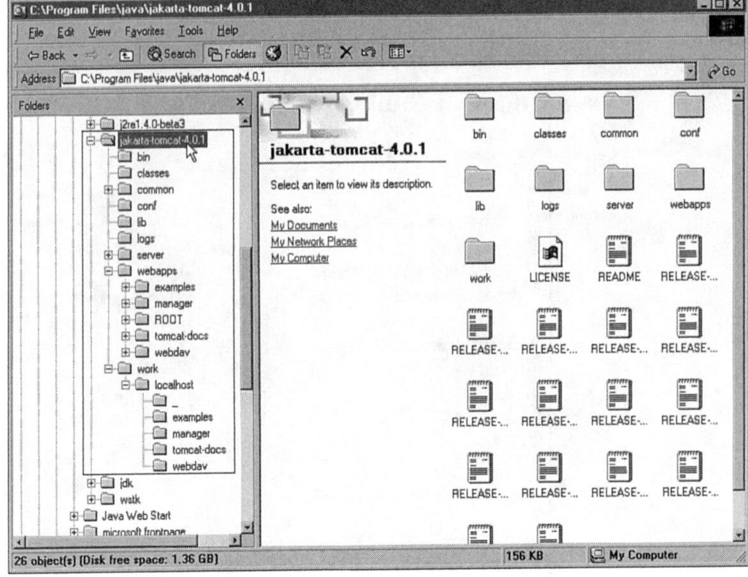

FIGURE 4.8
The directory structure for the Tomcat installation.

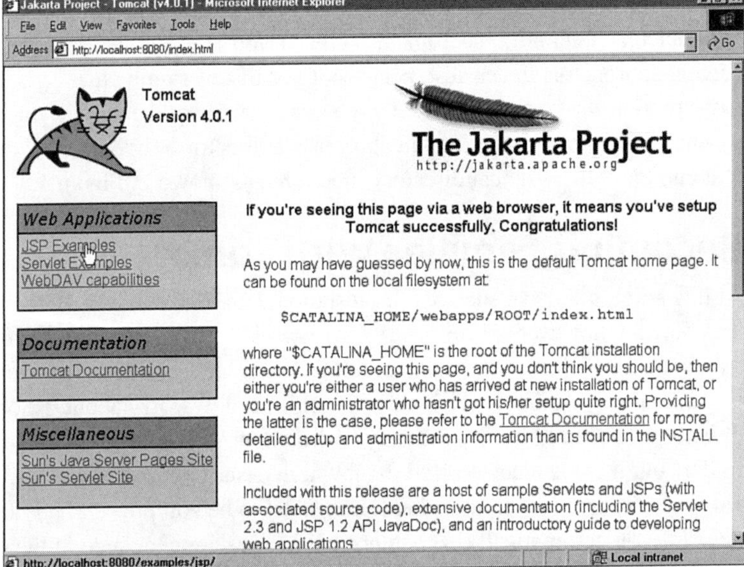

FIGURE 4.9
The Tomcat welcome page, showing that you have successfully installed and started the Tomcat server.

The Tomcat server comes with several JSP and servlet examples. If you follow the example links from the Tomcat welcome page, you can either test these examples out or see the example source code. Feel free to play with these examples; the actual source code is located in the `examples` subdirectory of the `webapps` folder. If you change a servlet after recompiling the Java file, you need to stop and restart the server so that the new classes are reloaded. You know all about starting the server; stopping it is just as easy. The shutdown script, also in the `bin` directory, shuts the server down properly and releases any acquired resources.

Note

When you run a server on a continuously live Internet connection—such as a cable modem or DSL connection—you are possibly opening yourself up to being attacked, especially if you are not behind a firewall. Unless you have taken proper security measures, don't leave a server, such as Tomcat, running for long periods of time unattended. Tomcat provides Web service functionality, so anyone with an Internet connection can connect to your server.

Building Services

After you have the Tomcat server installed, you can start to look at the Java technologies that enable Web services. This section first briefly mentions the Enterprise APIs that are relevant to building Web services, before focusing on both JavaServer pages and servlets.

If we focus on interfacing legacy applications, several Java technologies come to the forefront. First, if you need to connect to a database, Java provides several APIs. First is JDBC, which enables you to connect to a database, execute SQL, and process the results. If you need to utilize only static SQL statements, you should also look at SQLJ, which is an ANSI standard for embedding SQL into Java applications. A relative newcomer to this arena is the Java Data Objects (JDO) API. JDO supports what is known as *transparent persistence*. This enables a developer to work with Java objects, be they persistent or transient, in exactly the same manner, without worrying about persisting the Java objects and dealing with all the related complications.

If you need to integrate with an existing legacy application, you should investigate the Java Connector Architecture (JCA), Java Messaging Service (JMS), and Enterprise JavaBeans (EJB). JCA provides a standard interface to connect to legacy applications, hiding many of the difficulties in doing so, and thereby increasing productivity. JMS also is useful in this regard, but focuses more on the integration of messaging services. Finally, to minimize the interaction between your Java code and the legacy application, you can use EJBs to cache results.

Two other major concerns that you might have when developing Web services are security and internationalization. In both of these arenas, Java excels. First, Java is inherently safer than most other programming languages when you write secure applications. In addition, Java provides support for Secure Socket Layers (SSLs) with Java Secure Sockets Extension (JSSE), cryptographic communications with Java Cryptography Extension (JCE), as well as authentication and authorization with Java Authentication and Authorization Service (JAAS). And finally, Java itself is Unicode-compliant, and also provides a great deal of support for writing International applications.

Using JavaServer Pages and Servlets

Although all this is impressive, the two most important technologies for building and using Web services are JavaServer Pages (JSP) and servlets. Together with JavaBeans, which simplify the sharing of data among different server components, these two technologies enable developers to build powerful Web applications.

For example, consider the following demonstration of a login form, presented in different languages, depending on the Accept-Language HTTP header in the client request. Listing 4.1 provides an example of a simple JSP page that displays the login form, demonstrating how easy it is to use JSP technology to develop Web applications.

LISTING 4.1 `LogOn.jsp`

```
<%@ page
  contentType="text/html"
  import="java.util.*"
%>

<html>
  <head>
    <title> International JSP Login Page</title>
  </head>
<body>

<%
  Locale userLocale = request.getLocale() ;
  ResourceBundle loginBundle
    = ResourceBundle.getBundle("LogOn", userLocale) ;
%>

  <h1> <%= loginBundle.getString("welcome") %> </h1>
  <hr/>
  <h2> <%= loginBundle.getString("message") %> </h2>

  <form>
    <input type="text" name="user"/>
    <%= loginBundle.getString("user") %>
    <p/>
```

LISTING 4.1 continued

```
    <input type="text" name="pass"/>
    <%= loginBundle.getString("passwd") %>
    <p/>
  </form>

</body>
</html>
```

If you are familiar with JSP pages, you might notice that `Template` date was not used for the textfield labels. Instead, the labels are obtained from a `ResourceBundle`, which is selected at request-time via a `Locale` object, which is determined from the HTTP `Accept-Language` header. For this example to work, it's necessary to create `Property` files that define the necessary `Strings` for the different `Locales` that are to be supported. The first one is the `LogOn_en_US.properties` file, shown in Listing 4.2, which contains the `Strings` that normally would have just been placed into the JSP file as template data. After that, two more property files have the translated strings in Spanish (Listing 4.3), and German (Listing 4.4). Note that these were not translated professionally as would be done in a production environment.

LISTING 4.2 *LogOn_en_US.properties*

```
passwd=Password
user=Username
message=Please Login
welcome=Welcome
```

LISTING 4.3 `LogOn_es_MX.properties`

```
passwd=Palabra de paso
user=Username
message=Por favor conexi\u00F3n
welcome=Recepci\u00F3n
```

LISTING 4.4 `LogOn_de.properties`

```
passwd=Kennwort
user=Username
message=Bitte LOGON
welcome=Willkommen
```

To demonstrate this example, Figure 4.10 shows the result of viewing `LogOn.jsp` in Internet Explorer 6.0.

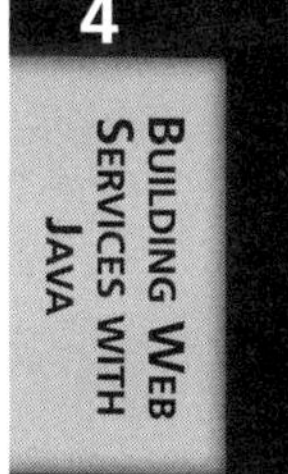

FIGURE 4.10
The LogOn JSP page shown for the U.S. locale.

Most browsers enable the user to change locales easily. For example, to change locales in Internet Explorer, open the Internet Options dialog, which is available from the Tools menu. The Internet Options window, shown in Figure 4.11, enables you to customize the behavior of the browser.

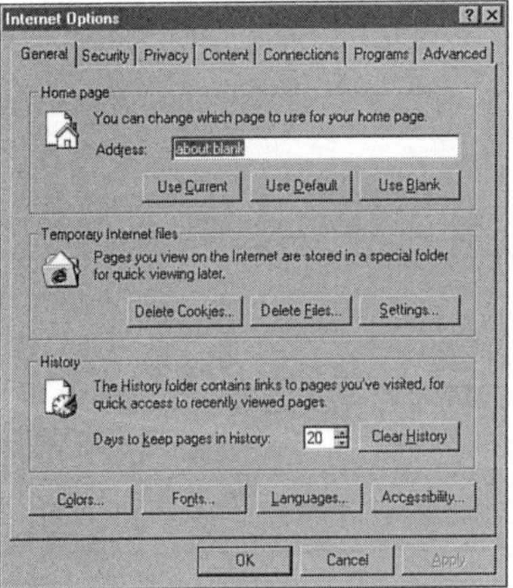

FIGURE 4.11
The Internet Options window, where a user can customize the behavior of the browser.

Near the bottom of the main panel is a Languages button. If you click this button, a new dialog opens, which enables you to set your language preferences. If you click Add, you are shown the window in Figure 4.12, which lists all the languages that IE supports.

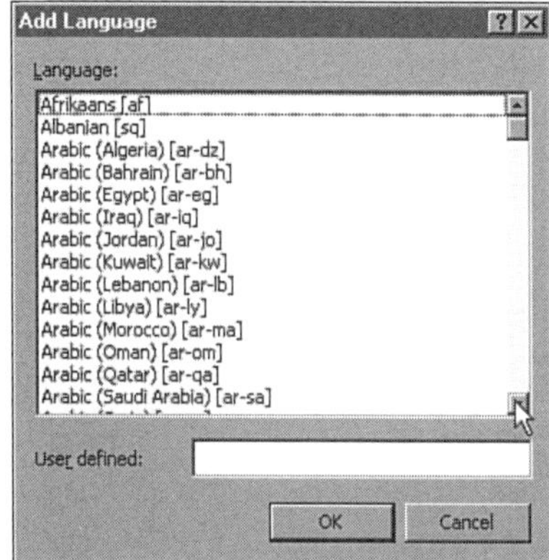

FIGURE 4.12
Languages supported by IE.

To test the `LogOn.jsp` page, follow these steps:

1. Select German (Germany) [de] from the list of languages and click OK.
2. Select the order of the languages. Click on German, and use the Move Up button to move it ahead of any other languages that are listed.
3. Click on OK to close the Add Language dialog, and also click on OK to close Internet Options.

If you reload the `LogOn.jsp` page, your Login form is now displayed in German, as shown in Figure 4.13.

FIGURE 4.13
The LogOn.jsp page showing the Login form in German.

If you repeat the previous process, but this time select Spanish (Mexican) [es_mx] from the list of languages, and move it to the top of the Preferred Languages, your browser now requests content with the Mexican Spanish locale. This time, `LogOn.jsp` displays the Login form in Spanish.

Two exciting new features have recently been added to the JSP and Servlets specification: custom actions and filters. They're discussed next.

Custom Actions

With JavaServer Pages, developers can now create and utilize custom actions, which are implemented as new tags in a JSP page. Custom tags enable JSP developers to remove Java code from JSP pages, which enables non-Java developers to generate dynamic JSP Web applications. Organizations such as Jakarta have also created custom tag libraries that enable a JSP developer to quickly add new functionality to a Web application with minimal coding. For example, Jakarta has a custom tag library that simplifies developing Internationalized JSP applications. Listing 4.5 shows how `LogOn.jsp` could be written using this tag library.

LISTING 4.5 `tagLogOn.jsp`

```
<%@ taglib prefix="logon" uri="http://java.sun.com/jstl/ea/fmt" %>

<html>
  <head>
    <title> International JSP Login Page</title>
  </head>
<body>

<logon:locale value="<%= request.getLocale() %>"/>
<logon:bundle basename="org.apache.taglibs.standard.examples.i18n.Resources">

  <h1> <logon:message key="welcome"/> </h1>
  <hr/>
  <h2> <logon:message key="message"/> </h2>

  <form>
    <input type="text" name="user"/>
    <logon:message key="user"/>
    <p/>

    <input type="text" name="pass"/>
    <logon:message key="passwd"/>
    <p/>
  </form>
```

LISTING 4.5 continued

```
</logon:bundle>

</body>
</html>
```

As you can see, this JSP page is almost completely free of Java code. The only remaining Java is in the setting of the locale for the i18n library.

Filters

The new concept of servlet filters enables you to preprocess client requests and to post-process server responses. As a simple example, consider the filter in Listing 4.6, which, when properly deployed, intercepts client requests and blocks any request that has a U.S. locale; see Figure 4.14.

LISTING 4.6 `LocaleFilter.java`

```
package com.sams ;

import java.util.* ;

import javax.servlet.*;
import javax.servlet.http.*;

public class LocaleFilter implements Filter {

  private ServletContext ctx ;
  private final static String msg = "English U.S. locale is currently blocked" ;

  public void init(FilterConfig config) throws ServletException {
    ctx = config.getServletContext() ;
    ctx.log("Initializing Locale Filter") ;
  }

  public void destroy() {
    ctx.log("Destroying Locale Filter") ;
  }

  public void doFilter(ServletRequest request,
  ServletResponse response,
  FilterChain chain) throws ServletException, java.io.IOException {

    HttpServletRequest req = (HttpServletRequest)request ;
```

LISTING 4.6 continued

```
    if(req.getLocale().equals(Locale.US)){
      HttpServletResponse res = (HttpServletResponse)response ;
      res.sendError(res.SC_SERVICE_UNAVAILABLE, msg) ;
    }
  }
}
```

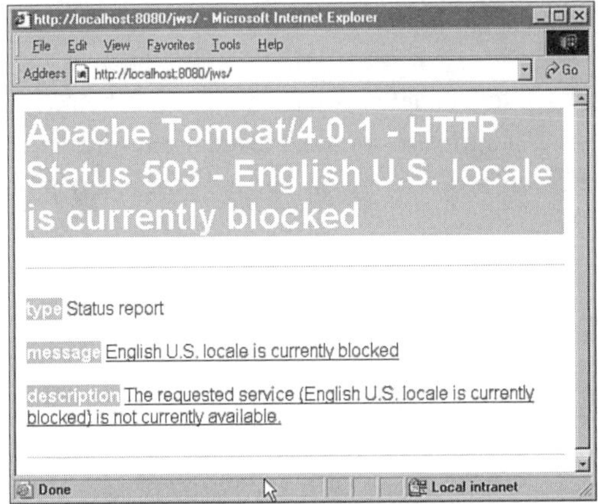

FIGURE 4.14
The effect of the `LocaleFilter` *on blocking those requests that have the Accept-Language HTTP header set to the U.S. locale.*

This capability to intercept requests and responses lends itself to many difficult tasks, including simplifying authentication, compressing content, or customizing responses.

User Interfaces

The actual Web service is only half the story, however; the other half is the client that accesses the Web service. Once again, Java is more than up to the task. Java supports the full range of potential clients, from Web browsers, which might actually be written in Java and that support the Java plug-in and now Java Web Start, to devices that utilize J2ME or PersonalJava, to smart cards. If a client exists, Java can probably run on it.

In fact, you can write Web clients in Java that perform double duty. For example, the application in Listing 4.7 can be executed as either a standalone application or as an applet. This simple application could be connected to a Web service, rather than a Web site, so that dynamic selection of contacts is supported. Executing this Java code as an application, shown in Figure 4.15, generates a GUI that displays a picture and enables the user to hear an audio recording.

LISTING 4.7 LoveZone.java

```
import javax.swing.*;
import java.applet.*;
import java.awt.*;
import java.awt.event.*;
import java.net.URL;
import java.net.MalformedURLException ;

public class LoveZone extends JApplet {

  private String soundFile = "hello.wav" ;
  private String imageFile = "rjb.jpg" ;

  private boolean inAnApplet = true;

  private JButton playButton ;
  private JButton stopButton;
  private JLabel label ;
  private JLabel lPhoto ;
  private AudioClip audioClip ;
  private ImageIcon icon ;

  public LoveZone() {
    this(true);
  }

  public LoveZone(boolean inAnApplet) {
    this.inAnApplet = inAnApplet;

    try{

      audioClip = newAudioClip(new URL("http://localhost:8080/jws/hello.wav")) ;
      icon = new ImageIcon(new URL("http://localhost:8080/jws/rjb.jpg")) ;

    }catch(MalformedURLException ex) {
      System.exit(0) ;
    }
  }

  public void init() {

    if(audioClip == null)
      audioClip = getAudioClip(getCodeBase(), soundFile);
    try{

      icon = new ImageIcon(new URL(getCodeBase(), imageFile)) ;

    }catch(MalformedURLException ex) {
      System.exit(0) ;
    }
```

LISTING 4.7 continued

```
    setContentPane(makeContentPane());
  }

  public Container makeContentPane() {

    label = new JLabel("Greetings from the LoveZone", JLabel.CENTER);

    playButton = new JButton("Play");
    playButton.addActionListener(new ActionListener() {
      public void actionPerformed(ActionEvent event) {
        audioClip.play() ;
        playButton.setEnabled(false);
        stopButton.setEnabled(true);
        return;
      }
    }) ;

    stopButton = new JButton("Stop");
    stopButton.addActionListener(new ActionListener() {
      public void actionPerformed(ActionEvent event) {
        audioClip.stop();
        playButton.setEnabled(true);
        stopButton.setEnabled(false);
        return;
      }
    }) ;

    stopButton.setEnabled(false);

    lPhoto = new JLabel("", icon, JLabel.CENTER) ;

    lPhoto.setToolTipText("Hi, I'm Robert") ;
    lPhoto.setPreferredSize(new Dimension(220, 300)) ;

    JPanel controlPanel = new JPanel();

    controlPanel.setLayout(new BorderLayout());

    controlPanel.add(label, BorderLayout.SOUTH) ;
    controlPanel.add(playButton, BorderLayout.WEST);
    controlPanel.add(stopButton, BorderLayout.EAST);
    controlPanel.add(lPhoto, BorderLayout.NORTH) ;

    controlPanel.setBackground(new Color(255,255,204));

controlPanel.setBorder(BorderFactory.createMatteBorder(1,1,2,2,Color.black));

    return(controlPanel) ;
  }
```

LISTING 4.7 continued

```
  public static void main(String[] args){

    try{

      UIManager.setLookAndFeel("javax.swing.plaf.metal.MetalLookAndFeel") ;

    }catch(Exception e){
      System.err.println("\nERROR When Setting the Metal Look and Feel: ");
      System.err.println(e.getMessage());
    }

    Frame frame = new Frame("Love Zone Example") ;

    frame.addWindowListener(new WindowAdapter() {
      public void windowClosing(WindowEvent e) {
        System.exit(0);
      }
    });

    LoveZone applet = new LoveZone(false);

    frame.add(applet.makeContentPane());
    frame.pack();
    frame.setVisible(true);
  }
}
```

FIGURE 4.15
The LoveZone application, showing how easy it is to combine images and audio for display in a Java application.

Java Tools

Although the Java programming language itself is starting to mature, native support for Web services within the Java language is only starting to emerge. This doesn't mean you can't implement Web services in Java; there are numerous different Java implementations for the different Web service standards. Eventually, the best attributes from these different efforts will be utilized to provide full native support for Web services in Java. Right now, however, you have to choose from the available commercial and open source products that are available.

Toolkits

For example, the Apache Software Foundation has developed the SOAP toolkit in Java, after an early code donation from IBM. Currently, a completely rewritten version, called AXIS, is available, which extends the communication to more protocols. Both these toolkits are discussed in more detail in Chapter 5, "A Simple Java Web Service."

Other toolkits are available for interacting with UDDI registries, including UDDI4J. Apache AXIS provides support for generating and interacting with WSDL documents. Likewise, a toolkit called WSDL4J also enables developers to work with WSDL documents.

Development Editors

With the maturation of the Java language, multiple vendors have developed powerful development editors that simplify the creation of Java applications, including Java Web services. This also helps the developer, because automatic generation of code and deployment information can improve productivity and shorten development cycles.

One example is the Forte for Java IDE, which comes in two versions. The first version is called the Community Edition, shown in Figure 4.16, and is free to use. The second version is the Enterprise Edition, and can be licensed from Sun. Both versions are based on the open source NetBeans project, available at `www.netbeans.org`.

IBM is another big player in the Java Web service development arena, having led the initial development of Java-based toolkits for working with SOAP, WSDL, and UDDI. IBM has developed a Web services toolkit, as well as a development editor, shown in Figure 4.17. IBM has donated a large quantity of IDE code to the eclipse project, available at `www.eclipse.org`.

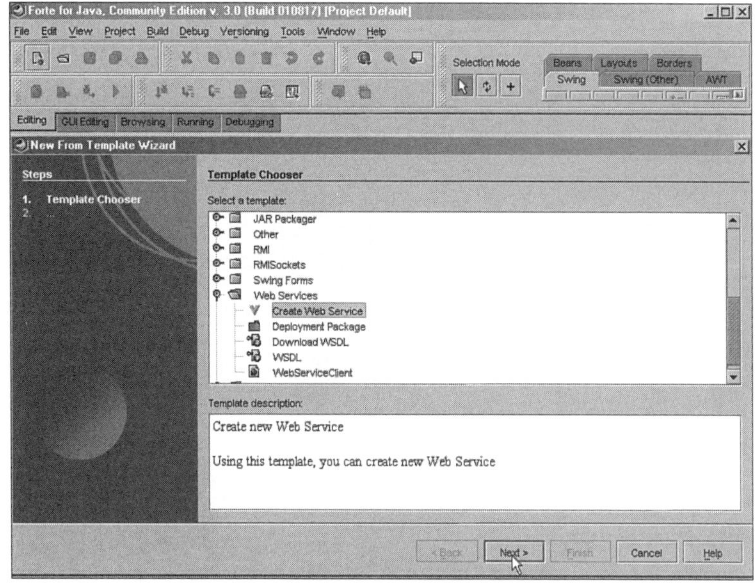

FIGURE 4.16
The Forte for Java Community Edition, showing the free Web Application Services Platform (WASP) plug-in from Systinet that provides support for Web services.

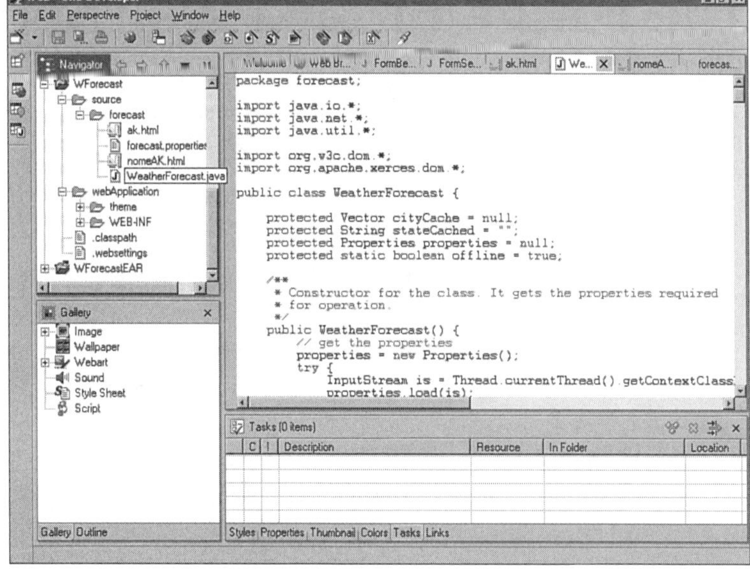

FIGURE 4.17
The Web Services Studio Development Editor from IBM, which can provide full Web service development, including SOAP, WSDL, and UDDI.

A surprise entrant is JDeveloper from Oracle, which is an enterprise Java development environment, written in Java. JDeveloper, shown in Figure 4.18, provides built-in support for Enterprise applications with Orcale9i application server. Further support for developing Web services is included as well.

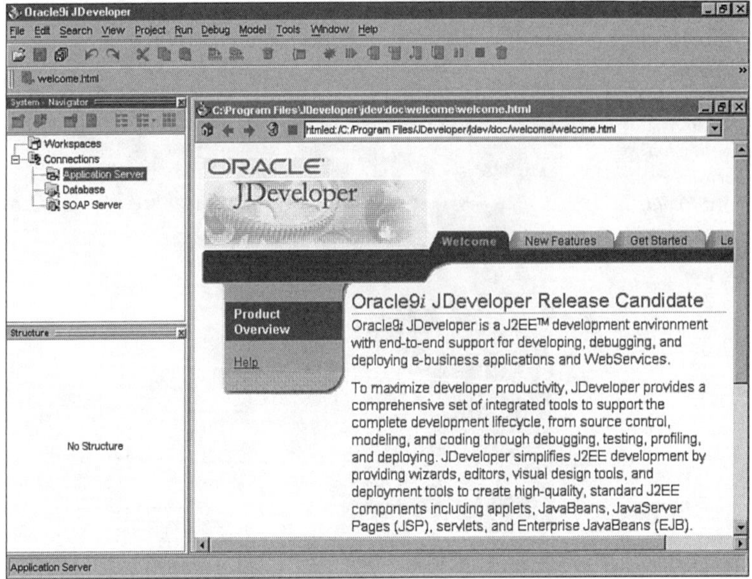

FIGURE 4.18
The JDeveloper IDE, which can be freely downloaded from the Oracle Technet Web site.

The Future of Java Web Services

Although the present situation for using Java to build Web services is pretty good, the future is even better. First, the first version of the entire JAX pack will soon be available. The JAX pack encompasses five different Java APIs for XML:

- JAXP, the Java API for XML parsing, discussed in Chapter 12. JAXP simplifies the parsing of XML documents with Java.
- JAXB, the Java API for XML Binding, discussed in Chapter 13. JAXB maps XML elements to Java classes.
- JAXR, the Java API for XML Registries, discussed in Chapter 14. JAXR provides a standard method for Java applications to access business registries, such as UDDI repositories.
- JAXM, the Java API for XML Messaging, discussed in Chapter 15. JAXM provides a standard method for using Java to send SOAP messages.
- JAX-RPC, the Java API for XML Remote Procedure Calls, discussed in Chapter 16. JAX-RPC enables a developer to send SOAP method calls over the Internet and receive the response in a standard manner.

But the story doesn't end there. The Java2 Enterprise Edition, version 1.4, is expected to provide significant built-in support for enabling Web services, including additions to both the servlet and JSP specifications. In addition, the following Java specification requests are currently underway, all impacting the native support for Web services in Java:

- JSR 104, "XML Trust Service APIs," provides a standard set of APIs for using XML Signatures.
- JSR 105, "XML Digital Signature APIs," provides a standard set of APIS for XML Digital Signature Services.
- JSR 106, "XML Digital Encryption APIs," provides a standard set of APIs for XML Digital Encryption services.
- JSR 109, "Implementing Enterprise Web Services," provides a model and architecture for developing Web services in Java.
- JSR 110, "Java APIs for WSDL," provides a standard API for working with WSDL documents from Java.
- JSR 111, "Java Services Framework," provides a specification for assembling service components into a Java Server application, including full lifecycle management.
- JSR 127, "JavaServer Faces," provides a standard method to simplify the creation and maintenance of JSP application GUIs. In essence, this enables developers to write JSP pages that work and look the same across all different Web browsers.
- JSR 153, "Enterprise JavaBeans version 2.1," provides additional support for EJBs to utilize Web services.
- JSR 154, "Java Servlet Specification," provides for additional built-in support for Web services in servlets.
- JSR 155, "Web Service Security Assertions," provides a set of APIs that enable Web services to exchange assertions.
- JSR 156, "XML Transactioning API for Java," provides an API for packaging and transporting ACID and extended transactions.
- JSR 157, "ebXML CPP/A APIs for Java," provides a standard set of APIS for working with ebXML CPP/A documents.

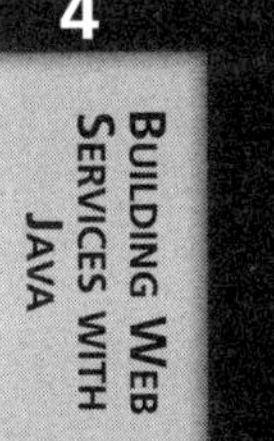

Summary

This chapter demonstrated the benefits of using Java to develop Web services. First, Java simplifies the development of servers, including those that need to provide Web services, either directly or by wrapping existing legacy applications. Second, Java is also an excellent language to use to develop Web service clients, because of both the breadth of support for Java across a range of hardware, as well as the rich GUI applications that Java enables.

Finally, the powerful Java development environments, many of which are free for development efforts, simplify the routine tasks that can be required in building and deploying Web services. In its current state, and given the incredible growth of new functionality, Java is poised to dominate the world of Web services.

The next two chapters build on this material, and use Java to actually create Web services and clients. First, Chapter 5 demonstrates how to put all the pieces together to create a Java HelloWorld Web service. Chapter 6 delves into a more complex example, showing how Web services can be used to connect businesses together.

CHAPTER 5

A Simple Java Web Service

by Robert Brunner

IN THIS CHAPTER

As you saw in Chapter 4, there are many advantages to using Java to build Web services. The main disadvantage, however, is that there currently isn't one Web service application programming interface that you can utilize. Similarly, there isn't one server to host your Web services, nor is there one toolkit or integrated development environment to build them.

Although some may see this as a serious detriment, it really goes back to one of the fundamental strengths of the Java programming language. That is, let different vendors compete with each other to satisfy the customer's needs. This happens naturally in Java, as vendors compete with different implementations of the various Java APIs, and even different Java virtual machines. Although Java-based Web services aren't quite to this level, as you will see throughout this book, they soon will be.

The Application

For your first Java Web service, you will create a very simple service: the traditional "Hello World" example. Maybe you are tired of seeing this as a first demonstration, but the reason it is so appropriate is that it forces you to understand the framework necessary to make such a simple example work, rather than worry about what bells and whistles to implement. In other words, it helps you to see the forest, rather than the trees.

Figure 5.1 lays out a schematic of this first Web service. As you can see from the figure, the "Hello World" Web service merely responds to all requests by sending the same greeting. The actual implementation of this service is shown in Listing 5.1.

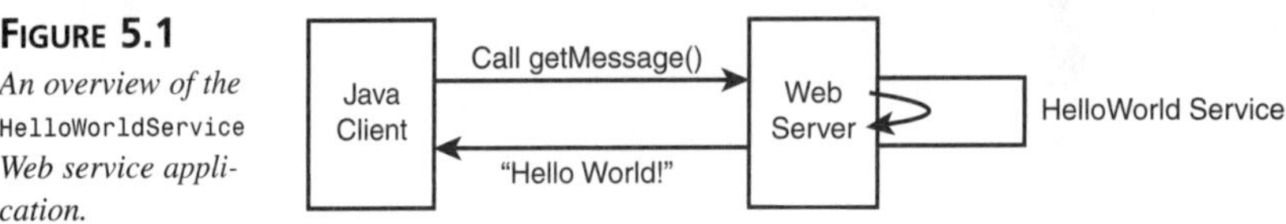

FIGURE 5.1 *An overview of the* `HelloWorldService` *Web service application.*

LISTING 5.1 `HelloWorldService.java`

```
//
// The class that implements the Web service.
//

public class HelloWorldService {

  // The greeting the service will send to the client.
  // You can change this to suit your own desires.

  private final static String sGreeting
    = "Hello World!" ;
```

LISTING 5.1 continued

```
  // Here is the method that implements the Web service.
  // As you can see, it is quite simple.

  public String getMessage() {

    return(sGreeting) ;
  }
}
```

As is rather obvious from this example, implementing a Web service in Java is quite easy. All that is required is the method that provides the service, which doesn't have to do anything fancy. As a result, it becomes very simple to wrap existing methods, be they in Java or a different programming language with Java wrappers, so that they can be exposed as Web services.

The Web Service Framework

To actually deploy a Web service in Java, however, a bit more work is required. Primarily this is a result of the fact that Java does not yet provide native support for Web services, something that, as you saw in Chapter 4, is being addressed through the Java community process.

The SOAP Toolkit

What you need to deploy the Web service is a server to host your service, and something that will direct incoming SOAP requests to your method. You took care of the server part in Chapter 4 by downloading and installing the Tomcat server. For the SOAP service, you also need to return to the Apache Software Foundation (ASF), which provides not one, but two different SOAP toolkits. Formally, these products are part of the XML project within the ASF, which is located at http://xml.apache.org, as shown in Figure 5.2.

The first toolkit is called Apache SOAP, and it's currently in version 2.2. Originally developed by IBM, it was eventually donated to the ASF as an open-source, Java-based implementation of the SOAP protocol. The Apache SOAP home page, shown in Figure 5.3, provides a great deal of background information, as well as download links to the actual SOAP libraries.

The second toolkit is called Apache AXIS, which stands for Apache eXtensible Interaction System. AXIS is a complete rewrite of the original Apache SOAP toolkit, designed to improve the overall performance, as well as support a wider range of messaging protocols. The AXIS project is still an alpha release; therefore the AXIS homepage at http://xml.apache.org/axis, as shown in Figure 5.4, isn't as full of information as the original SOAP toolkit.

AXIS is easy to use and provides all the functionality that you need. As a result, the examples in the next two chapters use AXIS to provide the SOAP service. To download the AXIS framework, click on the Releases link in the Download section of the table of contents on the left side of the AXIS Web site.

The examples in this chapter were tested with version 2.0 of the AXIS toolkit; however, feel free to try a more recent version if it exists. You probably want to download the binary version, as demonstrated in Figure 5.2; otherwise you need to build the Java ARchive files (JAR files) that provide the SOAP functionality. After you download the binary package, unzip the archive to a suitable workspace, such as `C:\projects` on Windows, or a Projects directory under your home directory in Linux.

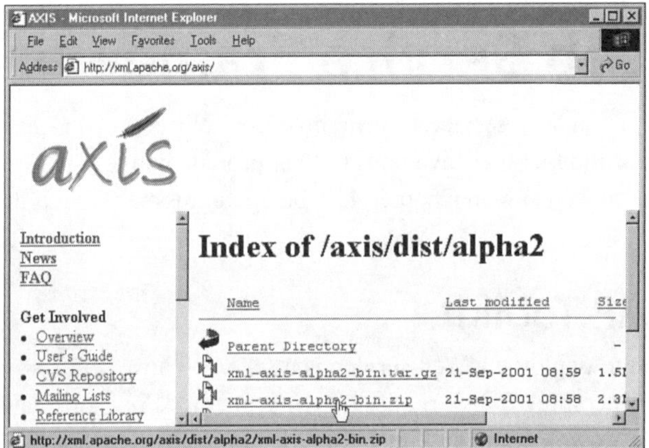

FIGURE 5.2
You will probably want to download the binary version of the AXIS package.

The XML Parser

Although AXIS provides the SOAP implementation, you still need to obtain one more item—an XML parser. Because SOAP is an XML application, you need an XML parser to read and write valid XML documents. AXIS utilizes the JAXP API to interact with an XML parser, thus any parser that implements the JAXP API can be used. In keeping with the ASF theme, the examples in the next two chapters utilize the Xerces for Java XML parser. However, you can use any JAXP-compliant parser, including the crimson parser that provides the reference implementation for the JAXP API.

> **Note**
>
> A parser is a software component that breaks a stream of characters, which might be a string or a file, into tokens that can be manipulated by other software components. The JAXP API, discussed in more detail in Chapter 12, provides an implementation-independent mechanism for interacting with Java XML parsers.

As was the case with the two SOAP toolkits, Xerces is a product of the ASF XML project. The Xerces for Java home page, seen Figure 5.6, provides information regarding the Xerces = Java-based XML parser. You can also download the Xerces parser by following the Download link on the table of contents at the left. The examples in this chapter were tested in the version 2.0 of the Xerces for Java parser.

As before, we recommend that you download the binary version of Xerces, so that you do not have to worry about building the Xerces JAR file. After you download the Xerces parser, unzip the distribution into the same folder as the one in which you placed the AXIS toolkit. If you unzipped the distribution packages with the Keep Folder Names flag checked, you should have the directory structure shown in Figure 5.3.

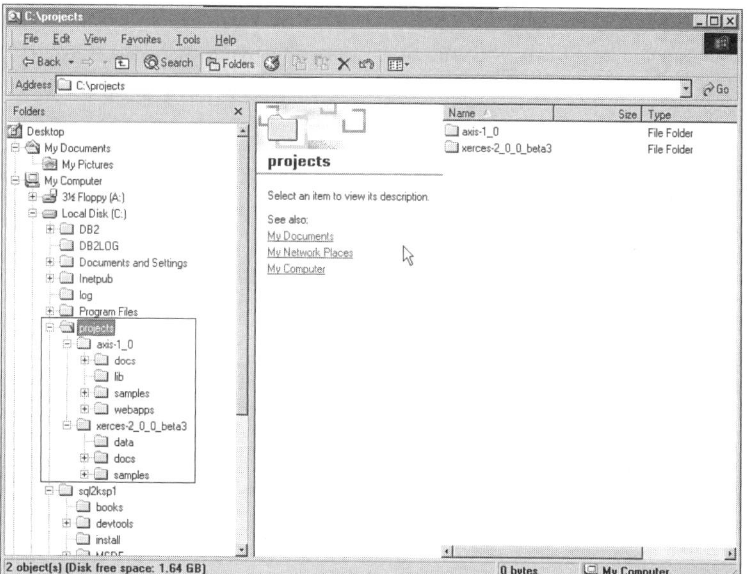

FIGURE 5.3
The directory structure after the AXIS and Xerces packages have been installed.

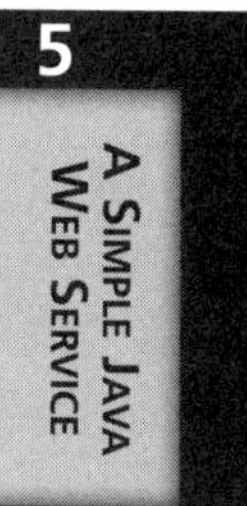

Testing the Installation

At this point, everything has been downloaded; now you just need to start everything up and test it out. One of the primary benefits of using AXIS, as opposed to Apache SOAP, is that installation and deployment of Java-based Web services is considerably easier with AXIS. To demonstrate, you will test your installation with the `HelloWorldService` shown earlier in this chapter in Listing 5.1.

First, however, you need to let the Tomcat server know that AXIS is a SOAP handler. To do so, you must install AXIS as a Web application within the Tomcat server. Fortunately, this is easier than it sounds. All you need to do is copy the contents of the `axis\webapps` folder into the Tomcat `webapps` folder:

```
C:\projects>xcopy /E axis-1_0\webapps jakarta-tomcat-4.0.1\webapps
```

This creates a new directory, named `axis`, in the Tomcat `webapps` directory structure, and installs the files necessary for AXIS to work with the Tomcat server. The next step is to install the Xerces, or other JAXP-compatible XML parser, so that AXIS can find and use it. Again, this is easy; all you need to do is copy the `xerces.jar` file into the installed AXIS `webapps` directory:

```
C:\projects>copy xerces-2_0_0_beta3\xerces.jar
  jakarta-tomcat-4.0.1\webapps\axis\WEB-INF\lib
```

At this point, you should start your Tomcat server, or restart it if it is already running. You can either do this with the Start icons that were installed if you downloaded the Windows executable version, or by explicitly calling the `startup.bat`, or `startup.sh` script on Linux.

First, change to the `bin` directory of your Tomcat installation, and then execute the appropriate startup script:

```
C:\projects>cd jakarta-tomcat-4.0.1\bin

C:\projects\jakarta-tomcat-4.0.1\bin>startup
Using CATALINA_BASE: ..
Using CATALINA_HOME: ..
Using CLASSPATH:     ..\bin\bootstrap.jar;C:\Program Files\java\jdk\lib\tools.jar
Using JAVA_HOME:     C:\Program Files\java\jdk
```

At this point, a command window should open that demonstrates that Tomcat is up and running, as shown in Figure 5.4.

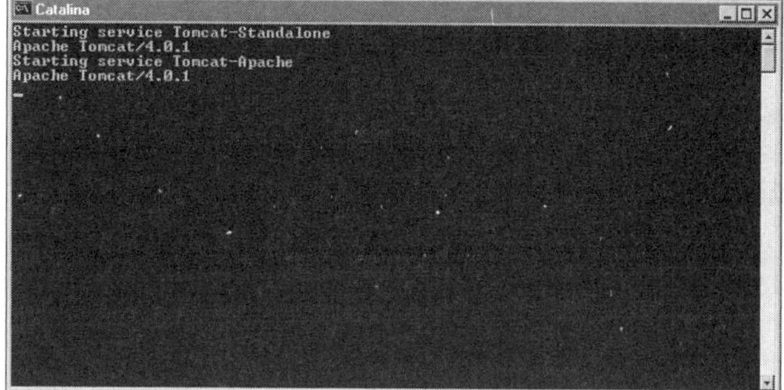

FIGURE 5.4
The Windows command window showing that Tomcat is running correctly.

Now that the framework is up and running, all you need to do is test it out. AXIS provides a very simple way to test new Java Web services that do not utilize advanced SOAP functionality, such as your simple HelloWorldService. To test a service, copy the source file to the AXIS `webapp` directory, renaming the file so that it has a .jws (for Java Web service) file extension. For example, if you saved Listing 5.1 in the `c:\project` directory, the following command would perform the appropriate action:

```
C:\projects>copy HelloWorldService.java
  jakarta-tomcat-4.0.1\webapps\axis\HelloWorldService.jws
```

Now all that is required is to explicitly call this Java Web service file, and AXIS will do the rest. Enter **`http://localhost:8080/axis/HelloWorldService.jws`** into your browser's address bar, and if you get the response seen in Figure 5.5, everything is working correctly.

FIGURE 5.5
The response from the AXIS Web application after `HelloWorldService.jws` *has been invoked.*

Invoking a SOAP Service

Okay, seeing the Web page that AXIS generates when you call the `HelloWorldService` isn't the most exciting thing, but you are almost all the way there when it comes to having a fully functioning, end-to-end Java Web service. All you really need to do is write the client. You can do this in two ways. First, you could write the Java client yourself, and second, you could have it generated for you. This section explores both approaches, starting with the generated version.

HelloWorldService WSDL

The Web Service Description Language, or WSDL, provides a language-independent technique for describing a Web service to any potential client. Although WSDL will be discussed in more detail in Chapter 11, "WSDL," for now you can just use AXIS to generate WSDL for you, and reap the benefits without having to go through all of the details first.

Generating the WSDL description for a Java Web service that uses AXIS is very simple, especially if the Web service is deployed as a jws file. All you need to do is append `?wsdl` to the URL of your Web service, and AXIS generates the WSDL document for you and returns it to your Web browser. For example, to see the WSDL for your `HelloWorldService`, just visit `http://localhost:8080/axis/HelloWorldService.jws?wsdl`, and you can browse the full WSDL document for your simple Java Web service, as shown in Figure 5.6.

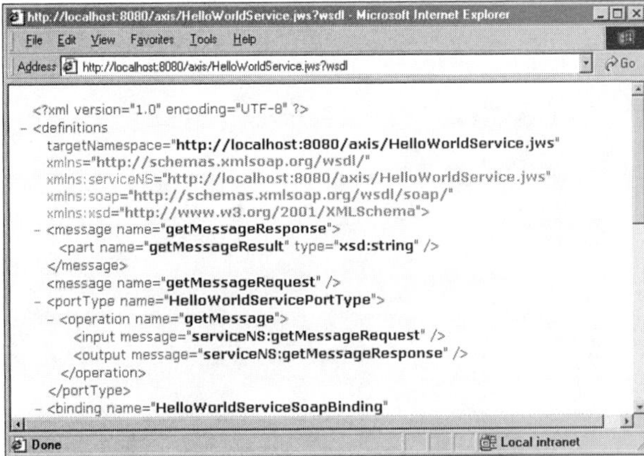

FIGURE 5.6
The WSDL document for HelloWorldService that is automatically generated by AXIS.

Although you may not fully understand all the WSDL terminology, the WSDL document that describes your `HelloWorldService` is actually not that complicated. If you take a look at Listing 5.2, which contains the complete WSDL document for `HelloWorldService`, you can quickly see the relevant sections for the simple Web service (which is yet another reason for starting with a simple example).

LISTING 5.2 HelloWorldService.wsdl

```
<?xml version="1.0" encoding="UTF-8" ?>
  <definitions
    targetNamespace="http://localhost:8080/axis/HelloWorldService.jws"
    xmlns="http://schemas.xmlsoap.org/wsdl/"
    xmlns:serviceNS="http://localhost:8080/axis/HelloWorldService.jws"
    xmlns:soap="http://schemas.xmlsoap.org/wsdl/soap/"
    xmlns:xsd="http://www.w3.org/2001/XMLSchema">
  <message name="getMessageResponse">
  <part name="getMessageResult" type="xsd:string" />
  </message>
  <message name="getMessageRequest" />
  <portType name="HelloWorldServicePortType">
  <operation name="getMessage">
  <input message="serviceNS:getMessageRequest" />
  <output message="serviceNS:getMessageResponse" />
  </operation>
  </portType>
  <binding name="HelloWorldServiceSoapBinding"
    type="serviceNS:HelloWorldServicePortType">
  <soap:binding style="rpc" transport="http://schemas.xmlsoap.org/soap/http" />
  <operation name="getMessage">
  <soap:operation soapAction="" style="rpc" />
  <input>
  <soap:body encodingStyle="http://schemas.xmlsoap.org/soap/encoding/"
    namespace="" use="encoded" />
  </input>
  <output>
  <soap:body encodingStyle="http://schemas.xmlsoap.org/soap/encoding/"
    namespace="" use="encoded" />
  </output>
  </operation>
  </binding>
  <service name="HelloWorldService">
  <port
    binding="serviceNS:HelloWorldServiceSoapBinding"
    name="HelloWorldServicePort">
  <soap:address location="http://localhost:8080/axis/HelloWorldService.jws" />
  </port>
  </service>
  </definitions>
```

First, the WSDL defines a Request and Response object, based on the HTTP communication model, for your service, which is called getMessage. The WSDL document goes on to define a HelloWorldService binding for the service, and indicates that it will function as a remote procedure call, or RPC. Finally, the service is defined and the URL for the service is defined. Don't worry if this is a little overwhelming—Chapter 12 explores WSDL in greater detail.

Generating the HelloWorldService Client

The WSDL document describing the HelloWorldService provides a complete representation of the service, in a language-independent manner. Because you are interested in Java Web services, the next step is to build a Java client that will invoke the HelloWorldService. AXIS comes with a special tool that generates a client stub that calls a service, given the WSDL representation of that service.

First, you need to set up your CLASSPATH appropriately, including the four JAR files that come with the AXIS distribution: axis.jar, clutil.jar, log4j-core, and wsdl4j.jar, as well as an XML parser that implements the JAXP API; in this case, that's xerces.jar. To simplify bookkeeping, we suggest you copy these files into a special lib directory in your project folder. After you have done that, setting your CLASSPATH appropriately is rather simple:

```
C:\projects>set CLASSPATH=.;lib\axis.jar
C:\projects>set CLASSPATH=%CLASSPATH%;lib\clutil.jar
C:\projects>set CLASSPATH=%CLASSPATH%;lib\log4j-core.jar
C:\projects>set CLASSPATH=%CLASSPATH%;lib\wsdl4j.jar
C:\projects>set CLASSPATH=%CLASSPATH%;lib\xerces.jar
```

After this is done, you can call the WSDL tool directly, passing in the URL for the appropriate WSDL document as a parameter:

```
C:\projects>java org.apache.axis.wsdl.Wsdl2java
  http://localhost:8080/axis/HelloWorldService.jws?wsdl
```

Or, to see everything that's going on, you can call the WSDL tool with the --verbose option right before the URL for the WSDL document:

```
C:\projects>java org.apache.axis.wsdl.Wsdl2java
  --verbose http://localhost:8080/axis/HelloWorldService.jws?wsdl
Parsing XML File: http://localhost:8080/axis/HelloWorldService.jws?wsdl
Generating portType interface: HelloWorldServicePortType.java
Generating client-side stub: HelloWorldServiceSoapBindingStub.java
Generating service class: HelloWorldService.java
```

As you can see, three new files are generated: HelloWorldServicePortType.java, shown in Listing 5.3, HelloWorldServiceSoapBindingStub.java, shown in Listing 5.4, and HelloWorldService.java, shown in Listing 5.5.

LISTING 5.3 HelloWorldServicePortType.java

```
/**
 * HelloWorldServicePortType.java
 *
 * This file was auto-generated from WSDL
 * by the Apache Axis Wsdl2java emitter.
 */

public interface HelloWorldServicePortType extends java.rmi.Remote {
    public String getMessage() throws java.rmi.RemoteException;
}
```

LISTING 5.4 HelloWorldServiceSoapBindingStub.java

```
/**
 * HelloWorldServiceSoapBindingStub.java
 *
 * This file was auto-generated from WSDL
 * by the Apache Axis Wsdl2java emitter.
 */

public class HelloWorldServiceSoapBindingStub
    extends org.apache.axis.wsdl.Stub
    implements HelloWorldServicePortType {

    private org.apache.axis.client.ServiceClient call
        = new org.apache.axis.client.ServiceClient(
            new org.apache.axis.transport.http.HTTPTransport()
          );

    private java.util.Hashtable properties = new java.util.Hashtable();

    public HelloWorldServiceSoapBindingStub(java.net.URL endpointURL)
      throws org.apache.axis.SerializationException {
         this();
         call.set(org.apache.axis.transport.http.HTTPTransport.URL,
           endpointURL.toString());
    }
    public HelloWorldServiceSoapBindingStub()
      throws org.apache.axis.SerializationException {
    }

    public void _setProperty(String name, Object value) {
        properties.put(name, value);
    }

    // From org.apache.axis.wsdl.Stub
    public Object _getProperty(String name) {
        return properties.get(name);
```

LISTING 5.4 continued

```
    }

    // From org.apache.axis.wsdl.Stub
    public void _setTargetEndpoint(java.net.URL address) {
        call.set(org.apache.axis.transport.http.HTTPTransport.URL,
          address.toString());
    }

    // From org.apache.axis.wsdl.Stub
    public java.net.URL _getTargetEndpoint() {
        try {
            return new java.net.URL(
              (String)call.get(org.apache.axis.transport.http.HTTPTransport.URL)
            );
        }
        catch (java.net.MalformedURLException mue) {
            return null; // ???
        }
    }

    // From org.apache.axis.wsdl.Stub
    public synchronized void setMaintainSession(boolean session) {
        call.setMaintainSession(session);
    }

    // From javax.naming.Referenceable
    public javax.naming.Reference getReference() {
        return null; // ???
    }

    public String getMessage() throws java.rmi.RemoteException{
        if (call.get(org.apache.axis.transport.http.HTTPTransport.URL)
            == null) {
            throw new org.apache.axis.NoEndPointException();
        }
        call.set(org.apache.axis.transport.http.HTTPTransport.ACTION, "");
        Object resp = call.invoke("", "getMessage", new Object[] {});

        if (resp instanceof java.rmi.RemoteException) {
            throw (java.rmi.RemoteException)resp;
        }
        else {
             return (String) resp;
        }
    }

}
```

LISTING 5.5 HelloWorldService.java

```
/**
 * HelloWorldService.java
 *
 * This file was auto-generated from WSDL
 * by the Apache Axis Wsdl2java emitter.
 */

public class HelloWorldService {

    // Use to get a proxy class for HelloWorldServicePort
    private final java.lang.String HelloWorldServicePort_address
      = "http://localhost:8080/axis/HelloWorldService.jws";
    public HelloWorldServicePortType getHelloWorldServicePort() {
       java.net.URL endpoint;
        try {
            endpoint = new java.net.URL(HelloWorldServicePort_address);
        }
        catch (java.net.MalformedURLException e) {
            return null; // unlikely as URL was validated in wsdl2java
        }
        return getHelloWorldServicePort(endpoint);
    }

    public HelloWorldServicePortType
      getHelloWorldServicePort(java.net.URL portAddress) {
        try {
            return new HelloWorldServiceSoapBindingStub(portAddress);
        }
        catch (org.apache.axis.SerializationException e) {
            return null; // ???
        }
    }
}
```

In addition, the `wsdl2java` tool generates a client configuration XML file, shown in Listing 5.6, that describes how the different pieces all fit together.

LISTING 5.6 client-config.xml

```
<?xml version="1.0" encoding="UTF-8"?>
<engineConfig>
 <handlers>
  <handler class="org.apache.axis.transport.http.HTTPSender" name="HTTPSender"/>
  <handler class="org.apache.axis.transport.local.LocalSender"
    name="LocalSender"/>
 </handlers>
 <services/>
```

LISTING 5.6 continued

```
 <transports>
  <transport name="http" pivot="HTTPSender"/>
  <transport name="local" pivot="LocalSender"/>
 </transports>
 <typeMappings/>
</engineConfig>
```

A Java client code can use these three Java files to connect to the remote Web service, hiding all the Web service details in the process. To test your Web service, however, you need to write a client. For simplicity, you will write a just simple class that calls the `HelloWorldService` Web service from the command line and prints out the response.

The client code, then, is rather simple. First, you create an instance of the desired service, which acts as a stub for the remote service. The generated stub acts as a factory object, generating a new connection to the desired Web service with each invocation:

```
HelloWorldService service = new HelloWorldService();
```

To actually establish a connection, you need to obtain the appropriate `PortType` object, which encapsulates the actual calling functionality:

```
HelloWorldServicePortType port = service.getHelloWorldServicePort();
```

Now all you need to do is call the appropriate method for your Web service and display the result:

```
String response = port.getMessage();

System.out.println(response);
```

For completeness, the full code for the client is shown in Listing 5.7.

LISTING 5.7 `HelloWorldClient.java`

```
//
// HelloWorldClient.java
//
// This class creates the client-side service factory
// for the desired service, makes the remote procedure call,
// and displays the response.
//

public class HelloWorldClient {

  public static void main(String [] args) throws Exception {
```

LISTING 5.7 continued

```
    // Create an instance of the desired service

    HelloWorldService service = new HelloWorldService();


    // Use the factory method on the service to get the portType stub.

    HelloWorldServicePortType port = service.getHelloWorldServicePort();

    // Make the actual call

    String response = port.getMessage();

    System.out.println(response);
  }
}
```

At this point, you should have four Java files: `HelloWorldClient.java`, `HelloWorldService.java`, `HelloWorldServicePortType.java`, and `HelloWorldServiceSoapBindingStub.java`. All that remains is to compile them, and execute the `HelloWorldClient` to test your first Web service:

```
C:\projects>javac *.java

C:\projects>java HelloWorldClient
Hello World!
```

Congratulations! You just tested your first Web service. Although you called the client stub from a simple command-line interface program, nothing prevents you from calling this stub from a Swing GUI application, a JavaServer Page (JSP) or servlet, or even from a Java2 Micro Edition (J2ME) application. That's the beauty of Web services: They make distributed programming rather easy.

Under the Covers

If the preceding section left you feeling a little empty, you might appreciate actually seeing what happened when you executed `HelloWorldClient`. Because SOAP is an XML application, which in this case operates directly over HTTP, watching the wire isn't very difficult.

In fact, the AXIS distribution comes with a TCP monitoring tool that enables you to see the SOAP request and the appropriate SOAP response when you invoke a Web service. You should either start this tool in the background, or better yet, start in it in a separate window. On Windows, the best way to do this is to use the `start` command, which creates a new command prompt window that uses the same environment variables as the parent window, including the CLASSPATH:

```
C:\projects>start java org.apache.axis.utils.tcpmon
```

This brings up the TCPMonitor application, which enables you to monitor the SOAP communication. To set it up properly, you need to specify which port the TCP monitor should listen to, the target machine, and the port number on the target machine with which you are trying to communicate. To use this tool with the HelloWorld Web service, type **8880** for local port, **localhost** for the target host, and **8080** for the target port, and click Add. Now you need to change the port number to which the client stub in HelloWorldServer.java will try to connect. All you need to do is change the port number in the address string from 8080 to 8880, so that your client first connects to the TCP monitor, which then forwards the request to the target service. In other words, change this:

```
private final java.lang.String HelloWorldServicePort_address
    = http://localhost:8080/axis/HelloWorldService.jws";
```

to this:

```
private final java.lang.String HelloWorldServicePort_address
    = http://localhost:8880/axis/HelloWorldService.jws";
```

Now just recompile the HelloWorldService class and execute the HelloWorldClient Java application. The SOAP request and response appear in different panels of the TCPMonitor tool, as shown in Figure 5.7. For completeness, the SOAP request is shown in Listing 5.8 and the SOAP response is shown in Listing 5.9.

LISTING 5.8 The SOAP Request

```
POST /axis/HelloWorldService.jws HTTP/1.0
Content-Length: 288
Host: localhost
Content-Type: text/xml; charset=utf-8
SOAPAction: ""

<?xml version="1.0" encoding="UTF-8"?>
<SOAP-ENV:Envelope
  xmlns:SOAP-ENV=http://schemas.xmlsoap.org/soap/envelope/
  xmlns:xsd="http://www.w3.org/2001/XMLSchema"
  xmlns:xsi="http://www.w3.org/2001/XMLSchema-instance">
 <SOAP-ENV:Body>
  <getMessage/>
 </SOAP-ENV:Body>
</SOAP-ENV:Envelope>
```

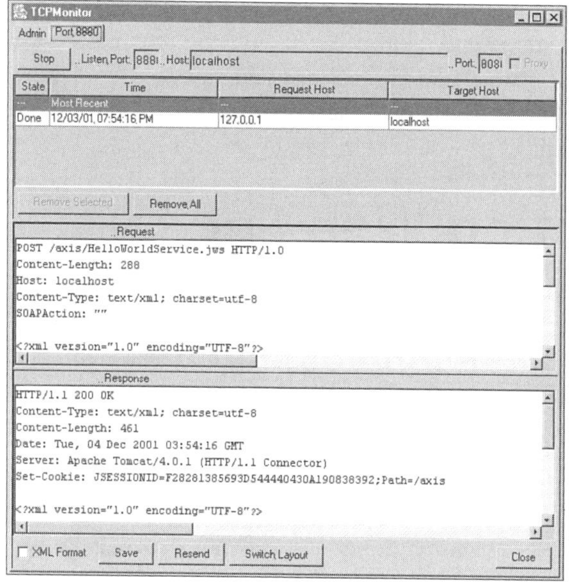

FIGURE 5.7
The TCP Monitor tool, showing the SOAP request and SOAP response when HelloWorldClient is invoked.

LISTING 5.9 The SOAP Response

```
HTTP/1.1 200 OK
Content-Type: text/xml; charset=utf-8
Content-Length: 461
Date: Sun, 02 Dec 2001 20:45:39 GMT
Server: Apache Tomcat/4.0.1 (HTTP/1.1 Connector)
Set-Cookie: JSESSIONID=709940D761F8752005509487D33532D9;Path=/axis

<?xml version="1.0" encoding="UTF-8"?>
<SOAP-ENV:Envelope
  SOAP-ENV:encodingStyle="http://schemas.xmlsoap.org/soap/encoding/"
  xmlns:SOAP-ENV="http://schemas.xmlsoap.org/soap/envelope/"
  xmlns:xsd="http://www.w3.org/2001/XMLSchema"
  xmlns:xsi="http://www.w3.org/2001/XMLSchema-instance">
 <SOAP-ENV:Body>
  <getMessageResponse>
   <getMessageResult xsi:type="xsd:string">Hello World!</getMessageResult>
  </getMessageResponse>
 </SOAP-ENV:Body>
</SOAP-ENV:Envelope>
```

If you look at the request and response, it is easy to grasp what is going on. In fact this is so simple, you can actually connect directly to the server that is accepting the SOAP request, in this case the Tomcat server, using a Telnet terminal and typing the request directly to the server. This shows the simplicity of SOAP, which is one of the main reasons for its popularity.

One of the other useful features of the TCPMonitor tool is the ability it gives you to edit the SOAP request and resend it directly. Although this won't affect your `HelloWorldService`, which doesn't take any parameters, you might want to try this out with other Web services. TCPMonitor also remembers requests, which means you can compare different requests when you're testing and debugging.

Generating Web Services

If you recall, when you first looked at the WSDL document that described the `HelloWorldService`, you saw how completely the WSDL document described your service. This enabled the `wsdl2java` tool to generate the client stubs that simplified the actual development of your client application. But how complete is the description?

You may be surprised to hear that you can use the WSDL document to generate a skeleton Java class file for the actual Web service. Why might this be interesting? Imagine you need to convert a Web service from some other language to Java. All you need to do is generate a WSDL document for the service, and then generate the skeleton class. Likewise, perhaps you want to participate in a business-to-business (or B2B) marketplace. If your partners provide you with the expected WSDL document defining the services that are required, you can easily generate the appropriate skeleton classes for the services and save considerable time and effort:

```
C:\projects>java org.apache.axis.wsdl.Wsdl2java
  --skeleton --verbose
  http://localhost:8080/axis/HelloWorldService.jws?wsdl
Parsing XML File: http://localhost:8080/axis/HelloWorldService.jws?wsdl
Generating portType interface: HelloWorldServicePortType.java
Generating client-side stub: HelloWorldServiceSoapBindingStub.java
Generating server-side skeleton: HelloWorldServiceSoapBindingSkeleton.java
Generating server-side impl template: HelloWorldServiceSoapBindingImpl.java
Generating service class: HelloWorldService.java
Generating deployment document: deploy.xml
Generating deployment document: undeploy.xml
```

As you can see, this generates both the client stubs, as well as the server skeleton. In this case, the `HelloWorldServiceSoapBindingSkeleton.java`, shown in Listing 5.10, provides the Web service skeleton file that is used by AXIS, whereas `HelloWorldServiceSoapBindingImpl.java`, shown in Listing 5.11, provides the actual implementation. To actually make this work, all you need to do is edit the implementation file and define the method that is actually made available as a Web service—in this case, `getMessage`.

LISTING 5.10 HelloWorldServiceSoapBindingSkeleton.java

```
/**
 * HelloWorldServiceSoapBindingSkeleton.java
 *
 * This file was auto-generated from WSDL
 * by the Apache Axis Wsdl2java emitter.
 */

public class HelloWorldServiceSoapBindingSkeleton {
    private HelloWorldServicePortType impl;

    public HelloWorldServiceSoapBindingSkeleton() {
        this.impl = new HelloWorldServiceSoapBindingImpl();
    }

    public HelloWorldServiceSoapBindingSkeleton(
      HelloWorldServicePortType impl) {
        this.impl = impl;
    }

    public Object getMessage() throws java.rmi.RemoteException
    {
        Object ret = impl.getMessage();
        return ret;
    }

}
```

LISTING 5.11 HelloWorldServiceSoapBindingImpl.java

```
/**
 * HelloWorldServiceSoapBindingImpl.java
 *
 * This file was auto-generated from WSDL
 * by the Apache Axis Wsdl2java emitter.
 */

public class HelloWorldServiceSoapBindingImpl
    implements HelloWorldServicePortType {

    public String getMessage() throws java.rmi.RemoteException {
        throw new java.rmi.RemoteException ("Not Yet Implemented");
    }
}
```

As you can see from Listing 5.11, all you need to do to implement the `getMessage` Web service is to delete the exception `throw` statement (because you're now providing the implementation) and add the statement that returns your greeting.

Along with generating the skeleton code, the `wsdl2java` tool also generates two XML files: `deploy.xml`, shown in Listing 5.12, and `undeploy.xml`, shown in Listing 5.13. A Web service provider, such as AXIS, can use these files to deploy or undeploy this particular Web service (as opposed to following the AXIS-specific JWS approach shown earlier in this chapter).

LISTING 5.12 `deploy.xml`

```
<!--                                                                  -->
<!--Use this file to deploy some handlers/chains and services       -->
<!--Two ways to do this:                                              -->
<!--  java org.apache.axis.utils.Admin deploy.xml                   -->
<!--     from the same dir that the Axis engine runs                  -->
<!--or                                                                -->
<!--  java org.apache.axis.client.AdminClient deploy.xml            -->
<!--     after the axis server is running                             -->
<!--This file will be replaced by WSDD once it's ready                -->

<m:deploy xmlns:m="AdminService">

   <!-- Services from HelloWorldService WSDL service -->

   <service name="HelloWorldServicePort" pivot="RPCDispatcher">
      <option name="className" value="HelloWorldServiceSoapBindingSkeleton"/>
      <option name="methodName" value=" getMessage"/>
   </service>
</m:deploy>
```

LISTING 5.13 `undeploy.xml`

```
<!--                                                                  -->
<!--Use this file to undeploy some handlers/chains and services       -->
<!--Two ways to do this:                                              -->
<!--  java org.apache.axis.utils.Admin undeploy.xml                   -->
<!--     from the same dir that the Axis engine runs                  -->
<!--or                                                                -->
<!--  java org.apache.axis.client.AdminClient undeploy.xml            -->
<!--     after the axis server is running                             -->
<!--This file will be replaced by WSDD once it's ready                -->

<m:undeploy xmlns:m="AdminService">

   <!-- Services from HelloWorldService WSDL service -->

   <service name="HelloWorldServicePort" pivot="RPCDispatcher">
   </service>
</m:undeploy>
```

As these listings show, deployment descriptors are rather simple. However, in AXIS, these are being phased out in favor of Web Service Deployment Descriptors, or WSDDs, which provide greater functionality and can be shared among different Web service providers.

Publishing and Finding Services

So far in this chapter, you have learned about building and describing Web services; but there is a third leg to the Web service tripod—Universal Discovery, Discovery and Integration, or UDDI. With UDDI, you can publish a Web service so others can see it, and you can find other Web services so you can call them. UDDI is discussed thoroughly in Chapters 9 and 10, "UDDI" and "UDDI in Depth."

Right now, the AXIS toolkit doesn't provide any basic UDDI services. So the discussion of UDDI in this chapter, is rather limited. However, other toolkits do, including WSTK, which is discussed in Chapter 23.

Summary

In this chapter, you built your first Java Web service, using the AXIS toolkit from the Apache Software Foundation. This Web service was a variant of the popular "Hello World!" example program, which, although not very extravagant, does demonstrate all the requisite basics. In Chapter 6, you will build on this simple example, to build a more complex JSP-based Web service.

CHAPTER 6

Building a JSP Web Service

by Robert Brunner

In This Chapter

In Chapter 5, "A Simple Java Web Service," you created a simple Web service, the mandatory Hello World application. Although it seems simple, it demonstrated all the machinery that has to be in place to build and deploy a Java Web Service. With that experience, you can now move on to a more advanced Web service.

The Application

The Web service that you will build in this chapter revolves around two fictitious companies: the ByteGourmet delivery service and the Thai Palace restaurant. ByteGourmet is in the business of providing a delivery service for restaurants in the local community, adding a small surcharge. The Thai Palace is the first restaurant in the area to sign up for this service.

The restaurants provide their menus to ByteGourmet via a Web service. ByteGourmet has its own Web site that calls the appropriate restaurant's Web service to obtain the relevant menu. The overall architecture, shown in Figure 6.1, involves JavaServer Pages, servlets, JavaBeans, and Java-based Web services. As it is written, the example application is easily extensible as well, because the menu has its own XML schema and XSL stylesheet.

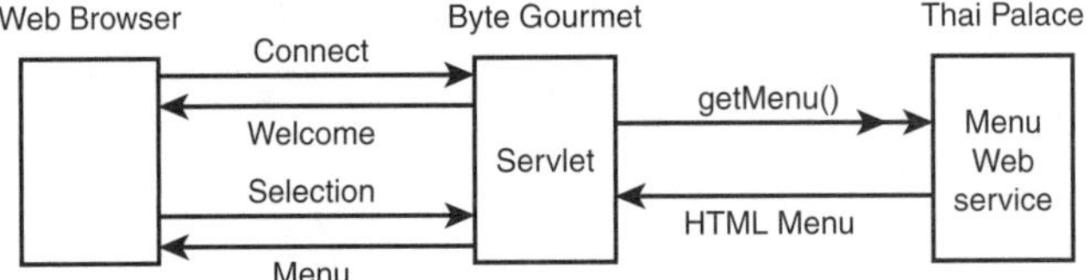

FIGURE 6.1 *An overview of the ByteGourmet Web service application.*

The Menu

To simplify the building of their business, the ByteGourmet developers first wrote an XML schema to describe allowable menu XML-based documents. Individual restaurants in the ByteGourmet architecture can extend this schema, shown in Listing 6.1, which enables all menus to be individually validated.

The schema is rather simple, defining several new types, and referencing them where appropriate.

LISTING 6.1 `menu.xsd`

```
<?xml version="1.0"?>
<xs:schema xmlns:xs="http://www.w3.org/2001/XMLSchema"
  elementFormDefault="qualified"
```

LISTING 6.1 continued

```
  attributeFormDefault="unqualified"
>

   <xs:annotation>
      <xs:documentation xml:lang="en">
         A sample XML Schema for a Restaurant Menu
      </xs:documentation>
   </xs:annotation>

   <xs:element name="menu" type="menuType" />

   <xs:complexType name="menuType">
      <xs:sequence>
         <xs:element name="name" type="nameType" />

         <xs:element name="fax" type="faxType" />

         <xs:element name="fax-order" type="fax-orderType" />

         <xs:element name="category" type="categoryType"
           minOccurs="1" maxOccurs="unbounded" />
      </xs:sequence>
   </xs:complexType>

   <xs:complexType name="categoryType">
      <xs:sequence>
         <xs:element name="name" type="nameType" />

         <xs:element name="item" type="itemType"
           minOccurs="1" maxOccurs="unbounded" />
      </xs:sequence>
   </xs:complexType>

   <xs:complexType name="itemType">
      <xs:sequence>
         <xs:element name="name" type="nameType" />

         <xs:element name="description" type="descriptionType" />

         <xs:element name="price" type="priceType" />
      </xs:sequence>

      <xs:attribute name="veggie" type="xs:boolean" />

      <xs:attribute name="spicy" type="xs:boolean" />

      <xs:attribute name="number" type="numberType" />
   </xs:complexType>
```

LISTING 6.1 continued

```
<xs:simpleType name="nameType">
   <xs:restriction base="xs:string">
      <xs:minLength value="1" />

      <xs:maxLength value="40" />
   </xs:restriction>
</xs:simpleType>

<xs:simpleType name="faxType">
   <xs:restriction base="xs:string">
      <xs:minLength value="8" />

      <xs:maxLength value="14" />
   </xs:restriction>
</xs:simpleType>

<xs:simpleType name="fax-orderType">
   <xs:restriction base="xs:string">
      <xs:minLength value="0" />

      <xs:maxLength value="240" />
   </xs:restriction>
</xs:simpleType>

<xs:simpleType name="numberType">
   <xs:restriction base="xs:decimal">
      <xs:totalDigits value="3" />

      <xs:fractionDigits value="0" />

      <xs:minExclusive value="0" />

      <xs:maxInclusive value="125" />
   </xs:restriction>
</xs:simpleType>

<xs:simpleType name="descriptionType">
   <xs:restriction base="xs:string">
      <xs:minLength value="4" />

      <xs:maxLength value="120" />
   </xs:restriction>
</xs:simpleType>

<xs:simpleType name="priceType">
   <xs:restriction base="xs:decimal">
      <xs:fractionDigits value="2" />

      <xs:minInclusive value="0" />
```

LISTING 6.1 continued

```
         <xs:maxExclusive value="10" />
      </xs:restriction>
   </xs:simpleType>
</xs:schema>
```

With this schema in hand, the individual restaurants can create XML documents that encode their menus. XML enables them to support multiple client types, including Web browsers that read HTML, mobile phones that read WAP, and local printers that prefer PDF.

The menu for the Thai Palace is shown in Listing 6.2, and includes different food categories, item identifiers, descriptions, and prices.

LISTING 6.2 menu.xml

```
<?xml version="1.0" encoding="UTF-8" ?>

<menu>

   <name>Thai Palace</name>

   <fax>(800) 867-5309</fax>

   <fax-order>Fax this menu back with your selections circled. If you want
➥more than one item, indicate the number of items in the number
➥column. Your order will be ready 30 minutes from when we receive
➥the fax.
   </fax-order>

   <category>      <name>appetizers</name>

      <item number="1" veggie="true" spicy="false">
         <name>Spring Roll</name>

         <description>Thai style egg roll with glass noodles and vegetables
➥served in a plum sauce</description>

         <price>1.75</price>
      </item>

      <item number="2" veggie="true" spicy="false">
         <name>Fried Tofu</name>

         <description>Deep-fried tofu served with a plum sauce</description>

         <price>2.25</price>
```

LISTING 6.2 continued

```
      </item>
   </category>

   <category>
      <name>soups</name>

      <item number="3" veggie="true" spicy="true">
         <name>Tom Yum</name>

         <description>
           Mushroom in hot and sour soup with a touch of lemon grass
         </description>

         <price>4.75</price>
      </item>

      <item number="4" veggie="false" spicy="false">
         <name>Wonton Soup</name>

         <description>
           Thai-style chicken dumpling soup, topped with chicken,
➥barbecued pork, and green onions
         </description>

         <price>5.25</price>
      </item>
   </category>

   <category>
      <name>salads</name>

      <item number="5" veggie="false" spicy="true">
         <name>Larb</name>

         <description>
           Ground meat mixed with lime juice, onion, chili, and mint leaves
➥served with cabbage
         </description>

         <price>4.75</price>
      </item>

      <item number="6" veggie="false" spicy="true">
         <name>Yum Yai</name>

         <description>
           Shrimp, chicken, cucumber, and onion served on a bed of lettuce
➥with sweet and sour dressing
```

LISTING 6.2 continued

```
            </description>

            <price>3.25</price>
        </item>
    </category>

    <category>
        <name>curry</name>

        <item number="7" veggie="false" spicy="true">
            <name>Prig King</name>

            <description>
              Green bean stir fry with chili paste
            </description>

            <price>5.75</price>
        </item>

        <item number="8" veggie="true" spicy="true">
            <name>Pa-Nang</name>

            <description>
              Ground peanut in curry with Thai spices and coconut milk
            </description>

            <price>5.25</price>
        </item>
    </category>

    <category>
        <name>rice</name>

        <item number="9" veggie="true" spicy="false">
            <name>House Fried Rice</name>

            <description>
              Fried rice with onion, tomato, peas, carrot, and egg
            </description>

            <price>4.75</price>
        </item>

        <item number="10" veggie="false" spicy="true">
            <name>spicy Fried Rice</name>

            <description>
              Fried rice with tomato, onion, bell pepper, and sweet basil
            </description>
```

LISTING 6.2 continued

```
            <price>5.25</price>
         </item>
      </category>

      <category>
         <name>noodles</name>

         <item number="11" veggie="true" spicy="false">
            <name>Pad Thai</name>

            <description>
              Pan-fried rice noodles with egg, onion, and bean sprouts topped
➥with crushed peanuts
            </description>

            <price>5.75</price>
         </item>

         <item number="12" veggie="true" spicy="true">
            <name>Phad-See-Yew</name>

            <description>
              Pan-fried flat noodles with egg and broccoli in brown sauce
            </description>

            <price>4.50</price>
         </item>
      </category>
</menu>
```

The next step for the ByteGourmet developers was to write an XSLT stylesheet that would transform the XML menu documents into HTML. Eventually, other stylesheets will be developed as well, to facilitate WML and XHTML formats.

The stylesheet shown in Listing 6.3 generates a simple HTML menu for any restaurant that implements an XML menu document. This stylesheet produces multiple HTML tables—one for each food category—and generates checks to indicate vegetarian or spicy selections.

LISTING 6.3 menu.xsl

```
<?xml version="1.0" encoding="UTF-8"?>
<xsl:stylesheet version="1.0"
xmlns:xsl="http://www.w3.org/1999/XSL/Transform"
>
```

LISTING 6.3 continued

```
<xsl:output method="html"/>

<xsl:template match="/" >
   <html>
      <xsl:apply-templates />
   </html>
</xsl:template>

<xsl:template match="menu">
   <head>
      <title>
         <xsl:value-of select="name" />
      </title>
   </head>

   <body>
      <h1>
      <xsl:value-of select="name" /> :
      <xsl:value-of select="fax" /> (FAX)
      </h1>

      <h4>
         <xsl:value-of select="fax-order" />
      </h1>

      <hr />

      <xsl:apply-templates />
   </body>
</xsl:template>

<xsl:template match="category">
   <h2 align="center">
      <xsl:value-of select="name" />
   </h2>

   <table border="2" width="100%">
      <tr>
         <th width="10%">Number</th>

         <th width="10%">Veggie</th>

         <th width="10%">Spicy</th>

         <th width="10%">Name</th>

         <th width="50%">Description</th>
```

LISTING 6.3 continued

```
            <th width="10%">Price</th>
         </tr>

         <xsl:apply-templates />
      </table>
   </xsl:template>

   <xsl:template match="item">
      <tr>
         <td align="center">
            <xsl:value-of select="@number" />
         </td>

         <td align="center">
            <xsl:choose>
               <xsl:when test="@veggie='true'">Yes</xsl:when>

               <xsl:when test="@veggie='false'">No</xsl:when>
            </xsl:choose>
         </td>

         <td align="center">
            <xsl:choose>
               <xsl:when test="@spicy='true'">Yes</xsl:when>

               <xsl:when test="@spicy='false'">No</xsl:when>
            </xsl:choose>
         </td>

         <td align="center">
            <xsl:value-of select="name" />
         </td>

         <td align="left">
            <xsl:value-of select="description" />
         </td>

         <td align="right">$
         <xsl:value-of select="price" />
         </td>
      </tr>
   </xsl:template>

   <xsl:template match="*" />
</xsl:stylesheet>
```

The rest of the application discussed in this chapter deals with only the HTML representation for the menu. To generate it, you can use any XSLT processor. The HTML menu shown in Listing 6.4 was generated with the open source, Instant Saxon XSLT processor, which is available at http://saxon.sourceforge.net.

LISTING 6.4 menu.html

```
<html>
   <head>
      <meta http-equiv="Content-Type" content="text/html; charset=utf-8">

      <title>Thai Palace</title>
   </head>
   <body>
      <h1>Thai Palace :
         (800) 867-5309 (FAX)
      </h1>
      <h4>Fax this menu back with your selections circled. If you want more
➥than one item, indicate the number of items in the number column.
➥Your order will be ready 30 minutes from when we receive the fax.
      </h4>
      <hr>

      <h2 align="center">appetizers</h2>
      <table border="2" width="100%">
         <tr>
            <th width="10%">Number</th>
            <th width="10%">Veggie</th>
            <th width="10%">Spicy</th>
            <th width="10%">Name</th>
            <th width="50%">Description</th>
            <th width="10%">Price</th>
         </tr>

         <tr>
            <td align="center">1</td>
            <td align="center">Yes</td>
            <td align="center">No</td>
            <td align="center">Spring Roll</td>
            <td align="left">Thai-style egg roll with glass noodles and
➥vegetables served in a plum sauce</td>
            <td align="right">$
               1.75
            </td>
         </tr>

         <tr>
            <td align="center">2</td>
            <td align="center">Yes</td>
            <td align="center">No</td>
```

LISTING 6.4 continued

```
            <td align="center">Fried Tofu</td>
            <td align="left">Deep-fried tofu served with a plum sauce</td>
            <td align="right">$
               2.25
            </td>
         </tr>

      </table>

      <h2 align="center">soups</h2>
      <table border="2" width="100%">
         <tr>
            <th width="10%">Number</th>
            <th width="10%">Veggie</th>
            <th width="10%">Spicy</th>
            <th width="10%">Name</th>
            <th width="50%">Description</th>
            <th width="10%">Price</th>
         </tr>

         <tr>
            <td align="center">3</td>
            <td align="center">Yes</td>
            <td align="center">Yes</td>
            <td align="center">Tom Yum</td>
            <td align="left">
                         Mushroom in hot and sour soup with a touch of lemon
➥grass

            </td>
            <td align="right">$
               4.75
            </td>
         </tr>

         <tr>
            <td align="center">4</td>
            <td align="center">No</td>
            <td align="center">No</td>
            <td align="center">Wonton Soup</td>
            <td align="left">
                         Thai-style chicken dumpling soup, topped with
➥chicken, barbecued pork, and green onions

            </td>
            <td align="right">$
               5.25
            </td>
```

LISTING 6.4 continued

```
      </tr>

   </table>

   <h2 align="center">salads</h2>
   <table border="2" width="100%">
      <tr>
         <th width="10%">Number</th>
         <th width="10%">Veggie</th>
         <th width="10%">Spicy</th>
         <th width="10%">Name</th>
         <th width="50%">Description</th>
         <th width="10%">Price</th>
      </tr>

      <tr>
         <td align="center">5</td>
         <td align="center">No</td>
         <td align="center">Yes</td>
         <td align="center">Larb</td>
         <td align="left">
                     Ground meat mixed with lime juice, onion, chili,
➥and mint leaves served with cabbage

         </td>
         <td align="right">$
            4.75
         </td>
      </tr>

      <tr>
         <td align="center">6</td>
         <td align="center">No</td>
         <td align="center">Yes</td>
         <td align="center">Yum Yai</td>
         <td align="left">
                     Shrimp, chicken, cucumber, and onion served on a
➥bed of lettuce with sweet and sour dressing

         </td>
         <td align="right">$
            3.25
         </td>
      </tr>

   </table>

   <h2 align="center">curry</h2>
```

LISTING 6.4 continued

```
      <table border="2" width="100%">
         <tr>
            <th width="10%">Number</th>
            <th width="10%">Veggie</th>
            <th width="10%">Spicy</th>
            <th width="10%">Name</th>
            <th width="50%">Description</th>
            <th width="10%">Price</th>
         </tr>

         <tr>
            <td align="center">7</td>
            <td align="center">No</td>
            <td align="center">Yes</td>
            <td align="center">Prig King</td>
            <td align="left">
                          Green bean stir fry with chili paste

            </td>
            <td align="right">$
               5.75
            </td>
         </tr>

         <tr>
            <td align="center">8</td>
            <td align="center">Yes</td>
            <td align="center">Yes</td>
            <td align="center">Pa-Nang</td>
            <td align="left">
                          Ground peanut in curry with Thai spices and coconut
➥milk

            </td>
            <td align="right">$
               5.25
            </td>
         </tr>

      </table>

      <h2 align="center">rice</h2>
      <table border="2" width="100%">
         <tr>
            <th width="10%">Number</th>
            <th width="10%">Veggie</th>
            <th width="10%">Spicy</th>
            <th width="10%">Name</th>
            <th width="50%">Description</th>
```

LISTING 6.4 continued

```
            <th width="10%">Price</th>
         </tr>

         <tr>
            <td align="center">9</td>
            <td align="center">Yes</td>
            <td align="center">No</td>
            <td align="center">House Fried Rice</td>
            <td align="left">
                           Fried rice with onion, tomato, peas, carrot, and egg

            </td>
            <td align="right">$
               4.75
            </td>
         </tr>

         <tr>
            <td align="center">10</td>
            <td align="center">No</td>
            <td align="center">Yes</td>
            <td align="center">spicy Fried Rice</td>
            <td align="left">
                           Fried rice with tomato, onion, bell pepper, and
➥sweet basil

            </td>
            <td align="right">$
               5.25
            </td>
         </tr>

      </table>

      <h2 align="center">noodles</h2>
      <table border="2" width="100%">
         <tr>
            <th width="10%">Number</th>
            <th width="10%">Veggie</th>
            <th width="10%">Spicy</th>
            <th width="10%">Name</th>
            <th width="50%">Description</th>
            <th width="10%">Price</th>
         </tr>

         <tr>
            <td align="center">11</td>
            <td align="center">Yes</td>
```

LISTING 6.4 continued

```
            <td align="center">No</td>
            <td align="center">Pad Thai</td>
            <td align="left">
                           Pan-fried rice noodles with egg, onion, and bean
➥sprouts topped with crushed peanuts

            </td>
            <td align="right">$
               5.75
            </td>
         </tr>

         <tr>
            <td align="center">12</td>
            <td align="center">Yes</td>
            <td align="center">Yes</td>
            <td align="center">Phad-See-Yew</td>
            <td align="left">
                           Pan-fried flat noodles with egg and broccoli
➥in brown sauce

            </td>
            <td align="right">$
               4.50
            </td>
         </tr>

      </table>

   </body>
</html>
```

These four files are saved in the `C:\projects\menu` directory, where the restaurant Web service accesses them.

Building the Web Service

With the preliminaries out of the way, you can now start building your Web service. In this case, the Web service reads the four files created in the last section from the `C:\projects\menu` directory and sends them to the Web service client. Thus your Web service will be very simple, requiring that you make only small changes to the `HelloWorldService` you developed in Chapter 5.

The Thai Palace Menu Service

The restaurant's Web service, shown in Listing 6.5, exposes four separate methods, one for each file that will be made available to the client. Although this Web service just reads the files directly, the client doesn't know this. In fact, as far as the client is concerned, the Web service could hide someone who is typing furiously at a keyboard. More likely, you might want to automatically generate the HTML when requested, or perhaps perform validation on the XML menu document.

LISTING 6.5 ThaiPalaceMenuService.jws

```
//
// The class that implements the Web service.
// This service is the Thai Palace Menu Web service.
// A client can receive the Menu XML document, the Menu
/// Schema document, and the Menu Stylesheet for generating
// an HTMLmenu representation. Other views can be supported
// by adding the appropriate methods, such as an XSL-FO
// method that returns an FO stylesheet that generates a PDF menu.
//

import java.io.* ;

public class ThaiPalaceMenuService {

  // The private class variables.

  // The buffer size is used for reading the relevant files.

  private final static int cBufferSize = 4096 ;

  // Menu Path

  private final static String sMenuPath = "C:\\projects\\menu\\" ;

  // The location of the Menu File

  private final static String sMenu = "menu.html" ;

  // The location of the Menu Schema File

  private final static String sMenuSchema = "menu.xsd" ;

  // The location of the Menu Document File

  private final static String sMenuDocument = "menu.xml" ;

  // The location of the Menu Stylesheet File
```

LISTING 6.5 continued

```
  private final static String sMenuStylesheet = "menu.xsl" ;

  // Here are the methods that implement the Web services.

  public String getMenu() throws IOException {

    return(fileToString(sMenuPath + sMenu)) ;
  }

  public String getMenuSchema() throws IOException {

    return(fileToString(sMenuPath + sMenuSchema)) ;
  }

  public String getMenuDocument() throws IOException {

    return(fileToString(sMenuPath + sMenuDocument)) ;
  }

  public String getMenuStylesheet() throws IOException {

    return(fileToString(sMenuPath + sMenuStylesheet)) ;
  }

  //
  // This method reads a File into a String. It is based on recipe 9.5
  // from Ian Darwin's Java Cookbook, published by O'Reilly.
  //

  private String fileToString(String filename) throws IOException {

    File fMenu= new File(filename) ;

    FileReader fr = new FileReader(fMenu) ;

    StringBuffer sb = new StringBuffer() ;
    char[] buffer = new char[cBufferSize] ;
    int n ;

    while((n = fr.read(buffer)) > 0){
      sb.append(buffer, 0, n) ;
    }

    return(sb.toString()) ;
  }
}
```

Because this application requires at least two servers—one each for the Web service and the ByteGourmet server—the different servers are deployed using different Web contexts. The Thai Palace Web service is deployed to the `tpmenu` context, whereas the ByteGourmet server is deployed to the `bg` context. In practice, this means that the Thai Palace Web service is located at `http://localhost:8080/axis/tpmenu/ThaiPalaceMenuService.jws`, whereas the ByteGourmet server is located at `http://localhost:8080/bg/ByteGourmetServer`. Of course, these context names are arbitrary; you can utilize whatever you want as long as you are consistent.

To make deployment easier, the Web service is saved as a JWS file in the `tpmenu` subdirectory of the `axis` directory. This enables AXIS to automatically deploy your Web service when it is first called.

As you can see, the most complex portion of the Web service is the task of reading each file into a `String`. Now that the Web service is written, you need to start up the server process that provides access to the Web service. In this case, this is the Tomcat server. All you need to do is execute the startup script (batch file on Windows, and shell script on Linux). Remember this JWS file should be saved in the `webapps\axis\tpmenu` subdirectory of your Tomcat installation.

The Menu WSDL

Before you can test out the Thai Palace Web service, you should first generate the WSDL document for it, which, if you remember from Chapter 5, can be obtained by appending`?wsdl` to the end of the desired Web service URL. Thus, the WSDL shown in Listing 6.6 was generated by the following URL: `http://localhost:8080/axis/tpmenu/ThaiPalaceMenuService.jws?wsdl`.

LISTING 6.6 ThaiPalaceMenuService.wsdl

```
<?xml version="1.0" encoding="UTF-8"?>
<definitions
  targetNamespace="http://localhost:8080/axis/tpmenu/ThaiPalaceMenuService.jws"
  xmlns="http://schemas.xmlsoap.org/wsdl/"
  xmlns:serviceNS="http://localhost:8080/axis/tpmenu/ThaiPalaceMenuService.jws"
  xmlns:soap="http://schemas.xmlsoap.org/wsdl/soap/"
  xmlns:xsd="http://www.w3.org/2001/XMLSchema">
  <message name="fileToStringRequest">
    <part name="arg0" type="xsd:string"/>
  </message>
  <message name="getMenuDocumentRequest">
  </message>
  <message name="getMenuStylesheetRequest">
```

Listing 6.6 continued

```
</message>
<message name="getMenuSchemaRequest">
</message>
<message name="getMenuStylesheetResponse">
  <part name="getMenuStylesheetResult" type="xsd:string"/>
</message>
<message name="getMenuDocumentResponse">
  <part name="getMenuDocumentResult" type="xsd:string"/>
</message>
<message name="getMenuRequest">
</message>
<message name="getMenuSchemaResponse">
  <part name="getMenuSchemaResult" type="xsd:string"/>
</message>
<message name="getMenuResponse">
  <part name="getMenuResult" type="xsd:string"/>
</message>
<message name="fileToStringResponse">
  <part name="fileToStringResult" type="xsd:string"/>
</message>
<portType name="ThaiPalaceMenuServicePortType">
  <operation name="fileToString">
    <input message="serviceNS:fileToStringRequest"/>
    <output message="serviceNS:fileToStringResponse"/>
  </operation>
  <operation name="getMenu">
    <input message="serviceNS:getMenuRequest"/>
    <output message="serviceNS:getMenuResponse"/>
  </operation>
  <operation name="getMenuDocument">
    <input message="serviceNS:getMenuDocumentRequest"/>
    <output message="serviceNS:getMenuDocumentResponse"/>
  </operation>
  <operation name="getMenuSchema">
    <input message="serviceNS:getMenuSchemaRequest"/>
    <output message="serviceNS:getMenuSchemaResponse"/>
  </operation>
  <operation name="getMenuStylesheet">
    <input message="serviceNS:getMenuStylesheetRequest"/>
    <output message="serviceNS:getMenuStylesheetResponse"/>
  </operation>
</portType>
<binding name="ThaiPalaceMenuServiceSoapBinding"
  type="serviceNS:ThaiPalaceMenuServicePortType">
  <soap:binding style="rpc" transport="http://schemas.xmlsoap.org/soap/http"/>
  <operation name="fileToString">
    <soap:operation soapAction="" style="rpc"/>
    <input>
```

LISTING 6.6 continued

```
      <soap:body encodingStyle="http://schemas.xmlsoap.org/soap/encoding/"
        namespace="" use="encoded"/>
    </input>
    <output>
      <soap:body encodingStyle="http://schemas.xmlsoap.org/soap/encoding/"
        namespace="" use="encoded"/>
    </output>
  </operation>
  <operation name="getMenu">
    <soap:operation soapAction="" style="rpc"/>
    <input>
      <soap:body encodingStyle="http://schemas.xmlsoap.org/soap/encoding/"
        namespace="" use="encoded"/>
    </input>
    <output>
      <soap:body encodingStyle="http://schemas.xmlsoap.org/soap/encoding/"
        namespace="" use="encoded"/>
    </output>
  </operation>
  <operation name="getMenuDocument">
    <soap:operation soapAction="" style="rpc"/>
    <input>
      <soap:body encodingStyle="http://schemas.xmlsoap.org/soap/encoding/"
        namespace="" use="encoded"/>
    </input>
    <output>
      <soap:body encodingStyle="http://schemas.xmlsoap.org/soap/encoding/"
        namespace="" use="encoded"/>
    </output>
  </operation>
  <operation name="getMenuSchema">
    <soap:operation soapAction="" style="rpc"/>
    <input>
      <soap:body encodingStyle="http://schemas.xmlsoap.org/soap/encoding/"
        namespace="" use="encoded"/>
    </input>
    <output>
      <soap:body encodingStyle="http://schemas.xmlsoap.org/soap/encoding/"
        namespace="" use="encoded"/>
    </output>
  </operation>
  <operation name="getMenuStylesheet">
    <soap:operation soapAction="" style="rpc"/>
    <input>
      <soap:body encodingStyle="http://schemas.xmlsoap.org/soap/encoding/"
        namespace="" use="encoded"/>
    </input>
    <output>
```

LISTING 6.6 continued

```
        <soap:body encodingStyle="http://schemas.xmlsoap.org/soap/encoding/"
          namespace="" use="encoded"/>
      </output>
    </operation>
  </binding>
  <service name="ThaiPalaceMenuService">
    <port binding="serviceNS:ThaiPalaceMenuServiceSoapBinding"
      name="ThaiPalaceMenuServicePort">
      <soap:address location="http://localhost:8080/axis/tpmenu/
➥ThaiPalaceMenuService.jws"/>
    </port>
  </service>
</definitions>
```

Although it's verbose, as most XML documents are, this WSDL document is rather straightforward. As you can see, it declares the four methods that you exposed: `getMenu()`, `getMenuDocument()`, `getmenuSchema()`, and `getMenuStylesheet()`. The WSDL also contains the server address that indicates where the Web service is hosted.

Thai Menu Web Service Client

Before allowing the world to see the Menu Web service, you need to test it out. Just as you did in Chapter 5 with the `HelloWorldService`, you can use the `wsdl2java` tool, along with the service WSDL document, to generate the client stub classes. First you need to set up your environment. If you create a new directory, called `thai` under the `projects` directory, you can add the appropriate `jar` files to your `CLASSPATH`, which should all be in the project's `lib` directory:

```
C:\projects\thai>set CLASSPATH=.
C:\projects\thai>set CLASSPATH=%CLASSPATH%;..\lib\axis.jar
C:\projects\thai>set CLASSPATH=%CLASSPATH%;..\lib\clutil.jar
C:\projects\thai>set CLASSPATH=%CLASSPATH%;..\lib\log4j-core.jar
C:\projects\thai>set CLASSPATH=%CLASSPATH%;..\lib\wsdl4j.jar
C:\projects\thai>set CLASSPATH=%CLASSPATH%;..\lib\xerces.jar
```

After you have set the `CLASSPATH`, all you need to do is call the `wsdl2java` tool, which does the hard part:

```
C:\projects\thai>java org.apache.axis.wsdl.Wsdl2java
  -verbose http://localhost:8080/axis/tpmenu/ThaiPalaceMenuService.jws?wsdl
Parsing XML File: http://localhost:8080/axis/tpmenu/
➥ThaiPalaceMenuService.jws?wsdl
Generating portType interface: ThaiPalaceMenuServicePortType.java
Generating client-side stub: ThaiPalaceMenuServiceSoapBindingStub.java
Generating service class: ThaiPalaceMenuService.java
Generating deployment document: deploy.xml
Generating deployment document: undeploy.xml
```

As the tool indicates, three new Java classes are generated: `ThaiPalaceMenuService.java`, shown in Listing 6.7, `ThaiPalaceMenuServicePortType.java`, shown in Listing 6.8, and `ThaiPalaceMenuServiceSoapBindingStub.java`, shown in Listing 6.9.

LISTING 6.7 ThaiPalaceMenuService.java

```
/**
 * ThaiPalaceMenuService.java
 *
 * This file was auto-generated from WSDL
 * by the Apache Axis Wsdl2java emitter.
 */

public class ThaiPalaceMenuService {

    // Use to get a proxy class for ThaiPalaceMenuServicePort
    private final java.lang.String
      ThaiPalaceMenuServicePort_address =
        "http://localhost:8080/axis/tpmenu/ThaiPalaceMenuService.jws";
    public ThaiPalaceMenuServicePortType getThaiPalaceMenuServicePort() {
       java.net.URL endpoint;
        try {
            endpoint = new java.net.URL(ThaiPalaceMenuServicePort_address);
        }
        catch (java.net.MalformedURLException e) {
            return null; // unlikely as URL was validated in wsdl2java
        }
        return getThaiPalaceMenuServicePort(endpoint);
    }

    public ThaiPalaceMenuServicePortType
      getThaiPalaceMenuServicePort(java.net.URL portAddress) {
        try {
            return new ThaiPalaceMenuServiceSoapBindingStub(portAddress);
        }
        catch (org.apache.axis.SerializationException e) {
            return null; // ???
        }
    }
}
```

LISTING 6.8 ThaiPalaceMenuServicePortType.java

```
/**
 * ThaiPalaceMenuServicePortType.java
 *
 * This file was auto-generated from WSDL
 * by the Apache Axis Wsdl2java emitter.
```

LISTING 6.8 continued

```
 */

public interface ThaiPalaceMenuServicePortType extends java.rmi.Remote {
    public String fileToString(String arg0) throws java.rmi.RemoteException;
    public String getMenu() throws java.rmi.RemoteException;
    public String getMenuDocument() throws java.rmi.RemoteException;
    public String getMenuSchema() throws java.rmi.RemoteException;
    public String getMenuStylesheet() throws java.rmi.RemoteException;
}
```

LISTING 6.9 ThaiPalaceMenuServiceSoapBindingStub.java

```
/**
 * ThaiPalaceMenuServiceSoapBindingStub.java
 *
 * This file was auto-generated from WSDL
 * by the Apache Axis Wsdl2java emitter.
 */

public class ThaiPalaceMenuServiceSoapBindingStub
  extends org.apache.axis.wsdl.Stub
  implements ThaiPalaceMenuServicePortType {

    private org.apache.axis.client.ServiceClient call = new
      org.apache.axis.client.ServiceClient(
        new org.apache.axis.transport.http.HTTPTransport()
      );

    private java.util.Hashtable properties = new java.util.Hashtable();

    public ThaiPalaceMenuServiceSoapBindingStub(java.net.URL endpointURL)
      throws org.apache.axis.SerializationException {
         this();
         call.set(org.apache.axis.transport.http.HTTPTransport.URL,
           endpointURL.toString());
    }
    public ThaiPalaceMenuServiceSoapBindingStub()
      throws org.apache.axis.SerializationException {
    }

    public void _setProperty(String name, Object value) {
        properties.put(name, value);
    }

    // From org.apache.axis.wsdl.Stub
    public Object _getProperty(String name) {
        return properties.get(name);
    }
```

LISTING 6.9 continued

```
    // From org.apache.axis.wsdl.Stub
    public void _setTargetEndpoint(java.net.URL address) {
        call.set(org.apache.axis.transport.http.HTTPTransport.URL,
          address.toString());
    }

    // From org.apache.axis.wsdl.Stub
    public java.net.URL _getTargetEndpoint() {
        try {
            return new java.net.URL((String)
              call.get(org.apache.axis.transport.http.HTTPTransport.URL));
        }
        catch (java.net.MalformedURLException mue) {
            return null; // ???
        }
    }

    // From org.apache.axis.wsdl.Stub
    public synchronized void setMaintainSession(boolean session) {
        call.setMaintainSession(session);
    }

    // From javax.naming.Referenceable
    public javax.naming.Reference getReference() {
        return null; // ???
    }

    public String fileToString(String arg0) throws java.rmi.RemoteException{
        if (call.get(org.apache.axis.transport.http.HTTPTransport.URL)
➥== null) {
            throw new org.apache.axis.NoEndPointException();
        }
        call.set(org.apache.axis.transport.http.HTTPTransport.ACTION, "");
        Object resp = call.invoke("", "fileToString", new Object[] {new
org.apache.axis.message.RPCParam("arg0", arg0)});

        if (resp instanceof java.rmi.RemoteException) {
            throw (java.rmi.RemoteException)resp;
        }
        else {
             return (String) resp;
        }
    }

    public String getMenu() throws java.rmi.RemoteException{
        if (call.get(org.apache.axis.transport.http.HTTPTransport.URL)
➥== null) {
            throw new org.apache.axis.NoEndPointException();
```

LISTING 6.9 continued

```
        }
        call.set(org.apache.axis.transport.http.HTTPTransport.ACTION, "");
        Object resp = call.invoke("", "getMenu", new Object[] {});

        if (resp instanceof java.rmi.RemoteException) {
            throw (java.rmi.RemoteException)resp;
        }
        else {
             return (String) resp;
        }
    }

    public String getMenuDocument() throws java.rmi.RemoteException{
        if (call.get(org.apache.axis.transport.http.HTTPTransport.URL)
➥== null) {
            throw new org.apache.axis.NoEndPointException();
        }
        call.set(org.apache.axis.transport.http.HTTPTransport.ACTION, "");
        Object resp = call.invoke("", "getMenuDocument", new Object[] {});

        if (resp instanceof java.rmi.RemoteException) {
            throw (java.rmi.RemoteException)resp;
        }
        else {
             return (String) resp;
        }
    }

    public String getMenuSchema() throws java.rmi.RemoteException{
        if (call.get(org.apache.axis.transport.http.HTTPTransport.URL)
➥== null) {
            throw new org.apache.axis.NoEndPointException();
        }
        call.set(org.apache.axis.transport.http.HTTPTransport.ACTION, "");
        Object resp = call.invoke("", "getMenuSchema", new Object[] {});

        if (resp instanceof java.rmi.RemoteException) {
            throw (java.rmi.RemoteException)resp;
        }
        else {
             return (String) resp;
        }
    }

    public String getMenuStylesheet() throws java.rmi.RemoteException{
        if (call.get(org.apache.axis.transport.http.HTTPTransport.URL)
➥== null) {
            throw new org.apache.axis.NoEndPointException();
        }
```

LISTING 6.9 continued

```
        call.set(org.apache.axis.transport.http.HTTPTransport.ACTION, "");
        Object resp = call.invoke("", "getMenuStylesheet", new Object[] {});

        if (resp instanceof java.rmi.RemoteException) {
            throw (java.rmi.RemoteException)resp;
        }
        else {
             return (String) resp;
        }
    }
}
```

These stub classes make writing the test client considerably easier. All you need to do is create an instance of the service, create a port type object, and call the appropriate methods. To show that you actually did get the menu, the test code, shown in Listing 6.10, prints the HTML menu to the console window.

LISTING 6.10 ThaiPalaceMenuClient.java

```
//
// ThaiPalaceMenuClient.java
//
// This class creates the client-side service factory
// for the desired service, makes the remote procedure call,
// and displays the response.
//

import java.io.*;


public class ThaiPalaceMenuClient {

  public static void main(String [] args) throws Exception {

    // Create an instance of the desired service

    ThaiPalaceMenuService service = new ThaiPalaceMenuService();

    // Use the factory method on the service to get the portType stub.

    ThaiPalaceMenuServicePortType port = service.getThaiPalaceMenuServicePort();

    // Make the actual calls

    String schema = port.getMenuSchema();
```

LISTING 6.10 continued

```
    String document = port.getMenuDocument();

    String stylesheet = port.getMenuStylesheet();

    String menu = port.getMenu() ;

    // What's for dinner?

    System.out.println(menu) ;

  }
}
```

If you compile and run this program, you get the HTML menu printed out in the console window—not the most exciting thing, but at least it works! If you are curious, the client code actually makes four separate SOAP calls, one for each of the four remote methods that it invokes. You can use the `tcpmon` tool included with the AXIS toolkit to see the SOAP communications.

All you need to do is change the port number to which the local service proxy connects, which in this case means editing the `ThaiPalaceMenuService.java` file, changing `localhost:8080` to `localhost:8880`. If you start the `tcpmon` tool in a new window, with the appropriate command line arguments, you can monitor the soap communication when you execute `ThaiPalaceMenuClient`:

```
C:\projects\menu\> start java org.apache.axis.utils.tcpmon 8880 localhost 8080
```

This statement first creates a new command window, and executes the `tcpmon` tool in the new window. The arguments to the tcpmon program tell the tool to listen for local connections on port 8880, and forward them to localhost, which is listening on port 8080 (in other words, your Tomcat Web server). The next two listings show the HTTP request that encapsulates the SOAP call for the `getMenu()` method invocation (Listing 6.11), and the HTTP response that encapsulates the response of the Web service (Listing 6.12).

LISTING 6.11 The `getMenu()` SOAP Request

```
POST /axis/tpmenu/ThaiPalaceMenuService.jws HTTP/1.0
Content-Length: 285
Host: localhost
Content-Type: text/xml; charset=utf-8
SOAPAction: ""

<?xml version="1.0" encoding="UTF-8"?>
<SOAP-ENV:Envelope
```

LISTING 6.11 continued

```
  xmlns:SOAP-ENV="http://schemas.xmlsoap.org/soap/envelope/"
  xmlns:xsd="http://www.w3.org/2001/XMLSchema"
  xmlns:xsi="http://www.w3.org/2001/XMLSchema-instance">
 <SOAP-ENV:Body>
  <getMenu/>
 </SOAP-ENV:Body>
</SOAP-ENV:Envelope>
```

LISTING 6.12 The `getMenu()` SOAP Response

```
HTTP/1.1 200 OK
Content-Type: text/xml; charset=utf-8
Content-Length: 11923
Date: Tue, 04 Dec 2001 00:59:17 GMT
Server: Apache Tomcat/4.0.1 (HTTP/1.1 Connector)
Set-Cookie: JSESSIONID=45F562F12463058514A0A33398F5A803;Path=/axis
<?xml version="1.0" encoding="UTF-8"?>
<SOAP-ENV:Envelope
  SOAP-ENV:encodingStyle="http://schemas.xmlsoap.org/soap/encoding/"
  xmlns:SOAP-ENV="http://schemas.xmlsoap.org/soap/envelope/"
  xmlns:xsd="http://www.w3.org/2001/XMLSchema"
  xmlns:xsi="http://www.w3.org/2001/XMLSchema-instance">
 <SOAP-ENV:Body>
  <getMenuResponse>
   <getMenuResult xsi:type="xsd:string">&lt;html&gt;
   &lt;head&gt;
      &lt;meta http-equiv=&quot;Content-Type&quot;
      content=&quot;text/html; charset=utf-8&quot;&gt;
      &lt;title&gt;Thai Palace&lt;/title&gt;
   &lt;/head&gt;
   &lt;body&gt;
      &lt;h1&gt;Thai Palace :
         (800) 867-5309 (FAX)
      &lt;/h1&gt;
      &lt;h4&gt;Fax this menu back with your selections circled. If you
➥want more than one item, indicate the number of items in the number
➥column. Your order will be ready 30 minutes from when we receive
➥the fax.
      &lt;/h4&gt;
      &lt;hr&gt;
…
   &lt;/body&gt;
&lt;/html&gt;</getMenuResult>
  </getMenuResponse>
 </SOAP-ENV:Body>
</SOAP-ENV:Envelope>
</SOAP-ENV:Envelope>
```

The SOAP response shown in Listing 6.12 is shortened; it really is much longer, because it encapsulates the entire HTML menu document.

Notice how the HTML entities have been quoted automatically. For example, < has been replaced with `<` and > has been replaced with `>`. If you think about it, SOAP is an XML application. If you use SOAP to pass XML documents, how do the SOAP server and client know how to properly handle the SOAP documents? The XML markup is quoted.

The ByteGourmet Server

Now that you have built and tested your `Menu` Web service, you can build the ByteGourmet server. The ByteGourmet Web site will be made available at `http://localhost:8080/bg/ByteGourmetServer`. You will build the server on the Model2 JSP design pattern, which is an MVC, or Model-View-Controller, pattern.

In this pattern, a servlet provides all controlling functionality. The model, which is the data of interest, is encapsulated in a JavaBean. Finally, the view, or the presentation, is handled by JavaServer Pages.

Deploying the Web Application

When deploying the ByteGourmet server in a real-world situation, a second Web server located on an entirely different machine would be used. Because you are just learning how this all works, however, you are limited to one machine. This means that you have two choices when it comes to deployment. First, you can start two separate Web servers on different ports. Second, you can use one Web server, and place the two servers in different contexts.

For simplicity, you will use the latter, as previously discussed. This means all the ByteGourmet software goes in a special subdirectory, `webapps\bg`, of the Tomcat installation directory. The standard servlet directory structure has all the JSP files in the main context directory. Inside this directory (the `bg` directory) is a directory called `WB_INF`. This directory contains two directories: `lib` and `classes`, as well as the context deployment descriptor, `web.xml`, which is shown in Listing 6.13.

LISTING 6.13 `web.xml`

```
<?xml version="1.0" encoding="ISO-8859-1"?>

<!DOCTYPE web-app
    PUBLIC "-//Sun Microsystems, Inc.//DTD Web Application 2.3//EN"
    "http://java.sun.com/dtd/web-app_2_3.dtd">
```

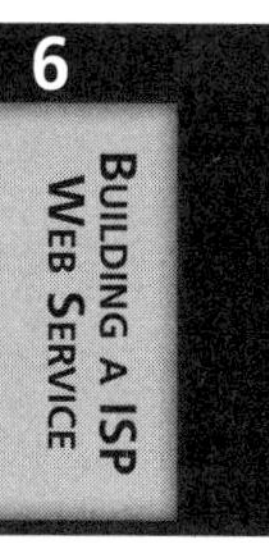

LISTING 6.13 continued

```
<web-app>

    <!-- Define servlets that are included in the ByteGourmet application -->

    <servlet>
        <servlet-name>ByteGourmetServer</servlet-name>
        <servlet-class>ByteGourmetServer</servlet-class>
    </servlet>

    <servlet-mapping>
        <servlet-name>
            ByteGourmetServer
        </servlet-name>
        <url-pattern>
            /ByteGourmetServer
        </url-pattern>
    </servlet-mapping>

</web-app>
```

In this deployment descriptor, you first define the servlet you will be exposing (the `ByteGourmetServer`), indicate what class actually provides the servlet implementation, and finally indicate what URL invokes the servlet.

Any `jar` files that the Web application needs go in the `lib` subdirectory, and the Web server automatically loads them. Because you are building a Web service client, you need to put the AXIS `jar` files (`axis.jar`, `clutils.jar`, `log4j-core.jar`, and `wsdl4j.jar`) in this directory, as well as `xerces.jar`.

The second subdirectory holds all Java classes, including the servlets. To simplify your Web application, you reuse the client stub classes discussed in the preceding section. All you need to do to use them in the Web application is copy the relevant class files into the `class` subdirectory.

The Servlet

The servlet that connects to the `Menu` Web service, shown in Listing 6.14, is rather straightforward after the test client has been built. Because this servlet provides all controlling functionality, you need a way to distinguish between the two possible states in which your Web application can exist.

LISTING 6.14 ByteGourmetServer.java

```
import java.io.*;
import java.util.*;
import javax.servlet.*;
import javax.servlet.http.*;

public class ByteGourmetServer extends HttpServlet {

    public void doGet(HttpServletRequest request,
      HttpServletResponse response) throws IOException, ServletException {
        processRequest(request, response) ;
    }

    public void doPost(HttpServletRequest request,
      HttpServletResponse response) throws IOException, ServletException {
        processRequest(request, response) ;
    }

    public void processRequest(HttpServletRequest request,
      HttpServletResponse response) throws IOException, ServletException
    {
        Enumeration e = request.getParameterNames();
        PrintWriter out = response.getWriter ();

        ByteGourmetMenuBean bgBean = new ByteGourmetMenuBean() ;

        while (e.hasMoreElements()) {
            String name = (String)e.nextElement();
            String value = request.getParameter(name);

        System.out.println(name + "\t" + value) ;

            if(name.equals("restaurant")) {
              if(value.equals("thaiPalace")) {

                ThaiPalaceMenuService service = new ThaiPalaceMenuService();
                ThaiPalaceMenuServicePortType port =
➥service.getThaiPalaceMenuServicePort();
                bgBean.setMenu(port.getMenu()) ;
                      request.setAttribute ("menuBean", bgBean);
                getServletConfig().getServletContext().
➥getRequestDispatcher("/menu.jsp").forward(request, response);
              }
            }
        }
        getServletConfig().getServletContext().
➥getRequestDispatcher("/welcome.jsp").forward(request, response);

    }
}
```

The first state is when a client initially connects. In this case, the servlet should provide the welcome screen to the client, where the client can decide which restaurant to visit. The second state is when a client has selected a restaurant and needs the appropriate menu. In this case, the servlet should connect to the `Menu` Web service and acquire the HTML menu document.

To determine the servlet's state, you use a servlet parameter called `restaurant`, which is set by the form in the welcome screen. When it is set, you invoke the appropriate Web service; otherwise, you show the welcome screen.

To keep things simple, you wrap the HTML menu in a JavaBean, `ByteGourmetMenuBean.java`, shown in Listing 6.15.

LISTING 6.15 `ByteGourmetMenuBean.java`

```
import java.io.Serializable;

public class ByteGourmetMenuBean implements Serializable {

  private String _menu ;

  public String getMenu() {
    return(_menu) ;
  }

  public void setMenu(String menu) {
    _menu = menu ;
  }
}
```

The JavaServer Pages

The two possible states for your Web application can be called New Client and Menu Request. Each state has its own view, and the two views are encapsulated by two separate JSP pages. For this example, they are both very simple.

The New Client State

The Welcome JSP page, shown in Listing 6.16, is actually an HTML page that enables the client to select from a list of restaurants. This JSP page, shown in Figure 6.2, is hard-wired to make sure nothing breaks, so that the value for the restaurant parameter is always `thaiPalace`. In production, these values would point to the different restaurant Web services. As you can see, the `FORM` element calls the `ByteGourmetServer`, which is easy because it is in the same Web application context. The `select` control, which is named `restaurant`, automatically sets the servlet parameter.

LISTING 6.16 welcome.jsp

```
<html>

<head>
<title> Welcome to ByteGourmet </title>
</head>

<body>

<h1> Welcome to the ByteGourmet </h1>
<hr />
<h4> Select your favorite restaurant from the list and you will be given
➥its menu. </h4>

<form method="POST" action="ByteGourmetServer">
<select name="restaurant">
<option value="thaiPalace" selected>The Thai Palace
<option value="thaiPalace">VeggieBurger Palace
<option value="thaiPalace">Pizza Palace
<option value="thaiPalace"> Nutty Palace
</select>
<input type="submit" value="Submit">

</form>

</body>
</html>
```

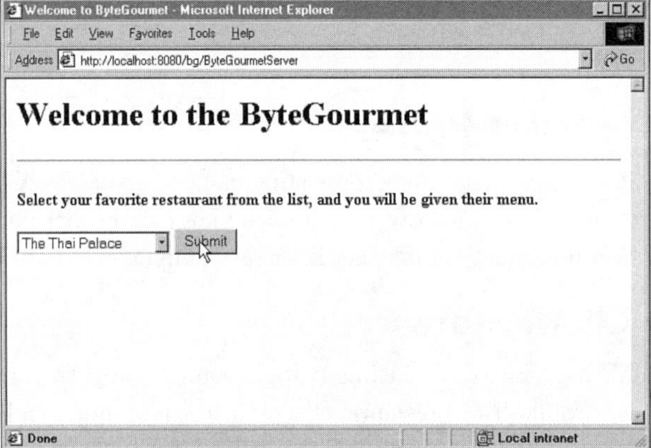

FIGURE 6.2
The ByteGourmet welcome screen. From here the client can select a menu to retrieve.

The Menu Request State

Your Web application is in the other state when it is processing a menu request. Because you have wrapped your HTML menu document in a JavaBean, the JSP page that needs to present the menu document is trivial, as shown in Listing 6.17. All you need to do is write out the contents of the JavaBean to the JSPWriter. The result, shown in Figure 6.3, is the HTML version of the Thai Palace menu.

LISTING 6.17 `menu.jsp`

```
<%@ page import = "ByteGourmetMenuBean" %>

<jsp:useBean id="menuBean" class="ByteGourmetMenuBean" scope="session"/>
<jsp:getProperty name="menuBean" property="menu"/>
```

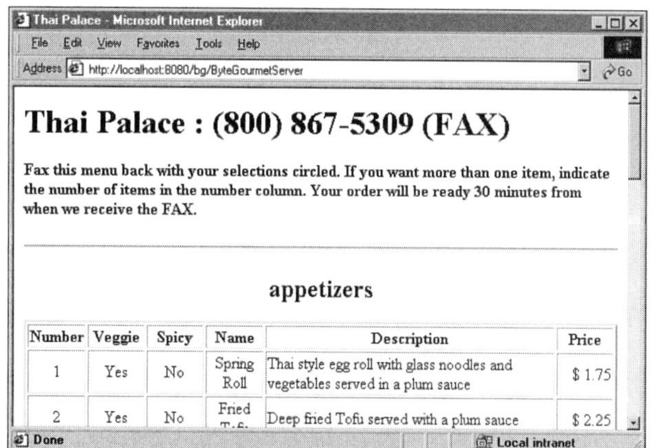

FIGURE 6.3
The ByteGourmet menu screen for the Thai Palace restaurant.

Summary

In this chapter, you used the AXIS toolkit and the Apache Software Foundation's Tomcat Web server to build and deploy a restaurant delivery service. Although this example is rather contrived, the fundamental principles behind it are not. Whether it is the ByteGourmet Server talking to the Thai Palace restaurant, or two Fortune 500 companies exchanging data in a B2B marketplace, the same principles apply. The rest of this book delves into the details of using Java to build Web services, including the basic technologies: SOAP, UDDI, WSDL, and the JAX pack.

Web Services Tools

Part II

In This Part

Understanding SOAP

by Benoît Marchal

In This Chapter

Some technologies, such as MP3, serve a very specific and well-defined purpose. MP3 is an audio file format specific for audio information, whereas XML, on the other hand, is a versatile technology that is used in a variety of solutions, including audio, voice, and data.

One of those solutions is the specific file format for application integration that is associated with Web services. As you will see, there have been several proposals to use XML in the field of Web services, but one of the most promising standards is SOAP, the Simple Object Access Protocol. This chapter introduces you to the SOAP protocol. In Chapter 8, "SOAP Basics," you learn how to develop applications with the Apache SOAP toolkit.

History of SOAP

SOAP connects two fields that were previously largely unrelated: application middleware and Web publishing.

Consequently, depending on whether your background is in middleware or Web publishing, you might understand SOAP slightly differently. Yet, it's important to realize that it is neither pure middleware nor is it pure Web publishing; it really is the convergence of the two.

The best approach to understanding the dual nature of SOAP is a historical one. If you review the concepts and trends that led to the development of SOAP, you will be better prepared to study it.

RPCs and Middleware

One of the goals of SOAP is to use XML to enable remote procedure calls (RPCs) over HTTP. Originally RPC was developed by the Open Group (`http://www.opengroup.org`) as part of its Distributed Computing Environment (DCE).

When writing distributed applications, programmers spend a disproportionate amount of time implementing network protocols: opening and closing sockets, listening on ports, formatting requests, decoding responses, and more. RPC offers an easier alternative. Programmers simply write regular procedure calls and a pre-compiler generates all the protocol-level code to call those procedures over a network.

Even if you have never used RPC, you might be familiar with its modern descendants: CORBA (Common Object Request Broker Architecture), DCOM (Distributed Component Object Model), and RMI (Remote Method Invocation). Although the implementations differ (and they are mostly incompatible), CORBA, DCOM, and RMI offer what is best described as an enhanced, object-oriented mechanism of implementing RPC functionality.

Listing 7.1 is the interface to a remote server object that uses RMI. As you can see, it's not very different from a regular interface. The only remarkable aspect is that it extends the `java.rmi.Remote` interface and every method can throw `java.rmi.RemoteException` exceptions.

LISTING 7.1 `RemoteBooking.java`

```
package com.psol.resourceful;

import java.util.Date;
import java.rmi.Remote;
import java.rmi.RemoteException;

public interface RemoteBooking
    extends Remote {
    public Resource[] getAllResources()
        throws RemoteException;
    public Resource[] getFreeResourcesOn(Date start,
                                         Date end)
        throws RemoteException;
    public void bookResource(int resource,
                             Date start,
                             Date end,
                             String email)
        throws RemoteException;
}
```

Where's the network code? There is none beyond what's necessary to extend the `Remote` interface. That's precisely the beauty of middleware: All you have to do is designate certain objects as remote and the middleware takes care of all the networking and protocol aspects for you. The way you designate remote objects varies depending on the actual technology (CORBA, RMI, or DCOM) you're using.

The Downside of Middleware

It's not all rosy with middleware, though. It has been successfully implemented on private networks (LANs, intranets, and the like) but has not been so successful on the Internet at large.

One of the issues is that middleware uses its own protocols and most firewalls are configured to block non-HTTP traffic. You have to reconfigure your firewall to authorize those communications. Oftentimes those changes prove incompatible with the corporate security policy.

Another issue is that middleware successfully addresses only one half of the equation: programming. It's not as good with the other half: deployment. Middleware significantly reduces the burden on the programmer writing distributed applications, but it does little to ease the deployment. In practice, it is significantly easier to deploy a Web site than to deploy a middleware-based application.

Most organizations have invested in Web site deployment. They have hired and trained system administrators that deal with the numerous availability and security issues. They are therefore reluctant to invest again in deploying another set of servers.

As you will see in a moment, SOAP directly addresses both issues. It borrows many concepts from middleware and enables RPC, but it does so with a regular Web server, which lessens the burden on system administrators.

RSS, RDF, and Web Sites

In parallel, the World Wide Web has evolved from a simple mechanism to share files over the Internet into a sophisticated infrastructure. The Web is universally available, and it is well understood and deployed in almost every company—small and large. The Web's success traces back to the ease with which you can join. You don't have to be a genius to build a Web site, and Web hosts offer a simple solution to deployment.

Obviously, the Web addresses a different audience than middleware, because it is primarily a publishing solution that targets human readers. RPC calls are designed for software consumption.

Gradually the Web has evolved from a pure human publishing solution into a mixed mode where some Web pages are geared toward software consumption. Most of those pages are built with XML.

RSS Documents

RSS is a good example of using XML to build Web sites for software rather than for humans. RSS, which stands for RDF Site Summary format, was originally developed by Netscape for its portal Web site. An RSS document highlights the main URLs in a Web vocabulary. Listing 7.2 is a sample RSS document.

LISTING 7.2 index.rss

```
<?xml version="1.0"?>
<rdf:RDF xmlns:rdf="http://www.w3.org/1999/02/22-rdf-syntax-ns#"
         xmlns="http://purl.org/rss/1.0/">
    <channel rdf:about="http://www.marchal.com/index.rss">
        <title>marchal.com</title>
        <link>http://www.marchal.com</link>
```

LISTING 7.2 continued

```
        <description>
            Your source for XML, Java and e-commerce.
        </description>
        <image rdf:resource="http://www.marchal.com/images/buttons/
➥              marchal.jpg"/>
        <items>
            <rdf:Seq>
                <rdf:li resource="http://www.marchal.com/go/xbe"/>
                <rdf:li resource="http://www.pineapplesoft.com/newsletter"/>
            </rdf:Seq>
        </items>
    </channel>
    <image rdf:about="http://www.marchal.com/images/buttons/marchal.jpg">
        <title>marchal.com</title>
        <link>http://www.marchal.com</link>
        <url>http://www.marchal.com/images/buttons/marchal.jpg</url>
    </image>
    <item rdf:about="http://www.marchal.com/go/xbe">
        <title>XML by Example</title>
        <link>http://www.marchal.com/go/xbe</link>
        <description>
            Introduction to XML. Discover the practical applications
            of XML, and see examples that include e-Commerce and SOAP.
        </description>
    </item>
    <item rdf:about="http://www.pineapplesoft.com/newsletter">
        <title>Pineapplesoft Link</title>
        <link>http://www.pineapplesoft.com/newsletter</link>
        <description>
            A free email magazine. Each month it discusses technologies,
            trends, and facts of interest to web developers.
        </description>
    </item>
</rdf:RDF>
```

As you can see, Listing 7.2 defines a channel with two items and one image. The two items are further defined with a link and a short description. The portal picks this document up and integrates it into its content.

Other applications of RSS include distributing newsfeeds. The items summarize the news and link to articles that have more details. See `http://www.moreover.com` for an example.

Although they are hosted on Web sites, RSS documents differ from plain Web pages. RSS goes beyond downloading information for browser rendering. A server downloads the RSS file and most likely integrates it in a database.

Making Requests: XML-RPC

The next logical step is to merge middleware with XML and the Web. How to best characterize the result depends on your point of view. To the Web programmer, adding XML to Web sites is like enhancing Web publishing with a query/response mechanism. But to the middleware programmer, it appears as if middleware had been enhanced to be more compatible with the Web and XML.

This is another illustration of XML being used to connect two fields (Web publishing and middleware) that were previously unrelated.

One of the earliest such implementations is probably XML-RPC. From a bird's-eye view, XML-RPC is similar to regular RPC, but the binary protocol used to carry the request on the network has been replaced with XML and HTTP.

Listing 7.3 illustrates an XML-RPC request. The client is remotely calling the `getFreeResourcesOn()`. The equivalent call in Java would have been written as:

```
BookingService.getFreeResourcesOn(startDate,endDate);
```

As you can see in Listing 7.3, XML-RPC packages the call in an XML document that is sent to the server through an HTTP `POST` request.

LISTING 7.3 An XML-RPC Request

```
POST /xmlrpc HTTP/1.0
User-Agent: Handson (Win98)
Host: joker.psol.com
Content-Type: text/xml
Content-length: 468

<?xml version="1.0"?>
<methodCall>
    <methodName>com.psol.resourceful.BookingService.
➥        getFreeResourcesOn</methodName>
    <params>
        <param>
            <value>
                <dateTime.iso8601>2001-01-15T00:00:00</dateTime.iso8601>
            </value>
        </param>
        <param>
            <value>
                <dateTime.iso8601>2001-01-17T00:00:00</dateTime.iso8601>
            </value>
        </param>
    </params>
</methodCall>
```

Without going into all the details, the elements in Listing 7.3 are

- `methodCall`, which is the root of the RPC call;
- `methodName`, which states which method is to be called remotely;
- `params`, which contains one `param` element for every parameter in the procedure call;
- `param`, to encode the parameters;
- `value`, an element that appears within `param` and holds its value;
- `dateTime.iso8601`, which specifies the type of the parameter value.

XML-RPC defines a handful of other types, including:

- `i4` or `int` for a four-byte signed integer;
- `boolean`, with the value of `0` (false) or `1` (true);
- `string`, a string;
- `double`, for double-precision signed floating point numbers;
- `base64`, for binary streams (encoded in base64).

XML-RPC also supports arrays and structures (also known as *records*) through the `array` and `struct` elements.

Note one major difference between Listing 7.3 and Listing 7.2: the former is a request made to a server. XML-RPC goes beyond downloading files; it provides a mechanism for the client to send an XML request to the server.

Obviously the server reply is also encoded in XML. It might look like Listing 7.4.

LISTING 7.4 An XML-RPC Encoded Response

```
HTTP/1.0 200 OK
Content-Length: 485
Content-Type: text/xml
Server: Jetty/3.1.4 (Windows 98 4.10 x86)

<?xml version="1.0"?>
<methodResponse>
    <params>
        <param>
            <value>
                <array>
                    <data>
                        <value><string>Meeting room 1</string></value>
                        <value><string>Meeting room 2</string></value>
                        <value><string>Board room</string></value>
```

LISTING 7.4 continued

```
                </data>
            </array>
        </value>
    </param>
  </params>
</methodResponse>
```

From XML-RPC to SOAP

XML-RPC is simple and effective, but early on its developers (Microsoft, Userland, and Developmentor) realized that they could do better.

Indeed XML-RPC suffers from four serious flaws:

- There's no clean mechanism to pass XML documents themselves in an XML-RPC request or response. Of course the request (or response) is an XML document, but what if you issue a call to, say, a formatter? How do you pass the XML document to the formatter? As you have seen, "XML document" is not a type for XML-RPC. In fact, to send XML documents, you would have to use strings or base64 parameters, which requires special encoding and is therefore suboptimal.
- There's no solution that enables programmers to extend the request or response format. For example, if you want to pass security credentials with the XML-RPC call, the only solution is to modify your procedure and add one parameter.
- XML-RPC is not fully aligned with the latest XML standardization. For example, it does not use XML namespaces, which goes against all the recent XML developments. It also defines its own data types, which is redundant with Part 2 of the XML schema recommendation.
- XML-RPC is bound to HTTP. For some applications, another protocol, such as Simple Mail Transfer Protocol (SMTP, the email protocol), is more sensible.

With the help of IBM, the XML-RPC designers upgraded their protocol. The resulting protocol, SOAP, is not as simple as XML-RPC, but it is dramatically more powerful. SOAP also broadens the field to cover applications that are not adequately described as remote procedure calls.

Note

Does SOAP make XML-RPC irrelevant? Yes and no. Most recent developments take advantage of SOAP's increased flexibility and power, but some developers still prefer the simpler XML-RPC protocol.

Listing 7.5 is the SOAP equivalent to Listing 7.3. Decoding the SOAP request is more involved than decoding an XML-RPC request, so don't worry if you can't read this document just yet. You learn how to construct SOAP requests in the next section.

LISTING 7.5 A SOAP Request

```
POST /soap/servlet/rpcrouter HTTP/1.0
Host: joker.psol.com
Content-Type: text/xml; charset=utf-8
Content-Length: 569
SOAPAction: "http://www.psol.com/2001/soapaction"

<?xml version='1.0' encoding='UTF-8'?>
<SOAP-ENV:Envelope xmlns:xsd="http://www.w3.org/1999/XMLSchema"
     xmlns:SOAP-ENV="http://schemas.xmlsoap.org/soap/envelope/"
     xmlns:xsi="http://www.w3.org/1999/XMLSchema-instance">
<SOAP-ENV:Body>
<ns1:getFreeResourcesOn xmlns:ns1="http://www.psol.com/2001/resourceful"
      SOAP-ENV:encodingStyle="http://schemas.xmlsoap.org/soap/encoding/">
<start xsi:type="xsd:timeInstant">2001-01-15T00:00:00Z</start>
<end xsi:type="xsd:timeInstant">2001-01-17T00:00:00Z</end>
</ns1:getFreeResourcesOn>
</SOAP-ENV:Body>
</SOAP-ENV:Envelope>
```

Listing 7.6 is the reply, so its the SOAP equivalent to Listing 7.4. Again, don't worry if you don't understand this listing; you will learn how to decode SOAP requests and responses in a moment.

LISTING 7.6 A SOAP Response

```
HTTP/1.0 200 OK
Server: Jetty/3.1.4 (Windows 98 4.10 x86)
Servlet-Engine: Jetty/3.1 (JSP 1.1; Servlet 2.2; java 1.3.0)
Content-Type: text/xml; charset=utf-8
Content-Length: 704

<?xml version='1.0' encoding='UTF-8'?>
<env:Envelope xmlns:xsd="http://www.w3.org/1999/XMLSchema"
     xmlns:env="http://schemas.xmlsoap.org/soap/envelope/"
     xmlns:xsi="http://www.w3.org/1999/XMLSchema-instance">
<env:Body>
<ns1:getFreeResourcesOnResponse
     xmlns:ns1="http://www.psol.com/2001/resourceful"
     env:encodingStyle="http://schemas.xmlsoap.org/soap/encoding/">
<return xmlns:ns2="http://schemas.xmlsoap.org/soap/encoding/"
         xsi:type="ns2:Array" ns2:arrayType="ns1:String[3]">
```

LISTING 7.6 continued

```
<item xsi:type="xsd:string">Meeting room 1</item>
<item xsi:type="xsd:string">Meeting room 2</item>
<item xsi:type="xsd:string">Board room</item>
</return>
</ns1:getFreeResourcesOnResponse>
</env:Body>
</env:Envelope>
```

SOAP Basics

This section reviews the basics of SOAP. After reading this section, you will be able to find your way through common SOAP interactions. The next section zooms in on some of these topics and provides the missing details.

At the time of writing, SOAP is not an official W3C standard. Two somewhat incompatible versions of SOAP coexist:

- SOAP 1.1 is defined in two W3C notes available from `http://www.w3.org/TR/SOAP` and `http://www.w3.org/TR/SOAP-attachments`.
- SOAP 1.2 is available as a W3C working draft from `http://www.w3.org/TR/soap12-part1` and `http://www.w3.org/TR/soap12-part2`. At the time of writing this version is still under development.

Note that SOAP 1.1 is not officially endorsed by W3C. It is available only on the W3C site as notes. Notes (as opposed to recommendations such as XML) are working documents prepared by W3C members and published for information only. Notes are intended to elicit comments.

The most visible difference between SOAP 1.1 and SOAP 1.2 is the use of XML namespaces. SOAP 1.1 builds all its namespaces from the `http://schemas.xmlsoap.org/soap` root, whereas SOAP 1.2 uses `http://www.w3.org/2001/09/soap`.

Caution

Because they use different namespaces, the two versions of SOAP are not directly compatible. Otherwise, they are mostly similar.

The remainder of this chapter concentrates on the similarities and highlights the differences only where relevant.

Other differences are mostly editorial. SOAP 1.2 is better written: it contains fewer ambiguities and is generally easier to read.

Tip

If you have problems when reading the SOAP 1.1 specification, look up the corresponding section in the SOAP 1.2 spec.

SOAP Architecture

The most striking difference between SOAP and XML-RPC is that SOAP leaves so many options open. XML-RPC provided a closed solution to one problem: sending RPC requests over HTTP.

SOAP, on the other hand, is more like a toolbox. It defines a messaging framework (the envelope), encoding rules and a binding to the HTTP protocol. RPC needs all three, but you can build SOAP requests with the envelope, the HTTP binding, and then use other encoding rules. Or you can use the envelope, the encoding rules, and another communication protocol.

Figure 7.1 illustrates this. At the bottom of the stack are HTTP and SMTP, two communication protocols developed independently from SOAP. They control sending and receiving files.

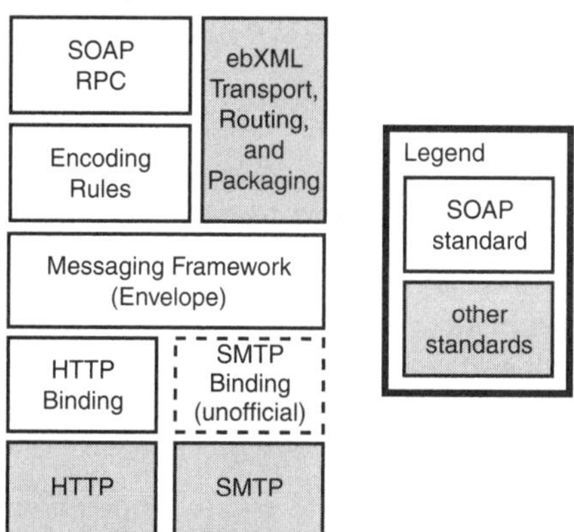

FIGURE 7.1
Logical view of SOAP.

SOAP attaches to those protocols through *bindings* (note that, at the time of writing, the SMTP binding is not official). On top of the binding comes the message framework that lays down the rules that organize SOAP messages. What goes in the messages? That's the role of the encoding rules. Finally the RPC uses the encoding rules to create a message, which is stored in an envelope (the message framework), and sent over HTTP.

Notice the ebXML Transport, Routing, and Packaging in Figure 7.1. The ebXML initiative develops e-commerce solutions with XML (see `http://www.ebxml.org` for more information). It uses the messaging framework and the SOAP bindings, but it has its own encoding rules. The ebXML initiative helps illustrate that SOAP is a toolbox from which you can pick and choose those elements that make sense for you.

Unfortunately, what is gained in flexibility is lost in simplicity. SOAP can be very confusing when you try to find your way through the maze of options. Also the options may result in incompatibilities. For example, although ebXML uses SOAP, it is not directly compatible with SOAP RPC because it does not use the same encoding rules.

Tip

If you ever get lost in the SOAP options, remember that, taken individually, each option is simple. Although the number of options may be confusing, they are not difficult to understand. If you understand how two options relate one to another, you should do fine.

SOAP Blocks and Elements

The messaging framework defines the basic XML elements you need to construct SOAP requests. SOAP defines the request in terms of *SOAP blocks* where a block is a single logical computational unit. The block is represented as an XML element identified by a qualified name, that is, a combination of local name and namespace.

XML Namespaces

A SOAP message contains elements defined by different sources: some are defined by the SOAP recommendation itself, others come from the XML schema recommendation and, finally, it is likely to also contain elements defined by the programmer.

The fact that different sources collaborate to create a document may cause conflicts and, in particular, naming conflicts.

XML namespaces is a standard mechanism (defined by the W3C) to avoid name conflicts. For example, if the programmer has defined a `Body` element, the namespace helps distinguish this `Body` element from the SOAP body. In that respect, namespaces are similar to Java packages.

To guarantee uniqueness, XML namespaces are URIs that are bound to prefixes through an `xmlns` attribute.

For example,

```
<env:Envelope xmlns:env="http://schemas.xmlsoap.org/soap/envelope/">
```

binds the `http://schemas.xmlsoap.org/soap/envelope/` namespace with the `env` prefix. Only the prefix appears in the remainder of the document. For example:

```
<env:Body>
```

The name after the prefix is said to be the *local name*. Again, note the similarity with Java packages that also use domain names to guarantee the uniqueness of names.

Unfortunately, because SOAP uses HTTP, SOAP nodes are also identified by URIs and this creates some confusion. To avoid confusion, remember that URIs to `xmlsoap.org` and `w3.org` are likely to be namespaces.

SOAP defines four XML elements:

- `env:Envelope` is the root of the SOAP request. At the minimum, it defines the SOAP namespace (`http://schemas.xmlsoap.org/soap/envelope/` for SOAP 1.1 and `http://www.w3.org/2001/09/soap-envelope` for SOAP 1.2; the latter URI is likely to change). It may define additional namespaces.
- `env:Header` contains auxiliary information as SOAP blocks, such as authentication, routing information, or transaction identifier. The header is optional.
- `env:Body` contains the main information in one or more SOAP blocks. An example would be a SOAP block for RPC call. The body is mandatory and it must appear after the header.
- `env:Fault` is a special block that indicates protocol-level errors. If present, it must appear in the body.

Caution

The SOAP 1.1 specification uses `SOAP-ENV` for the prefix throughout the specification. Consequently most SOAP 1.1 libraries use the `SOAP-ENV` prefix. This chapter uses `env`, as in the SOAP 1.2 recommendation. Bear in mind that the prefix is irrelevant as long as the URI remains correct.

Figure 7.2 illustrates the physical organization of a SOAP message. Notice that the header appears before the body.

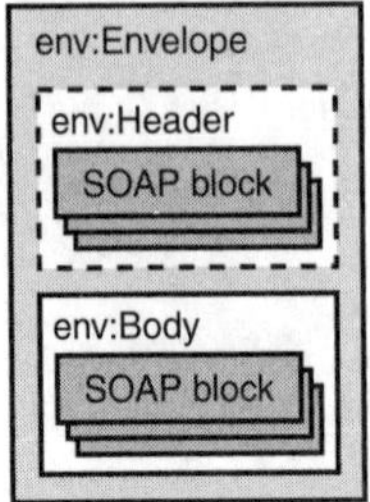

FIGURE 7.2
Physical layout of a SOAP message.

SOAP requests may be sent directly to the server or they may be routed through one or more so-called SOAP nodes. A typical example is when a message is routed through proxies on its way to the final recipient, as Figure 7.3 illustrates.

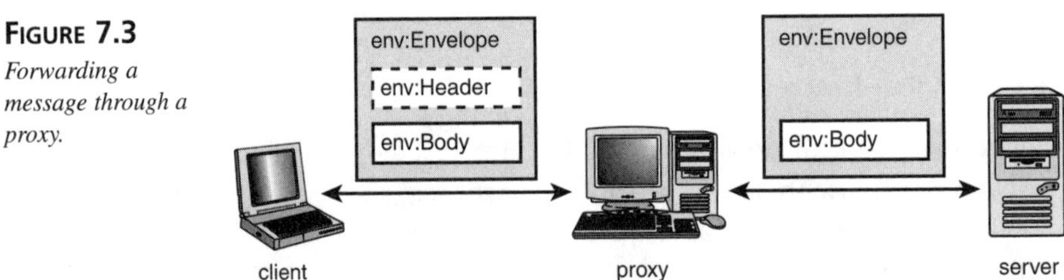

FIGURE 7.3
Forwarding a message through a proxy.

Some or all the SOAP blocks in the headers may be targeted to intermediary SOAP nodes, as was shown in Figure 7.3. In this example, the header contains routing information that is intended for the proxy only. Notice that the proxy has processed and removed the information from the message it forwards to the ultimate recipient. Unlike the header, the body is always routed to the ultimate SOAP node unmodified.

Encoding Styles

With the exception of the `env:Fault` element, which signals protocol errors, SOAP leaves it up to you to decide what goes in the header and body. Still, SOAP defines a so-called *encoding style* to create XML documents from data structures. The SOAP encoding style defines XML equivalents for data structures commonly found in programming languages: simple types (integer, string, and the like), arrays, and structures.

For arrays and structures, SOAP defines an *accessor*, which is an identifier for the data. In an array, the accessor is the position of the element; in a structure, the accessor is the name field.

SOAP maps all the information to XML elements. For example, a `name` field will become a `name` element in the XML document. Instances of the Java class in Listing 7.7 are represented with the XML document in Listing 7.8 (using SOAP 1.2 namespaces).

LISTING 7.7 Resource.java

```
package com.psol.resourceful;

public class Resource
{
   public int id = -1;
   public String name = null,
                 description = null;
}
```

LISTING 7.8 SOAP Encoding for a Resource

```
<?xml version="1.0"?>
<rs:Resource xmlns:rs="http://www.psol.com/2001/resourceful"
             xmlns:xsi="http://www.w3.org/2001/XMLSchema-instance"
             xmlns:xsd="http://www.w3.org/2001/XMLSchema"
             xmlns:env="http://www.w3.org/2001/09/soap-envelope"
             env:encodingStyle="http://www.w3.org/2001/09/soap-encoding">
    <id xsi:type="xsd:int">0</id>
    <name>Auditorium</name>
    <description>Our largest meeting room</description>
</rs:Resource>
```

SOAP defines the `env:encodingStyle` attribute to indicate the rules used to create a document. The value of `env:encodingStyle` is a list of URIs that identify the rules to decode the document. The attribute may be attached to any element and its scope extends to the descendant of the element (not unlike XML namespaces).

The URIs for SOAP's own encoding rules are `http://schemas.xmlsoap.org/soap/encoding/` for SOAP 1.1 and `http://www.w3.org/2001/09/soap-envelope` for SOAP 1.2. You can see the `env:encodingStyle` attribute on line 6 of Listing 7.8.

Transport Options

SOAP defines an HTTP binding. Essentially a SOAP message is sent using the `POST` verb. HTTP also supports `GET`, `HEAD`, and `PUT`, but SOAP does not use them.

SOAP with attachments is an extension to SOAP 1.1 that supports sending attachments next to the SOAP body. Attachments are similar to mail attachments and may include images or other files.

Although it only defines the binding for HTTP, the SOAP recommendation makes it clear that binding SOAP to other protocols is possible. In practice, there's great interest in binding SOAP over SMTP, the email protocol. Obviously, when bound over SMTP, SOAP provides one-way communication only: A message is sent but there is no response. If the recipient wants to reply, it needs to send another request.

RPC

Armed with encoding rules, an envelope, and HTTP binding, it's not difficult to support RPC. For SOAP, an RPC request is a structure where each `in` and `in/out` parameter is given its own accessor. For example, a call to the Java method `getFreeResourcesOn(Date start,Date end)` is encoded as the following structure:

```
struct GetFreeResourcesOn {
    TimeInstant start;
    TimeInstant end;
}
```

or, using the SOAP encoding rules introduced in the earlier "Encoding Styles" section (using SOAP 1.1 namespaces):

```
<?xml version='1.0'?>
<rs:getFreeResourcesOn
    xmlns:rs="http://www.psol.com/2001/resourceful"
    env:encodingStyle="http://schemas.xmlsoap.org/soap/encoding/"
    xmlns:env="http://schemas.xmlsoap.org/soap/envelope/"
    xmlns:xsi="http://www.w3.org/1999/XMLSchema-instance"
    xmlns:xsd="http://www.w3.org/1999/XMLSchema">
<start xsi:type="xsd:timeInstant">2001-01-15T00:00:00Z</start>
<end xsi:type="xsd:timeInstant">2001-01-17T00:00:00Z</end>
</rs:getFreeResourcesOn>
```

The response is also a `struct` with one accessor for the return value and one accessor for each of the `out` and `in/out` parameters.

Caution

Java does not support `in/out` or `out` parameters. It supports only `in` parameters.

Messaging Framework

Now that you have a basic understanding of SOAP, it's time to zoom in and fill in the blanks. The last section provided an overview of SOAP; this section gives you more technical details that the basic introduction left out.

Version Compatibility

SOAP uses the namespace for version control. If the SOAP envelope is in the `http://schemas.xmlsoap.org/soap/envelope/` namespace, then the request is SOAP 1.1. If the SOAP envelope is in the `http://www.w3.org/2001/09/soap-envelope` namespace, then the request is draft SOAP 1.2.

> **Caution**
>
> The URI for SOAP 1.2 is likely to change between the draft and the release of the actual recommendation. If anything, the URI should drop the month indicator and be of the following form (assuming the recommendation is published in 2002):
>
> `http://www.w3.org/2002/soap-envelope`
>
> Check the W3C Web site for the most recent URI.

If a SOAP 1.2 node receives a SOAP 1.1 request, it can either process it as SOAP 1.1 or reject it with a `VersionMismatch` fault message. In any case, a `VersionMismatch` fault message is always returned with the SOAP 1.1 URI so that older clients can decode the response.

SOAP 1.2 defines an optional `Upgrade` element, in the `http://www.w3.org/2001/09/soap-upgrade` namespace, that lets the server specify which versions it recognizes. If present, `Upgrade` must appear in the header, not the body. See Listing 7.9 for an example.

LISTING 7.9 `VersionMismatch` fault with the `Upgrade` element.

```
<env:Envelope xmlns:env="http://schemas.xmlsoap.org/soap/envelope/">
    <env:Header>
        <upg:Upgrade
           xmlns:upg="http://www.w3.org/2001/09/soap-upgrade">
            <envelope qname="ns1:Envelope"
                xmlns:ns1="http://www.w3.org/2001/09/soap-envelope"/>
        </upg:Upgrade>
    </env:Header>
    <env:Body>
        <env:Fault>
            <faultcode>env:VersionMismatch</faultcode>
            <faultstring>Requires SOAP 1.2</faultstring>
        </env:Fault>
    </env:Body>
</env:Envelope>
```

Header

Recall from the earlier discussion that the header is the place to put auxiliary information. Typically it provides storage for options on how to process the call.

The header is similar to email headers: It is not the message itself, but it provides information that may be useful (or even essential) in decoding the payload. For example, ebXML uses the header to store routing information in an ebXML-defined `MessageHeader`. (This is the smallest ebXML message possible. Indeed, ebXML defines many other elements, but their use is optional.)

Listing 7.10 is an example of an ebXML header. Because ebXML is outside the scope of this chapter, we encourage you to turn to `http://www.ebxml.org` if you want specific information on these elements. However, you are sure to recognize routing information (`From`, `To`, `Service`, `Action`), as well as message identifiers (`MessageData`). The `CPAId` element points to the Collaboration Protocol Agreement that details how the partners ("partner" is ebXML jargon for the parties in the transaction) work together.

LISTING 7.10 An ebXML Header

```
<env:Header xmlns:env="http://schemas.xmlsoap.org/soap/envelope/"
            xmlns:eb="http://www.ebxml.org/namespaces/messageHeader">
    <eb:MessageHeader env:mustUnderstand="1" eb:version="1.0">
        <eb:From><eb:PartyId>urn:duns:374950798</eb:PartyId></eb:From>
        <eb:To><eb:PartyId>urn:duns:912345678</eb:PartyId></eb:To>
        <eb:CPAId>http://www.psol.com/cpas/default.xml</eb:CPAId>
        <eb:ConversationId>20011115-122303-28572</eb:ConversationId>
        <eb:Service>urn:services:SupplierOrderProcessing</eb:Service>
        <eb:Action>NewOrder</eb:Action>
        <eb:MessageData>
            <eb:MessageId>20011115-122303-28572@psol.com</eb:MessageId>
            <eb:Timestamp>2001-11-15T11:12:12Z</eb:Timestamp>
        </eb:MessageData>
    </eb:MessageHeader>
</env:Header>
```

SOAP defines two attributes specifically for the header: `env:mustUnderstand` and `env:actor`. A client attaches the `env:mustUnderstand` attribute (with a value of `1` for true) to elements that are essential for processing the call.

A node should not attempt to process a request if it does not recognize one or more elements flagged with `env:mustUnderstand`. In Listing 7.10, the `MessageHeader` is flagged with `env:mustUnderstand` because servers should not attempt to process ebXML requests unless they support the `MessageHeader`.

The other attribute is `env:actor`. It signals that the element is intended for a given node. Remember Figure 7.3, which shows that the proxy does not pass the header to the ultimate node. The proxy uses the `env:actor` to decide which header elements, if any, are for its own consumption.

The `env:actor` attribute contains the URI of the node or the special URI `http://schemas.xmlsoap.org/soap/actor/next` for SOAP 1.1. For SOAP 1.2 it contains `http://www.w3.org/2001/09/soap-envelope/actor/next`, which stands for the next node.

SOAP Fault

In most cases, SOAP lets the application define the content of the body. The one exception is when there's an error for which SOAP defines the `env:Fault`. The SOAP fault provides minimal common ground between different SOAP implementations in case of a protocol error.

The content of `env:Fault` is detailed in the following list. Note that the `Fault` element is prefixed with a namespace but its content is not (in an XML schema the content would be written as local elements):

- `faultcode` is a code that indicates the error. This element is required.
- `faultstring` is an human-readable error message. It is required.
- `faultactor` is the URI of the node that reports the error. It is required only if the node reporting the error is not the ultimate node.
- `detail` contains additional, application-specific information on the error. It is required if the error took place in the body; it is forbidden otherwise.

SOAP defines the following error codes for the `faultcode` field:

- `VersionMismatch` indicates the node does not recognize the version of SOAP used; see Listing 7.9 for an example.
- `MustUnderstand` indicates the node does not recognize a block flagged with `mustUnderstand`.
- `Client` indicates the node cannot process the message because of the client's fault, for example, when the message is not formatted correctly.
- `Server` indicates the error is not due to the message itself but rather the state in which the server was.
- `DataEncodingUnknown` indicates the node does not recognize the `encodingStyle`. This is defined only in SOAP 1.2.

The codes should be placed in the envelope namespace. It is possible to extend the code to provide a more detailed error message if you use the dot (`.`) as a separator. For example, a error code for Java exceptions could be defined as `Server.Exception`. The server would return this error:

```
<env:Envelope xmlns:env="http://www.w3.org/2001/09/soap-envelope">
    <env:Body>
        <env:Fault>
            <faultcode>env:Server.Exception</faultcode>
            <faultstring>Null pointer exception</faultstring>
            <detail>                <stackTrace>
                  java.lang.NullPointerException:                     at
com.psol.jws.TroubleMaker(TroubleMaker.java:148)                     at
java.lang.Thread.run(Thread.java:484)               </stackTrace>
</detail>         </env:Fault>
    </env:Body>
</env:Envelope>
```

The SOAP Encoding

The specification goes on at great length over the encoding. In this chapter, we can point out only the most important rules; turn to the specification itself if you need more details.

Caution

Unlike traditional middleware, SOAP does not explicitly map its encoding to programming languages. In other words, there is no standard SOAP mapping for Java. Therefore, two different implementations of SOAP may produce different encoding for the same objects.

Encoding Fields

The most basic rule is that values are always encoded in elements. For example, a `name` field is encoded as:

```
<name>Board room</name>
```

but not as:

```
<item name="Board room"/>
```

SOAP uses attributes exclusively to modify the default processing of an element. For example, the `env:actor` attribute indicates which node should process the element.

Simple Types

SOAP supports the simple types defined in the XML schema, Part 2: Datatypes recommendation (`http://www.w3.org/TR/2001/REC-xmlschema-2-20010502`). The most commonly used types are as follows:

- `string`
- `base64Binary`
- `integer`, `byte`, `short`, `int`, `long`
- `decimal`, `float`, `double`
- `boolean`
- `dateTime`, `time`, `date`, `duration`

Note that `base64Binary` supports binary objects.

Caution

SOAP 1.1 uses an earlier draft of XML schema that is identified with the `http://www.w3.org/1999/XMLSchema-instance` namespace URI.

Simple types are encoded as XML elements. If required, the `xsi:type` attribute may disambiguate the type. For example, a date might be encoded as:

```
<start xmlns:xsi="http://www.w3.org/2001/XMLSchema-instance"
       xmlns:xsd="http://www.w3.org/2001/XMLSchema"
       xsi:type="xsd:dateTime">2001-01-15T00:00:00Z</start>
```

SOAP states that the `xsi:type` must be used when the type of the element cannot be deduced from its name. In practice, this is a major source of interoperability problems between SOAP implementations.

Indeed, different programming languages have different needs for the use of `xsi:type`. For example, Java is strongly typed and Java implementations use the `xsi:type` attribute liberally. Languages with less restrictive type systems may ignore the `xsi:type` attribute, which leads to conflicts.

Note that using valid XML documents (that is, documents with an XML schema) may help reduce ambiguities. However, as of this writing, no SOAP implementation uses schemas.

Compound Types: `Structs`

The encoding recognizes two compound types:

- A *structure* (`struct`) is a list of elements logically grouped together. The elements are identified by their names. (The element accessor is its name.)
- The *array* is a group of values identified not by their names but by their ordinal positions. (The accessor of the element is the position of the element in the array.)

Structures are encoded as accessor elements. (In most cases, the element borrows its name from the name of the `struct` in the programming language.) The fields are encoded as accessor elements. Having accessors whose names are local to their containing types results in unqualified elements; other elements are always qualified with a namespace.

You already saw how to encode a structure in Listing 7.8 (reproduced here for your convenience):

```
<?xml version="1.0"?>
<rs:Resource xmlns:rs="http://www.psol.com/2001/resourceful"
             xmlns:xsi="http://www.w3.org/2001/XMLSchema-instance">
    <id xsi:type="xsd:int">0</id>
    <name xsi:type="xsd:string">Auditorium</name>
    <description xsi:type="xsd:string">Our largest meeting room
➥        </description>
</rs:Resource>
```

Compound Type: Arrays

Arrays are encoded as elements of type `enc:Array` (or a type derived from `enc:Array`) where `enc` is bound to `http://schemas.xmlsoap.org/soap/encoding/` or `http://www.w3.org/2001/09/soap-encoding`, respectively, for SOAP 1.1 and SOAP 1.2.

The `array` element has an additional attribute, `enc:arrayType`, which declares the content of the array. Array type declarations are of the form

```
type[size]
```

This is very close to Java. An array of three strings has an `enc:arrayType` value of `xsd:string[3]`; an array with 25 integers has an `enc:arrayType` value of `xsd:integer[25]`. A multi-dimensional array is of the form `xsd:decimal[5][10]`.

The array content is encoded as a sequence of XML elements. The names of the elements are irrelevant because, for arrays, the position of the element is the accessor. Listing 7.11 is an array of strings.

LISTING 7.11 An Array of Strings

```
<array xmlns:enc="http://schemas.xmlsoap.org/soap/encoding/"
       xmlns:xsi="http://www.w3.org/2001/XMLSchema-instance"
       xmlns:xsd="http://www.w3.org/2001/XMLSchema"
       xsi:type="enc:Array"
       enc:arrayType="xsd:String[3]">
    <item xsi:type="xsd:string">Board room</item>
    <item xsi:type="xsd:string">Meeting room 1</item>
    <item xsi:type="xsd:string">Meeting room 2</item>
</array>
```

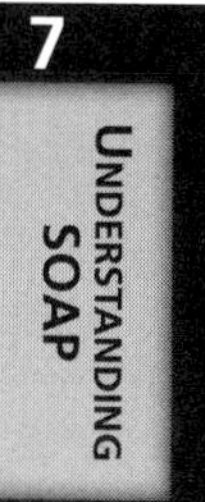

For obvious reasons, the elements must appear in the order of the array.

Array elements are not limited to simple types; compound types are acceptable, as Listing 7.12, an array of `Resource` objects, illustrates. The `Resource` class was defined in Listing 7.7.

LISTING 7.12 An Array of Compound Types

```
<array xmlns:enc="http://schemas.xmlsoap.org/soap/encoding/"
       xsi:type="enc:Array" enc:arrayType="rs:Resource[3]"
       xmlns:rs="http://www.psol.com/2001/resourceful"
       xmlns:xsi="http://www.w3.org/1999/XMLSchema-instance"
       xmlns:xsd="http://www.w3.org/1999/XMLSchema">
    <item xsi:type="rs:Resource">
        <id xsi:type="xsd:int">1</id>
        <name xsi:type="xsd:string">Board room</name>
        <description xsi:type="xsd:string">Mid-sized room,
➥             quality furniture</description>
    </item>
    <item xsi:type="rs:Resource">
        <id xsi:type="xsd:int">2</id>
        <name xsi:type="xsd:string">Meeting room 1</name>
        <description xsi:type="xsd:string">Mid-sized room</description>
    </item>
    <item xsi:type="rs:Resource">
        <id xsi:type="xsd:int">3</id>
        <name xsi:type="xsd:string">Meeting room 2</name>
        <description xsi:type="xsd:string">Small room</description>
    </item>
</array>
```

To support multidimensional arrays, SOAP uses references to arrays. A *reference* is an `href` attribute. An `href` attribute is a URI that points to another element in the same document. The original element is identified with an `id` attribute. The `id` attribute is of type `ID` as defined in XML schema and DTD.

The multidimensional array is encoded as an array of reference items pointing to the actual column data. In other words, a multidimensional array is an array whose elements point to other arrays.

Listing 7.13 is a multidimensional array. Note that this is a document fragment because it does not have a root element. In practice, with SOAP, it is never a problem to use document fragments since `env:Envelope` is the root.

LISTING 7.13 A multidimensional array

```
<matrix xmlns:xsi="http://www.w3.org/2001/XMLSchema-instance"
        xmlns:xsd="http://www.w3.org/2001/XMLSchema"
        xmlns:enc="http://www.w3.org/2001/09/soap-encoding"
        xsi:type="enc:Array"
        enc:arrayType="xsd:int[][2]" >
   <item href="#array-1"/>
   <item href="#array-2"/>
</matrix>
<array xmlns:xsi="http://www.w3.org/2001/XMLSchema-instance"
       xmlns:xsd="http://www.w3.org/2001/XMLSchema"
       xmlns:enc="http://www.w3.org/2001/09/soap-encoding"
       id="array-1"
       enc:arrayType="xsd:int[3]">
   <item>10</item>
   <item>20</item>
   <item>30</item>
</array>
<array xmlns:xsi="http://www.w3.org/2001/XMLSchema-instance"
       xmlns:xsd="http://www.w3.org/2001/XMLSchema"
       xmlns:enc="http://www.w3.org/2001/09/soap-encoding"
       id="array-2"
       enc:arrayType="xsd:int[2]">
   <item>15</item>
   <item>25</item>
</array>
```

Because arrays can grow very large, the encoding has two optimizations for partially transmitted arrays and sparse arrays. In a *partially transmitted array*, not every element is sent. Typically it would be used when the recipient knows some sections of the array. The `env:offset` attribute specifies the zero-origin offset of the elements being transmitted in the array:

```
<enc:Array enc:arrayType="xsd:int[7]" enc:offset="[3]"
           xmlns:enc="http://schemas.xmlsoap.org/soap/encoding/"
           xmlns:xsd="http://www.w3.org/1999/XMLSchema">
   <item>4</item>
   <item>5</item>
   <item>6</item>
</enc:Array>
```

Likewise, the `enc:position` encodes *sparse arrays*, in other words, arrays where most elements are null or not present:

```
<enc:Array enc:arrayType="xsd:string[10,10]"
           xmlns:enc="http://schemas.xmlsoap.org/soap/encoding/"
           xmlns:xsd="http://www.w3.org/1999/XMLSchema">
   <item enc:position="[2,2]">Third row, third col</item>
   <item enc:position="[7,2]">Eighth row, third col</item>
</enc:Array>
```

Transport Options

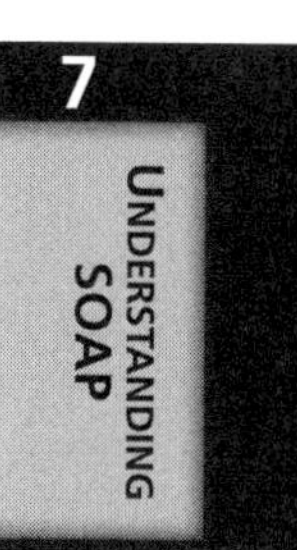

SOAP request/response maps nicely in HTTP, but SOAP has been used with other protocols and, in particular, SMTP. We are also aware of FTP implementations of SOAP.

HTTP Binding

If you remember Listings 7.5 and 7.6, a SOAP request is sent with the POST order. The SOAP response is transmitted with the HTTP response.

HTTP requests and responses contain one or more headers (not to be confused with the SOAP header that appears in the XML document) and one payload. SOAP imposes the use of two headers: `Content-Type` and `SOAPAction`.

The `Content-Type` must be set to `text/xml`, which is expected because it is the regular type for XML documents. `SOAPAction`, however, is new. Early in the development of SOAP, it was foreseen that proxies and firewalls might handle RPC requests differently from regular Web browsing. The `SOAPAction` header was introduced to alert proxies and firewalls on which requests are SOAP requests. You might argue that they could recognize SOAP requests from the `env:Envelope` element but, for increased efficiency, it's best if proxies and firewalls work on the headers only.

The `SOAPAction` content is a URI that supposedly identifies the intent of the call. In practice, most SOAP implementations ignore `SOAPAction`. It was introduced primarily for proxies.

The server uses the HTTP response code to indicate errors. A 2xx code accepts the request, whereas a 500 code signals the server could not process the request (the response includes a fault).

As a final note on HTTP binding, what about HTTP extension? The HTTP protocol offers an extension mechanism that was originally intended for special orders such as RPC. How come SOAP does not use it? The earliest drafts of SOAP mandated the use of the extension mechanism but experience showed that few HTTP libraries were compatible with it. By the time SOAP 1.0 was published, the standard was no longer recommending HTTP extension. With SOAP 1.1 and SOAP 1.2, HTTP extension remains as an option that is largely not implemented or used.

SMTP Bindings

The only official SOAP binding is for HTTP, but the SOAP 1.2 working draft has a section on "SOAP Transport Binding Framework." The framework lays down the rules to bind SOAP to non-HTTP protocols. In the meantime, many SOAP implementations offer an SMTP binding. Most are based on the ebXML Transport, Routing, and Packaging specification (see `http://www.ebxml.org`).

Because HTTP and SMTP headers are similar, an SMTP binding is easily derived from the HTTP binding. SOAP emails include the `SOAPAction` header; the `Content-Type` header is set to `text/xml`. The `To` and `From` are set according to the SMTP rules.

Obviously, SMTP does not support synchronous calls (where the client waits for a immediate response from the server). It works in asynchronous mode, wherein the client sends a request and forgets about it. If the server sends a response, it comes in a different message.

SOAP with Attachments

Some applications of SOAP require that more than just the envelope be sent. The SOAP with Attachments note (available from `http://www.w3.org/TR/SOAP-attachments`) proposes a solution to send several documents in a SOAP 1.1 request. At the time of writing, no equivalent exists for SOAP 1.2.

SOAP with Attachments is defined as a special binding that uses the `multipart/related` MIME encoding rather than `text/xml`. As the name implies, `multipart/related` breaks the content of the HTTP request into several parts. By convention, the first part contains the SOAP envelope and is of type `text/xml`.

Each part includes a few headers, such as the `Content-Type` and a document. The parts may contain more XML documents, images, text, or any other files. In practice, they are similar to email attachments. This solution is attractive because it leaves the SOAP intact. In fact, the SOAP document is not aware of the multipart binding.

Listing 7.14 is an ebXML SOAP request with attachment. The SOAP envelope contains the now familiar `MessageHeader` and a new `Manifest`. The manifest lists the attachments. Note the use of XLink links to point to parts. MIME defines the `Content-ID` and `Content-Name` header to attach identifiers or names to the parts.

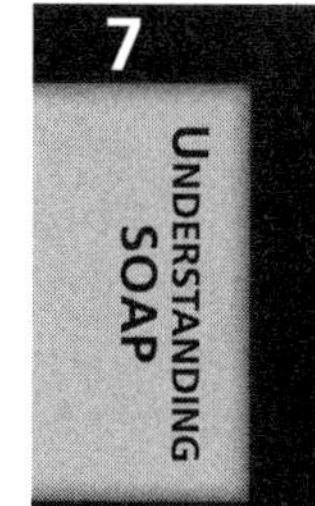

LISTING 7.14 An ebXML Multipart Request

```
POST /soap/servlet/rpcrouter HTTP/1.0
Host: joker.psol.com
Content-Type: multipart/related; boundary=MIME_boundary; type=text/xml;
        start="<ebxhmheader-143@example.com>"
Content-Length: 1682
SOAPAction: "ebXML"

--MIME_boundary
Content-ID: <ebxhmheader-143@example.com>
Content-Type: text/xml

<?xml version="1.0" encoding="UTF-8"?>
<env:Envelope xmlns:env="http://schemas.xmlsoap.org/soap/envelope/"
              xmlns:eb="http://www.ebxml.org/namespaces/messageHeader">
<env:Header xmlns:eb="http://www.ebxml.org/namespaces/messageHeader">
    <eb:MessageHeader env:mustUnderstand="1" eb:version="1.0">
        <eb:From><eb:PartyId>urn:duns:374950798</eb:PartyId></eb:From>
        <eb:To><eb:PartyId>urn:duns:912345678</eb:PartyId></eb:To>
        <eb:CPAId>http://www.psol.com/cpas/default.xml</eb:CPAId>
        <eb:ConversationId>20011115-122303-28572</eb:ConversationId>
        <eb:Service>urn:services:SupplierOrderProcessing</eb:Service>
        <eb:Action>NewOrder</eb:Action>
        <eb:MessageData>
            <eb:MessageId>20011115-122303-28572@psol.com</eb:MessageId>
            <eb:Timestamp>2001-11-15T11:12:12Z</eb:Timestamp>
        </eb:MessageData>
    </eb:MessageHeader>
</env:Header>
<env:Body>
    <eb:Manifest env:mustUnderstand="1" eb:version="1.0">
        <eb:Reference xlink:href="cid:ebxmlpayload-143@psol.com"
                      xlink:role="XLinkRole"
                      xlink:type="simple"
                      xmlns:xlink="http://www.w3.org/1999/xlink">
        </eb:Reference>
    </eb:Manifest>
</env:Body>
</env:Envelope>

--MIME_boundary
Content-ID: <ebxmlpayload-143@psol.com>
Content-Type: text/xml

<?xml version="1.0"?>
<Order xmlns="http://www.psol.com/2001/order">
    <Reference>53</Reference>
    <ISBN>0-7897-2504-5</ISBN>
    <Title>XML by Example, Second Edition</Title>
```

LISTING 7.14 continued

```
</Order>

--MIME_boundary--
```

Note that according to the rules for MIME encoding, a boundary string separates the parts. The boundary string is defined in the `boundary` property (`boundary=MIME_boundary`, as shown in Listing 7.14).

Summary

This chapter discussed the SOAP protocol. Specifically, you have learned how to construct RPC requests with XML and HTTP. You have also learned about other SOAP options such as using SOAP to send regular XML documents, using SOAP over SMTP, and using SOAP with attachments.

I hope this chapter has convinced you that SOAP is a technology worth studying further. In Chapter 8, you will learn how to write SOAP applications.

CHAPTER

SOAP Basics

by Benoît Marchal

In This Chapter

In Chapter 7, "Understanding SOAP," you learned about the Simple Object Access Protocol (SOAP). SOAP offers RPC (Remote Procedure Calls) with XML and HTTP.

As you have seen, SOAP is not a monolith. On the contrary, it is designed in a highly modular fashion and you can use subsets of the standard such as the envelope to exchange XML documents. One example of using subsets is the ebXML transport, routing, and packaging specification that was introduced in Chapter 7.

In this chapter, you will learn more about using SOAP and, in particular, you will learn how to develop with SOAP.

Writing SOAP Nodes

When working with SOAP, the first decision is whether you will use a SOAP library or roll up your sleeves and write your own SOAP handling. SOAP is a lightweight protocol, so it's relatively easy to write a SOAP node with JSP and servlets, or even with CGI, PHP, ASP, and other server-side scripting languages.

Do-It-Yourself

Although you are more likely to use SOAP libraries, it's interesting to review how to write a SOAP node in JSP. Listing 8.1 implements one of the easiest services: It accepts calls of the form `String reverse(String st)`. It simply reverses the string given as the parameter, so *Java* becomes *avaJ*.

Caution

Listing 8.1 needs the `org.apache.xpath` package to use Xalan 2.0's proprietary XPath API. You have to install Xalan 2.0 (or a compatible version) in your classpath to run this JSP.

You can download Xalan 2.0 from `http://xml.apache.org`.

LISTING 8.1 soapreverse.jsp

```
<?xml version="1.0"?>
<%@page contentType="text/xml"%>
<%@page import="org.w3c.dom.*,javax.xml.parsers.*"%>
<%@page import="org.apache.xpath.*"%>
<env:Envelope xmlns:xsd="http://www.w3.org/1999/XMLSchema"
     xmlns:env="http://schemas.xmlsoap.org/soap/envelope/"
     xmlns:xsi="http://www.w3.org/1999/XMLSchema-instance">
<env:Body>
<%
```

LISTING 8.1 continued

```
DocumentBuilderFactory factory =
    DocumentBuilderFactory.newInstance();
factory.setNamespaceAware(true);
DocumentBuilder builder = factory.newDocumentBuilder();
Document document = builder.parse(request.getInputStream());
Element root = document.getDocumentElement(),
        namespaces = document.createElement("namespaces");
namespaces.setAttribute("xmlns:env",
                    "http://schemas.xmlsoap.org/soap/envelope/");
namespaces.setAttribute("xmlns:rv",
                        "http://www.psol.com/2001/reverse");
boolean versionMismatch =
    root.getLocalName().equals("Envelope") &&
    !root.getNamespaceURI().equals(
                    "http://schemas.xmlsoap.org/soap/envelope/");
XPathAPI xpath = new XPathAPI();
Node node = xpath.selectSingleNode(document,
         "/env:Envelope/env:Header/*[@env:mustUnderstand = '1']",
         namespaces);
Text text = (Text)xpath.selectSingleNode(document,
               "/env:Envelope/env:Body/rv:reverse/string/text()",
               namespaces);
if(!versionMismatch && node == null && text != null) {
    StringBuffer st = new StringBuffer(text.getData());
    st = st.reverse();
%>
<rv:reverseResponse xmlns:rv="http://www.psol.com/2001/reverse"
   env:encodingStyle="http://schemas.xmlsoap.org/soap/encoding/">
    <return xsi:type="xsd:string"><%= st.toString() %></return>
</rv:reverseResponse>
<%
}
else {
%>
<env:Fault>
<faultcode><%= versionMismatch ? "env:VersionMismatch" :
                   node != null ? "env:MustUnderstand" :
                                  "env:Client" %></faultcode>
<faultstring>Sorry, I cannot process your request.</faultstring>
</env:Fault>
<%
}
%>
</env:Body>
</env:Envelope>
```

As you can see, the listing is not very long, yet it implements a workable subset of SOAP. This is possible because the SOAP request arrives as a regular HTTP request.

Caution

Listing 8.1 is a SOAP end node. You would need to write a SOAP client to access it. You will learn how to write clients in a moment, but for this discussion, it is sufficient to compare Listings 8.1 and 8.2.

Compare this page with a regular JSP page. Listing 8.2 implements the same functionality but as an HTML form.

LISTING 8.2 formreverse.jsp

```
<html>
<head><title>Reverse</title></head>
<body>
<h1>Reverse</h1>
<%
String st = request.getParameter("string");
if(st != null) {
    StringBuffer bf = new StringBuffer(st);
    String rv = bf.reverse().toString();
%>
<p>The reverse of  <%= st %> is <%= rv %>.</p>
<%
}
else {
%>
<form action="<%= request.getRequestURI() %>">
<p>String: <input type="text" name="string"><br>
<input type="submit"></p>
</form>
<%
}
%>
</body>
</html>
```

Although Listing 8.2 is smaller, the two listings are remarkably similar. The only significant difference is in how they retrieve the string parameter. Listing 8.2 uses the servlet-provided `getParameter()` method, whereas Listing 8.1 has to decode the SOAP request. Note that because the service is so simple (it takes only one line to reverse the string), decoding the SOAP request appears proportionally longer than it really is.

Let's review salient aspects of Listing 8.1 and compare them with Listing 8.2. Listing 8.1 first sets the content type to `text/xml`, with an `@page` directive, as required by the SOAP specification. Listing 8.2 uses the default content type, `text/html`.

Tip

If present, the XML declaration (`<?xml version="1.0"?>`) must appear as the first character of the XML document's first line. Always include JSP directives immediately after the XML declaration.

Next, Listing 8.1 issues the SOAP envelope and body where Listing 8.2 issues an HTML body.

The next section has the most differences between listings 8.1 and 8.2. Listing 8.1 parses the request with an XML parser and extracts three pieces of information:

- It tests the namespace of the `Envelope` element (`getNamespaceURI()`) for a version mismatch. This test enables a backward compatibility mode that will be handy when SOAP 1.2 is more widely deployed.
- With the first call to `selectSingleNode()`, it validates that the header contains no elements marked with `env:mustUnderstand`.
- It extracts the string parameter with a second call to `selectSingleNode()`.

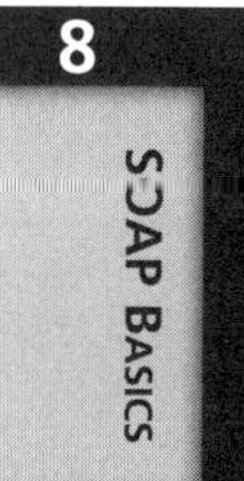

Caution

You might be tempted to skip the tests for version mismatch and `env:mustUnderstand` parameters. Don't. They define the bare bones minimum requirements to guarantee compatibility with SOAP clients.

Next, both listings reverse the string and return the result. If everything goes well, Listing 8.1 marks the result with XML elements, whereas Listing 8.2 uses HTML. In case of errors, Listing 8.1 returns an `env:Fault` element, whereas Listing 8.2 creates an HTML form.

So should you use this technique and write SOAP nodes in raw JSP? Most likely not, but this section shows that SOAP is a lightweight protocol. In fact, it takes only a dozen lines of JSP code to implement it.

Tip

You might want to use this method if you need to quickly port JSP pages to Web services. In the long term, it is more cost-effective to redesign your application, implement the logic in JavaBeans (or EJB), and use a SOAP library to expose the beans.

SOAP Libraries

The alternative to writing JSP pages is to turn to a SOAP library such as Apache SOAP. A library provides three important benefits:

- It makes it even easier to write SOAP nodes. As you will see, with Apache SOAP, writing a SOAP node is as easy as writing an XML file.
- The library should simplify the migration from SOAP 1.1 to SOAP 1.2.
- A library may support more advanced options such as SSL, authentication, and the like.

In this chapter, I use Apache SOAP. Apache SOAP was originally an IBM alphaWorks project, but IBM gave it to the Apache Foundation. It is now distributed as open source. Apache SOAP is arguably one of the most popular implementations of SOAP, but other toolkits for Java include:

- XSOAP, which conforms to the RMI interface. It is available from `http://www.extreme.indiana.edu/soap`.
- Orbix E2A XMLBus Edition from Iona. It builds on the company's years of experience writing CORBA implementations. More information is available at `http://www.xmlbus.com`.

Vendors increasingly offer SOAP implementations. For an up-to-date list, turn to `http://www.soapware.org`.

Caution

Theoretically, SOAP implementations are interoperable. In practice, as I explained in Chapter 7, problems do occur, mostly because of typing errors. Although we can hope that SOAP 1.2 will help reduce the problems, it is prudent to test compatibility when using different libraries on both the client and the server.

A Simple Web Service: Booking Service

The underlying project for this chapter is a room booking service. Such a service would be useful for business centers, business hotels, or a multinational company with offices in various locations. (If you're unfamiliar with business centers, they rent meeting rooms for short duration, sometimes as little as half a day.)

Because it's not possible to hold two meetings in the same room at the same time, you need to track room usage. You also need a mechanism to reserve rooms for a date.

In both cases (business center or multinational), it is useful to make the booking system available on the Internet. Obviously, the business center benefits if travel agencies and others can book its rooms. The multinational may want to let employees in other countries book, as well.

For example, Figure 8.1 shows a business center in London. Through a SOAP node, it lets local travel agencies book offices. This will be handy next time you're in London for business!

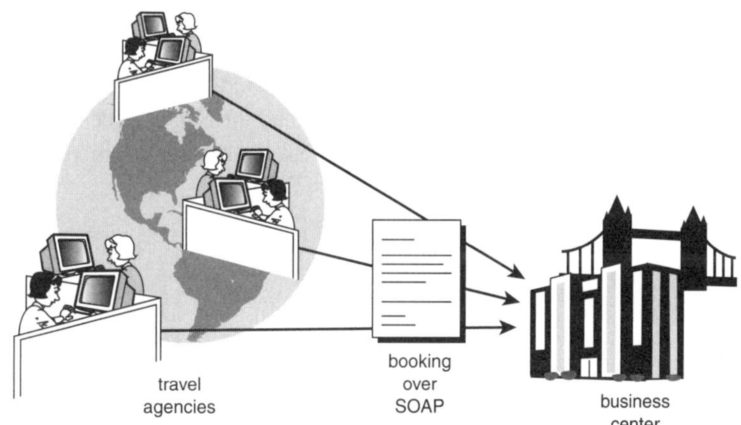

FIGURE 8.1
A SOAP booking service.

You'll use this example throughout the rest of this chapter. Note that I have made several simplifications so as to let SOAP shine through and not spend too much time on the business of room booking, which is not directly relevant to the theme.

The booking service responds to the following RPC methods:

- `getAllResources()` returns an array with all the rooms.
- `getFreeResourcesOn()`returns an array with only those rooms still free between two dates.
- `bookResource()` lets the user book a room for a certain period of time.

A true room booking service would offer more services, such as the capability to free a room you've booked previously. I chose those methods primarily to illustrate interesting options in SOAP, not to build a production-grade Web service.

Organization

You'll be coding three different elements and it's important for you to understand how they relate to each other:

- The SOAP node offers its services through a Web server.
- The SOAP client accesses the SOAP node to mediate between the end user and the service.
- The administrator, which is not related to SOAP, provides minimal number of services to create and review the database.

For demonstration purposes, you will run all three services on one machine, but in reality the SOAP client and the SOAP node would be on different machines. Figure 8.2 highlights this. The client is at the travel agency and the SOAP node is with the business center. The administrator is local to the SOAP node, so it resides there as well.

FIGURE 8.2
Client and server would run on different computers.

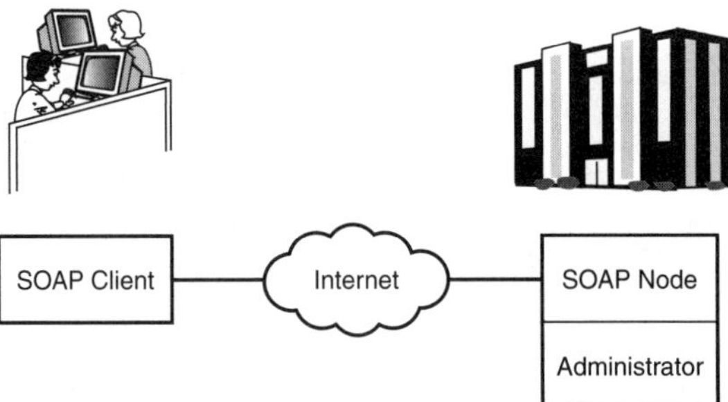

Installing the Example

I encourage you to download the booking service application, run it, and study how it works. It will be easier for you to follow this chapter if you have seen the booking service running. The easiest option is to download a ready-to-run package from either http://www.samspublishing.com or http://www.marchal.com. Follow the links to this book's page and download the listings from there.

The ready-to-run package comes in Zip file or self-installing archive. Uncompress it and install it in the directory of your choice. This package is complete with a Web server and a database, so you have nothing else to install.

Under Windows, go to the directory where you uncompressed the archive and first edit the launch.bat file:

```
@echo off
set JAVA_HOME=c:\jdk1.3
call jetty
```

Change the JAVA_HOME variable to point to the JDK on your system. Save your changes and double-click launch.bat. The Web server starts.

With other operating systems, you start the Web server by selecting the directory where you uncompressed the archive and then issuing the following command:

```
java -classpath lib/resourceful.jar;lib/hsqldb.jar;lib/xalan.jar;
➥lib/xcommerce.jar;%JAVA_HOME%/lib/tools.jar;lib/javax.servlet.jar;
➥lib/org.mortbay.jetty.jar;lib/activation.jar;lib/mail.jar;
➥lib/org.apache.jasper.jar;lib/xerces.jar;lib/soap.jar
➥-Dorg.xml.sax.parser=org.apache.xerces.parsers.SAXParser
➥org.mortbay.jetty.Server etc/jetty.xml
```

where %JAVA_HOME% is bound to the directory where the JDK is installed on your system.

Caution

To run this application, you need to install a JDK 1.3 or above. A JRE, in particular, will not suffice because JSP needs a compiler.

What should you do if you see an error message?

- Check the readme file included in the Zip file. It contains last-minute updates and might point to a solution.
- Under Windows, make sure you edited the launch.bat file as explained earlier.
- By default, the Web server runs on port 5401. Make sure you do not have another service running on port 5401.

Walking Through the Example

Having launched the server, as explained in the preceding section, point your browser to `http://localhost:5401/resourceful/index.jsp`. The screen should be similar to Figure 8.3.

FIGURE 8.3
Opening screen.

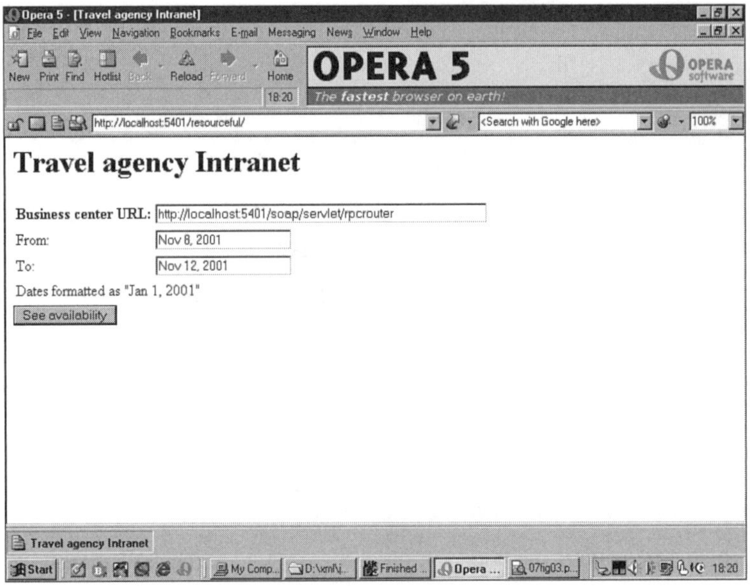

Note that the title is "Travel agency Intranet." You're on a JSP server that acts as a SOAP client. This application runs at the travel agency, outside the business center. Also note the field labeled "Business Center URL." That's the URL to the SOAP node. The SOAP node is with the business center.

In the rest of this section, you'll be interacting with the travel agency application, the SOAP client. This application makes regular calls to the SOAP node.

Caution

Be patient. The first time you run Apache SOAP, it may take up to one minute to warm up.

If you enter dates and hit the See Availability button, a screen similar to Figure 8.4 should appear. Although the screen is rendered by a local JSP, the data is coming from the SOAP.

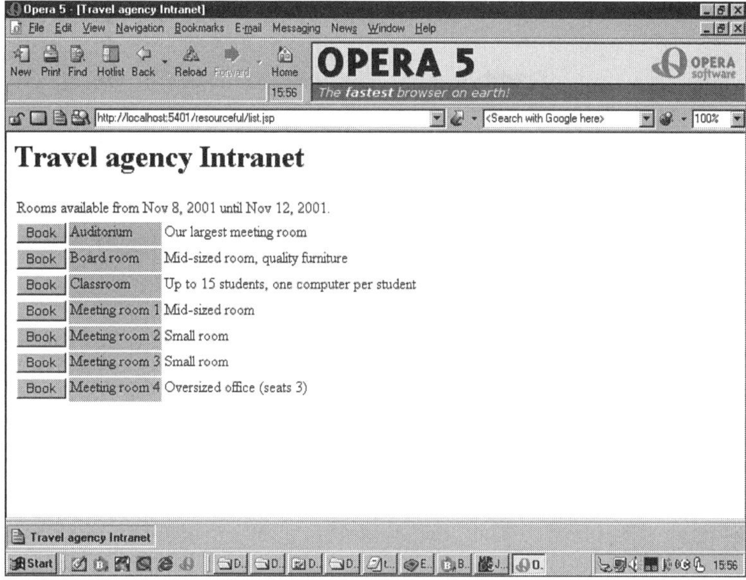

FIGURE 8.4
Room availabilities as reported by the SOAP node.

Click the Book button and you will be taken to the booking screen, seen in Figure 8.5. The dates should be pre-filled, enter your email address and hit Book Now to book your room. For simplicity, you do not need to enter your name, address, and phone number; the email address suffices. It's not difficult to modify the service to collect more data.

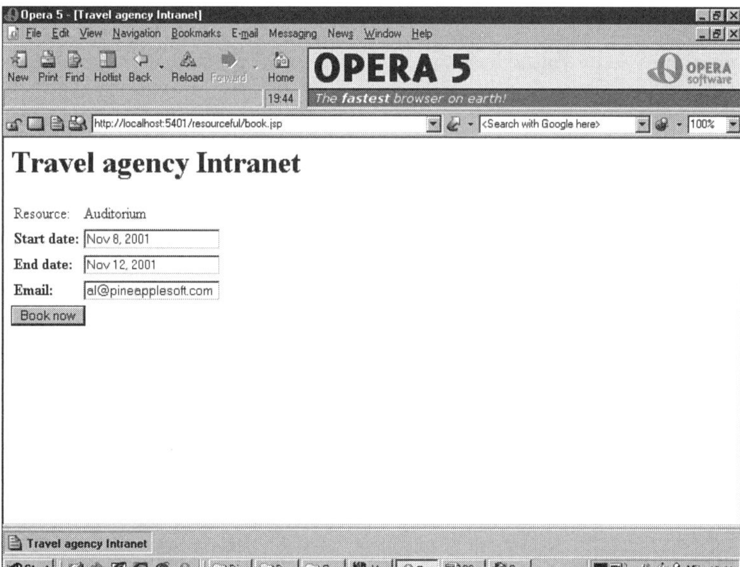

FIGURE 8.5
Booking a room at the agency.

A confirmation screen, shown in Figure 8.6, appears next.

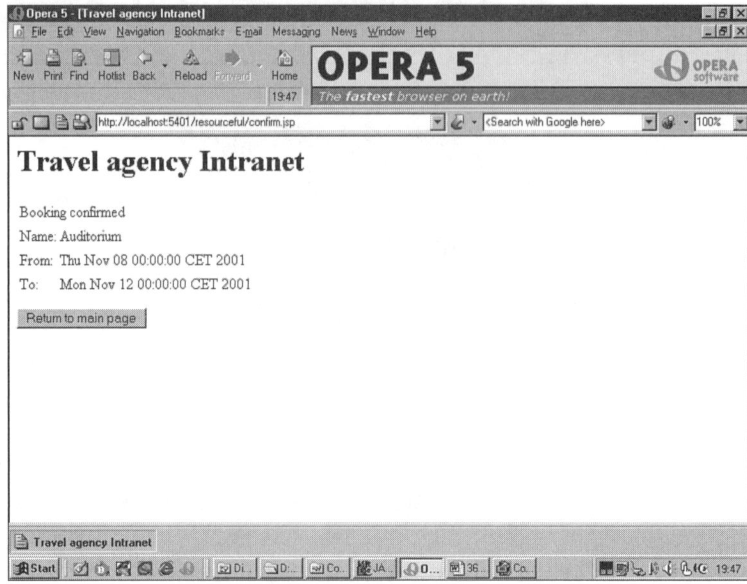

FIGURE 8.6
The room is booked.

I would encourage you to run the SOAP node on a different computer of your network. It's easy: First launch a copy of the application on another machine connected to your network. Next, return to the front and replace `localhost` in the `Business Center URL` with the name of the computer. If the remote computer is called `joker.psol.com`, you edit the URL in Figure 8.3 to read:

```
http://joker.psol.com:5401/soap/servlet/rpcrouter
```

Caution

Note that this is the URL for the SOAP end point. Because your browser is not a SOAP client, you should not enter it in the address field of your browser. Rather, this is the URL for the SOAP client to connect to. In this case, you can change it through the Business Center URL field in the client's screen, as explained before.

Book another room, as you saw previously. The requests are now being sent through to the remote SOAP node. This more closely mimics the setup you saw in Figure 8.2.

Tip

When you're finished, you can stop the server by going to `http://localhost:5401/jetty/admin` and clicking Exit All Servers. The server then reports that it is no longer available.

Tracing SOAP Messages

Apache SOAP comes with a handy tool called TCP Tunnel. This lets you see what goes over the wire, including the SOAP requests and responses. TCP Tunnel is a proxy that listens to one port and forwards the request, unmodified, to another port. In the process, it displays the request on screen.

You'll be using TCP Tunnel between the JSP server (the SOAP client) and the SOAP node (see Figure 8.7). Two Web interactions are running on your computer. The JSP server interacts with your browser in a classic HTML mode. That's not the dialogue you're interested in.

What you are interested in is the communication between the JSP Server acting as a SOAP client and the SOAP node.

FIGURE 8.7
Listening to the SOAP exchange.

To start TCP Tunnel under Windows, just double-click the `tcptunnel.bat` file to start TCP Tunnel. `tcptunnel.bat` listens on port 5403. Make sure no other servers are active on that port or you'll get a conflict. You might also edit `tcptunnel.bat` to use another port.

Under another operating system, the command is the following:

```
@java -classpath lib\soap.jar org.apache.soap.util.net.TcpTunnelGui
➥ 5403 localhost 5401
```

Now start the server, as explained in the section "Installing the Example," and go to `http://localhost:5401/resourceful/index.jsp`. Change the Business center URL to use the TCP Tunnel port, 5403 (the URL should read `http://localhost:5403/soap/servlet/rpcrouter`). Note that two URLs are on the screen; make sure you change the SOAP one as shown in Figure 8.8, not your browser URL. Book yourself a room as you did in the previous section.

> **Caution**
>
> Again note that `http://localhost:5403/soap/servlet/rpcrouter` is the URL to the SOAP endpoint. You should enter it in the Business center URL field, not in your browser address field.

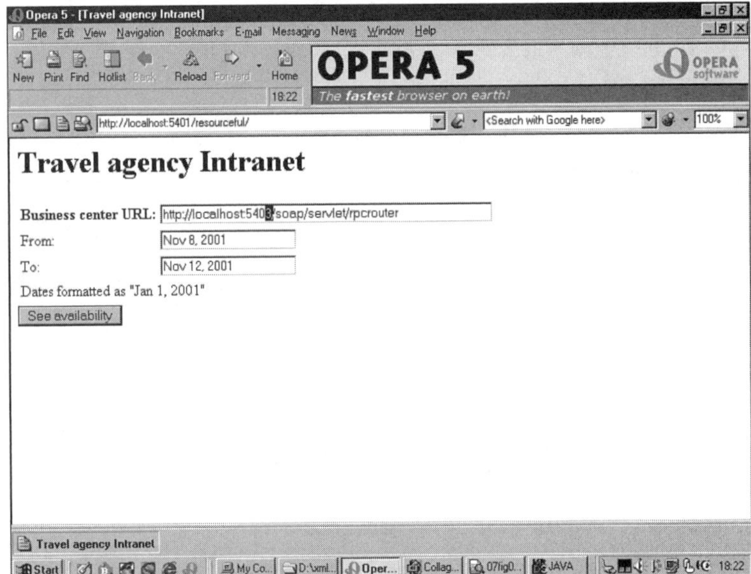

FIGURE 8.8
Changing the URL to go through the proxy.

Immediately you see the RPC call in the TCP Tunnel window. If you review the information in TCP Tunnel, you will recognize the SOAP request and SOAP response that were introduced in Chapter 6, "Building a JSP Web Service." Figure 8.9 is an excerpt from the SOAP dialogue.

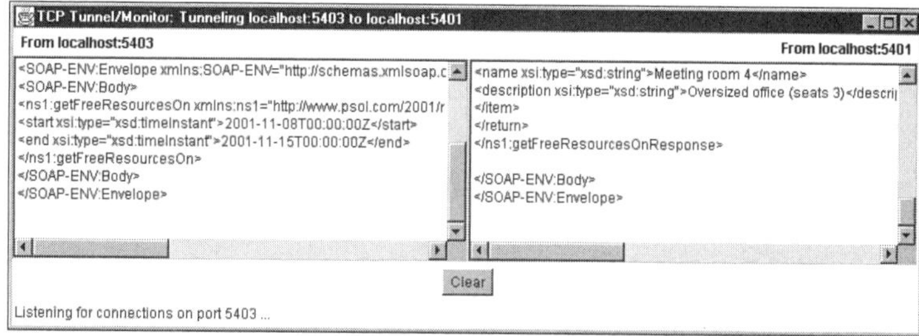

FIGURE 8.9
TCP Tunnel lets you look under the hood.

Recompiling the Project

This section contains useful information if you would like to recompile the project. If you use the ready-to-run package, you do not have to recompile the project, so you may skip this section. If you would like to modify the project, you need the following information.

> **Caution**
>
> The project has been tested with the version of the libraries listed in this section. A more recent version should work fine, but ensuring backward compatibility is not always a priority for developers.

This Web service uses the following libraries:

- Jetty 3.1.4. Jetty is an efficient open-source Web server that supports JSP and servlets. Porting the project to another JSP-compliant Web server should not be too much work. Jetty is available from `http://jetty.mortbay.com`;
- hsql Database Engine 1.6.1 RC1, a lightweight open-source database that implements JDBC. I tried to stick to standard SQL as much as possible, so porting to another database should not be too much work. The hsql Database Engine is available from `http://www.hsqldb.org`.
- Apache SOAP 2.2, an open-source SOAP toolkit. At the time of writing, this is the closest thing to a reference implementation of SOAP for Java. Apache SOAP is available from `http://xml.apache.org`.

Be warned that Jetty and SOAP have dependencies on other libraries. If you update one of the libraries, make sure you read the documentation and download all the JARs.

Listing 8.3 is the configuration file for Jetty. It enables a minimalist Web server with just enough options to run this application.

The line you are most likely to edit in Listing 8.3 is:

```
<Set name="Port">5401</Set>
```

This line sets the Web server port. If port 5401 is already in use on your computer (or if you'd rather use another port), change this line and restart the server.

LISTING 8.3 jetty.xml

```
<?xml version="1.0" encoding="ISO-8859-1"?>

<!DOCTYPE Configure PUBLIC
   "-//Mort Bay Consulting//DTD Configure 1.0//EN"
   "http://jetty.mortbay.com/configure_1_0.dtd">

<Configure class="org.mortbay.jetty.Server">

<!-- starts the Web server -->
<Call name="addListener">
    <Arg>
        <New class="org.mortbay.http.SocketListener">
            <!-- change port here -->
            <Set name="Port">5401</Set>
            <Set name="MinThreads">5</Set>
            <Set name="MaxThreads">255</Set>
            <Set name="MaxIdleTimeMs">60000</Set>
            <Set name="MaxReadTimeMs">60000</Set>
        </New>
    </Arg>
</Call>

<Set name="RequestLogSink">
    <New class="org.mortbay.util.OutputStreamLogSink">
        <Arg>etc/logs/yyyy_mm_dd.request.log</Arg>
        <Set name="RetainDays">90</Set>
        <Set name="Append">true</Set>
    </New>
</Set>

<!-- enables online administration
     add authentication for a server facing the Internet -->
<Call name="addContext">
    <Arg>/jetty/*</Arg>
    <Call name="addServlet">
        <Arg>admin</Arg>
        <Arg>/</Arg>
        <Arg>org.mortbay.servlet.AdminServlet</Arg>
    </Call>
</Call>
```

LISTING 8.3 continued

```
<!-- enables SOAP -->
<Call name="addWebApplication">
    <Arg>/soap/*</Arg>
    <Arg>./webapps/soap</Arg>
    <Arg>./webapps/soap/WEB-INF/web.xml</Arg>
    <Arg type="boolean">false</Arg>
    <Call name="addServlet">
        <Arg>JSP</Arg>
        <Arg>*.jsp</Arg>
        <Arg>org.apache.jasper.servlet.JspServlet</Arg>
    </Call>
</Call>

<Call name="addContext">
    <Arg>/soap/*</Arg>
    <Set name="ResourceBase">./soap/</Set>
    <Set name="ServingResources">true</Set>
    <Set name="HttpServerAccess">true</Set>
</Call>

<Call name="addContext">
    <Arg>/soap/admin/*</Arg>
    <Set name="ResourceBase">./soap/admin/</Set>
    <Set name="ClassPath">./soap/admin/</Set>
    <Set name="ServingResources">true</Set>
    <Call name="addServlet">
        <Arg>JSP</Arg>
        <Arg>/soap/admin/*.jsp</Arg>
        <Arg>org.apache.jasper.servlet.JspServlet</Arg>
    </Call>
    <Set name="HttpServerAccess">true</Set>
</Call>

<!-- enable JSP -->
<Call name="addContext">
    <Arg>/resourceful/*</Arg>
    <Call name="addHandler">
      <Arg type="int">0</Arg>
      <Arg>
        <New class="org.mortbay.http.handler.ForwardHandler">
          <Arg>index.jsp</Arg>
        </New>
      </Arg>
    </Call>
    <Call name="addServlet">
        <Arg>JSP</Arg>
        <Arg>*.jsp</Arg>
        <Arg>org.apache.jasper.servlet.JspServlet</Arg>
    </Call>
```

LISTING 8.3 continued

```
    <Set name="ResourceBase">./docroot/</Set>
    <Set name="ServingResources">true</Set>
</Call>

</Configure>
```

Listing 8.4 is the Ant 1.2 build file for this project. It recompiles the SOAP node only. Because the client is written in JSP, the server recompiles it when appropriate.

LISTING 8.4 build.xml

```
<?xml version="1.0"?>

<!-- Ant 1.2 build file: jakarta.apache.org -->

<project name="resourceful" default="jar" basedir=".">
    <property name="classpath"
              value="lib/xerces.jar;lib/soap.jar;lib/mail.jar"/>

    <target name="jar" depends="compile">
        <jar jarfile="lib/resourceful.jar"
             basedir="classes"/>
    </target>
    <target name="compile" depends="prepare">
        <javac srcdir="src"
               destdir="classes"
               classpath="${classpath}"/>
    </target>
    <target name="prepare">
        <mkdir dir="classes"/>
        <mkdir dir="lib"/>
    </target>
</project>
```

The Administration Interface

The project comes with an administration interface. The interface gives you direct access to the database for the SOAP node. For administrative tasks, it is more effective to connect directly through the database than to write more methods on the SOAP node.

Caution

It might even be dangerous to provide database administration as a group of Web services because doing so gives more people administrative privileges over your database.

Strictly speaking, this is not SOAP programming, but it is useful nevertheless! The administration interface is designed to run on the same computer as the SOAP node, and it enables you to create and delete the database tables, create new rooms, and review all the bookings.

You access the administration at `http://localhost:5401/resourceful/admin.jsp`. The screen is similar to Figure 8.10.

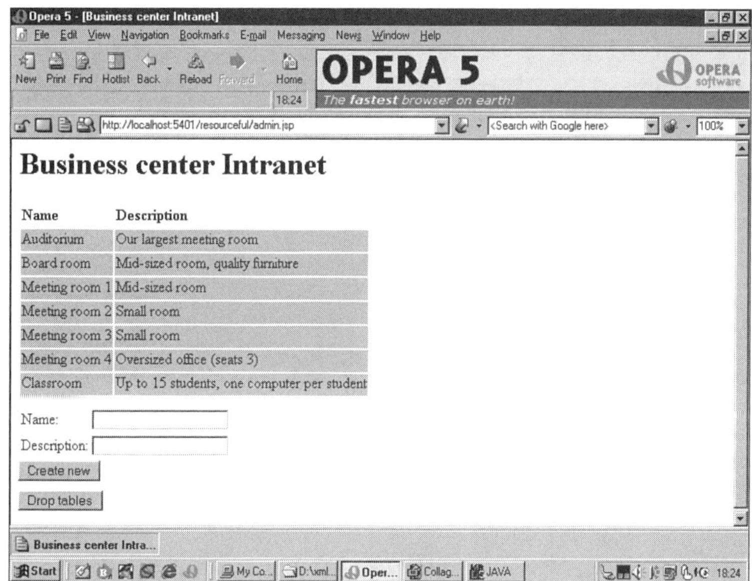

FIGURE 8.10
Administering the SOAP node.

The bulk of the page lists the rooms available in the database with their bookings. It is followed by a form where you can enter new rooms.

The last button gives you a chance to drop the tables in the database. Use it with care because you will lose all your data! When you reconnect after dropping the tables, however, you'll be given a chance to recreate them.

Listing 8.5 is the page listing. It is large as far as JSP pages go because it supports all the administrative functions. This approach may produce less readable code, but it helps separate the administrative tasks from the SOAP client itself.

LISTING 8.5 admin.jsp

```
<%@page import="java.sql.*,java.util.*,java.text.*"%>
<% response.setHeader("Cache-Control","no-cache"); %>
<%!
```

LISTING 8.5 continued

```
private boolean isSchemaCreated(Connection connection)
    throws SQLException
{
    // ask the name of all the tables in the database
    // compare against a list of known tables
    DatabaseMetaData meta = connection.getMetaData();
    ResultSet rs =
        meta.getTables(null,null,null,new String[] { "TABLE" });
    int found = 0;
    while(rs.next()) {
        String tableName = rs.getString("TABLE_NAME");
        if(tableName.equalsIgnoreCase("resource")
            || tableName.equalsIgnoreCase("booking"))
            found++;
    }
    rs.close();
    return 2 == found;
}

protected void doUpdates(Connection connection,
                         String[] statements)
    throws SQLException
{
    Statement stmt = connection.createStatement();
    SQLException e = null;
    try {
        for(int i = 0;i < statements.length;i++)
           try {
               stmt.executeUpdate(statements[i]);
           }
           catch(SQLException x)
               { e = e != null ? e : x; }
        if(null != e) {
            throw e;
        }
    }
    finally {
        stmt.close();
    }
}

private boolean isEmpty(String st)
{
   if(null != st)
       return st.trim().length() == 0;
   else
       return true;
}
```

LISTING 8.5 continued

```
private void doInsertResource(Connection connection,
                              String name,
                              String description)
    throws SQLException
{
    PreparedStatement stmt =
        connection.prepareStatement(
           "insert into resource (name, description) values (?,?)");
    try {
        stmt.setString(1,name);
        stmt.setString(2,description);
        stmt.executeUpdate();
    }
    finally {
        stmt.close();
    }
}
%>
<%
DateFormat dateFormat =
    DateFormat.getDateInstance(DateFormat.MEDIUM,
                               Locale.US);
Class.forName("org.hsqldb.jdbcDriver");
Connection connection =
    DriverManager.getConnection("jdbc:hsqldb:db/resourceful",
                                "sa",
                                null);
try
{
    connection.setAutoCommit(true);
%>
<html>
<head>
<title>Business center Intranet</title>
</head>
<body>
<h1>Business center Intranet</h1>
<%
    String todo = request.getParameter("todo"),
           message = null;
    if(todo != null) {
        if(todo.equals("drop"))
            doUpdates(connection,new String[] {
               "drop index resource.idx_name",
               "drop index booking.idx_start",
               "drop index booking.idx_end",
               "drop table resource",
               "drop table booking",
            });
```

LISTING 8.5 continued

```
        else if(todo.equals("create"))
            doUpdates(connection,new String[]
            {
               "set ignorecase true",
               "create table resource (id integer not null " +
                  "identity primary key, name varchar(50) not " +
                  "null, description varchar(100) not null, " +
                  "unique (name))",
               "create table booking (id integer not null " +
                  "identity primary key, resourceid integer not " +
                  "null, email varchar(80), start datetime not " +
                  "null, end datetime not null, foreign key " +
                  "(resourceid) references resource (id))",
               "create index idx_name on resource (name)",
               "create index idx_start on booking (start)",
               "create index idx_end on booking (end)",
            });
        else if(todo.equals("insert"))
            doInsertResource(connection,
                             request.getParameter("name"),
                             request.getParameter("description"));
    }
%>
<%
    if(isSchemaCreated(connection)) {
%>
<%-- a table with the list of data --%>
<table>
<tr><td><b>Name</b></td>
    <td><b>Description</b></td></tr>
<%
        Statement stmt = connection.createStatement();
        PreparedStatement pstmt =
            connection.prepareStatement("select id, start, end, " +
                      "email from booking where resourceid = ?");
        try {
           ResultSet resources =
               stmt.executeQuery("select id, name, " +
                                 "description from resource");
           while(resources.next()) {
%>
<tr><td bgcolor="#bbbbbb"
    valign="top"><%= resources.getString(2) %></td>
    <td valign="top" bgcolor="#bbbbbb"
       colspan="2"><%= resources.getString(3) %></td></tr>
<%
               pstmt.setInt(1,resources.getInt(1));
               try {
```

LISTING 8.5 continued

```
                  ResultSet bookings = pstmt.executeQuery();
                  while(bookings.next()) {
%>
<tr><td colspan="2">booked by
    <%= bookings.getString(4) %>
    (<%= dateFormat.format(bookings.getTimestamp(2)) %> -
    <%= dateFormat.format(bookings.getTimestamp(3)) %>)</td></tr>
<%
                 }
              }
              finally {
                 pstmt.close();
              }
%>
<%
           }
       }
       finally {
           stmt.close();
       }
%>
</table>
<%-- a form to create entries --%>
<form action="<%= request.getRequestURI() %>" method="post">
<table>
<tr><td>Name:</td><td>
<input type="text" name="name"></td></tr>
<tr><td>Description:</td><td>
<input type="text" name="description"></td></tr>
</table>
<input type="hidden" name="todo" value="insert">
<input type="submit" value="Create new">
</form>
<%
    }
%>
<%-- a small form to create/drop tables in the database --%>
<form action="<%= request.getRequestURI() %>" method="post">
<%
    if(isSchemaCreated(connection)) {
%>
<input type="hidden" name="todo" value="drop">
<input type="submit" value="Drop tables"><br>
<%
    }
    else {
%>
<input type="hidden" name="todo" value="create">
<input type="submit" value="Create tables"><br>
```

LISTING 8.5 continued

```
<%
    }
%>
</form>
<%
}
finally {
   connection.close();
}
%>
</body>
</html>
```

I won't go into great detail over this page, because it mostly collects data from forms and issues the appropriate SQL request.

Figure 8.11 is the database schema. Suffice it to say that the database contains two tables:

- `resource` records the rooms available at the location with their `names` and `descriptions`. Resources are identified by their `ids`.
- `booking` records the bookings made so far. For simplicity, it identifies users by their `email` addresses only. A booking has an `id` identifier, and a `start` and `end` date. A booking is attached to a resource through the `resourceid` foreign key.

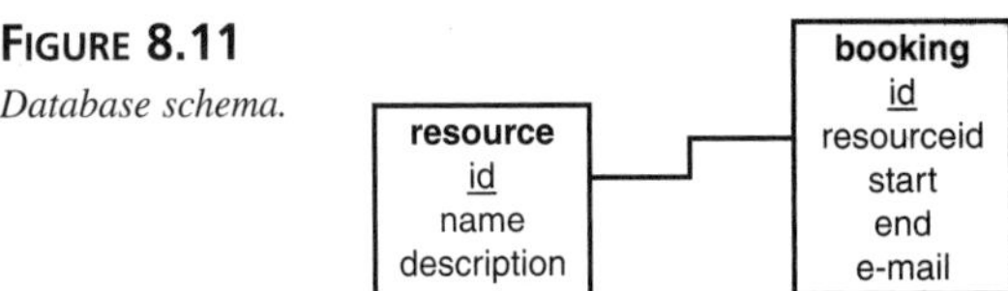

FIGURE 8.11
Database schema.

The database uses hsql's proprietary `identity` type. An identity column auto-increments itself when a record is added. Every database offers auto-increment columns, but the syntax differs, so you may have to change the statements.

The page creates several forms for inserting a new resource or dropping or creating the tables. Each form includes a hidden `todo` parameter:

```
<input type="hidden" name="todo" value="insert">
```

When the page loads, it retrieves the `todo` parameter that indicates which form, if any, was called. The page also queries the list of tables in the database. If it cannot find `resource` and `booking`, it assumes that the tables have been dropped and prompts you to re-create them.

Public Interface: Design Considerations

When you design a Web service, you have to consider two aspects:

- The public interface to the service, which prescribes how clients can interface with your SOAP node
- The internal implementation of the node that implements the public interface

Be careful to keep in mind the distinction between the two as you design your service. You do not necessarily want the public interface to directly reflect the internal implementation.

For example, if the Web service is built on top of a legacy system, you might decide to not expose a slightly modified version of the service. Alternatively, you might decide to not make every local service available remotely—for security reasons, for example.

This section is concerned with the public interface only. As you design the public interface to your SOAP node, pay special attention to the following aspects:

- Security
- Network latency
- Responsiveness
- Independence

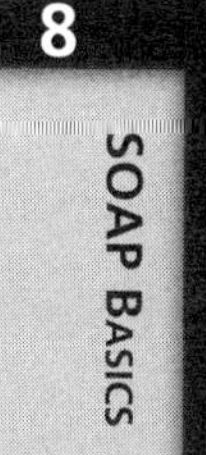

Security Considerations

We want to open this section with a word of warning. Security is not limited to encryption. Encryption may be a component of security, but security goes further then deciding whether you should use SSL or not.

During the design phase, you want to consider carefully which services and what information is being exposed. Just because SOAP lets you take any object and turn it into a remotely callable object doesn't mean it's a good idea to do so. For example, the booking service does not offer administrative tasks. Those are available through a completely different interface whose access, presumably, would be limited to local users.

Generally speaking, you don't want to give too much power to the service. Among other things, it's a good idea to limit the tables and files to which it has access.

Obviously, there will be conflicts between usability and security: You might have to forego features for security reasons. That's largely a judgment call, but keep in mind it's better to be safe than sorry. I advise you to challenge every feature against security requirements.

The Replay Attack

There's work in progress to build security features in SOAP. One option is to use HTTP basic authentication, but because the password is sent in clear over the network, this provides only the most basic level of security.

A W3C note available at `www.w3.org/TR/soap-DSIG` explains how to digitally sign SOAP requests with the XML digital signature. The signature information is added to the SOAP header.

However, signing does not protect you from the pernicious replay attack. In a replay attack, a hacker intercepts communication between client and server and simply resends the same message to the server.

A replay attack is easier for the hacker than breaking the digital signature. Depending on your service, though, a replay attack can have dramatic consequences. Imagine a hacker intercepting a valid order and repeatedly sending it. You'd end up producing a large number of unwanted products. You'd also pay to ship goods that the customer only returns again.

Fortunately, SSL provides a good protection against the replay attack. Because SSL encodes the communication, the hacker cannot intercept the message.

Network Latency

Network latency has a profound impact on the design of the public interface of SOAP nodes. Study Figures 8.12 and 8.13 to understand its effects.

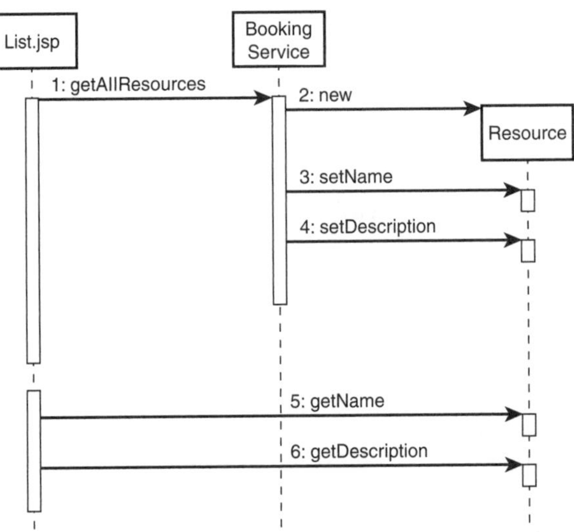

FIGURE 8.12
UML sequence diagram with a local call.

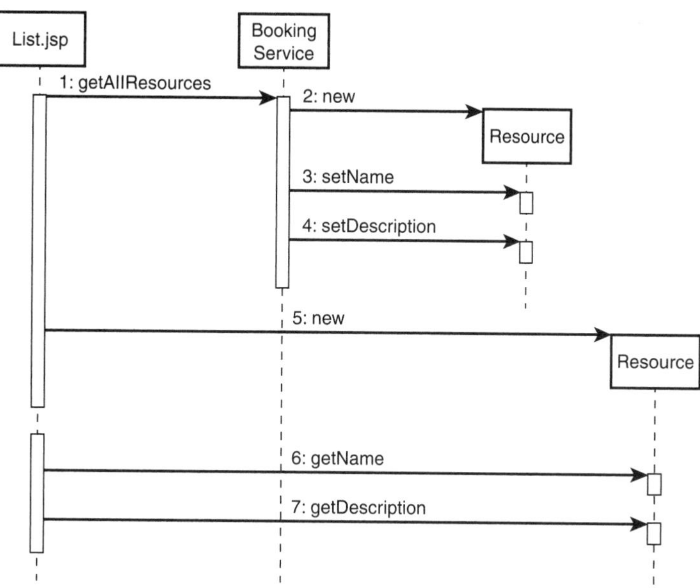

FIGURE 8.13
UML sequence diagram with RPC.

Figure 8.12 decomposes a call to `getAllResources()` in a standalone version of the application. The JSP page requests a list of `Resources` from the `BookingService`, which creates the object and returns them. The JSP page issues further calls directly on the `Resource` objects to extract the information it needs.

Figure 8.13 is the same sequence diagram where local calls have been replaced with SOAP RPCs. In response to a `getAllResources()` call, the `BookingService` still creates `Resource` objects. The rest of the call differs. `BookingService` compiles a SOAP response with the `Resource` objects and returns it to the client. The client decodes the request and creates its own set of `Resource` objects with which it then interacts as previously.

On the surface there's little difference between an RPC call and a regular procedure call but, as Figure 8.13 shows, there is one important difference: The client ends up working with copies of the `Resource` objects. So, for example, if it modifies the object, it does not affect the server.

Why is that so? Why not turn `Resources` into remote objects and use RPC to query their names and descriptions? Because it would not be efficient, that's why.

As discussed in Chapter 7, RPC was designed to hide some of the complexity in writing distributed applications. The trick is only cosmetic, though. RPC requests are coded more or less like regular procedure calls, but they still go over the network. They are inherently slower than local calls: no matter how fast the network, it will always be slower to send an RPC request than to access a memory zone. So for the sake of practicality, just be aware that you should minimize the interaction between the client and the server or you will bring both the network and the server to its knees.

Therefore, designing SOAP nodes requires a different set of rules than designing standalone applications. The granularity is different: Standalone applications have many small- to medium-sized objects, but a SOAP node exposes fewer (and comparatively larger) objects.

Tip

Those design rules apply to the SOAP node's public interface. They do not necessarily impact the implementation of node. In other words, even your SOAP node may appear as a monolith; it's a good idea to break down the implementation in discrete objects.

Efficiency

Efficiency takes on a whole new meaning with Web services. Specifically, from the user standpoint, it is measured not by your service alone but by a combination of your service, its local application, and the pipe between the two. You might think that a 50ms response time is great for the service, but it might lead to terrible performance when combined with the other elements.

What can you do about this when designing your Web service? Obviously, you cannot guarantee the efficiency of the client, but you can control how often it needs to interact with your service. You need to carefully consider the interaction between your service and the client and make sure you provide the most pertinent information or service in the most useful format.

For example, the booking service provides two different methods to return a list of resources: `getAllResources()` and `getResourcesFreeOn()`. I could have added availability information in the result of `getAllResources()`, but it puts more work on the client, not to mention that it sends more data over the wire.

Also, you should provide enough information so that the client can predict the result of a request and, maybe, decide not to issue it. For example, to find a free room on November 8, the client can either call `getResourcesFreeOn()` or repetitively try to book a room until it succeeds (failure to book a room indicates that it is not free on the chosen date). In most cases, it's more efficient to call `getResourcesFreeOn()` first.

Independence

There are two kinds of concepts in a model: what I would call business concepts, which model real-world concepts, and technical concepts, which exist solely to make the implementation more efficient. To ensure the maintainability of your service, you should minimize technical concepts in the public interface.

Again `BookingService` illustrates this. The database uses numbers to identify rooms internally. Those identifiers are known as *technical identifiers* because they do not model a real-world concept: businesspeople book the rooms by their names, not their database id.

The public interface carefully avoids exposing the technical identifier and sticks with names. Indeed, technical concepts exist only because of technical choices made during the development of the node (in this case, the use of a relational database). Unfortunately, because they have no reality outside the technical implementation, clients may not be able to manage them efficiently.

My own experience with system integration is that most of the time is spent working on identifiers and other technical concepts that exist to serve a particular implementation of one system.

Tip

In practice, you may have to override this rule for increased efficiency. Unfortunately, design often implies balancing conflicting interests.

Apache SOAP for RPC

Apache SOAP's strongest capability is in writing SOAP nodes. Literally all you need to do is write a so-called deployment descriptor (an XML document that outlines which methods are exposed on the network) to turn regular Java classes in SOAP nodes.

Unfortunately, it is less effective for writing clients. The library requires too many steps for a simple call. We hope that future versions of the library will address this problem, perhaps with an RMI binding or by generating the code from WSDL files.

Writing the Service Provider

Listing 8.6 is `BookingService`, the SOAP node you have used so far. It implements the three methods defined on the service. Remember they are:

- getAllResources()
- getFreeResourcesOn()
- bookResource()

LISTING 8.6 BookingService.java

```
package com.psol.resourceful;

import java.io.*;
import java.sql.*;
import java.util.*;
import javax.mail.*;
import org.w3c.dom.*;
import org.apache.soap.*;
import org.apache.soap.rpc.*;

public class BookingService
{
    protected Connection makeConnection()
        throws SQLException
    {
        try {
            Class.forName("org.hsqldb.jdbcDriver");
            Connection connection =
               DriverManager.getConnection(
                                     "jdbc:hsqldb:db/resourceful",
                                     "sa",
                                     null);
            connection.setAutoCommit(false);
            return connection;
        }
        catch(ClassNotFoundException e) {
            e.printStackTrace();
            return null;
        }
    }

    public Resource[] getAllResources()
        throws SQLException
    {
        Vector vector = new Vector();
        Connection connection = makeConnection();
        try {
            Statement stmt = connection.createStatement();
            try {
                ResultSet rs = stmt.executeQuery("select name," +
                    "description from resource");
                while(rs.next()) {
                    Resource resource = new Resource();
                    resource.setName(rs.getString(1));
```

LISTING 8.6 continued

```
                    resource.setDescription(rs.getString(2));
                    vector.addElement(resource);
                }
            }
            finally {
                stmt.close();
            }
        }
        finally {
            connection.close();
        }
        Resource[] resourceList = new Resource[vector.size()];
        vector.copyInto(resourceList);
        return resourceList;
    }

    public Resource[] getFreeResourcesOn(java.util.Date start,
                                        java.util.Date end)
        throws SQLException
    {
        if(start.compareTo(end) > 0)
            throw new IllegalArgumentException(
                               "start date must be before end date");
        Vector vector = new Vector();
        Connection connection = makeConnection();
        try {
            PreparedStatement stmt =
                connection.prepareStatement("select distinct " +
                    "name,description from resource where " +
                    "id not in (select resourceid from booking " +
                    "where not(end < ?) and not(start > ?))");
            try {
                stmt.setTimestamp(1,new Timestamp(start.getTime()));
                stmt.setTimestamp(2,new Timestamp(end.getTime()));
                ResultSet rs = stmt.executeQuery();
                while(rs.next()) {
                    Resource resource = new Resource();
                    resource.setName(rs.getString(1));
                    resource.setDescription(rs.getString(2));
                    vector.addElement(resource);
                }
            }
            finally {
                stmt.close();
            }
        }
        finally {
            connection.close();
        }
```

LISTING 8.6 continued

```
        Resource[] resourceList = new Resource[vector.size()];
        vector.copyInto(resourceList);
        return resourceList;
    }

    protected void doBookResource(Connection connection,
                                  String resource,
                                  java.util.Date start,
                                  java.util.Date end,
                                  String email)
        throws SQLException
    {
        if(start.compareTo(end) > 0)
            throw new IllegalArgumentException(
                           "start date must be before end date");
        Timestamp tstart = new Timestamp(start.getTime()),
                  tend = new Timestamp(end.getTime());
        PreparedStatement qstmt =
           connection.prepareStatement("select count(*) " +
                "from resource where name like ? and id not in" +
                "(select resourceid from booking where not(end < ?) " +
                "and not(start > ?))");
        try {
            qstmt.setString(1,resource);
            qstmt.setTimestamp(2,tstart);
            qstmt.setTimestamp(3,tend);
            ResultSet rs = qstmt.executeQuery();
            if(!rs.next() || rs.getInt(1) < 1)
            {
               System.out.println(rs.getInt(1));
               throw new IllegalArgumentException(
                             "resource is already booked");
            }
        }
        finally {
            qstmt.close();
        }
        PreparedStatement ustmt =
            connection.prepareStatement("insert into " +
                "booking (resourceid, start, end, email) " +
                "values((select id from resource where " +
                "name like ?),?,?,?)");
        try {
            ustmt.setString(1,resource);
            ustmt.setTimestamp(2,tstart);
            ustmt.setTimestamp(3,tend);
            ustmt.setString(4,email);
            ustmt.executeUpdate();
        }
```

LISTING 8.6 continued

```
        finally {
            ustmt.close();
        }
    }

    public void bookResource(String resource,
                             java.util.Date start,
                             java.util.Date end,
                             String email)
        throws SQLException
    {
        Connection connection = makeConnection();
        try {
            doBookResource(connection,resource,start,end,email);
            connection.commit();
        }
        catch(SQLException e) {
            connection.rollback();
            throw e;
        }
        finally {
           connection.close();
        }
    }
}
```


The two `getXXXResources()` methods are very similar. They query the database, with different criteria, and convert the `ResultSet` into an array of `Resource` objects. Both methods return the array.

Note that there is nothing specific to SOAP in these two methods. They do need to take special arguments; they do not need to throw special exceptions. They can, however, throw exceptions, and indeed, both throw `SQLException`.

Each method opens and closes a database connection, but this is not related to SOAP; it's a side effect of using the hsql Database Engine. Unlike other databases, there is virtually no cost to open a connection with hsql but you cannot open more than one connection to the database at any given time. Consequently, it's easier to have each method grab its own database connection.

Listing 8.7 is the `Resource` class. The class has only two fields for name and description. It also has getter and setter methods.

LISTING 8.7 Resource.java

```
package com.psol.resourceful;

public class Resource
{
   protected String name = null,
                    description = null;

   public Resource()
   {
   }

   public void setName(String name)
   {
      this.name = name;
   }

   public String getName()
   {
      return name;
   }

   public void setDescription(String description)
   {
      this.description = description;
   }

   public String getDescription()
   {
      return description;
   }
}
```

Look at the `bookResource()` method. Again, unless you know it, you'd be hard-pressed to recognize a SOAP RPC implementation. This method takes four parameters and returns no value, but may throw an exception.

The private `doBookResource()` method does the actual database insert. The `doBookResource()` method executes two SQL statements. The first query tests that the room is still free at the requested dates. (It counts the number of free rooms; if the result is less than one, the room is no longer free.) The second query inserts the new booking.

Deploying the Service Provider

As you have seen, nothing in `BookingService` identifies the RPC method implementations. As far as Apache SOAP goes, a SOAP node is just a regular Java class.

The secret to turn a regular Java class into a SOAP node is to write deployment descriptors. Listing 8.8 is the deployment descriptor for `BookingService`.

LISTING 8.8 ddservice.xml

```
<isd:service
    xmlns:isd="http://xml.apache.org/xml-soap/deployment"
    id="http://www.psol.com/2001/resourceful"
    checkMustUnderstands="true">
    <isd:provider scope="Application"
                  type="java"
                  methods="getAllResources getFreeResourcesOn
➥                          bookResource">
        <isd:java class="com.psol.resourceful.BookingService"
                  static="false"/>
    </isd:provider>
    <isd:faultListener>org.apache.soap.server.
➥               DOMFaultListener</isd:faultListener>
    <isd:mappings>
        <isd:map
            encodingStyle="http://schemas.xmlsoap.org/
➥                            soap/encoding/"
            xmlns:rful="http://www.psol.com/2001/resourceful"
            qname="rful:Resource"
            javaType="com.psol.resourceful.Resource"
            java2XMLClassName="org.apache.soap.encoding.soapenc.
➥                               BeanSerializer"
            xml2JavaClassName="org.apache.soap.encoding.soapenc.
➥                               BeanSerializer"/>
    </isd:mappings>
</isd:service>
```

As the name implies, the deployment descriptor is an XML document that describes the SOAP node. The most important elements are:

- `isd:service` is the root of the document.
- `isd:provider` defines the service implementation.
- `isd:faultListener` associates one or more error handlers to the service.
- `isd:mappings` is an optional element. It controls the mapping of Java objects to XML. If present, it contains one or more `isd:map`.

`isd:service` declares the `http://xml.apache.org/xml-soap/deployment` namespace. It has one required attribute, `id`, that defines the namespace URI of your service. That's the namespace used to encode the request. In the following example, it is bound to `ns1`:

```
<?xml version='1.0' encoding='UTF-8'?>
<SOAP-ENV:Envelope
```

```
   xmlns:SOAP-ENV="http://schemas.xmlsoap.org/soap/envelope/">
<SOAP-ENV:Body>
<ns1:getAllResources
    xmlns:ns1="http://www.psol.com/2001/resourceful"
    SOAP-ENV:encodingStyle="http://schemas.xmlsoap.org/soap/encoding/">
</ns1:getAllResources>
</SOAP-ENV:Body>
</SOAP-ENV:Envelope>
```

As always, do not confuse namespace URIs with the address of your server. This is particularly important for the `id` attribute (the namespace URI of your service). It can (but does not have to) match the actual URL of the service.

> **Tip**
>
> If you are confused by namespaces, try to forget that they are URIs for a moment.
>
> The namespace is just one half of the name of an element (the other half is the local name). At the syntax level, `http://xml.apache.org/xml-soap/deployment` is not different from `service` in `isd:service`. The fact that the namespace is a URI is largely irrelevant.

Obviously, the Apache-defined namespaces such as `http://xml.apache.org/xml-soap/deployment` cannot be modified.

`isd:service` also has two optional attributes: `type`, which takes the value `message` if the service is document-oriented (instead of RPC), and `checkMustUnderstands`, which takes the values `true` and `false`. If `true`, it generates a SOAP fault if a header entry is flagged with `env:mustUnderstand`.

> **Tip**
>
> Setting `checkMustUnderstands` to false is mostly used with message-oriented services where your application decodes the header.

The `isd:provider` tag has several required attributes:

- `type`, whose value is set to `java` for Java classes (Apache SOAP also supports EJB and scripting languages).

- `scope`, which indicates the lifecycle of the object. It accepts the following values: `Request`, for objects that are destroyed at the request; `Session`, for objects that survive until the end of the HTTP session; and `Application`, for objects that are destroyed only when the servlet is unloaded.
- `methods`, which is a space-separated list of methods to be made available for RPC.

The `isd:java` tag points to the Java class. Its two attributes are `class`, with the name of the Java class implementing the SOAP node, and `static`, which is set to `true` if the implementing methods are static methods and `false` otherwise.

When there's an error, Apache SOAP generates a fault element, but it does not know how to report application-specific error data. The `isd:faultListener` registers a class to provide the missing information.

The `org.apache.soap.server.DOMFaultListener` class is the default fault listener. You can write your own by implementing the `org.apache.soap.server.SOAPFaultListener` interface. The tag can be repeated to register several fault listeners.

The most important section is `isd:mappings`. Recall from the previous chapter that SOAP proposes, but does not impose its default encoding. Also, it does not fully specify how to map Java classes (or classes in any other language) to SOAP compound types. Among other things, it does not specify which URI and element name to use.

The `isd:mappings` section fills in the blank. It contains as many `isd:map` entries as there are classes. The `isd:map` has the following parameters:

- `encodingStyle` is the URI for the encoding method. In most cases, you want to stick to SOAP encoding or `http://schemas.xmlsoap.org/soap/encoding/`.
- `qname` is the qualified name of the XML element. Note that the name is qualified with a namespace prefix that must have been declared.
- `javaType` is the Java class for which the map is being defined.
- `java2XMLClassName` specifies the serializer (that turn Java objects into XML equivalent); it can be any class that implements the `org.apache.soap.util.xml.Serializer` interface. In most cases, it's the Apache-provided default: `org.apache.soap.encoding.soapenc.BeanSerializer`.
- `xml2JavaClassName` is the deserializer. It must implement the `org.apache.soap.util.xml.Deserializer` interface and you can use the same Apache-provided default.

Apache SOAP knows how to map only simple types (`string`, `number`, and the like) and arrays. You need to define an `isd:map` entry for every class that you use in the input parameter or the return value.

Caution

Failing to define maps for one or more classes is one of the most common errors users make with Apache SOAP. Unfortunately, the error message does not always point to a faulty map. If you experience unexpected errors, double-check the mapping section.

When the deployment descriptor is written, you are ready to deploy your service. The command is the following:

```
java -classpath lib/xerces.jar;lib/soap.jar;lib/mail.jar;
➥lib/activation.jar org.apache.soap.server.ServiceManagerClient
➥http://localhost:5401/soap/servlet/rpcrouter deploy etc/ddservice.xml
```

where

- `http://localhost:5401/soap/servlet/rpcrouter` is the URL to your SOAP node.
- `deploy` is the command (another useful command is `list`).
- `etc/ddservice.xml` is the path to your deployment descriptor.

Caution

If you change the deployment descriptor (for example, to declare a new method or a new map), you have to re-deploy the service. If in doubt, re-deploy—it never hurts.

Apache SOAP also offers a Web-based interface at `http://localhost:5401/soap/admin`. Unless you love typing, you don't want to deploy services through the Web interface, but it's handy to check the configuration of your server. See Figure 8.14.

Caution

The Web-based interface is a major security risk on servers facing the Internet. You want to disable it on those machines or, at least, password-protect it.

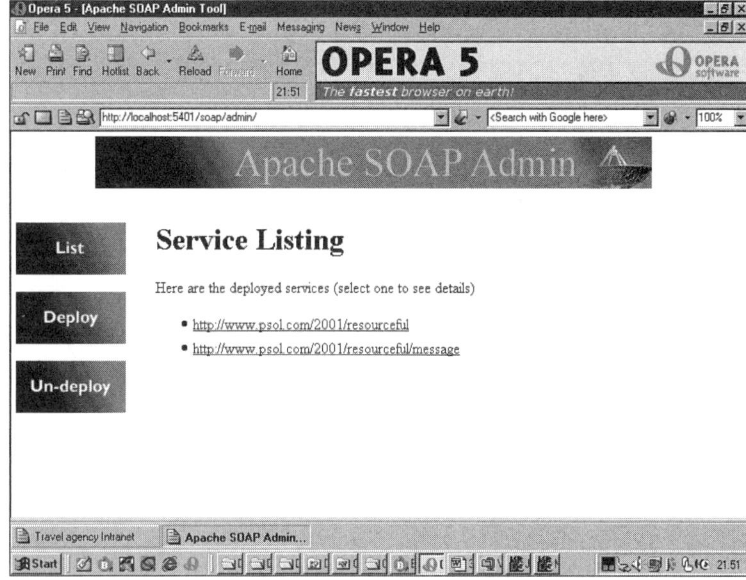

FIGURE 8.14
The Web administrator lists two services.

Calling the Service Provider

Now that you've successfully deployed a SOAP node, take a look at the other side of the transaction by moving to the travel agency application. Have a look at Listing 8.9, `confirm.jsp`. It is not the first JSP page in the application, but it is one of the cleanest.

This page calls `bookResource()` on the SOAP node. The calling page (`book.jsp` in Listing 8.13) passes the URL to the SOAP node (in the `rpcrouter` parameter), the booking period (`start` and `end`), and the email address. For simplicity, it does not validate its parameters.

LISTING 8.9 `confirm.jsp`

```
<%@include file="utils.jsp"%>
<html>
<head><title>Travel agency Intranet</title></head>
<body>
<h1>Travel agency Intranet</h1>
<%
URL rpcRouter = new URL(request.getParameter("rpcrouter"));
DateFormat dateFormat =
     DateFormat.getDateInstance(DateFormat.MEDIUM,Locale.US);
dateFormat.setLenient(true);
Date start = dateFormat.parse(request.getParameter("start")),
     end = dateFormat.parse(request.getParameter("end"));
```

LISTING 8.9 continued

```
String resource = request.getParameter("resource"),
       email = request.getParameter("email");
Vector params = new Vector();
params.addElement(new Parameter("name",
                                String.class,resource,null));
params.addElement(new Parameter("start",
                                Date.class,start,null));
params.addElement(new Parameter("end",
                                Date.class,end,null));
params.addElement(new Parameter("email",
                                String.class,email,null));
Response rsp = rpcCall(rpcRouter,"bookResource",params);
if(!rsp.generatedFault()) {
%>
<table>
<tr><td colspan="2" valign="top">Booking confirmed</td></tr>
<tr><td valign="top">Name:</td>
    <td valign="top"><%= resource %></td></tr>
<tr><td valign="top">From:</td>
    <td valign="top"><%= start %></td></tr>
<tr><td valign="top">To:</td>
    <td valign="top"><%= end %></td></tr>
</table>
<%
}
else {
   Fault fault = rsp.getFault();
%>
<table>
<tr><td>Error:</td><td><%= fault.getFaultString() %></td></tr>
<tr><td>Code:</td><td><%= fault.getFaultCode() %></td></tr>
</table>
<%
}
%>
<form action="index.jsp" method="post">
<input type="hidden" name="rpcrouter"
   value="<%= rpcRouter.toExternalForm() %>">
<input type="submit" value="Return to main page">
</form>
</body>
</html>
```

The page collects the parameters for the RPC in a `Vector` of `Parameter` objects. Each `Parameter` object takes the name of the parameter, its type, its value, and the encoding to use (null for SOAP encoding).

Next it calls `rpcCall()`, a method defined in Listing 8.10, which returns a `Response` object. A call to `generateFault()` on the `Response` object returns true if the server replied with a SOAP fault; it returns false otherwise.

Depending on whether there's been an error, the page proceeds to display a confirmation message or an error message. `Response.getFault()` returns a `Fault` object that represents the fault element. `Fault.getFaultCode()` and `Fault.getFaultString()` return, respectively, the `faultcode` and `faultstring` elements' values.

Listing 8.10 is the `utils.jsp` page. As you can see, issuing an RPC call is a lot of work.

LISTING 8.10 `utils.jsp`

```
<%@page import="java.io.*,java.net.*,java.util.*,java.text.*"%>
<%@page import="javax.mail.internet.*"%>
<%@page import="com.psol.resourceful.*"%>
<%@page import="org.apache.soap.transport.*"%>
<%@page import="org.apache.soap.messaging.*"%>
<%@page import="javax.xml.parsers.*,org.w3c.dom.*"%>
<%@page import="org.apache.soap.*,org.apache.soap.encoding.*"%>
<%@page import="org.apache.soap.rpc.*,org.apache.soap.util.xml.*"%>
<%@page import="org.apache.soap.encoding.soapenc.*"%>
<%!
private Response rpcCall(URL rpcRouter,
                         String methodName,
                         Vector params)
   throws SOAPException
{
   BeanSerializer serializer = new BeanSerializer();
   SOAPMappingRegistry registry = new SOAPMappingRegistry();
   registry.mapTypes(Constants.NS_URI_SOAP_ENC,
                     new QName(
                        "http://www.psol.com/2001/resourceful",
                        "Resource"),
                     Resource.class,serializer,serializer);
   Call call = new Call();
   call.setSOAPMappingRegistry(registry);
   call.setTargetObjectURI("http://www.psol.com/2001/resourceful");
   call.setEncodingStyleURI(Constants.NS_URI_SOAP_ENC);
   call.setMethodName(methodName);
   if(params != null)
      call.setParams(params);
   return call.invoke(rpcRouter,
                      "http://www.psol.com/2001/soapaction");
}
%>
```

The method starts by creating a `SOAPMappingRegistry`. This object is the equivalent of the deployment descriptor on the client. For every `isd:map` entry, you call `mapTypes()` with the encoding style URI (`Constants.NS_URI_SOAP_ENC` is a handy reference to SOAP encoding), a `QName` object for the qualified name (namespace URI and local name) of the XML element, the Java class, and finally the serializer and deserializer.

> **Caution**
>
> I cannot stress enough that the maps in the `SOAPMappingRegistry` must match the values in the deployment descriptor.

Next, the method creates a `Call` object, sets its mapping registry, sets its target URI (the `id` parameter in the deployment descriptor), sets its encoding style, sets the method name, sets the parameters to the Vector created previously, and finally invokes the method.

`invoke()` accepts two parameters: a `URL` object that points to the SOAP node and a string with the SOAP action URI. Remember from Chapter 7 that the value of the SOAP action URI is largely irrelevant.

Clearly Apache SOAP does a better job with service writing than with clients. You literally have to build the RPC request step by step, being sure to include an array with the parameters and decode the response.

The remainder of this section reviews the other pages in the travel agency application in the order in which the user encounters them. The first page is `index.jsp`, shown in Listing 8.11. This page is a regular HTML form.

LISTING 8.11 `index.jsp`

```
<html>
<head><title>Travel agency Intranet</title></head>
<body>
<h1>Travel agency Intranet</h1>
<form action="list.jsp" method="post">
<table>
<%
String rpcRouter = request.getParameter("rpcrouter");
if(rpcRouter == null)
    rpcRouter = "http://localhost:5401/soap/servlet/rpcrouter";
%>
<tr><td><b>Business center URL:</b></td>
    <td><input type="text" name="rpcrouter" size="50"
        value="<%= rpcRouter %>"></td></tr>
```

LISTING 8.11 continued

```
<tr><td>From:</td><td><input type="text" name="start"></td></tr>
<tr><td>To:</td><td><input type="text" name="end"></td></tr>
<tr><td colspan="2">Dates formatted as "Jan 1, 2001"</td></tr>
</table>
<input type="submit" value="See availability">
</form>
</body>
</html>
```

Listing 8.12 is `list.jsp`. It calls the `getAllResources()` or `getFreeResourcesOn()` RPC method and presents the result in an HTML table. You are already familiar with building the RPC call, but note that the page retrieves the response by calling `getReturnValue().getValue()` on the `Response` object.

LISTING 8.12 `list.jsp`

```
<%@include file="utils.jsp"%>
<html>
<head><title>Travel agency Intranet</title></head>
<body>
<h1>Travel agency Intranet</h1>
<table>
<%
URL rpcRouter = new URL(request.getParameter("rpcrouter"));
String stStart = request.getParameter("start"),
       stEnd = request.getParameter("end");
Vector params = null;
if(stStart != null && stEnd != null) {
    params = new Vector();
    DateFormat dateFormat =
         DateFormat.getDateInstance(DateFormat.MEDIUM,Locale.US);
    dateFormat.setLenient(true);
    try {
        Date start = dateFormat.parse(stStart),
             end = dateFormat.parse(stEnd);
        params.addElement(new Parameter("start",
                                        Date.class,start,null));
        params.addElement(new Parameter("end",
                                        Date.class,end,null));
    }
    catch(java.text.ParseException e) {
        params = null;
    }
}
Response rsp = null;
if(params == null) {
    rsp = rpcCall(rpcRouter,"getAllResources",null);
```

LISTING 8.12 continued

```
%>
<tr><td colspan="3">All rooms, regardless of
    availability.</td></tr>
<%
}
else {
    rsp = rpcCall(rpcRouter,"getFreeResourcesOn",params);
%>
<tr><td colspan="3">Rooms available from <%= stStart %>
    'till <%= stEnd %>.</tr></td>
<%
}
if(!rsp.generatedFault()) {
    Resource[] resources =
        (Resource[])rsp.getReturnValue().getValue();
    for(int i = 0;i < resources.length;i++) {
%>
   <tr><td valign="top"><form action="book.jsp" method="post">
         <input type="hidden" name="resource"
          value="<%= resources[i].getName() %>">
         <input type="hidden" name="rpcrouter"
          value="<%= rpcRouter.toExternalForm() %>">
         <input type="hidden" name="start" value="<%= stStart %>">
         <input type="hidden" name="end" value="<%= stEnd %>">
         <input type="submit" value="Book"></form></td>
      <td valign="top"
        bgcolor="#bbbbbb"><%= resources[i].getName() %></td>
      <td valign="top"><%= resources[i].getDescription() %></td>
   </tr>
<%
    }
}
else {
    Fault fault = rsp.getFault();
%>
<tr><td>Error:</td><td><%= fault.getFaultString() %></td></tr>
<tr><td>Code:</td><td><%= fault.getFaultCode() %></td></tr>
<%
}
%>
</table>
</body>
</html>
```

From `list.jsp`, the user jumps to `book.jsp` (in Listing 8.13), a plain HTML form that points to `book.jsp` (Listing 8.9).

LISTING 8.13 book.jsp

```
<html>
<head><title>Travel agency Intranet</title></head>
<body>
<h1>Travel agency Intranet</h1>
<form action="confirm.jsp" method="post">
<table>
    <tr><td>Resource:</td>
    <td><%= request.getParameter("resource") %></td></tr>
    <tr><td><b>Start date:</b></td><td><input type="text"
        value="<%= request.getParameter("start") %>"
        name="start"></td></tr>
    <tr><td><b>End date:</b></td><td><input type="text"
        value="<%= request.getParameter("end") %>"
        name="end"></td></tr>
    <tr><td><b>Email:</b></td><td><input type="text"
        name="email"></td></tr>
</table>
<input type="hidden" name="resource"
 value="<%= request.getParameter("resource") %>">
<input type="hidden" name="rpcrouter"
 value="<%= request.getParameter("rpcrouter") %>">
<input type="submit" value="Book now">
</form>
```

Summary

In this chapter you've learned how to use Apache SOAP to build a simple Web service. The sample application puts some flesh over the material covered in the last chapter. You have also learned about important design issues you need to consider when building SOAP nodes.

In the next chapter, you will learn how to advertise your Web services through UDDI.

CHAPTER 9

UDDI

By Mark Wutka

IN THIS CHAPTER

The Universal Description, Discovery, and Integration protocol, or UDDI, is a directory service that enables Web service clients to locate Web services. The problem that UDDI solves is very common and very well-known. This chapter introduces you to the basics of UDDI.

UDDI in Web Services: Why Is It Needed?

The goal behind Web services is really to use XML and the various Internet protocols as more of a communications device. Although the Internet itself is really just a big communications network, the World Wide Web is more like a giant book. It is great at presenting specific content to a human reader, but programs have trouble extracting data from the pages.

The great promise of XML is that the Web can now provide data in a form that is both human- and computer-readable. In essence, Web services help transform the Web into something as widespread and useful as the telephone system. UDDI is the equivalent of the phone book for this next-generation phone system. It enables businesses—specifically business applications—to locate service providers and services on the Web.

Think about how difficult the phone system would be for you if you didn't have a phone book. If you want to order a pizza and don't have the number for the pizza place, you're stuck. If one of your friends moves and neglects to give you his new number ahead of time, you have lost contact with that friend. Or imagine the turmoil when, after accumulating your own personal list of local numbers, you suddenly move and find that many of the numbers on your list are no good anymore. The same problem exists for Web services. Without UDDI, the only way two applications can communicate is if they already know about each other.

Basic UDDI

Like many other Web services protocols, UDDI is a layer on top of SOAP, as shown in Figure 9.1.

Just like the phone book, UDDI has two main users: clients and publishers. A *publisher* is a company that offers Web services—in the phone book analogy, it's someone who publishes his or her number in the book. A *client* is someone who is searching for a Web service—the person thumbing through the phone book. Figure 9.2 shows the high-level view of the UDDI world.

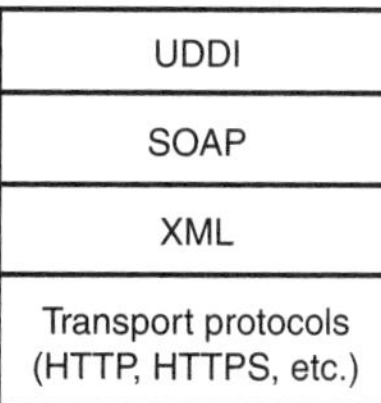

FIGURE 9.1
UDDI uses SOAP, XML, and lower-level Internet protocols.

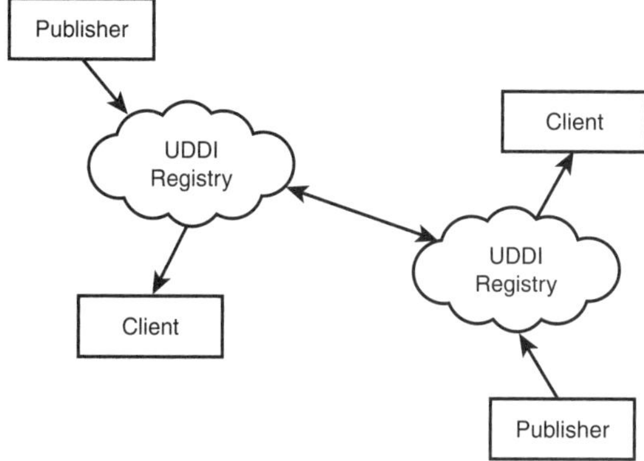

FIGURE 9.2
Clients, publishers, and UDDI registries make up the UDDI world.

In many ways, UDDI is also like the Internet's Domain Name Service (DNS), which is the phone book for Internet hosts. Every computer connected to the Internet has a unique address, which is usually of the form *number.number.number.number*, as in 192.168.19.47. When you enter a URL in your Web browser, such as `http://www.samspublishing.com`, the browser uses DNS to translate `www.samspublishing.com` into the address 63.69.111.193.

Of course, DNS operates at a lower level than UDDI. DNS resolves IP addresses, while UDDI resolves services—which themselves may have host names that are resolved via DNS.

UDDI has a deeper similarity to DNS that goes beyond the notion of a simple phone book, however. Before the days of online phone books, if you wanted to call someone in another city, you either had to dial the information operator or you needed a phone book for a particular city. Although the Internet is present around the world and features many different naming schemes—such as `.com`, `.edu`, `.gov`, `.uk`, `.jp`, and so on—you don't need different DNS services. In other words, DNS is basically a single worldwide service.

Of course, no single server contains all the addresses for the entire Internet. Instead, several well-known root servers contain many common addresses. For example, one server contains `.com` addresses, and knows the address of `samspublishing.com`, but not `www.samspublishing.com`. Instead, `samspublishing.com` has a separate DNS server that contains `www.samspublishing.com`. Figure 9.3 shows an example DNS tree.

FIGURE 9.3
The Domain Name Service is actually a tree of servers.

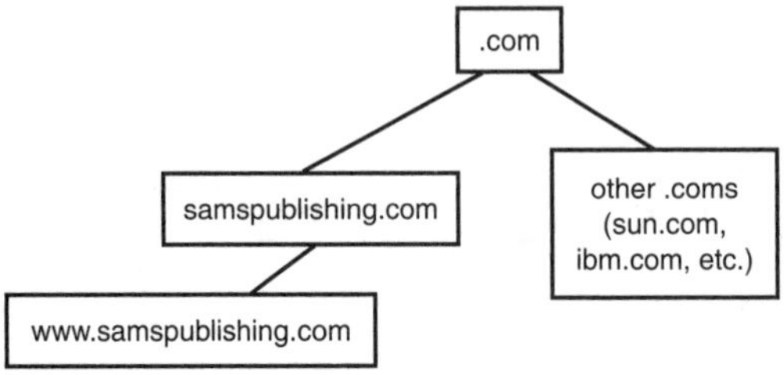

UDDI is also meant to be a single worldwide service consisting of a number of servers, although UDDI isn't arranged in a tree structure. Instead, servers share data through a replication protocol, ensuring that a service registered on one server will be visible from all of them. You will learn more about UDDI replication in Chapter 10, "UDDI in Depth."

Using UDDI

When two applications use UDDI to locate each other, they begin with one application publishing itself to UDDI, as shown in Figure 9.4.

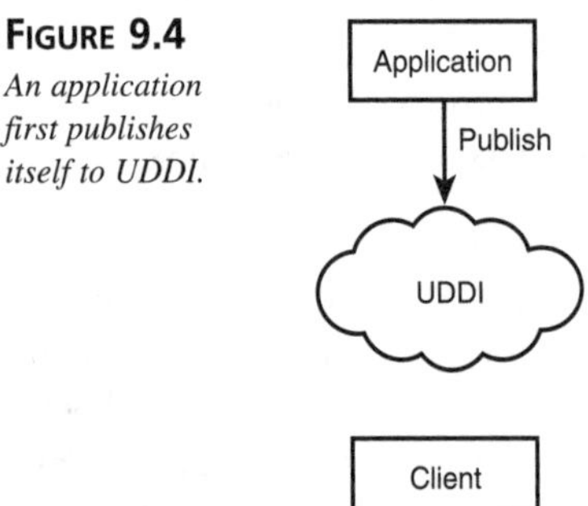

FIGURE 9.4
An application first publishes itself to UDDI.

Next, a client queries UDDI to locate a service matching a specific set of criteria, as shown in Figure 9.5.

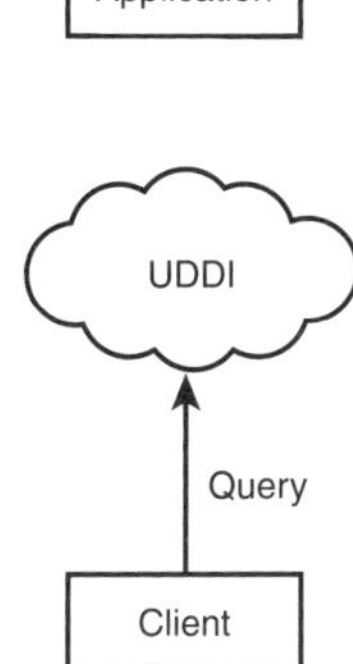

FIGURE 9.5
A client queries UDDI.

After the client receives the information about the published service, it is free to communicate with the service without any further interaction with UDDI, as shown in Figure 9.6.

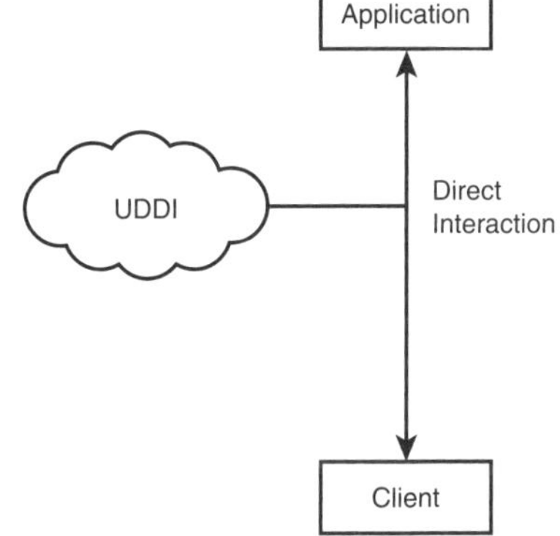

FIGURE 9.6
The client communicates directly with the service.

Ideally, the interaction between the client, the publisher, and UDDI all take place at the time that the client wishes to perform the service. Such immediate interaction, however, requires a great deal of up-front work and standardization.

Standardization

The evolution of XML clearly shows that although a standard format for representing data is certainly useful, it's standardized content that really accelerates information exchange. If your company communicates with five others, all using XML, you get some benefit just by using XML, but unless all the customers use the same XML schema, you still have to write special code to handle each customer.

With Web services, the problem is somewhat magnified, because in addition to data, you now have operations (functions, methods—whatever you prefer to call them). The Web Services Description Language (WSDL) described in Chapter 11, "WSDL," is the emerging standard for describing the operations a Web service offers.

To make things even more complex, certain applications may require you to perform several different tasks, which brings the concept of workflow into the mix. If you think it takes companies a long time to decide on a common data model, wait until they start debating operations and workflow! The Web Services Flow Language (WSFL), described in Chapter 18, "Web Services Flows (WSFL)," is the emerging standard for describing the workflow of a Web service.

Typical Usage

Fortunately, UDDI is useful without everyone agreeing to a standard set of operations or workflow. It just requires a little more manual intervention. The initial usage model for UDDI starts with a manager, business analyst, or programmer browsing through UDDI, looking for a particular service as shown in Figure 9.7. Eventually, applications will use UDDI to automatically locate services, bypassing the current manual process.

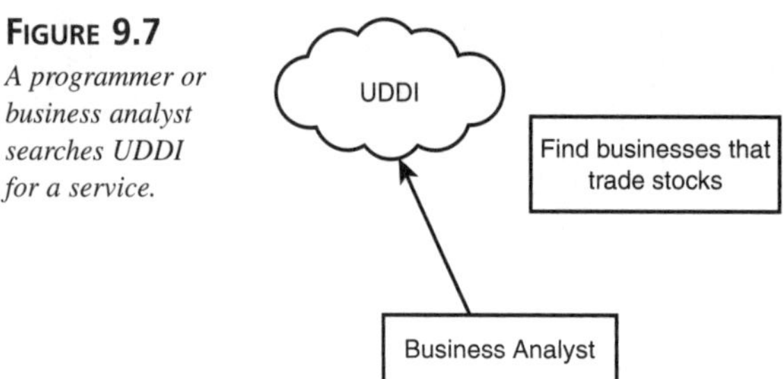

FIGURE 9.7
A programmer or business analyst searches UDDI for a service.

After you locate a service, you may need to make arrangements with the service provider for payment information or any special configuration needs. (Again, in the future, when things have been better standardized, this may become a more automated process.) Eventually, your company decides on a service provider.

Next, a programmer consults UDDI for implementation information—the operations and data the service uses, as shown in Figure 9.8.

Using the implementation information, possibly with help from the service provider, the programmer develops an application that accesses the service, and the companies are ready to do business.

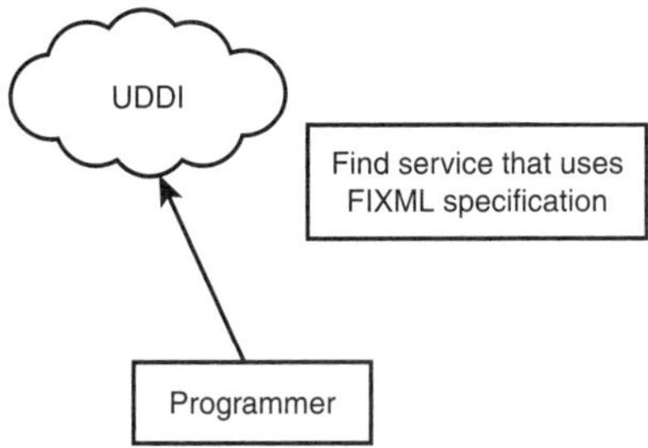

FIGURE 9.8
A programmer gets implementation information from UDDI.

At some point, a publisher may decide to remove a service from UDDI, which it can do by sending a delete request. When it comes to modifying or deleting UDDI data, there is the additional problem of potential mischief. What if a competitor tries to delete your service from UDDI, or replace yours with theirs? Fortunately, the UDDI designers have already considered that problem.

UDDI servers authenticate publishers, keeping track of who is allowed to publish and what they have published. Only a service's original publisher is allowed to modify or delete the service.

UDDI Roles

The phone book analogy for UDDI is so appropriate that the UDDI designers actually use phone book terminology to refer to the kinds of data stored in UDDI. Basically, there are three "roles" for UDDI data:

- White pages contain technical contact information and addresses so that potential Web service customers know how to reach the publishers to do any up-front negotiations or to obtain technical support.
- Yellow pages contain information about the various services available from businesses. If you want a kind of service but don't know of any specific companies, you search the yellow pages.
- Green pages contain technical information about the Web service itself, and may even include the WSDL description of the service.

These roles are really just conceptual ways of looking at the functions UDDI provides. Except in technical overviews, you won't find any mention of white, yellow, or green pages in the UDDI specifications.

White Pages

The main white pages portion of UDDI is the `businessEntity` data structure, which stores contacts, addresses, and various other pieces of information for a business. Although the contacts and addresses have a specific format, UDDI can't anticipate everything that a business may want to store. The `businessEntity` structure contains something called the `identifierBag`, which is a list of name-value pairs. The `identifierBag` may contain information such as the company's Dun & Bradstreet Number (D-U-N-S) or its Federal Taxpayer ID.

The white pages portion of the UDDI registry is intended mostly for human consumption, and is typically used during the initial setting up of a business relationship.

The `businessEntity` structure is defined as:

```
<element name = "businessEntity">
    <complexType>
        <sequence>
            <element ref = "discoveryURLs" minOccurs = "0"/>
            <element ref = "name" maxOccurs = "unbounded"/>
            <element ref = "description" minOccurs = "0"
                maxOccurs = "unbounded"/>
            <element ref = "contacts" minOccurs = "0"/>
            <element ref = "businessServices" minOccurs = "0"/>
            <element ref = "identifierBag" minOccurs = "0"/>
            <element ref = "categoryBag" minOccurs = "0"/>
    </sequence>
    <attribute ref = "businessKey" use = "required"/>
    <attribute ref = "operator"/>
    <attribute ref = "authorizedName">
    </complexType>
</element>
```

Yellow Pages

The yellow pages portion of the UDDI registry enables companies to locate each other's services. Eventually, programs may use UDDI to locate each other at runtime. Initially, however, the main users of the yellow pages are people—both programmers and business analysts.

Unlike the regular yellow pages, which are grouped only by business category, UDDI enables you to search on business category, business name, services provided, as well as many other ways. In fact, you can even use a business as the basis for a search—the `find_relatedBusinesses` structure returns a list of businesses related to another business, usually by business category.

Because you can search for both businesses and services based on different options, it's difficult to classify some data structures as belonging to white pages or yellow pages. For example, the `businessEntity` information you saw in the previous section is still appropriate for a yellow pages search; except rather than search for a business by name or some well-known identifier, you search by other attributes of the business.

Taxonomies

The `categoryBag` portion of the `businessEntity` structure is closely related to yellow pages searches, because it contains general categories related to the business. One of the words you often hear in discussions of UDDI categories is *taxonomies*, or classifications. Because different people have different ways of categorizing things, UDDI supports different taxonomies that allow you to group businesses and services in different ways. For example, a U.S. government standard, called NAICS (North American Industry Classification System), categorizes businesses by assigning numeric codes to different types of businesses. There is also a product-based taxonomy called UNSPSC (United Nations Standard Product and Services Classification code). When you register a business or a service, you can specify the different attributes for each taxonomy.

Each taxonomy has a unique `tModel`—a detailed description of data in the UDDI registry. You can think of the *t* in `tModel` as meaning *type* or *technical*; a `tModel` gives specific details for implementation. The `tModel` isn't just for labeling taxonomies, of course; it is also useful for describing various services. UDDI registry entries, including `tModels`, have a universally unique ID (UUID) that serves as the key for that data item. The UUID (not to be confused with UDDI) is a 128-bit number of the form nnnnnnnn-nnnn-nnnn-nnnn-nnnnnnnnnnnn.

Strangely, when you use the UUID as a key for a `tModel`, you must include the prefix `uuid:`, whereas for other keys, you simply specify the UUID itself. Obviously, UDDI is paving the way for using identifiers other than the UUID for a `tModel`.

In addition to searching for business entities, you can also search the UDDI registry for services. The `businessService` structure contains information about a specific service a business offers. The structure is defined this way:

```
<element name = "businessService">
    <complexType>
        <sequence>
            <element ref = "name" maxOccurs = "unbounded"/>
            <element ref = "description" minOccurs = "0" maxOccurs =
"unbounded"/>
            <element ref = "bindingTemplates"/>
            <element ref = "categoryBag" minOccurs = "0"/>
        </sequence>
        <attribute ref = "serviceKey" use = "required"/>
```

```
        <attribute ref = "businessKey"/>
    </complexType>
</element>
```

Green Pages

The green pages portion of the UDDI registry provides specific technical information for developers who need to write services or configure software to use specific services. The two main structures that make up the green pages portion of the UDDI registry are the `bindingTemplate` and the `tModel`.

The `bindingTemplate`

The `bindingTemplate` structure contains information used to locate a particular service, as well as a technical footprint of the service in the form of `tModel` keys. The technical footprint specifies the various methods implemented by the service, along with their parameters and data structures. The `bindingTemplate` structure is very important for services at runtime, because it provides the Web address of the service, via the `accessPoint` attribute.

Although your application may cache the Web address of a service, you should also give it the capability to query UDDI for an updated location. For example, suppose a business has a fire at its main server site and moves to its disaster recovery site. Your application will suddenly find that it can't connect to the service any more. If your application checks the UDDI registry again, however, it can locate the new address for the service and continue with only a minimal interruption.

The `bindingTemplate` structure is defined this way:

```
<element name = "bindingTemplate">
    <complexType>
        <sequence>
            <element ref = "description" minOccurs = "0" maxOccurs =
                "unbounded"/>
            <choice>
                <element ref = "accessPoint" minOccurs = "0"/>
                <element ref = "hostingRedirector" minOccurs = "0"/>
            </choice>
            <element ref = "tModelInstanceDetails"/>
        </sequence>
        <attribute ref = "bindingKey" use = "required"/>
        <attribute ref = "serviceKey"/>
    </complexType>
</element>
```

The tModel

The tModel structure is the last of the main UDDI data types, and is defined this way:

```
<element name = "tModel">
    <complexType>
        <sequence>
            <element ref = "name"/>
            <element ref = "description" minOccurs = "0" maxOccurs =
"unbounded"/>
            <element ref = "overviewDoc" minOccurs = "0"/>
            <element ref = "identifierBag" minOccurs = "0"/>
            <element ref = "categoryBag" minOccurs = "0"/>
        </sequence>
        <attribute ref = "tModelKey" use = "required"/>
        <attribute ref = "operator"/>
        <attribute ref = "authorizedName"/>
    </complexType>
</element>
```

Although the tModel structure doesn't appear to contain much detail, it is still a significant part of UDDI, if only because of the tModelKey attribute, which is a UUID. At the lowest level, all services have a unique tModel key. You can use a set of tModel keys as a fingerprint for required services. For example, if your application needs both UDDI inquiry and UDDI publishing capabilities, you can use the tModel keys for each of these capabilities when you search for services, weeding out those services that don't have both capabilities.

Summary

In this chapter, you have seen only the data types stored in the UDDI registry. In the next chapter, you'll see how to use various SOAP requests to retrieve and store UDDI registry data.

CHAPTER

UDDI in Depth

By Mark Wutka

In the Chapter

Now that you understand the various types of data stored in UDDI and the general categories for the data, you can examine the various SOAP message calls the UDDI API provides. The UDDI API consists of three main parts: inquiry, publishing, and replication.

The inquiry API is for clients who want to locate businesses, services, or contact information. It provides methods to perform general searches, as well as specific queries for a known item.

The publishing API enables services to publish information about themselves and to delete entries from the UDDI registry. Only the original publisher of a UDDI entry may delete or modify the entry.

The replication portion of the API is really intended for server-to-server communication within the network of UDDI servers. In other words, neither the publisher nor the client actually use the replication API.

Inquiry: Finding Items

The inquiry portion of the UDDI API consist of two types of requests: find and detail. When you first search for a particular business or service, you use one of the find requests. After you locate a specific business or service, you use one of the detail requests to obtain more information.

Performing a UDDI query is a little like using a web search engine such as Google. You first do a find based on some keywords, then the search engine returns a list of matching items, often with a small summary of each item. When you use Google, you click on an item to see it. When you use UDDI, you send a detail request.

Although only four types of data are stored in a UDDI registry, there are actually five different find requests: `find_binding`, `find_business`, `find_relatedBusinesses`, `find_service` and `find_tModel`.

`find_business`

The `find_business` request lets you use different search criteria to search for a business. You can search by business name, business category, supported models, or other attributes. The general format of the `find_business` soap request is as follows:

```
<find_business [maxRows="nn"] generic="2.0" xmlns="um:uddi-org:api_v2">
    [<find-qualifiers/>]
    [<name/>[<name/>]..]
    [<discoveryURLs/>]
    [<identifierBag/>]
    [<categoryBag/>]
    [<tModelBag/>]
</find_business>
```

The items in brackets are optional. You can, for example, search for a business just by name. The `name` parameter appears to support several names; in reality, version 2.0 of the UDDI specification allows up to five names, but they are really just multi-language versions of the same name. For example, you might provide a template for matching English names, and a similar one for matching German names. If you use multiple names, you must label each name with an `xml:lang` adornment. The choice of languages is up to you; the only limitation is that you can have a maximum of five.

The `identifierBag`, `categoryBag`, and `discoveryURLs` parameters are just like the structures found in the `BusinessEntity` data structure you saw in Chapter 9. The `tModelBag` parameter is a list of `tModel` UUID values, in case you want to locate all businesses that support a specific UDDI model.

The `find_business` request returns a `businessList` structure, which has the following format:

```
<businessList>
    <businessInfos>
        <businessInfo businessKey="1234..">
            <name>business name</name>
            <serviceInfos>
                <serviceInfo serviceKey="1234..">
                    <name>service name</name>
                </serviceInfo>
                    .
                    .
            </serviceInfos>
        </businessInfo>
            .
            .
    </businessInfos>
</businessList>
```

You can use the `businessKey` or `serviceKey` values to obtain more detail with one of the `get_xxxDetail` requests.

Listing 10.1 shows a SOAP request that looks for businesses named "Microsoft."

LISTING 10.1 Source Code for `findms.soap`

```
<?xml version="1.0" encoding="UTF-8"?>
<Envelope xmlns="http://schemas.xmlsoap.org/soap/envelope/">
    <Body>
        <find_business generic="2.0" xmlns="urn:uddi-org:api_v2">
            <name>Microsoft</name>
        </find_business>
    </Body>
</Envelope>
```

Listing 10.2 shows the response returned by IBM's UDDI registry.

LISTING 10.2 Response from UDDI Search for Microsoft


```
<?xml version="1.0" encoding="UTF-8" ?>
<Envelope xmlns="http://schemas.xmlsoap.org/soap/envelope/">
  <Body>
    <businessList generic="1.0" xmlns="urn:uddi-org:api"
    operator="www.ibm.com/services/uddi" truncated="false">
      <businessInfos>
        <businessInfo
        businessKey="0076B468-EB27-42E5-AC09-9955CFF462A3">
          <name>Microsoft Corporation</name>

          <description xml:lang="en">Empowering people through
          great software - any time, any place and on any device is
          Microsofts vision. As the worldwide leader in software
          for personal and business computing, we strive to produce
          innovative products and services that meet our
          customer's</description>

          <serviceInfos>
            <serviceInfo
            serviceKey="86E46AAD-82A5-454F-8957-381C2F724D6F"
            businessKey="0076B468-EB27-42E5-AC09-9955CFF462A3">
              <name>UDDI Web Sites</name>
            </serviceInfo>

            <serviceInfo
            serviceKey="33C3D124-E967-4AB1-8F51-D93D95FAC91A"
            businessKey="0076B468-EB27-42E5-AC09-9955CFF462A3">
              <name>UDDI Web Services</name>
            </serviceInfo>

            <serviceInfo
            serviceKey="17B29861-2F33-402C-98F0-FD16CF5B8E9C"
            businessKey="0076B468-EB27-42E5-AC09-9955CFF462A3">
              <name>Home Page</name>
            </serviceInfo>

            <serviceInfo
            serviceKey="491E8F93-E90F-42E3-A048-726744453659"
            businessKey="0076B468-EB27-42E5-AC09-9955CFF462A3">
              <name>Online Shopping</name>
            </serviceInfo>

            <serviceInfo
            serviceKey="4DE36949-E757-4DE1-A3BD-B3F1D4350325"
            businessKey="0076B468-EB27-42E5-AC09-9955CFF462A3">
              <name>Microsoft Developer Network</name>
            </serviceInfo>
```

LISTING 10.2 continued

```
            <serviceInfo
            serviceKey="F9D39C6F-AA09-4C5C-BC7B-6B26B0BA016D"
            businessKey="0076B468-EB27-42E5-AC09-9955CFF462A3">
              <name>Technet</name>
            </serviceInfo>

            <serviceInfo
            serviceKey="367DF918-7D5E-4B00-8CF6-AFE56367C2D6"
            businessKey="0076B468-EB27-42E5-AC09-9955CFF462A3">
              <name>Volume Licensing Select Program</name>
            </serviceInfo>

            <serviceInfo
            serviceKey="BD9B1A10-4668-42E9-AC69-D3DA905C314D"
            businessKey="0076B468-EB27-42E5-AC09-9955CFF462A3">
              <name>Electronic Business Integration Services</name>
            </serviceInfo>

            <serviceInfo
            serviceKey="A97EF39E-853B-47BD-985A-1EB0FAB7D342"
            businessKey="0076B468-EB27-42E5-AC09-9955CFF462A3">
              <name>Web services for smart searching</name>
            </serviceInfo>
          </serviceInfos>
        </businessInfo>
      </businessInfos>
    </businessList>
  </Body>
</Envelope>
```

Taxonomies

Although searching for a particular business name might be useful, most of the time you don't know the name of the business ahead of time. Instead, you may want to search for companies in a particular line of business.

Because there are many different ways to classify businesses, UDDI supports multiple taxonomies—classification methods. For example, the standard business taxonomy is called NAICS (North American Industry Classification System), and has various code numbers for different industries. Likewise, the UNSPSC (United Nations Standard Product and Services Classification code) taxonomy classifies products. Each of these taxonomies has a unique `tModel` UUID, which you must use when performing a search.

The `tModel` UUID for NAICS is C0B9FE13-179F-413D-8A5B-5004DB8E5BB2. Likewise, the `tModel` UUID for UNSPSC is DB77450D-9FA8-45D4-A7BC-04411D14E384. You can find the `tModel` values for various taxonomies in the UDDI API specification.

Listing 10.3 shows an example search for an airline reservations system, which has an NAICS code number of 561599. The NAICS database at `http://www.naics.com` lists the various code numbers.

LISTING 10.3 SOAP Request for Searching by NAICS Number

```
<Envelope xmlns="http://schemas.xmlsoap.org/soap/envelope/">
    <Body>
        <find_business xmlns="urn:uddi-org:api" generic="1.0">
            <categoryBag>
                <keyedReference
                tModelKey="uuid:C0B9FE13-179F-413D-8A5B-5004DB8E5BB2"
                     keyName=""
                     keyValue="561599"/> </categoryBag>
        </find_business>
    </Body>
</Envelope>
```

find_relatedBusinesses

If you want to find a related business—for instance, a business that has some sort of relationship with another one—you can use the `find_relatedBusinesses` request. All you need is the business key, which you can find in the response from `find_business`. The general format for `find_relatedBusinesses` is as follows:

```
<find_relatedBusinesses generic="2.0" xmlns="um:uddi-org:api_v2">
    [<find-qualifiers/>]
    <businessKey/>
    [<keyedReference/>]
</find_relatedBusinesses>
```

The optional keyed reference enables you to focus on a particular aspect, such NAICS category, to narrow the search further.

For example, if you refer back to Listing 10.2, you can see that the business key for Microsoft is 0076B468-EB27-42E5-AC09-9955CFF462A3. Listing 10.4 shows a SOAP request to find businesses related to Microsoft.

LISTING 10.4 SOAP Request for `find_relatedBusinesses`

```
<Envelope xmlns="http://schemas.xmlsoap.org/soap/envelope/">
    <Body>
        <find_relatedBusiness xmlns="urn:uddi-org:api_v2" generic="2.0">
            <businessKey>0076B468-EB27-42E5-AC09-9955CFF462A3</businessKey>
        </find_relatedBusiness>
    </Body>
</Envelope>
```

find_binding

The find_binding request enables you to find a binding template for a particular service that matches a specific fingerprint. The idea here is that you may already have software that works with a particular set of SOAP requests, so you want to find a service that is compatible with your software. The format for the find_binding request is as follows:

```
<find_binding serviceKey="1234.." [maxRows="nn"] generic="2.0"
    xmlns="um:uddi-org:api_v2">
   <tModelBag/>
</find_binding>
```

This request returns a bindingDetail message, which is simply a list of bindingTemplate structures, like this:

```
<bindingDetail generic="2.0" operator="uddi.xxxxoperator"
    truncated="true" xmlns="urn:uddi-org:api_v2">
    <bindingTemplate bindingKey="1234.." serviceKey="1234..">
    </bindingTemplate>
        .
        .
</bindingDetail>
```

find_service

The find_service request enables you to find services a business provides, using many of the same options as the find_business request. The format for the request is as follows:

```
<find_service businessKey="1234.." [maxRows="nn"]
    generic="2.0" xmlns="um:uddi-org:api_v2">
    [<find-qualifiers/>]
    [<name/>]
    [<categoryBag/>]
    [<tModelBag/>]
</find_service>
```

Listing 10.5 shows a sample find_service request that displays a list of all services registered by Microsoft.

LISTING 10.5 find_service SOAP Request for Microsoft

```
<?xml version="1.0" encoding="UTF-8"?>
<Envelope xmlns="http://schemas.xmlsoap.org/soap/envelope/">
    <Body>
        <find_service businessKey="0076B468-EB27-42E5-AC09-9955CFF462A3"
            generic="2.0" xmlns="urn:uddi-org:api_v2">
        </find_service>
    </Body>
</Envelope>
```

Listing 10.6 shows the response returned by IBM's UDDI registry.

LISTING 10.6 Response from `find_service` SOAP Request

```
<?xml version="1.0" encoding="UTF-8" ?>
<Envelope xmlns="http://schemas.xmlsoap.org/soap/envelope/">
  <Body>
    <serviceList generic="1.0" xmlns="urn:uddi-org:api"
    operator="www.ibm.com/services/uddi" truncated="false">
      <serviceInfos>
        <serviceInfo
        serviceKey="BD9B1A10-4668-42E9-AC69-D3DA905C314D"
        businessKey="0076B468-EB27-42E5-AC09-9955CFF462A3">
          <name>Electronic Business Integration Services</name>
        </serviceInfo>

        <serviceInfo
        serviceKey="17B29861-2F33-402C-98F0-FD16CF5B8E9C"
        businessKey="0076B468-EB27-42E5-AC09-9955CFF462A3">
          <name>Home Page</name>
        </serviceInfo>

        <serviceInfo
        serviceKey="4DE36949-E757-4DE1-A3BD-B3F1D4350325"
        businessKey="0076B468-EB27-42E5-AC09-9955CFF462A3">
          <name>Microsoft Developer Network</name>
        </serviceInfo>

        <serviceInfo
        serviceKey="491E8F93-E90F-42E3-A048-726744453659"
        businessKey="0076B468-EB27-42E5-AC09-9955CFF462A3">
          <name>Online Shopping</name>
        </serviceInfo>

        <serviceInfo
        serviceKey="F9D39C6F-AA09-4C5C-BC7B-6B26B0BA016D"
        businessKey="0076B468-EB27-42E5-AC09-9955CFF462A3">
          <name>Technet</name>
        </serviceInfo>

        <serviceInfo
        serviceKey="33C3D124-E967-4AB1-8F51-D93D95FAC91A"
        businessKey="0076B468-EB27-42E5-AC09-9955CFF462A3">
          <name>UDDI Web Services</name>
        </serviceInfo>

        <serviceInfo
        serviceKey="86E46AAD-82A5-454F-8957-381C2F724D6F"
        businessKey="0076B468-EB27-42E5-AC09-9955CFF462A3">
          <name>UDDI Web Sites</name>
        </serviceInfo>
```

LISTING 10.6 continued

```
        <serviceInfo
        serviceKey="367DF918-7D5E-4B00-8CF6-AFE56367C2D6"
        businessKey="0076B468-EB27-42E5-AC09-9955CFF462A3">
          <name>Volume Licensing Select Program</name>
        </serviceInfo>

        <serviceInfo
        serviceKey="A97EF39E-853B-47BD-985A-1EB0FAB7D342"
        businessKey="0076B468-EB27-42E5-AC09-9955CFF462A3">
          <name>Web services for smart searching</name>
        </serviceInfo>
      </serviceInfos>
    </serviceList>
  </Body>
</Envelope>
```

find_tModel

The `find_tModel` request enables you to search for `tModel` structures based on a name or other criteria. The result is a list of `tModels`. The general format of the request is as follows:

```
<find_tModel businessKey="1234.." [maxRows="nn"]
    generic="2.0" xmlns="um:uddi-org:api_v2">
    [<find-qualifiers/>]
    [<name/>]
    [<identifierBag/>]
    [<categoryBag/>]
</find_tModel>
```

Listing 10.7 shows a request that displays all `tModels` whose names begin with *Microsoft*.

LISTING 10.7 `find_tModel` SOAP Request

```
<?xml version="1.0" encoding="UTF-8"?>
<Envelope xmlns="http://schemas.xmlsoap.org/soap/envelope/">
    <Body>
        <find_tModel generic="2.0" xmlns="urn:uddi-org:api_v2">
            <name>Microsoft</name>
        </find_tModel>
    </Body>
</Envelope>
```

Listing 10.8 shows the results that the IBM UDDI registry returns.

LISTING 10.8 Results from `find_tModel` Request

```
<?xml version="1.0" encoding="UTF-8" ?>
<Envelope xmlns="http://schemas.xmlsoap.org/soap/envelope/">
  <Body>
    <tModelList generic="1.0" xmlns="urn:uddi-org:api"
    operator="www.ibm.com/services/uddi" truncated="false">
      <tModelInfos>
        <tModelInfo
        tModelKey="UUID:7CDAFF56-6034-4A97-81C5-E36E3993B0CB">
          <name>Microsoft for Partners Sales Readiness
          Training</name>
        </tModelInfo>

        <tModelInfo
        tModelKey="UUID:9D36EE1C-6897-4E9B-923F-886A1795B1B6">
          <name>Microsoft software development and
          consultancy</name>
        </tModelInfo>

        <tModelInfo
        tModelKey="UUID:3D4992AA-2779-4E8C-AC02-E42B0A0BE602">
          <name>microsoft-com:ID:businessEntity:child</name>
        </tModelInfo>

        <tModelInfo
        tModelKey="UUID:7D345114-49D6-48E0-849B-8C0E4696EB82">
          <name>microsoft-com:ID:businessEntity:parent</name>
        </tModelInfo>

        <tModelInfo
        tModelKey="UUID:81C87FAA-9BF1-43B5-BDE6-EF1EEBAF8020">
          <name>microsoft-com:ID:marketplace</name>
        </tModelInfo>

        <tModelInfo
        tModelKey="UUID:9353124F-4DC3-4614-8CB4-B30C83865420">
          <name>microsoft-com:ID:marketplace:buyer</name>
        </tModelInfo>

        <tModelInfo
        tModelKey="UUID:2B9EE746-D799-4C17-A825-E8E713BF3BDF">
          <name>microsoft-com:ID:marketplace:supplier</name>
        </tModelInfo>

        <tModelInfo
        tModelKey="UUID:C95F02D4-38BC-48D2-9827-5AAF58D68E5B">
          <name>microsoft-com:ID:tax_authority</name>
        </tModelInfo>
```

LISTING 10.8 continued

```
        <tModelInfo
        tModelKey="UUID:C90D731D-777D-4130-9DE3-5303371170C2">
          <name>microsoft-com:disco</name>
        </tModelInfo>

        <tModelInfo
        tModelKey="UUID:297AAA47-2DE3-4454-A04A-CF38E889D0C4">
          <name>microsoft-com:geoweb:2000</name>
        </tModelInfo>
      </tModelInfos>
    </tModelList>
  </Body>
</Envelope>
```

Inquiry: Getting Details

The various find requests help you locate items when you aren't sure what you're looking for, or if you just need a brief summary. When you need a fully-detailed record, however, you use `get_bindingDetail`, `get_businessDetail`, `get_businessDetailExt`, `get_serviceDetail`, or `get_tModelDetail`.

Because the detail requests locate specific items by their key, the requests are all very simple—just a single key as a parameter.

get_bindingDetail

The `get_bindingDetail` request takes a `bindingKey` parameter and returns a `bindingDetail` structure. The general format for the request is as follows:

```
<get_bindingDetail  generic="2.0" xmlns="um:uddi-org:api_v2">
    <bindingKey/>[<bindingKey/>...]
</get_bindingDetail>
```

Notice that you can send multiple binding keys in the request. Be aware, though, that the UDDI registry may truncate the results if you ask for too much data.

Listing 10.9 shows a sample request that retrieves the binding detail for Microsoft's UDDI Inquiry service.

LISTING 10.9 `get_bindingDetail` SOAP Request

```
<?xml version="1.0" encoding="UTF-8"?>
<Envelope xmlns="http://schemas.xmlsoap.org/soap/envelope/">
    <Body>
        <get_bindingDetail generic="2.0" xmlns="urn:uddi-org:api_v2">
```

LISTING 10.9 continued

```
            <bindingKey>ED223839-4A96-482C-86BF-FED8AE6427E4</bindingKey>
        </get_bindingDetail>
    </Body>
</Envelope>
```

Listing 10.10 shows the response from the `get_bindingDetail` request.

LISTING 10.10 Response from `get_bindingDetail`

```
<?xml version="1.0" encoding="UTF-8" ?>
<Envelope xmlns="http://schemas.xmlsoap.org/soap/envelope/">
  <Body>
    <bindingDetail generic="1.0" xmlns="urn:uddi-org:api"
    operator="www.ibm.com/services/uddi" truncated="false">
      <bindingTemplate
      bindingKey="ED223839-4A96-482C-86BF-FED8AE6427E4"
      serviceKey="33C3D124-E967-4AB1-8F51-D93D95FAC91A">
        <description xml:lang="en">Production UDDI server, Inquiry
        interface</description>

        <accessPoint URLType="http">
        http://uddi.microsoft.com/inquire</accessPoint>

        <tModelInstanceDetails>
          <tModelInstanceInfo
          tModelKey="UUID:4CD7E4BC-648B-426D-9936-443EAAC8AE23">
            <description xml:lang="en">UDDI SOAP Inquiry
            Interface</description>
          </tModelInstanceInfo>
        </tModelInstanceDetails>
      </bindingTemplate>
    </bindingDetail>
  </Body>
</Envelope>
```

`get_businessDetail` and `get_businessDetailExt`

The `get_businessDetail` and `get_businessDetailExt` requests return information about a specific business. The `get_businessDetailExt` request returns the same information as `get_businessDetail`, along with some additional attributes.

The general format for the `get_businessDetail` request is as follows:

```
<get_businessDetail  generic="2.0" xmlns="um:uddi-org:api_v2">
    <businessKey/>[<businessKey/>...]
</get_businessDetail>
```

The `get_businessDetailExt` request uses identical syntax, except for the name of the request. Also, notice that you can send multiple business keys in the request, although the server may truncate the response if it is too long—you'll still get a valid XML document, but it won't list all the available items.

Listing 10.11 shows an example `get_businessDetail` request that returns information about Microsoft.

LISTING 10.11 `get_businessDetail` SOAP Request

```
<?xml version="1.0" encoding="UTF-8"?>
<Envelope xmlns="http://schemas.xmlsoap.org/soap/envelope/">
    <Body>
        <get_businessDetail generic="2.0" xmlns="urn:uddi-org:api_v2">
            <businessKey>0076B468-EB27-42E5-AC09-9955CFF462A3</businessKey>
        </get_businessDetail>
    </Body>
</Envelope>
```

Listing 10.12 shows a portion of the response from the `get_businessDetail` request.

LISTING 10.12 Response from `get_businessDetail` Request

```
<?xml version="1.0" encoding="UTF-8" ?>
<Envelope xmlns="http://schemas.xmlsoap.org/soap/envelope/">
  <Body>
    <businessDetail generic="1.0" xmlns="urn:uddi-org:api"
    operator="www.ibm.com/services/uddi" truncated="false">
      <businessEntity authorizedName="Martin Kohlleppel"
      operator="Microsoft Corporation"
      businessKey="0076B468-EB27-42E5-AC09-9955CFF462A3">
        <discoveryURLs>
          <discoveryURL useType="businessEntity">
          http://uddi.microsoft.com/discovery?
          businessKey=0076B468-EB27-42E5-AC09-9955CFF462A3
          </discoveryURL>
        </discoveryURLs>

        <name>Microsoft Corporation</name>

        <description xml:lang="en">Empowering people through great
        software - any time, any place and on any device is
        Microsoft's vision. As the worldwide leader in software for
        personal and business computing, we strive to produce
        innovative products and services that meet our
        customer's</description>
```

LISTING 10.12 continued

```
        <contacts>
          <contact useType="Corporate Addresses and telephon">
            <description xml:lang="en">Corporate Mailing
            Addresses</description>

            <personName>
            </personName>

            <phone useType="Corporate Headquarters">(425)
            882-8080</phone>

            <address useType="Corporate Headquarters" sortCode="~">
              <addressLine>Microsoft Corporation</addressLine>

              <addressLine>One Microsoft Way</addressLine>

              <addressLine>Redmond, WA 98052-6399</addressLine>

              <addressLine>USA</addressLine>
            </address>
          </contact>

          <contact useType="Technical Contact - Corporate UD">
            <description xml:lang="en">World Wide
            Operations</description>

            <personName>Martin Kohlleppel</personName>

            <email>martink@microsoft.com</email>
          </contact>
        </contacts>

        <businessServices>
          <businessService
          serviceKey="86E46AAD-82A5-454F-8957-381C2F724D6F"
          businessKey="0076B468-EB27-42E5-AC09-9955CFF462A3">
            <name>UDDI Web Sites</name>

            <description xml:lang="en">UDDI Registry Web
            Sites</description>

            <bindingTemplates>
              <bindingTemplate
              bindingKey="98A459BF-1E5C-489E-AD65-61B7ECBCB333"
              serviceKey="86E46AAD-82A5-454F-8957-381C2F724D6F">
                <description xml:lang="en">Microsoft Production
                UDDI Registry Web Site</description>
```

LISTING 10.12 continued

```
                <accessPoint URLType="http">
                http://uddi.microsoft.com</accessPoint>

                <tModelInstanceDetails>
                  <tModelInstanceInfo
                  tModelKey="UUID:68DE9E80-AD09-469D-8A37-088422BFBC36">

                    <description xml:lang="en">HTTP Web site
                    URL</description>
                  </tModelInstanceInfo>
                </tModelInstanceDetails>
              </bindingTemplate>

              <bindingTemplate
              bindingKey="FEBDD4AD-3870-4B40-AC3F-9AE73E640C33"
              serviceKey="86E46AAD-82A5-454F-8957-381C2F724D6F">
                <description xml:lang="en">Microsoft Test UDDI
                Registry Web Site</description>

                <accessPoint URLType="http">
                http://test.uddi.microsoft.com</accessPoint>

                <tModelInstanceDetails>
                  <tModolInotanooInfo
                  tModelKey="UUID:68DE9E80-AD09-469D-8A37-088422BFBC36">

                    <description xml:lang="en">HTTP Web site
                    URL</description>
                  </tModelInstanceInfo>
                </tModelInstanceDetails>
              </bindingTemplate>
            </bindingTemplates>
          </businessService>
...
      </businessEntity>
    </businessDetail>
  </Body>
</Envelope>
```

The full response from the `get_businessDetail` request for Microsoft is quite long, but full of interesting information, such as the Microsoft D-U-N-S number (the Dun & Bradstreet unique identifying number) and its NAICS classification.

get_serviceDetail

The `get_serviceDetail` request returns a detailed description of a specific service, based on the service key. The general format of the request is as follows:

```
<get_serviceDetail  generic="2.0" xmlns="um:uddi-org:api_v2">
    <serviceKey/>[<serviceKey/>...]
</get_serviceDetail>
```

Once again, you can send multiple keys, but the request may be truncated if it is too long.

Listing 10.13 shows an example `get_serviceDetail` request for Microsoft's UDDI service.

LISTING 10.13 `get_serviceDetail` SOAP Request

```
<?xml version="1.0" encoding="UTF-8"?>
<Envelope xmlns="http://schemas.xmlsoap.org/soap/envelope/">
    <Body>
        <get_serviceDetail generic="2.0" xmlns="urn:uddi-org:api_v2">
            <serviceKey>33C3D124-E967-4AB1-8F51-D93D95FAC91A</serviceKey>
        </get_serviceDetail>
    </Body>
</Envelope>
```

Listing 10.14 shows the response from the `get_serviceDetail` request.

LISTING 10.14 Response from `get_serviceDetail` Request

```
<?xml version="1.0" encoding="UTF-8" ?>
<Envelope xmlns="http://schemas.xmlsoap.org/soap/envelope/">
  <Body>
    <serviceDetail generic="1.0" xmlns="urn:uddi-org:api"
    operator="www.ibm.com/services/uddi" truncated="false">
      <businessService
      businessKey="0076B468-EB27-42E5-AC09-9955CFF462A3"
      serviceKey="33C3D124-E967-4AB1-8F51-D93D95FAC91A">
        <name>UDDI Web Services</name>

        <description xml:lang="en">UDDI SOAP/XML message-based
        programmatic web service interfaces.</description>

        <bindingTemplates>
          <bindingTemplate
          bindingKey="48F2BC6B-A6DE-4BE8-9F2B-2342AEAFAAAC"
          serviceKey="33C3D124-E967-4AB1-8F51-D93D95FAC91A">
            <description xml:lang="en">Production UDDI server,
            Publishing interface</description>

            <accessPoint URLType="https">
            https://uddi.microsoft.com/publish</accessPoint>
```

LISTING 10.14 continued

```
            <tModelInstanceDetails>
              <tModelInstanceInfo
              tModelKey="UUID:64C756D1-3374-4E00-AE83-EE12E38FAE63">

                <description xml:lang="en">UDDI SOAP Publication
                Interface</description>
              </tModelInstanceInfo>
            </tModelInstanceDetails>
          </bindingTemplate>

          <bindingTemplate
          bindingKey="ED223839-4A96-482C-86BF-FED8AE6427E4"
          serviceKey="33C3D124-E967-4AB1-8F51-D93D95FAC91A">
            <description xml:lang="en">Production UDDI server,
            Inquiry interface</description>

            <accessPoint URLType="http">
            http://uddi.microsoft.com/inquire</accessPoint>

            <tModelInstanceDetails>
              <tModelInstanceInfo
              tModelKey="UUID:4CD7E4BC-648B-426D-9936-443EAAC8AE23">

                <description xml:lang="en">UDDI SOAP Inquiry
                Interface</description>
              </tModelInstanceInfo>
            </tModelInstanceDetails>
          </bindingTemplate>

          <bindingTemplate
          bindingKey="3C2272AF-5002-415C-AB8D-B659FD5FF657"
          serviceKey="33C3D124-E967-4AB1-8F51-D93D95FAC91A">
            <description xml:lang="en">Test UDDI server, Publishing
            interface</description>

            <accessPoint URLType="https">
            https://test.uddi.microsoft.com/publish</accessPoint>

            <tModelInstanceDetails>
              <tModelInstanceInfo
              tModelKey="UUID:64C756D1-3374-4E00-AE83-EE12E38FAE63">

                <description xml:lang="en">UDDI SOAP Publication
                Interface</description>
              </tModelInstanceInfo>

              <tModelInstanceInfo
              tModelKey="UUID:F372E009-F372-429C-A09A-794113A5C5F9">
```

LISTING 10.14 continued

```
            <description xml:lang="en">
            urn:microsoft-com:test-signature-element -
            signifies that this is a testing version of the
            service</description>
          </tModelInstanceInfo>
        </tModelInstanceDetails>
      </bindingTemplate>

      <bindingTemplate
      bindingKey="4A495A47-F125-4437-8757-C61B9355483D"
      serviceKey="33C3D124-E967-4AB1-8F51-D93D95FAC91A">
        <description xml:lang="en">Test UDDI server, Inquiry
        interface</description>

        <accessPoint URLType="http">
        http://test.uddi.microsoft.com/inquire</accessPoint>

        <tModelInstanceDetails>
          <tModelInstanceInfo
          tModelKey="UUID:4CD7E4BC-648B-426D-9936-443EAAC8AE23">

            <description xml:lang="en">UDDI SOAP Inquiry
            Interface</description>
          </tModelInstanceInfo>

          <tModelInstanceInfo
          tModelKey="UUID:F372E009-F372-429C-A09A-794113A5C5F9">

            <description xml:lang="en">
            urn:microsoft-com:test-signature-element -
            signifies that this is a testing version of the
            service</description>
          </tModelInstanceInfo>
        </tModelInstanceDetails>
      </bindingTemplate>
    </bindingTemplates>

    <categoryBag>
      <keyedReference
      tModelKey="UUID:A035A07C-F362-44DD-8F95-E2B134BF43B4"
      keyName="KEYWORD" keyValue="SOAP">
      </keyedReference>

      <keyedReference
      tModelKey="UUID:A035A07C-F362-44DD-8F95-E2B134BF43B4"
      keyName="KEYWORD" keyValue="API">
      </keyedReference>
```

LISTING 10.14 continued

```
          <keyedReference
          tModelKey="UUID:A035A07C-F362-44DD-8F95-E2B134BF43B4"
          keyName="KEYWORD" keyValue="XML">
          </keyedReference>
        </categoryBag>
      </businessService>
    </serviceDetail>
  </Body>
</Envelope>
```

get_tModelDetail

The `get_tModelDetail` request returns information about a specific `tModel` or set of `tModels`. The general format of the request is as follows:

```
<get_tModelDetail  generic="2.0" xmlns="um:uddi-org:api_v2">
    <tModelKey/>[<tModelKey/>...]
</get_tModelDetail>
```

Listing 10.15 shows a `get_tModelDetail` request that retrieves the `tModel` for Microsoft's UDDI inquiry service.

LISTING 10.15 `get_tModelDetail` SOAP Request

```
<?xml version="1.0" encoding="UTF-8"?>
<Envelope xmlns="http://schemas.xmlsoap.org/soap/envelope/">
    <Body>
        <get_tModelDetail generic="2.0" xmlns="urn:uddi-org:api_v2">
            <tModelKey>uuid:64C756D1-3374-4E00-AE83-EE12E38FAE63</tModelKey>
        </get_tModelDetail>
    </Body>
</Envelope>
```

Listing 10.16 shows the response from the `get_tModelDetail` request.

LISTING 10.16 Response from `get_tModelDetail` Request

```
<?xml version="1.0" encoding="UTF-8" ?>
<Envelope xmlns="http://schemas.xmlsoap.org/soap/envelope/">
  <Body>
    <tModelDetail generic="1.0" xmlns="urn:uddi-org:api"
    operator="www.ibm.com/services/uddi" truncated="false">
      <tModel authorizedName="0100000M99"
      operator="www.ibm.com/services/uddi"
      tModelKey="UUID:64C756D1-3374-4E00-AE83-EE12E38FAE63">
        <name>uddi-org:publication</name>
```

LISTING 10.16 continued

```
        <description xml:lang="en">UDDI Publication API - Core
        Specification</description>

        <overviewDoc>
          <description xml:lang="en">This tModel defines the
          publication API calls for interacting with the UDDI
          registry.</description>

          <overviewURL>
          http://www.uddi.org/wsdl/publish_v1.wsdl</overviewURL>
        </overviewDoc>

        <categoryBag>
          <keyedReference
          tModelKey="UUID:C1ACF26D-9672-4404-9D70-39B756E62AB4"
          keyName="types" keyValue="specification">
          </keyedReference>

          <keyedReference
          tModelKey="UUID:C1ACF26D-9672-4404-9D70-39B756E62AB4"
          keyName="types" keyValue="xmlSpec">
          </keyedReference>

          <keyedReference
          tModelKey="UUID:C1ACF26D-9672-4404-9D70-39B756E62AB4"
          keyName="types" keyValue="soapSpec">
          </keyedReference>

          <keyedReference
          tModelKey="UUID:C1ACF26D-9672-4404-9D70-39B756E62AB4"
          keyName="types" keyValue="wsdlSpec">
          </keyedReference>
        </categoryBag>
      </tModel>
    </tModelDetail>
  </Body>
</Envelope>
```

Publishing

One of the big differences between the inquiry and publishing APIs is that whereas anyone can inquire, only specific users can publish information to the registry. This means that unless you have a private UDDI registry program on your system, you may not be able to publish data without going through a signup process with one of the UDDI service providers.

The limitation on who can publish also puts a constraint on the UDDI publishing API. It needs some way to verify that a user is authorized to make a request. Unfortunately, the SOAP protocol doesn't have a standard authentication mechanism, so UDDI must do authentication on its own.

Authentication

A publisher must obtain an authentication token from the UDDI server before publishing any information. The `get_authToken` request takes a user ID and some kind of credential (such as a password) and returns an `authToken` message that can be used with other requests. In other words, the `get_authToken` request is the login mechanism for the UDDI publishing framework.

The general structure for `get_authToken` is as follows:

```
<get_authToken generic="2.0" xmlns="urn:uddi-org:api_v2"
   userID="someLoginName" cred="someCredential" />
```

The `authInfo` structure you get back is usually just a single string, like `<authInfo>897324875245</authInfo>`. You must pass this structure as a parameter to all the other publishing API requests.

When you have finished interacting with the server, you should invoke `discard_authToken` to tell the server you no longer need the token. The general structure for `discard_authToken` is as follows:

```
<discard_authToken generic="2.0" xmlns="urn:uddi-org:api_v2" >
    <authInfo/>
</discard_authToken>
```

Saving and Deleting UDDI Data Types

The bulk of the publishing work lies in storing and removing the four main UDDI data types: businesses, services, bindings, and `tModels`. The rest of the publishing calls are mainly for simple housekeeping chores.

Most of the publishing requests are very simple, much like the detail requests in the inquiry API. Basically, the various `save` requests take one or more data items (`save_business` takes one or more `businessEntity` objects, for example) and the `delete` requests take a list of one or more key values.

Note

Whenever you add an object that has a key—a business, service, and so on—if you leave the `key` field blank, the UDDI registry automatically generates a UUID for the key value. In other words, if you don't want to generate your own UUIDs ahead of time, you don't have to.

Saving and Deleting Businesses

The general format for the `save_business` request is as follows:

```
<save_business generic="2.0" xmlns="urn:uddi-org:api_v2">
    <authInfo/>
    <businessEntity/> [<businessEntity/>..]
</save_business>
```

The format for the `delete_business` request is as follows:

```
<delete_business generic="2.0" xmlns="urn:uddi-org:api_v2">
    <authInfo/>
    <businessKey/> [<businessKey/>..]
</delete_business>
```

Saving and Deleting Services

The general format for the `save_service` request is as follows:

```
<save_service generic="2.0" xmlns="urn:uddi-org:api_v2">
    <authInfo/>
    <businessService/> [<businessService/>..]
</save_service>
```

The format for the `delete_service` request is as follows:

```
<delete_service generic="2.0" xmlns="urn:uddi-org:api_v2">
    <authInfo/>
    <serviceKey/> [<serviceKey/>..]
</delete_service>
```

Saving and Deleting Bindings

The general format for the `save_binding` request is as follows:

```
<save_binding generic="2.0" xmlns="urn:uddi-org:api_v2">
    <authInfo/>
    <bindingTemplate/> [<bindingTemplate/>..]
</save_binding>
```

The format for the `delete_binding` request is as follows:

```
<delete_binding generic="2.0" xmlns="urn:uddi-org:api_v2">
    <authInfo/>
    <bindingKey/> [<bindingKey/>..]
</delete_binding>
```

Saving and Deleting tModels

The general format for the `save_tModel` request is as follows:

```
<save_tModel generic="2.0" xmlns="urn:uddi-org:api_v2">
    <authInfo/>
    <tModel/> [<tModel/>..]
</save_tModel>
```

The format for the `delete_tModel` request is as follows:

```
<delete_tModel generic="2.0" xmlns="urn:uddi-org:api_v2">
    <authInfo/>
    <tModelKey/> [<tModelKey/>..]
</delete_tModel>
```

Assertions

For two businesses to appear as being related (that is, related when you call `find_relatedBusinesses`), both businesses must assert the relationship in the UDDI registry. The idea here is that although businesses may want to make their relationships visible, a business shouldn't be allowed to claim a relationship with another business without that other business' consent. After all, you don't want Billy Bob's Bait, Tackle, & Software to claim itself as a holding company for Microsoft.

To assert a relationship, each side of the relationship must store an assertion, either through `add_publisherAssertion` or `set_publisherAssertions`. The general format for `add_publisherAssertion` is as follows:

```
<add_publisherAssertions generic="2.0" xmlns="urn:uddi-org:api_v2" >
    <authInfo/>
    <publisherAssertion>
        <fromKey/>
        <toKey/>
        <keyedReference/>
    </publisherAssertion> [<publisherAssertion/> ..]
</add_publisherAssertions>
```

The general format for `set_publisherAssertions` is as follows:

```
<set_publisherAssertions generic="2.0" xmlns="urn:uddi-org:api_v2" >
    <authInfo/>
    <publisherAssertion>
        <fromKey/>
```

```
        <toKey/>
        <keyedReference/>
    </publisherAssertion> [<publisherAssertion>..]
</set_publisherAssertions>
```

Only the original publisher of a business can assert an association from that business, and for the association to be visible from `find_relatedBusinesses`, both sides must assert the relationship.

You can also delete an assertion with the `delete_publisherAssertions`, which has this general format:

```
<delete_publisherAssertions generic="2.0" xmlns="urn:uddi-org:api_v2" >
    <authInfo/>
    <publisherAssertion>
        <fromKey/>
        <toKey/>
        <keyedReference/>
    </publisherAssertion> [<publisherAssertion/> ..]
</delete_publisherAssertions>
```

Either one of the two parties mentioned in an assertion can delete the assertion.

Replication

When it comes to replication, you don't really need to know any of the associated SOAP messages, because unless you are writing your own UDDI registry server, you don't do any replication yourself. As a UDDI user, the only thing you need to know about replication is that a group of UDDI servers occasionally exchange replication messages, exchanging new entries and deleting old entries.

The servers keep track of who originally registered the information, to make sure you can't trick a server into deleting another user's information.

Summary

Although you can use UDDI to locate services and examine some of the details about the services, you can't always get as much detail from UDDI as you need. In Chapter 11, you'll learn about the Web Services Description Language (WSDL), which describes services in greater detail and is an excellent companion to UDDI.

CHAPTER 11

WSDL

By Joe Weber

In This Chapter

This chapter discusses the Web Services Description Language. It explains how to tell the world how to use your Web service, or find out how to use a third party's Web service.

Welcome to WSDL

Welcome to the world of WSDL, the Web Services Definition Language. WSDL was designed by IBM, Microsoft, and Ariba to provide a standard mechanism to describe Web services. It was then submitted to the W3C for standardization. The need for this definition is akin to the need for distributed systems to define an IDL (Interface Definition Language).

As you have been reading until now, finding Web services can be as simple as thumbing through the yellow pages. After you've found a service, though, what do you do with it? You could call up the provider of the Web service and ask for the names of all its services and what SOAP messages you need to invoke them. This would obviously be rather inefficient and would really stymie your work. So what is needed is a way for the service provider to describe the nature of the service it provides in a way that your program can plug into it—something similar to the way an RMI stub or CORBA IDL describes the methods available in its environment.

This is where WSDL comes in. WSDL is the standard for describing the processes needed to utilize a service. WSDL goes a couple of steps further by defining not only what the service parameters are but also the transport protocol. As you will see later, this means that you can describe that one service uses HTTP, another uses SMTP, and yet a third uses the FTP protocol. WSDL leaves the decision about transport up to the service's developer.

By being fairly agnostic about the transport mechanism, WSDL can bring together groups working in disparate environments such as SOAP, WDDX, XML-RPC, RSS, and others.

At the same time, WSDL seeks to provide a definition that is relatively easy for developers on both sides of the wire to deal with. Service providers need a system that enables them to make updates to the interface that will have a minimal impact on the consumers. Consumers need a definition that enables them to easily make assessments and comparisons about the nature of competitive services.

Communication Processes

A WSDL document comprises essentially seven different XML elements, which correspond to different parts of your specification. The elements are:

- Types
- Messages
- Operations
- Port Types
- Bindings
- Ports
- Services

Each of these elements serves to describe one segment of the entire service. As you read through this chapter, it may be useful to refer to Figure 11.1, which shows one way the elements might be modeled.

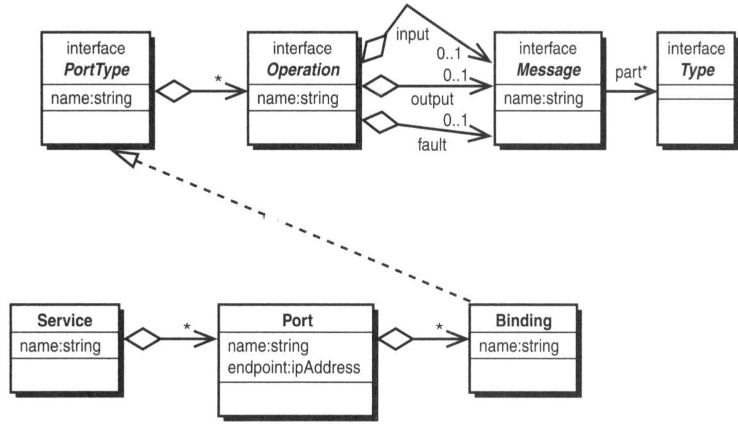

FIGURE 11.1
UML class diagram of WSDL, putting it all together.

In Figure 11.1, notice that the WSDL design first defines abstract elements and then defines elements that will realize those. This accomplishes two things:

- The generalized version of the elements is flexible and subject to extension (just like inheritance and polymorphism in Java).
- The end points (the actual IP addresses involved) are specified only in the service, and the actual transport protocol (such as SOAP, SMPT, HTTP, FTP etc) are defined only in the bindings. This means that the basic definition elements are consistent regardless of the transport or the end points.

Caution

It's important to note that Figure 11.1 represents only the author's rendering of the WSDL; it should not be taken as definitive.

Figure 11.2 provides a complete outline of the elements in WSDL. The nodes in the figure represent the elements as seen from the XML schema. As you continue reading the chapter, you may want to refer back to Figure 11.2 to better understand how the elements work together.

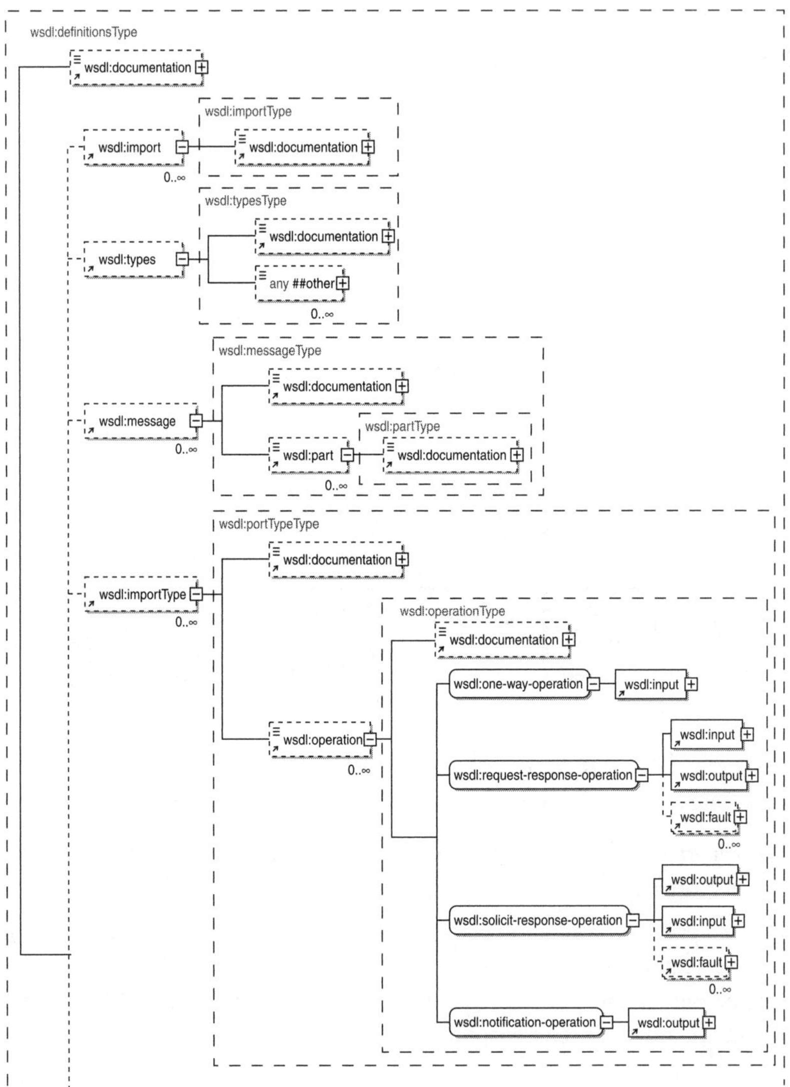

FIGURE 11.2

WSDL schema outline.

continued

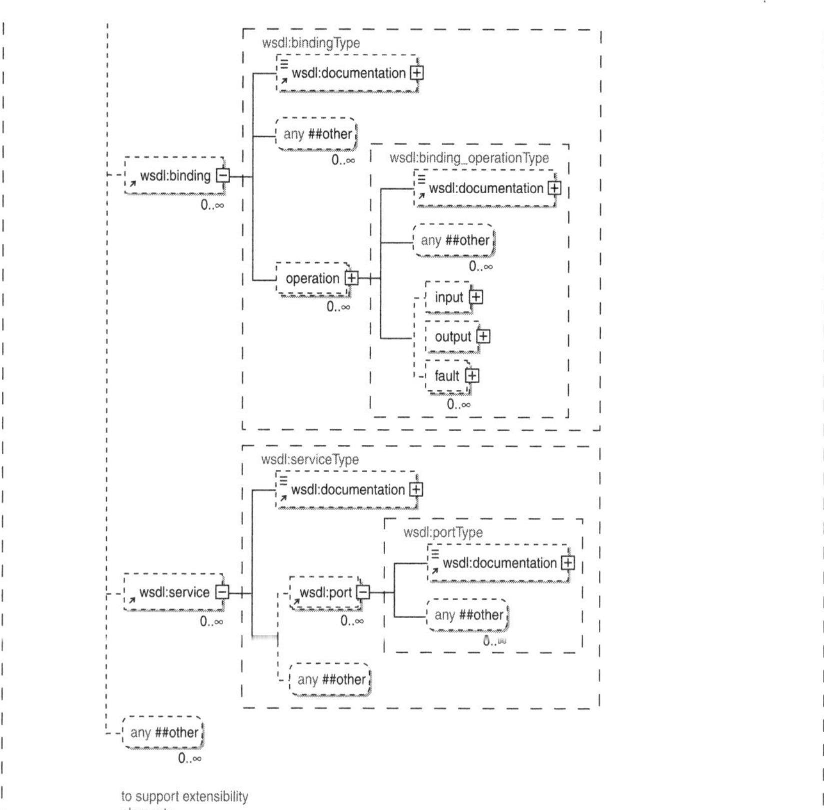

Types

A *type* is the most basic form of an element in WSDL. A type is very closely related to a type in an XSD (XML Schema) document. In fact, if you describe the type in XSD form they are identical. For this reason schema is the preferred mechanism for description.

You can think of a type as a struct in C/C++. Java has no direct parallel, but it would be the equivalent of a class with variables but no methods. In fact, the most basic types are directly analogous to primitive values in Java.

Types are needed to describe the fundamental elements of a method call. For instance, consider the following Java method:

```
public void myMethod(String parameter){
//do something
}
```

In the most basic sense, to be able to call the method `myMethod()`, you must be able to define the nature of a String. That seems completely obvious and you're probably wondering why String isn't predefined. Well, `String` *is* predefined. The `Types` construct is something you will be most concerned about when your methods require more complex entries.

Now consider the Java code in Listing 11.1.

LISTING 11.1 Passing Address as a Class

```
public class Address {
  public String name;
  public String address1;
  public String address2;
  public String city;
  public String state;
  public String zip;
}

public class MyClass{
   public void myMethod(Address myAddress){
     //do something
   }
}
```

Clearly `Address` isn't something you'd find predefined somewhere. Types enable you to encapsulate the entire structure of the `Address`. In Java you certainly wouldn't want to pass each of the atomic elements of the `Address` separately, as in the following:

```
public class MyClass{
   public void myMethod(String name, String address1, String address2,
                        String city, String state, String zip){
     //do something
   }
}
```

You know you want to pass all the elements as a unit, as one encapsulated object. Types fill the bill.

Brief Overview of XML Schema

Types are generally created with XML Schema, often called Schema for short. Schema is the W3C standard for defining XML data. If you are familiar with DTDs, Schema fills a similar role and adds significantly greater capability to architect, control, and detail XML data.

A full tutorial of Schema is beyond the scope of this book. However, to make sure that you have a general sense of Schema, go through some quick examples.

Defining the XML

Let's say that you want to create a schema document for the following XML, a sample that contains an address:

```
<address>
    <name>Bob Smith</name>
    <address1>123 W. Wisconsin</address1>
    <address2>Apt. 4</address2>
    <city>Milwaukee</city>
    <state>WI</state>
    <zip>53222</zip>
</address>
```

Clearly you could make the `state` element limited to just one of the valid 50 state abbreviations, or limit the zip code to a valid 5 digit number. But for simplicity's sake, we're going to skip over these issues. For the time being, we'll also skip over the issue of international addresses.

Opening a `Schema` Element

A Schema document always begins with a `schema` node. In general, you can do this in two ways. The simplest case would be similar to the following:

```
<schema targetNamespace="http://www.fluidimagination.com/sams/address.xsd"
       xmlns="http://www.w3.org/2001/XMLSchema"
       xmlns:addr="http://www.fluidimagination.com/sams/address.xsd" />
```

In the `schema` element you see three attributes:

- The `targetNamespace` attribute effectively defines the location where the schema is going to be located.
- The `xmlns` or XML Name Space attribute defines the schema document that actually provides the definition for the schema itself. In this case we show the utilization of the XMLSchema document published in 2001. Presented this way, the `xmlns` attribute defines the source of all the elements. In other words, all the elements in this element are considered to be sourced from the `xmlns` document.
- The final attribute is the `xmlns` for this document. More on this next.

The alternative definition is to give the `xmlns` for schema a more specific name. You can do this by defining a prefix for elements and their source. This leads to the following definition, which shows a standard `schema.xsd` with `XMLSchema` having a qualified name space:

```
<xsd:schema targetNamespace="http://www.fluidimagination.com/sams/address.xsd"
      xmlns:xsd="http://www.w3.org/2001/XMLSchema"
      xmlns:addr="http://www.fluidimagination.com/sams/address.xsd" />
```

In this case, the `xmlns` for the schema reference includes the name `:xsd`. All the elements that are from the schema namespace now have a prefix of `xsd`. In this case, the only element is the `schema` element, and if you look at the beginning of the element you can see that has become `xsd:schema`.

Now look again at the final attribute `xmlns:addr`. This attribute defines the namespace within which the current document will reside. Note that the `targetNamespace` and `xmlns:addr` attributes point to the same document. The result is that whenever you refer to elements defined within the current document you must refer to them as `addr:theValue` rather than just `theValue`. You will see an example of this later in Listing 11.2.

A list of the common namespace elements, and their traditional prefixes, are listed in Table 11.1. Note that it's good to use a prefix for consistency, but whether you do so is in fact entirely up to you.

TABLE 11.1 Namespace Elements

Prefix	*Namespace URI*	*Definition*
`wsdl`	`http://schemas.xmlsoap.org/wsdl/`	WSDL namespace for WSDL framework.
`soap`	`http://schemas.xmlsoap.org/wsdl/soap/`	WSDL namespace for WSDL SOAP binding.
`http`	`http://schemas.xmlsoap.org/wsdl/http/`	WSDL namespace for WSDL HTTP GET & POST binding.
`mime`	`http://schemas.xmlsoap.org/wsdl/mime/`	WSDL namespace for WSDL MIME binding.
`soapenc`	`http://schemas.xmlsoap.org/soap/encoding/`	Encoding namespace as defined by SOAP 1.1 [8].
`soapenv`	`http://schemas.xmlsoap.org/soap/envelope/`	Envelope namespace as defined by SOAP 1.1 [8].
`xsi`	`http://www.w3.org/2000/10/XMLSchema-instance`	Instance namespace as defined by XSD [10].

TABLE 11.1 continued

Prefix	*Namespace URI*	*Definition*
xsd	http://www.w3.org/2000/10/XMLSchema	Schema namespace as defined by XSD [10].
tns	(various)	The "this namespace" (tns) prefix is used as a convention to refer to the current document.

Creating the address Element

Now consider an even simpler XML document :

```
<address>some address</address>
```

In this extraordinarily simple case, the address is limited to just a single element. To define the element in the schema, you need to add an element element, as shown here:

```
<?xml version="1.0" encoding="us-ascii"?>
 <schema targetNamespace="http://www.fluidimagination.com/sams/address.xsd"
           xmlns:addr="http://www.fluidimagination.com/sams/address.xsd"
           xmlns="http://www.w3.org/2001/XMLSchema">
        <element name="address"  type="string"/>
</schema>
```

As you can see, the element has two attributes: name, which is the name of the element, and type, which details the nature of the contents of the <address> element.

In the following example, one additional modification has been made to the document to specify the namespace for the schema:

```
<?xml version="1.0" encoding="us-ascii"?>
 <xsd:schema targetNamespace="http://www.fluidimagination.com/sams/address.xsd"
           xmlns:addr="http://www.fluidimagination.com/sams/address.xsd"
           xmlns:xsd="http://www.w3.org/2001/XMLSchema">
        <xsd:element name="address"  type="xsd:string"/>
</xsd:schema>
```

Note that this code and the previous example produce identical results. You will use this form as you move forward because the more xmlns elements you add, the more important it is to have clarity with regard to element sources.

Notice that element became xsd:element in the same way that earlier, schema became xsd:schema. At the same time the value of the type parameter changed from string to xsd:string. The string type is actually a standard type, defined in the XMLSchema document, so when the namespace of the XML Schema changed to include a qualified name of xsd the reference to Schema's "string" also changed.

Creating the Address Type

The next step in the evolution of the address.xsd document is to be able to include sub-nodes to the address element. In the preceding example, the address element's type is set to be a simple string. To include the additional elements in address you need to define a new type that has these elements. Take a look at Listing 11.2.

LISTING 11.2 address2.xsd

```
<xsd:schema targetNamespace="http://www.fluidimagination.com/sams/address.xsd"
    xmlns:xsd="http://www.w3.org/2001/XMLSchema"
     xmlns:addr="http://www.fluidimagination.com/sams/address.xsd">
    <xsd:element name="address" type="addr:addressType" />

    <xsd:complexType name="addressType">
        <xsd:sequence>
            <xsd:element name="name" type="xsd:string"/>
            <xsd:element name="address1" type="xsd:string"/>
            <xsd:element name="address2" type="xsd:string"/>
            <xsd:element name="city" type="xsd:string"/>
            <xsd:element name="state" type="xsd:string"/>
            <xsd:element name="zip" type="xsd:string"/>
        </xsd:sequence>
    </xsd:complexType>
</xsd:schema>
```

Listing 11.2 shows several new concepts. Notice that the address element is now defined to be of the type addr:addressType rather than xsd:string. The addressType is then defined immediately after the address element. Setting the type to addr:addressType indicates that instead of following the string format, address is going to take its lead from the newly defined addressType type.

Note

The addr prefix used in type="addr:addressType" comes from the xmlns:addr attribute in the enclosing schema entry. The document's namespace is determined by finding the xmlns whose value matches the targetNamespace.

To define addressType you can see the use of the <xsd:complexType> element. The <xsd:complexType> element is used to define types that will include attributes, elements, or both.

The `sequence`, `all`, and `choice` Tags

Notice the `<xsd:sequence>` tag inside the `<xsd:complexType>` element. A sequence is used to indicate that an instance of this type must contain all the included elements, and they must be in the order specified. So, for instance, the following would *not* be legal because the `address1` and `address2` elements do not follow the `name` element:

```
<address>
    <name>Bob Smith</name>
    <city>Milwaukee</city>
    <state>WI</state>
    <zip>53222</zip>
    <address1>123 W. Wisconsin</address1>
    <address2>Apt. 4</address2>
</address>
```

On the other hand, if you want to allow the elements to be in any order, you can substitute the `<all>`tag for `<sequence>`. An `<all>` tag indicates only that all the elements within the set must be included, but does not impose an ordering.

In addition to `all` and `sequence`, you will see one other element frequently: the `choice` tag. If you replace the `sequence` with `choice`, an XML instance based on the schema needs to include one (and only one) of the elements. In the case of an address, including only one of the elements wouldn't make a lot of sense. Assume, however, that you have a situation where you are defining data for a cash register. At the register you can scan books with ISBN numbers or regular products with standard UPC symbols on them. (Books tend to have UPC symbols too, but bear with the example.) In this case, you would probably define two types: one for UPC symbols, and one for ISBN numbers. After you did that, you would want to create a situation where either the UPC symbol or the ISBN symbol could be entered in the XML, such as in the following example:

```
<xsd:complexType name="scannerType">
     <xsd:choice>
         <xsd:element name="upc" type="upcType"/>
         <xsd:element name="isbn" type="isbnType"/>
     </xsd:choice>
</xsd:complexType>
```

Creating a Complex Element Using an Anonymous Type

One other way to create the `address` element is to define the schema type for the `address` element anonymously. In the examples up until now, the types have all been given names. You can also define a type directly within the body of an element and skip the naming step, as shown in Listing 11.3.

LISTING 11.3 address.xsd with the Type Defined Anonymously

```
<xsd:schema targetNamespace="http://www.fluidimagination.com/sams/address.xsd"
    xmlns:xsd="http://www.w3.org/2001/XMLSchema"
     xmlns:addr="http://www.fluidimagination.com/sams/address.xsd">
    <xsd:element name="Address">
        <xsd:complexType>
            <xsd:sequence>
                <xsd:element name="name" type="xsd:string"/>
                <xsd:element name="address1" type="xsd:string"/>
                <xsd:element name="address2" type="xsd:string"/>
                <xsd:element name="city" type="xsd:string"/>
                <xsd:element name="state" type="xsd:string"/>
                <xsd:element name="zip" type="xsd:string"/>
            </xsd:sequence>
        </xsd:complexType>
    </xsd:element>
</xsd:schema>
```

Anonymous definitions work only when you are defining the type for a single purpose. If you want to reuse the type for several elements, you must declare the type separately with its own name.

Note

The information provided here is extremely limited. For the sake of brevity there is no coverage of attributes, restrictions, and a host of other options. For more information on schema please visit `http://www.w3.org/XML/Schema`.

Creating the `Address` Type for the WSDL Document

Now that you understand how to define an `address` type in schema, it's time to look at how to create a WSDL type for `address`. All WSDL documents start with a `definition` element as their root, just as XML Schema documents all start with `schema` as their root element.

As you will see throughout the rest of this chapter, the rest of the WSDL elements are defined within the `definition`. The `type` element can contain any type of referenceable name space, but in practice it's almost always a schema entry. Listing 11.4 shows how the type for the address is defined in WSDL.

LISTING 11.4 Address Type in WSDL

```
<?xml version="1.0"?>
<definitions name="AddressType"
        targetNamespace="http://www.fluidimagination.com/sams/addressType.wsdl"
        xmlns:tns="http://www.fluidimagination.com/sams/addressType.wsdl"
        xmlns="http://schemas.xmlsoap.org/wsdl/">
    <types>
      <schema
         targetNamespace=http://www.fluidimagination.com/sams/addressType.xsd
         xmlns="http://www.w3.org/2001/XMLSchema">
         <element name="Address">
            <complexType>
               <all>
                  <element name="name" type="string"/>
                  <element name="address1" type="string"/>
                  <element name="address2" type="string"/>
                  <element name="city" type="string"/>
                  <element name="state" type="string"/>
                  <element name="zip" type="string"/>
               </all>
            </complexType>
         </element>
      </schema>
    </types>
</definitions>
```

Notice that in Listing 11.4, the default `xmlns` has been changed to be `http://schemas.xmlsoap.org/wsdl/`. This means that all the elements without specified prefixes are coming from the WSDL schema definition. Then later in the `schema` tag, the default `xmlns` is redefined to be `http://www.w3.org/2001/XMLSchema`. This means that elements defined after that point are considered to be part of the schema namespace. Although this is entirely legitimate, altering the default namespace can cause some confusion for future readers of your schema. To make it easier on your schema's consumers, the document could be rewritten to look like Listing 11.5.

LISTING 11.5 Address Type in WSDL with all Namespaces Identified

```
<?xml version="1.0"?>
<wsdl:definitions name="AddressType"
        targetNamespace="http://www.fluidimagination.com/sams/addressType.wsdl"
        xmlns:tns="http://www.fluidimagination.com/sams/addressType.wsdl"
        xmlns:wsdl="http://schemas.xmlsoap.org/wsdl/">
    <wsdl:types>
      <xsd:schema
         targetNamespace="http://www.fluidimagination.com/sams/addressType.xsd"
         xmlns:xsd="http://www.w3.org/2001/XMLSchema">
         <xsd:element name="Address">
```

LISTING 11.5 continued

```
            <xsd:complexType>
               <xsd:all>
                  <xsd:element name="name" type="xsd:string"/>
                  <xsd:element name="address1" type="xsd:string"/>
                  <xsd:element name="address2" type="xsd:string"/>
                  <xsd:element name="city" type="xsd:string"/>
                  <xsd:element name="state" type="xsd:string"/>
                  <xsd:element name="zip" type="xsd:string"/>
               </xsd:all>
            </xsd:complexType>
         </xsd:element>
      </xsd:schema>
   </wsdl:types>
</wsdl:definitions>
```

Again, Listings 11.4 and 11.5 are completely identical in function.

Sidebar

Until now we have shown all the values of the address as elements. The values have not been attributes of the address. There is, in fact, a reason for this: Because types are an abstract definition of the data, and they do not detail the actual wire format of the data, elemental form—not attribute form—is highly recommended for WSDL documents. The elemental form can be translated to non-XML wire formats, whereas the attribute form cannot.

There are a couple of other standard rules for creating types in WSDL. These rules are also based on the abstract nature of the type system:

- Use element form, not attributes.
- Do not use values that are specific to a specific wire format, such as `soap:root` or `soap:encodingStyle`.
- If you are representing an array, at least at the time of this writing, you should use the SOAP array encoding (`soap:Array`). This would seem to fly in the face of the preceding point, but it stems out of the fact that XSD does not currently have a complete set of support for arrays. For instance, the default value of the array entry cannot be specified in the current XML Schema definition. When Schema catches up, the standard will reverse and at that time arrays should then be represented using the resulting Schema standard that is created.
- If the element's type isn't actually controlled (that is, it could really be any type) use `xsd:anyType`.

Messages

The next part of a WSDL document is the *message*. Messages have no real direct parallel within Java. However, you can think of a message this way: Consider a system wherein each method can have only one input parameter, one output parameter, and perhaps one parameter for throwing an exception. As you will see later, this is exactly how WSDL is constructed.

Now that you have this type of a system, you want a way to collect those items you'd normally place as an enumeration on a method. Go back to the address example, but this time assume that the method `order()` actually takes two addresses:

```
public void order(Address shipTo, Address billTo){
  //do something
}
```

At this point you could declare yet another type for each of the two addresses (shipTo and billTo), but the odds are there is nothing different about the two addresses that would cause you to want to go through the process of declaring a new type.

A far more logical process would be to group the two addresses together. Messages are just such a construction.

Using Elemental Form to Create Messages

In WSDL, a message includes a `message` element, which then contains `part` elements. The `part` elements each represent what would be called a parameter to a method in Java. So in the case of the `order()` method, where you have the `shipTo` and `billTo` address elements, each address gets its own part, as shown in Listing 11.6.

LISTING 11.6 Adding the `Address` Message

```
<?xml version="1.0"?>
<definitions name="addresses"
        targetNamespace="http://www.fluidimagination.com/sams/addressType.wsdl"
        xmlns:tns="http://www.fluidimagination.com/sams/addressType.wsdl"
        xmlns="http://schemas.xmlsoap.org/wsdl/">
    <types>
        <schema
         targetNamespace="http://www.fluidimagination.com/sams/addressType.wsdl"
         xmlns="http://www.w3.org/2001/XMLSchema">
            <element name="address">
                <complexType>
                    <all>
                        <element name="name" type="string"/>
                        <element name="address1" type="string"/>
```

LISTING 11.6 continued

```
                        <element name="address2" type="string"/>
                        <element name="city" type="string"/>
                        <element name="state" type="string"/>
                        <element name="zip" type="string"/>
                    </all>
                </complexType>
            </element>
        </schema>
    </types>
    <!-- Adding a message that has two addresses -->
    <message name="purchase">
        <part name="billTo" element="tns:address"/>
        <part name="shipTo" element="tns:address"/>
    </message>
</definitions>
```

Pay special attention to the `message` element. Notice that there are two parts, and each part references the `tns:address` element defined in the type section.

Using Types to Create Messages

Referencing the `address` element in the `part` works fine in many cases. However, there are other situations in which it is more appropriate to reference the type directly. To do this, you must ensure that the `part` tag has a `type` attribute rather than an `element` attribute. Consider the situation in Listing 11.7 which continues the ISBN and UPC example discussed earlier in the chapter.

LISTING 11.7 Creating a `Part` with a Specified Type

```
<?xml version="1.0"?>
<definitions name="AddressType"
         targetNamespace="http://www.fluidimagination.com/sams/addressType.wsdl"
        xmlns:tns=http://www.fluidimagination.com/sams/addressType.wsdl
        xmlns="http://schemas.xmlsoap.org/wsdl/">
    <types>
        <xsd:schema
         targetNamespace="http://www.fluidimagination.com/sams/addressType.wsdl"
                  xmlns:xsd="http://www.w3.org/2001/XMLSchema">
            <xsd:complexType name="scannerType">
                <xsd:all>
                    <xsd:element name="upc" type="upcType"/>
                    <xsd:element name="isbn" type="isbnType"/>
                </xsd:all>
            </xsd:complexType>
            <xsd:simpleType name="upcType">
                <xsd:restriction base="xsd:string">
```

LISTING 11.7 continued

```
                    <xsd:pattern value="[0-9]{12}"/>
                </xsd:restriction>
            </xsd:simpleType>
            <xsd:simpleType name="isbnType">
                <xsd:restriction base="xsd:string">
                    <xsd:pattern value="([0-9]- ){13}"/>
                </xsd:restriction>
            </xsd:simpleType>
        </xsd:schema>
    </types>
    <!-- Adding message which has two addresses -->
    <message name="purchase">
        <part name="productCode" type="tns:scannerType"/>
    </message>
</definitions>
```

Notice that in this example the `productCode` part refers to the type and not the element. This is similar to declaring a new element in schema.

Note

In Listing 11.7 you see an example of creating a restricted entry. The restriction means that a value entered into the element is valid only if it complies with the restriction. In the case of the `upcType`, values are legitimate only if they are 12 characters long and consist of the numbers 0-9. In the case of `isbnType`, 13 characters—0-9, a space, or a hyphen will work. In truth, a more complex regular expression can be created for ISBN numbers that more accurately reflects the requirement to have exactly 3 spaces or 3 hyphens. The expression here is intended to be only a sample.

Operations

The next element, `operation`, is perhaps the easiest of all the WSDL elements to understand. An operation is, as its name pretty clearly suggests, a parallel to a Java method. There are several key differences, of course. One of them is that an `operation` has three and only three messages. They are:

- Input message
- Output message
- Fault message

This isn't a great stretch from Java methods. After all, a Java method has only one return object, and it is not uncommon for a method to throw only one type of exception. The main difference here lies in the fact that an operation has just one input message, rather than a list of input parameters.

Types of Operations

Operations generally fall into four forms, based on the nature of the communication. They include:

- **One-way**. Characterized by a message from the client to the service, as shown in Figure 11.3.
- **Request/response**. Characterized by a message from the client and a response from the service, as shown in Figure 11.4.
- **Notification**. The opposite of one-way, it is characterized by a message from the service to the client, as shown in Figure 11.5.
- **Solicit/response**. The opposite of request/response. With solicit/response, the original message is from the service and it's the client that responds, as shown in Figure 11.6.

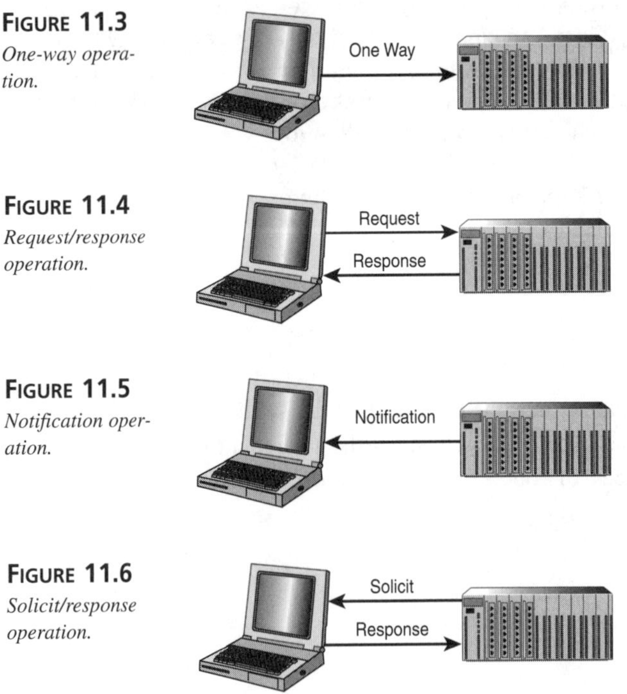

FIGURE 11.3
One-way operation.

FIGURE 11.4
Request/response operation.

FIGURE 11.5
Notification operation.

FIGURE 11.6
Solicit/response operation.

Creating a One-Way Operation

Operations in general consist of an operation element, and the operation element can contain one or more of the messages: input, output, and fault. The fault message is akin to Java's exception mechanism. The other two (input and output) are the messages that determine the nature of the operation. In the case of the one-way operation, the operation has only an input message. The simple operation for sending a purchase would be:

```
<operation name="submitPurchase">
   <input message="purchase"/>
</operation>
```

Note that the name parameter refers back to the message created in Listing 11.6 (and Listing 11.7).

Creating a Request/Response Operation

Request/response operations are declared exactly like one-way operations, plus they add an output message. If you want to send back a confirmation message when the purchase is completed, the operation might look like this:

```
<operation name="submitPurchase">
   <input message="purchase"/>
   <output message="confirmation"/>
</operation>
```

Note that with request/response and solicit/response operations you can also have fault messages. You might use a fault message if, for example, the purchase was supposed to be shipped to a location for which you don't have service. To do this you just need to add one or more fault messages, as in the following:

```
<operation name="submitPurchase">
   <input message="purchase"/>
   <output message="confirmation"/>
   <fault message="faultMessage"/>
</operation>
```

Creating a Notification Operation

A notification operation is the logical opposite of a one-way operation. A one-way operation is sent from the client to the service; a notification operation originates from the service and goes out to the client. Take, for instance, the situation where you want to actively notify the client of the shipping state of a purchase. You might have an operation such as this:

```
<operation name="deliveryStatus">
   <output message="trackingInformation"/>
</operation>
```

Notice that the notification operation does not have an `input` operation; it has just an `output`.

Note

Note that notification and one-way operations are not allowed to have `fault` messages.

Creating a Solicit/Response Operation

The last operational form is the solicit/response. The solicit/response is used in the case where a service wants to request information from the client. The simple example for this is when you want to request further information about the client's status. If you were building a high bandwidth/low bandwidth site, for instance, you might define an operation that looks like this:

```
<operation name="clientQuery">
    <output message="bandwidthRequest"/>
    <input message="bandwidthInfo"/>
    <fault message="faultMessage"/>
</operation>
```

It should be noted that although you have seen operations appear as standalone elements so far, in reality they are defined within the body of a port type.

Port Type

A *port type* is defined in W3C terms this way: "A port type is a named set of abstract operations and the abstract messages involved." What this really means is that it is the equivalent of an interface. A port type is used to define a group of operations, along with their messages.

As with all of the elements you have seen so far, the port type is not directly realizable. Instead, the port type only provides abstract definitions and requires some of the elements we will cover later to actually be realized. On the other hand, as a consumer of a service, much like the consumer of an interface, the port type provides all the information you will need once you are actually talking to the service.

Creating a Port Type with a One-Way Operation

A port type is really just a <portType> element enclosing one or more operations. The following example shows a port type for the submitPurchase operation:

```
<portType name="submitPurchaseType">
        <operation name="submitPurchase">
        <input message="purchase"/>
    </operation>
</portType>
```

Binding

Up until this point in the chapter you have been dealing with elements that, in UML terms, would be called unrealizable. In other words, you can't actually realize the port type by itself. The port type is like an interface. After you actually have an instance of a port type object, you have all the information you need to use it, but you can't take the port type and instantiate it directly. This is the same situation that prevents you from instantiating a new interface; you can only instantiate an Object that implements the interface. So you can't write the following:

```
public interface SomeInterface(){
    public submitPurchase(Address billTo, Address sendTo);
}
public class SomeClass{
    public void myMethod(){
       //This is illegal
       SomeInterface si = new SomeInterface();
    }
}
```

To realize a port, you must provide some concrete information about how to talk to the port—in particular, the methods the port will use for transport. So, for instance, when you define a port type for the submitPurchase operation, you don't deal with any of the wire format issues. So up to this point the port type could be carried over SOAP, SMTP, standard HTML, or a variety of other forms. The binding provides the implementation details for the port type.

Binding myMethod to SOAP over HTTP

To utilize the SOAP binding schema, it's necessary to first expand the list of schemas you include in the definition header. In particular, you must now include the xmlns for the WSDL SOAP schema at http://www.schemas.xmlsoap.org/wsdl/soap/.

With that said, it's time to look at a simple binding:

```
<wsdl:binding name="purchaseBinding" type="tns:purchaseType">
    <soap:binding style="document"
          transport="http://schemas.xmlsoap.org/soap/http"/>
    <wsdl:operation name="tns:purchaseOperation">
        <wsdl:input>
             <soap:body use="literal"/>
        </wsdl:input>
    </wsdl:operation>
</wsdl:binding>
```

Binding myMethod to Multiple Transports

Just because you have created a binding to HTTP/SOAP does not mean that the port type cannot also be used for a SOAP message sent over SMTP. To accomplish that you simply bind the port type to SMTP in addition to HTTP as shown in Listing 11.8.

LISTING 11.8 Multiple Bindings

```
<?xml version="1.0" encoding="UTF-8"?>
<wsdl:definitions name="PurchaseExample"
    targetNamespace="http://www.fluidimagination.com/sams/PurchaseExample.wsdl"
    xmlns:tns="http://www.fluidimagination.com/sams/PurchaseExample.wsdl"
    xmlns:soap="http://www.schemas.xmlsoap.org/wsdl/soap/"
    xmlns:wsdl="http://schemas.xmlsoap.org/wsdl/">

    <wsdl:types>
        <xsd:schema

targetNamespace="http://www.fluidimagination.com/sams/productType.wsdl"
                  xmlns:xsd="http://www.w3.org/2001/XMLSchema">
            <xsd:complexType name="scannerType">
                <xsd:all>
                    <xsd:element name="upc" type="upcType"/>
                    <xsd:element name="isbn" type="isbnType"/>
                </xsd:all>
            </xsd:complexType>
            <xsd:simpleType name="upcType">
                <xsd:restriction base="xsd:string">
                    <xsd:pattern value="[0-9]{12}"/>
                </xsd:restriction>
            </xsd:simpleType>
            <xsd:simpleType name="isbnType">
                <xsd:restriction base="xsd:string">
                    <xsd:pattern value="([0-9]- ){10}"/>
                </xsd:restriction>
            </xsd:simpleType>
        </xsd:schema>
    </wsdl:types>
```

LISTING 11.8 continued

```
    <!-- Adding a message that has two addresses -->
    <wsdl:message name="purchaseMessage">
        <wsdl:part name="productCode" element="tns:scannerType"/>
    </wsdl:message>
    <!--create a port type with one operation -->
    <wsdl:portType name="purchaseType">
        <wsdl:operation name="purchaseOperation">
            <wsdl:input name="tns:purchaseMessage"/>
        </wsdl:operation>
    </wsdl:portType>
    <!--Bind the message to SOAP using HTTP -->
    <wsdl:binding name="purchaseBinding" type="tns:purchaseType">
        <soap:binding style="document"
              transport="http://schemas.xmlsoap.org/soap/http"/>
        <wsdl:operation name="tns:purchaseOperation">
            <wsdl:input>
                 <soap:body use="literal"/>
            </wsdl:input>
        </wsdl:operation>
    </wsdl:binding>
    <!--Bind the message to SOAP over  SMTP -->
    <wsdl:binding name="purchaseBindingSMTP" type="tns:purchaseType">
        <soap:binding style="document"
              transport="http://schemas.xmlsoap.org/soap/smtp"/>
        <wsdl:operation name="tns:purchaseOperation">
            <wsdl:input>
                 <soap:body use="literal"/>
            </wsdl:input>
        </wsdl:operation>
    </wsdl:binding>
</wsdl:definitions>
```

It should be clearer now why each element is handled separately. If you allow the port type to be bound to several protocols, you can reuse the work needed in the production of the port across multiple bindings.

It's further worth noting that for most developers the nature of the bindings will be nearly transparent except when you are scripting the WSDL, because almost all the architectures out there allow you to switch out the binding almost transparently.

Port

Now that you have defined the method of the transport, you can finally start to tie the whole thing to a specific IP address. The binding identified that you were using SOAP over HTTP or SOAP over SMTP, but did not yet define what the network address was of the machine that was hosting the service. The `port` element adds that information.

Defining a Port

A port consists primarily of a name, a binding, and the wire-specific address information. The port name must be unique among the entire WSDL document and represents the name by which the port will be known. The binding name is, of course, the name of the binding you created in the earlier section. Finally, the specific wire format you are using provides the address information via extension. The next example shows the purchaseBinding defined in Listing 11.8 bound to the address of the Apache SOAP server at www.fluidimagination.com:

```
<port binding="tns:purchaseBinding" name="Purchase_ServicePort">
     <soap:address
       location="http://www.fluidimagination.com:8080/soap/servlet/rpcrouter"/>
</port>
```

Service

The service element ties all the previous elements together into a single offering. In general, the service element can be thought of as an entire Java class. The service element is the element that your customers see first when they obtain your WSDL document.

The service element is designed to bring all the related ports together into a one solid group. If the complete list is provided, a consumer can go through and determine all the port types a particular service supports. The service allows a client to determine whether a particular service supports all the operations that the client needs.

There is one rule about combining ports within the service: The ports within the service cannot communicate between each other. In other words, they can't be chained so that one port's output is the input to another port.

Declaring the Service

A service consists of just a service element, its name, and the ports included in the service. Listing 11.9 shows the previous Purchase_ServicePort port as part of the Purchase_Service service.

LISTING 11.9 The Complete WSDL

```
<?xml version="1.0" encoding="UTF-8"?>
<wsdl:definitions name="PurchaseExample"
targetNamespace="http://www.fluidimagination.com/sams/PurchaseExample.wsdl"
         xmlns:tns="http://www.fluidimagination.com/sams/PurchaseExample.wsdl"
         xmlns:soap="http://www.schemas.xmlsoap.org/wsdl/soap/"
```

LISTING 11.9 continued

```
      xmlns:wsdl="http://schemas.xmlsoap.org/wsdl/">

  <wsdl:types>
      <xsd:schema
       targetNamespace="http://www.fluidimagination.com/sams/productType.xsd"
       xmlns:xsd="http://www.w3.org/2001/XMLSchema">
          <xsd:complexType name="scannerType">
              <xsd:all>
                  <xsd:element name="upc" type="upcType"/>
                  <xsd:element name="isbn" type="isbnType"/>
              </xsd:all>
          </xsd:complexType>
          <xsd:simpleType name="upcType">
              <xsd:restriction base="xsd:string">
                  <xsd:pattern value="[0-9]{12}"/>
              </xsd:restriction>
          </xsd:simpleType>
          <xsd:simpleType name="isbnType">
              <xsd:restriction base="xsd:string">
                  <xsd:pattern value="([0-9]- ){10}"/>
              </xsd:restriction>
          </xsd:simpleType>
      </xsd:schema>
  </wsdl:types>
  <!-- Adding a message that has two addresses -->
  <wsdl:message name="purchaseMessage">
      <wsdl:part name="productCode" element="tns:scannerType"/>
  </wsdl:message>
  <!--create a port type with one operation -->
  <wsdl:portType name="purchaseType">
      <wsdl:operation name="purchaseOperation">
          <wsdl:input name="tns:purchaseMessage"/>
      </wsdl:operation>
  </wsdl:portType>
  <!--Bind the message to SOAP over  HTTP -->
  <wsdl:binding name="purchaseBinding" type="tns:purchaseType">
      <soap:binding style="document"
            transport="http://schemas.xmlsoap.org/soap/http"/>
      <wsdl:operation name="tns:purchaseOperation">
          <wsdl:input>
               <soap:body use="literal"/>
          </wsdl:input>
      </wsdl:operation>
  </wsdl:binding>
  <!--Bind the message to SOAP over SMTP -->
  <wsdl:binding name="purchaseBinding" type="tns:purchaseType">
      <soap:binding style="document"
            transport="http://schemas.xmlsoap.org/soap/smtp"/>
```

LISTING 11.9 continued

```
        <wsdl:operation name="tns:purchaseOperation">
            <wsdl:input>
                 <soap:body use="literal"/>
            </wsdl:input>
        </wsdl:operation>
    </wsdl:binding>

    <service name="Purchase_Service">
        <documentation>Purchase service,
                       offering purchase of ISBN or UPC based matterials
                       to the world!</documentation>
        <port binding="tns:purchaseBinding" name="Purchase_ServicePort">
            <soap:address
       location="http://www.fluidimagination.com:8080/soap/servlet/rpcrouter"/>
        </port>
    </service>

</wsdl:definitions>
```

Notice that in the service you also see the use of the `<documentation>` element. In truth, it is a good idea to include `documentation` elements throughout your WSDL. It's a good practice to document all your elements. For the sake of conserving a few trees we've left these elements out of the rest of this chapter, but the `documentation` element is shown here so you don't forget about it.

Combining Port Types Within a Service

Within the same service, you can place several of the same port type elements that each use a different binding (service), or a different port (address). If you do this, each port must have semantically equivalent behavior. The idea here is to allow consumers to choose the best type of communication for their situation. So, for instance, you may want to publish your service where the most ideal performance would come from a binding to FTP, but you also want to make the service available to users behind a firewall that need to use an HTTP proxy. You accomplish this by providing two different ports: one for the FTP and another for HTTP.

Creating WSDL Documents from a Java Class

The effort involved in laying out a WSDL document by hand is clearly not trivial. You might understandably wish for a way to create the WSDL document simply by introspecting your Java class. Fortunately, most application servers provide a tool to do just

this. In addition, there is a Java Community Process group working on Java Specification Request 110 to provide a standardized set of tools and APIs called JWSDL (`javax.wsdl`).

Unfortunately, JWSDL is not yet available at the time of this writing. Most of the various application servers such as IONA, Bea, IBM's Websphere, and others contain tools to create proxies. For the purposes of this book, we'll use the Axis from Apache. (For information about obtaining and installing these tools, see Chapters 4 and 5, "Building Web Services with Java" and "A Simple Java Web Service.")

Declare `HelloWorldWSDL`

To begin the example you must first declare a Java class. You will then create a WSDL document from this class. For the purposes of this example, declare the following very simple Java class:

```
/*
 * HelloWorldWSDL.java
 *
 */

package sams;

public class HelloWorldWSDL {

    public String helloWorld(){
       return "HelloWorld!";
    }
}
```

Obtaining the WSDL File from the Axis Server

Perhaps the easiest way to obtain a WSDL file based on `HelloWorldWSDL` is to deploy the class file to Axis and get the automatically generated WSDL file. As discussed in Chapter 5, "A Simple Java Web Service," a WSDL file can be obtained for any service deployed through Axis by simply appending `?wsdl` to the service's URL.

Using the `Java2WSDL` Tool

The WSDL file that is obtained automatically from Axis using the `?wsdl` method can also be obtained using the `Java2WSDL` tool. This is very useful because it gives you greater control of the WSDL file.

To begin, compile `HelloWorldWSDL.java` using javac or your favorite IDE. After you have compiled `HelloWorldWSDL.java`, you can then utilize the `Java2WSDL` tool to create the WSDL document for it.

Note

When you compile the Java files it's useful to compile with debug information turned on. If debug information is available, Java2WSDL can use the parameter names you've provided as the names of the parameters in the WSDL file.

Next, make sure that you have all the necessary Axis JAR files in your classpath. In addition, make sure that you have also included the directory where the HelloWorldWSDL class can be found.

Note

HelloWorldWSDL is in the sams package. When specifying the classpath make sure that you specify the path where Sams is located; do not include /sams in the path. In other words, the virtual machine will be looking for the HelloWorldWSDL class file in the location CLASSPATH/sams/HelloWorldWSDL.class.

The program you want to run is contained in the class org.apache.axis.wsdl.Java2WSDL. It requires a number of parameters that are outlined in Table 11.2. To create the WSDL file run the following command line:

```
java -cp %classpath% org.apache.axis.wsdlgen.Java2Wsdl -n
"http://www.fluidimagination.com/wsdl/HelloWorldWSDL"
     -o HelloWorldWSDL.wsdl -O HelloWorldWSDL-impl.wsdl sams.HelloWorldWSDL
```

Caution

If you get the following message after executing the command line, it means that you have not included the necessary JAR files in your classpath:

```
Exception in thread "main" java.lang.NoClassDefFoundError:
org/apache/axis/wsdlgen/Java2Wsdl
```

If you see the following message you have either mistyped the name of the input class or you do not have the classpath correctly pointing to the location of the sams.HelloWorldWSDL class file:

```
java.lang.ClassNotFoundException: sams.HelloWordlWSDL
```

This command line causes the `org.apache.axis.wsdlgen.Java2Wsdl` class to be executed. The command line options here are really the minimum ones you need. The `-n` option specifies the namespace of the schema file. This is directly related to the namespace parameters discussed earlier in the section "Opening a `Schema` Element." The `-o` (small O) parameter specifis the name of the output file (the resulting WSDL file). The `-O` (capital O) parameter defines the implementation class. Finally, the last parameter is the name of the classfile that `Java2Wsdl` should inspect.

Results of Running Java2WSDL

After you have executed `Java2WSDL`, you should find two output files called `HelloWorldWSDL.wsdl` and `HelloWorldWSDL-impl.wsdl`, which look like Listing 11.10 and 11.11 respectively. The generator conveniently separates the abstract definitions (that is, types, messages, port types, and the SOAP binding) from the realization elements (that is, service and port).

LISTING 11.10 HelloWorldWSDL.wsdl: All the Abstract Definitions

```
<?xml version="1.0" encoding="UTF-8"?>
<wsdl:definitions
targetNamespace="http://www.fluidimagination.com/wsdl/HelloWorldWSDL"
xmlns="http://schemas.xmlsoap.org/wsdl/"
xmlns:impl="http://www.fluidimagination.com/wsdl/HelloWorldWSDL-impl"
    xmlns:intf="http://www.fluidimagination.com/wsdl/HelloWorldWSDL"
    xmlns:soap="http://schemas.xmlsoap.org/wsdl/soap/"
xmlns:soapenc="http://schemas.xmlsoap.org/soap/encoding/"
xmlns:wsdl="http://schemas.xmlsoap.org/wsdl/"
xmlns:xsd="http://www.w3.org/2001/XMLSchema">

   <wsdl:message name="helloWorldResponse">

      <wsdl:part name="helloWorldResult" type="xsd:string"/>

   </wsdl:message>

   <wsdl:message name="helloWorldRequest">

   </wsdl:message>

   <wsdl:portType name="HelloWorldWSDLPortType">

      <wsdl:operation name="helloWorld">

         <wsdl:input message="intf:helloWorldRequest"/>

         <wsdl:output message="intf:helloWorldResponse"/>
```

LISTING 11.10 continued

```
      </wsdl:operation>

   </wsdl:portType>

   <wsdl:binding name="HelloWorldWSDLSoapBinding"
         type="intf:HelloWorldWSDLPortType">

      <soap:binding style="rpc"
            transport="http://schemas.xmlsoap.org/soap/http"/>

      <wsdl:operation name="helloWorld">

         <soap:operation soapAction="" style="rpc"/>

         <wsdl:input>

            <soap:body
             encodingStyle="http://schemas.xmlsoap.org/soap/encoding/"
             namespace="http://www.fluidimagination.com/wsdl/HelloWorldWSDL"
             use="encoded"/>

         </wsdl:input>

         <wsdl:output>

            <soap:body
             encodingStyle="http://schemas.xmlsoap.org/soap/encoding/"
             namespace="http://www.fluidimagination.com/wsdl/HelloWorldWSDL"
             use="encoded"/>

         </wsdl:output>

      </wsdl:operation>

   </wsdl:binding>

</wsdl:definitions>
```

LISTING 11.11 `HelloWorldWSDL-impl.wsdl`: Service and Port Definitions

```
<?xml version="1.0" encoding="UTF-8"?>
<wsdl:definitions targetNamespace=
        "http://www.fluidimagination.com/wsdl/HelloWorldWSDL-impl"
    xmlns="http://schemas.xmlsoap.org/wsdl/"
    xmlns:impl="http://www.fluidimagination.com/wsdl/HelloWorldWSDL-impl"
    xmlns:intf="http://www.fluidimagination.com/wsdl/HelloWorldWSDL"
    xmlns:soap="http://schemas.xmlsoap.org/wsdl/soap/"
    xmlns:soapenc="http://schemas.xmlsoap.org/soap/encoding/"
```

LISTING 11.11 continued

```
    xmlns:wsdl="http://schemas.xmlsoap.org/wsdl/"
    xmlns:xsd="http://www.w3.org/2001/XMLSchema">

   <wsdl:import namespace=
        "http://www.fluidimagination.com/wsdl/HelloWorldWSDL"/>

   <wsdl:service name="HelloWorldWSDL">

      <wsdl:port binding="intf:HelloWorldWSDLSoapBinding"
          name="HelloWorldWSDLPort">

         <soap:address/>

      </wsdl:port>

   </wsdl:service>

</wsdl:definitions>
```

Other Java2WSDL options

Java2WSDL has a myriad of options to help you fine-tune the WSDL creation. The list in Table 11.2 is based on the Alpha 3 release of Axis and may differ slightly from the release you have.

TABLE 11.2 Java2WSDL Options

Option	*Description*
-h, --help	Prints the help message.
-o, --output *<wsdl file>*	Indicates the name of the output WSDL file. If not specified, a suitable default WSDL file is written into the current directory.
-l, --location *<location>*	Indicates the URL of the location of the service. The name after the last slash or backslash is the name of the service port (unless overriden by the -s option). The service port address location attributed is assigned the specified value.
-s, -service *<name>*	Indicates the name of the service. If not specified, the service name is derived from the --location value. The names of the WSDL binding, service, and port elements are derived from the service name as indicated in the "Details" section above.

TABLE 11.2 continued

Option	*Description*
`-n, --namespace <target namespace>`	Indicates the name of the WSDL's target namespace.
`-p, --PkgToNS <package> <namespace>`	Indicates the mapping of a package to a namespace. If a package is encountered that does not have a namespace, the `Java2WSDL` emitter generates a suitable namespace name. This option may be specified multiple times.
`-m, --methods <arguments>`	If this option is specified, only the indicated methods in your interface class will be exported into the WSDL file. The methods list must be comma separated. If not otherwise specified, all methods declared in the interface class are exported into the WSDL file.
`-a, --all`	If this option is specified, the `Java2WSDL` parser looks into extended classes to determine the list of methods to export into the WSDL file.
`-w, --outputWSDLMode <mode>`	Indicates the kind of WSDL to generate. Accepted values are: `All` (default)—Generates WSLD containing both interface and implementation WSDL constructs. `Interface`—Generates a WSDL containing the interface constructs (no service element). `Implementation`—Generates a WSDL containing the implementation. The interface WSDL is imported via the `-L` option.
`-L, --locationImport <url>`	Used to indicate the location of the interface WSDL when generating an implementation WSDL.
`-N, --namespaceImpl <namespace>`	Namespace of the implementation WSDL.
`-O, --outputImpl <wsdl file>`	Use this option to indicate the name of the output implementation WSDL file. If specified, Java2WSDL produces interface and implementation WSDL files. If this option is used, the `-w` option is ignored.
`-f, --factory <class>`	Use this expert option to extend and customize the `WSDL2Java` tool.

TABLE 11.2 continued

Option	*Description*
`-i, --implClass <impl-class>`	The `Java2WSLD` tool uses method parameter names to construct the WSDL message `part` names. The message names are obtained from the debug information of the `<class-of-portType>` class file. If that class file was compiled without debug information or if `<class-of-portType>` is an interface, the method parameter names are not available. In these cases, you can use the `--implClass` option to provide an alternative class from which to obtain method parameter names. The `<impl-class>` could be the actual implementation class, a stub class, or a skeleton class.

Accessing a Web Service via a WSDL Document

The whole reason for declaring a WSDL document is, of course, to allow consumers to access your Web service. As a client of a Web service you want to be able to read the WSDL document and produce Java code to interact with it. You can do this in several ways. Clearly, one way is to read the WSDL document and produce by hand the code necessary to talk to the WSDL document. The process you work through here is similar to the processes you learned about in the SOAP chapters earlier.

Creating WSDL Proxy Classes

It seems unlikely that, as a Java developer, you will go through the whole process of creating the access to the service manually. Doing so would be time consuming, and it is fortunately not necessary. Most of the application providers provide tools to create a proxy class. As an example, look at `Java2WSDL`'s sister: `Wsdl2Java`. At the time of this writing, a fair amount of standardization work is going on in the Java Community Process under the initiative called JSR-110, which will be called JWSDL. It seems likely that the Axis implementation is a reasonable reflection of what JWSDL will end up looking like.

Using WSDL2Java to Create a Proxy to HelloWorldWSDL

To run WSDL2Java on the HelloWorldWSDL file you created in the preceding section, execute the following command line:

```
java -cp %classpath% org.apache.axis.wsdl.Wsdl2java HelloWorldWSDL.wsdl
```

The only parameter needed to execute WSDL2java is the URL for the WSDL file for which you wish to create the class files. In this case, that's just the local HelloWorldWSDL.wsdl file. You can use any standard URL as well.

Results

The result of running the WSDL2Java is the creation of the source code for the class com.fluidimagination.www.HelloWorldWSDLSoapBindingStub and the interface com.fluidimagination.www.HelloWorldWSDLPortType.java. The actual source code is shown in Listings 11.12 and 11.13, respectively.

LISTING 11.12 HelloWorldWSDLSoapBindingStub

```
/**
 * HelloWorldWSDLSoapBindingStub.java
 *
 * This file was auto-generated from WSDL
 * by the Apache Axis Wsdl2java emitter.
 */

package com.fluidimagination.www;

public class HelloWorldWSDLSoapBindingStub extends javax.xml.rpc.Stub
        implements com.fluidimagination.www.HelloWorldWSDLPortType {
    private org.apache.axis.client.Service service = null ;
    private org.apache.axis.client.Call call = null ;
    private java.util.Hashtable properties = new java.util.Hashtable();

    public HelloWorldWSDLSoapBindingStub(java.net.URL endpointURL)
        throws org.apache.axis.AxisFault {
         this();
         call.setTargetEndpointAddress( endpointURL );
         call.setProperty(org.apache.axis.transport.http.HTTPTransport.URL,
             endpointURL.toString());
    }
    public HelloWorldWSDLSoapBindingStub() throws org.apache.axis.AxisFault {
        try {
            service = new org.apache.axis.client.Service();
            call = (org.apache.axis.client.Call) service.createCall();
        }
```

LISTING 11.12 continued

```
        catch(Exception t) {
            throw org.apache.axis.AxisFault.makeFault(t);
        }
    }

    public void _setProperty(String name, Object value) {
        properties.put(name, value);
    }

    // From javax.xml.rpc.Stub
    public Object _getProperty(String name) {
        return properties.get(name);
    }

    // From javax.xml.rpc.Stub
    public void _setTargetEndpoint(java.net.URL address) {
        call.setProperty(org.apache.axis.transport.http.HTTPTransport.URL,
            address.toString());
    }

    // From javax.xml.rpc.Stub
    public java.net.URL _getTargetEndpoint() {
        try {
            return new java.net.URL((String)

call.getProperty(org.apache.axis.transport.http.HTTPTransport.URL));
        }
        catch (java.net.MalformedURLException mue) {
            return null; // ???
        }
    }

    // From javax.xml.rpc.Stub
    public synchronized void setMaintainSession(boolean session) {
        call.setMaintainSession(session);
    }

    // From javax.naming.Referenceable
    public javax.naming.Reference getReference() {
        return null; // ???
    }

    public java.lang.String helloWorld() throws java.rmi.RemoteException{
        if (call.getProperty(org.apache.axis.transport.http.HTTPTransport.URL)
                == null) {
            throw new org.apache.axis.NoEndPointException();
        }
        call.removeAllParameters();
        call.setReturnType(new org.apache.axis.encoding.XMLType(
            new
```

LISTING 11.12 continued

```
javax.xml.rpc.namespace.QName("http://www.w3.org/2001/XMLSchema",
            "string")));

        call.setProperty(org.apache.axis.transport.http.HTTPTransport.ACTION,
"");
        call.setProperty(call.NAMESPACE,
            "http://www.fluidimagination.com/wsdl/HelloWorldWSDL");
        call.setOperationName( "helloWorld");
        Object resp = call.invoke(new Object[] {});

        if (resp instanceof java.rmi.RemoteException) {
            throw (java.rmi.RemoteException)resp;
        }
        else {
             return (java.lang.String) resp;
        }
    }
}
```

LISTING 11.13 HelloWorldWSDLPortType

```
/**
 * HelloWorldWSDLPortType.java
 *
 * This file was auto-generated from WSDL
 * by the Apache Axis Wsdl2java emitter.
 */

package com.fluidimagination.www;

public interface HelloWorldWSDLPortType extends java.rmi.Remote {
    public java.lang.String helloWorld() throws java.rmi.RemoteException;
}
```

A casual glance at Listing 11.13 reveals several interesting facts. First, `HelloWorldWSDLPortType` looks just like any remote object over RMI. Second, if you compare Listing 11.13 to 11.10, you can see that the operation exposed in the WSDL document in Listing 11.10 is exactly represented in the `HelloWorldWSDLPortType` interface.

The class `HelloWorldWSDLSoapBindingStub` in Listing 11.12 contains all the implementation details needed to transfer the SOAP messages to and from the server.

Other WSDL2Java Options

As with Java2WSDL, WSDL2Java contains several additional options. The options listed in Table 11.3 are from Alpha 3 of the Axis implementation and may differ slightly from your installation.

TABLE 11.3 WSDL2Java Options

Option	*Description*
`-h, --help`	Print the usage statement and exit.
`-v, --verbose`	See what the tool is generating as it generates it.
`-s, --skeleton`	In addition to generating the client-side classes, `WSDL2Java` can also create the server-side classes for you. The result is two additional class files. The the resulting `Impl` and `Skeleton` classes can be edited to provide you with a framework on which to develop your server. This is useful if you are part of a trading group and need to create a server class that conforms to a standard WSDL file.
`-m, --messageContext`	The AXIS runtime contains a `MessageContext` that is normally not available to the server-side implementation. Turning on this option adds a `MessageContext` argument to each operation in the server-side interface so that the implementation can be given the context.
`-N, --NStoPkg` *<argument>=<value>*	By default, package names are generated from the namespace strings in the WSDL document. Users can provide their own mapping with the `--NStoPkg` argument, which can be repeated as often as necessary: once for each unique namespace mapping. For example, if there is a namespace in the WSDL document called `urn:AddressFetcher2`, and you want files generated from the objects within this namespace to reside in the package `samples.addr`, you would provide the following option to Wsdl2java: `--NStoPkg urn:AddressFetcher2=samples.addr`. If a number of namespaces are in the WSDL document, listing a mapping for them all could become tedious. To help keep the command line terse, Wsdl2java also looks for mappings in a file called `NStoPkg.properties`, which resides in the default

TABLE 11.3 continued

Option	*Description*
	package (that is, no package). The entries in this file are of the same form as the arguments to the --NStoPkg command line option. For example, instead of providing the command line option as above, you could provide the same information in NStoPkg.properties: urn\:AddressFetcher2= samples.addr. (Note that the colon must be escaped in the Properties file.) If an entry for a given mapping exists both on the command line and in the Properties file, the command line entry takes precedence.
-p, --package <argument>	This is a shorthand option to map all namespaces in a WSDL document to the same Java package name. This can be useful, but dangerous. You must make sure that you understand the effects of doing this. For instance, there may be multiple types with the same name in different namespaces. It is an error to use the --NStoPkg switch and --package at the same time.
-o, --output *<argument>*	The root directory for all emitted files.
-d, --deployScope *<argument>*	Add scope to deploy.wsdd: Application, Request, or Session. If this option does not appear, no scope tag appears in deploy.wsdd, which the AXIS runtime defaults to Request.
-t, --testCase	Generate a client-side JUnit test case.
-n, --noImports	Generate code for only the WSDL document that appears on the command line. The default behavior is to generate files for all WSDL documents—the immediate one and all imported ones.

Summary

As you have seen, the Web Services Definition Language (WSDL) is extraordinarily useful for defining the implementation details between the participants in a Web services transation. WSDL forms one of the cornerstones of Web services.

In the next chapter, you begin your exploration of the JAX Pack.

The JAX Pack

Part III

In This Part

CHAPTER 12

JAXP

By Steve Haines

In This Chapter

Throughout this book you have been learning the facets that make up Web services. The key to Web services' success is their inherent platform and language independence; and the key to their platform and language independence is XML.

By defining a specific set of XML files, a Web services client running on any platform in any programming language can locate and communicate with a Web services server, again running on any platform and written in any programming language.

As a Web services developer, therefore, you are going to have to become versed in using XML files inside your code. Sun has provided a set of tools to make working with XML an easier task: the Java API for XML Processing (JAXP) and the Java Architecture for XML Binding (JAXB). JAXP is the subject of this chapter and JAXB is the subject of the next chapter.

XML Components

Before you dive into using JAXP to manipulate XML files, we need to define the components that make up XML documents.

XML Document

The core of an XML document is the document itself. It consists of the following components:

- **Prolog**. Contains version information, comments, and references to Document Type Definition (DTD) files.
- **Body**. Contains a document root and sub-elements.
- **Epilog**. Contains comments and processing instructions.

Listing 12.1 shows a simple XML file that might be used in a bookstore to define a set of books.

LISTING 12.1 books.xml<?xml version="1.0"?>

```
<!DOCTYPE books SYSTEM "Books.dtd">
<books>
  <book category="computer-programming">
    <author>Steven Haines</author>
    <title>Java 2 From Scratch</title>
    <price>39.95</price>
  </book>
  <book category="fiction">
    <author>Tim LaHaye</author>
    <title>Left Behind</title>
  </book>
</books>
```

The first two lines define the header. The line

```
<?xml version="1.0"?>
```

notes that this XML document is written against the 1.0 version of the XML specification; the next line references a Document Type Definition (DTD) file that defines the syntax rules for this XML file.

The rest of the code defines the body of the XML document. Most XML documents that you will encounter, as well as this one, will not have an epilog, but the specification allows for it.

Document Type Definition (DTD)

Document Type Definition files, or DTD for short, define the syntactical rules by which XML files are written. They define things such as:

- The name of the root element in the document (for example, `<books>`).
- The elements that can be contained inside other elements (for example, `<book>` can be contained within `<books>`).
- The multiplicity of elements (for example, `<book>` can appear multiple times).
- The order of elements (for example, `<author>` must precede `<title>`, which must precede `<price>`).
- Optional elements (for example, `<price>` appears in the first `<book>` but not in the second `<book>`).
- The type of data that is contained in the element's content(for example, all elements are text elements).
- The attributes that can appear in an element (`<book>` contains the attribute category—and it is a text string).

The origin of DTD files dates back to XML's forefather markup language, SGML, so it may initially appear cryptic, but its conventions are pretty straightforward. The following lines show the DTD that defines the `books.xml` file in Listing 12.1:

```
<!ELEMENT books (book*)>

<!ELEMENT book (author, title, price?)>

<!ATTLIST book category CDATA>

<!ELEMENT author (#PCDATA)>
<!ELEMENT title (#PCDATA)>
<!ELEMENT price (#PCDATA)>
```

The first line defines the element `<books>` as containing zero or more `<book>` elements:

```
<!ELEMENT books (book*)>
```

The `<books>` element is defined as an element, denoted by the `<!ELEMENT` prefix. The parentheses contain a comma-separated list of sub-elements that the `<books>` element can contain; in this case it can contain only the element `<book>`, but because an asterisk follows `book`, it denotes that it can contain zero or more instances of the `<book>` element. Note that if `book` was followed by a plus sign it would denote that `<books>` could contain one or more `<book>` elements (but it must contain at least one).

Similarly, the next line defines the sub-elements that the `<book>` element can contain:

```
<!ELEMENT book (author, title, price?)>
```

That is, `<author>`, followed by `<title>`, followed by an optional `<price>` element. The question mark following `price` notes that `price` is optional and can appear zero or one time as a sub-element of the `<book>` element. Note that the DTD enforces the order; if `<price>` appears, it must be after `<title>`, which must be after `<author>`.

The next line defines one of the attributes of the `<book>` element as `category` and notes its type: `CDATA`:

```
<!ATTLIST book category CDATA>
```

`CDATA` (character data) and its counterpart `PCDATA` (parsed character data) both refer to character data or text.

The remaining lines define the elements `<author>`, `<title>`, and `<price>` as containing character data. Note that if you were to consider an XML document as a tree, the `<book>` element would be a branch that contained other elements, and the `<author>`, `<title>`, and `<price>` elements would be considered leaf nodes. (They do not have any children of their own.)

Document Validation

Why all these rules? The answer lies in document validation. When an XML document is parsed (or read) the parser (the process that is responsible for reading the document) can validate the XML document's syntax against its DTD file and report back whether the document is well formed; a document is said to be well formed if it properly adheres to its DTD. If it is well formed, you can trust that you will be able to extract its data according to the rules in the DTD file; if not, you can reject the document. This is a valuable asset to you as the programmer.

Parsing Techniques

Sun, through JAXP, provides two mechanisms for reading XML documents:

- An event model
- A tree model

The Simple API for XML (SAX) Parser is event-driven: a program using the SAX parser registers a listener with the parser and the parser streams through the file, firing notifications when it encounters XML elements. The Document Object Model (DOM), on the other hand, constructs a tree representation of the XML document and provides an Application Programmers Interface (API) for accessing and manipulating the data in the tree.

SAX and DOM both exist for different application purposes and both have their advantages and disadvantages. The SAX parser maintains a very small memory footprint because it does not store any information in memory: it simply streams through the document and fires notifications of what it finds. It is extremely fast, but it requires the developer to build his own data structure representation of the document for in-memory use of the data. The DOM is slow to build and consumes a lot of memory, but it maintains an in-memory representation of the data, provides an API to access and manipulate that data, and even allows for complex searching and reporting based off that data.

If you are reading an XML file to load data into your own data structures, then you should use SAX. If you need a subset of the information or are simply trying to compute a value based off what is contained in the XML file (for example, how many books are in my document), then you should use SAX. Furthermore, if you are reading huge XML documents, the memory overhead in using the DOM may be prohibitive.

On the other hand, if you want to access the entire document in memory, you should use DOM. If you want to manipulate the document and then output the modified document to a destination (for example, save it to a file), then you should use DOM.

The choice is all a matter of how you are going to use the data obtained from the XML document.

Getting Started

Before you get started you are going to have to obtain a copy of JAXP from Sun's website at `http://java.sun.com/xml/jaxp`.

When you download JAXP, decompress it to a directory on your computer and you are ready to go. The files of interest in the distribution are the following:

- **`docs` subdirectory**. This contains all the javadocs for all the classes provided in the JAXP; it is the resource that you are going to make most use of in your XML development.
- **`crimson.jar`**. This archive contains all the World Wide Web Consortium (W3C) DOM and SAX classes along with the Apache Crimson JAXP implementation classes.
- **`jaxp.jar`**. This archive contains all the JAXP interfaces.

You need to add these two archives to your `CLASSPATH` when compiling and running Java applications that make use of the JAXP. Be cognizant of the version of JAXP you are using and other versions that may be in your existing `CLASSPATH`; incompatible versions in the `CLASSPATH` have been an endless frustration to many developers!

Simple API for XML (SAX) Parser

The main advantages of the SAX parser over the DOM include:

- It can parse documents of any size.
- Useful when you want to build your own data structures.
- Useful when you want only a small subset of information contained in the XML document.
- It is simple.
- It is fast.

Its main disadvantages include:

- It does not provide random access to the document; it starts at the beginning and reads through serially to the end.
- Complex searches can be difficult to implement.
- Lexical information is not available.
- It is read-only.

The first thing you need to read an XML document is a SAX parser that reads the document and a document handler that makes meaningful use of the data the SAX parser reads. JAXP provides a SAX parser in its distribution (`javax.xml.parsers.SAXParser`); the SAX parser is made available to you through the SAX parser factory (`javax..xml.parsers.SAXParserFactory`). The `SAXParserFactory` class is an API for obtaining SAX-based parsers. Call its `newSAXParser()` method to obtain a preconfigured SAX parser (based off the settings you define in the factory). Note that both these classes are abstract and are provided as base classes so that you, the developer, have a consistent programming interface regardless of the underlying implementation.

Creating a Document Handler

Your job now is to create a document handler. A document handler is defined by the class `org.xml.sax.helpers.DefaultHandler`. It implements several interfaces, but the one that you will be most interested in is the `org.xml.sax.ContentHandler` interface.

Table 12.1 displays all the methods defined in the `org.xml.sax.ContentHandler` interface. The document parser calls these methods on the class that implements this interface; for example, when the document starts, the `startDocument()` method is called, and when the `<books>` element is found, the `startElement()` method is called with a qName value of `book (see table 1).`

TABLE 12.1 `ContentHandler` Interface

Method	*Description*
`void characters(char[] ch, int start, int length)`	Receive notification of character data
`void endDocument()`	Receive notification of the end of a document
`void endElement(String namespaceURI, String localName, String qName)`	Receive notification of the end of an element
`void endPrefixMapping(String prefix)`	End the scope of a prefix-URI mapping
`void ignorableWhitespace(char[] ch, int start, int length)`	Receive notification of ignorable whitespace in element content
`void processingInstruction(String target, String data)`	Receive notification of a processing instruction
`void setDocumentLocator(Locator locator)`	Receive an object for locating the origin of SAX document events
`void skippedEntity(String name)`	Receive notification of a skipped entity
`void startDocument()`	Receive notification of the beginning of a document
`void startElement(String namespaceURI, String localName, String qName, Attributes atts)`	Receive notification of the beginning of an element
`void startPrefixMapping(String prefix, String uri)`	Begin the scope of a prefix-URI Namespace mapping

The `DefaultHandler` class also implements the `org.xml.sax.DTDHandler`, `org.xml.sax.EntityResolver`, and `org.xml.sax.ErrorHandler` interfaces to help the SAX parser resolve symbols it does not understand and to handle errors. When you create a handler it is best to extend the `DefaultHandler`.

Using the SAX Parser

With that said, here are the steps to parsing and handling the content of an XML document when you use the SAX parser:

1. Import the SAX classes, handler class, and parser classes into your Java program.
2. Get an instance of the `org.xml.sax.SAXParserFactory` by calling its static method `newInstance()`.
3. Configure the `SAXParserFactory`'s options (whether it is aware of namespaces and whether it is validating).
4. Obtain a `org.xml.sax.SAXParser` by calling the `SAXParserFactory`'s `newSAXParser()` method.
5. Create an instance of your `org.xml.sax.helpers.DefaultHandler` class.
6. Open a stream to your XML source.
7. Ask the SAX parser to parse your XML stream by calling one of its `parse()` methods (see Table 12.2).
8. Handle all the SAX parser notifications in your `DefaultHandler` class.

TABLE 12.2 SAX Parser `parse()` methods

Method	*Description*
`void parse(java.io.File f, DefaultHandler dh)`	Parse the content of the file specified as XML using the specified `DefaultHandler`
`void parse(org.xml.sax.InputSource is, DefaultHandler dh)`	Parse the content given `InputSource` as XML using the specified `DefaultHandler`
`void parse(java.io.InputStream is, DefaultHandler dh)`	Parse the content of the given `InputStream` instance as XML using the specified `DefaultHandler`
`void parse(java.io.InputStream is, DefaultHandler dh, String systemId)`	Parse the content of the given `InputStream` instance as XML using the specified `DefaultHandler`
`void parse(String uri, DefaultHandler dh)`	Parse the content described by the given Uniform Resource Identifier (URI) as XML using the specified `DefaultHandler`

Table 12.2 shows the `SAXParser`'s various `parse()` methods; the basic variation is that the source can be a file, a stream, a URI pointing to the file, or an `InputSource` (which can be an `InputStream` or a `Reader`—see the javadoc that accompanies the JAXP for more information). When looking at the javadoc for the `SAXParser` class, you may notice

reference to the deprecated `HandlerBase` class in addition to the `DefaultHandler` class: this is a remnant of the original SAX implementation, but with the advent of SAX2, which is what we are studying, it is no longer supported.

As an example, consider the `books.xml` file in Listing 12.1. To read that XML file and do something meaningful with it, you will need to create a couple of classes to represent an individual book and a collection of books. To realize this in software you will create two helper classes: `SAXBook` and `SAXBooks`; see Figure 12.1.

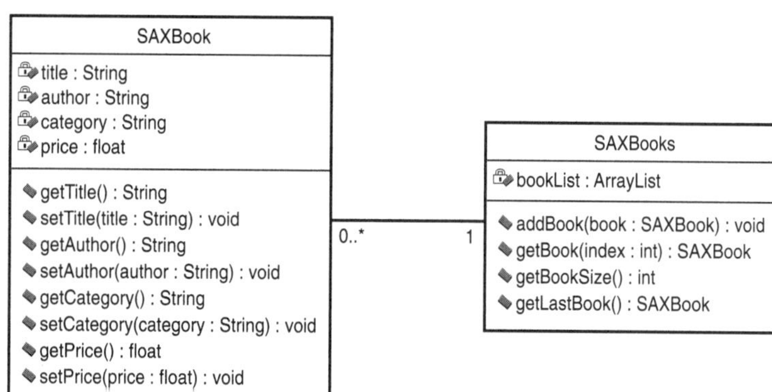

FIGURE 12.1
SAXBook And SAXBooks class diagram.

Listings 12.2 and 12.3 show the code for the `SAXBook` and `SAXBooks` classes.

LISTING 12.2 `SAXBook.java`

```
public class SAXBook {
   private String title;
   private String author;
   private String category;
   private float price;

   public SAXBook() {
   }

   public SAXBook( String title,
                   String author,
                   String category,
                   float price ) {
      this.title = title;
      this.author = author;
      this.category = category;
      this.price = price;
   }
```

LISTING 12.2 continued

```
    public String getTitle() {
        return this.title;
    }

    public void setTitle( String title ) {
        this.title = title;
    }

    public String getAuthor() {
        return this.author;
    }

    public void setAuthor( String author ) {
        this.author = author;
    }

    public String getCategory() {
        return this.category;
    }

    public void setCategory( String category ) {
        this.category = category;
    }

    public float getPrice() {
        return this.price;
    }

    public void setPrice( float price ) {
        this.price = price;
    }

    public String toString() {
        return "Book: " + title + ", " + category + ", " + author + ", " +
price;
    }
}
```

Listing 12.2 has simple code to provide standard JavaBean-esque access to the four fields defined in the class: title, author, category, and price. It also overloads the `toString()` method to return the values contained in all the fields.

LISTING 12.3 SAXBooks.java

```
import java.util.ArrayList;

public class SAXBooks {
   private ArrayList bookList = new ArrayList();
```

LISTING 12.3 continued

```
   public SAXBooks() {
   }

   public void addBook( SAXBook book ) {
          this.bookList.add( book );
   }

   public SAXBook getBook( int index ) {
          if( index >= bookList.size() ) {
                 return null;
          }
          return( SAXBook )bookList.get( index );
   }

   public SAXBook getLastBook() {
          return this.getBook( this.getBookSize() - 1 );
   }

   public int getBookSize() {
          return bookList.size();
   }
}
```

Listing 12.3 shows that the `SAXBooks` class maintains its collection of `SAXBook` objects in a `java.util.ArrayList` and provides methods to add a book, retrieve a book, and retrieve the total number of books in the `ArrayList`. One additional method, `getLastBook()`,returns the last book in the `ArrayList`; the reason for that becomes apparent in the `MyHandler.java` file you'll see in Listing 12.5.

Listing 12.4 shows the code for the `SAXSample` class; this is the main class that opens your XML file, creates a parser, and asks the parser to notify your handler.

LISTING 12.4 `SAXSample.java`

```
import java.io.*;
import org.xml.sax.*;
import org.xml.sax.helpers.DefaultHandler;
import javax.xml.parsers.SAXParserFactory;
import javax.xml.parsers.ParserConfigurationException;
import javax.xml.parsers.SAXParser;

public class SAXSample {
   public static void main( String[] args ) {
          try {
                 File file = new File( "book.xml" );
                 if( !file.exists() ) {
```

Listing 12.4 continued

```
                System.out.println( "Couldn't find file..." );
                return;
            }

            // Use the default (non-validating) parser
            SAXParserFactory factory = SAXParserFactory.newInstance();

            // Create an instance of the handler
            MyHandler handler = new MyHandler();

            // Parse the file
            SAXParser saxParser = factory.newSAXParser();
            saxParser.parse( file, handler );
            SAXBooks books = handler.getBooks();

            for( int i=0; i<books.getBookSize(); i++ ) {
                SAXBook book = books.getBook( i );
                System.out.println( book );
            }

        }
        catch( Throwable t ) {
            t.printStackTrace();
        }
    }
}
```

The following lines create a `java.io.File` object that points to the `book.xml` file that it expects to find in the same directory as the one from which this program is launched:

```
File file = new File( "book.xml" );
if( !file.exists() ) {
    System.out.println( "Couldn't find file..." );
    return;
}
```

It validates that the file exists and quits out of the program if it does not exist.

```
SAXParserFactory factory = SAXParserFactory.newInstance();
```

This line creates a new instance of the `SAXParserFactory` class by calling the `SAXParserFactory` class's static `newInstance()` method:

```
SAXParserFactory factory = SAXParserFactory.newInstance();
```

Recall that the `SAXParserFactory` is responsible for configuring a `SAXParser` and returning it upon request.

```
MyHandler handler = new MyHandler();
```

The following line creates an instance of the `MyHandler` class that will be described in Listing 12.5:

```
MyHandler handler = new MyHandler();
```

This line asks the `SAXParserFactory` to create a new `SAXParser` by calling its `newSAXParser()` method:

```
SAXParser saxParser = factory.newSAXParser();
```

The next line uses the `SAXParser` to parse the `book.xml` file and provide notifications to the `MyHandler` instance:


```
saxParser.parse( file, handler );
```

The next several lines retrieve the `SAXBooks` from the `MyHandler` instance and then iterate over all the `SAXBook` instances it contains, displaying the books to the screen. (Passing the `SAXBook` instance to `System.out.println` invokes the `toString()` that was overridden in Listing 12.2.)

```
SAXBooks books = handler.getBooks();

for( int i=0; i<books.getBookSize(); i++ ) {
       SAXBook book = books.getBook( i );
       System.out.println( book );
}
```

The `MyHandler` class in listing 12.5 is the most complicated class in the sample and is responsible for handling all the `SAXParser` notifications and building the data structures from those notifications.

LISTING 12.5 MyHandler.java

```
import org.xml.sax .*;
import org.xml.sax.helpers.DefaultHandler;

public class MyHandler extends DefaultHandler {
   private SAXBooks books;
   private boolean readingAuthor;
   private boolean readingTitle;
   private boolean readingPrice;

   public SAXBooks getBooks() {
          return this.books;
   }

   public void startElement( String uri,
                             String localName,
                             String qName,
                             Attributes attributes ) {
```

LISTING 12.5 continued

```
        System.out.println( "Found element: " + qName );
        if( qName.equalsIgnoreCase( "books" ) ) {
              books = new SAXBooks();
        }
        else if( qName.equalsIgnoreCase( "book" ) ) {
              SAXBook book = new SAXBook();
              for( int i=0; i<attributes.getLength(); i++ ) {
                    if( attributes.getQName( i ).equalsIgnoreCase(
➥ "category" ) ) {
                          book.setCategory( attributes.getValue( i ) );
                    }
              }
              books.addBook( book );
        }
        else if( qName.equalsIgnoreCase( "author" ) ) {
              this.readingAuthor = true;
        }
        else if( qName.equalsIgnoreCase( "title" ) ) {
              this.readingTitle = true;
        }
        else if( qName.equalsIgnoreCase( "price" ) ) {
              this.readingPrice = true;
        }
        else {
              System.out.println( "Unknown element: " + qName );
        }
  }

  public void startDocument() {
        System.out.println( "Starting..." );
  }

  public void endDocument() {
        System.out.println( "Done..." );
  }

   public void characters( char[] ch,
                           int start,
                           int length ) {
       String chars = new String( ch, start, length).trim();
       if( chars.length() == 0 ) {
           return;
       }

       SAXBook book = books.getLastBook();
       if( readingAuthor ) {
           book.setAuthor( chars );
       }
```

LISTING 12.5 continued

```
        else if( readingTitle ) {
            book.setTitle( chars );
        }
        else if( readingPrice ) {
            book.setPrice( Float.parseFloat( chars ) );
        }
    }

    public void endElement( String uri,
                            String localName,
                            String qName ) {
        System.out.println( "End Element: " + qName );
        if( qName.equalsIgnoreCase( "author" ) ) {
            this.readingAuthor = false;
        }
        else if( qName.equalsIgnoreCase( "title" ) ) {
            this.readingTitle = false;
        }
        else if( qName.equalsIgnoreCase( "price" ) ) {
            this.readingPrice = false;
        }
    }
}
```

The following line shows that the `MyHandler` class extends the `org.xml.sax.helpers.DefaultHandler` class:

```
public class MyHandler extends DefaultHandler {
```

This class has methods that can be overloaded to respond to `SAXParser` notifications. The notifications of interest are

- `startDocument()`
- `endDocument()`
- `startElement()`
- `endElement()`
- `characters()`

The `startDocument()` and `endDocument()` methods in the `MyHandler` class simply print out debug statements; all the real work happens in the `startElement()`, `endElement()`, and `characters()` methods. Because the SAX model deals with message notifications, the handler cannot run serially; it must instead run as a state machine.

The order of events in the SAX model is that the handler receives a `startElement()` notification for the `book` element, at which time you can get its attributes (category), then a `startElement()` for the `author` element, then a `characters()` call containing the text for the `author` element, and then an `endElement()` for `authors`. The process continues through `title` and `price`, and finally you get an `endElement()` call on `book`; at this point you have a complete book.

When the `MyHandler` class gets a `startElement()` call for `book`, it creates a new book, retrieves its `category` attribute, and adds it to the `SAXBooks` class:

```
        if( qName.equalsIgnoreCase( "books" ) ) {
                books = new SAXBooks();
        }
        else if( qName.equalsIgnoreCase( "book" ) ) {
                SAXBook book = new SAXBook();
                for( int i=0; i<attributes.getLength(); i++ ) {
                        if( attributes.getQName( i ).equalsIgnoreCase(
➥ "category" ) ) {
                                book.setCategory( attributes.getValue( i ) );
                        }
                }
                books.addBook( book );
        }
```

The `MyHandler` class maintains three variables to help it keep track of what element it is reading:

```
private boolean readingAuthor;
private boolean readingTitle;
private boolean readingPrice;
```

Invocations of `startElement()` for `author`, `title`, and `price` modify these variables to note what element a subsequent `characters()` method can be applied to:

```
        else if( qName.equalsIgnoreCase( "author" ) ) {
                this.readingAuthor = true;
        }
        else if( qName.equalsIgnoreCase( "title" ) ) {
                this.readingTitle = true;
        }
        else if( qName.equalsIgnoreCase( "price" ) ) {
                this.readingPrice = true;
        }
        else {
                System.out.println( "Unknown element: " + qName );
        }
```

In a larger example, you might want to use one integer variable and define some constant states in which that variable could be. When the `endElement()` method is called for each element, the handler resets the appropriate variable:

```
        if( qName.equalsIgnoreCase( "author" ) ) {
            this.readingAuthor = false;
        }
        else if( qName.equalsIgnoreCase( "title" ) ) {
            this.readingTitle = false;
        }
        else if( qName.equalsIgnoreCase( "price" ) ) {
            this.readingPrice = false;
        }
```

The following lines define the `characters()` method:

```
    public void characters( char[] ch,
                            int start,
                            int length ) {
        String chars = new String( ch, start, length).trim();
        if( chars.length() == 0 ) {
            return;
        }

        SAXBook book = books.getLastBook();
        if( readingAuthor ) {
            book.setAuthor( chars );
        }
        else if( readingTitle ) {
            book.cotTitlo( oharo );
        }
        else if( readingPrice ) {
            book.setPrice( Float.parseFloat( chars ) );
        }
    }
```


This method retrieves the last book added (which is the reason the `SAXBooks` class has the `getLastBook()` method), which was added in the `startElement()` for the `book` element and is the book for which this `characters()` method is applicable. The `characters()` method has three parameters: a character array containing the entire contents of the XML file, the start index, and the length into that character array to which this element's character text is applicable. The method builds a new `String` from this subsection of the character array, trimming off white space, and then ensuring that it has some characters; the reason for checking the length is that elements such as `book`, which contain other elements, still may have some white space between the end of the `<book>` tag and the beginning of the `<author>` tag. After it verifies that it has data, it checks the state variables defined earlier, accesses the last book added to the `SAXBooks` instance, and updates the appropriate book property (author, title, or price).

The `MyHandler` classes took a fair amount of work, but the end result is that the `MyHandler` instance has a complete `SAXBooks` property that maintains an in-memory representation of the XML file that can now be used elsewhere in the application.

Document Object Model (DOM)

The Document Object Model presents a tree representation of an XML document through a standards-based API that the World-Wide-Web Consortium (W3C) maintains. The DOM is better suited for applications that want to read information from an XML file, manipulate the XML data, and then eventually write the data out to a destination. Additionally, it offers the benefit over SAX that the document can be accessed randomly (the program does not have to read through the document sequentially).

The DOM does have a serious limitation in that it must read the entire XML document into memory. This is not a problem for the small example in the chapter, but in some real life applications, such as B2B e-commerce, XML files can get considerably large. (In B2B e-commerce applications that mapped EDI to XML, XML files could exceed 100MB in size!) But if your application's architecture can make use of the DOM, it does not require all the code to build an in-memory representation of an XML file using the SAX.

Building an XML Tree in Memory

Building a DOM XML tree in memory is actually a fairly trivial task. Similar to the SAX model, the DOM has a factory that creates parsers: `javax.xml.parsers.DocumentBuilderFactory`. This class enables the programmer to define the parser parameters available in a parser created by the factory (see the javadoc documentation for more information). You can obtain a `DocumentBuilderFactory` by calling its static `newInstance()` method. After the `DocumentBuilderFactory` is configured, its `newDocumentBuilder()` method returns an instance of the `javax.xml.parsers.DocumentBuilder` class, This is the DOM parser. The `DocumentBuilder` class has several `parse()` methods that construct a DOM document, shown in Table 12.3.

TABLE 12.3 `DocumentBuilder parse()` Methods

Method	*Description*
`Document parse(java.io.File f)`	Parse the content of the given file as an XML document and return a new DOM `Document` object
`Document parse(org.xml.sax.InputSource is)`	Parse the content of the given input source as an XML document and return a new DOM `Document` object
`Document parse(java.io.InputStream is)`	Parse the content of the given `InputStream` as an XML document and return a new DOM `Document` object

TABLE 12.3 continued

Method	*Description*
`Document parse(java.io.InputStream is, String systemId)`	Parse the content of the given `InputStream` as an XML document and return a new DOM `Document` object
`Document parse(String uri)`	Parse the content of the given URI as an XML document and return a new DOM `Document` object

These `parse()` methods are very similar to their SAX counterparts, but the bottom line is that they build an `org.w3c.dom.Document` object from varying input sources. For example, consider building a DOM document from a file:

```
File f = new File( "myfile.xml" );
DocumentBuilderFactory factory = DocumentBuilderFactory.newInstance();
DocumentBuilder builder = factory.newDocumentBuilder();
Document doc = builder.parse( f );
```

Reading from the XML Tree

A DOM tree is an in-memory representation of an XML file; and just as it sounds, it is in the form of a tree. Figure 12.2 shows how the `book.xml` file might appear in a DOM.

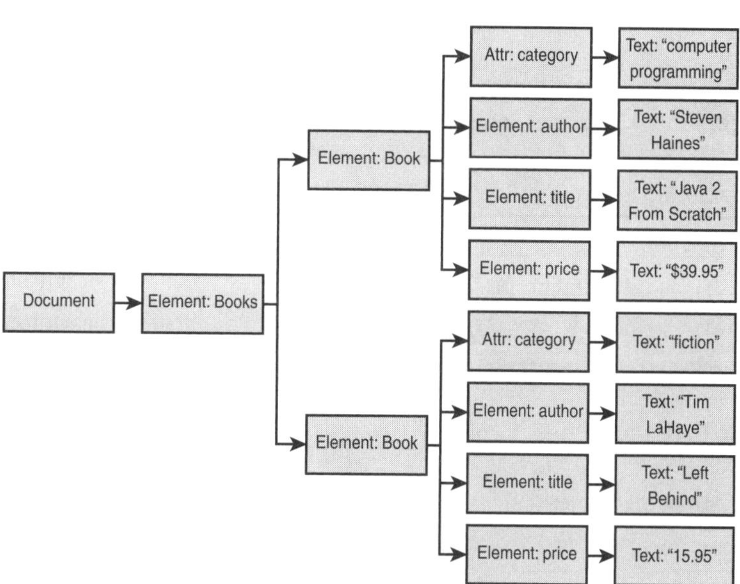

FIGURE 12.2
DOM tree diagram.

Observe from Figure 12.2 that the `<books>` root element contains two `<book>` elements. Each `<book>` element has an attribute node named `category` and has three elements: `<author>`, `<title>`, and `<price>`. Each element has a child text node that contains the element's value.

After a `Document` object is obtained from the `DocumentBuilder`, its root node can be accessed through the `DocumentBuilder`'s `getDocumentElement()` method; this method returns an instance of a class implementing the `org.w3c.com.Element` interface. Table 12.4 describes some of the more useful retrieval methods of the `Document` class.

TABLE 12.4 Document Retrieval Methods

Method	*Description*
`DocumentType getDoctype()`	The DTD (see `org.w3c.dom.DocumentType`) associated with this document
`Element getDocumentElement()`	This convenience attribute offers direct access to the child node that is the root element of the document
`NodeList getElementsByTagName(String tagname)`	Returns a `NodeList` of all the `Elements` with a given tag name in the order in which they are encountered in a preorder traversal of the `Document` tree

The `org.w3x.dom.Element` interface defines a set of methods for traversing the DOM tree. Table 12.5 shows some of the more useful `Element` retrieval methods.

TABLE 12.5 Element Retrieval Methods

Method	*Description*
`String getAttribute(String name)`	Retrieves an attribute value by name
`Attr getAttributeNode(String name)`	Retrieves an attribute node by name
`NodeList getElementsByTagName(String name)`	Returns a `NodeList` of all descendant `Elements` with a given tag name, in the order in which they are encountered in a preorder traversal of this `Element` tree
`String getTagName()`	The name of the element

The `Element` interface is derived from the `org.w3c.dom.Node` interface that offers the addition methods shown in Table 12.6.

TABLE 12.6 Element Retrieval Methods

Method	*Description*
`NamedNodeMap getAttributes()`	A `NamedNodeMap` containing the attributes of this node (if it is an `Element`) or null otherwise
`NodeList getChildNodes()`	A `NodeList` that contains all children of this node
`Node getFirstChild()`	The first child of this node
`Node getLastChild()`	The last child of this node
`String getNodeName()`	The name of this node, depending on its type
`short getNodeType()`	A code representing the type of the underlying object
`String getNodeValue()`	The value of this node, depending on its type

Together, the `Element` methods and the `Node` methods offer you a way to discover the node's type (element node, text node, attribute node, and so on—see the javadoc for the `org.w3c.dom.Node` interface), retrieve a list of child nodes, retrieve a list of attributes, retrieve the name of the node, and retrieve its value. Listing 12.6 shows a sample application that reads the same `book.xml` file into a DOM object and traverses it, using the methods just discussed.

LISTING 12.6 `DOMSample.java`

```
import javax.xml.parsers.DocumentBuilder;
import javax.xml.parsers.DocumentBuilderFactory;
import javax.xml.parsers.FactoryConfigurationError;
import javax.xml.parsers.ParserConfigurationException;

import org.xml.sax.SAXException;
import org.xml.sax.SAXParseException;

import java.io.FileInputStream;
import java.io.File;
import java.io.IOException;

import org.w3c.dom.Document;
import org.w3c.dom.Element;
import org.w3c.dom.NodeList;
import org.w3c.dom.Node;
import org.w3c.dom.DOMException;
```

LISTING 12.6 continued

```
public class DOMSample
{
    public static void main( String[] args )
    {
        try
        {
            File file = new File( "book.xml" );
            if( !file.exists() )
            {
                System.out.println( "Couldn't find file..." );
                return;
            }

           // Parse the document
            DocumentBuilderFactory factory =
➥ DocumentBuilderFactory.newInstance();
            DocumentBuilder builder = factory.newDocumentBuilder();
            Document document = builder.parse( file );

            // Walk the document
            Element root = document.getDocumentElement();
            System.out.println( "root=" + root.getTagName() );

            // List the children of <books>; a set of <book> elements
            NodeList list = root.getChildNodes();
            for( int i=0; i<list.getLength(); i++ )
            {
                Node node = list.item( i );
                if( node.getNodeType() == node.ELEMENT_NODE )
                {
              // Found a <book> element
              System.out.println( "Handling node: " + node.getNodeName() );
              Element element = ( Element )node;
              System.out.println( "\tCategory Attribute: " +
➥ element.getAttribute( "category" ) );

          // Get its children: <author>, <title>, <price>
              NodeList childList = element.getChildNodes();
               for( int j=0; j<childList.getLength(); j++ )
               {
                 // After one of these nodes is attained, the next
                     // step is to locate its text element
                  Node childNode = childList.item( j );
                 if( childNode.getNodeType() == childNode.ELEMENT_NODE )
                 {
                     NodeList childNodeList = childNode.getChildNodes();
                     for( int k=0; k<childNodeList.getLength(); k++ )
                     {
```

LISTING 12.6 continued

```
                            Node innerChildNode = childNodeList.item( k );
                            System.out.println( "\t\tNode=" +
➥ innerChildNode.getNodeValue() );
                        }
                    }
                }
            }
        }
    } catch( Exception e )
    {
        e.printStackTrace();
    }
  }
}
```

The following lines obtain a reference to the book.xml file and verify that it exists:

```
File file = new File( "book.xml" );
if( !file.exists() )
{
    System.out.println( "Couldn't find file..." );
    return;
}
```

These lines use the DocumentBuilderFactory to obtain a DocumentBuilder and then have the DocumentBuilder parse the XML file:

```
DocumentBuilderFactory factory =
    DocumentBuilderFactory.newInstance();
DocumentBuilder builder = factory.newDocumentBuilder();
Document document = builder.parse( file );
```

The return value is an instance of a class implementing the org.w3c.dom.Document interface.

The following line gets the root element of the document as an org.w3c.dom.Element; this is the <books> element:

```
Element root = document.getDocumentElement();
```

This line gets all the child nodes of the <books> element:

```
NodeList list = root.getChildNodes();
```

This list contains the <book> elements as well as a set of empty text elements (which you ignore). The result is an instance of a class that implements the org.w3c.dom.NodeList interface. This interface defines two methods, as shown in Table 12.7.

TABLE 12.7 NodeList Methods

Method	*Description*
`int getLength()`	The number of nodes in the list
`Node item(int index)`	Returns the *index*-th item in the collection

The following line takes the node from the child node list and determines whether it is an element node (in this case it is the <book> node):

```
if( node.getNodeType() == node.ELEMENT_NODE )
```

If it is and element node, then these lines extract the `category` attribute:

```
Element element = ( Element )node;
System.out.println( "\tCategory Attribute: " + {
{ic:ccc} element.getAttribute( "category" ) );
```

The following lines iterate over all the <book> node's children: <author>, <title>, and <price>:

```
// Get its children: <author>, <title>, <price>
    NodeList childList = element.getChildNodes();
     for( int j=0; j<childList.getLength(); j++ )
     {
       // After a child node is found,
       // the next stepis to find its
       // text element
        Node childNode = childList.item( j );
       if( childNode.getNodeType() == childNode.ELEMENT_NODE )
       {
           NodeList childNodeList = childNode.getChildNodes();
           for( int k=0; k<childNodeList.getLength(); k++ )
           {
              Node innerChildNode = childNodeList.item( k );
              System.out.println( "\t\tNode=" +
➥ innerChildNode.getNodeValue() );
           }
       }
     }
```

Remember that these nodes do not contain the values of the aforementioned tags, but they instead contain text nodes that contain the values, which is extracted here:

```
 Node childNode = childList.item( j );
if( childNode.getNodeType() == childNode.ELEMENT_NODE )
{
    NodeList childNodeList = childNode.getChildNodes();
    for( int k=0; k<childNodeList.getLength(); k++ )
    {
```

```
                        Node innerChildNode = childNodeList.item( k );
                        System.out.println( "\t\tNode=" +
➥ innerChildNode.getNodeValue() );
                    }
```

As you experiment with the DOM, you will notice that every node that has children also has a set of text nodes containing only white space. The reason for this is that unless the elements in the document do not have spaces between them, the DOM builds a node to hold them. The example carefully avoided printing blank text nodes because it understood the nature of the XML document. The results of this sample application should resemble the following:


```
root=books
Handling node: book
        Category Attribute: fiction
                Node=Left Behind
                Node=Tim Lahaye
                Node=14.95
Handling node: book
        Category Attribute: Computer Programming
                Node=Java 2 From Scratch
                Node=Steven Haines
                Node=39.95
```

Outputting the XML Tree

After all the work involved in parsing through the DOM tree, outputting the DOM tree to a stream is a very simple thing. The DOM implementation of the `Element` interface in the JAXP has overridden the `toString()` method to display the tree in XML form. Therefore, to display the entire DOM tree to the screen, you can pass the element to `System.out.println()`, as follows:

```
System.out.println( root );
```

Manipulating the XML Tree

After a DOM tree is constructed in memory, you may want to modify the tree by adding nodes, changing values, or deleting nodes.

Adding an Element to the XML Tree

When you add nodes to a DOM tree, recall the internal structure of the DOM tree (Figure 12.2). An element in the DOM tree is a node that is the composition of other nodes, including attribute nodes, text nodes, and other element nodes. Therefore, to add a new `<book>` to the `<books>` root element node, `<author>`, `<title>`, and `<price>` nodes must be created that contain text nodes with their respective values and then added to a new `<book>` node.

The `Document` class offers some helpful methods that create new nodes; see Table 12.8.

TABLE 12.8 Document Node Creation Methods

Method	*Description*
`Attr createAttribute(String name)`	Creates an `Attr` of the given name
`CDATASection createCDATASection(String data)`	Creates a `CDATASection` node whose value is the specified string
`Comment createComment(String data)`	Creates a `Comment` node given the specified string
`DocumentFragment createDocumentFragment()`	Creates an empty `DocumentFragment` object
`Element createElement(String tagName)`	Creates an element of the type specified
`EntityReference createEntityReference(String name)`	Creates an `EntityReference` object
`ProcessingInstruction createProcessingInstruction(String target, String data)`	Creates a `ProcessingInstruction` node, given the specified name and data strings
`Text createTextNode(String data)`	Creates a `Text` node, given the specified string

The `Element` and `Node` interfaces offer additional help in document creation through the methods described in Table 12.9.

TABLE 12.9 Element and Node Document Creation Methods

Method	*Description*
`Node appendChild(Node newChild)`	Adds the node `newChild` to the end of the list of children of this node
`void setAttribute(String name, String value)`	Adds a new attribute
`Attr setAttributeNode(Attr newAttr)`	Adds a new attribute node

Listing 12.7 shows a sample application that adds a new book to the DOM and then displays the new document to the standard output.

LISTING 12.7 DOMSample2.java

```
import javax.xml.parsers.DocumentBuilder;
import javax.xml.parsers.DocumentBuilderFactory;
import javax.xml.parsers.FactoryConfigurationError;
import javax.xml.parsers.ParserConfigurationException;

import org.xml.sax.SAXException;
import org.xml.sax.SAXParseException;

import java.io.FileInputStream;
import java.io.File;
import java.io.IOException;

import org.w3c.dom.Document;
import org.w3c.dom.Element;
import org.w3c.dom.NodeList;
import org.w3c.dom.Node;
import org.w3c.dom.DOMException;
import org.w3c.dom.Text;

public class DOMSample2
{
    public static void main( String[] args )
    {
        try
        {
            File file = new File( "book.xml" );
            if( !file.exists() )
            {
                System.out.println( "Couldn't find file..." );
                return;
            }

           // Parse the document
            DocumentBuilderFactory factory =
➥ DocumentBuilderFactory.newInstance();
            DocumentBuilder builder = factory.newDocumentBuilder();
            Document document = builder.parse( file );

            // Get the root of the document
            Element root = document.getDocumentElement();

        // Build a new book
        Element newAuthor = document.createElement( "author" );
        Text authorText = document.createTextNode( "Tim Lahaye" );
        newAuthor.appendChild( authorText );
        Element newTitle = document.createElement( "title" );
        Text titleText = document.createTextNode( "Desecration" );
        newTitle.appendChild( titleText );
        Element newPrice = document.createElement( "price" );
```

Listing 12.7 continued

```
        Text priceText = document.createTextNode( "19.95" );
        newPrice.appendChild( priceText );
        Element newBook = document.createElement( "book" );
        newBook.setAttribute( "category", "fiction" );
        newBook.appendChild( newAuthor );
        newBook.appendChild( newTitle );
        newBook.appendChild( newPrice );

        // Add the book to the root
        root.appendChild( newBook );

        // Display the document
        System.out.println( root );
         } catch( Exception e )
         {
             e.printStackTrace();
         }
    }
}
```

The output from Listing 12.7 should appear similar to the following:

```
<books>

    <book category="fiction">
        <title>Left Behind</title>
        <author>Tim Lahaye</author>
        <price>14.95</price>
    </book>

    <book category="Computer Programming">
        <title>Java 2 From Scratch</title>
        <author>Steven Haines</author>
        <price>39.95</price>
    </book>

<book category="fiction"><author>Tim
LaHaye</author><title>Desecration</title><price>19.95</price></book></books>
```

Notice that the XML content is correct, but why is the added node formatted so poorly? Remember all those aforementioned text nodes? Without those nodes this is how the output looks.

Removing an Element from the XML Tree

Removing an element from the DOM tree is a simple operation:

1. Obtain a reference to the node that is to be deleted.
2. Call the `Node` interface's `removeChild( Node node )` method from the parent node, passing it the child to delete.

   For example:

```
// Get document root into variable books
// Find the book we are looking for: oldBook
books.removeChild( oldBook );
```

Modifying an `Element` in the XML Tree

Modifying an `Element` involves retrieving the `Element` and calling one of the `Element` or `Node` document modification methods, see Table 12.10.

TABLE 12.10 `Element` and `Node` Document Modification Methods

Method	*Description*
`void removeAttribute(String name)`	Removes an attribute by name
`Attr removeAttributeNode(Attr oldAttr)`	Removes the specified attribute node
`void setAttribute(String name, String value)`	Adds a new attribute
`Attr setAttributeNode(Attr newAttr)`	Adds a new attribute node
`void setNodeValue(String nodeValue)`	Sets the value of a node

From the `Element` interface, there are methods to remove and set attributes, and the `Node` interface offers a method that sets or replaces the value of a node.

XSLT

The XML Style Sheet Language (XSL) Transformation (XSLT) API is used for transforming an XML document into any other form; the most common use of XSLT for Web development is for transforming XML documents into HTML for presentation in a Web browser.

The JAXP defines an XSLT Transformer that reads an XML document and applies to it the rules specified in a style sheet to produce a resultant document. Figure 12.3 shows this graphically.

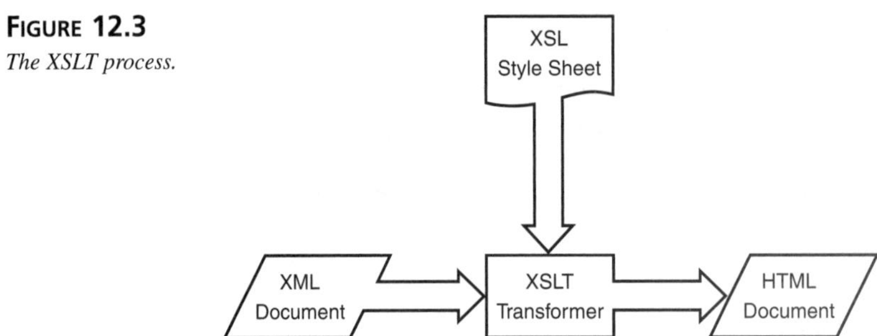

FIGURE 12.3
The XSLT process.

The JAXP provides XSLT support through the `javax.xml.transform` package. The `javax.xml.Transformer` class performs the actual transformation and, in a similar fashion to the way a SAX parser or a DOM document builder is obtained, a Transformer is obtained through a factory, or more specifically a `javax.xml.TransformerFactory`. An instance of the `TransformerFactory` class can be obtained by calling the `TransformerFactory`'s `newInstance()` method:

```
TransformerFactory factory = TransformerFactory.newInstance();
```

From the `TransformerFactory`, a `Transformer` can be obtained by calling one of its `newTransformer()` methods (see Table 12.11).

TABLE 12.11 `TransformerFactory newTransformer()` Methods

Method	*Description*
`Transformer newTransformer()`	Create a new `Transformer` object that performs a copy of the source to the result
`Transformer newTransformer(javax.xml.transform.Source source)`	Process the `Source` into a `Transformer` object

The latter of the `newTransformer()` methods is used when an XML document is transformed into another form. It accepts a style sheet in the form of a class implementing the `javax.xml.transform.Source` interface; three classes are provided as sources in the JAXP:

- `javax.xml.transform.DOMSource`
- `javax.xml.transform.SAXSource`
- `javax.xml.transform.StreamSource`

Together these source objects allow a `Transformer` to be built with an XML style sheet from an existing DOM document, a SAX parser, or a stream, which includes a file, a `java.io.InputStream`, or a `java.io.Reader`.

To use the `Transformer`, call its `transform()` method to transform a source document to a result document:

```
void transform( Source xmlSource, Result outputTarget )
```

The XML source document is another instance of a class implementing the `javax.xml.transform.Source` interface (which includes SAX, DOM, or Stream inputs), and the output target is an instance of a class implementing the `javax.xml.transform.Result` interface. Similar to the `Source` interface, the `Result` interface has three implementations:

- `javax.xml.transform.SAXResult`
- `javax.xml.transform.DOMResult`
- `javax.xml.transform.StreamResult`

The resultant transformation can be in the form of SAX events, a DOM document, or any `java.io.OutputStream`, `java.io.File`, or `java.io.Writer` variation.

The steps involved in using XSLT to transform an XML document to another form can be summarized as follows:

1. Get an instance of the `TransformerFactory` by calling its static `newInstance()` method.
2. Create a `javax.xml.transform.Source` reference to the stylesheet used in the transformation by building a `SAXSource`, `DOMSource`, or `StreamSource`.
3. Get a `Transformer` from the `TransformerFactory` by calling the XSL source's `newTransformer()` method.
4. Create a `javax.xml.transform.Source` reference to the source XML document.
5. Create a `javax.xml.transform.Result` reference to the output target.
6. Call the `Transformer`'s `transform()` method.

XSL Style Sheets

The Java code to apply a style sheet to an XML document to produce an output document is trivial; the real work is in defining the style sheet. Exhaustive references to XSL and the corresponding XPath specification can be found both in print (see *Professional XSLT*, by Wrox Press) and on the World Wide Web at `http://www.w3c.org`.

At its core, XSL files contain processing instructions that are organized by XPath expressions; the XSLT processor traverses the source XML document looking for matching XPath expressions defined in the style sheet. An XSL style sheet always starts by defining the XSL namespace and version:

```
<xsl:stylesheet version="1.0" xmlns:xsl="http://www.w3.org/1999/XSL/Transform">
```

This header defines the XSL style sheet language and fully qualifies the `xsl` prefix that will be used later in the document with the qualifying URL: `http://www.w3.org/1999/XSL/Transform`.

From this point forward, XSL-specific tags will be represented with the `xsl` prefix: `<xsl:command>`.

The most common XSL command is the `match` command; this is used to match patterns in the XML file. For example, the following statement matches the root of the XML file:

```
<xsl:template match="/">
  ...
</xsl:template>
```

The statements enclosed between the `<xsl:template>` start and end tags will be written to the result document. Another common tag is the `<xsl:apply-templates>` tag; this tag tells the XSLT transformer to execute the other template match expressions and place their output at the location of the `<xsl:apply-templates>` tag. For example:

```
<xsl:template match="/">
  <HTML>
    <BODY>
      <table>
        <xsl:apply-templates/>
      </table>
    </BODY>
  </HTML>
</xsl:template>

<xsl:template match="books/book">
  <tr><td>...</td></tr>
</xsl:template>
```

This example creates a new HTML document that contains a table when it sees the root of the XML document. Other patterns handle the contents of the table; in this case the pattern books/book looks for all `<book>` tags that appear inside of a `<books>` tag. The `"books/book"` handler creates table rows and table cells that presumably describe a book. For more information on XPath, XSL, and XSLT fundamentals, please refer to the World Wide Web Consortium Web Site at `http://www.w3c.org`.

Example

This example transforms the `book.xml` file that you have been working with throughout this chapter and generates an HTML representation of it. The HTML is purposely simple so as not to confuse the technical issues. Listing 12.8 shows the contents of the XSL file that contains the instructions for the transformation, and Listing 12.9 shows the Java code that performs the transformation.

LISTING 12.8 book.xsl

```
<xsl:stylesheet version="1.0" xmlns:xsl="http://www.w3.org/1999/XSL/Transform">

<xsl:template match="/">
  <HTML>
    <HEAD>
      <TITLE>My Books</TITLE>
    </HEAD>
    <BODY>
      <TABLE>
        <TR>
     <TH>Category</TH>
     <TH>Title</TH>
       <TH>Author</TH>
     <TH>Price</TH>
        </TR>
        <xsl:apply-templates select="books/book">
          <xsl:sort select="@category"/>
        </xsl:apply-templates>
      </TABLE>
    </BODY>
  </HTML>
</xsl:template>

<xsl:template match="books/book">
  <TR>
    <TD><xsl:value-of select="@category" /></TD>
    <TD><xsl:value-of select="./title" /></TD>
    <TD><xsl:value-of select="./author" /></TD>
    <TD><xsl:value-of select="./price" /></TD>
  </TR>
</xsl:template>

</xsl:stylesheet>
```

The first line defines the version of XSL style sheet that this style sheet is using, and it defines the `xsl` namespace.

The following lines handle the root element:

```
<xsl:template match="/">
  <HTML>
    <HEAD>
      <TITLE>My Books</TITLE>
    </HEAD>
    <BODY>
      <TABLE>
        <TR>
     <TH>Category</TH>
     <TH>Title</TH>
       <TH>Author</TH>
     <TH>Price</TH>
        </TR>
        <xsl:apply-templates select="books/book">
          <xsl:sort select="@category"/>
        </xsl:apply-templates>
      </TABLE>
    </BODY>
  </HTML>
</xsl:template>
```

This code creates an HTML document with a table, a table header, and then it delegates the contents of the table to the `books/book` element. The `select` clause in the `<xsl:apply-template>` tag tells the XSLT transformer what patterns to match; if it is omitted, then it matches all patterns. This line tells the transformer to sort the results by the `<book>` element's `category` attribute (the at sign [@] denotes category):

```
<xsl:sort select="@category"/>
```

The following lines handle the `<book>` nodes by creating a table record and four table rows:

```
<xsl:template match="books/book">
  <TR>
    <TD><xsl:value-of select="@category" /></TD>
    <TD><xsl:value-of select="./title" /></TD>
    <TD><xsl:value-of select="./author" /></TD>
    <TD><xsl:value-of select="./price" /></TD>
  </TR>
</xsl:template>
```

The code obtains the value of the `category` attribute by using the `<xsl:value-of>` tag and passing its `select` clause the value `"@category"` (again the @ means *attribute*). Similarly, it uses the `<xsl:value-of>` tag, passing its select clause of the child nodes to get the title, author, and price.

LISTING 12.9 XSLTTest.java

```
import javax.xml.transform.*;
import javax.xml.transform.stream.*;
import java.io.File;

public class XSLTTest
{
    public static void main( String[] args )
    {
        try
        {
            StreamSource source = new StreamSource( new File( "book.xml" ) );
            StreamResult result = new StreamResult( System.out );
            TransformerFactory factory = TransformerFactory.newInstance();
            Transformer transformer = factory.newTransformer(
➥ new StreamSource( new File( "books.xsl" ) ) );
            transformer.transform( source, result );
        }
        catch( Exception e )
        {
            e.printStackTrace();
        }
    }
}
```


The following line creates a `StreamSource` to the file `book.xml`:

```
StreamSource source = new StreamSource( new File( "book.xml" ) );
```

The next line creates a `StreamResult` to the standard output; this application transforms the `book.xml` file to the screen:

```
StreamResult result = new StreamResult( System.out );
```

The next two lines obtain a new instance of the `TransformerFactory` and use it to create a new `Transformer` for the `books.xsl` file (as a `StreamSource`):

```
TransformerFactory factory = TransformerFactory.newInstance();
Transformer transformer = factory.newTransformer(
➥ new StreamSource( new File( "books.xsl" ) ) );
```

Finally, the following line transforms the source document to the result (screen):

```
transformer.transform( source, result );
```

The output should look something like the following:

```
<HTML>
<HEAD>
<META http-equiv="Content-Type" content="text/html; charset=UTF-8">
```

```
<TITLE>My Books</TITLE>
</HEAD>
<BODY>
<TABLE>
<TR>
<TH>Category</TH><TH>Title</TH><TH>Author</TH><TH>Price</TH>
</TR>
<TR>
<TD>Computer Programming</TD>
<TD>Java 2 From Scratch</TD>
<TD>Steven Haines</TD><TD>39.95</TD>
</TR>
<TR>
<TD>fiction</TD><TD>Left Behind</TD><TD>Tim Lahaye</TD><TD>14.95</TD>
</TR>
</TABLE>
</BODY>
</HTML>
```

JAXP and Web Services

Now that you understand how to use the SAX parser to parse an XML document, how to use the DOM to read an XML document into a memory tree, and how to use XSLT to transform an XML document into another document format, how can you use this knowledge in developing Web services?

The answer to this question is that all the interactions between Web services and their clients are in the form of an XML document. For example, the Web Services Description Language (WSDL) file describes all the capabilities of a Web service; see Listing 12.10 for a sample WSDL file that describes the Stock Quote Web service.

LISTING 12.10 Stock Quote WSDL File

```
<?xml version="1.0"?>
  <definitions name="StockQuote"
               targetNamespace="http://sample.com/stockquote.wsdl"
               xmlns:tns="http://sample.com/stockquote.wsdl"
               xmlns:xsd="http://www.w3.org/2000/10/XMLSchema"
               xmlns:xsd1="http://sample.com/stockquote.xsd"
               xmlns:soap="http://schemas.xmlsoap.org/wsdl/soap/"
               xmlns="http://schemas.xmlsoap.org/wsdl/">
      <message name="GetStockPriceInput">
          <part name="symbol" element="xsd:string"/>
      </message>
      <message name="GetStockPriceOutput">
          <part name="result" type="xsd:float"/>
      </message>
```

LISTING 12.10 continued

```
    <portType name="StockQuotePortType">
        <operation name="GetLastStockQuote">
           <input message="tns:GetStockPriceInput"/>
           <output message="tns:GetStockPriceOutput"/>
        </operation>
    </portType>
    <binding name="StockQuoteSoapBinding" type="tns:StockQuotePortType">
        <soap:binding style="rpc"
                      transport="http://schemas.xmlsoap.org/soap/http"/>
        <operation name="GetLastStockQuote">
           <soap:operation soapAction="http://sample.com/GetLastStockQuote"/>
           <input>
             <soap:body use="encoded"
                 namespace="http://sample.com/stockquote"
             encodingStyle="http://schemas.xmlsoap.org/soap/encoding/"/>
           </input>
           <output>
           <soap:body use="encoded" namespace="http://sample.com/stockquote"
            encodingStyle="http://schemas.xmlsoap.org/soap/encoding/"/>
           </output>
        </operation>>
    </binding>
    <service name="StockQuoteService">
        <documentation>My first service</documentation>
        <port name="StockQuotePort" binding="tns:StockQuoteSoapBinding">
           <soap:address location="http://sample.com/stockquote"/>
        </port>
    </service>
</definitions>
```

From what you have learned in this chapter, you should be able to traverse this XML file and extract any piece of information you want. For example, the service name, the port binding (which will lead you to the operations), and the address of the service. Most Web services platforms provide an easy-to-use abstraction of the details contained in the WSDL file, but if you ever need to delve deeper, the SAX and DOM will help you greatly.

Summary

This chapter discussed the Java API for XML Parsing (JAXP). There are two models for reading XML documents: the Simple API for XML (SAX) parser and the Document Object Model (DOM). The SAX parser is event-driven, whereas the DOM maintains an in-memory tree representation of the XML document. Each has its advantages, depending on the application being developed. Finally, this chapter discussed the XML

Stylesheet Language Transformation (XSLT) API that is used for transforming an XML document into any form; in Web applications the most dominant use for XSLT is the transformation of XML data into an HTML presentation.

The next chapter takes what you have learned and wraps it up with another Java XML technology: Java API for XML Binding (JAXB).

CHAPTER 13

JAXB

By Steve Haines

IN THIS CHAPTER

Java provides an API for reading, writing, and modifying XML documents, known as the Java API for XML Parsing (JAXP). It is effective, but it is not necessarily very intuitive to use. When you know absolutely the rules or the Data Type Definition (DTD) that define a specific category of XML documents, you can leverage that information to greatly simplify your development efforts. The Java API for XML Binding (JAXB) provides a two-way mapping between XML documents and Java objects.

The JAXB takes a DTD file and a binding schema (something you write that defines variable types and how classes are defined) and generates a set of classes that can read from, write to, and modify XML documents that adhere to that DTD. After you have this set of classes and a knowledge of the XML file, they are intuitive to use; rather than blindly traversing a tree in a DOM looking for a specific node name, you can go directly to the node you are looking for by name!

Prerequisites

Download the JAXB implementation from Sun's web site at:

```
http://java.sun.com/xml/jaxb
```

After you decompress the files in the JAXB implementation archive, you will find the following two JAR files in the lib folder:

```
jaxb-rt-{version}.jar
jaxb-xjc-{version}.jar
```

When you use the JAXB to generate classes, you need to have the `xjc` JAR file in your `CLASSPATH`, and when you use the classes that the JAXB generates for you, you need the `rt` JAR file in your `CLASSPATH`.

JAXB Terminology

Before you can jump into using JAXB, there are a few terms that you must understand:

- *Marshalling* is the act of packaging your XML document and sending it to some destination; the Java object representing the XML document can marshal the contents of the XML document to some destination, such as a file on the file system, for example.
- *Unmarshalling* is the act of building an XML Java object from a data source; the data source contains a representation of an XML document (such as an XML document stored on the file system, for example), and unmarshalling is the process of reading that XML document from the data source and constructing its Java representation.

- *Validating* is the act of determining whether an XML document properly adheres to the DTD that the JAXB Java object represents; an XML document is said to be well-formed if it properly adheres to the DTD. This is necessary because the classes are built only to support that DTD.

Binding an XML Schema to a Class

Using the `xjc` JAR file in the JAXB `lib` folder and passing it a DTD and a binding schema performs binding. The `xjc` JAR file can be used as follows:

```
java -jar jaxb-xjc-{version}.jar books.dtd books.xjs
```

The two inputs to the `xjc` JAR file are the DTD and the binding schema (commonly with the extension `xjs`). The DTD used for this chapter is shown in Listing 13.1.

LISTING 13.1 `books.dtd`

```
<!ELEMENT books (book*) >
<!ELEMENT book (title, author, price) >
<!ATTLIST book category CDATA #REQUIRED >
<!ELEMENT title (#PCDATA) >
<!ELEMENT author (#PCDATA) >
<!ELEMENT price (#PCDATA) >
```

This DTD defines a root `<books>` node that has zero or more `<book>` nodes; a sample XML document is shown in Listing 13.2.

LISTING 13.2 `books.xml`

```
<?xml version="1.0"?>
<!DOCTYPE books SYSTEM "Books.dtd">
<books>
  <book category="computer-programming">
    <author>Steven Haines</author>
    <title>Java 2 From Scratch</title>
    <price>39.95</price>
  </book>
  <book category="fiction">
    <author>Tim LaHaye</author>
    <title>Left Behind</title>
  </book>
</books>
```

The binding schema defines what classes to build and what data types to assign to what variables within each class. In its simplest form, an XJS file for the `books.dtd` file simply needs to define the root element; see Listing 13.3.

LISTING 13.3 books.xjs

```
<?xml version="1.0" encoding="ISO-8859-1" ?>
<xml-java-binding-schema version="1.0ea">
    <element name="books" type="class" root="true" />
</xml-java-binding-schema>
```

Line 2 defines the main node of the binding schema `<xml-java-binding-schema>`; all the rules in the binding schema are defined as children of this node. Line 3 defines the root element of the XML document to be `<books>`.

XJC in Action

Launching the XJC JAR against the `books.dtd` file with the aforementioned binding schema generates two files:

- `Books.java`
- `Book.java`

The `Books` class contains a `java.util.List` object containing `Book` instances and a set of methods for managing the list; see Table 13.1.

TABLE 13.1 `Books.java` Public Methods

Method	*Description*
`List getBook()`	Returns the list of `Book` objects.
`void deleteBook()`	Deletes the list of `Book` objects; note that this method does not delete one book from the list, but the entire list.
`void emptyBook()`	Empties out the contents of the list of `Book` instances.
`void validateThis()`	Placeholder used to validate the contents of this class instance.
`void validate(javax.xml.bind.Validator v)`	Uses the specified `Validator` to validate each `Book` in the `List` of `Book` instances.
`void marshal(javax.xml.bind.Marshaller m)`	Uses the specified `Marshaller` to marshal each `Book` in the `List` of `Book` instances.
`void unmarshal(javax.xml.bind.Unmarshaller u)`	Uses the specified `Unmarshaller` to unmarshal each `Book` in the `List` of `Book` instances.

TABLE 13.1 continued

Method	*Description*
`static Books unmarshal(java.io. InputStream in)`	Unmarshals, or builds a Java object representation of an XML document, from the specified `InputStream`.
`static Books unmarshal(javax.xml.marshal. XMLScanner xs)`	Unmarshals, or builds a Java object representation of an XML document, from the specified `XMLScanner`.
`static Books unmarshal(javax.xml.marshal. XMLScanner xs, javax.xml.bind.Dispatcher d)`	Unmarshals, or builds a Java object representation of an XML document, from the specified `XMLScanner` and uses the specified `Dispatcher` to build an element to class name map.
`boolean equals(Object ob)`	Denotes whether a `Books` element is equal to another object.
`int hashCode()`	Generates a hash code for use in collection classes.
`String toString()`	Builds a string representation of the `Books` object.
`static Dispatcher newDispatcher()`	Creates a new dispatcher.

The `Book` class maintains four member variables, one for each of its sub-elements and one for its attribute. Each member is defined as a `String`; the binding schema has to be modified to change a data type. Table 13.2 shows the methods defined in the `Book` class.

TABLE 13.2 `Book.java` Methods

Method	*Description*
`String getCategory()`	Returns the value of the `category` attribute.
`void setCategory(String _Category)`	Sets the value of the `category` attribute.
`String getTitle()`	Returns the value of the `title` sub-element.
`void setTitle(String _Title)`	Sets the value of the `title` sub-element.
`String getAuthor()`	Returns the value of the `author` sub-element.

TABLE 13.2 continued

Method	*Description*
`void setAuthor(String _Author)`	Sets the value of the `author` sub-element.
`String getPrice()`	Returns the value of the `price` sub-element.
`void setPrice(String _Price)`	Sets the value of the `price` sub-element.
`void validateThis()`	Validates the `Book` object; checks whether the `Book` object has valid values for all its sub-elements and attributes. Will throw either a `MissingAttributeException` or a `MissingContentException` if anything is missing.
`void validate(Validator v)`	Placeholder for validation code.
`void marshal(Marshaller m)`	Builds an XML document representing the `<book>` element using the specified marshaller.
`void unmarshal(Unmarshaller u)`	Builds the Java `Book` object from the XML document provided by the specified unmarshaller.
`static Book unmarshal(InputStream in)`	Builds the Java `Book` object from the XML document provided by the specified `InputStream`.
`static Book unmarshal(XMLScanner xs)`	Builds the Java `Book` object from the XML document provided by the specified `XMLScanner`.
`static Book unmarshal(XMLScanner xs, Dispatcher d)`	Builds the Java `Book` object from the XML document provided by the specified `XMLScanner` and `Dispatcher`.
`boolean equals(Object ob)`	Compares the value of a `Book` object to this book; all attributes and sub-elements must match.
`int hashCode()`	Computes a hash value for this `Book` for its use in collection classes.
`static Dispatcher newDispatcher()`	Constructs a new `Dispatcher` that understands the `Book` and `Books` classes.

The first few methods are the standard get/set methods that you would expect to find in any Java class. The `validateThis()` method validates that all the member variables in the `Book` class (attributes and sub-elements) are not null. Listing 13.4 shows the code for the `validateThis()` method; note that the variables starting with an underscore (_) are member variables in the `Book` class.

LISTING 13.4 Book Class's `validateThis()` Method

```
public void validateThis() throws LocalValidationException
{
    if (_Category == null) {
        throw new MissingAttributeException("category");
    }
    if (_Title == null) {
        throw new MissingContentException("title");
    }
    if (_Author == null) {
        throw new MissingContentException("author");
    }
    if (_Price == null) {
        throw new MissingContentException("price");
    }
}
```


Marshalling

The `marshal()` method builds an XML document node representing this `Book` by using an `javax.xml.marshal.XMLWriter` obtained from the specified marshaller. The `XMLWriter` class provides a very simple and intuitive mechanism for building an XML node. Table 13.3 shows the constructors and methods provided by the `XMLWriter` class.

TABLE 13.3 `XMLWriter` Methods

Method	*Description*
`XMLWriter(OutputStream out)`	Creates a new writer that uses the UTF-8 encoding to write to the given byte-output stream.
`XMLWriter(OutputStream out, String enc)`	Creates a new writer that uses the given encoding to write to the given byte-output stream.
`XMLWriter(OutputStream out, String enc, boolean declare)`	Creates a new writer that uses the given encoding to write to the given byte-output stream.

TABLE 13.3 continued

Method	*Description*
`void attribute(String name, String value)`	Writes an attribute for the current element.
`void attributeName(String name)`	Writes an attribute name for the current element.
`void attributeValue(String value)`	Writes a value for the current attribute.
`void attributeValueToken(String token)`	Writes one token of the current attribute's value.
`void chars(String chars)`	Writes some character data.
`void close()`	Flushes the writer and closes the underlying byte-output stream.
`void doctype(String root, String dtd)`	Writes a `DOCTYPE` declaration.
`void end(String name)`	Writes an end tag for the named element.
`void flush()`	Flushes the writer.
`void leaf(String name)`	Writes an empty leaf element.
`void leaf(String name, String chars)`	Writes a leaf element with the given character content.
`void setQuote(char quote)`	Sets the quote character to be used by this writer when writing attribute values.
`void start(String name)`	Writes a start tag for the named element.

An instance of the `XMLWriter` class can be created from a `java.io.OutputStream` or any variation thereof, (such as a `java.io.FileOutputStream`, for example), and can optionally specify an encoding scheme and output the XML declaration header (if this is the root element). Listing 13.5 shows how the `marshal()` method makes use of the `XMLWriter` class to build a `Book` node.

LISTING 13.5 Book Class's `marshal()` Method

```
public void marshal(Marshaller m)
    throws IOException
{
    XMLWriter w = m.writer();
    w.start("book");
    w.attribute("category", _Category.toString());
```

LISTING 13.5 continued

```
    w.leaf("title", _Title.toString());
    w.leaf("author", _Author.toString());
    w.leaf("price", _Price.toString());
    w.end("book");
}
```

The `start()`method call starts the `book` node. The attribute() method call sets the `category` attribute to the value of the `category` member variable. The leaf() method calls create the `title`, `author`, and `price` sub-elements from the values of their respective member variables. Finally, line 10 ends the `book` node.

Unmarshalling

The `unmarshal()` methods`()` use the `javax.xml.marshal.XMLScanner` class to build a `Book` node from an XML document. The `XMLScanner` class is not based off a SAX parser, but instead iterates over the contents of the XML document one attribute and one subelement at a time. An `XMLScanner` can be built from a DOM tree or directly from a `java.util.InputStream`. The `XMLScanner` can be in one of several states at any given time; the `XMLScanner` states are shown in Table 13.4.

TABLE 13.4 `XMLScanner` States

State	*Description*
`Start`	The scanner is positioned at a start tag. This state may be followed by the `AttributeName`, `Chars`, `Start`, or `End` states. An empty tag—that is, a tag of the form `<foo/>`—yields the `Start` state followed by the `End` state, possibly with some intervening attribute states.
`AttributeName`	The scanner is positioned at an attribute name. This state may be followed by only the `AttributeValue` state. This state is entered exactly once for each attribute that is read. Attributes are read in the order in which they appear in the input document.
`AttributeValue`	The scanner is positioned at an attribute value. This state may be followed by the `AttributeName`, `Chars`, `Start`, or `End` states. If the `tokenizeAttributeValue` method is invoked, then this state may also be followed by the `AttributeValueToken` state.

13 JAXB

TABLE 13.4 continued

State	*Description*
`AttributeValueToken`	The scanner is positioned at one of the tokens of a tokenized attribute value. This state may be followed by the `AttributeValueToken`, `AttributeName`, `Chars`, `Start`, or `End` states.
`Chars`	The scanner is positioned at some character content. This state may be followed by the `Start` or `End` states.
`End`	The scanner is positioned at an end tag. This state may be followed by the `Chars`, `Start`, `End`, or `EndOfDocument` states.
`EndOfDocument`	The scanner has reached the end of the input document, at which point it closes itself. The state of the scanner does not change after it reaches this state.

XML Scanner

The `XMLScanner` class operates off a set of `at` methods to determine where the scanner is positioned, and a set of `take` methods to take the content of the given element. Table 13.5 shows the methods defined in the `XMLScanner` class.

TABLE 13.5 `XMLScanner` Methods

Method	*Description*
`boolean atAttribute()`	Tests whether the scanner is positioned at an attribute name.
`boolean atAttributeValue()`	Tests whether the scanner is positioned at an attribute value.
`boolean atAttributeValueToken()`	Tests whether the scanner is positioned at an attribute-value token.
`boolean atChars(int whitespace)`	Tests whether the scanner is positioned at some character data.
`boolean atEnd()`	Skips whitespace, if any, and then tests whether the scanner is positioned at an end tag.
`boolean atEnd(String name)`	Skips whitespace, if any, and then tests whether the scanner is positioned at an end tag with the given name.

TABLE 13.5 continued

Method	*Description*
`boolean atEndOfDocument()`	Skips whitespace, if any, and then tests whether the scanner has reached the end of the input document.
`boolean atStart()`	Skips whitespace, if any, and then tests whether the scanner is positioned at a start tag.
`boolean atStart(String name)`	Skips whitespace, if any, and then tests whether the scanner is positioned at a start tag with the given name.
`void close()`	Closes this scanner.
`static XMLScanner open(org.w3c.dom. Document doc)`	Creates a new scanner that scans the given DOM tree.
`static XMLScanner open(InputStream in)`	Creates a new scanner that reads an XML document from the given input stream.
`String peekStart()`	Skips whitespace, if any, and then reads the current start tag.
`ScanPosition position()`	Returns a new scan-position object reporting the scanner's current position.
`String takeAttributeName()`	Reads the current attribute name and then advances the scanner to the next state.
`String takeAttributeValue()`	Reads the current attribute value, collapsing whitespace, and then advances the scanner to the next state.
`String takeAttributeValue(int whitespace)`	Reads the current attribute value and then advances the scanner to the next state.
`String takeAttributeValueToken()`	Reads the current attribute-value token and then advances the scanner to the next state.
`String takeChars(int whitespace)`	Reads the current character data and then advances the scanner to the next state.
`void takeEmpty(String name)`	Takes an empty tag.

TABLE 13.5 continued

Method	*Description*
`String takeEnd()`	Skips whitespace, if any, reads the current end tag, and then advances the scanner to the next state.
`void takeEnd(String name)`	Skips whitespace, if any, checks that the current end tag's name is equal to the given name, and then advances the scanner to the next state.
`void takeEndOfDocument()`	Skips whitespace, if any, and then checks that the scanner has reached the end of the input document.
`String takeLeaf(String name, int whitespace)`	Takes a simple leaf element.
`String takeStart()`	Skips whitespace, if any, reads the current start tag, and then advances the scanner to the next state.
`void takeStart(String name)`	Skips whitespace, if any, checks that the current start tag's name is equal to the given name, and then advances the scanner to the next state.
`void tokenizeAttributeValue()`	Reads the current attribute's value as a sequence of non-whitespace tokens, returning them in succeeding `AttributeValueToken` states.

Listing 13.6 shows a good example of how to use the `XMLScanner` class as the `Book` class's `unmarshal()` method uses it.

LISTING 13.6 `Book` Class's `unmarshal()` Method

```
public void unmarshal(Unmarshaller u)
    throws UnmarshalException
{
    XMLScanner xs = u.scanner();
    Validator v = u.validator();
    xs.takeStart("book");
    while (xs.atAttribute()) {
        String an = xs.takeAttributeName();
        if (an.equals("category")) {
            if (_Category!= null) {
                throw new DuplicateAttributeException(an);
            }
```

LISTING 13.6 continued

```
        _Category = xs.takeAttributeValue();
        continue;
    }
    throw new InvalidAttributeException(an);
}
if (xs.atStart("title")) {
    xs.takeStart("title");
    String s;
    if (xs.atChars(XMLScanner.WS_COLLAPSE)) {
        s = xs.takeChars(XMLScanner.WS_COLLAPSE);
    } else {
        s = "";
    }
    try {
        _Title = String.valueOf(s);
    } catch (Exception x) {
        throw new ConversionException("title", x);
    }
    xs.takeEnd("title");
}
if (xs.atStart("author")) {
    xs.takeStart("author");
    String s;
    if (xs.atChars(XMLScanner.WS_COLLAPSE)) {
        s = xs.takeChars(XMLScanner.WS_COLLAPSE);
    } else {
        s = "";
    }
    try {
        _Author = String.valueOf(s);
    } catch (Exception x) {
        throw new ConversionException("author", x);
    }
    xs.takeEnd("author");
}
if (xs.atStart("price")) {
    xs.takeStart("price");
    String s;
    if (xs.atChars(XMLScanner.WS_COLLAPSE)) {
        s = xs.takeChars(XMLScanner.WS_COLLAPSE);
    } else {
        s = "";
    }
    try {
        _Price = String.valueOf(s);
    } catch (Exception x) {
        throw new ConversionException("price", x);
    }
```

LISTING 13.6 continued

```
        xs.takeEnd("price");
    }
    xs.takeEnd("book");
}
```

The unmarshalmethod starts the XMLScanner by positioning it at the <book> tag.

It then iterates through all the attributes at the <book> node by calling the atAttribute() method to step through the attributes. The method looks for the category attribute and saves it to the _Category member variable by calling the takeAttributeValue() method.

It then calls the atStart() method to advance the scanner to the <title> node, uses the takeChars() method to read in the characters in the <title> node, stores the value in the _Title member variable, and then uses the atEnd() method to advance the scanner to the end of the <title> node.

Similar actions are performed for the <author> and <price> nodes.

Finally, the unmarshal() method calls the takeEnd() method to position the scanner at the end of the <book> node.

Using JAXB-Built Classes

As soon as the JAXB has built classes that represent an XML document, it is a simple matter to use them. The operations that make XML processing complete include:

- Reading an XML document
- Modifying an XML document (adding, removing, and updating nodes)
- Writing an XML document

Reading an XML Document

Recall from earlier in the chapter that the process of building a Java object representation of an XML document in JAXB terms is referred to as *unmarshalling*. Therefore, the process for reading an XML document that adheres to the chosen DTD is to call the Java class representing the root node's unmarshal() method.

In the example, the root node is <books> and is represented by the Books class. The Books class has four unmarshal() variations:

```
void unmarshal(Unmarshaller u)
static Books unmarshal(InputStream in)
static Books unmarshal(XMLScanner xs)
static Books unmarshal(XMLScanner xs, Dispatcher d)
```

Developing from outside the JAXB classes, the simplest way to build the `Books` object is to obtain a `java.io.InputStream` reference to the XML document and use that `unmarshal()` method:

```
File file = new File( "book.xml" );
FileInputStream fis = new FileInputStream( file );
Books books = Books.unmarshal( fis );
fis.close();
```

At this point you have a `Books` instance that represents the `book.xml` file.

Modifying an XML Document

The second aspect of working with XML documents is the modification of the document: adding nodes, removing nodes, and updating existing nodes. The `Books` class provides several methods to help you out:

- `List getBook()`. Return a list of `Book` instances
- `void deleteBook()`. Delete the entire list of `Book` instances
- `void emptyBook()`. Empty out the entire list of `Book` instances

Therefore, modifying `Book` instances is a rather trivial task: obtain the `java.util.List` of `Book` instances and modify it directly. Recall that the `List` class has methods to add, remove, and retrieve individual elements.

The following code adds a new `Book` node to the `Books` node:

```
// Construct a new book
Book newBook = new Book();
newBook.setAuthor( "Tim Lahaye" );
newBook.setTitle( "Desecration" );
newBook.setCategory( "Fiction" );
newBook.setPrice( "19.95" );

// Add the book to the list
List bookList = books.getBook();
booklist.add( newBook );
```

The underlying JAXB infrastructure handles all the work of building the XML document for you.

To remove a `Book`:

```
// Remove the first <book>
List bookList = books.getBook();
bookList.remove( 0 );
```

```
// Remove all books by Steven Haines (why would we do that!?)
for( Iterator i = bookList.iterator; i.hasNext(); ) {
  Book book = ( Book )i.next();
  if( book.getAuthor().equals( "Steven Haines" ) ) {
    bookList.remove( book );
  }
}
```

Finally, to modify a Book, recall that all Java local variables are references to one memory space unless an explicit copy is performed. Therefore, after a reference is obtained, modifications to it affect the original:

```
// Change all "Steven Haines" authors to "Steven E. Haines"
List bookList = books.getBook();
for( Iterator i = bookList.iterator; i.hasNext(); ) {
  Book book = ( Book )i.next();
  if( book.getAuthor().equals( "Steven Haines" ) ) {
    // Update this <book> node's <author> sub-element
    book.setAuthor( "Steven E. Haines" );
  }
}
```

Writing an XML Document

Recall that the process of outputting an XML document in JAXB terms is referred to as *marshalling*. To output a root node, all that is required is to call the Java class's (in this case Books) marshal() method, passing it one of the following:

```
javax.xml.marshal.Marshaller
java.io.OutputStream
javax.xml.marshal.XMLWriter
```

The latter two are obtained from the Books class's parent class: javax.xml.bind.MarshallableRootElement. The former is provided in the Books class implementation, but presents a bit of a problem: A Marshaller cannot be constructed (its constructors are disabled); it must be obtained from within the JAXB infrastructure.

To write an XML document to any destination, an OutputStream can be constructed to that destination and passed directly to the marshal() method or to the marshal() method through the XMLWriter construct (this allows the specification of encoding and XML header outputting). For example:

```
// Output the XML document directly to the screen
books.marshal( System.out );

// Output the XML document to a file
FileOutputStream fos = new FileOutputStream( "books.xml" );
XMLWriter writer = new XMLWriter( fos, "US-ASCII", true );
books.marshal( writer );
```

Example

This example opens the `book.xml` file, displays its contents to the screen, adds a new `<book>` node, displays the updated contents to the screen, and then outputs the XML document to the screen. Listing 13.7 shows the listing for the `TestClient.java` file.

LISTING 13.7 TestClient.java

```
import java.io.*;
import java.util.*;
import javax.xml.bind.*;
import javax.xml.marshal.*;

public class TestClient
{
    public static void showBooks( List bookList )
    {
        for( Iterator i=bookList.iterator(); i.hasNext(); )
        {
            Book book = ( Book )i.next();
            System.out.println( "Book: " +
                                book.getTitle() + ", " +
                                book.getAuthor() + ", " +
                                book.getPrice() + ", " +
                                book.getCategory() );
        }
    }

    public static void main( String[] args )
    {
        try
        {
            // Open the book.xml file
            File file = new File( "book.xml" );
            if( !file.exists() )
            {
                System.out.println( "Couldn't find file..." );
                return;
            }
            FileInputStream fis = new FileInputStream( file );
            Books books = Books.unmarshal( fis );
            fis.close();

            // Show the initial contents of the file
            showBooks( books.getBook() );

            // Add a Book
            System.out.println( "\nAdding a book" );
            Book book = new Book();
            book.setTitle( "Web Services Unleashed" );
```

LISTING 13.7 continued

```
            book.setAuthor( "Buncha Guys..." );
            book.setPrice( "49.95" );
            book.setCategory( "Computer Programming" );
            books.getBook().add( book );

            // Show the updated contents of the XML document
            showBooks( books.getBook() );

            // Display the complete document to the screen
            XMLWriter writer = new XMLWriter( System.out, "US-ASCII", true );
            books.validate();
            books.marshal( writer );
        }
        catch( Exception e )
        {
            e.printStackTrace();
        }
    }
}
```

The `main()` method starts by verifying that the `book.xml` file exists and opens a `java.io.FileInputStream` to it. It then reads the file into the `Books` Java object by calling the `Books` class's static `unmarshal()` method and passing it the `FileInputStream`.

The `showBooks()` helper method iterates over all the `Book` instances in a `java.util.List` and displays each Book's values by calling the various `Book` class `get` methods.

The `main()` method continues by displaying the initial contents of the XML document.

It next creates a new `Book` instance and adds it to the `Books` instance's `List` of `Book` elements. Note that all this is facilitated through obtaining the `Books` instance's `Book List` (`getBook()`) and modifying that `List` directly.

Finally, it displays the XML document to the standard output stream. Note that no matter what marshalling mechanism you choose (either to an `OutputStream` or to an `XMLWriter`), the marshalling process requires that the content be validated. The class does not want to try to marshal its contents to any destination unless it is sure that the contents are valid and do not violate any of the rules defined in the DTD.

Advanced Binding Schemas

The previous example demonstrated how easy JAXB can be to use, but in turn it hid all the details of the binding scheme. To become proficient in using JAXB, you must understand how binding schemes work and what default values are used when you do not specify them explicitly.

The sample binding scheme used previously in the chapter is as follows:

```
<?xml version="1.0" encoding="ISO-8859-1" ?>
<xml-java-binding-schema version="1.0ea">
    <element name="books" type="class" root="true" />
</xml-java-binding-schema>
```

It defines a single element, <books>, as the root element. The JAXB code generator then looks at the DTD:

```
<!ELEMENT books (book*) >
<!ELEMENT book (title, author, price) >
<!ATTLIST book category CDATA #REQUIRED >
<!ELEMENT title (#PCDATA) >
<!ELEMENT author (#PCDATA) >
<!ELEMENT price (#PCDATA) >
```

It can see that <books> has a collection (asterisk) of <book> elements. Because the <book> element has attributes and sub-elements, it decides to create a class for it; if an element has one or more attributes or one or more sub-elements, the generator creates a class for it. When it looks at the title, author, and price elements, they contain only character data, so it creates `String` fields in the <book> element for them. For all elements that contain only character data, the generator treats them as fields of the parent element; for all elements that contain anything other than character data—for example, attributes or sub-elements—it treats them as classes.

The <books> element has the root attribute set to true, denoting that it is the root of the XML document, causing the generator to derive that class from `javax.xml.bind.MarshallableRootElement`. The <book> element is not a root, so it is derived from `javax.xml.bind.MarshallableElement`.

The complete expanded version of the binding scheme displaying the default values for this example is shown in Listing 13.8.

LISTING 13.8 books2.xjs—Explicit Binding Scheme

```
<?xml version="1.0" encoding="ISO-8859-1" ?>
<xml-java-binding-schema version="1.0ea">
    <element name="books" type="class" root="true">
            <content>
                    <element-ref name="book"/>
            </content>
    </element>
    <element name="book" type="class">
            <attribute name="category"/>
             <content>
                    <element-ref name="author"/>
                    <element-ref name="title"/>
```

13

JAXB

LISTING 13.8 continued

```
                <element-ref name="price"/>
            </content>
    </element>
    <element name="author" type="value"/>
    <element name="title" type="value"/>
    <element name="price" type="value"/>
</xml-java-binding-schema>
```

The listing defines this binding schema as a binding schema for version 1.0ea (early access, which was the most current at the time of this writing).

Then it defines the `<books>` element at the root of the XML document as a class. The content of the `<books>` element is a reference to the `<book>` element, and the JAXB processor knows from the DTD file that this is a list.

Next, it defines the `<book>` element as a class. It has a category attribute that is a `String`, and the content contains references to three elements: `<author>`, `<title>`, and `<price>`.

Finally, it defines the three aforementioned elements as `Strings` (the default type for variables).

Defining Primitive Types

`String` types are great from an XML perspective, but from a Java perspective, `Strings` are not always preferable; some variables are better represented by more explicit types. For example, a number might better represent the price of a book.

To convert a variable to a primitive type, you only need to add the `convert` attribute to the `element` node and specify the primitive type to convert it to. To make that change to the `price` element, add `convert="float"` to the `price` element; refer to Listing 13.9.

LISTING 13.9 `books3.xjs`—Defining a Primitive Type

```
<?xml version="1.0" encoding="ISO-8859-1" ?>
<xml-java-binding-schema version="1.0ea">
    <element name="books" type="class" root="true">
            <content>
                    <element-ref name="book"/>
            </content>
    </element>
    <element name="book" type="class">
            <attribute name="category"/>
             <content>
                     <element-ref name="author"/>
                     <element-ref name="title"/>
                     <element-ref name="price"/>
```

LISTING 13.9 continued

```
            </content>
     </element>
     <element name="author" type="value"/>
     <element name="title" type="value"/>
     <element name="price" type="value" convert="float"/>
</xml-java-binding-schema>
```

The resultant `Book.java` file now has price defined as a float and defines the following two methods:

```
public float getPrice()
public void setPrice( float _Price )
```

Defining Non-Primitive Types

Variable types can be mapped to non-primitive types as well; you can accomplish this by defining a conversion node and then referencing that conversion node in your element's `convert` attribute. A conversion node can be added anywhere in the top level of the binding schema and has the following form:

```
<conversion name="ReferenceName" type="fully.qualified.ClassName" />
```

Then the element's `convert` attribute can reference the reference name:

```
<element name="myelement" type="value" convert="ReferenceName" />
```

To complete the example and convert the price to a `java.math.BigDecimal` type, which is much more appropriate for performing mathematical operations on monetary elements, see Listing 13.10.

LISTING 13.10 books4.xjs—Defining a Non-Primitive Type

```
<?xml version="1.0" encoding="ISO-8859-1" ?>
<xml-java-binding-schema version="1.0ea">
    <element name="books" type="class" root="true">
          <content>
                <element-ref name="book"/>
          </content>
    </element>
    <element name="book" type="class">
          <attribute name="category"/>
           <content>
                 <element-ref name="author"/>
                 <element-ref name="title"/>
                 <element-ref name="price"/>
           </content>
     </element>
```

LISTING 13.10 continued

```
     <element name="author" type="value"/>
     <element name="title" type="value"/>
     <element name="price" type="value" convert="BigDecimal"/>
     <conversion name="BigDecimal" type="java.math.BigDecimal" />
</xml-java-binding-schema>
```

The <conversion> node defines the reference type BigDecimal to be the type java.math.BigDecimal, and the <price> element tells the JAXB processor to convert the price element to a BigDecimal.

The resultant Book.java file now imports the java.math.BigDecimal class, has price defined as a BigDecimal, and defines the following two methods:

```
public BigDecimal getPrice()
public void setPrice( BigDecimal _Price )
```

Defining Enumerated Types

Sometimes nodes are going to be able to accept the value of one of a fixed set of values; you could define your book category to be defined by an enumeration rather than by a string. Consider limiting the values of the category attribute to:

- fiction
- computer programming

Type-safe enumerations are defined in Java as separate classes. To instruct the JAXB processor to generate a new class, an <enumeration> tag is added to the binding schema. It takes the following form:

```
<enumeration name="EnumerationType" members="value1 value2 ... valuen" />
```

And then you can define a variable to accept one of these enumerations by adding to its element tag a convert attribute that references the enumeration type. Listing 13.11 shows how this might be accomplished by modifying the book category to an enumerated type.

LISTING 13.11 books5.xjs—Defining an Enumerated Type

```
<?xml version="1.0" encoding="ISO-8859-1" ?>
<xml-java-binding-schema version="1.0ea">
    <element name="books" type="class" root="true">
           <content>
                  <element-ref name="book"/>
           </content>
    </element>
```

LISTING 13.11 continued

```
    <element name="book" type="class">
           <attribute name="category" convert="CategoryType" />
            <content>
                   <element-ref name="author"/>
                   <element-ref name="title"/>
                   <element-ref name="price"/>
            </content>
     </element>
     <element name="author" type="value"/>
     <element name="title" type="value"/>
     <element name="price" type="value" convert="BigDecimal"/>
     <conversion name="BigDecimal" type="java.math.BigDecimal" />
     <enumeration name="CategoryType" members="fiction computer-programming" />
</xml-java-binding-schema>
```

The listing defines the enumeration tag named `CategoryType` to permit the following values (members):

- `fiction`
- `computer-programming`

The <book> node's category <attribute> node marks the category as being of the `CategoryType` type.

The result of executing the JAXB processor is the modification of the `Book.java` file and the creation of a `CategoryType.java` file. Listing 13.12 shows the contents of the `CategoryType` class.

LISTING 13.12 `CategoryType.java`

```
import javax.xml.bind.IllegalEnumerationValueException;

public final class CategoryType {

    private String _CategoryType;
    public final static CategoryType FICTION = new CategoryType("fiction");
    public final static CategoryType COMPUTER_PROGRAMMING =
➥new CategoryType("computer-programming");

     private CategoryType(String s) {
         this._CategoryType = s;
     }

     public static CategoryType parse(String s) {
         if (s.equals("computer-programming")) {
             return COMPUTER_PROGRAMMING;
         }
```

LISTING 13.12 continued

```
        if (s.equals("fiction")) {
            return FICTION;
        }
        throw new IllegalEnumerationValueException(s);
    }

    public String toString() {
        return _CategoryType;
    }
}
```

The `CategoryType` class maintains a `String` in its `_CategoryType` member variable. It defines one private constructor that initializes the `_CategoryType` member variable; this means that `CategoryType` instances can be created only within the `CategoryType` class itself.

The listing defines two `CategoryType` instances for the two categories that were defined in the binding schema:

```
FICTION = "fiction"
COMPUTER_PROGRAMMING = "computer-programming"
```

These instances are static and final, meaning that only one instance exists for all classes that use the `CategoryType` class and that their values cannot change.

The `Book.java` file now defines the `_Category` member variable as a `CategoryType` instance and provides the following methods:

```
public CategoryType getCategory()
public void setCategory( CategoryType _Category )
```

From a programmatic perspective, the category must be updated as follows:

```
book.setCategory( CategoryType.FICTION );
```

The string `fiction` can no longer be used.

If you want to obtain a `CategoryType` from the actual string, for example, `fiction` or `computer-programming`, you can use the `CategoryType.parse()` method.

Subclassing a Generated Class

The classes that the JAXB generates are not final, so you are free to extend them to add any application-specific behavior. Follow the standard rules for subclassing any of the generated classes. For example, consider a `SaleableBook` class that adds in a markup to the price of a `Book` before reporting it to the user.

Summary

This chapter discussed the Java API for XML Binding (JAXB). If the DTD for an XML document type is known, that information can offer a much more intuitive interface to the XML document than that provided by the JAXP. The JAXB provides a compile time tool that generates Java class objects from a DTD and a binding schema that defines how the classes are to be built. At its simplest level, the binding schema need only define the root node of the XML document, but the binding schema is much more powerful. The binding schema can change variables from their default `String` type to any primitive, non-primitive, or enumerated type. Finally, the classes the JAXB generates can be extended to add application-specific functionality.

With JAXB under your belt, you have a pretty clean way to develop Web services. The next chapter looks at how you use the Java API for XML Registration (JAXR) to locate Web services.

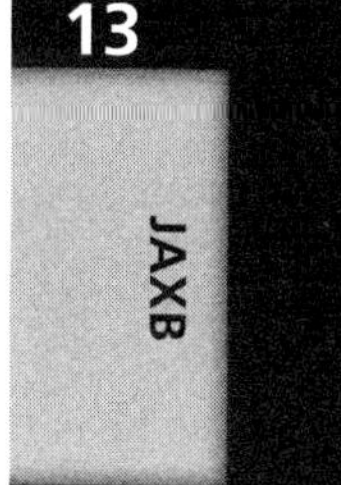

CHAPTER 14

JAXR

By Mark Wutka

IN THIS CHAPTER

The JAXR API gives you a standard way to access various XML-based registries in a platform-neutral way. Just as JDBC frees you from dependence on specific database implementations, JAXR frees you from dependence on specific registry implementations.

The Need for a Registry API

Registries such as UDDI are SOAP-based, so you can always access them with a generic SOAP library. Java-specific APIs, such as `UDDI4J`, make it even easier to access these registries, but in the end, these access methods lock you into a specific registry. It would be much better if you could write web services that could store and retrieve registry information without tying yourself to a particular kind of registry.

The Java API for XML Registries (JAXR) solves this problem by providing an implementation-independent way to access registries, similar to the way JDBC enables you to access different databases. JAXR consists of two parts: a JAXR provider and a JAXR client.

A JAXR provider provides the connection between the generic JAXR API and a particular registry implementation. A provider is the JAXR equivalent of a JDBC driver: it understands the specifics of a particular registry protocol.

A JAXR client is really not part of JAXR itself, but is instead a user of the JAXR API. A client uses the JAXR interfaces and classes to communicate with a JAXR provider, which then accesses a registry. Figure 14.1 shows the relationship between a client, a provider, and a registry.

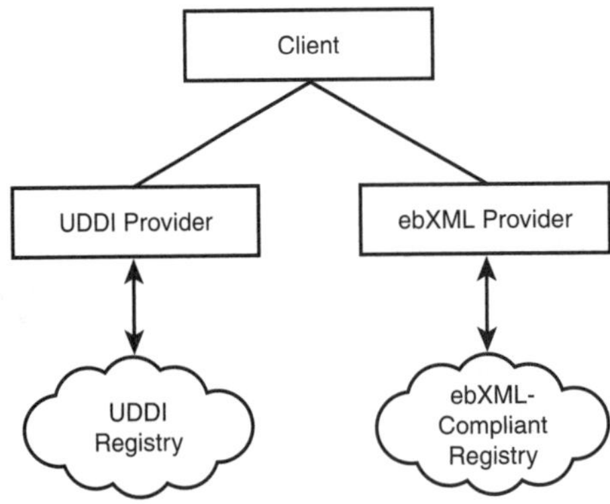

FIGURE 14.1
A client communicates with a provider to access a registry.

Basic JAXR Classes

You do most of your JAXR work through the `RegistryService` interface, which provides methods for querying and updating the registry. To get a `RegistryService` object, you must first use JNDI to locate a `ConnectionFactory`, then use the factory's `createConnection` method to create a `Connection` object. Finally, you use the `Connection`'s `getRegistryService` method to create a `RegistryService` object.

Connection

The `Connection` interface is your link to the underlying registry provider. Usually, you just use the `Connection` to create a `RegistryService` object, but you can also perform a few housekeeping chores.

First, you can specify your security credentials with the `setCredentials` method, which takes a `Set` object as a parameter. You will probably need to set credentials in order to update a registry, because most registries won't let just anyone modify data.

You can also specify a locale with the `setLocale` method, in case the registry requires a different locale than the rest of your application.

You may also call the `setSynchronous` method to tell the `Connection` whether it should operate synchronously. When the connection is synchronous, the `RegistryService` method waits for responses from the registry. For graphical applications that may hang while waiting for data, synchronous operations are difficult to deal with. When you perform asynchronous operations, you receive responses through a `RegistryClient` interface.

RegistryClient

When you create a `Connection`, you pass two parameters to the `createConnection` method: one is a `Properties` object, specifying various connection properties, and the other is a `RegistryClient` reference, which may be `null`. The `RegistryClient` interface is a set of callbacks that the `Connection` class uses to notify you about a request's completion.

The `RegistryClient` interface consists of two methods: `onException` and `onResponse`. Obviously, the `onException` method notifies you when an exception occurs, whereas the `onResponse` method notifies you when a response is ready.

Although JAXR permits you to use a single `RegistryClient` object with multiple connections, you should ensure that the `onException` and `onResponse` methods are thread-safe. You may have a situation where two different `Connection` objects try to invoke one of these two methods at the same time.

RegistryService

The `RegistryService` interface is your central gateway to the various capabilities that JAXR supports. The interface doesn't really contain methods to access registries, however. Instead, it provides methods to access other interfaces that access a registry. JAXR makes the assumption that registries may provide drastically different sets of services, making it difficult to define a "least common denominator" set of methods. Instead, JAXR groups capabilities into various categories, such as "query" or "life-cycle management," and provides standard interfaces, such as `BusinessQueryManager` and `BusinessLifecycleManager`. You access these interfaces through the `RegistryService` interface.

After you have a JAXR `Connection` object, you obtain the `RegistryService` by calling `getRegistryService`:

```
RegistryService resService = conn.getRegistryService();
```

From the `RegistryService` object, you can call methods such as `getBusinessQueryManager` and `getBusinessLifeCycleManager` to obtain interfaces to various JAXR services.

The JAXR Data Model

The JAXR data model is based on the Registry Information Model (RIM) defined by ebXML, which itself is meant as a generic interface to specific registry implementations. The names that JAXR uses for various items may not always match the names used by a different registry service, of course. The classes in the data model are as follows:

- `RegistryEntry`. The `RegistryEntry` class is an abstract base class that contains information about each item in the registry. Most other classes in the information model are subclasses of `RegistryEntry`.
- `Organization`. The `Organization` class contains information about an organization, such as a submitting organization (that is, a company that has stored an entry in the registry).
- `Service`. The `Service` class represents information about services an organization provides. The `Organization` class maintains a collection of `Service` objects, so after you have an instance of `Organization`, you can immediately determine what services it offers.
- `ServiceBinding`. The `ServiceBinding` class represents specific technical information describing how to access a service. Each service has a collection of `ServiceBinding` objects.
- `Concept`. A `Concept` is a class that helps classify a registry entry. It can represent almost anything, but is intended to help identify an entity's position in a taxonomy.

- Classification. A Classification relates a RegistryEntry to a particular Concept; in other words, it represents the entry's classification.
- Association. An Association simply associates one RegistryEntry with another. JAXR uses this mechanism to allow almost any possible relationship instead of trying to figure out all the possible relationships ahead of time.
- Package. A Package is a group of related registry entries. It enables you to perform operations over a group of entries rather than perform them on each entry individually.
- ExternalIdentifier. An ExternalIdentifier identifies a registry entry by some external naming scheme, such as a social security number or federal tax ID.
- ExternalLink. An ExternalLink contains a link to information outside the registry. Although you can't use the registry to change the external information, you should be aware that the information could change at any time.
- Slot. A Slot is a generic information holder that enables you to add arbitrary information to a RegistryEntry without defining a whole new class. In essence, it makes the RegistryEntry work like a Hashtable or Properties object.
- ExtensibleObject. The ExtensibleObject interface defines the methods required to support the addition and removal of Slot objects.
- AuditableEvent. The AuditableEvent class contains audit trail information that describes any changes made to objects in the registry. Obviously, the registry must support audit trails and the object must be auditable before this class has any significance.
- User. A User object represents a registry user and is typically associated with an AuditableEvent.
- PostalAddress. The PostalAddress class contains a postal address, and may be associated with either an Organization or a User.

Using JAXR

The JAXR API is very simple to use, although you must do a few housekeeping chores before you can actually access a registry.

Creating a Connection

Before you create a connection, you must use the Java Naming and Directory Interface (JNDI) to locate a ConnectionFactory. After you obtain the factory object, you must specify the factory implementation to use, as well as the URLs for the query manager and life cycle manager (in UDDI terms, the inquiry and publish APIs).

Listing 14.1 shows a program that creates a connection to IBM's UDDI registry. (It doesn't do anything with the connection, however.)

LISTING 14.1 GetConn.java

```
import javax.xml.registry.*;
import javax.naming.*;
import java.util.*;

public class GetConn
{
    public static void main(String[] args)
    {
        try
        {

            ConnectionFactory factory =
                ConnectionFactory.newInstance();

            Properties props = new Properties();

// Specify the implementation for the actual
// connection factory
            props.put("javax.xml.registry.factoryClass",
        "com.sun.xml.registry.uddi.ConnectionFactoryImpl");

// Specify the location of the inquiry and publish APIs
            props.put("javax.xml.registry.queryManagerURL",
    "www-3.ibm.com/services/uddi/testregistry/inquiryapi");
            props.put("javax.xml.registry.lifeCycleManagerURL",
    "www-3.ibm.com/services/uddi/testregistry/publish");

// Store the properties in the factory
            factory.setProperties(props);

// Create the Connection
            Connection conn = factory.createConnection();

// Get the RegistryService
            RegistryService regService =
                conn.getRegistryService();

        }
        catch (Exception exc)
        {
            exc.printStackTrace();
        }
    }
}
```

Note

To use the JAXR APIs, you must download and install the JAXR libraries from `http://java.sun.com/xml`. The examples use Sun's reference implementation. If you use a different JAXR implementation, you must change the `factoryClass` property in the examples to match the factory class for your implementation.

Querying a Registry

The `BusinessQueryManager` interface enables you to use many different options to query for various types of objects. Because there are so many possible options for a query, the `BusinessQueryManager` allows you to provide collections that contain various query parameters. The most common collections include the following:

- `findQualifiers`, which contains constants from the `FindQualifier` interface, specifying options such as `caseSensitiveMatch`, `exactNameMatch` and `andAllKeys`.
- `namePatterns` is a set of possible names, including wildcard patterns. Normally, the query matches any of the patterns (such as a logical `OR`), but if you specify `andAllKeys` in your list of `findQualifiers`, the search must match all the names.
- `classifications` is a set of `Classification` objects that describes what you are searching for. In UDDI terms, this is like the category bag.
- `specifications` is a set of `RegistryObject` objects containing technical information about the objects. In UDDI terms, this is like the `tModelBag`.
- `externalIdentifiers` is a set of `ExternalIdentifier` objects containing other descriptions of the object, such as a Federal Tax ID number or a D-U-N-S number (the Dun & Bradstreet numbering standard).
- `externalLinks` is a set of `ExternalLink` objects referring to content outside the registry.

The query methods that the `BusinessQueryManager` interface provides are as follows:

```
BulkResponse findAssociations(
                        Collection findQualifiers,
                        Collection associationTypes,
                        boolean sourceObjectConfirmed,
                        boolean targetObjectConfirmed
                        ) throws JAXRException;

 BulkResponse findOrganizations( Collection findQualifiers,
                        Collection namePatterns,
                        Collection classifications,
```

```
                                Collection specifications,
                                Collection externalIdentifiers,
                                Collection externalLinks
                                ) throws JAXRException;

BulkResponse findServices(Key orgKey,
                                Collection findQualifiers,
                                Collection namePatterns,
                                Collection classifications,
                                Collection specifications
                                ) throws JAXRException;

BulkResponse findServiceBindings( Key serviceKey,
                                Collection findQualifiers,
                                Collection classifications,
                                Collection specifications
                                ) throws JAXRException;

BulkResponse findClassificationSchemes(
                                Collection findQualifiers,
                                Collection namePatterns,
                                Collection classifications,
                                Collection externalLinks
                                ) throws JAXRException;

ClassificationScheme findClassificationSchemeByName(
                                String namePattern)
                                throws JAXRException;

BulkResponse findConcepts(Collection findQualifiers,
                                Collection namePatterns,
                                Collection classifications,
                                Collection externalIdentifiers,
                                Collection externalLinks
                                ) throws JAXRException;

Concept findConceptByPath(String path)
                    throws JAXRException;

BulkResponse findRegistryPackages(
                                Collection findQualifiers,
                                Collection namePatterns,
                                Collection classifications,
                                Collection externalLinks
                                ) throws JAXRException;
```

The `BulkResponse` object that most of the query methods return enables the query manager to return a subset of the entire response. Sometimes your query returns so much data that the query manager can't reasonably fit it all into memory. In these cases, it gives you a partial response and sets a flag indicating that you have a partial response.

To get the data from a `BulkResponse` object, use the `getCollection` method, which returns a `Collection` containing the response.

Listing 14.2 shows a program that displays all the services and service bindings for Microsoft.

LISTING 14.2 DoQueries.java

```
import javax.xml.registry.*;
import javax.xml.registry.infomodel.*;
import javax.naming.*;
import java.util.*;

public class DoQueries
{
    public static void main(String[] args)
    {
        try
        {

            ConnectionFactory factory =
               ConnectionFactory.newInstance();

            Properties props = new Properties();

// Specify the implementation for the actual
// connection factory
            props.put("javax.xml.registry.factoryClass",
     "com.sun.xml.registry.uddi.ConnectionFactoryImpl");

// Specify the location of the inquiry and publish APIs
            props.put("javax.xml.registry.queryManagerURL",
    "http://www-3.ibm.com/services/uddi/testregistry/inquiryapi");
            props.put("javax.xml.registry.lifeCycleManagerURL",
    "http://www-3.ibm.com/services/uddi/testregistry/publish");

// Store the properties in the factory
            factory.setProperties(props);

// Create the Connection
            Connection conn = factory.createConnection();

// Get the RegistryService
            RegistryService regService = conn.getRegistryService();

// Get the BusinessQueryManager
            BusinessQueryManager query =
                regService.getBusinessQueryManager();
```

LISTING 14.2 continued

```
// Look for companies named Microsoft
            ArrayList namePatterns = new ArrayList();
            namePatterns.add("Microsoft");

// Perform the query
            BulkResponse response = query.findOrganizations(
                null, namePatterns, null, null, null, null);

// Get the collection of responses
            Collection respData = response.getCollection();

            Iterator iter = respData.iterator();

            System.out.println("Organizations matching Microsoft:");
// Loop through the responses
            while (iter.hasNext())
            {
// Get the next organization
                Organization org = (Organization) iter.next();

                System.out.println("Organization: "+org.getName());
                System.out.println(org.getDescription());
                System.out.println();

// Get the key for this organization
                Key orgKey = org.getKey();

// Find all services offered by this organization
                BulkResponse servResp =
                    query.findServices(orgKey, null, null, null, null);

// Get the list of services
                Collection services = servResp.getCollection();

                Iterator servIter = services.iterator();

                System.out.println("Services:");

// Loop through the services
                while (servIter.hasNext())
                {
                    Service service = (Service) servIter.next();

                    System.out.println("Service: "+service.getName());

                    Collection bindings = service.getServiceBindings();

                    Iterator bindIter = bindings.iterator();
```

LISTING 14.2 continued

```
// Loop through the service bindings
                    while (bindIter.hasNext())
                    {
                        ServiceBinding binding =
                            (ServiceBinding) bindIter.next();

                        System.out.println(binding.getAccessURI());
                    }
                    System.out.println();
                }

            }

        }
        catch (Exception exc)
        {
            exc.printStackTrace();
        }
    }
}
```

Updating a Registry

To save an object in a registry, you simply call the `saveObjects` method in the `BusinessLifeCycleManager` class, passing a collection of the objects you want to save. To delete objects, you call `deleteObjects`, again passing a collection of the objects you want to save.

If you are just modifying an existing object, you can modify the objects the query manager returns and then use the life-cycle manager to save them. If you want to create new objects, you must use the life-cycle manager to create the instances. After you create an instance, you must still save the object.

The life-cycle methods for creating objects are as follows:

```
public Object createObject(String className)
    throws JAXRException, InvalidRequestException,
    UnsupportedCapabilityException;

public Association createAssociation(
    RegistryObject targetObjet,
    Concept associationType
    ) throws JAXRException;

public Classification createClassification(
    ClassificationScheme scheme,
    String name,
```

```
    String value
    ) throws JAXRException;

public Classification createClassification(
    Concept concept
    ) throws JAXRException, InvalidRequestException;

public ClassificationScheme createClassificationScheme(
    String name, String description
    ) throws JAXRException, InvalidRequestException;

public ClassificationScheme createClassificationScheme(
    Concept concept
    ) throws JAXRException, InvalidRequestException;

public Concept createConcept(
    RegistryObject parent,
    String name,
    String value
    ) throws JAXRException;

public EmailAddress createEmailAddress(
    String address
    ) throws JAXRException;

public EmailAddress createEmailAddress(
    String address,
    String type
    ) throws JAXRException;

public ExternalIdentifier createExternalIdentifier(
    ClassificationScheme identificationScheme,
    String name,
    String value
    ) throws JAXRException;

public ExternalLink createExternalLink(
    String externalURI,
    String description
    ) throws JAXRException;

public ExtrinsicObject createExtrinsicObject(
    ) throws JAXRException;

public InternationalString createInternationalString(
    ) throws JAXRException;

public InternationalString createInternationalString(
    String s
    ) throws JAXRException;
```

```
public InternationalString createInternationalString(
    Locale l,
    String s
    ) throws JAXRException;

public Key createKey(
    String id
    ) throws JAXRException;

public LocalizedString createLocalizedString(
    Locale l,
    String s
    ) throws JAXRException;

public Organization createOrganization(
    String name
    ) throws JAXRException;

public PersonName createPersonName(
    String firstName,
    String middleName,
    String lastName
    ) throws JAXRException;

public PersonName createPersonName(
    String fullName
    ) throws JAXRException;

public PostalAddress createPostalAddress(
    String streetNumber,
    String street,
    String city,
    String stateOrProvince,
    String country,
    String postalCode,
    String type
    ) throws JAXRException;

public RegistryPackage createRegistryPackage(
    String name
    ) throws JAXRException;

public Service createService(
    String name
    ) throws JAXRException;

public ServiceBinding createServiceBinding(
    ) throws JAXRException;

public Slot createSlot(
    String name,
```

```
    String value,
    String slotType
    ) throws JAXRException;

public Slot createSlot(
    String name,
    Collection values,
    String slotType
    ) throws JAXRException;


public SpecificationLink createSpecificationLink(
    ) throws JAXRException;

public TelephoneNumber createTelephoneNumber()
    throws JAXRException;

public User createUser()
    throws JAXRException;
```

One of the issues you may remember from UDDI is that each object has a unique key. If you create an object without saving it, the registry automatically generates a unique key for the object. When you use `saveObjects` to save an object, you receive a collection of `Key` objects, which are the keys for each object you saved. This way, you can find out what key the registry assigned to your new object.

Listing 14.3 shows a program that creates a new organization and adds it to the registry.

LISTING 14.3 `CreateOrg.java`

```
import javax.xml.registry.*;
import javax.xml.registry.infomodel.*;
import javax.naming.*;
import java.util.*;

public class CreateOrg
{
    public static void main(String[] args)
    {
        try
        {

            ConnectionFactory factory =
                ConnectionFactory.newInstance();

            Properties props = new Properties();

// Specify the implementation for the actual connection factory
            props.put("javax.xml.registry.factoryClass",
                "com.sun.xml.registry.uddi.ConnectionFactoryImpl");
```

LISTING 14.3 continued

```
// Specify the location of the inquiry and publish APIs
            props.put("javax.xml.registry.queryManagerURL",
                "www-3.ibm.com/services/uddi/testregistry/inquiryapi");
            props.put("javax.xml.registry.lifeCycleManagerURL",
                "www-3.ibm.com/services/uddi/testregistry/publish");

// Store the properties in the factory
            factory.setProperties(props);

// Create the Connection
            Connection conn = factory.createConnection();

// Get the RegistryService
            RegistryService regService = conn.getRegistryService();

// Get the BusinessQueryManager
            BusinessLifeCycleManager lifeCycle =
                regService.getBusinessLifeCycleManager();

// Create a new organization
            Organization newOrg = lifeCycle.createOrganization(
                "WebServCorp");

// Describe the organization (must use an international string)
            newOrg.setDescription(
                lifeCycle.createInternationalString(
                    "Providing Web services to the world"));

            ArrayList save = new ArrayList();

// Add the organization to a collection
            save.add(newOrg);

// Save the collection
            BulkResponse resp = lifeCycle.saveObjects(save);

// Get the response data
            Collection respColl = resp.getCollection();

            Iterator iter = respColl.iterator();

// Get the key generated for the new organization
            Key key = (Key) iter.next();

            System.out.println("The organization's key is "+
                key.getId());
        }
        catch (Exception exc)
        {
```

LISTING 14.3 continued

```
            exc.printStackTrace();
        }
    }
}
```

Summary

The JAXR API gives you a simple, standard way to access XML registries. You should be able to adapt to new registry formats with few or no code changes. Because JAXR is one of the newest XML APIs, you may see some significant changes as it stabilizes, but overall it should already be sufficient for most applications. JAXR gives you a standard way to access XML registries, whereas the JAXM API gives you a standard way to send XML messages, such as SOAP messages. In Chapter 15, you'll learn how to use the JAXM API.

CHAPTER 15

JAXM

By K. Scott Morrison

IN THIS CHAPTER

There is tremendous enthusiasm and hype surrounding Web services. And legitimately so: It's satisfying to envision a world where we have finally organized our disparate systems into dynamic, flexible, and loosely coupled relationships made possible through the exchange of XML documents—the *lingua franca* of future business computing. It's exciting because it seems very close. Much of the infrastructure—HTTP transport, Web servers, XML parsers—is available and is familiar.

This chapter shows you how to use an important new piece of the Web services puzzle: the Java API for XML Messaging (JAXM). JAXM is the new Java-based standard for SOAP messaging. It provides a standard API for message producers and consumers, thus decoupling your application from dependency on a particular messaging infrastructure.

Introduction to JAXM

Many of the most successful projects within the Java Community Process (JCP), such as the definition of the Java API for XML Parsing (JAXP), which is described in Chapter 12, have been motivated by the need for a single, consistent Java API that unifies a number of different, rapidly evolving approaches to a problem. In the case of JAXP, the challenge was to define an API that would accommodate the large number of different implementations that were appearing for processing XML documents, either using a tree-style (such as DOM) or event-style (such as SAX) approach. Document transformation was another area where individual APIs diverged greatly. JAXP quite successfully set out to unite these based on the TrAX Java API. With the publication of a crisp API definition, a developer writing a new SAX parser or XSLT engine has a collection of very specific interfaces that he or she must implement to achieve compliance with the standards set by the Java language. XML messaging—that is, the exchange of XML-based business documents between applications—is another domain where a similar approach is needed. A number of standardization efforts are currently underway, including ebXML, RosettaNet, and a handful of Web services standards; all are evolving at different rates and all are under the control of standards organizations operating outside the JCP's sphere of influence. The JCP recognized that a single model to access these messaging standards must be defined in Java—one that can accommodate a number of different approaches to building loosely coupled, message-based systems, yet that at the same time can address the particular needs of the Java community first and foremost.

JAXM is the project within the JCP to define Java APIs that facilitate XML document exchange. The goal is not to define message formats (at least beyond SOAP, which is discussed later in this chapter), but to create a means to compose and examine messages, as well as send and receive them. JAXM should support a number of different message formats and exchange paradigms, and accommodate the higher-level protocols that will inevitably see widespread use in the B2B world. The ebXML specification (`http://www.ebxml.org`) is a good example of this. UN/CEFACT and OASIS are developing ebXML to provide a means to conduct global electronic business. The standard defines message content, orchestration of document exchange, publication standards, and so on, all within the messaging envelope defined by SOAP. JAXM can provide the standard interface to different ebXML implementations; indeed, the JAXM distribution includes a rudimentary ebXML profile right now.

The JAXM project began officially in June 2000, under the designation JSR-67. You can find the full specification on the JCP Web site, at `http://www.jcp.org/jsr/detail/67.jsp`. JAXM is also the foundation technology of another proposal, JSR-109: "Implementing Enterprise Web Services" (`http://www.jcp.org/jsr/detail/109.jsp`). JSR-109 is concerned with addressing issues such as programming model, standard object lifecycle, how to define transactional boundaries, and so on—all details that fall outside of the scope of JAXM, but which will ultimately draw on JAXM as a means of creating, manipulating, and transporting messages.

What JAXM Is, and What It Is Not

JAXM is specifically an abstraction of SOAP messaging infrastructure. It exclusively supports SOAP-style messages, as described in the W3C notes *Simple Object Access Protocol (SOAP) 1.1* (`http://www.w3.org/TR/SOAP/`) and *SOAP Messages with Attachments* (`http://www.w3.org/TR/2000/NOTE-SOAP-attachments-20001211`). However, JAXM mandates nothing about transport, which could be HTTP, SMTP, commercial Message-Oriented Middleware (MOM, which includes products such as IBM's MQSeries or Microsoft's MSMQ), and so on. Thus, although JAXM provides a rich set of interfaces for composing and examining SOAP messages, its interface to the transport system remains deliberately abstract.

JAXM does not define specific protocols for business messaging. For example, suppose a company publishes a particular message schema and a set of orchestration rules to which its partners must conform to conduct business. JAXM simply provides the generic API to create and manipulate messages, to send them, and to receive them. The actual business process (including message format), however, could potentially be accommodated through JAXM's application-specific, pluggable *profiles*—a concept which we will examine shortly.

JAXM does not try to define a reliability layer for SOAP messaging. However, a JAXM *provider* might define this as its distinguishing feature. A provider is the JAXM term for the infrastructure that is responsible for transporting messages and dispatching them to services. A provider could be as simple as a SOAP server hosted in a servlet container;

however, it could also be an asynchronous messaging infrastructure, composed of complex routings across multiple intermediaries. In the past, these similar, but functionally different messaging paradigms demanded very dissimilar APIs, such as Apache SOAP and the Java Messaging Service (JMS). JAXM is unique in that it defines a very clear interface to interact with all providers, so it's generally easy to substitute one for another. To get reliable messaging, one might replace a provider that uses unreliable HTTP with a provider based on robust, commercial message-oriented middleware (or a provider that adds a reliability layer over HTTP). JAXM approaches security in the same way: it does not define how to implement security, but rather delegates security to be a characteristic of a provider, or potentially a feature of a message profile.

JAXM also does not define a marshalling/unmarshalling framework for transforming graphs of Java objects to or from XML documents. This may come as a surprise to developers whose experience with Web services is with Apache SOAP, which does provide a marshalling framework. Generalized data binding between Java and XML is actually a complex topic that is defined separately in JSR-31, *the Java API for XML Binding* (JAXB, `http://www.jcp.org/jsr/detail/31.jsp`), described in Chapter 13.

JAXM has no functionality for service publication or discovery and utilization. This is the domain of UDDI and WSDL; however, clients communicate with UDDI repositories using SOAP messages. Thus, a client can use JAXM as an API to query or update a WSDL description residing in a remote UDDI registry. The JAXM distribution provides some good examples of this.

You might be thinking that if JAXM is the API for SOAP messaging, then it's in conflict with its JAX brother, *the Java API for XML RPCs* (JAX-RPC, `http://www.jcp.org/jsr/detail/101.jsp`), which is evolving in a similar direction with its support for SOAP messaging (see Chapter 16). Well, it is and it isn't. The orientation of JAX-RPC is very much toward synchronous, request/response-style messaging. Although JAXM certainly supports this paradigm (and indeed, most of this chapter's examples will showcase this), it also supports other, more generalized messaging patterns involving the exchange of XML documents, such as asynchronous inquiry or update and send-and-forget messaging. It is likely, though, that as the JAXM and JAX-RPC standards evolve, JAX-RPC will become the primary interface for synchronous, RPC-style client/server communication, with JAXM acting as the API for all other messaging applications.

Finally, how does JAXM compare with Apache SOAP? Apache SOAP is an implementation of SOAP-based Web services that happens to make a Java API available; however, there is no intent to make it the standard Java API for all styles of SOAP messaging. Apache SOAP has the advantage of a considerable head start on JAXM, so it does have some very advanced and rich functionality that is still missing in JAXM. Apache SOAP supports both an RPC-style invocation (which hides SOAP message details), and a lower-level message-oriented interface (which exposes SOAP packaging and thus is more similar to JAXM in its current form). It is likely in the future that JAXM and JAX-RPC will both have providers for Apache SOAP infrastructure, because this particular technology is now seeing such widespread use.

When to Use JAXM

This is a time of great technological change, which makes adhering to a recognizable standard a very attractive proposition. Nevertheless, it is difficult to make a blanket architectural statement about when you should use JAXM. As with most technologies, there are tradeoffs, and right now, most of these don't have to do just with availability, but—more importantly—with maturity.

If you are building a SOAP messaging application and you are concerned about adhering to standards, you should very seriously consider JAXM. If you do only synchronous RPC-style client/server communication, you should look at JAX-RPC; however, any application needing asynchronous exchange or messaging models of greater complexity is better suited for JAXM. If you need true reliability (as defined by most MOM vendors), then consider JAXM if a profile that uses MOM transport is available. (Or consider a profile with a reliability layer built over unreliable transport such as HTTP or SMTP. Keep an eye on efforts around IBM's HTTPR at `http://www-106.ibm.com/developerworks/library/ws-phtt/`.) Alternatively, use JMS and conventional XML tools. At the time of writing, no MOM JAXM providers are obtainable, but this situation will likely change before long.

Finally, the existence of a JAXM profile supporting a particular XML protocol might make the decision for you. The emerging ebXML standard is a good example. The JAXM group has always maintained that supporting ebXML is a high priority, and a rudimentary ebXML profile—one that implements the mandatory message fields in the ebXML spec—is included in the JAXM distribution kit.

Architecture

The following section examines the basic architecture of JAXM. First, it describes typical messaging patterns. Then it introduces the concepts of providers and messaging profiles.

Messaging Patterns

One of JAXM's distinguishing features is that the API supports both synchronous and asynchronous communications. The Web has made us all familiar with synchronous communication: An application sends a message, usually over a socket, and blocks indefinitely until it receives a reply. (As with Web browsers, most well-behaved applications set a timeout limit on how long they will wait for a reply before signaling an exception.) In contrast, an application using asynchronous communication does not block when it sends a message, because it can respond at any time to message arrival, whether expected or not. The actual implementation can be either event-based or polling-oriented. If polling-oriented, the sender sends a message and then periodically checks a queue to ascertain whether the response has returned. If event-based, the sender sends a message and registers a handler routine to process the response when it arrives. In the meantime, the sender can continue processing other tasks. A variation on this is the send-and-forget paradigm, in which the sender never expects a response (so blocking would not make a lot of sense).

Clearly, event-based asynchronous communication is the harder of these to implement. It requires an activation framework to listen for a message and dispatch it to the appropriate handler. Although it sounds simple, there is actually some tricky thread management and pooling involved to do it well. In the next section, you will see how JAXM delegates this task to existing J2EE infrastructure.

Providers

Suppose you have an XML document that you need to exchange on a regular basis with a remote application. What are your options for transport? HTTP is an obvious option. Lately, it has been increasing in popularity because of the well-defined SOAP binding to it, the abundance of infrastructure and experience supporting it, and the ease with which it can pass through existing firewalls. SMTP is less well supported, but is attractive for similar reasons, and because its store and forward architecture contributes to loose coupling between applications (consider that the receiving application does not need to be available for you to send the document). Commercial MOM systems extend this concept, implementing genuine reliable messaging (meaning that the infrastructure can guarantee that a message will be delivered to its destination, and that only one copy will be delivered—a claim that neither HTTP nor SMTP can match without considerable additional support code).

JAXM supports this diversity of transports through the concept of a *provider*. A provider is the abstract representation of a message exchange infrastructure. It provides an interface to send messages, as well as receive them asynchronously. A provider could encapsulate HTTP, a mail system, MOM, and so on. Different providers necessarily feature different capabilities. For example, a MOM-based provider may implicitly implement reliability, security, and provide finely grained access to transactional boundaries, making it much more attractive than HTTP for many mission-critical applications.

Applications that make use of a JAXM provider are called *clients* of JAXM. It is important to recognize that this usage does not imply that there exists a subordinate relationship between a message sender and a message receiever, as there is with the phrase "client/server." Here, *client* simply implies that the application is making use of a JAXM provider's services. The application could be a producer of messages for other applications, a consumer of messages, or both. In other words—and using the more conventional interpretation—it could be a client, a server, or, as is the case with some messaging applications, a peer of many applications.

There are two principal deployment scenarios for JAXM clients: as a J2EE application running in a Web container, or as a J2EE application running as a message-driven bean. Both these deployments rely on their containers' listen-and-dispatch frameworks to perform asynchronous message receipts.

In Figure 15.1, the standalone application does not use a provider, but uses the JAXM APIs and a thin HTTP interface. Without a container, it cannot receive asynchronous messages, although it can synchronously send and receive. Applications like A and B are the focus of this chapter, because these have the most well-developed implementations at publication time.

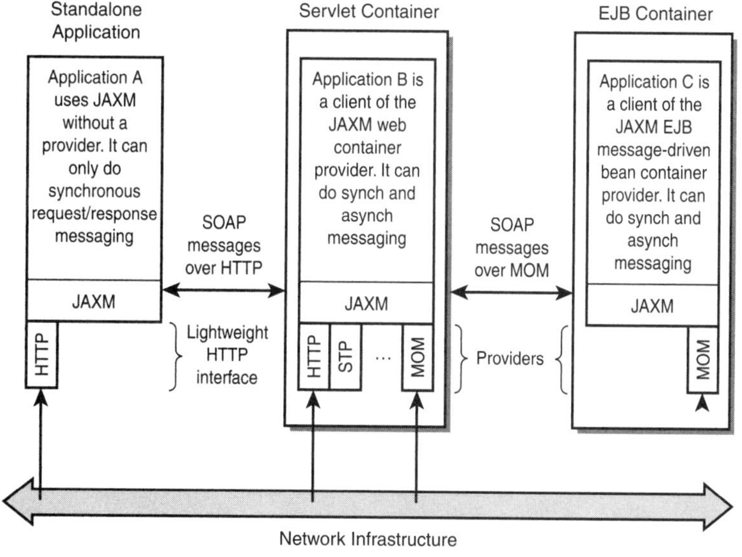

FIGURE 15.1
Three clients of JAXM.

It is also possible to create a J2SE JAXM application that makes no use of a provider. This application simply uses thin JAXM wrappers around the transport interface to implement synchronous, request/response-style communications. Logically, such an application cannot receive messages asynchronously because there is not a container to receive a message and dispatch it to a service. Nevertheless, it is still a powerful application of JAXM's capabilities, and one that this chapter demonstrates extensively.

Messaging Profiles

SOAP is simply a wire protocol—that is, it's a packaging format for sending business documents across a computer network. It does not attempt to say what headers need to be available for a particular operation. SOAP is overt in its avoidance of making a statement about how to deal with object activation or lifecycle on a server. It does not attempt to describe how to approach security, reliability, or transactions. These are all details promoted to higher-level protocols, which remain largely undefined. Instead, SOAP describes a simple and extensible format for message headers and body contents, a method to render faults, and recently an approach to include attachments. The JAXM interfaces, designed specifically to act on SOAP messages, echo the elegant simplicity of this design.

To accommodate higher-level protocols defined in SOAP, JAXM provides the concept of pluggable *profiles*. Profiles define a contract under which business messaging is to be conducted. If two applications share a profile, they can exchange messages. Profiles add the additional, higher-level messaging features that SOAP does not provide. Some of these things may be implementations of generic messaging concepts, such as a message timestamp, a transaction ID, or the correlation ID for a response. Others may be industry- or application-specific. For example, suppose that protocol X demands that all its SOAP messages contain a specific field, such as a `<To>addressee</To>` element in the header, where `addressee` is a unique DUNS number. A developer could write a specific profile for protocol X that would provide a means to set or inspect this in a manner consistent with the protocol's rules. But beyond simple message format and contents, protocols also define message orchestration, or choreography—that is, the dialog of messages through which a business purpose is realized. JAXM ships with two profiles that extend simple SOAP message containers and provide a good example of the versatility of the profile system: one for ebXML and one for SOAP-RP. Although ebXML mandates the use of SOAP 1.1 and SOAP with attachments to package messages, it includes a number of new fields that are necessary to implement reliable messaging, transmission across intermediates, message timeout, request/response correlation, and so on. Examination of messages produced by the JAXM ebXML profile reveals a number of ebXML-specific headers; these include PartyId, To, From, and a `MessageData` container holding MessageId, Timestamp, and RefId.

SOAP-RP is an implementation of the standard now called the Web Services Routing Protocol (WS Routing) proposed by Microsoft (have a look at `http://msdn.microsoft.com/library/default.asp?url=/library/en-us/dnglobspec/html/ws-routing.asp`). WS Routing defines a protocol for one-way message exchange between applications via intermediates. Much like a mail protocol, it accommodates recording of a reverse path, allowing routing of responses back to an initial sender.

Of course, the profile is only half of the reliability equation. The design of both the ebXML and SOAP-RP messages suggests a provider that has the capability of doing asynchronous messaging, not simply direct point-to-point synchronous messaging. To this end, the distribution includes a remote provider that features simple message queuing, using the file system to queue messages for delivery to JAXM services running under the Web container.

Implementation

The next section explores the packaging model for JAXM, and highlights its dependencies.

Packaging

The JAXM distribution consists of two main packages. The package `javax.xml.messaging` contains high-level APIs used to interact with providers, which are the interfaces to the transport system. This is where you will find the implementations of connections, listeners, and endpoints. (The following sections will examine each of these objects in detail.) The package `javax.xml.soap` contains APIs for working with SOAP messages. Also in this package is the connection class for standalone J2SE applications that implement direct, point-to-point communications. That is, all of the applications that could be characterized as not making use of a messaging provider.

Examination of the JAXM examples will also reveal two additional packages: `com.sun.xml.messaging.ebxml`, and `com.sun.xml.messaging.soaprp`. These contain implementations of the profiles for ebXML style, and WS Routing style messaging, respectively.

Dependencies

JAXM makes use of a number of Java technologies that may not be present in the standard distribution kit, but are nonetheless available at `http://www.javasoft.com`. Check the classpaths of your standalone JAXM applications and of your servlet container carefully, because this is a common source of errors. Be careful also of package version mismatches (particularly for the servlet container), and watch out for sealing violations caused by sealed Java Archive (JAR) files. You may have to extract the file tree from the archive, and then re-archive it, this time without a sealing attribute in the manifest.

You should consult the current documentation for an up-to-date list of JAR file dependencies. At the time of writing, JAXM made use of JavaMail for packaging MIME contents, the JavaBeans Activation Framework for handling arbitrary content, DOM4J to manipulate XML documents internally, JAXP for external representations of XML documents, JNDI for provider lookups (now part of the JDK), and Log4j for servlet logging.

Focus of the Examples

The JAXM distribution is rich in functionality—and richer still in potential; however, at the time of writing, much of the functionality remains immature and incomplete. Although it is tempting to try to cover all the features that are available today, it is also unrealistic. To do so well would easily fill a book rather than a single chapter.

The examples in this chapter center around the direct, point-to-point SOAP messaging, using a standalone J2SE client and a local provider that implements services in a J2EE Web container. At present, this is well-developed technology, and it serves to illustrate the major features of JAXM that are common to all applications. After you have mastered these, by all means explore the nooks and crannies of the distribution on your own: You will find great rewards there, including a rudimentary remote messaging provider, profiles for ebXML and WS Routing, and examples of how to invoke JAXM services from custom tags in JSP pages.

Basic Steps

Probably the best way to introduce JAXM is to examine a simple, synchronous request/response-style interaction. Here is the algorithm from the perspective of a sender, or message producer:

1. Create a connection. This encapsulates the message transport.
2. Create an endpoint. An endpoint represents a service. They describe the ultimate destination of a message.
3. Create a message factory. This is a simple factory-pattern object. Message factories create empty message templates that implement different profiles.
4. Construct a request message requesting a service. The application populates the message template with relevant data, using interfaces the profile implements.

5. Send the request message to its destination; synchronously receive an associated response. Asynchronous replies require a provider to implement a container as a dispatch mechanism. If you are not using a provider, then you are limited to synchronous, request/response-style messaging.
6. Process the reply message. The SOAP profile provides a DOM-like interface for visiting each XML node—often called tree-walking—as well as interfaces to extract attachments and MIME headers.
7. Close the connection. It is always advisable to clean up gracefully. Closing may release resources such as sockets that the connection maintains (although as you will see for point-to-point messaging this is not an issue).

Building a receiver, or message consumer, is even simpler:

1. Receive the message. In the point-to-point scenario, the J2EE Web container receives a message and dispatches it to your receiver service's `onMessage()` method. As JAXM matures, expect to see J2EE application servers as common messaging providers. In this scenario, JAXM implements services as message-driven EJBs.
2. Get a message factory. A typical design pattern is to preallocate this in an initialization routine.
3. Process the request message. The service creates a response message and populates it appropriately.
4. The service returns the response as a return value of the `onMessage()` method. In point-to-point messaging, this response returns on an existing, open-socket connection with the implicit understanding that the sender is at the other end. Consider, though, a more complex messaging system that uses a message provider with a shared communications channel (a very common messaging scenario). The message itself would have to contain endpoint information for routing and correlation identification to ensure that a sender could recognize which response goes with which request.

The following sections realize these operations in Java.

Connections

Connections encapsulate the underlying communication with a remote service. They are conceptually similar to the abstractions defined in JDBC's `java.sql.Connection`, or JMS's `javax.jms.Connection`. Generally speaking, connections tend to be heavyweight objects to instantiate, often requiring expensive operations such as creating socket pools, performing authentication, building up sessions on remote servers, and so on. It frequently makes sense for multiple threads to share a connection (assuming that the implementation is thread safe), instead of having each hold nearly identical resources. One of the examples you will develop near the end of this chapter demonstrates this.

JAXM has provided three special classes to implement simple HTTP transport: `SOAPConnectionFactory`, `SOAPConnection`, and `URLEndpoint`. `SOAPConnectionFactory` is an abstract class with a static `newInstance()` method—essentially the common factory pattern used in much of the JAX technologies. The `SOAPConnectionFactory` instantiates concrete implementations of the abstract `SOAPConnection` class. Perhaps not surprisingly, these implementations delegate to `java.net.HttpURLConnection` to provide much of the HTTP transport. Here's what it looks like:

```
import javax.xml.soap.SOAPConnectionFactory;
import javax.xml.soap.SOAPConnection;
import javax.xml.soap.SOAPException;
...
try {
    SOAPConnectionFactory soapConnectionFct =
SOAPConnectionFactory.newInstance();
    SOAPConnection soapConnection = soapConnectionFct.createConnection();
} catch (SOAPException e) {
    e.printStackTrace();
}
```

Connections provide an interface to send a message to its destination, but we will defer examination of this until you have learned more about endpoints and message creation.

After you have finished with the connection, it should be closed. The `SOAPConnection` class defines a `close()` method:

```
try {
    soapConnection.close();
} catch (SOAPException e) {
    e.printStackTrace();
}
```

The SOAPConnection class doesn't really hold on to many resources, but it is easy to imagine that future implementations might pool connections, perhaps with a `Keep-Alive` attribute in the HTTP `Connection` header, so it is best to clean up under all circumstances.

SOAPConnection and Generalized Messaging

Is SOAPConnection, and its associated classes, appropriate for generalized messaging applications? Not really. In fact, the SOAPConnection class sits somewhat uneasily as a special case in the wider model of messaging as defined in JAXM. JAXM defines a general ProviderConnectionFactory abstract class; from this one can instantiate objects that implement the ProviderConnection interface. A ProviderConnectionFactory can instantiate itself, but what's more interesting is that one can retrieve ProviderConnectionFactory instances from a directory with JNDI. There is a real advantage to this: Now changes to a provider become an *administration* issue, not a *code* issue. Rather than recompiling to accommodate a new provider implementation, one needs only to change the registered entry in the repository:

```
import javax.xml.messaging.ProviderConnectionFactory;
import javax.xml.messaging.ProviderConnection;
import javax.xml.messaging.JAXMException;
import javax.naming.InitialContext;
import javax.naming.NamingException;
...
String providerURI = "someURI";
try {
    InitialContext initialContext = new InitialContext();
    ProviderConnectionFactory providerConnectionFactory =
       (ProviderConnectionFactory) initialContext.lookup(providerURI);
    ProviderConnection providerConnection =
       providerConnectionFactory.createConnection();
} catch (NamingException e) {
    e.printStackTrace();
} catch (JAXMException e) {
    e.printStackTrace();
}
```

But there are other significant differences between the generalized ProviderConnection class and a SOAPConnection. ProviderConnection supplies a method called send() that is asynchronous: It does not block and it returns void. (You will see shortly that the SOAPConnection analog is get(), which is strictly synchronous—it blocks and returns a reply.) Furthermore, SOAPConnection.send() does not accept a separate endpoint object. Instead, it relies on endpoint information to be present in the message. This is a logical assumption when you consider that the message could traverse multiple intermediaries as it travels to its ultimate destination. In contrast, SOAPConnection assumes a direct socket connection between sender and recipient.

Endpoints

Endpoints define an ultimate destination for a message. Thus, endpoints are tied intimately to the messaging profile as well as to the provider. An endpoint could be a URI, or it could be very specialized address notation peculiar to a certain application, such as an industry-standard business identification number.

In true messaging applications, the endpoint is embedded within a message itself—as in the relationship between a letter and its address. A messaging provider can route internally addressed messages effectively between intermediates. This contributes greatly to loose coupling, because it implies that the sender and recipient never have to maintain a direct, end-to-end communications channel. Consider the enormous advantage this offers for traversing unreliable networks.

Alternatively, an endpoint may be an integral part of setting up a point-to-point communications channel used for exchange of multiple messages—as in the relationship between a telephone conversation and the phone number used to establish it. Obviously, this demands that both systems (and any transparent intermediates, such as a Web proxy) remain available for the duration of the connection.

JAXM supports both models. In the examples offered here, where you use JAXM without a messaging provider, endpoints are simply URLs, distinct from the message and provided at transmission time. This is logical, because the base SOAP HTTP binding does not define any additional routing information in the message itself. (Indeed, SOAP does not even attempt to make a definitive statement about how a URL may be ultimately mapped to a service.)

For point-to-point SOAP messaging, JAXM provides a special class, `URLEndpoint`, which extends the JAXM `Endpoint` base class. Both these classes have concrete implementations in the `javax.xml.messaging` package. In the current distribution, `URLEndpoint` simply wraps the `String` URL provided to its constructor:

```
import javax.xml.soap.URLEndpoint;
...
urlEndpoint = new URLEndpoint("http://jws.sams.com/someServiceName");
```

`URLEndpoint` is an immutable, supplying only an accessor in addition to the `toString()` method inherited from the Endpoint super class:

```
String url = urlEndpoint.getURL();
```

Messages

Messages are the vehicles that contain data exchanged between systems. JAXM bases its message format on the *SOAP 1.1* and *SOAP with Attachments* standards. It accommodates extensions to these specifications—such as the ebXML and WS Routing message formats—through pluggable profiles.

JAXM quite explicitly keeps messages and transport independent from a class perspective, but there is some logical interdependence. The instantiation chain from providers to messages illustrates this. For example, from a `ProviderConnection`, you can obtain a `MessageFactory`; this object is in turn responsible for instantiating empty `SOAPMessage` instances appropriate for the profile in use. `SOAPMessage` contains any additional attributes or functionality that makes the profile unique.

Alternatively, the abstract class MessageFactory can create a MessageFactory instance that is independent of a specific profile—in other words, simply a factory for unadorned SOAP messages:

```
import javax.xml.soap.MessageFactory;
…
try {
    MessageFactory messageFactory = MessageFactory.newInstance();
} catch (SOAPException e) {
    e.printStackTrace();
}
```

Before examining how to create and manipulate messages, it is important to understand first how messages are structured.

A Tour of the Message Hierarchy

JAXM provides a fundamental, abstract `SOAPMessage` class, which represents the "root" message unit. `SOAPMessage` objects decompose into a number of constituent parts, representing the by-now familiar SOAP message components, together with optional MIME multipart/related attachment parts. The simplified class diagram in Figure 15.2 attempts to show the containment relationships rooted at the `SOAPMessage`. The actual physical internal class relationships are different from this, but conceptually they follow a similar model.

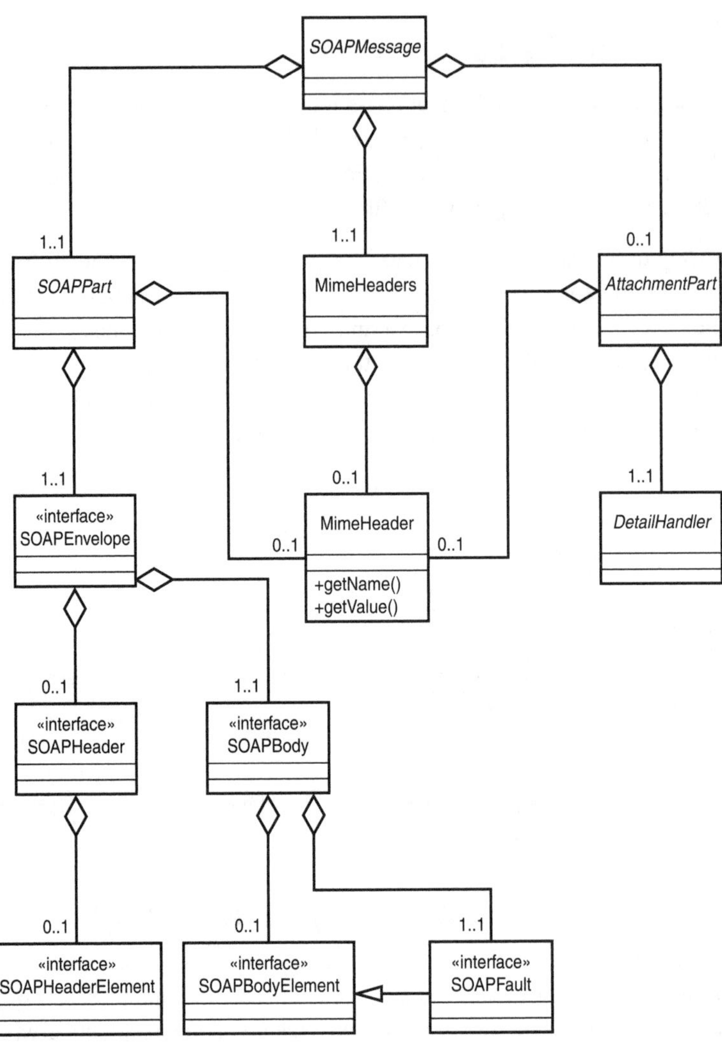

FIGURE 15.2
Containment model for principal JAXM document types.

Later sections of this chapter explore a number of these classes and interfaces.

Message Creation

The `MessageFactory` class supplies a `createMessage()` method that returns an empty `SOAPMessage` template, appropriate for the profile (or, as in most examples here, a base SOAP. `SOAPMessage` is actually an abstract class from the `javax,xml.soap` package. Contrast this to most of the components that a `SOAPMessage` contains (components such as the header and body, which are covered in the next section); JAXM defines these exclusively as interfaces, which is logical because they are simply references to source data the SOAPMessage manages.

All SOAPMessage objects contain a single SOAPPart instance (described in the following section) at creation, and can contain multiple attachments and MIME headers:

```
import javax.xml.soap.SOAPMessage;
...
try {
    SOAPMessage requestSoapMsg = messageFactory.createMessage();
} catch (SOAPException e) {
    e.printStackTrace();
}
```

An empty SOAPMessage can immediately be sent to a recipient, although without content it really isn't too interesting.

The SOAPMessage class also has an extremely useful writeTo() method, which accepts an object that extends java.io.OutputStream (such as System.out, a FileOutputStream, and so on):

```
import java.io.IOException;
...
try {
    requestSoapMsg.writeTo(System.out);
} catch (SOAPException e) {
    e.printStackTrace();
} catch (IOException e) {
    e.printStackTrace();
}
```

This writes the entire message to the stream, including attachment content and boundary markers. A godsend for debugging, this method is especially useful because of the XML document that makes up the SOAPPart of the message. Anyone who has struggled with the difficulty of using the DOM to output parsed XML documents will appreciate this enormously!

You will create and modify messages in the following sections, within the context of exploring a message's constituent parts. However, the SOAPMessage class has one more important method that is convenient to cover here. After alterations are made to a message, always call the saveChanges() method. This pulls in all MIME content, sets boundaries, and may set profile-specific attributes such as message ID. This method is invoked automatically when a message is passed to the send() method of a SOAPConnection, or if the SOAPMessage.writeTo() method is called:

```
try {
    requestSoapMsg.saveChanges();
} catch (SOAPException e) {
    e.printStackTrace();
}
```

You may also check whether a save is called for by using the `SOAPMessage.changeRequired()` inquiry, which returns a boolean.

The `SOAPPart` Class

`SOAPPart` is an abstract class that acts as a container for the SOAP envelope. It exists to disambiguate the primary part of a MIME message, which is an XML document, from any other attachments, which can be of varied types. The `SOAPMessage` can provide a reference to the `SOAPPart` directly:

```
import javax.xml.soap.SOAPPart;
…
try {
    SOAPPart requestSoapPart = requestSoapMsg.getSOAPPart();
} catch (SOAPException e) {
    e.printStackTrace();
}
```

Because in a multipart message the `SOAPPart` is a legitimate MIME part of the message, `SOAPPart` has methods to access its MIME-specific headers. JAXM encapsulates MIME headers with a utility class called `MIMEHeader`, which is simply a wrapper for a MIME header name and value:

```
import java.util.Iterator;
import javax.xml.soap.MimeHeader;
…
Iterator iterator = soapPart.getAllMimeHeaders();
while (iterator.hasNext()) {
    MimeHeader mh = (MimeHeader) iterator.next();
    System.out.println("HEADER NAME=" + mh.getName());
    System.out.println("HEADER VALUE=" + mh.getValue());
}
```

The `SOAPPart` can return its envelope contents as a JAXM envelope, which is the topic of the next section. More interestingly, though, it also provides accessor and mutator (that is, getter and setter) methods for an object instance that implements `javax.xml.transform.Source`, a class defined in the JAXP distribution:

```
import javax.xml.transform.Source;
…
try {
    Source source = soapPart.getContent();
} catch (SOAPException e) {
    e.printStackTrace();
}
```

This is the only API in JAXM that provides a means for developers to cross over to JAXP tools that provide more conventional DOM, SAX, and transform (XSLT at present) implementations. If there is a manipulation tool developed in JAXP—such as XPath—that you cannot live without, then this is the place you can make use of it.

XML Components

Because the `SOAPPart` is a container for XML content, JAXM provides a number of utilities to navigate these data in their tree representation. The model is deliberately similar to the W3C DOM, including interfaces such as `Node` and methods such as `getElementName()` and `getChildElements()`. But it should be emphasized that it is not the DOM. All the interfaces—including `Node`, a name that also appears in the DOM specification—are defined in the `javax.xml.soap` namespace, and are not compatible with DOM types. In fact, internally JAXM uses DOM4J, and its own model borrows freely from this. DOM4J provides a much more Java-friendly interface to DOM and SAX functionality.

Figure 15.3 illustrates the interface hierarchy for these JAXM XML types. This deliberately shows only the inheritance relationships for clarity. A complete class diagram would actually be quite a bit more complicated.

FIGURE 15.3
Inheritance hierarchy of principal JAXM XML interfaces.

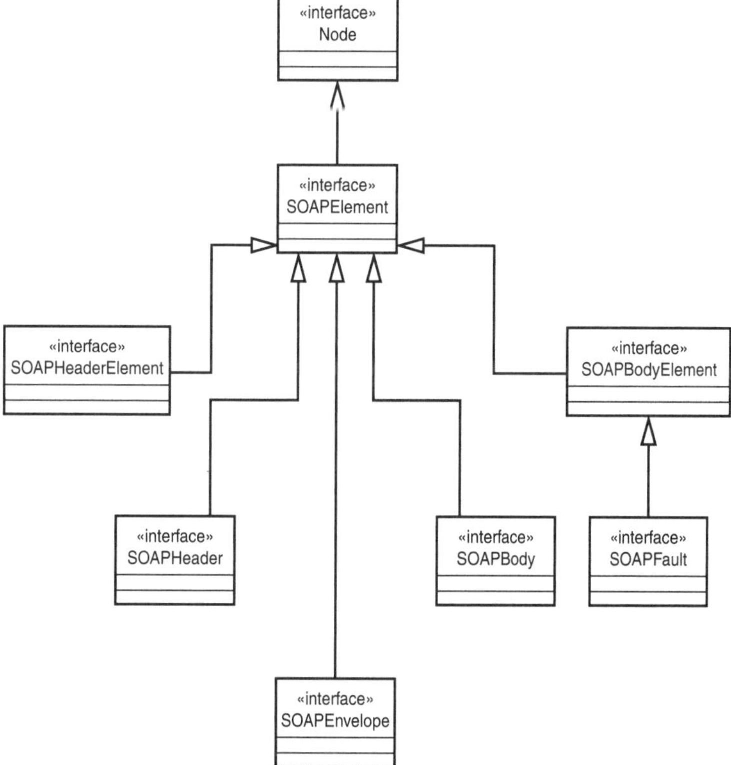

The following sections explore each of these important fundamental types.

Name

Name is an interface providing accessors to an XML name's components, such as the local name, the namespace prefix, the URI of the namespace, or the fully qualified name. It is an important input argument used when you create new child nodes:

```
import javax.xml.soap.Name;
...
try {
    String localName = "Route";
    String prefix = "sams";
    String uri = "http://www.jws.sams.com";
    Name name = soapEnvelope.createName(localName, prefix, uri);
} catch (SOAPException e) {
    e.printStackTrace();
}
```

The createName() method is overloaded to include versions with just localName, or with just localName and prefix as arguments.

Node and SOAPElement

Node and SOAPElement are two interfaces that are widely extended by most of the XML subtypes you will use in the following sections. They provide the basic interfaces for navigating and manipulating a document in a DOM tree.

Node represents the fundamental XML element in a tree representation. It contributes methods to get or set its parent element, detach itself from the document, or get the value of its immediate child if that child is a text node:

```
String childValue = node.getValue();
```

SOAPElement is the basic representation of an XML element in a SOAP message. It extends Node, and further contributes methods to navigate a document through its child elements, to add new child elements or text nodes, to get and set the element namespace, and to get and set individual attributes. You will see how to use these in the context of SOAPBody, described in the following section.

The SOAPEnvelope

The SOAPEnvelope is an interface that provides access to the SOAP header and body elements. SOAPPart supplies a method to obtain a reference to the envelope:

```
import javax.xml.soap.SOAPEnvelope;
...
try {
    SOAPEnvelope requestSoapEnv = requestSoapPart.getEnvelope();
} catch (SOAPException e) {
    e.printStackTrace();
}
```

Note that SOAPMessages produced by the MessageFactory come with SOAPEnvelope, the header, and the body elements allocated but empty.

Headers

The SOAPHeader interface extends SOAPElement and Node, adding methods to introduce specialized header elements—called SOAPHeaderElements—and to examine or detach header fields based on the value of their actor attributes:

```
import javax.xml.soap.SOAPHeader;
import javax.xml.soap.SOAPHeaderElement;
import javax.xml.soap.Name;
…
String actor = "someURI";
try {
    SOAPHeader requestSoapHdr = requestSoapEnv.getHeader();
    // Create a header element called <NewHeader>
    Name hdrName = requestSoapEnv.createName("NewHeader");
    SOAPHeaderElement soapHeaderEl = requestSoapHdr.addHeaderElement(hdrName);
    soapHeaderEl.setMustUnderstand(true);
    String actorUri = "http://www.jws.sams.com/receiverDemo";
    msgPurposeElement.setActor(actorUri);
    soapHeaderEl.addTextNode("Simple header example");
} catch (SOAPException e) {
    e.printStackTrace();
}
```

Note that the argument provided to construct the new SOAPHeaderElement is a JAXM Name instance. In the example, this is not qualified with a namespace, although as has earlier been pointed out, Name certainly provides overloaded constructors with this capability. The SOAPHeaderElement reference provides accessors and mutators for the optional actor and mustUnderstand attributes associated with regular SOAP message header elements.

In this example, the code is adding a single header element containing a text leaf node, leaving a message that looks like the following (looking only at the envelope down, and adding some tabbing and linefeeds for clarity):

```
<soap-env:Envelope xmlns:soap-env="http://schemas.xmlsoap.org/soap/envelope/">
    <soap-env:Header>
        <MsgPurpose soap-env:mustUnderstand="1"
➥soap-env:actor="http://www.jws.sams.com/receiverDemo">Simple header example
➥</MsgPurpose>
    </soap-env:Header>
    <soap-env:Body/>
</soap-env:Envelope>
```

Consider, however, that the intent of SOAP headers is that they be entirely extensible; it is perfectly acceptable for there to be multiple headers, and any of these header elements can of course contain nested XML.

In addition to a method to add a new header, as you have already seen, `SOAPHeader` provides a method to examine existing headers, indexed by actor:

```
import java.util.Iterator;
...
// Iterate through all headers, echoing element name and value
Iterator iterator = requestSoapHdr.examineHeaderElements(actor);
while (iterator.hasNext()) {
    SOAPHeaderElement soapHdrEl = (SOAPHeaderElement) iterator.next();
    System.out.println("Header: "+soapHdrEl.getElementName().getLocalName());
    System.out.println("Value: "+SoapHdrEl.getValue()+"\n");
}
```

Extraction of header elements, indexed by actor, is similar:

```
Iterator iterator = requestSoapHdr.extractHeaderElements(actor);
```

Unlike the previous example, this disengages each `SOAPHeaderElement` that the `Iterator` contains. This functionality is particularly useful for intermediaries that, by SOAP conventions, must remove and process all headers marked for their consumption before forwarding the resulting altered message to the next system.

The SOAPBody

The `SOAPBody` is a container for body elements and SOAP faults. Its organization mirrors that of the header, with both a `SOAPBody` interface and a `SOAPBodyElement` interface:

```
import javax.xml.soap.SOAPBody;
import javax.xml.soap.SOAPBodyElement;
import javax.xml.soap.Name;
...
try {
    SOAPBody requestSoapBody = requestSoapEnv.getBody();
    // Add simple body element with the name <Stock>
    Name stockName = requestSoapEnv.createName("Stock");
    SOAPBodyElement stockElement = requestSoapBody.addBodyElement(stockName);
    stockElement.addTextNode("SAMS");
} catch (SOAPException e) {
    e.printStackTrace();
}
```

This code snippet, if applied to an empty message, would build the following message:

```
<soap-env:Envelope xmlns:soap-env="http://schemas.xmlsoap.org/soap/envelope/">
    <soap-env:Header/>
    <soap-env:Body>
        <Stock>SAMS</Stock>
    </soap-env:Body>
</soap-env:Envelope>
```

Unlike SOAPHeaderElement, which has two clearly defined—though optional—attributes, the SOAP specification does not offer any attributes for elements in the SOAP body, so the SOAPBodyElement interface does not actually contribute any additional methods.

Recall that the SOAPHeader interface defines methods to return all headers it contains, indexed by a particular actor attribute. This is a logical specialization for headers, because intermediaries are required to remove and process all headers that explicitly identify them as actors. SOAP has no such requirement for the body elements, and thus there are no specialized accessors in the SOAPBody interface. Consider, though, that SOAPBody extends the SOAPElement interface, which has a number of useful methods for walking the XML tree:

```
import java.util.Iterator;
…
// Iterate through all body elements, echoing element name and value
Iterator iterator = requestSoapBody.getChildElements();
while (iterator.hasNext()) {
    SOAPBodyElement requestSoapBdyEl = (SOAPBodyElement) iterator.next();
    System.out.println("Body element: " + requestSoapBdyEl.getElementName()
                                                    .getLocalName());
    System.out.println("Value: "+requestSoapBdyEl.getValue()+"\n");
}
```

Faults

SOAP encapsulates faults in the body element, mandating that there can be at most a single fault element in a message. JAXM provides the SOAPBody.addFault() method to introduce a fault into the message and return a reference to it:

```
import javax.xml.soap.SOAPFault;
…
try {
    SOAPFault soapFault = requestSoapBody.addFault();
} catch (SOAPException e) {
    e.printStackTrace();
}
```

Messages can be tested for faults, and an existing fault can be extracted for examination:

```
if (requestSoapBody.hasFault()){
    SOAPFault soapFault = requestSoapBody.getFault();
    System.out.println("Fault code: "+soapFault.getFaultCode());
    System.out.println("Fault string: "+soapFault.getFaultString());
}
```

JAXM models a SOAPFault as an interface that extends SOAPBodyElement. SOAPFault provides an accessor for a Detail interface, which is a container for DetailEntries. This is intended as a means of communicating additional information about a fault—

such as a stack trace describing where it occurred—that cannot be accommodated within the fault code or fault string. The actual contents, of course, are application-specific and not mandated by SOAP.

Attachments

One of the initial criticisms leveled at SOAP, as well as other XML-based messaging proposals, was that XML is not well suited for encapsulating a large number of commonly encountered data types. Binary content, such as images, sounds, or movies, require conversion to a text representation so that XML elements can contain the content with no risk of making the document itself invalid. Ironically, even XML documents themselves are problematic. Consider the following well-formed and valid XML document:

```
<?xml version="1.0" encoding="UTF-8"?>
<!DOCTYPE SalesFigures [
<!ELEMENT QuarterlyTotal (#PCDATA)>
<!ATTLIST QuarterlyTotal quarter (Q1|Q2|Q3|Q4) #REQUIRED>
<!ELEMENT SalesFigures (QuarterlyTotal+)>
]>

<SalesFigures>
    <QuarterlyTotal quarter="Q1">123.00</QuarterlyTotal>
    <QuarterlyTotal quarter="Q2">456.00</QuarterlyTotal>
    <QuarterlyTotal quarter="Q3">789.00</QuarterlyTotal>
    <QuarterlyTotal quarter="Q4">987.00</QuarterlyTotal>
</SalesFigures>
```

How would a SOAP message transport this? Certainly not like this:

```
<Envelope xmlns="http://schemas.xmlsoap.org/soap/envelope/">
<Header/>
<Body>
<!-- This is wrong! -->
<?xml version="1.0" encoding="UTF-8"?>
<!DOCTYPE SalesFigures [
<!ELEMENT QuarterlyTotal (#PCDATA)>
<!ATTLIST QuarterlyTotal quarter (Q1|Q2|Q3|Q4) #REQUIRED>
<!ELEMENT SalesFigures (QuarterlyTotal+)>
]>

<SalesFigures>
    <QuarterlyTotal quarter="Q1">123.00</QuarterlyTotal>
    <QuarterlyTotal quarter="Q2">456.00</QuarterlyTotal>
    <QuarterlyTotal quarter="Q3">789.00</QuarterlyTotal>
    <QuarterlyTotal quarter="Q4">987.00</QuarterlyTotal>
</SalesFigures>
</Body>
</Envelope>
```

This is invalid XML. In addition to the havoc the now embedded DTD would cause, the XML specification quite clearly states that the XML declaration has to begin at the first character of the document.

One solution to this problem would be to wrap the document in an XML `CDATA` section. This is a common, though inelegant and unsatisfying, approach to this problem. The more conventional solution to this problem, which is also applicable to binary content, is to apply a base-64 transform to the offending data, mapping everything to nice, XML-friendly hex characters. Unfortunately, there are flaws with this, too. Base-64 increases the content size by about 30%, which for large binary attachments may be an issue, especially if network bandwidth is constrained, as you might encounter with wireless networking. Furthermore, for text content such as XML documents, you unfortunately loose all legibility on the wire, which defeats much of the value of XML messaging.

But lurking in this proposed solution is a much more significant problem: You are introducing a massive parser burden. Remember that parsers such as DOM create `Node` objects up front and hold them in memory. (There are some exceptions to this, such as the lazy DOM implementation of Apache Xerces and some of the newer "pull" parsers.) So running a DOM-based parser on an XML document that contains a base-64 transformed object as a value of some element can be enormously wasteful of resources. For a messaging application, where parsing speed is a particular concern, this is simply unacceptable.

The XML community recognized this problem early on, and about eight months after the SOAP 1.1 specification was released, a proposal for attachment handling—that is, a strategy for managing content such as that just described—was submitted to the W3C. It leverages the existing and mature standards for Internet mail attachment handling, in particular RFC 2387, which describes the Multi-Purpose Internet Mail Extensions (MIME) Multipart/Related Content-type. (You can download this RFC at `http://www.ietf.org/rfc/rfc2387.txt`.) SOAP with attachments actually defines a completely different packaging model for SOAP messages on the wire. It introduces an optional outer MIME envelope; this contains the SOAP envelope as its primary part, but can also include any number of attached objects of arbitrary type, each separated by a conventional MIME boundary. Later, this chapter examines what these messages look like by capturing some SOAP messages exchanged between a client and a server.

One great advantage of using JAXM is that it provides an implementation of this proposal. One can add any number of attachments to the SOAP message—and these attachments can be pictures, PDF files, MP3s, serialized Java objects, or even simple plain text. It opens up a number of interesting possibilities for Web services. For example, applications could exchange Java byte code for a new class inside SOAP calls, making use of them with the local Java class loader.

JAXM attachment handling delegates much of the heavy lifting to the existing JavaBeans Activation Framework (JAF), which was originally designed as a supplement to JavaMail. JAF is described in detail at `http://java.sun.com/products/javabeans/glasgow/jaf.html`. JAF is valuable because it can automatically identify content (which may reside in a file, in a `java.lang.Object`, or at a URL) based on inspection of the content (typically through registered magic numbers). This is in contrast to simple identification through file extension bindings (for example, .jpg is a JPEG image), which might not be accurate. Using a standard `DataHandler` interface, JAF provides a means to acquire the handler appropriate for the content type, and to determine what methods are available in this handler to act on this type of content. As an example, suppose you have a JPEG picture. JAF would identify its MIME type based on content inspection, instantiate the specific data handler for JPEGs, and make its unique methods available through the `DataHandler`. The JPEG handler might have a method called `edgeDetect()`, which would apply an edge detection filter to the image. An application that uses JAF could discover and use this property dynamically.

JAXM provides an `AttachmentPart` class that encapsulates the content of an attachment, its content type (named as the MIME header `Content-Type`), and any additional application-specific MIME headers that are present. Attachments are created from a factory method of the `SOAPMessage` class. This takes either a JAF data handler (which implicitly knows its own MIME type), or a `java.lang.Object` and `String` MIME type as arguments. Here is an example that creates an attachment out of a GIF image of Duke, the Java mascot:

```
import javax.xml.soap.AttachmentPart;
import javax.activation.DataHandler;
import javax.activation.FileDataSource;
...
String fileName = "duke.gif";
DataHandler dataHandler = new DataHandler(new FileDataSource(fileName));
AttachmentPart attachmentPart = requestSoapMessage.createAttachmentPart(
➥dataHandler);
attachmentPart.setContentType(dataHandler.getContentType());
requestSoapMessage.addAttachmentPart(attachmentPart);
```

The `AttachmentPart` class provides methods to add additional, application-specific MIME headers:

```
attachmentPart.addMimeHeader("FileName", fileName);
attachmentPart.addMimeHeader("Custom-Header", "Some text");
```

This is useful as an indexing mechanism, so that elements in the SOAP message can refer to particular attachments in a multi-attachment message. Retrieval of custom headers is just as easy. Most JAXM MIME header access methods make use of two JAXM utility classes first encountered in the `SOAPPart` class: `MIMEHeader`, which is little more than a structure encapsulating the header name and value; and `MIMEHeaders`, which is a container for `MIMEHeader` instances:

```
import javax.xml.soap.MimeHeader;
import java.util.Iterator;
…
Iterator iterator = attachmentPart.getAllMimeHeaders();
while (i2.hasNext()) {
    MimeHeader mh = (MimeHeader) iterator.next();
    System.out.println("HEADER NAME=" + mh.getName());
    System.out.println("HEADER VALUE=" + mh.getValue());
}
```

It is also possible to retrieve a unique MIME header directly by its name:

```
String target = "FileName";
String[] hdrValues = attachmentPart.getMimeHeader(target);
System.out.println("HEADER NAME="+target);
for (int j = 0; j < hdrValues.length; j++) {
    System.out.println("HEADER VALUE=" + hdrValues[j]);
}
```

Note that multiple headers can share the target name, which is why it returns a `String` array of values.

There is an option to find all the headers that match a `String` array of targets:

```
String[] mimeTargets = new String[]{ "FileName", "Custom-Header" };
Iterator iterator = attachmentPart.getMatchingMimeHeaders(mimeTargets);
while (iterator.hasNext()) {
    MimeHeader mh = (MimeHeader) iterator.next();
    System.out.println("HEADER NAME=" + mh.getName());
    System.out.println("HEADER VALUE=" + mh.getValue());
}
```

And finally, there is the converse of the above, which returns all the headers not found in the `String` array:

```
Iterator iterator = attachmentPart.getNonMatchingMimeHeaders(mimeTargets);
```

The `SOAPMessage` provides a number of useful methods to extract attachments:

```
int attNo = 1;
Iterator iterator = requestSoapMessage.getAttachments();
while (iterator.hasNext()) {
    AttachmentPart attachmentPart = (AttachmentPart) iterator.next();
    System.out.println("Attachment no: " + attNo++);
    System.out.println("Content-Type="+ attachmentPart.getContentType());
    System.out.println("Content size="+ attachmentPart.getSize());
}
```

You can also retrieve only those attachments that contain headers named in a MIMEHeaders object:

```
MimeHeaders mimeHeaders = new MimeHeaders();
mimeHeaders.addHeader("FileName", fileName);
Iterator iterator = requestSoapMessage.getAttachments(mimeHeaders);
```

The AttachmentPart can also return its content encapsulated in a JAF DataHandler. This brings all the advantages of JAF, including implicit recognition of the MIME type of the content, and some useful utility functions, such as the capability to write to a java.io.OutputStream:

```
import java.io.IOException;
javax.activation.DataHandler;
...
DataHandler dataHandler=null;
try {
    dataHandler = attachmentPart.getDataHandler();
    System.out.println("MIME type is: "+dataHandler.getContentType());
} catch (SOAPException e) {
    e.printStackTrace();
}
try {
    dataHandler.writeTo(System.out);
} catch (IOException e) {
    e.printStackTrace();
}
```

Observe that DataHandler.writeTo() throws a java.io.IOException if a problem occurs.

Naturally, the OutputStream could be a java.io.FileOutputStream if you were intent on extracting the attachment content to a file:

```
import java.io.FileNotFoundException;
...
try {
    String fname = "someFile";
    FileOutputStream fileOutputStream = new FileOutputStream(fname);
    dh.writeTo(fileOutputStream);
} catch (FileNotFoundException e) {
    e.printStackTrace();
} catch (IOException e) {
    e.printStackTrace();
}
```

Message Producers and Consumers

Now that you have an understanding of the basic types, you can see how to use them to send and receive messages.

Sending a Message

When you make use of JAXM without a provider, the `SOAPConnection` object instance, which encapsulates the underlying HTTP transport semantics, provides an interface to send messages. Because neither this `SOAPConnection`, nor the message itself, is bound to any destination, an `URLEndpoint` object wrapping an URL is also required input:

```
try {
    // Message, endpoint, and connection initialization not shown.
    SOAPMessage responseSoapMsg = soapConnection.call(requestSoapMsg,
                                                      urlEndpoint);
} catch (SOAPException e) {
    e.printStackTrace();
}
```

You can use the methods described in detail in the previous sections to examine the response message.

Receiving a Message

Receiving a message asynchronously requires a provider to implement a multithreaded listening and dispatch framework. The server infrastructure used in this chapter's examples consists of a servlet 2.3 container with supporting JAXM classes. The distribution kit often calls this the local provider, as a way of distinguishing it from the remote provider, which the ebXML and WS Routing examples use. The remote provider implements more traditional messaging server functionality, such as allowing intermediaries and persistence of messages if a receiver is unavailable.

To create a new JAXM service, simply extend the abstract class `JAXMService`, and implement one of two marker interfaces: either `OneWayListener` or `ReqRespListener`. The `JAXMService` class provides the link between the Java servlet model and JAXM. It overrides the `HttpServlet.doPost()` method, converts the post data contained in `javax.servlet.http.HTTPServletRequest` into a JAXM `SOAPMessage`, and calls the service's `onMessage(SOAPMessage)` method with this transformed argument. The interfaces contribute `onMessage()`. The method `onMessage()` defined in the `AsyncListener` interface returns `void`; this is intended for true asynchronous, one-way messaging, where a sender does not expect any kind of acknowledgement. In contrast, `SyncListener` marks the request/response paradigm. Its `onMessage()` returns a `SOAPMessage`, which is a response that the provider must return to the sender.

The following example demonstrates a loopback server, just about the most straightforward message consumer you can create. It simply echoes whatever message it receives back to the sender:

```
package com.sams.jws.chapter15;

/*
 * MinimalMessageConsumer
 * Echo received messages back to sender.
 */
// JAXM
import javax.xml.soap.SOAPMessage;
import javax.xml.messaging.JAXMServlet;
import javax.xml.messaging.ReqRespListener;

public class MinimalMessageConsumer
extends JAXMServlet
implements ReqRespListener {
public SOAPMessage onMessage(SOAPMessage requestSoapMsg) {

    return requestSoapMsg;

}    // onMessage()
}    // HelloWorldReceiver
```

`JAXMServlet` is doing most of the real work for you here. Note that the reply is a JAXM `SOAPMessage`; `JAXMServlet` renders this into the content type `text/xml` and returns it to the caller as a response to its initial post. (Bear in mind that there is no implementation of `doGet()`; as with most servlets that leave this out, if you use `GET` to call the URL, you will receive an `HTTP Status 405 - HTTP method GET is not supported by this URL` response. However, this also means that `doGet()` is available if you want to create a conventional servlet that renders HTML but can also respond to asynchronous SOAP requests.)

In contrast to the simplistic loopback example, most real applications construct a new response message from the ground up. In many circumstances, it is advisable to pre-allocate frequently used, stateless objects such as factories. Because `JAXMServlet` extends `HTTPServlet`, you can certainly override the `init()` method to add initialization processing when the servlet is loaded; however, you should delegate to `super.init()` at the outset to ensure that all JAXM initialization is carried out:

```
public void init(ServletConfig servletConfig) throws ServletException {
    super.init(servletConfig);
    try {
        messageFactory = MessageFactory.newInstance();
    } catch (SOAPException e) {
        System.err.println("Exception instantiating MessageFactory:");
        e.printStackTrace();
    }
}
```

Here you are creating an instance variable—albeit a *servlet* instance variable, with all the concurrency implications that this entails—that references a JAXM `MessageFactory` instance. An added benefit of this design is that it provides an opportunity to access the `javax.servlet.ServletConfig` instance.

Notice that unlike the other classes and interfaces you have examined up to now, which reside in the package `javax.xml.soap`, `JAXMServlet`, `ReqRespListener`, and `OnewayListener` are defined in the more generalized JAXM package `javax.xml.messaging`.

Tying It All Together

Now it's time to apply what you have learned to some real examples. As a first step, let's build that computing classic, the Hello World application. Following that, you will develop a simple file server application to demonstrate the use of attachments and reveal some more sophisticated XML document processing techniques.

Both these examples have been tested with JAXM 1.0.1 Early Edition 1 and Java 1.3.1_01. The provider for the message consumers is Jakarta Tomcat 4.0.

Hello World

So maligned, yet so crucial; where would we be without HelloWorld? With that simple message comes reassurance that our infrastructure, our access to code, and our compilers are all functioning the way we intend them to. In this example, illustrated in Figure 15.4, you will use the SOAP message profile to build a very simple sender and receiver pair. The sender application is completely standalone, not relying on any provider. Thus, it is restricted to simple, point-to-point, request/response-style synchronous communication with receivers. The receiver, however, is deployed in a servlet container.

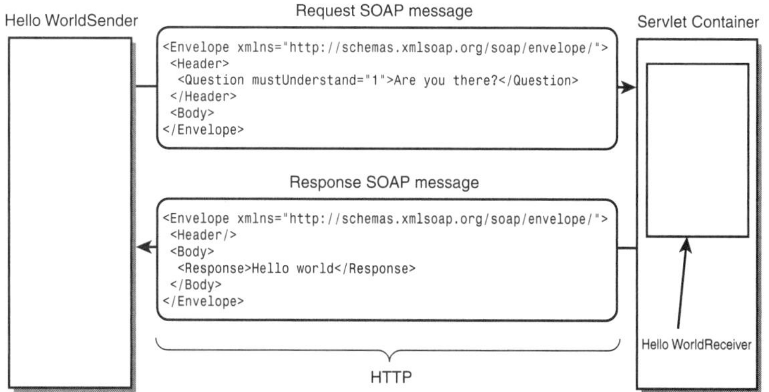

FIGURE 15.4
Deployment for the simple HelloWorld example.

First, take a look at the sender, shown in Listing 15.1.

LISTING 15.1 HelloWorldSender.java: A Simple JAXM Client Without a Provider

```
package com.sams.jws.chapter15;

/*
 * HelloWorldSender
 * Very basic demonstration of JAXM SOAP profile with no provider.
 * This shows synchronous, client/server-style call.
 */
// General JDK
import java.io.IOException;
// JAXM
import javax.xml.soap.SOAPConnectionFactory;
import javax.xml.soap.SOAPConnection;
import javax.xml.soap.MessageFactory;
import javax.xml.soap.SOAPMessage;
import javax.xml.soap.SOAPElement;
import javax.xml.soap.SOAPPart;
import javax.xml.soap.SOAPEnvelope;
import javax.xml.soap.SOAPHeader;
import javax.xml.soap.SOAPHeaderElement;
import javax.xml.soap.Name;
import javax.xml.soap.SOAPException;
import javax.xml.messaging.URLEndpoint;

public class HelloWorldSender {

    public static void main(String args[]) {

        URLEndpoint urlEndpoint = null;
        if (args.length == 1)
            urlEndpoint = new URLEndpoint(args[0]);
        else {
            System.err.println("Usage: java HelloWorldSender targetURL");
            System.exit(0);
        } // Else

        try {
            // Initialize connection and SOAP Profile.
            System.out.println("Opening connection...");
            SOAPConnectionFactory soapConnFct =
                SOAPConnectionFactory.newInstance();
            SOAPConnection soapConnection = soapConnFct.createConnection();

            System.out.println("Creating message...");
            MessageFactory messageFactory = MessageFactory.newInstance();
            SOAPMessage requestSoapMsg = messageFactory.createMessage();
```

LISTING 15.1 continued

```
            // Create references to SOAP message components
            SOAPPart requestSoapPart = requestSoapMsg.getSOAPPart();
            SOAPEnvelope requestSoapEnv = requestSoapPart.getEnvelope();
            SOAPHeader requestSoapHdr = requestSoapEnv.getHeader();

            // Add header field. Header fields are optional.
            Name questionName = requestSoapEnv.createName("Question");
            SOAPHeaderElement questionElement =
                requestSoapHdr.addHeaderElement(questionName);
            questionElement.setMustUnderstand(true);
            questionElement.addTextNode("Are you there?");

            /*
            * Note that a body element is not defined here.
            * Because this is a required field, JAXM
            * implicitly creates an empty body.
            */

            // Save all changes to message before printing.
            // Sending will also implictly save changes.
            requestSoapMsg.saveChanges();

            System.out.println(
                "HelloWorldSender is sending the following message:");
            try {
                requestSoapMsg.writeTo(System.out);
            } catch (IOException e) {
                System.err.println(
➥"Encountered IOException trying to write SOAPMessage to System.out: ");
                e.printStackTrace();
            }
            System.out.println("\nTo URL: ");
            System.out.println(urlEndpoint.getURL() + "\n");

            // Send request and block until reply appears.
            SOAPMessage responseSoapMsg = soapConnection.call(requestSoapMsg,
                                                              urlEndpoint);

            System.out.println(
                "HelloWorldSender received the following reponse message:");
            try {
                responseSoapMsg.writeTo(System.out);
                System.out.println("\n");
            } catch (IOException e) {
                System.err.println(
➥"Encountered IOException trying to write SOAPMessage to System.out: ");
                e.printStackTrace();
            }
```

LISTING 15.1 continued

```
            // Clean up
            soapConnection.close();
            System.out.println("Connection closed.");

        } catch (SOAPException e) {
            System.err.println("Encountered general SOAPException: ");
            e.printStackTrace();
        }
        System.out.println("Done.");
    } // main()
} // HelloWorldSender
```

Although this looks like a lot of code, it's actually very straightforward—something that attests to the power of JAXM, because there is in fact quite a lot going on here. Notice that the code is deliberately verbose, echoing request and response message contents to `System.out` by leveraging the powerful `SOAPMessage.writeTo(java.io.OutputStream)` method. Consider also that in your request message, you explicitly include a header field, but no body. The SOAP specification requires the `body` element, so JAXM conveniently creates an empty body for you.

Listing 15.2 shows the receiver code, to be deployed in the servlet container.

LISTING 15.2 `HelloWorldReceiver.java`: A Very Simple JAXM Server

```
package com.sams.jws.chapter15;

/*
 * HelloWorldReceiver
 * Receive a JAXM message and reply in the time-honored fashion.
 */

// General JDK
import java.io.IOException;
// JAXM
import javax.xml.soap.MessageFactory;
import javax.xml.soap.SOAPMessage;
import javax.xml.soap.SOAPElement;
import javax.xml.soap.SOAPPart;
import javax.xml.soap.SOAPEnvelope;
import javax.xml.soap.SOAPBody;
import javax.xml.soap.SOAPBodyElement;
import javax.xml.soap.SOAPException;
import javax.xml.messaging.JAXMServlet;
import javax.xml.messaging.ReqRespListener;
// Servlet
import javax.servlet.ServletConfig;
```

LISTING 15.2 continued

```
import javax.servlet.ServletException;

public class HelloWorldReceiver
    extends JAXMServlet
    implements ReqRespListener {
    MessageFactory messageFactory = null;
    public void init(ServletConfig servletConfig) throws ServletException {
        super.init(servletConfig);
        try {
            messageFactory = MessageFactory.newInstance();
        } catch (SOAPException e) {
             System.err.println("Exception instantiating MessageFactory:");
            e.printStackTrace();
        } // Catch
    }
    public SOAPMessage onMessage(SOAPMessage requestSoapMsg) {
        System.out.println(
            "HelloWorldReceiver recv the following JAXM msg in onMessage():");
        try {
            requestSoapMsg.writeTo(System.out);
            System.out.println("\n");

            SOAPMessage responseSoapMsg = messageFactory.createMessage();

            /*
             * Note that a header element is not defined here.
             * Although this is an optional element, JAXM will implicitly
             * nevertheless create an empty header.
             */
            // Create Body element containing response.
            SOAPEnvelope responseSoapEnv = responseSoapMsg.getSOAPPart()
                                                          .getEnvelope();
            SOAPBody responseSoapBody = responseSoapEnv.getBody();
            SOAPBodyElement responseSoapBodyEl =
➥responseSoapBody.addBodyElement(responseSoapEnv.createName("Response"));
            responseSoapBodyEl.addTextNode("Hello world");

            responseSoapMsg.saveChanges();
            System.out.println(
➥"HelloWorldReceiver responding with the following JAXM message:");
            responseSoapMsg.writeTo(System.out);
            System.out.println("\n");

            return responseSoapMsg;

        } catch (SOAPException e) {
            System.err.println("Error in processing or replying to a message");
            e.printStackTrace();
            return null;
```

LISTING 15.2 continued

```
        } catch (IOException e) {
            System.err.println(
                "Encountered IOException writing SOAPMessage to System.out: ");
            e.printStackTrace();
            return null;
        }
    } // onMessage()
} // HelloWorldReceiver
```

As in your sender, here you are also being quite verbose, writing status messages to the standard output stream. These should show up in the console running your servlet container, although this may depend on which container you are running. Check your documentation to be sure.

Deploying and Running Hello World

To start with, deploy both the sender and the receiver on one machine. Deployment for the sender is no different from any Java application—just don't forget that all the classes reside in the package, `com.sams.jws.chapter15`! Also, make sure you don't leave out any of the JAR files that JAXM needs. This will probably change with different versions, but at publication time the list is fairly long and includes the following:

- `activation.jar`
- `dom4j.jar`
- `jaxm.jar`
- `jaxm-client.jar`
- `log4j.jar`
- `mail.jar`
- `xalan.jar`
- `xerces.jar`

Obviously, not all archives are needed for every JAXM program, but if you're just experimenting with code it's a good habit to include them all in any run template that you may have. These all reside in `{`*`JAXM_HOME`*`}\lib`, except for `jaxm-client.jar`, which you find in `{`*`JAXM_HOME`*`}\jaxm`, and xalan and xerces, which come with the JAXP distribution. The `jam-client` archive is important, because it includes the classes the Java interpreter needs to run the JAXM application standalone in the absence of a provider.

Deploy the receiver as you would any Web application. For Tomcat, this is simple. First create a new Web application, called jaxm. This can be as simple as creating the directories `jaxm`, `jaxm\WEB_INF`, and `jaxm\WEB-INF\classes` underneath `{TOMCAT_HOME}\webapps`. Finally, place the `HelloWorldReceiver.class` file in the directory `{TOMCAT_HOME}\webapps\jaxm\WEB-INF\classes\com\sams\jws\chapter15` and cycle the server.

Run the sender with the receiver URL as an argument:

```
java com.sams.jws.chapter15.HelloWorldSender
➥http://localhost:8080/jaxm/servlet/com.sams.jws.chapter15.HelloWorldReceiver
```

substituting whatever port number your servlet container is bound to. The output should look similar to the following:

```
Opening connection...
Creating message...
HelloWorldSender is sending the following message:
<soap-env:Envelope xmlns:soap-env="http://schemas.xmlsoap.org/soap/envelope/">
➥<soap-env:Header><Question soap-env:mustUnderstand="1">Are you there?
➥</Question></soap-env:Header><soap-env:Body/></soap-env:Envelope>
To URL:
http://localhost:8080/jaxm/servlet/com.sams.jws.chapter15.HelloWorldReceiver

HelloWorldSender received the following reponse message:
<soap-env:Envelope xmlns:soap-env="http://schemas.xmlsoap.org/soap/envelope/">
➥<soap-env:Header/><soap-env:Body><Response>Hello world</Response>
➥</soap-env:Body></soap-env:Envelope>

Connection closed.
Done.
```

One of the more persuasive arguments for using HTTP and XML as a basis for distributed computing is that both use regular text that is plainly visible on the wire. This can be of enormous benefit when you have to track a nasty protocol bug. Yet even in the absence of problems, it can be constructive to examine the wire protocol to better understand precisely how JAXM renders messages.

One approach would be to use a network sniffer to grab the message exchange directly off the network; however, most of these tools operate at too low a level for your needs. Instead, you can explicitly set up an HTTP-aware, transparent proxy that has been designed to echo all HTTP dialogs to the screen. A number of these are available, such as TcpTunnelGui, which comes with the Apache SOAP distribution. But if you are using a Windows-based computer, I would recommend TcpTrace, from `http://www.pocketsoap.com`, because it's simple, standalone, and best of all, free (see Figure 15.5).

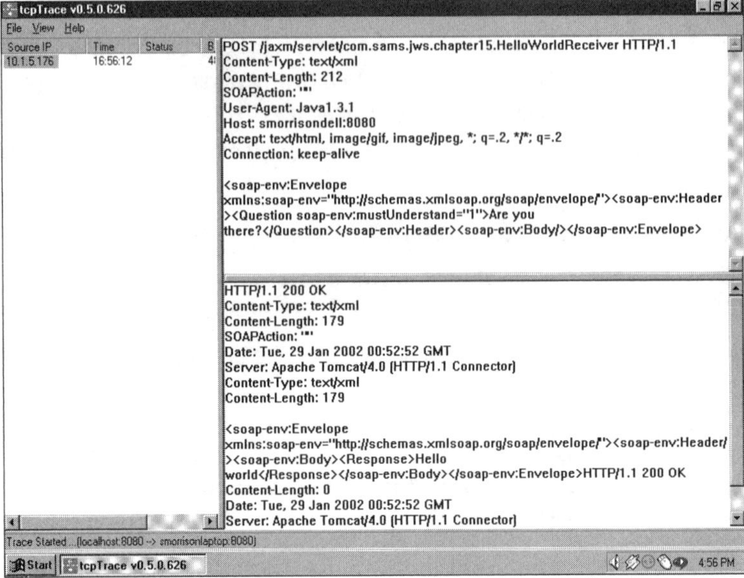

FIGURE 15.5
TcpTrace captures the dialog between HelloWorldSender and HelloWorld-Receiver.

Notice here that JAXM's SOAP messages set the usual SOAP namespace as a default, and that the HTTP `SOAPAction` header is an empty string.

Simple File Server

For the second example, you will try something a little more complicated, and build a simple, Web-based file server. Before you begin, an important word of caution: Deploy this example only on a secure system that is inaccessible from the Internet and any other systems that you do not trust. To simplify the example, this file server performs virtually no security checks, so do not deploy it on any machine that other users can access.

The file server is actually quite simple. The user enters the name of a file into a text entry box displayed in a Web browser. The browser posts this parameter to a servlet, which in turn uses it in a query it sends to a remote file service. The file server is a Web service that you implement with JAXM. The servlet also uses JAXM client calls to access the service. If the file exists on the file server relative to the Web root of the servlet container, the server returns it to the calling servlet and ultimately to the browser with the HTTP `Content-Type` set appropriately. The server derives the `Content-Type` from an examination of the file itself, as opposed to making a guess based on file extension bindings, which may be inaccurate. If the file is a directory, the browser should display a listing of the contents of the directory, including file modification times, access permissions, and so on. And finally, if a problem is encountered, the user should receive a reasonable explanation describing why the request could not be fulfilled.

Don't be surprised if this sounds familiar—most Web servers will do this already. The key difference here is that you will actually build file services as a Web service, making use of SOAP and JAXM. This enables you to make use of the expressive power of XML to contain file metadata, and enables you to use the SOAP attachment extension to transport non-XML content. In contrast to a Web server, your file server does not mix presentation tags (that is, HTML) into its content—such as when it returns a directory listing. This makes it much more appropriate as a server for non-browser clients. After you have file retrieval capability, a simple extension is all that's required to implement file upload capability. Thus, you can easily begin to approach some of the functionality that WebDAV provides (WebDAV is the Web Distributed Authoring and Versioning standard, a technology that enables distributed and collaborative production of Web content).

To showcase your file Web service, you will build a physically separate presentation service layer to render the results in a form appropriate for HTML-aware browser clients. This is a transformation service. It acts as an intermediary: a client of the file service, but a server for your browser. To simplify the example, you actually keep this code fairly thin; however, you could very easily render to a different presentation markup—such as WML or cHTML—based on client identification from the HTTP `User-Agent` field. Because your file service uses XML to respond to queries, the presentation server could use a technology such as XSLT to transform this content directly into presentation markup. But we will leave that as an exercise for you.

Figure 15.6 depicts the basic architecture.

FIGURE 15.6
The file server architecture. `FileRetrieverServlet` *demonstrates how a servlet can consume Web services, and render their results for browser-based clients.*

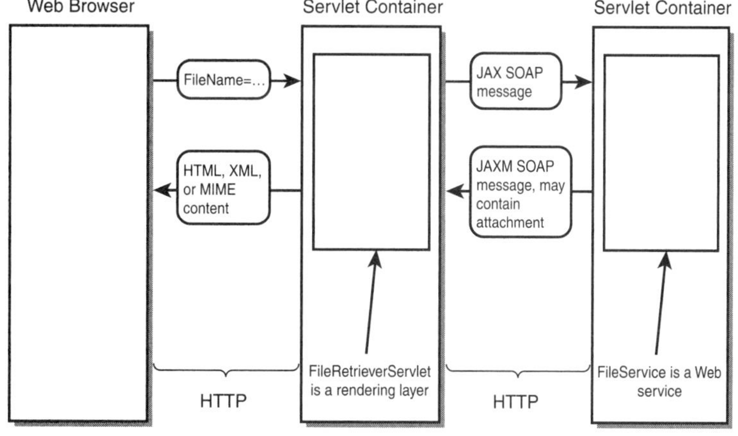

You begin with the code for the `FileService` Web service. Adopt the following query syntax to request files:

```
<soap-env:Envelope xmlns:soap-env="http://schemas.xmlsoap.org/soap/envelope/">
   <soap-env:Header>
      <CmdName soap-env:mustUnderstand="1">FileService</CmdName>
   </soap-env:Header>
   <soap-env:Body>
      <FileName> file to retrieve </FileName>
   </soap-env:Body>
</soap-env:Envelope>
```

You are explicitly including a header element `CmdName` here. This is a little redundant for the SOAP binding for HTTP, because the URL endpoint names the service you are obtaining. This could be an application-level routing field—a subservice, perhaps. In this example, it is included simply to clearly label message intent during logging.

The response semantics should include both the attached file and metadata about the file (or simply a directory listing, if your file request names a directory). For example, assume that you have a subdirectory of your Web root called `\directory`, which consists of a single file, `textFile.txt`. This file contains the string `"This is a textFile.txt."` A request for `\directory` should yield a SOAP response like the following (to improve readability, we have removed the HTTP fields and added extra line feeds and white space in the XML):

```
<soap-env:Envelope xmlns:soap-env="http://schemas.xmlsoap.org/soap/envelope/">
   <soap-env:Header>
      <ResponseType>directoryListing</ResponseType>
   </soap-env:Header>
   <soap-env:Body>
      <List>
         <File>
            <Name>textFile.txt</Name>
            <Path>{WEBROOT}\directory\textFile.txt</Path>
            <AbsolutePath>{WEBROOT}\directory\textFile.txt</AbsolutePath>
            <CanonicalPath>{WEBROOT}\directory\textFile.txt</CanonicalPath>
            <IsDirectory>false</IsDirectory>
            <IsFile>true</IsFile>
            <LastModified>Wed Nov 07 22:31:26 PST 2001</LastModified>
            <Length>20</Length>
            <CanRead>true</CanRead>
            <CanWrite>true</CanWrite>
            <IsHidden>false</IsHidden>
      </File>
      </List>
   </soap-env:Body>
</soap-env:Envelope>
```

where the `File` element is repeated for every file in the directory, and `{WEBROOT}` is the resolved path to the Web root of your servlet container. You might recognize the fields in the `file` element as mirroring the attributes of the `java.io.File` class.

A request for the actual file `\directory\textFile.txt` should return both the `file` element described in the preceding paragraph and the attachment as a MIME type (again reformatting the XML a little for clarity and dropping HTTP fields, but retaining the MIME fields):

```
------=_Part_4_491844.1012257832888
Content-Type: text/xml

<soap-env:Envelope xmlns:soap-env="http://schemas.xmlsoap.org/soap/envelope/">
   <soap-env:Header>
      <ResponseType>attachedFile</ResponseType>
   </soap-env:Header>
   <soap-env:Body>
      <File>
         <Name>textFile.txt</Name>
         <Path>{WEBROOT}\directory\textFile.txt</Path>
         <AbsolutePath>{WEBROOT}\directory\textFile.txt</AbsolutePath>
         <CanonicalPath>{WEBROOT}\directory\textFile.txt</CanonicalPath>
         <IsDirectory>false</IsDirectory>
         <IsFile>true</IsFile>
         <LastModified>Wed Nov 07 23:04:12 PST 2001</LastModified>
         <Length>20</Length>
         <CanRead>true</CanRead>
         <CanWrite>true</CanWrite>
         <IsHidden>false</IsHidden>
      </File>
   </soap-env:Body>
</soap-env:Envelope>
------=_Part_4_491844.1012257832888
Content-Type: text/plain
FileName: textFile.txt

This is textFile.txt
------=_Part_4_491844.1012257832888--
```

Note now that MIME boundaries delimit the MIME multipart/related types. You have also added an additional MIME header in the attachment, `FileName`, as a marker so that eventually you can include multiple attachments.

Listing 15.3 shows the server code.

LISTING 15.3 `FileService.java`: The Entry Point for a Web Services File Server

```
package com.sams.jws.chapter15;
/*
 * FileService
 * Process JAXM requests for files named in a SOAP message. If the file is
 * a directory, then list its contents--including characteristics of files in
 * the directory--in the SOAP body. If the file is a regular file, return it
 * as an attachment and include its characteristics in the SOAP body.
 * Typical requests look like the following:
 * <Envelope xmlns="http://schemas.xmlsoap.org/soap/envelope/">
 * <Header><CmdName mustUnderstand="1">FileService</CmdName></Header>
 * <Body><FileName>C:\temp\dir\a.txt</FileName></Body>
 * </Envelope>
 */
// General JDK
import java.io.IOException;
import java.io.File;
import java.util.Iterator;
import java.util.Hashtable;
// JAXM
import javax.xml.soap.MessageFactory;
import javax.xml.soap.SOAPMessage;
import javax.xml.soap.SOAPElement;
import javax.xml.soap.SOAPEnvelope;
import javax.xml.soap.SOAPHeader;
import javax.xml.soap.SOAPHeaderElement;
import javax.xml.soap.SOAPBody;
import javax.xml.soap.SOAPFault;
import javax.xml.soap.SOAPException;
import javax.xml.soap.AttachmentPart;
import javax.xml.messaging.JAXMServlet;
import javax.xml.messaging.ReqRespListener;
// JAF
import javax.activation.DataHandler;
import javax.activation.FileDataSource;
// Servlet
import javax.servlet.ServletConfig;
import javax.servlet.ServletContext;
import javax.servlet.ServletException;

public class FileService extends JAXMServlet implements ReqRespListener {
    static final boolean DEBUG = true;
    MessageFactory messageFactory = null;
    private ServletContext servletContext = null;
    private static Hashtable errorCodes = new Hashtable();
    static {
        // Initialize all error codes and messages here.
        errorCodes.put("100", "Incorrect command name sent to FileService.");
        errorCodes.put("200", "Missing FileName tag or illegal content.");
        errorCodes.put("300", "File does not exist.");
        errorCodes.put("400", "Cannot read file.");
    }
```

LISTING 15.3 continued

```
    public void init(ServletConfig servletConfig) throws ServletException {
        super.init(servletConfig);
        servletContext = servletConfig.getServletContext();
        try {
            messageFactory = MessageFactory.newInstance();
        } catch (SOAPException e) {
            System.err.println(
                "FileService caught exception instantiating MessageFactory:");
            e.printStackTrace();
        }
    }   // init()
    /*
     * renderFault
     * A fault has occured. Return fault details as response.
     */
    public void renderFault(
        SOAPHeaderElement responseType,
        SOAPBody responseSoapBody,
        String code,
        String param)
        throws SOAPException {

        System.err.println("ERROR Code: " + code);
        System.err.println("ERROR Desc: " + errorCodes.get(code)
                                          + " " + param);

        responseType.addTextNode("fault");
        SOAPFault soapFault = responseSoapBody.addFault();
        soapFault.setFaultCode(code);
        soapFault.setFaultString((String) errorCodes.get(code) + " " + param);
    }    // renderFault()
    // Version of renderFault() without additional param (eg: file name).
    public void renderFault(
        SOAPHeaderElement responseType,
        SOAPBody responseSoapBody,
        String code)
        throws SOAPException {
        renderFault(responseType, responseSoapBody, code, "");
    }    // renderFault()

    /*
     * onMessage
     * Process JAX request to retrieve file.
     */
    public SOAPMessage onMessage(SOAPMessage requestSoapMsg) {

        try {
            if (DEBUG) {
                System.out.println(
➥"FileService received the following message in onMessage():");
```

LISTING 15.3 continued

```
        requestSoapMsg.writeTo(System.out);
        System.out.println("\n");
    }

    // Create response.
    SOAPMessage responseSoapMsg = messageFactory.createMessage();
    SOAPEnvelope responseSoapEnv = responseSoapMsg.getSOAPPart()
                                                  .getEnvelope();
    SOAPHeader responseSoapHdr = responseSoapEnv.getHeader();
    SOAPBody responseSoapBody = responseSoapEnv.getBody();

    SOAPHeaderElement responseType =
        responseSoapHdr.addHeaderElement(
            responseSoapEnv.createName("ResponseType"));

    // Extract contents of query, validating in process.
    SOAPEnvelope requestSoapEnv = requestSoapMsg.getSOAPPart()
                                                .getEnvelope();
    SOAPHeader requestSoapHdr = requestSoapEnv.getHeader();
    SOAPBody requestSoapBody = requestSoapEnv.getBody();

    // Validate the CmdName header.
    String cmd = DocumentUtils.findValueOfChild(requestSoapHdr,
                                                "CmdName");
    if ((cmd == null) || (!cmd.equals("FileService"))) {
        // Could not locate CmdName tag
        renderFault(responseType, responseSoapBody, "100");
        return responseSoapMsg;
    }

    // Get filename parameter.
    String fileName = DocumentUtils.findValueOfChild(requestSoapBody,
                                                     "FileName");
    if ((fileName == null) || (fileName.indexOf("..") > -1)) {
        // No parameter, or attempt to navigate out of web root.
        renderFault(responseType, responseSoapBody, "200");
        return responseSoapMsg;
    }

    // Translate to absolute path with respect to web root.
    fileName = servletContext.getRealPath(fileName);
    System.out.println("Opening local fileName: " + fileName);
    File file = new File(fileName);
    if (!file.exists()) {
        // File doesn't exist.
        renderFault(responseType, responseSoapBody, "300",
                    file.getName());
        return responseSoapMsg;
    }
```

LISTING 15.3 continued

```
            if (!file.canRead()) {
                // File is inaccessible.
                renderFault(responseType, responseSoapBody, "400",
                            file.getName());
                return responseSoapMsg;
            }

            if (file.isDirectory()) {
                // List directory contents in SOAP body.
                responseType.addTextNode("directoryListing");
                SOAPElement listElement =
                    responseSoapBody.addChildElement("List");

                File[] fileList = file.listFiles();
                for (int j = 0; j < fileList.length; j++) {
                    FileElement fileElement = new FileElement(fileList[j]);
                    fileElement.marshalFile(listElement);
                }
                return responseSoapMsg;

            }

            if (file.isFile()) {
                // Return file contents as attachment and file characteristics
                // in SOAP body.
                responseType.addTextNode("attachedFile");
                FileElement fileElement = new FileElement(file);
                fileElement.marshalFile(responseSoapBody);

                // Add an attachment to the message.
                DataHandler dataHandler = new DataHandler(
➥new FileDataSource(file));
                AttachmentPart attachmentPart =
                    responseSoapMsg.createAttachmentPart(dataHandler);
                attachmentPart.setContentType(dataHandler.getContentType());
                // Add extra MIME header with file name.
                attachmentPart.addMimeHeader("FileName", file.getName());
                responseSoapMsg.addAttachmentPart(attachmentPart);
                return responseSoapMsg;

            }

            // General exceptions potentially thrown when working
            // with SOAPMessages.
        } catch (SOAPException e) {
            System.err.println(
➥"FileService encountered error in processing or replying to msg");
            e.printStackTrace();
            return null;
```

LISTING 15.3 continued

```
        } catch (IOException e) {
            System.err.println(
➥"FileService IOException when trying to write SOAPMessage: ");
            e.printStackTrace();
            return null;
        }
        return null;
    } // onMessage
} // Class FileService
```

`FileService` uses SOAP faults here to communicate when a problem has occurred. For example, if someone tries to navigate outside the Web root, using a path like `\..`, the server returns a fault signifying an illegal file name. This remains a weak security check, so to reiterate once more, you do not want to run this on a machine that is accessible to anyone you don't trust.

Notice that this service is not using any kind of schema to validate the XML message explicitly; however, you are validating implicitly by throwing faults if a necessary field is missing. This is actually one of the critical tradeoffs in any messaging application. Explicit validation to a schema (such as a DTD or W3C Schema) is desirable from a robustness and maintainability perspective, but it does incur a performance penalty. Unfortunately, JAXM does not provide any validating parsing functions. Thus, the only way to validate against a schema is with other tools, such as JAXP. There are two approaches to this. You can use the `SOAPPart.getContent()` method to extract the core SOAP message as a JAXP object. This returns an instance of an object that implements `javax.xml.transform.Source`. This interface encapsulates an XML document source under the JAXP abstraction for XML transformation. An object implementing `Source` can ultimately provide input to a validating SAX or DOM parser in JAXP. An alternative approach is to use the `SOAPMessage(java.io.OutputStream)` method to create a text representation of the SOAP message in a buffer that could then be fed to an appropriate JAXP parser. Neither option is particularly fast.

`FileService` makes use of some simple utility classes. The first of these is an XML document navigational aid. JAXM provides a DOM-like interface to access nodes, but tree walking is one of those tedious DOM operations that are best automated through utility classes, such as the `DocumentUtils` class shown in Listing 15.4.

LISTING 15.4 DocumentUtils.java: A Simple Utility Class

```
package com.sams.jws.chapter15;

/**
 * DocumentUtils
 * Utility methods for working with JAXM SOAP documents
 */
import java.util.Iterator;
import javax.xml.soap.SOAPElement;

public class DocumentUtils {
/**
 * Private constructor ensures that util class can't be instantiated
 * or extended.
 */
private DocumentUtils() {}
/**
 * findChild
 * Return the SOAPElement representing direct decendant of root
 * named by childName. This is case-sensitive.
 */
public static SOAPElement findChild(SOAPElement root, String childName) {
    Iterator i = root.getChildElements();
    while (i.hasNext()) {
        SOAPElement soapElement = (SOAPElement) i.next();
        if (soapElement.getElementName().getLocalName().equals(childName))
            return soapElement;
    }
    return null;
}    // findChild()
/**
 * findValueOfChild
 * Find the SOAPElement representing direct decendant of root
 * named by childName. If the immediate decendant of this is a text node,
 * return the value of this node. Otherwise return null.
 *
 * For example, given: <Foo> bar </Foo> where Foo is the root, return bar.
 * Note that childName is case-sensitive
 */
public static String findValueOfChild(SOAPElement root, String childName) {
    SOAPElement childElement = findChild(root, childName);
    if (childElement == null) {
        return null;
    }
    return childElement.getValue();
}    // findValueOfChild()
}    // DocumentUtils
```

This is useful enough that you will call it both in the servlet FileRetrieverServlet and in the Web service FileService. To enforce the point of this being a utility class, the constructor is private. The only way to use it is to call the class methods.

The purpose of the `FileElement` class is to marshal `java.io.File` Java object instances to an XML document representation. One of the goals of the JAXB project, discussed elsewhere in this book, is to provide an automated method to generate such bindings between graphs of Java objects (with their rich typing system) and XML documents (with a type system enforced though W3C Schema). This time, you will do it manually; see Listing 15.5.

LISTING 15.5 `FileElement.java`: An Extension of `java.io.File` that Uses Delegation.

```
package com.sams.jws.chapter15;

/**
 * FileElement
 * Wrapper class for the java.io.File type. The wrapper knows how to
 * marshal itself into a JAXM XML document.
 */
import java.io.File;
import java.io.IOException;
import java.util.Date;
import javax.xml.soap.SOAPElement;
import javax.xml.soap.SOAPException;

public class FileElement {
    private java.io.File file = null;
public FileElement(File file) {
    this.file=file;
}   // FileElement constructor
public File getFile() {
    return file;
}   // getFile
/**
 * marshalFile
 * Build XML representation of file based at soapElement.
 */
public void marshalFile(SOAPElement soapElement) throws SOAPException {

    // Create an XML subdocument describing the characteristics
    // of the file, as represented by the File object.
    SOAPElement fileElement = soapElement.addChildElement("File");
    fileElement.addChildElement("Name").addTextNode(file.getName());
    fileElement.addChildElement("Path").addTextNode(file.getPath());
    fileElement.addChildElement("AbsolutePath")
            .addTextNode(file.getAbsolutePath());
```

LISTING 15.5 continued

```
    try {
        fileElement.addChildElement("CanonicalPath")
                   .addTextNode(file.getCanonicalPath());
    } catch (IOException e){
    // Just leave out CanonicalPath element if the IOException is thrown.
    }
    fileElement.addChildElement("IsDirectory")
               .addTextNode(String.valueOf(file.isDirectory()));
    fileElement.addChildElement("IsFile")
               .addTextNode(String.valueOf(file.isFile()));
    fileElement.addChildElement("LastModified")
               .addTextNode(new Date(file.lastModified()).toString());
    fileElement.addChildElement("Length")
               .addTextNode(String.valueOf(file.length()));
    fileElement.addChildElement("CanRead")
               .addTextNode(String.valueOf(file.canRead()));
    fileElement.addChildElement("CanWrite")
               .addTextNode(String.valueOf(file.canWrite()));
    fileElement.addChildElement("IsHidden")
               .addTextNode(String.valueOf(file.isHidden()));
}    // marshalFile
public void setFile(File newFile) {
    file = newFile;
}    // setFile
}    // FileElement
```

That's all you need for the Web service `FileService`. Place these three class files under your Web application root. I reused the JAXM Web application from the last example and placed these files in the directory: `{TOMCAT_HOME}\webapps\jaxm\WEB-INF\classes\com\sams\jws\chapter15`. Note that the evaluation of all of the file requests is relative to the Web root, `{TOMCAT_HOME}\webapps\jaxm`. I created a subdirectory underneath this called `directory`, and populated it with files of various types to download, including text, GIF files, PDFs, and so on.

Testing the File Server

At this point, you should test the `FileService` Web service. One of the great attractions of Web services is that they are basically coarsely grained, late-bound objects that are very loosely coupled to clients—and most importantly, coupled through human-understandable text streams. This contributes to making Web services very easy to exercise individually with very simple test harnesses. In fact, you can test your application directly using little more than Telnet:

```
telnet localhost 8080
```

Copy and paste the following HTTP message into the session:

```
POST /jaxm/servlet/com.sams.jws.chapter15.FileService HTTP/1.1
Content-Type: text/xml
Content-Length: 253
SOAPAction: ""
User-Agent: Telnet
Host: localhost:8080
Accept: text/xml

<soap-env:Envelope xmlns:soap-env="http://schemas.xmlsoap.org/soap/envelope/">
➥<soap-env:Header>
➥<CmdName soap-env:mustUnderstand="1">FileService</CmdName>
➥</soap-env:Header>
➥<soap-env:Body><FileName>\directory</FileName></soap-env:Body>
➥</soap-env:Envelope>
```

Make sure that the XML SOAP message is all on a single line. We have had to break it up here to get everything on a single page. If you add any similar line feeds, you will need to increase the `Content-length` HTTP header accordingly.

If everything is working, you should receive an XML listing of the files residing in `{WEBROOT}\directory`.

The awkward part of debugging with Telnet is getting the HTTP `Content-Length` header right. As an alternative, you could build a standalone JAXM test driver. We will leave this for you to discover as a personal exercise, but a good place to start is with `HelloWorldSender` from the previous section. You can lift most of the code you will need to modify this from `FileRetrieverServlet`, which is developed next.

Web browsers cannot communicate directly with Web services, so you need to create a service between the browser and `FileService` to link the two. The source for this is in Listing 15.6:

LISTING 15.6 `FileRetrieverServlet.java`: A Simple Servlet that Demonstrates Use of the Web File Service

```
package com.sams.jws.chapter15;

/**
 * FileRetrieverServlet
 * Servlet to demonstrate use of JAXM. Calls a remote file
 * server Web service, and renders the results appropriately
 * for browser consumption.
 */
// General JDK
import java.io.IOException;
import java.util.Iterator;
```

LISTING 15.6 continued

```
// JAXM
import javax.xml.soap.SOAPConnectionFactory;
import javax.xml.soap.SOAPConnection;
import javax.xml.soap.MessageFactory;
import javax.xml.soap.SOAPMessage;
import javax.xml.soap.SOAPElement;
import javax.xml.soap.SOAPPart;
import javax.xml.soap.SOAPEnvelope;
import javax.xml.soap.SOAPHeader;
import javax.xml.soap.SOAPHeaderElement;
import javax.xml.soap.SOAPBody;
import javax.xml.soap.SOAPBodyElement;
import javax.xml.soap.SOAPFault;
import javax.xml.soap.Name;
import javax.xml.soap.SOAPException;
import javax.xml.soap.AttachmentPart;
import javax.xml.messaging.URLEndpoint;
// JAF
import javax.activation.DataHandler;
// Servlet
import javax.servlet.*;
import javax.servlet.http.*;

public class FileRetrieverServlet extends HttpServlet {
    private final static boolean DEBUG = true;
    private final static String FILE_SERVICE_URL =
       "http://localhost:8080/jaxm/servlet/com.sams.jws.chapter15.FileService";
    public URLEndpoint urlEndpoint = new URLEndpoint(FILE_SERVICE_URL);
    private final static String DEFAULT_TARGET = "/";
    public SOAPConnection soapConnection = null;
    /**
     * doGet()
     * Respond to browser request for file listing from remote FileService.
     * Render results of retrieval appropriately, either by passing the
     * file directly to the browser, returning a directory listing if
     * the file names a directory, or returning an error
     * page explaining that a problem was encountered.
     * File to list is variable FileName in get query string.
     */
    public void doGet(
        HttpServletRequest httpServletRequest,
        HttpServletResponse httpServletResponse)
        throws ServletException {

        ServletOutputStream outputStream = null;
        try {
            outputStream = httpServletResponse.getOutputStream();
```

LISTING 15.6 continued

```
        String targetFile = httpServletRequest.getParameter("FileName");
        if ((targetFile == null) || (targetFile == ""))
            targetFile = DEFAULT_TARGET;

        if (DEBUG)
            System.out.println(
                "FileRetrieverServlet has retrieval request for file: " +
                 targetFile);

        // Send file retrieval request to FileService.
        SOAPMessage responseSoapMsg = sendRequestMsg(targetFile);

        // Get some utility references parts of response message.
        SOAPEnvelope responseSoapEnv = responseSoapMsg.getSOAPPart()
                                                      .getEnvelope();
        SOAPHeader responseSoapHdr = responseSoapEnv.getHeader();
        SOAPBody responseSoapBody = responseSoapEnv.getBody();

        // Determine response type and render accordingly.
        String responseType =
            DocumentUtils.findValueOfChild(responseSoapHdr,
                                           "ResponseType");
        if ((responseType != null) &&
            (responseType.equals("directoryListing"))) {
            // Return message as is to browser. Ultimately, this could be
            // replaced with a transform step that creates an HTML listing
            // of the directory contents, with appropriate links to each
            // file.
            httpServletResponse.setContentType("text/xml");
            responseSoapMsg.writeTo(outputStream);
        } else if (responseType.equals("attachedFile")) {
            // Return attachment.
            Iterator iterator = responseSoapMsg.getAttachments();
            if (iterator.hasNext()) {
                // We are assuming that the first attachment part is
                // the file we are after. A better solution is to
                // look for a particular MIME header.
                AttachmentPart attachmentPart =
                    (AttachmentPart) iterator.next();
                DataHandler dataHandler = attachmentPart.getDataHandler();
                httpServletResponse.setContentType(
                    dataHandler.getContentType());
                dataHandler.writeTo(outputStream);
            } else {
                renderErrorPage(outputStream,
                                "Could not locate attached file",
                                targetFile);
            } // Else
        } else if (responseType.equals("fault")) {
```

LISTING 15.6 continued

```
            SOAPFault soapFault = responseSoapBody.getFault();
            httpServletResponse.setContentType("text/html");
            renderErrorPage(
                outputStream,
                "<B>Code:</B> " + soapFault.getFaultCode(),
                "<B>Description:</B> " + soapFault.getFaultString());
        } else {
            // Unidentifiable response
            httpServletResponse.setContentType("text/html");
            renderErrorPage(
                outputStream,
                "Received corrupted response from server.",
                "<B>Could not retrieve file:</B> " + targetFile);
        }
        // General SOAPMessage manipulation exceptions.
    } catch (SOAPException e) {
        System.err.println("Encountered general SOAPException: ");
        e.printStackTrace();
    } catch (IOException e) {
        System.err.println(
            "Encountered IOException when trying to write SOAPMessage: ");
        e.printStackTrace();
    }
} // doGet()
public void init(ServletConfig servletConfig) throws ServletException {
    super.init(servletConfig);
    try {
        // Initialize connection so that all instances can use it.
        SOAPConnectionFactory soapConnFct =
            SOAPConnectionFactory.newInstance();
        soapConnection = soapConnFct.createConnection();
    } catch (SOAPException e) {
        System.err.println("Encountered general SOAPException: ");
        e.printStackTrace();
    }
} // init()
/**
 * renderErrorPage
 * Return an HTML formatted error page to the ServletOutputStream
 */
public void renderErrorPage(
    ServletOutputStream outputStream,
    String line1,
    String line2)
    throws IOException {
    outputStream.println("<HTML>");
    outputStream.println(
        "Error encountered trying to fullfil request.<P>");
    outputStream.println(line1 + "<P>");
```

LISTING 15.6 continued

```
        outputStream.println(line2 + "<P>");
        outputStream.println("</HTML>");
    } // renderErrorPage()
    /**
     * sendRequestMsg
     * Call the FileService remote file access Web service, requesting
     * a retrieval of the file targetFile. Return SOAPMessage response.
     */
    public SOAPMessage sendRequestMsg(String targetFile)
        throws SOAPException, IOException {

        // Initialize connection and SOAP Profile
        MessageFactory messageFactory = MessageFactory.newInstance();

        SOAPMessage requestSoapMsg = messageFactory.createMessage();

        SOAPPart requestSoapPart = requestSoapMsg.getSOAPPart();
        SOAPEnvelope requestSoapEnv = requestSoapPart.getEnvelope();
        SOAPHeader requestSoapHdr = requestSoapEnv.getHeader();
        SOAPBody requestSoapBody = requestSoapEnv.getBody();

        // Add header field
        Name msgPurposeName = requestSoapEnv.createName("CmdName");
        SOAPHeaderElement msgPurposeElement =
            requestSoapHdr.addHeaderElement(msgPurposeName);
        msgPurposeElement.setMustUnderstand(true);
        msgPurposeElement.addTextNode("FileService");

        // Add namespace-qualified body field
        Name fileName = requestSoapEnv.createName("FileName");
        SOAPBodyElement fileNameElement =
            requestSoapBody.addBodyElement(fileName);
        fileNameElement.addTextNode(targetFile);

        // Save all changes to message before printing.
        // Sending will also implictly save changes.
        requestSoapMsg.saveChanges();

        if (DEBUG) {
            System.out.println("FileRetrieverServlet is sending message:");
            requestSoapMsg.writeTo(System.out);
            System.out.println("\n");
        }

        // Send request and block until reply appears.
        SOAPMessage responseSoapMsg = soapConnection.call(requestSoapMsg,
                                                           urlEndpoint);
```

LISTING 15.6 continued

```
        if (DEBUG) {
            System.out.println(
                "FileRetrieverServlet received response message:");
            responseSoapMsg.writeTo(System.out);
            System.out.println("\n");
        }

        return responseSoapMsg;

    } // sendRequestMsg()
} // FileRetrieverServlet
```

This servlet has two hardwired settings you may want to modify—or better yet, extract into external resource bundles or XML files. The first is the DEBUG flag, which simply controls the verbosity of the servlet. The second is the FILE_SERVICE_URL, which defines the URL where the FileService Web service resides. Don't forget to update the latter if your deployment differs from the one described here.

As an initial deployment, place the `FileRetrieverServlet` in the same directory as the `FileService`. Note that the `FileRetrieverServlet` also uses the `DocumentUtils` class, so make sure it accompanies the servlet if you move things around.

Finally, Listing 15.7 contains a very simple Web page to get things started. This can be loaded into your browser directly from the file system, or you can serve it from your Web server/servlet container.

LISTING 15.7 `FileRetriever.html`: A Simple Web Page to Access the Web File Services

```
<!DOCTYPE HTML PUBLIC "-//W3C//DTD HTML 3.2 Final//EN">
<HTML>
<HEAD>
<TITLE>File Retriever Application</TITLE>
</HEAD>

<BODY>
<H2>File Retriever Application</H2>

<FORM name=FileRetriever action=
➥"http://localhost:8080/jaxm/servlet/
➥com.sams.jws.chapter15.FileRetrieverServlet"
➥ method=get>
<TABLE cellspacing=0 cellpadding=5>
<TR align=left>
<TD>
   Enter file to retrieve:
```

LISTING 15.7 continued

```
</TD>
<TD>
   <input type=text value="\dir" name="FileName" size=25 maxlength=50>
</TD>
<TD>
   <input type=submit value="Retrieve File">
</TD>
</TR>
</TABLE>
</FORM>
<P>
Must include path and filename. For example:
<P>
\dir
<P>
\dir\a.txt
<P>
</BODY>
</HTML>
```

You will have to change the value of the `action` attribute in the `Form` element if you move `FileRetrieverServlet`.

To run this, enter a file or directory name into the text entry box on the Web page. If the target is a directory, the servlet returns the `SOAPPart` of the JAXM message—an XML document describing the directory contents—to the browser. The browser renders this document using the standard stylesheet for XML, which indents elements and colors tags, attributes, and content. If the target is a file, the servlet returns the file contents to the browser directly, setting the `Content-Type` based on the MIME-type header in the JAXM message. Recall that the file service used the Java Activation Framework to derive the `Content-Type`. In this case, the presentation layer discards the additional file metadata. A good extension would be to direct the file metadata to a different frame. The browser displays the returned file contents if it is able (for example, if its content type is image/gif, text/xml, text/html, and so on); otherwise, it may delegate display to an external application if it has an appropriate binding for the MIME type (for example, `application/msword`, which is a Microsoft Word file). As an exercise, you can write a stylesheet to transform the XML directory listing into nicely formatted HTML with links referencing each individual file in a directory.

A Note on Security

Is the `FileService` Web service ready for production? Of course not—in the interest of simplicity, this example has largely ignored the security implications surrounding a service like `FileService`. Remember that by deploying `FileService`, you are publishing an API, so you need to consider controlling access to it, as well as the potential consequences of unencrypted file transmission.

The good thing about SOAP is that when used with the HTTP binding, firewall traversal is generally pretty easy. The bad thing about SOAP is that when used with the HTTP binding, firewall traversal is generally pretty easy. In effect, SOAP breaks down the fundamental security model of the Internet protocol, wherein applications are bound to port numbers, thus making ports the basis for packet filtering. (Source and destination port are each 16-bit fields in every TCP or UDP packet.) By hosting all applications within the context of an HTTP provider, you lose that detail at the Internet Protocol transport layer, making filtering packets at a firewall much more complex. Now you need stateful inspection of messages at the application layer (that is, assembly of multiple sequential packets to reconstruct the application-layer message), plus the capability to parse and interpret application protocols such as HTTP—ultimately not difficult, but nonetheless complicated given the capabilities many existing firewall tools.

`FileService` is exactly the kind of application that scares people about Web services, and it's wide open applications like this that may be this technology's downfall in a number of security-conscious organizations. At present, `FileService` makes no attempt to authenticate the client calling it. With no credentials, there can be no authorization for access to a particular resource; `FileService` lets everyone see everything. The client is similarly naive. It makes no attempt to authenticate the server, leaving it open to impersonations and man-in-the-middle attacks. The HTTP stream is completely plain text: an advantage for debugging, but a similar advantage to unauthorized users intent on capturing sensitive information in transit.

One of the goals of SOAP is to leverage existing infrastructure as much as is reasonably possible. HTTP, of course, provides a rich legacy of security infrastructure. Server-side certificates can provide two important things: server authentication to the client, and the server's public key. This enables secure exchange of asymmetric cipher key needed for stream encryption. HTTP has facilities for authentication of clients, including basic authentication, digest (which has the advantage of not transmitting passwords), embedded within the URL, and a number of proprietary vendor methods such as Microsoft's NTLM or RSA's SecureID secondary authentication mechanism. A number of resource authorization frameworks are available for servlets. These are typically associated with commercial containers, such as those provided with IBM's WebSphere or BEA's WebLogic.

At the time of writing, the JAXM distribution supports SSL connections to secure transmission and authenticate servers, and URL-based authentication of clients to servers (which should never be used without SSL). As JAXM matures, it safe to assume that commercial-grade HTTP providers with a more sophisticated security model will appear, as well as commercial profiles that employ element-level document encryption.

Summary

This chapter really had two goals: to introduce JAXM as the standardized Java API for SOAP messaging, and to highlight some of the capabilities that JAXM has now. As you can appreciate, the implementations are undergoing considerable change; however, the API itself is quite stable, well thought out, and ready to use. If you are building Web services with Java, and you are concerned about adhering to the standards of the language, then you should very seriously consider adopting JAXM.

CHAPTER

JAX-RPC

by Benoît Marchal

In This Chapter

In this chapter you'll learn about JAX-RPC, the Java API for XML-based RPC. JAX-RPC is one of the XML APIs for Java and it promises to simplify writing Web services.

Note, however, that at the time of writing, JAX-RPC was still very early in its development cycle. This chapter presents what you are likely to find in the final version of JAX-RPC.

Why Another API?

In Chapter 7, "Understanding SOAP," you learned the basics of Simple Object Access Protocol (SOAP), a simple XML-based protocol for RPC (Remote Procedure Call). In Chapter 8, "SOAP Basics," you learned how to develop SOAP Web services with Apache SOAP. In Chapter 11, you learned about WSDL (Web Services Definition Language).

SOAP defines a simple and elegant protocol to implement remote procedure calls over HTTP with XML. SOAP also supports XML message passing, which is covered in Chapter 15, "JAXM." but this chapter concentrates on RPCs only.

WSDL is an XML vocabulary to describe Web services: which services are available, over which transport, what are the expected parameters, or return values, and more.

From Proprietary APIs to Open Ones

Together SOAP and WSDL provide the technical foundation for building Web services. Java developers working on Web services therefore need to learn them both.

In practice, however, as you saw in Chapters 6 and 10, few developers write to the raw protocol any more than RMI developers would write directly to JRMP or IIOP. Application programmers should be writing to APIs—not directly to wire protocols. It simply is not effective to repetitively develop the same low-level protocol-oriented code.

Instead, developers use libraries and tools that shield them from the most technical aspects. They enable them to concentrate on the business aspects of their Web services. Ultimately, libraries and tools make developers more productive.

Obviously, unless a standard API is agreed upon, library and tool vendors will develop their own and they will be incompatible. The unfortunate result would be to lock developers with vendors. For example, code written with Apache SOAP cannot easily be migrated to a competing product. Ultimately this disparity also makes it harder for developers to learn the new protocols. For example, one cannot lift code from an XSOAP example and apply it to another product.

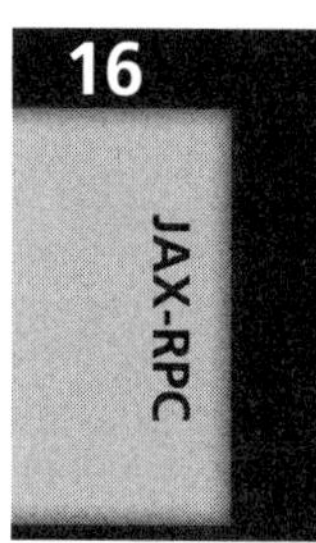

Essentially the situation is similar to APIs in other areas such as databases (JDBC), email (JavaMail) or Web servers (servlets and JSP). It is expected that a standard API will foster adoption.

The new API is called JAX-RPC, the Java API for XML-based RPC.

Scope of JAX-RPC

It is important to understand that the name was selected purposefully as JAX-RPC rather than JAX-SOAP. In other words, the API is not a SOAP API in at least two ways:

- It is not limited to SOAP implementations.
- It leaves out certain options in SOAP (amongst other things, it does not support message-oriented transactions).

Let's first look at other implementations. The current draft is divided into two sections: a generic section that works with any XML-based protocol for RPC, and a more specific one for SOAP. This is similar to the servlet API that also combines a generic section (the `javax.servlet` package) and a more specific one (the `javax.servlet.http` package).

At the time of writing, it is unclear whether JAX-RPC will ever be adapted to other XML-based protocols such as XML-RPC (introduced in Chapter 7, "Understanding SOAP").

As for SOAP and WSDL support, remember that SOAP is organized around the following modules (see also Figure 16.1):

- Protocol bindings and, in particular, HTTP binding
- Messaging framework with the SOAP envelope
- Encoding rules that specify how to construct XML content
- RPC that uses all the above to implement procedure calls.

JAX-RPC concentrates on the RPC support only. In particular, it offers only limited access to the underlying messaging framework. Access to messages is further limited to an RPC context.

Likewise, JAX-RPC gives you no control over WSDL files. To the contrary, one of its goals is to shield the programmer from the intricacies of WSDL. If you nevertheless need to manipulate WSDL files, a separate API has been proposed.

FIGURE 16.1
SOAP builds on different modules.

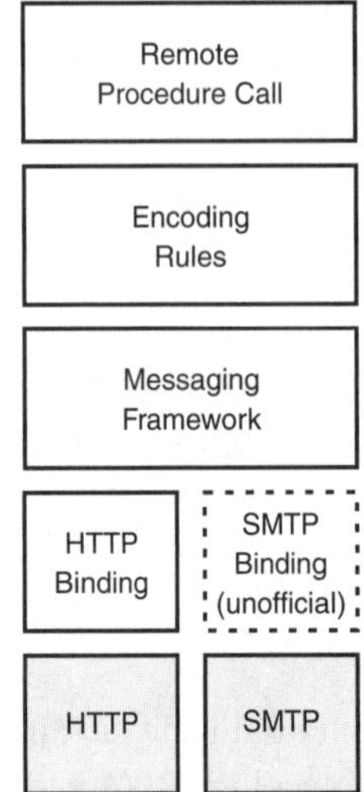

Status of JAX-RPC

At the time of writing, JAX-RPC is still under development through the Java Community Process (JCP). JCP is an open standardization process, organized by Sun, for the development of Java APIs. You can find more details on JCP at `http://www.jcp.org`.

The draft for JAX-RPC at the time of writing is at version 0.6, so it's very early. Therefore, this chapter can only highlight trends and explain what JAX-RPC might look like. The final version may differ, maybe significantly, from what is presented in this chapter.

Tip

Make sure you visit `http://java.sun.com/xml` for an update on the latest version of JAX-RPC.

For more practical details on programming with the final version of JAX-RPC, turn to `http://www.marchal.com` where I will post links.

Also, unfortunately, at the time of writing there are no implementations of JAX-RPC. The closest thing is probably a combination of XSOAP (`http://www.extreme.indiana.edu/soap`) that implements the RMI (Remote Method Invocation) mapping, (more details on the RMI mapping soon) and Apache SOAP (`http://xml.apache.org`) that implements dynamic invocation (more details soon).

Data Mapping

JAX-RPC fills in two holes in the SOAP specification:

- It defines a standard Java mapping for the SOAP encoding.
- It tries to shield the Java developer from the specifics of XML coding.

A Standard Java Mapping

The SOAP encoding specifies how to write, in XML, data types commonly found in programming languages: simple types (strings, numbers, Booleans, and more), as well as compound types (structs and arrays). What it does not specify, however, is the Java equivalent.

The same holds true for WSDL. It uses XML schemas to specify XML structures as input or output of operations, but it does not specify how to map those structures to Java (or any other programming language) objects.

Although it's obvious that a `java.lang.String` in Java should map to an `xsd:string` in XML, other types are less obvious. For example, Java has no structs. Is the best mapping a JavaBean (with getter and setter methods), or a simple class with fields and no methods?

Even simple types may be worth discussing. How do you map an XML `xsd:integer` that has no upper limit? The Java `int`, which is probably the easiest mapping, is limited to 32-bit numbers.

Of course, unless there's a standard Java mapping, implementations will vary in how they map between Java types and XML types. JAX-RPC proposes a standard mapping.

Note

SOAP is unique because it lacks a standard mapping for programming languages. Other distributed computing architectures, such as CORBA, RMI, DCOM, and even the original RPC, go to great lengths to define a programming language mapping for their constructs.

CORBA, DCOM, and RPC define an IDL (Interface Definition Language), a special-purpose language, that plays a role similar to WSDL. However, the IDL also defines standard mappings from specific programming languages to RPCs.

For example, there are standard mappings between the CORBA IDL and Java, C++, Ada, and other languages. In practice, the availability of standard mappings means that Java implementations of CORBA map network objects to Java coherently.

SOAP and WSDL lacks those standard mappings. It is mostly left to the implementers to decide which Java concepts best represent an XML concept.

Mapping of Element Names

JAX-RPC defines rules for the mapping of XML names into Java. The rules may appear complex, but they attempt to bridge cultural differences between the Java and XML communities.

Compared with Java names, there are very few constraints on XML names. The XML syntax supports more punctuation characters than Java. For example, the minus character (`-`) and the dot (`.`) are often used to separate words in XML element names, but they are illegal in Java names.

Java has a small set of reserved keywords such as `for`, `if`, and `private`. The XML specification has only two reserved keywords: `xml:space` and `xml:lang`. However, the XML specification does reserve every name starting with `xml`.

XML also has no universal convention to build names. For Java, Sun has published a strict set of rules that are used almost uniformly. Java recommends the camel case rule (it capitalizes the first letter of each word in multi-word names) for class and method names. The first letter of class and interface names is further capitalized; the first letter of method names and local variables is lower-case:

```
public interface TheaterOperations {
    public int bookASeat(int category);
    public int[] bookSeats(int category,int groupSize);
    // ...
}
```

Only constants follow a different rule. They are written in all uppercase with the underscore as the word separator:

```
public int CATEGORY_STALLS = 1;
```

XML has no such naming convention. The XML recommendation offers no guidance, and the W3C itself has used many diverging conventions in subsequent recommendations.

For example, XSL has only lowercase names. Multi-word names use the minus as separator:

```
<xsl:template match="article">
    <xsl:for-each select="title">
        <!-- ... -->
    </xsl:for-each>
</xsl:template>
```

XML schema, however, follows the camel case convention, but it never capitalizes the first letter of elements names and attributes:

```
<xsd:complexType name="Seat">
    <xsd:sequence>
        <xsd:element name="number" type="xsd:int"/>
        <xsd:element name="row"    type="xsd:int"/>
    </xsd:sequence>
</xsd:complexType>
```

A popular variation on the latter is to use camel case but capitalize the first letter in the names of elements, sticking to lowercase for attributes. RDF is a prime example of this:

```
<RDF xmlns="http://www.w3.org/1999/02/22-rdf-syntax-ns#">
    <Description about="http://www.marchal.com">
        <ps:Writer xmlns:ps="http://www.psol.com/2001/writer">
            Beno&#238;t Marchal
        </ps:Writer>
    </Description>
</RDF>
```

Unfortunately, it gets more complex when you combine XML vocabularies that do not strictly adhere to the same conventions. Listing 16.1 is a signed DocBook document. It combines elements from the digital signature and the DocBook vocabularies. Digital signature follows the camel case convention, whereas DocBook is all lowercase, with no word separator.

> **Caution**
>
> I had to reformat the Listing 16.1 for printing. The original file had longer lines in the certificate section.

LISTING 16.1 A Signed DocBook Document

```
<?xml version='1.0' encoding='UTF-8'?>
<Signature xmlns="http://www.w3.org/2000/09/xmldsig#">
  <SignedInfo>
    <CanonicalizationMethod
     Algorithm="http://www.w3.org/TR/2000/WD-xml-c14n-20000119"/>
    <SignatureMethod
     Algorithm="http://www.w3.org/2000/09/xmldsig#dsa-sha1"/>
    <Reference URI="#Res0">
      <Transforms>
        <Transform
     Algorithm="http://www.w3.org/TR/2000/WD-xml-c14n-20000119"/>
      </Transforms>
      <DigestMethod
```

Listing 16.1 continued

```
       Algorithm="http://www.w3.org/2000/09/xmldsig#sha1"/>
      <DigestValue>EnjbDLqPu+IJvjobZ0KnvL30k0M=</DigestValue>
    </Reference>
  </SignedInfo>
  <SignatureValue>
    lzJVXLLvTPEOWm89JxJfDr2UBDh8eD6cy+LbeiRj1m9vRlwxAT3erg==
  </SignatureValue>
  <KeyInfo>
    <KeyValue>
      <DSAKeyValue>
<P>
/X9TgR11EilS30qcLuzk5/YRt1I870QAwx4/gLZRJmlFXUAiUftZPY1Y+r/F9bow9s
ubVWzXgTuAHTRv8mZgt2uZUKWkn5/oBHsQIsJPu6nX/rfGG/g7V+fGqKYVDwT7g/bT
xR7DAjVUE1oWkTL2dfOuK2HXKu/yIgMZndFIAcc=
</P>
<Q>l2BQjxUjC8yykrmCouuEC/BYHPU=</Q>
<G>
9+GghdabPd7LvKtcNrhXuXmUr7v6OuqC+VdMCz0HgmdRWVeOutRZT+ZxBxCBgLRJFn
Ej6EwoFhO3zwkyjMim4TwWeotUfI0o4KOuHiuzpnWRbqN/C/ohNWLx+2J6ASQ7zKTx
vqhRkImog9/hWuWfBpKLZl6Ae1UlZAFMO/7PSSo=
</G>
<Y>
ExRJP2t4T0h07oLAqlgv9mXNFKX8X+tIgjA6860srebYoWLaxFTdEV6dq0DM5ffejf
1tkmPYS5wIsUXMrILPJpTpp/4c/AROv2dqnqAch4KqE7sJ16hKUxJyB8r2Rw6LIZmZ
m80S5nWt2UxC3rLy/lBmSTLCHBbx3/lGR+gfiOs=
</Y>
      </DSAKeyValue>
    </KeyValue>
    <X509Data>
      <X509IssuerSerial>
        <X509IssuerName>
           CN=Benoï¿_t Marchal, O=Pineapplesoft, L=Namur, C=BE
        </X509IssuerName>
        <X509SerialNumber>982695798</X509SerialNumber>
      </X509IssuerSerial>
      <X509SubjectName>
         CN=Benoï¿_t Marchal, O=Pineapplesoft, L=Namur, C=BE
      </X509SubjectName>
      <X509Certificate>
MIIC0DCCAo4CBDqSv3YwCwYHKoZIzjgEAwUAME4xCzAJBgNVBAYTAkJFMQ4wDAYDVQQHEwVOYW11
cjEWMBQGA1UEChMNUGluZWFwcGxlc29mdDEXMBUGA1UEAxMOQmVub690IE1hcmNoYWwwHhcNMDEw
MjIwMTkwMzE4WhcNMDEwNTIxMTkwMzE4WjBOMQswCQYDVQQGEwJCRTEOMAwGA1UEBxMFTmFtdXIx
FjAUBgNVBAoTDVBpbmVhcHBsZXNvZnQxFzAVBgNVBAMTDkJlbm+vdCBNYXJjaGFsMIIBtzCCASwG
ByqGSM44BAEwggEfAoGBAP1/U4EddRIpUt9KnC7s5Of2EbdSPO9EAMMeP4C2USZpRV1AIlH7WT2N
WPq/xfW6MPbLm1Vs14E7gB00b/JmYLdrmVClpJ+f6AR7ECLCT7up1/63xhv4O1fnxqimFQ8E+4P2
08UewwI1VBNaFpEy9nXzrith1yrv8iIDGZ3RSAHHAhUAl2BQjxUjC8yykrmCouuEC/BYHPUCgYEA
9+GghdabPd7LvKtcNrhXuXmUr7v6OuqC+VdMCz0HgmdRWVeOutRZT+ZxBxCBgLRJFnEj6EwoFhO3
zwkyjMim4TwWeotUfI0o4KOuHiuzpnWRbqN/C/ohNWLx+2J6ASQ7zKTxvqhRkImog9/hWuWfBpKL
Zl6Ae1UlZAFMO/7PSSoDgYQAAoGAExRJP2t4T0h07oLAqlgv9mXNFKX8X+tIgjA6860srebYoWLa
```

LISTING 16.1 continued

```
xFTdEV6dq0DM5ffejf1tkmPYS5wIsUXMrILPJpTpp/4c/AROv2dqnqAch4KqE7sJ16hKUxJyB8r2
Rw6LIZmZm80S5nWt2UxC3rLy/1BmSTLCHBbx3/1GR+gfiOswCwYHKoZIzjgEAwUAAy8AMCwCFG/V
auq62IHCx0o2wCqWb6x0hXRNAhQ8wEQ0yznxVqcVZ60bxOuCr5V30Q==
      </X509Certificate>
    </X509Data>
  </KeyInfo>
  <dsig:Object Id="Res0" xmlns=""
   xmlns:dsig="http://www.w3.org/2000/09/xmldsig#"><article>
<articleinfo>
 <title>XSL -- First Step in Learning XML</title>
 <author><firstname>BenoÃ®t</firstname>
  <surname>Marchal</surname></author>
</articleinfo>
<sect1><title>The Value of XSL</title>
 <para>This is an excerpt from the September 2000 issue of
  Pineapplesoft Link. To subscribe free visit
  <ulink url="http://www.marchal.com">marchal.com</ulink>.</para>
 <para>Where do you start learning XML? Increasingly my answer
  is with XSL. XSL is a very powerful tool with many
  applications. Many XML applications depend on it. Let's take
  two examples.</para>
</sect1>
<sect1>
 <title>XSL and Web Publishing</title>
 <para>As a webmaster you would benefit from using XSL.</para>
 <para>Let's suppose that you decide to support smartphones.
  You will need to redo your web site using WML, the
  <emphasis>wireless markup language</emphasis>, instead of
  HTML. While learning WML is easy, it can take days if not
  months to redo a large web site. Imagine having to edit every
  single page by hand!</para>
 <para>In contrast with XSL, it suffices to update one style
  sheet the changes flow across the entire web site.</para>
</sect1>
<sect1>
 <title>XSL and Programming</title>
 <para>The second facet of XSL is the scripting language. XSL
  has many features of scripting languages including loops,
  function calls, variables and more.</para>
 <para>In that respect, XSL is a valuable addition to any
  programmer toolbox. Indeed, as XML popularity keeps growing,
  you will find that you need to manipulate XML documents
  frequently and XSL is the language for so doing.</para>
</sect1>
<sect1>
 <title>Conclusion</title>
 <para>If you're serious about learning XML, learn XSL. XSL is
  a tool to manipulate XML documents for web publishing or
  programming.</para>
```

LISTING 16.1 continued

```
</sect1>
</article></dsig:Object>
</Signature>
```

JAX-RPC Mapping Rules

JAX-RPC attempts to formulate universal rules to map from the XML diversity into Java well-ordered names. The Java convention and most XML conventions attempt to improve readability by identifying word breaks into multi-word names.

> **Note**
>
> At first sight, this discussion on naming appears futile: Because JAX-RPC is concerned with only RPC, it seems that procedure names will follow Java naming conventions, if only because they are written in Java.
>
> However, SOAP nodes may be written with any programming language. Indeed, the capability to bridge different programming languages and even different operating systems is one of the highest-rated features of SOAP.

JAX-RPC defines the following mapping rules for names. They are inspired by the JAXB (Java API for XML Binding):

- Parse the element name into words, by searching for punctuation characters, to build a list of words.
- Construct the identifier by grouping the words according to the camel case convention.
- If the target name is a classname, leave the name as is (that is, the first letter is capitalized).
- if the target name is a getter or setter method, prepend the `get` or `set` verb to the name.
- If the target name is a method name, turn the first letter into its lowercase equivalent.

For example, the XML name `seat-information` is broken down into two words: `seat` and `information`. It is rebuilt into the `SeatInformation` identifier. If the XML element is mapped to a Java class, the name of the class will be `SeatInformation`.

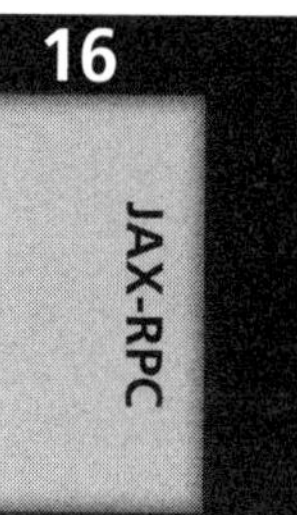

If it is mapped to a method, it becomes `seatInformation()`. If mapped to a getter or a setter method (a JavaBean property), it becomes `getSeatInformation()` and `setSeatInformation()`.

Note that the mapping rules do not break names that already follow the camel case convention. For example, the XML name `SeatInformation` may be mapped to `SeatInformation`, `seatInformation()`, `getSeatInformation()` or `setSeatInformation()` for a classname, a method name or `getter` and `setter` methods, respectively.

Caution

The actual mapping rules are more sophisticated because they account for an XML name that maps to a Java keyword. They also take care of conflicts while mapping names.

Note that the mapping of XML elements to Java names is a one-way function: from an XML name, it is always possible to construct the corresponding Java name, but from a Java name it is not always possible to recover the original XML name.

For example, does the Java name `SeatInformation` stand for `seat-information`, `SeatInformation`, or `seatInformation`? You can't tell without looking at the XML document first. This is not a problem because, as you have seen, XML rules for names are more flexible than their Java counterpart. In practice, any valid Java name will result in a valid XML name.

Mapping of XML Types

Table 16.1 lists the most useful mappings between XML simple types and Java types (as of version 0.6 of JAX-RPC).

TABLE 16.1 Mapping of XML Simple Types to Java

XML type	*Java type*
`xsd:string`	`java.lang.String`
`xsd:integer`	`java.math.BigInteger`
`xsd:int`	`int`
`xsd:long`	`long`
`xsd:short`	`short`

TABLE 16.1 continued

XML type	*Java type*
xsd:decimal	java.math.BigDecimal
xsd:float	float
xsd:double	double
xsd:boolean	boolean
xsd:byte	byte
xsd:QName	javax.xml.rpc.namespace.QName
xsd:dateTime	java.util.Calendar
xsd:base64Binary	byte[]

JAX-RPC defines a special-purpose class, `QName`, to map the `xsd:QName` type. A `QName` is a qualified name—that is, a name with a namespace. The class `QName` defines a JavaBean with two read-only properties: `LocalPart` and `NamespaceURI`.

SOAP arrays are mapped to Java arrays with the corresponding type. JAX-RPC 0.6 supports only the `soapenc:Array`, which is consistent with array support in WSDL.

XML complex type (declared as `xsd:sequence` or `xsd:all` in the XML schema) and SOAP structs are mapped to JavaBeans that implement the `java.io.Serializable` interface. Each element in the sequence becomes a JavaBean property. In practice, there's one `getter` and a `setter` method for each element in the sequence. The property's type is deduced from the XML element's type.

The bean has to implement the `Serializable` interface to indicate that it can be serialized or deserialized to and from XML documents. The interface defines no methods; it serves only as a flag that the method can be serialized and deserialized.

Caution

Java serialization provides a default binary serialization format with which you might be familiar. However, the API is modular and developed in such a way that other formats or even other serialization mechanisms can be used too.

The JAX-RPC reference implementation (RI) offers many useful classes to serialize and deserialize Java classes as XML documents. Although not part of the standard API (they are defined in the `com.sun.xml.rpc.streaming` and `com.sun.xml.rpc.encoding.soap` packages), they will prove useful to programmers.

One of the most useful such classes is the XMLWriter and XMLReader that are similar to java.io.ObjectInputStream and java.io.ObjectOutputStream, but use XML rather than a binary format.

The reference implementation is particularly flexible in that respect because it lets you register special classes to control how objects are serialized and deserialized to and from XML streams. The mechanism is similar to the isd:map entries in Apache SOAP.

Service Mapping

The second goal of JAX-RPC is to simplify writing SOAP nodes and SOAP clients. As you saw in Chapter 7, writing nodes may not be difficult with a library such as Apache SOAP. The clients, though, require more work.

Mapping Services to Java

As of version 0.6, JAX-RPC maps WSDL services as Java classes that extend javax.xml.rpc.Service. Service is a new interface that is equivalent to the wsdl:service tag.

Service offers a few generic methods to retrieve a service port and create Call objects (more on call objects in the next section).

The generated service interface takes this form:

```
public interface <ServiceName>
    extends javax.xml.rpc.Service {
    public <ServiceDefInterface> get<Name of the wsdl:port>()
        throws JAXRPCException;
    // more get<ServiceDefInterface> methods
}
```

For example, a hypothetical TheaterService interface may be of the form:

```
public interface TheaterService
    extends javax.xml.rpc.Service {
    public TheaterPort getTheaterPort();
}
```

Mapping Ports to Java

WSDL ports are mapped as RMI remote interfaces. RMI, which stands for Remote Method Invocation, was introduced in the JDK 1.1 as a Java-specific mechanism for RPC.

JAX-RPC does not use the entire RMI package. Indeed, RMI defines its own binary protocol, which is incompatible with SOAP and of no use in this case. RMI also defines a common representation for remote objects in Java and JAX-RPC builds upon it.

You can think of this remote object representation as the Java equivalent to WSDL: It specifies the interface to remote objects but, rather than do so in XML, it uses the Java language itself. JAX-RPC specifies how to map from one to the other.

RMI defines the `java.rmi.Remote` interface for, as the name implies, remote objects. Like the `Serializable` interface, `Remote` defines no method, but acts as a flag. It is used only with interfaces.

Figure 16.2 illustrates why `Remote` can be used with interfaces only. It shows the division of work between the client and the server.

FIGURE 16.2
The interface is common to both the client and the server.

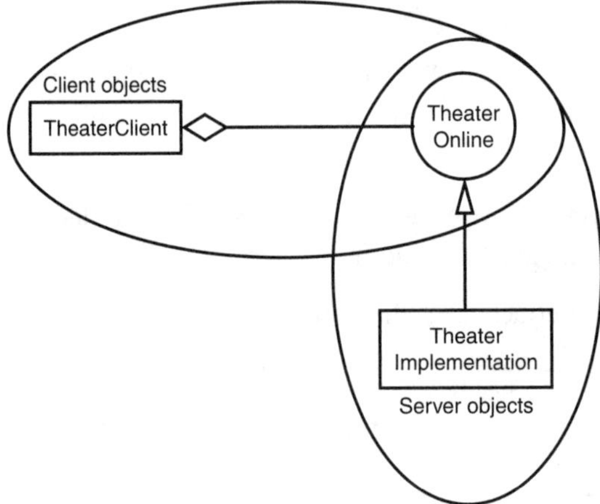

The client needs access to a definition of the remote object so it can call the object's methods. As a Web service is defined, however, the client does not have access to the actual implementation of the object (which may require access to resources unavailable on the client). Otherwise, it would not be necessary to bother with remote objects.

A Java interface is the natural implementation because interfaces can define methods, but they have no implementation. In practice, the interface is common to the client and the server, so as to make sure they use the same methods. The client sees the interface only while the server implements it.

For example, the following specifies a hypothetical Web service for a theater booking service:

```
public interface TheaterPort
    extends Remote {
    public int bookASeat(int category)
        throws RemoteException;
    public int[] bookSeats(int category,int groupSize)
        throws RemoteException;
    // ...
}
```

The `TheaterPort` interface extends `Remote` to signal that it's a Web service. Because remote calls may fail in unexpected ways, they must throw `java.rmi.RemoteException`.

Caution

The WSDL pre-processor discussed in the preceding section automatically generates the remote interface. This is in sharp contrast with RMI, where the programmer starts by writing the interface. With JAX-RPC, the programmer starts with a WSDL file.

JAX-RPC for Client Coding

JAX-RPC clients typically run in a J2EE environment (although JAX-RPC also defines a J2SE configuration for lightweight clients). The J2EE container provides a `Context` object that you can use to access the service object for the WSDL service. On the service object, retrieve the port object and use it for remote procedure calls:

```
Context ctx = new InitialContext();
TheaterService ts = ctx.lookup("java:comp/env/TheaterService");
TheaterPort tp = ts.getTheaterPort();
int seatNumber= tp.bookASeat(Constants.CATEGORY_STALLS);
```

Note that there is no XML-specific code and that, unlike Apache SOAP, you do not need to painfully create the call one parameter at a time.

In that respect, JAX-RPC is similar to RMI: A pre-processor removes much of the complexity by generating stub classes. The pre-processor effectively hides the complexity of SOAP RPC.

Figure 16.3 summarizes the role of the pre-processor. From the WSDL description of the Web service, it generates the service class, one or more remote classes (for the WSDL ports), and as many stubs (for clients) and skeletons (for servers) as required.

FIGURE 16.3
The pre-processor takes the pain out of SOAP programming.

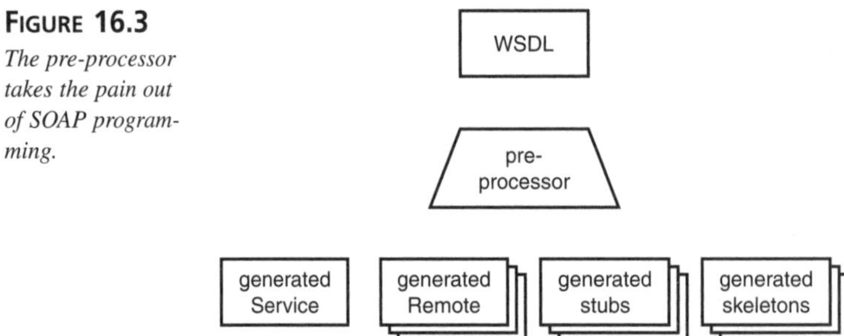

Dynamic Invocation

The example introduced in the preceding section is valid only if the client knows about the Web service beforehand. However, that is not always the case.

For example, the client may have just discovered the service in a UDDI registry. It would download the WSDL service description and use it to invoke the service. JAX-RPC supports this through the dynamic invocation interface (DII). The word *dynamic* refers to the capability for the client to construct the call dynamically.

The concept of DII is borrowed from CORBA. It makes it possible to write Web service browsers, or clients that discover servers at run-time and dynamically learn how to query them.

Note

RMI does not support dynamic invocation because it does not need to. When RMI clients hit an unknown server, they can download the stubs. This is not possible with Web services, if only because the server may not be written in Java.

Using DII is not unlike writing Apache SOAP clients. DII uses a `javax.xml.rpc.Call` object to manually construct the call. You obtain the `Call` object from the `Service` interface:

```
QName intType = new QName("http://www.w3.org/2001/XMLSchema",
                          "int");
Call call = service.createCall(portName,"bookASeat");
call.addParameter("category",intType, Call.PARAM_MODE_IN);
call.setReturnType(intType);
Object[] params = new Object[]
    { new Integer(Constants.CATEGORY_STALLS) };
Integer result = (Integer)call.invoke(params);
```

Unlike Apache SOAP, the `addParameter()` method does not set the parameter value, but does set its name and type. Likewise the `setReturnType()`sets only the return type. The parameters are passed as a vector of objects.

Writing SOAP Nodes

This section of JAX-RPC is still very much in development at the time of writing. It aims to integrate with an upcoming standard on Web service development.

Figure 16.4 summarizes the concept, which is not unlike writing servlets. In particular, writing a SOAP node requires preparing a WAR file (Web Archive) that will ultimately be executed in a servlet container. JAX-RPC defines a new deployment file: `jaxrpc.xml`. The file must appear in the `WEB-INF` directory, next to the more familiar `web.xml`.

FIGURE 16.4
Writing a JAX-RPC server or SOAP node.

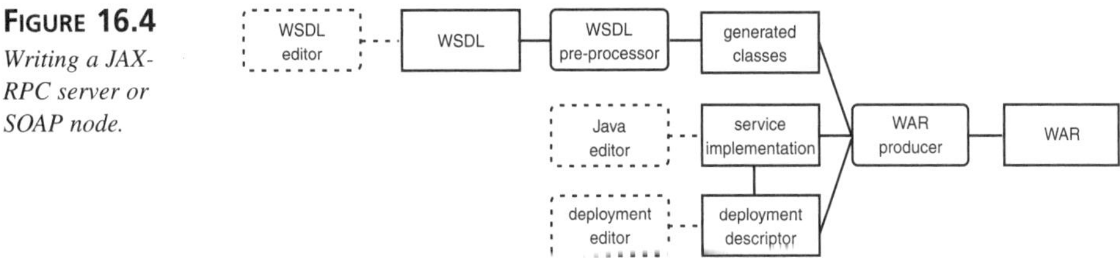

The `jaxrpc.xml` file contains the following entries:

- `service-definition` is the root element.
- `display-name` gives a name for the service. This is primarily used by the deployment tool. This element is optional.
- `description` is essentially a comment for the WAR user. This element is optional.
- `service-definition-name` is an identifier for the service definition.
- `service-definition-interface` specifies the fully qualified name of the service definition interface.
- `service-definition-class` specifies the fully qualified name of the service definition class that implements the service definition interface.
- `wsdl-document-location` specifies a URL that points to the WSDL document that contains the description of this service definition. This element is optional.
- `binding-name` specifies the qualified name of the binding that should be used for this service definition. For namespace resolution, this element is within the scope of the WSDL document, which is at the location `wsdl-document-location`.

In Figure 16.4, you prepare a WSDL file to describe the service. You may write the descriptor directly in XML, although it might be more sensible to use a WSDL editor. Using the pre-processor, you generate the `Service` interface, the `Remote` interface, and appropriate stubs and skeletons. The next step is to implement the business logic for the RPC requests and the deployment descriptor. Finally, using a WAR producer, you package all the information in a WAT file. The result is deployed on a servlet container.

Tip

In practice, IDEs and other tools will automate most of these tasks. You are unlikely to have to write WSDL files explicitly, manually pre-process them, and prepare the `jaxrpc.xml` file. IDEs will offer wizards and other visual gadgetry that perform most of those tasks for you.

Beware of the Simplicity

JAX-RPC defines tools that will greatly simplify writing Web services, but the design considerations introduced in Chapter 7 are as valid as ever, if not more.

Let's briefly review them in light of JAX-RPC:

- **Security**. JAX-RPC supports basic authentication, SSL, and SOAP security extensions. But do not make the mistake of confusing security with cryptography. Evaluate carefully which services are being offered in light of security considerations.
- **Network latency**. By definition, RPCs are less efficient than local calls. Carefully design your system to minimize the number of remote calls you have to perform.
- **Responsiveness**. Always bear in mind that your service will integrate with clients and possibly other services. Take the time to offer an interface that is efficient and minimizes the work on the client.
- **Independence**. This remains as critical as ever. Try to free your interface from technical considerations so as to minimize the dependencies between your service and the clients.

Caution

JAX-RPC makes it almost too easy to write Web services. Yet a good Web service must be open and flexible, so take the time to design and test your service, taking into consideration the listed criteria.

Comparing JAX-RPC with Other Distributed Technologies

This section points out the difference between JAX-RPC and other technologies for distributed computing, more specifically RMI, CORBA, and DCOM. It also discusses when to use JAX-RPC as opposed to JAXM.

Differences between JAX-RPC, RMI, DCOM, and CORBA.

RMI stands for Remote Method Invocation. RMI is a Java-specific technology for RPCs. RMI's strongest point is that it is a Java-only technology, meaning it is very well integrated into the Java language and platform.

This is also its greatest constraint because it means that RMI does not work with applications written in other programming languages such as C++. If you're in a Java shop, RMI is a good solution; otherwise it is simply not usable.

DCOM is Distributed COM. It's a Microsoft technology to enable remote communication between Windows processes. DCOM's strengths mimic RMI strengths, but on the Windows platform.

More specifically, DCOM is a Windows-only solution. It is available in every Windows programming language, but it is not available on other platforms. This makes it the best solution for applications built on Windows only, but it also means it is useless with applications deployed on other platforms (including the Java platform).

CORBA is an open standard that is almost totally agnostic: It works across all languages and all platforms. CORBA designers went to great lengths to make sure their solution would be compatible with any languages (from Cobol to Java) and any platform (from Palm handhelds to 390 mainframes). The downside is complexity. It is so open that it is never optimal. Although useful on heterogeneous projects, CORBA is not as popular as RMI and DCOM.

RMI, DCOM, and CORBA are currently the most popular technologies for RPC. Still, it is important to realize that they were designed primarily for LANs—local networks.

For example, they depend on specific, binary protocols that Internet firewalls love to block. Therefore deploying a CORBA client/server application over the Internet, for example, is not a trivial task. You will most likely need to install special firewalls or gateways.

JAX-RPC offers similar services, but it builds on SOAP, and ultimately HTTP and XML. The tradeoffs are therefore different. JAX-RPC is comparatively less efficient and less powerful than its LAN siblings.

For example, the textual nature of XML messages is less efficient than binary protocols. Also, SOAP does not support distributed garbage collecting, transaction, and the like. If you are used to CORBA programming, you'll have to lower your ambitions.

That's what you lose, but what you gain is invaluable: openness and increased connectivity. Precisely because it offers a minimal set of services, SOAP is a totally universal solution. Because it builds on HTTP and XML, it is compatible with all the firewalls. Therefore SOAP is ideal for open applications that are to be accessed outside the firewall.

Figure 16.5 summarizes where to use which solution:

- DCOM is ideal in the subset of Windows-based applications running on a LAN.
- RMI is perfect for those Java applications running on a LAN.
- CORBA works with Windows, Java, and other platforms available on LANs.
- SOAP and JAX-RPC is the first solution to break free from the LAN. It caters to the needs of Web services developers.

FIGURE 16.5
When to use RMI, DCOM, CORBA and SOAP?

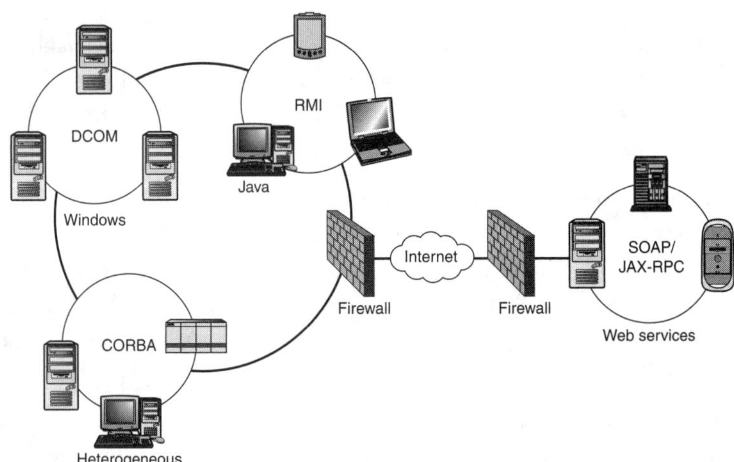

When to Use JAX-RPC and When to Prefer JAXM

JAX-RPC and JAXM are both Java APIs built on top of SOAP. As discussed in Chapter 15, they support different subsets of the SOAP specification:

- JAXM offers message-oriented services.
- JAX-RPC offers RPC over the Internet.

As a Web service developer, you must ask yourself when to use which. The obvious answer is to use JAXM for message-orientated applications and JAX-RPC otherwise, but that doesn't help much. You still need to decide what makes a message-oriented application.

One criterion that you might want to use is to search for the most stable aspect in the project. When you offer new services on the Internet, the last thing you want to do is have to support users that connect to your service. Indeed, if the service becomes popular, they may number in the thousands.

Consider a small example. Imagine you build a Web service and it becomes popular. Imagine that a year after building the service you have thousands of clients connecting to it.

Now, how do you go about modifying your service? Unless you want to be inundated with emails from users and client developers, you need to modify the service in a way that is compatible with the existing solution.

Therefore, from the onset, you should choose the most stable solution for your problem. Examine your Web service—does it revolve around data or procedures?

- Electronic invoicing is an example of a service that revolves around data. The most stable aspect is the invoice itself: You might later decide to change what you do with the invoice, but the data is unlikely to change soon.
- Data-oriented services are first-class candidates for message-oriented services and therefore JAXM.
- Checking the availability of a product in the inventory is an example of a procedural service. The stable aspect is the process to check the availability. The data you need for that control may change, but not the checking process.

  Procedure-oriented services are best suited for RPC and they would be written with JAX-RPC.

Unfortunately, the difference is not always clean-cut, but try to identify the most stable aspects of your system: What is likely to remain unchanged 3, 5, 10 years from now? That should give you a clue.

Summary

In this chapter you learned about work in progress to simplify writing SOAP applications (as well as applications that use other XML-based protocols). At the time of writing, the specification is not final, but enough details were available to give the flavor of JAX-RPC.

Now that you have a firm understanding of the theoretical background for Web services, you'll turn to security in the next chapter.

Completing Web Services

Part IV

In This Part

Handling Security in Web Services

By Mark Wutka

IN THIS CHAPTER

Because the Internet is essentially a public network, electronic commerce can be a scary proposition. You don't want to send credit card numbers electronically when there is the possibility that someone could intercept them. The common solution to this problem, of course, is data encryption—encoding the data in such a way that only the intended recipient can decode it.

When it comes to browsing the Web, the most common encryption mechanism is through a protocol called SSL—the Secure Sockets Layer. When you see a URL that starts with `https:`, it means that the Web site uses SSL to encrypt data. SSL isn't an encryption method itself; it is just a framework for sending encrypted messages over a network. This chapter discusses SSL and encryption mechanisms that can help secure your Web services.

Why Is Encryption Important?

Security is a tricky business, and it is difficult to anticipate the clever ways people can circumvent your security measures. When it comes to online shopping, there are ways that someone could trick an unsuspecting user. For example, someone could trick your browser into going to `amazzon.com` rather than `amazon.com`, taking your credit card number and saving it for future use. There is really nothing `amazon.com` could to do to prevent this either; it's up to you to look at the address line on your browser to make sure you're where you expect to be.

Although an application can't be fooled by simple spelling changes, there is still the danger that it can be tricked. An application doesn't have any intuition, so it must rely on programmatic means to thwart potential mischief. An application must rely on encryption and digital signatures (a special kind of encryption) to solve many problems.

Private Key Encryption

Private key encryption is actually what most people think of when they think of encryption. You have some kind of private password that only you and your intended recipient know. You encrypt a message with the private password, or key, and send it along. The recipient takes the encrypted message and decodes it with the same key you used to encrypt it. Obviously, anyone who knows the key can read the message, and that's why it must be kept private—hence the term *private key*.

Private key encryption actually dates back thousands of years. The Greeks and Romans were known to have used various kinds of encryption to hide messages. Private key encryption even played a big role in World War II, when the Allies were able to decode critical German and Japanese messages that were thought to be unbreakable.

The computer age put a new twist on encryption, because the primitive pencil-and-paper encryption and simple encryption machines were no match for a determined computer. Cryptographers developed new computer-specific encryption algorithms, and also discovered ways to break these algorithms. Digital cryptography is now a very complex field, with plenty of algorithms and amazingly clever ways to attack those algorithms.

Public Key Encryption

Compared to private key encryption, public key encryption is very young. It was invented in the mid-1970s to solve a very important problem: the exchange of private keys. When you use private key encryption, how do you give the recipient your private key? In the past, military organizations had to rely on code books and couriers to pass keys around. In the computer age, you need a way to send a private key to someone else almost instantaneously.

The solution for this problem is the use of a public-private key pair. Basically, when you want to receive encrypted messages, you use a complex mathematical process to create a special pair of keys. One half of this pair is a private decryption key that you must keep secret. The other half is called a public key, because you can give it to everyone in the world if you want to. Whenever someone wants to send you a secret message, they simply encrypt the message with your public key. The trick here is that because of the mathematical properties of the key and the encryption process, the only person who can decode the message is the person with the private key. You can't compute the private key from the public key, and you can't use the public key to decrypt the message.

This form of encryption is also referred to as *asymmetric key encryption* because the encryption key is different from the decryption key. Typical private key encryption is symmetric—you use the same key to encrypt and decrypt. It is theoretically possible to have an asymmetric private key algorithm, where you use different keys that must both be private, but that is almost unheard of. It is impossible to have useful symmetric public key encryption, however. If everyone has the public key and that key can be used to decode the message, everyone can read the message.

The Secure Sockets Layer

The Secure Sockets Layer (SSL) is a great example of public key and private key encryption. It is a protocol for exchanging encrypted data over a network. An SSL client connects to an SSL server, which then sends the client a certificate containing the server's public key.

The client then creates a random private symmetric key, and then uses the server's public key to encrypt the private key. Next, the client sends the encrypted key to the server, which decrypts it. Now, the client and server both know the private symmetric key and they can exchange data.

Figure 17.1 shows a typical SSL key exchange.

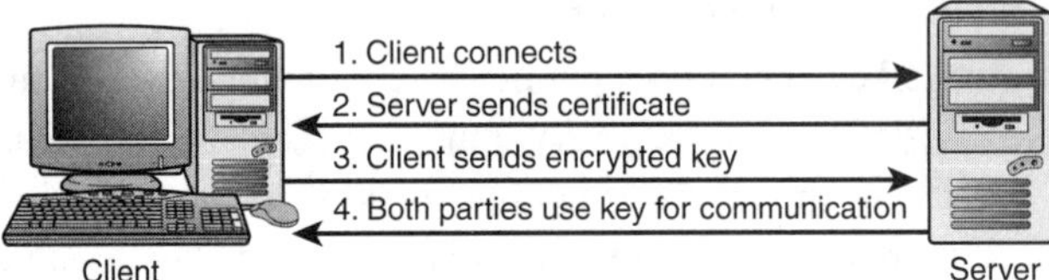
1. Client connects
2. Server sends certificate
3. Client sends encrypted key
4. Both parties use key for communication
Client
Server

FIGURE 17.1
SSL uses a public key to transmit a private key.

You might wonder why the client and server even bother with the private key encryption. Why don't they just use public key encryption to exchange data? There's no technical reason why they can't, in that they know each other's public keys. The problem is that the public key encryption algorithms are very complex and require many more computations than private key algorithms. Most public key algorithms are based on raising a number to a very large power. Imagine raising a number to a power that is over 300 digits long!

Digital Signatures

Public key encryption gives rise to another kind of encryption that is absolutely crucial for electronic commerce: digital signatures. A digital signature is basically a snapshot of data that is encoded in such a way that someone can tell who signed the data and whether the data has been modified.

To create a digital signature, you first use an algorithm called a *secure hash*. A secure hash is a small fingerprint of the data—usually around 1024 bits or so. The hashing algorithm must ensure that it is extremely difficult to modify the original data and retain the same hash value. With a typical secure hashing algorithm, changing the value of even one bit radically changes the value of the hash. You are unlikely to be able to change some small number of bits to get back to the original value.

After you compute the secure hash, you use a public key encryption algorithm, but this time, you encrypt the hash with your *private* key. The neat thing about the relationship between a matched public-private key pair is that not only can you use the public key to encrypt a message that only the private key can decrypt, but you can also do the reverse. You can encrypt something with the private key that only the public key can decrypt. Obviously, for sending private messages, the second technique is useless. Who wants to encrypt a message that everyone else in the world can decrypt?

As it turns out, this is exactly what you want for a digital signature. Everyone in the world can decrypt your encrypted secure hash. When you send out a digitally signed document, the recipient computes the secure hash of the document, and compares it against the encrypted signature you sent. Because you are the only one with the private half of the key, only you could have encrypted the secure hash that has been decrypted with your public key, which verifies that you are the person who sent the document.

Because the secure hashing algorithm can't be fooled by subtle changes to the document, if the secure hash of the document matches the one you sent, then it is extremely likely that the document hasn't been tampered with.

Digital signatures enable you to verify both the integrity of data and its origin—at least to the extent that you trust the sender of the information and its ability to keep the private key secret. The one thing that digital signatures don't ensure is privacy. Although digital signature algorithms include encryption, they don't actually encrypt the data. The digital signature always accompanies the original data. If you want the data to be private, you must encrypt it.

Certificate Authorities

Digital signatures also play a role in SSL. When the server sends its public key to the client, it sends it in the form of a digital certificate. This certificate is actually a public key and a digital signature. When you set up a secure Web server, you generate a public-private key pair. You then send the public key to a company known as a Certificate Authority (CA). Usually, you must also send some form of identification along with the key so that the CA can verify your identity. The CA then digitally signs the key and gives you back a certificate containing your key and the CA's signature of your key.

The Web browser, or your SSL library, maintains a list of trusted CAs. When your server sends its certificate, the browser not only verifies the signature in the certificate, but also checks to make sure it was signed by a trusted CA. Without the CA, your browser has no way of verifying the identify of a Web server. For example, someone could trick your Web browser into thinking that his or her site is really amazon.com, and even present a certificate stating that this site is amazon.com. Without relying on a CA, the browser has no way to determine whether the certificate is authentic. Although a malicious person can still trick your browser, no one should be able to obtain a certificate stating that another site is amazon.com—although people have fooled CAs in the past!

The reason the CA mechanism works is that the browser or SSL library has a list of valid CAs ahead of time. If the browser relies on only that information it gets from the network, it is vulnerable to something called a man-in-the-middle attack, where someone feeds phony information to the browser to trick it. Because the browser has a piece of data that didn't come from the network, however (the list of trusted CAs), it can avoid such attacks.

Encryption in Java

Until the Java-XML libraries have built-in encryption, you'll have to use the Java Cryptography Extensions to do any encryption. The JDK already supports digital signatures, and JDK 1.4 supports SSL for secure networking.

Digitally Signing Data

To digitally sign data with Java, you need a `Signature` object, which you obtain by calling the `Signature.getInstance` method with the appropriate security algorithm name. The algorithm names for the signing algorithms are actually combinations of secure hashing algorithms and public key encryption algorithms.

The two most common secure hashing algorithms are SHA1 (Secure Hash Algorithm 1) and MD5 (Message Digest 5). The most common public key encryption algorithms are RSA (named for its inventors—Rivest, Shamir, and Adleman) and DSA (Digital Signature Algorithm). The general format for the full algorithm name is *HHHwithCCC* where *HHH* is the name of the secure hashing algorithm and *CCC* is the public key cipher. For example, you might pick SHA1withDSA or MD5withRSA as potential algorithms. Because Java allows you to use different cryptographic software providers, there is no single list of supported algorithms. Instead, each software provider chooses which algorithms and hashing method to implement. The cryptographic software built into JDK 1.3 supports SHA1withDSA, SHA1withRSA, MD5withRSA and MD2withDSA.

In addition to the data you want to sign, you also need a private key. Typically, you load this key from a special key database called the *keystore*. The JDK comes with a keystore management tool called `keytool`.

Listing 17.1 shows a simple program that loads a key from the key store and then uses the key to digitally sign the data from a file.

LISTING 17.1 Source Code for `SignData.java`

```
import java.security.*;
import java.security.interfaces.*;
import java.io.*;

/** Computes a digital signature for a file */

public class SignData
{
```

LISTING 17.1 continued

```
    public static void main(String[] args)
    {
        try
        {
            String keystorePassword = "changeit";
            String testAlias = "signkey";
            String testKeyPassword = "changeit";

// Create a keystore.
            KeyStore keystore = KeyStore.getInstance("JKS");

// Figure out where the user's keystore is located.
            String keystoreFilename = System.getProperty("user.home")+
                File.separator+".keystore";

// Load the keystore from the keystore file.
            keystore.load(new FileInputStream(keystoreFilename),
                keystorePassword.toCharArray());

// Locate the key with the specified alias and password.
            Key testkey = keystore.getKey(testAlias,
                testKeyPassword.toCharArray());

// Assume that the key is an RSA key.
            RSAPrivateKey pvtKey = (RSAPrivateKey) testkey;

// Get the certificate for the key (not for computing the signature,
// just for writing out to a separate file for later signature verification).
            java.security.cert.Certificate cert =
                keystore.getCertificate(testAlias);

// Create and initialize a signer to use MD5 and RSA.
            Signature signer = Signature.getInstance("MD5withRSA");
            signer.initSign(pvtKey);

// Open the data file.
            FileInputStream in = new FileInputStream(args[0]);

// Create a block of bytes for reading the file.
            byte[] buffer = new byte[4096];
            int len;

// Read a block of the file and add it to the signature object.
            while ((len = in.read(buffer)) > 0)
            {
                signer.update(buffer, 0, len);
            }
            in.close();
```

LISTING 17.1 continued

```
// Compute the digital signature.
            byte signatureBytes[] = signer.sign();

// Write the signature out to a file.
            FileOutputStream out = new FileOutputStream(args[0]+".sig");
            out.write(signatureBytes);
            out.close();

// Write the certificate out to the file in encoded format.
            out = new FileOutputStream(args[0]+".cer");
            out.write(cert.getEncoded());
            out.close();
        }
        catch (Exception exc)
        {
            exc.printStackTrace();
        }
    }
}
```

Before you can run the signing program, you must create a new public-private key pair named *signkey* (the name used in the SignData program). Notice, too, that `SignData` uses RSAwithMD5 as the signing algorithm, so when you create the key pair, you must specify RSA as the algorithm. Finally, you can protect keys with a password (the keystore is also protected with a password) and because `SignData` expects a key password, you must specify the password at key creation time. The following command creates the key as needed by the `SignData` program:

```
keytool -genkey -alias signkey -keyalg RSA -keypass mykeypass
```

When you run `keytool` for the first time, it asks you for a keystore password. Make sure you enter **changeit** for the password, or change the password in the `SignData` program to match whatever password you choose. If you try to run the SSL-encrypted SOAP example later in this chapter, you must use a keystore password of **changeit**.

Listing 17.2 shows a simple program that verifies a digital signature, again using the keystore and the `Signature` object.

LISTING 17.2 Source Code for `VerifyData.java`

```
import java.io.*;
import java.security.*;
import java.security.cert.*;
import java.security.interfaces.*;
```

LISTING 17.2 continued

```
/** Uses the public key from a certificate (that is, it uses the
 *  original data file and the two files generated by the SignData
 *  program) to verify a digital signature against a file.
 */
public class VerifyData
{
    public static void main(String[] args)
    {
        try
        {
            if (args.length < 3)
            {
                System.out.println(
                    "Please supply the data file, the sig file "+
                    "and the cert file.");
                System.exit(1);
            }

            FileInputStream certFile = new FileInputStream(args[2]);

// Create a certificate factory to read an X.509 certificate
            CertificateFactory certFact = CertificateFactory.
                getInstance("X.509");

// Load the certificate from the certificate file
            java.security.cert.Certificate cert =
                certFact.generateCertificate(certFile);

            certFile.close();

// Extract the public key from the certificate (assume it's an RSA key)
            RSAPublicKey pubKey = (RSAPublicKey) cert.getPublicKey();

// Create and initialize a Signature object for MD5 and RSA
            Signature sigVerifier = Signature.getInstance("MD5withRSA");
            sigVerifier.initVerify(pubKey);

// Open the data file
            FileInputStream dataFile = new FileInputStream(args[0]);

// Create a buffer for reading the file
            byte[] buffer = new byte[4096];

            int len;

// Read block of bytes from the file and add them to the signature
            while ((len = dataFile.read(buffer)) > 0)
            {
```

LISTING 17.2 continued

```
                sigVerifier.update(buffer, 0, len);
            }

            dataFile.close();

// Create a byte buffer for the original signature
            File sigFile = new File(args[1]);
            byte sigBytes[] = new byte[(int) sigFile.length()];

// Read the signature from a file
            FileInputStream sigIn = new FileInputStream(sigFile);
            sigIn.read(sigBytes);
            sigIn.close();

// Compare the signature from the file with the data file
// and the public key from the certificate
            if (sigVerifier.verify(sigBytes))
            {
                System.out.println("The signature matches.");
            }
            else
            {
                System.out.println(
                    "The signature doesn't match.");
            }
        }
        catch (Exception exc)
        {
            exc.printStackTrace();
        }
    }
}
```

Encrypting Data

If you want to use the Java Cryptography Extensions (JCE) to encrypt data, you may want to go ahead and upgrade to JDK 1.4. Otherwise, you must download and install JCE separately, and the installation is a little more complicated than just adding files to your CLASSPATH.

If you need to use JCE with JDK 1.2 or 1.3, download and unpack the latest version of JCE. In JCE's `lib` directory, you should see four files: `jce1_2_1.jar`, `subjce_provider.jar`, `local_policy.jar`, and `US_export_policy.jar`. Copy these four files to the `jre/lib/ext` directory of your JDK installation. Finally, edit your `jre/lib/security/java.security` file. The `java.security` file has a section that should look something like this:

```
security.provider.1=sun.security.provider.Sun
security.provider.2=com.sun.rsajca.Provider
```

Add the following line after the `security.provider.2` line:

```
security.provider.3=com.sun.crypto.provider.SunJCE
```

If your `java.security` file has fewer than two, or more than two providers, just add the new line after the highest numbered provider. If you already have a `security.provider.5`, make the new one `security.provider.6`.

After you save the `java.security` file, JCE should be available from your JDK. As you can see, the installation is a little cumbersome, making JDK 1.4 with its built-in JCE look much more attractive.

Just as you use a `Signature` object to digitally sign data, you use a `Cipher` object to encrypt data. Basically, you just use `Cipher.getInstance` to create the `Cipher` and then use the `update` and `doFinal` methods to pass data to the `Cipher`. The `doFinal` method then returns the encrypted or decrypted data as an array of bytes.

The `Cipher` object performs both encryption and decryption. You specify which operation you want by calling the `init` method, passing either `Cipher.ENCRYPT_MODE` or `Cipher.DECRYPT_MODE` along with the key.

Listing 17.3 shows a simple encryption program that reads a file and then encrypts it.

LISTING 17.3 Source Code for `EncryptData.java`

```
import java.io.*;
import javax.crypto.*;
import javax.crypto.spec.*;

public class EncryptData
{

/* This program uses Triple-DES (DESede) to encrypt a file.
   You pass the filename as a command-line parameter. The result
   is placed in a file with the same name as the original, but with
   ".enc" appended to it. */

    public static void main(String[] args)
    {
        try
        {
// Create an array to hold the key.
            byte[] encryptKey = "This is a test DESede key".getBytes();
```

LISTING 17.3 continued

```
// Create a DESede key spec from the key.
            DESedeKeySpec spec = new DESedeKeySpec(encryptKey);

// Get the secret key factory for generating DESede keys.
            SecretKeyFactory keyFactory = SecretKeyFactory.getInstance(
                "DESede");

// Generate a DESede SecretKey object.
            SecretKey theKey = keyFactory.generateSecret(spec);

// Create a DESede Cipher.
            Cipher cipher = Cipher.getInstance("DESede/ECB/PKCS5Padding");

// Initialize the cipher and put it into encrypt mode.
            cipher.init(Cipher.ENCRYPT_MODE, theKey);

// Open the file to encrypt.
            FileInputStream in = new FileInputStream(args[0]);

// Open the output file.
            FileOutputStream out = new FileOutputStream(args[0]+".enc");

            byte[] buffer = new byte[7];
            int len;

// Read one DES block at a time.
            while ((len = in.read(buffer)) > 0)
            {
                // Add the bytes to the cipher
                byte[] encrypted = cipher.doFinal(buffer, 0, len);
                out.write(encrypted);
            }

            in.close();
            out.close();
        }
        catch (Exception exc)
        {
            exc.printStackTrace();
        }
    }
}
```

Listing 17.4 shows a program that decrypts the file encrypted by the program in Listing 17.3.

LISTING 17.4 Source Code for `DecryptData.java`

```
import java.io.*;
import javax.crypto.*;
import javax.crypto.spec.*;

public class DecryptData
{

/* This program uses Triple-DES (DESede) to decrypt a file.
   You pass the filename as a command-line parameter without
   the .enc appended to it. */

    public static void main(String[] args)
    {
        try
        {
// Create an array to hold the key.
            byte[] encryptKey = "This is a test DESede key".getBytes();

// Create a DESede key spec from the key.
            DESedeKeySpec spec = new DESedeKeySpec(encryptKey);

// Get the secret key factory for generating DESede keys.
            SecretKeyFactory keyFactory = SecretKeyFactory.getInstance(
                "DESede");

// Generate a DESede SecretKey object.
            SecretKey theKey = keyFactory.generateSecret(spec);

// Create a DESede Cipher.
            Cipher cipher = Cipher.getInstance("DESede/ECB/PKCS5Padding");

// Initialize the cipher and put it into encrypt mode.
            cipher.init(Cipher.DECRYPT_MODE, theKey);

// Open the file to encrypt.
            FileInputStream in = new FileInputStream(args[0]+".enc");

// Open the output file.
            FileOutputStream out = new FileOutputStream(args[0]);

            byte[] buffer = new byte[8];
            int len;

// Read one DES block at a time.
            while ((len = in.read(buffer)) > 0)
            {
                // Add the bytes to the cipher
                byte[] encrypted = cipher.doFinal(buffer, 0, len);
                out.write(encrypted);
            }
```

LISTING 17.4 continued

```
            in.close();
            out.close();
        }
        catch (Exception exc)
        {
            exc.printStackTrace();
        }
    }
}
```

Using Secure Sockets with SOAP

Although JCE gives you the power to encrypt and decrypt any data you choose, the Secure Sockets Layer (SSL) provides a simple way to send encrypted data over a network connection. The advantage of SSL is that you no longer encrypt the data yourself—you transmit data over a secure socket just as you do with a regular socket. The SSL implementation takes care of the encryption for you. Because secure sockets work just like regular sockets, they work with all of Java's built-in networking classes. For example, you can use the `URL` and `URLConnection` classes with `HTTPS` URLs as long as your JDK supports SSL.

The Java Secure Sockets Extension implements secure sockets for Java and is built into JDK 1.4. If you need JSSE for JDK 1.2 or 1.3, you must download and install it yourself. Unfortunately, the installation procedure for JSSE is as cumbersome as the JCE installation procedure. You must download JSSE from `http://java.sun.com/products/jsse` and then unpack the installation file. Next, copy `jsse.jar`, `jcert.jar`, and `jnet.jar` from JSSE's `lib` directory to your JDK's `jre/lib/ext` directory. Finally, you must edit the `jre/lib/security/java.security` file, just as you did for JCE. The security provider line for JSSE is:

```
security.provider.5=com.sun.net.ssl.internal.ssl.Provider
```

Again, change the number of the security provider line to fit your own `java.security` file (it should be one higher than the current highest provider number). Again, if you use JDK 1.4, JSSE is already installed.

Usually, a SOAP implementation relies on a Web server to handle any SSL interaction. If you want to use SSL with SOAP, you must enable SSL within your Web server. Many commercial Web servers support SSL automatically. Apache's Tomcat 4.0 supports SSL if you already have JSSE installed. You simply edit the `server.xml` file in the `conf` directory. The default `server.xml` file comes with a commented-out section that enables SSL. The section looks like this:

```
<!--
<Connector className="org.apache.catalina.connector.http.HttpConnector"
    port="8443" minProcessors="5" maxProcessors="75"
    enableLookups="true"
    acceptCount="10" debug="0" scheme="https" secure="true">
    <Factory className="org.apache.catalina.net.SSLServerSocketFactory"
             clientAuth="false" protocol="TLS"/>
</Connector>
-->
```

Simply remove the `<!-- -->` comment tags to activate SSL. Before Tomcat can use SSL, however, it needs its own encryption key. Use the following command to create an encryption key in your keystore for Tomcat:

```
keytool -genkey -alias tomcat -keyalg RSA
```

Tomcat expects the keystore and the key to have a password of `changeit`. After you generate the key, restart your Tomcat server and it should be SSL-enabled. To verify that it is working, access your Tomcat server with a URL like `https://`*`tomcathostname`*`:8443`. The default SSL configuration for Tomcat uses port 8443. You can change to the standard port 443 by editing the `server.xml` file; you can see the port number in the SSL section. Keep in mind, however, that if you are running Unix or Linux, you must be root to run a server on port numbers less than 1024

Listing 17.5 shows a very simple Java class that you can call using SOAP.

LISTING 17.5 Source Code for *SubmitOrder.java*

```
public class SubmitOrder
{
    public SubmitOrder()
    {
    }

    public String submit(String customerName, String address,
        String partNumber, int quantity, String creditCard,
        String creditCardNumber)
    {
// Insert your code here to store an order. For this example, just
// print out the values.
        System.out.println("Order from: "+customerName);
        System.out.println(address);
        System.out.println("Part: "+partNumber);
        System.out.println("Quantity: "+quantity);
        System.out.println("Credit card: "+creditCard+" "+creditCardNumber);

        return "Order Submitted";
    }
}
```

As you can see, this class doesn't have any SSL-specific code. It relies on the Web server to handle the secure sockets. Listing 17.6 shows an Apache SOAP client that uses an `https` URL to access a SOAP object with SSL.

LISTING 17.6 Source Code for *SendOrder.java*

```
import java.util.*;
import java.net.*;
import org.apache.soap.*;
import org.apache.soap.encoding.*;
import org.apache.soap.encoding.soapenc.*;
import org.apache.soap.rpc.*;
import org.apache.soap.util.xml.*;

public class SendOrder
{
    public static void main(String[] args)
    {
// Create a URL for the SOAP server, use https instead of the normal http.
        URL url = null;

        try
        {
            url = new URL("https://localhost:8443/soap/servlet/rpcrouter");
        }
        catch (Exception exc)
        {
            exc.printStackTrace();
            System.exit(0);
        }

// Create a new call.
        Call call = new Call();

// Tell SOAP which object to use.
        call.setTargetObjectURI("urn:OrderApp");

// Tell SOAP which method to invoke.
        call.setMethodName("submit");

// Tell SOAP to use the regular SOAP encoding style.
        call.setEncodingStyleURI(Constants.NS_URI_SOAP_ENC);

// Create a vector to hold the parameters.
        Vector params = new Vector();

// Add the parameters to the vector.
        params.addElement(new Parameter("customerName", String.class,
            "Kaitlynn Tippin", null));
```

LISTING 17.6 continued

```
        params.addElement(new Parameter("address", String.class,
            "321 Barbie Ln., Ethere, AL, 37373", null));
        params.addElement(new Parameter("partNumber", String.class,
            "BD-015", null));
        params.addElement(new Parameter("quantity", Integer.class,
            new Integer(8), null));
        params.addElement(new Parameter("creditCard", String.class,
            "SamCard", null));
        params.addElement(new Parameter("creditCardNumber", String.class,
            "40123-557799-12", null));

// Store the parameters in the request.
        call.setParams(params);

        Response resp = null;

// Invoke the method.
        try
        {
            resp = call.invoke(url, "");
        }
        catch (SOAPException exc)
        {
            exc.printStackTrace();
            System.exit(0);
        }

// See if the response contains an error.
        if (!resp.generatedFault())
        {
// If not, get the return value
            Parameter retValue = resp.getReturnValue();

            System.out.println(retValue.getValue());
        }
        else
        {
            Fault fault = resp.getFault();

            System.err.println("Generated fault:");
            System.err.println("  Fault Code = "+fault.getFaultCode());
            System.err.println("  Fault String = "+fault.getFaultString());
        }
    }
}
```

The important part of the `SendOrder` class is that the URL uses the SSL-based `https` prefix rather than `http`. You should be able to run this program under JDK 1.4 with no problem, but for JDK 1.2 and 1.3, you must include a special system property (using the `-D` option) to tell Java about `https`. You can run the program with the following command:

```
java -Djava.protocol.handler.pkgs=com.sun.net.ssl.internal.www.protocol
➥SendOrder
```

Java's `URL` and `URLConnection` classes don't actually implement any of the common network protocols such as HTTP and FTP. Instead, they rely on special protocol handler classes. Whenever the `URL` class sees a request for a particular protocol, it searches through a list of Java packages to find a handler for that protocol. The `java.protocol.handler.pkgs` adds more packages to the search list.

You may discover that you receive an I/O error when you try to run the `SendOrder` program with SOAP implementation running under Tomcat. When you activate SSL for Tomcat, you generate a public-private key pair using the `keytool` command. The certificate is initially untrusted—it hasn't been signed by a recognized certificate authority (CA). You have two choices: You can send your public key off to a CA to have it signed, or you can force your JDK to recognize your certificate anyway.

To force the JDK to recognize a certificate, use `keytool` to export the certificate to a file, like this:

```
keytool -export -file tomcat.cert -alias tomcat
```

You should now have a file called `tomcat.cert` that contains the digital certificate that Tomcat uses. Now you must import this certificate into the JDK's trusted CA keystore. The trusted CA keystore is in the JDK's `jre/lib/security/cacerts` file. On my Linux machine, for example, I use the following command to import the certificate into the `cacerts` file:

```
keytool -import -keystore /usr/java/jre/lib/security/cacerts -file tomcat.cert
```

On my Windows machine, I use the following command:

```
keytool -import -keystore c:\jdk1.3.1\jre\lib\security\cacerts -file
➥tomcat.cert
```

After you import the certificate, your SOAP client should have no trouble accessing Tomcat with SSL.

The important thing to remember with SSL and SOAP is that you don't need to do anything different for SSL—you just change the URL from `http` to `https`.

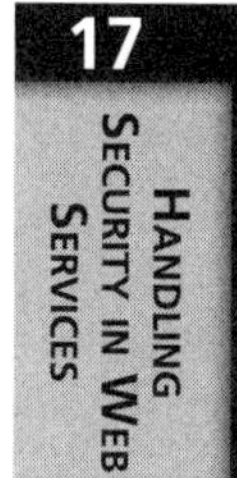

Encryption in XML

One problem with using encryption with XML is that XML was designed to be more of a human-readable format, and encrypted data is anything but readable. Any encrypted data appears as a big block of random text.

When it comes to digital signatures, things are even worse. Remember that changing even a single bit in the original data causes the secure hash to change. When you send an XML file from one system to another, or run it through a parser first, you may find that some subtle changes have taken place. For example, some systems use the newline character as a line terminator, whereas others use a carriage return followed by newline. If the original signature is based on having only newlines at the end, but the recipient receives it with carriage-return and newline, the signature won't match. Also, the order of attributes in a tag may not matter to most programs, but again it throws off the signature.

The XML Digital Signature (DSIG) specification aims to solve this problem by specifying a special canonical form of XML that includes the following restrictions:

- Remove all whitespace that isn't part of text data (that is, all unnecessary whitespace inside the tags themselves).
- Provide default values for all missing attributes.
- Use only newline as a line terminator.
- Expand any entity references as well as any special character references.

After you come up with the canonical form of a document, you can compute the digital signature. The XML-DSIG specification defines the format for a `<Signature>` tag, which contains all the information needed to verify a signature.

The basic format for an XML signature is:

```
<Signature>
   <SignedInfo>
      (CanonicalizationMethod)
      (SignatureMethod)
      (<Reference (URI=)? >
          (Transforms)?
          (DigestMethod)
          (DigestValue)
       </Reference>)+
     </SignedInfo>
(SignatureValue)
    (KeyInfo)?
    (Object)*
</Signature>
```

The `SignedInfo` section describes the various algorithms used to generate the signature. For example, you may use different canonicalization methods to preprocess the XML. A canonicalization method is a way to transform an XML document into a common format. Although XML is already a common format, the various canonicalization methods contain rules about whitespace and other items to ensure that two XML documents that contain the same data are actually identical byte-for-byte. You must also specify the secure hashing (digest) method and the signature method (RSA, DSA, and so on). You must also, of course, specify the actual value of the signature—that is, the final result of the signing algorithm. Notice, too, that the `<SIGNATURE>` tag does not contain the actual data being signed, just the signature itself.

The signature value, digest value, and key info are usually specified in a special format called base-64, which represents binary data that uses only 64 different printable characters. You encode 3 8-bit binary values with 4 characters, making the final data block size grow by about 33%.

You use references to W3C specifications to specify the various encoding methods. Listing 17.7 shows a Java program that reads an XML document, then produces a signature for the document.

LISTING 17.7 Source Code for `SignXML.java`

```
import java.security.*;
import java.security.interfaces.*;
import java.io.*;

/** Computes a digital signature for an XML file */

public class SignXML
{
    public static void main(String[] args)
    {
        try
        {
            String keystorePassword = "changeit";
            String testAlias = "signkey";
            String testKeyPassword = "changeit";

// Create a keystore.
            KeyStore keystore = KeyStore.getInstance("JKS");

// Figure out where the user's keystore is located.
            String keystoreFilename = System.getProperty("user.home")+
                File.separator+".keystore";
```

LISTING 17.7 continued

```
// Load the keystore from the keystore file.
            keystore.load(new FileInputStream(keystoreFilename),
                keystorePassword.toCharArray());

// Locate the key with the specified alias and password.
            Key testkey = keystore.getKey(testAlias,
                testKeyPassword.toCharArray());

// Assume that the key is an RSA key.
            RSAPrivateKey pvtKey = (RSAPrivateKey) testkey;

// Get the certificate for the key (not for computing the signature,
// just for writing out to a separate file for later signature verification).
            java.security.cert.Certificate cert =
                keystore.getCertificate(testAlias);

// Get the public key from the certificate.
            RSAPublicKey pubKey = (RSAPublicKey) cert.getPublicKey();

// Create and initialize a signer to use MD5 and RSA.
            Signature signer = Signature.getInstance("MD5withRSA");
            signer.initSign(pvtKey);

// Create a message digest, because the XML signature must contain
// the message digest
            MessageDigest digest = MessageDigest.getInstance("MD5");

// Open the XML file
            FileInputStream in = new FileInputStream(args[0]);

// Create a block of bytes for reading the file
            byte[] buffer = new byte[4096];
            int len;

// Read a block of the file and add it to the signature object
            while ((len = in.read(buffer)) > 0)
            {
                signer.update(buffer, 0, len);
                digest.update(buffer, 0, len);
            }
            in.close();

// Compute the digital signature
            byte signatureBytes[] = signer.sign();

            byte digestBytes[] = digest.digest();

// Write the signature out to a file
            PrintWriter ps = new PrintWriter(
```

LISTING 17.7 continued

```
                new BufferedWriter(
                new FileWriter(args[0]+".sig.xml")));

            ps.println("<?xml version=\"1.0\" encoding=\"UTF-8\"?>");
            ps.println("<Signature Id=\"SampleSignature\"
➥xmlns=\"http://www.w3.org/2000/09/xmldsig#\">");
            ps.println("  <SignedInfo>");
            ps.println("    <CanonicalizationMethod
Algorithm=\"http://www.w3.org/TR/2001/
➥REC-xml-c14n-20010315\"/>");
            ps.println("    <Reference URI=\"http://www.w3.org/TR/2000/
➥REC-xhtml1-2000-126/\">");
            ps.println("      <Transforms>");
            ps.println("        <Transform
Algorithm=\"http://www.w3.org/TR/2001/
➥REC-xml-c14n-20010315\"/>");
            ps.println("      </Transforms>");
            ps.println("      <DigestMethod
Algorithm=\"http://www.w3.org/2000/09/
➥xmldsig#md5\"/>");
            ps.println("      <DigestValue>"+Base64.toBase64(digestBytes)+
                "</DigestValue>");
            ps.println("    </Reference>");
            ps.println("  </SignedInfo>");
            ps.println("  <SignatureValue>");
            ps.println("    "+Base64.toBase64(signatureBytes));
            ps.println("  </SignatureValue>");
            ps.println("  <KeyInfo>");
            ps.println("    <KeyValue>");
            ps.println("      <RSAKeyValue>");
            ps.println("        <Exponent>");
            ps.println("
"+Base64.toBase64(pubKey.getPublicExponent().toByteArray()));
            ps.println("        </Exponent>");
            ps.println("        <Modulus>");
            ps.println("          "+Base64.toBase64(pubKey.getModulus().
                toByteArray()));
            ps.println("        </Modulus>");
            ps.println("      </RSAKeyValue>");
            ps.println("    </KeyValue>");
            ps.println("  </KeyInfo>");
            ps.println("</Signature>");
            ps.close();
        }
        catch (Exception exc)
        {
            exc.printStackTrace();
        }
    }
}
```

Listing 17.8 shows the output from SignXML for a simple XML file.

LISTING 17.8 Output from `SignXML.java`

```
<?xml version="1.0" encoding="UTF-8"?>
<Signature Id="SampleSignature" xmlns="http://www.w3.org/2000/09/xmldsig#">
  <SignedInfo>
    <CanonicalizationMethod Algorithm="http://www.w3.org/TR/2001/REC-xml-c14n-
20010315"/>
    <Reference URI="http://www.w3.org/TR/2000/REC-xhtml1-2000-126/">
      <Transforms>
        <Transform Algorithm="http://www.w3.org/TR/2001/REC-xml-c14n-20010315"/>
      </Transforms>
      <DigestMethod Algorithm="http://www.w3.org/2000/09/xmldsig#md5"/>
      <DigestValue>tYL+Xgo3exn7dEta8gTW2A==</DigestValue>
    </Reference>
  </SignedInfo>
  <SignatureValue>
    TTdqAXD83GzdyBa6XB8HVMDckb4+zM4oxhgnvePMOIY8zI9WXnHx+FuF4a/
➥SNHJxoHuMv0N51MMrzOwJwsCQAZ6GKfKiebMCyZINXbctKPCXJ+fjiY
➥TXeYa5fg5rJsmwCMv8NYVZiynxItk8uAHzgIJmarU3JBeIjOc/dkp1dU4=
  </SignatureValue>
  <KeyInfo>
    <KeyValue>
      <RSAKeyValue>
        <Exponent>
          AQAB
        </Exponent>
        <Modulus>
          /7KpRkbNo3y35VzK4RraLcuG4kdaRWlIT4lpMRkDMxchICNhm43pIVokRmWQl43bov
➥IHZmaoK7660BGzIaylXeK4z5FXaiUOb6edmtzkgSdQLPskthwZWaDCS6W9iUkgbAyTZ6
➥ZSABApxMJ75XlbryRdlfOVInLNqEJ1kOvoUY+J
        </Modulus>
      </RSAKeyValue>
    </KeyValue>
  </KeyInfo>
</Signature>
```

The XML-DSIG standard is fairly new and is still evolving. After it settles down, you should expect to see Java libraries that make it easy to sign XML and verify XML signatures.

Summary

As you can see, you have several options for improving the security of your application. You can use SSL for encrypted transmission; you can use the JCE to encrypt data before sending it in a SOAP request; or you can use JCE to encrypt your entire XML request.

In Chapter 18, you will learn about WSFL, the Web Services Flow Language, which enables you to specify how various SOAP methods work together.

CHAPTER 18

Web Services and Flows (WSFL)

By Francisco Curbera and Matthias Kloppmann

In This Chapter

The overall aim of Web services is to provide a standards-based framework to enable application-to-application interaction. Simple interactions, in particular stateless ones, can be modeled as single operation invocations or message exchanges with a service; WSDL and SOAP provide convenient support for this type of basic interaction. Richer interactions typically involve multiple invocations flowing between two or more services in a peer-to-peer setting—that is, a scenario in which all participants potentially act as both clients and servers. This is the model of interaction prevalent even in simple business transactions, both in the business-to-consumer and (especially) in the business-to-business scenarios. Even a process as simple as ordering merchandise online involves at least three parties—a customer, an e-commerce retailer, and a shipper—as well as direct interactions between the three of them.

The full potential of the Web services framework will not be realized until complex interactions of this kind are properly supported. Although no single standard has yet emerged, Web services flow (or process) languages, such as the Web Services Flow Language (WSFL) and XLANG), provide the means to deal with them. This chapter reviews the basic concepts underlying these languages, drawing mainly from WSFL.

Service Flow and Service Composition

Complete representations of complex service interactions rely on two basic concepts: service flow and service composition. The service flow is a description of how the service operates. In business environments, the service flow is a representation of the business process that it implements. By revealing the internal operation of the service, the flow lets users and possible business partners know how the service should be used. In particular, the flow describes the order in which the operations the service provides should be used, and the logic the service follows to process requests. Following a long-standing tradition in the field of business process modeling, WSFL uses a flow model to represent service flows. The flow model itself is presented in the section "Flow Modeling Concepts."

A flow's individual steps can be realized through a multitude of possible implementations, from manual realizations performed by people to automatic implementations performed by software. The usage of Web services as particular realizations of the individual steps of a flow is described in the section "Flows as Compositions of Web Services."

Flows themselves are of course services, too, though more complex ones. It must therefore be possible to make them available as Web services. The section "Exposing Flows as Web Services" shows how this can be done.

Flows can provide different levels of description of the business process followed by a Web service. The complete description allows a flow language interpreter (a *flow engine*) to actually implement all the service functionality with no other input than the service flow specification itself. Typically, this level of description is not published, because it may reveal details of the hosting enterprise's operation or its trade secrets. The complete flow is in this case referred to as the *private flow* of the service. A simplified flow is published instead, containing just the information partners need to interact with the service. This *public flow* differs from the private one only in the level of detail provided, not in the underlying representation model. The section "Public and Private Flows" deals with public flows.

Service composition is the second fundamental concept that is required to represent complex service interactions. *Composition* refers to the act of putting together two or more existing services to provide new functionality not present in the original ones, either in the form of a new service or in the form of a distributed service interaction. A flow typically accesses other Web services in the course of its operation, thus becoming a composition of services itself: It defines a usage pattern for existing services and optionally offers the composed functionality as a new service. A second type of composition occurs when multiple services interact following a certain interaction pattern to achieve some business goal. The nature of this composition is intrinsically distributed: Unlike the flow-based composition, these compositions are not orchestrated from a single point of control or flow engine. Service composition in WSFL is described in some detail in "Flows as Compositions of Web Services" and "Global Models."

The rest of this chapter develops the themes outlined here in some detail, using the flow depicted in Figure 18.1 to introduce the basic concepts of service process and service composition. You will notice a significant difference between this and other chapters in the book: There is no Java code provided here. The reason, obviously, is that there is no support available yet for any of the proposed Web services flow languages. The goal of this chapter is thus limited to introducing the fundamental concepts of service flows and compositions.

FIGURE 18.1
Cell phone ordering service sample flow.

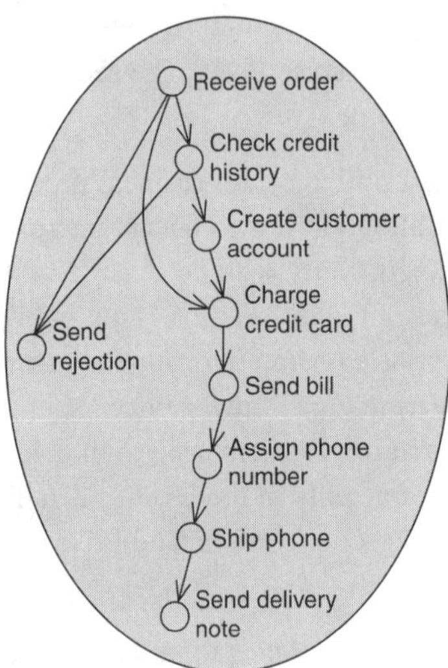

Flow Modeling Concepts

In WSFL, flow models are used for the specification of complex interactions of services. A flow model describes a usage pattern of a collection of available services, so that the composition of those services provides the functionality needed to achieve a certain business goal—that is, the composition describes a business process. The flow model specifies precisely how those services (steps in the flow) are combined, specifying in which order they have to be performed (including the possibility of concurrent execution), the conditional logic deciding whether an individual step or a group of steps have to be performed at all or should be looped, and the passing of data between the involved steps.

Figure 18.1 shows an example of a flow model describing a simplified ordering process for a cell phone that continues and evolves throughout this chapter. It consists of a set of business tasks that are executed in a certain order, although some tasks may be skipped. The example flow starts with the receipt of an order for a new cell phone. If the requestor is not known as a customer, the credit history is checked first, and then a customer account is created. Neither of these tasks need to be done for an existing customer. Depending on retrieved knowledge about the requestor, the order might be rejected. Otherwise, the order is processed. The credit card is charged, a bill is sent, a new phone number is assigned, the phone is sent, and so is a note informing of its delivery.

Data produced by a certain task in the flow may be used by a subsequent task; for example, the customer account data is used to send the bill.

From the example, you can already see that the key ingredients for the description of a flow model are the individual business tasks that have to be executed, the specification of the control flow describing the order of their execution and the conditional logic, and the specification of the associated data flow describing the passing of data between them. In WSFL, those three concepts are described by activities, control links, and data links.

Activities

An *activity* is a single step in a flow. It represents a business task that potentially has to be performed as part of the business process the flow model describes. Whether it is actually performed during the execution of a specific flow depends on the conditional logic of the control flow into which it is embedded.

WSFL distinguishes between an activity and its implementation. The *implementation* describes an actual operation that is invoked when the activity is reached during execution of the flow. The activity, on the other hand, describes how this operation is embedded into the flow. An *operation* in this context can be anything needed to realize the particular business task. The most obvious realization is the invocation of a piece of code. Another very common realization in existing workflow products is the involvement of human beings performing a task manually.

In the example, the CheckCreditHistory activity is described by the following WSFL fragment:

```
<activity name="CheckCreditHistory">
  <input name="CustomerData" message="tns:Customer"/>
  <output name="Result" message="tns:CreditWorthiness"/>
  <implement>
    <internal>
      <!-- Implementation is provided by check method of
           an EJB -- outside WSFL scope -->
      <ns1:ejbMethod xmlns:ns1="..."
                     ejbNameJndiName="/finance/creditHistory"
                     operation="check" />
    </internal>
  </implement>
  <!-- Other properties describing embedding into
       (control and data) flow -->
</activity>
```

The fragment specifies that the `CheckCreditHistory` task expects a message of type `Customer` and produces a message of type `CreditWorthiness`. Both messages are WSDL messages as described Chapter 11.

Note

The `tns` (this name space) prefix is needed because messages are actually XML-qualified names that are qualified by associated name spaces.

For the example, we assume that the activity is implemented by a certain EJB's `check` method. Note that the specification of the actual implementation is from a different name space, because WSFL addresses this as an extensibility element outside the WSFL scope.

Additional properties of the activity relate to its embedding into the control and data flow, which is covered in the following section.

Control Flow

The *control flow* of a flow model specifies the execution order of the individual business tasks to be performed, and the conditional logic specifying whether they should be performed at all, or possibly looped. The need for executing two business tasks in a certain order follows from logical dependencies between them; if no such dependency exists, they can be performed concurrently, thus speeding up the execution of the flow.

In WSFL, a control link is a relationship between two activities, A_1 and A_2,that prescribes an execution order: A_1 has to be completed before A_2 can be started. In WSFL, the set of all activities and the set of all control links together describe a directed, acyclic graph.

Figure 18.2 has more control flow detail for the first part of the example flow model. Here, the control link between the `ReceiveOrder` activity and `CheckCreditHistory` activity indicates that the latter cannot be started until the former has completed. Whether it is actually started depends on the control link's optional transition condition attribute, which is evaluated at the flow's run-time. Depending on that evaluation, control is either passed along the control link, or the control link marks the start of a dead path, which is eliminated from the flow during its run-time.

WSFL doesn't distinguish between alternate branches where one is taken depending on a certain condition (switch) and parallel branches that are all taken concurrently (fork). In the WSFL model, multiple control links originating from the same activity always denote a fork, possibly followed by a dead-path elimination of some of the parallel branches.

FIGURE 18.2

Flow model: control links, transition conditions, and join conditions.

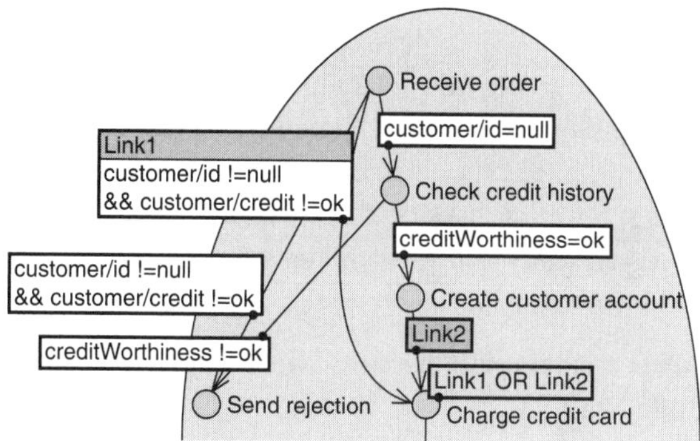

In the example, the following lines specify that this path is to be taken only if the activity ReceiveOrder returned no customer ID, that is, when nothing is known about the customer:

```
<controlLink source="ReceiveOrder" target="CheckCreditHistory"
  transitionCondition="customer/id=null" />
```

The two control links leading to the `ChargeCreditCard` activity specify a control join, stating that this activity can be started only after both the `ReceiveOrder` and `CreateCustomerAccount` activities are complete. Completion is achieved either by successful execution or by dead path elimination. When an activity is the target of more than one control link, a WSFL join element associated with the activity describes how the activity is dealt with.

In the example, the following lines state that the `ChargeCreditCard` activity is executed only after all its incoming control links have been evaluated, synchronizing the parallel paths (deferred evaluation of the join element, the only option currently offered by WSFL), and only if at least one of those control links evaluated to true:

```
<activity name="ChargeCreditCard">
  <input name="CreditCardData" message="tns:CreditCard"/>
  <output name="Result" message="tns:CreditCardChargeRecord"/>
  <implement>...</implement>
  <join condition="link1 OR link2" when="deferred" />
</activity>
<controlLink name="link1"
  source="ReceiveOrder" target="ChargeCreditCard"
  transitionCondition="customer/id != null &amp;&amp;
                       customer/credit=ok " />
<controlLink name="link2"
  source="CreateCustomerAccount" target="ChargeCreditCard" />
```

Data Flow

A flow model's data flow specifies how the output message of a given business task is used by one or more (subsequent) business tasks. Put the other way round, the data flow specifies how the input message of a given business task is created from the results of one or more (preceding) business tasks or the input message of the flow itself. In that the involved message types typically don't match, the mapping from an output message to a subsequent input can involve transformations such as the renaming of message parts.

In WSFL, a data link is a relationship between two activities, A_1 andA_2, that describes that A_2 uses the result data of A_1.

Figure 18.3 shows the signatures of the first few activities involved in the example flow model. The dashed arrows represent data links.

The following lines specify that the field `customerInfo` from the data part of the Order message, which was the result of the `ReceiveOrder` activity, is mapped to the `record` part of the `Customer` message that is the input to the `ChargeCreditCard` activity:

```
<dataLink source="ReceiveOrder" target="ChargeCreditCard">
  <map sourceMessage="tns:Order" targetMessage="tns:Customer"
       sourcePart="data" sourceField="customerInfo"
       targetPart="record"/>
</dataLink>
```

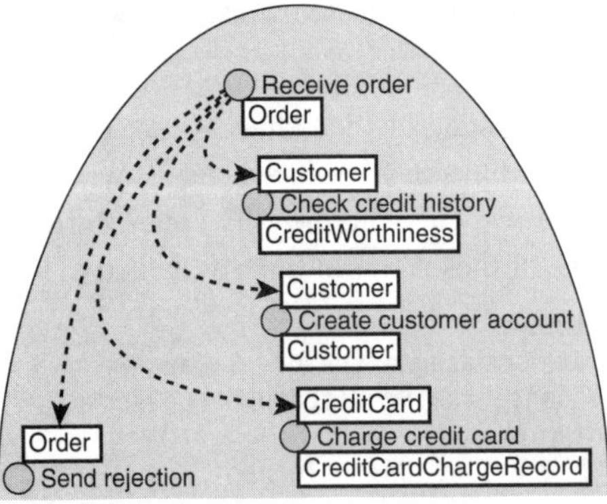

FIGURE 18.3
Flow model: inputs, outputs, and data links.

As the example shows, WSFL allows the data flow to be specified independent from the control flow, as long as the execution order constraints still guarantee that a message is produced before it is used by another activity. Generally speaking, the data flow has to be parallel to the control flow.

It is possible that an activity receives data from multiple other activities (a *data join*). In this situation, WSFL allows for the detailed specification of the materialization of that activity's input message, using either an override technique such as "last writer wins," or a merge technique that can be specified via an XSL transformation with multiple inputs. This kind of elaborate container materialization is not needed for the current example, and so it is not detailed further here.

Flow

If you put the ingredients described in the previous sections together, you have already completed the specification of a simple flow model involving activities that are implemented by internal operations, like this:

```
<flowModel name="cellPhoneOrder">
  ...
  <activity name="CheckCreditHistory">
    <input name="CustomerData" message="tns:Customer"/>
    <output name="Result" message="tns:CreditWorthiness"/>
    <implement>
      <internal>...</internal>
    </implement>
  </activity>
  ...
  <controlLink source="ReceiveOrder" target="CheckCreditHistory"
               transitionCondition="customer/id=null" />
  ...
  <dataLink source="ReceiveOrder" target="CheckCreditHistory">
    <map sourceMessage="Order" targetMessage="Customer"
         sourcePart="data" sourceField="customerInfo"
         targetPart="record"/>
  </dataLink>
  ...
</flowModel>
```

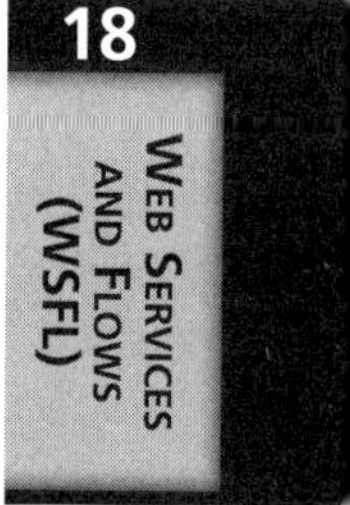

Flows as Compositions of Web Services

The previous sections introduced the basic building blocks of a flow, without focusing too much on the actual realizations of the flow's activities. Although those realizations could be anything from manual realizations by human beings to an assembler program, the goal of WSFL is obviously not so much the composition of flows that coordinate internal implementations, but rather the composition of flows that perform the coordination of Web services, where the Web services implement individual activities.

For that, WSFL first introduces the notion of a service provider as an abstraction for a business partner that offers one or more WSDL services that are used within the flow model. Second, a WSFL activity can then refer to a specific operation that a specific service provider provides, as an alternative to the internal implementation you already saw in the previous sections.

Service Providers and Service Provider Types

Service providers are abstractions for the concrete business partners with which a flow model interacts. Service providers are declared in a WSFL flow in the same way that variables are declared in a Java program. A type ("service provider type") is assigned to each service provider. The type is essentially nothing but a predefined list of WSDL portTypes, and it gives a formal representation of the service or services that each service provider must offer to participate in the flow. The actual binding between a service provider variable of a given type and a concrete business partner is a separate step, which is described by the locator element.

The distinction between a service provider and a service is an important one: Flow models specify the usage of a service instance of a given type, rather than the service itself. Several flows can use a single Web service simultaneously, whereas a single flow model can use more than one provider of a given service type. (Whether or not the service type is supported or bound to the same service is in principle irrelevant; see the section "Locators," however). Coming back to the example, Figure 18.4 shows an updated version of the flow model, where three steps have been outsourced to business partners.

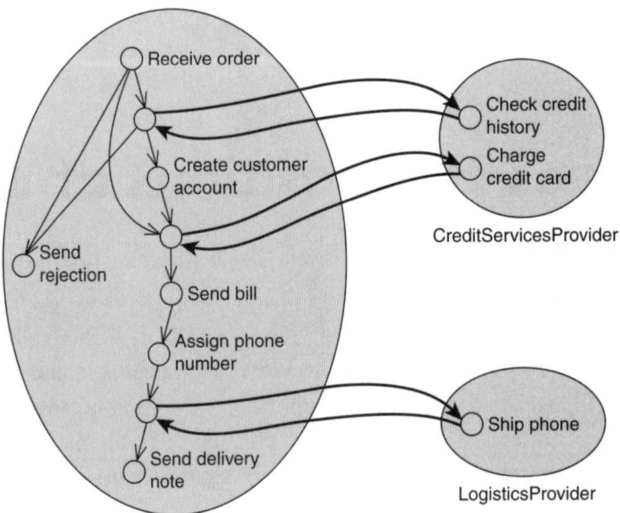

FIGURE 18.4
Flow model using Web services.

WSFL requires that the business partners with which the flow model interoperates are declared as service providers (of the appropriate type). In the example, there are two, which are made available at the flow model level as follows:

```
<flowModel name="cellPhoneOrder">
  <serviceProvider name="Partner1" type="CreditServicesProvider"/>
  <serviceProvider name="Partner2" type="LogisticsProvider"/>
  ...
</flowModel>
```

This simply declares two global variables at the flow level to be service providers of the specified service provider type. A service provider type in WSFL describes the external interface a business partner makes available, which can consist of multiple port types and multiple operations.

The specification of service provider types is also part of the WSFL definitions, in an element preceding the flow model.

In the example, the following lines indicate that the `CreditServicesProvider` offers two operations from two port types (and a similar definition for the `LogisticsProvider`, which is not shown here):

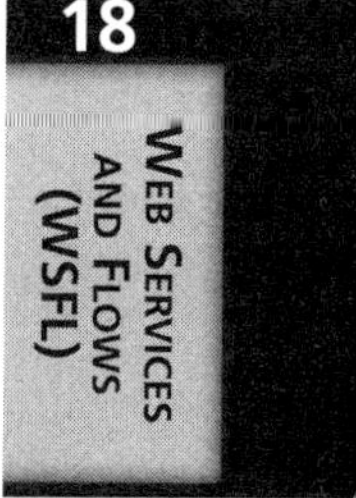


```
<serviceProviderType name="CreditServicesProvider"
  <portType name="creditHistoryHandler">
    <operation name="check"/>
  </portType>
  <portType name="creditCardHandler">
    <operation name="charge"/>
  </portType>
</serviceProviderType>
```

Locators

The declaration of the service providers with which a flow interacts is separated from binding those service providers to actual business partners that offer the required services (according to the associated service provider type). Although it is possible and often desirable to always use the same business partner as a certain service provider, sometimes more dynamic binding mechanisms are needed. A foremost example is UDDI lookup: Service providers of a given type are looked up in a UDDI directory according to some criteria, then the most suitable service among the retrieved set (according to some quality of service criterion) is selected and bound.

In WSFL, the locator element covers the entire range of possible bindings, locating the actual business partner that acts as a specific service provider—either statically or dynamically.

The example has so far declared two global variables at the flow level that represent business partners with which the flow is interacting, and has defined the required interface the partners have to provide, described by their service provider type. It has not yet specified the concrete partners, that is, how these variables are bound. A WSFL locator element specified this as part of the service provider declaration.

The simplest kind of locator in WSFL is a static locator, which directly refers to a WSDL service that provides the required operations. Observe that the service is then identified by its namespace-qualified name, as defined in the corresponding WSDL file. It appears in the example as follows:

```
<flowModel name="cellPhoneOrder">
  <serviceProvider name="Partner1" type="CreditServicesProvider">
    <locator type="static" service="abc:qualityCreditServices"/>
  </serviceProvider>
  ...
</flowModel>
```

A second possibility is a dynamic locator that uses UDDI (see Chapter 9) to dynamically find a suitable service provider of the required type:

```
<flowModel name="cellPhoneOrder">
  ...
  <serviceProvider name="Partner2" type="LogisticsProvider">
    <locator type="uddi" bindTime="firstHit"
             selectionPolicy="user-defined" invoke="leastcost.wsdl">
      <uddi-api:find_service businessKey="uuid_key" generic="1.0"
                             xmlns:uddi-api="urn:uddi-org:api">

           ...
      </uddi-api:find_service>
    </locator>
  </serviceProvider>
  ...
</flowModel>
```

In this example, the flow engine uses UDDI to locate `Partner2`, the logistics provider, when an operation this partner provides is needed for the first time (`firstHit`). The flow engine executes the specified UDDI query, which returns a list of possible providers, which the flow engine then filters using a user-defined routine to return the cheapest provider. This locator type provides for many more options not detailed here.

There are other locator types. Internal activity implementations (as described in the "Flow Modeling Concepts" section) are actually represented as operations a service provider implements with a locator type of `local` (The earlier discussion omitted that detail.) Finally, with a locator of type `mobility` it is possible to use a data field from a message to locate a service provider.

Note

A more thorough description of locators and their options is in section 4.4.3 of *Web Services Flow Language (WSFL)* (see the "References" section).

Outsourcing Activity Implementations: Export

After the service providers the flow model uses are declared, and given the definition of their associated service provider types, the implementation of an outsourced activity simply needs to reference an operation a service provider offers, as shown in the following example:

```
<activity name="CheckCreditHistory">
  ...
  <performedBy serviceProvider="Partner1"/>
  <implement>
    <internal>
      <target portType="creditHistoryHandler" operation="check"/>
    </internal>
  </implement>
</activity>
```

Thus, the Check operation that is part of partner 1's `CreditHistoryOperations` port type implements the flow model's `CheckCreditHistory` operation. This is well defined, because partner 1 has been declared to be of type `CreditServicesProvider`, and thus is guaranteed to provide that operation.

Note

The model WSFL uses for outsourcing an implementation is in fact more complicated than presented here. The concept, however, is essentially the one that is presented here. It would not make sense in this short overview to go over the details of WSFL activity implementations. See Section 4.6 in the *Web Services Flow Language (WSFL)* (see the "References" section).

Exposing Flows as Web Services

Having built a flow model implementing the cell phone ordering process, the next step is to make it available so others can use it. To do this, the flow model itself is defined as a service provider implementing a particular service provider type.

You can denote the flow's individual activities that implement this service's operations by "exporting" them, that is, by making them available for direct interactions with service clients. Still left open is how a flow's concrete instance actually comes to life and vanishes again after it is completed—this is addressed by the flow model's life cycle operations.

After you have these ingredients together, it is possible to use WSDL services and other WSFL flows to recursively compose flows.

Flow Model as Service Provider

Figure 18.5 highlights the interface to which the flow model's client connects. The flow's interface contains four operations, one inbound and three outbound, depicted as arrows that are graphically connected to the activities they implement via dashed lines. Initially, the client using that interface sends a request for a new cell phone, upon which he receives either a rejection or a bill, which eventually is followed by a delivery note (and the physical delivery of the phone, which is outside the scope of a software solution).

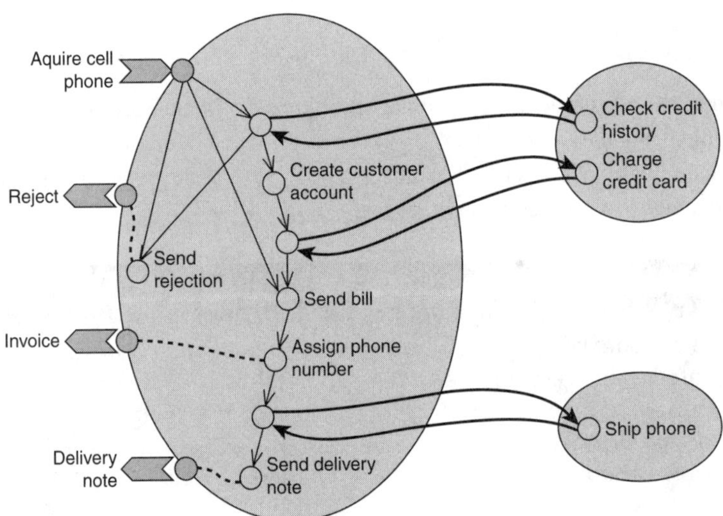

FIGURE 18.5
Externalizing a flow as a Web service.

For this, you can define a port type and service provider type as follows:

```
<portType name="cellPhoneOrderHandler">
  <operation name="acquireCellPhone">
    <input name="theOrder" message="tns:Order"/>
  </operation>
  <operation name="reject">
    <output name="theRejection" message="tns:RejectionNotice" />
```

```
  </operation>
  ...
</portType>
<serviceProviderType name="cellPhoneOrderProvider">
  <portType name="cellPhoneOrderHandler"/>
</serviceProviderType>
```

Given these definitions, the flow model can be defined to be a service provider of that service provider type by the actual flow model declaration:

```
<flowModel name="cellPhoneOrder"
           serviceProviderType="cellPhoneOrderProvider">
  ...
```

Exported Activities

You have previously seen (in the section "Outsourcing Activity Implementations: Export") how you can outsource an activity's implementation to an external service provider by using the `internal` element to specify an activity's implementation. The use of the `internal` element is necessary when the connection to the external provider is kept private to the service, in the sense that it is not carried through a public WSDL interface; that is, it is not mediated by an operation in the service provider type that the flow declares.

Alternatively, an activity's implementation can be provided by exporting it. Exporting an activity makes it visible to the flow's clients in the form of an operation on the flow's service interface. In this case, an `export` element replaces the `internal` element used before, and a nested `target` element identifies the operation in the flow's own interface that is mapped to this activity.

Detailing the Reject activity to make use of `export` produces the following WSFL fragment:

```
<activity name="Reject">
  <input name="orderData" message="tns:Order"/>
  <implement>
    <export>
      <target portType="cellPhoneOrderHandler" operation="reject"/>
      ...
    </export>
  </implement>
  ...
</activity>
```

When an activity's implementation is exported, the flow engine executes the activity by either receiving an invocation from a client (if the operation to which the activity is exported is one-way or request-response—that is, an inbound operation), or by invoking an operation on a partner (when the operation mapped to the activity is an outbound operation—that is, notification or solicit-response). For example, the reject operation in the preceding example is a notification operation on the phone ordering service interface, but corresponds to the invocation of a one-way operation in the customer interface (which is to say that the customer must be able to receive the rejection, and implies a peer-to-peer interaction model, see "Global Models"). Because of the uniform treatment that WSDL gives to inbound and outbound operations, WSFL deals with both cases in the same way.

Note

In WSFL, a plug link can be provided inside the `export` element to indicate the operation in the target provider that is actually being invoked. You do not need to be concerned with this level of detail at this point. Plug links are introduced in the section "Plug Links"; additional details can be found in sections 4.5 and 4.6 of the WSFL specification (see the "References" section).

Note that in the example the message types of the activity and the exported operation don't match. In this case, an additional `map` element is required to perform the message transformation. The full specification of the export element from the preceding example would then be as follows:

```
<export>
  <target portType="cellPhoneOrderHandler" operation="reject"/>
  <map sourceMessage="tns:Order" targetMessage="tns:RejectionNotice"
       sourcePart="data" sourceField="customerInfo"
       targetPart="customerData"/>
</export>
```

Life Cycle Operations, Flow Input, and Output

Many instances of a given flow model can execute at the same time on the associated run-time infrastructure. In WSFL, a new instance of a flow is created with either the `call` or `spawn` operation.

`Call` is defined as a WSDL request-response operation where the input message is the input of the flow, and the output message is the result from the flow. `Spawn` is defined as a WSDL one-way operation where the input message is the input of the flow. Both operations can be exported (that is, exposed to clients) with a different name and signature.

Thus, the more precise definition of the sample flow model doesn't represent the AcquireCellPhone operation as the flow's first activity, but as an exported spawn operation, creating the flow instance and passing input data. It also introduces a node representing said flow input data (a flow source), replacing the previously present ReceiveOrder activity:

```
<flowModel name="cellPhoneOrder">
           serviceProviderType="cellPhoneOrderProvider">
  <flowSource name="ReceiveOrder">
    <output name="orderData" message="tns:Order"/>
  </flowSource>
  <export lifecycleAction="spawn">
    <target portType="cellPhoneOrderHandler" operation="acquireCellPhone"/>
  </export>
  <activity name="CheckCreditHistory">
    ...
  </activity>
  ...
  <controlLink source="ReceiveOrder" target="CheckCreditHistory"
               transitionCondition="customer/id=null" />
  ...
```

Additional life cycle operations are available:

- A flow can be suspended through the use of the suspend operation. When suspended, the flow's execution is discontinued, but the flow still exists in its current state.
- A suspended flow can be resumed through the use of the resume operation. Execution of the flow continues from the state where it was suspended.
- The current state of a running flow can be queried through the use of the inquire operation. This enables a business partner to find out how far a given business process's execution (seen via its public flow interface, as described in the "Public and Private Flows" section) has already progressed.
- A running flow can be terminated. This aborts the flow's execution at its current state.

All the life cycle operations are offered as WSDL operations taking a flow instance ID as a parameter. The operations can be exported via an export element, as in the example in "Exported Activities" section.

Recursive Composition

You have seen that a flow utilizes operations provided by several other services as the implementation of its activities. Another way to put this is to say that a flow defines a *composition of services* by specifying a certain usage pattern of its service providers' functionality. That is, the flow combines the operations made available by its providers to achieve a given compositional goal. You have also seen that a flow model itself can implement a certain service provider type—that is, it can become a service itself, offering a set of WSDL interfaces to possible clients. In particular, the flow could become part of yet another service composition itself. The result is a mechanism by which services can be recursively composed following a *flow composition* model.

In general, this form of composition assumes a peer-to-peer interaction model between services, in which the flow can invoke and be invoked by other services. However, the compositional model provided by flows is a centralized model, in which the composition is fully orchestrated from a single control point: the executing flow engine. Fully distributed compositions of services are introduced in the section "Plug Links."

A special case of flow composition is based on hierarchical interactions between services, as opposed to the more flexible peer-to-peer model. In this case, an entire flow model can provide the implementation of a single activity of another flow—that is, it becomes a sub-flow of the invoking flow. You can achieve this kind of composition by using the flow model's `Call` operation to implement the other flow's activity. Input data from the activity is then passed to the `flowSource` of the sub-flow, and data from the sub-flow's `flowSink` is passed back to become the output of the activity.

Public and Private Flows

The introduction to this chapter mentioned the important fact that flow languages are used both to provide users of the service with a description of its behavior, and to actually implement the service. When used to describe service behavior, the information provided is strictly limited to what partners need to know to successfully interact with the service; implementations, on the other hand, must contain all the details that would enable a compatible interpreter to execute the service on behalf of requesters.

This section briefly reviews these two requirements and shows how a service's public and private behavior are related in a typical case.

Defining Service Behavior

The behavioral description of a service is the first and most important task of a flow language in the Web services space. It is intended for the service customer and provides the information that enables the customer to effectively use the service and understand how its requests will be processed. In particular, this includes:

- The correct order in which the operations of the service need to be invoked.
- The alternative paths that the execution of the service may follow based on the received information.
- The set of steps that represent the possible states in the execution of the service, which the requester could possibly need to query in the course of a long-running interaction (as when using a lifecycle `inquire` operation; see the section "Life Cycle Operations, Flow Input, and Output").
- The data flow between steps, as needed to support the flow of control.

All this information can be easily encoded through the use of the flow model described in previous sections. A service description based on a flow model, on the other hand, does not imply anything about the actual implementation of the service. Implementation independence is a foremost concern in designing the Web services framework. Many services are likely to be implemented using technologies that don't rely on flow models, such as traditional object oriented languages. Regardless of the implementation technology, these services require a standards-based description of their behavior to facilitate their use and integration with other services.

Implementing a Service as a Flow: Private Versus Public Flows

On the other hand, the language necessary to provide a behavioral description is fundamentally enough to describe the full execution of that behavior on a compatible interpreter such as a traditional workflow engine. You just need to make sure that the language allows the specification of additional implementation details, such as what program or service to invoke at each activity in the flow and a set of endpoint and quality-of-service properties (such as security, transactionality, timing, and so on.) You have already seen that the WSFL model enables you to do this within the same language that you use for public flows.

There are two advantages to having a single language for both purposes: First, a common language enables developers to easily transform existing business processes (which are commonly encoded as flows) into actual Web services; second, a flow language capable of encoding actual implementations defines a platform-independent, standard, portable execution language for Web services. This implementation language relies on Web service standards (basically, WSDL and related specifications) to provide implementation details, and can be executed on any vendor's standardized flow engine.

A flow that provides the service implementation is usually not suitable as a public description of service behavior; on one hand, it may reveal information private to the service provider or even trade secrets, whereas on the other hand, the actual implementation flow is usually too complex and cluttered with details that have no relevance to customers. To highlight this difference, it's common to refer to the actual implementation flow as the *private flow* of the service, and to its simplified public description as the *public flow*.

Defining a Public Flow

The difference between a private flow (one with complete implementation information) and a simplified (or customer-facing) public flow is thus fundamentally one of authoring style. Consider now the cell phone ordering service that has served as an example.

The original process was depicted in Figure 18.5. A simplified flow is shown in Figure 18.6. Here, only the steps that are relevant to the interaction with the ordering customer are shown. Note, for instance, that the steps of checking credit history or creating a new account are not present in the simplified flow. The service user needs to know only that his request will be either rejected (resulting in a rejection message being sent back to him), or accepted (resulting in his credit card being charged and a bill sent). Likewise, if you proceed downstream through the flow, you will see that the activity `AssignPhoneNumber` is missing in the public flow, which is explained by the fact that this operation has internal relevance to the cell phone company but not to the customer.

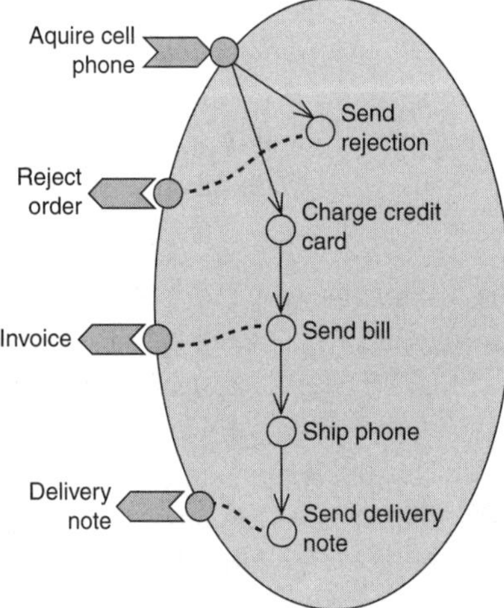

FIGURE 18.6
Public flow.

The simplification of the flow is not limited to revealing fewer internal steps to the customer. First, observe the modification of the control flow, as the double control dependencies at `SendRejection` and `ChargeCreditCard` are removed. Note also that the relationship established with a shipper service in activity `ShipPhone` is not reflected in the flow of Figure 18.6, because this is a private detail that the service does not want to reveal to customers or competitors. In terms of the definition of the corresponding activities, you would have in this case an activity without an implementation block.

Drawing from this example, the typical relationship between the private and the public flow can be summarized as follows:

- Public flows have only a subset of all the activities present in the private flow. The activities present in the public flow are those needed to support the proper flow of control and to provide users with information on the execution state.
- Public flows have simpler flow of data and control, but provide full information about the sequencing of service operations.
- The implementation of certain activities is not exposed in public flows.
- A private flow and its corresponding public version both support the same customer-facing interfaces. From the customer perspective, both flows show the same service provider type.

Regardless of the differences between a service's private and public flows, both should match the observable behavior of the service: The same external interactions with the customer need to be present in both representations, and the sequencing and control dependencies between them must be equivalent, in the sense that the two descriptions should accept as valid the same sequences of message exchanged between a client and the service. Making sure that this type of equivalence holds can be hard to show in the case of complex flows. The important point to keep in mind, however, is that from a service user's perspective, both flows should behave in exactly the same way.

Global Models

Up until now you've been dealing with the problem of specifying the behavior of a single Web service, either in executable form (private flow) or as a public contract (public flow). In practice, every transaction involves at least two parties, each of which can be characterized in general as a Web service. Complex transactions can typically involve three and more participants directly interacting with each other. Using the flow model described in the previous sections, you can represent the behavior of each one of the parties involved in a transaction. This, however, is not enough to fully specify how the interaction is carried out. What is still missing is a specification of the way in which all these parties need to interact to carry out a certain transaction. Global models are used in WSFL to specify the form of multiparty interactions.

To begin, consider the simplest case: an interaction between two services. A new service must be added to the example, representing an automated cell phone requester service—or customer—of the ordering service. The customer service and its interactions with the cell phone order services are shown in Figure 18.7.

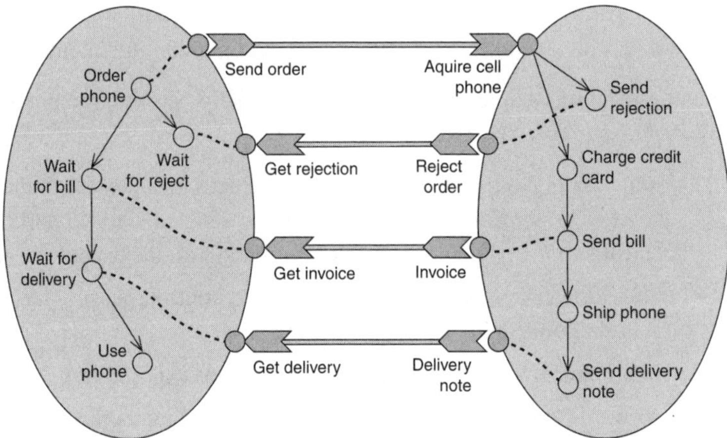

FIGURE 18.7
Global model involving two parties.

Observe that the customer is modeled as a service itself, with a WSDL interface and a flow representing its behavior, in just the same way as the phone ordering service. In non-trivial interactions both the provider and the requester of a service need to send and receive messages at different points in their interaction; that is, both effectively behave as clients and servers simultaneously. The Web services interaction paradigm is thus naturally a peer-to-peer interaction model.

In WSDL terms, the customer interface includes one notification operation (`sendOrder`) and three in-only operations (`getRejection`, `getInvoice`, and `getDelivery`). The customer's public flow specifies the steps that need to follow the sending of the order before the customer's ordering process can be considered terminated: receiving the bill and receiving a note informing of the phone delivery. The customer can also receive a rejection message informing it that the request was not accepted.

Plug Links

In addition to the public flows of two services, Figure 18.7 depicts the interactions between the two in the form of connections between the two services. WSFL refers to these connections as *plug links*. Plug links are directional connections that represent the invocation of an operation of the target service by the source. WSFL models invocations as an ordered pair consisting of an outbound operation at the source (that is, a WSDL notification or solicit-response operation) followed by an inbound operation (WSDL one-way or request-response) at the target.

It is important to note here that WSFL makes the assumption that outbound operations in a WSDL interface represent a service's ability to invoke the corresponding inbound operation—that is, one whose signature is obtained by exchanging the input and output elements in the operation definition. Thus, WSFL interprets outbound operations by as proxies of the corresponding inbound operation, and a plug link is basically a symbolic representation of connection that exists between the proxy and the operation that it actually invokes on a given service.

The following is an example of a plug link as specified in WSFL syntax:

```
<plugLink>
   <source serviceProvider="customer" portType="customerPortType"
           operation="sendOrder"/>
   <target serviceProvider="cellPhoneOrderService" portType="orderPortType"
           operation="receiveOrder"/>
</plugLink>
```

In this example, the assumption is that `sendOrder` and `receiveOrder` have dual but matching signatures, as in the sample `portTypes` below:

```
<portType name="customerPortType">
   <operation name="sendOrder">
      <output message="tns:phoneOrder"/>
   </operation>
   ...
</portType>
<portType name="orderPortType">
   <operation name="receiveOrder">
      <input message="tns:phoneOrder"/>
   </operation>
   ...
</portType>
```

Provision must be made, however, for the case in which the types of the messages sent and received by the source and the target do not match, because in practice the connected services may have not been developed from a common design. WSFL allows for simple adaptation of the messages exchanged by means of a mapping mechanism similar to the one used with data links (see the section "Data Flow"). Thus, if the message that `sendOrder` sends has a different type from the message that `receiveOrder` accepts, a `map` specification can be included in the plug link to provide for the necessary data mapping:

```
<plugLink>
   <source serviceProvider="customer" portType="customerPortType"
           operation="sendOrder"/>
   <target serviceProvider="cellPhoneOrderService" portType="orderPortType"
           operation="receiveOrder"/>
```

```
   <map sourceMessage="sendOrderOutput" sourcePart="personalInfo"
        targetMessage="receiveOrderInput" targetPart="customerData"/>
</plugLink>
```

Global Models in WSFL

To describe a multiparty transaction, WSFL uses a new construct: the *global model*. A global model identifies the set of service instances that participate in the transaction (these are the service providers you saw in the section "Flows as Compositions of Web Services") and uses plug links to define the interactions between them.

The customer-to-phone order service transaction has a very simple global model with two providers and four plug links:

```
<globalModel name="phoneOrder">
   <serviceProvider name="customer"
                    serviceProviderType="abc:customerType"/>
   <serviceProvider name="cellPhoneOrderService"
                    serviceProviderType="cde:phoneOrderType"/>
   <plugLink>
      <source serviceProvider="customer" portType="abc:customerPortType"
              operation="sendOrder"/>
      <target serviceProvider="cellPhoneOrderService"
              portType="cde:orderPortType" operation="receiveOrder"/>
   </plugLink>
   <plugLink>
      <source serviceProvider="cellPhoneOrderService"
              portType="cde:orderPortType" operation="rejectOrder"/>
      <target serviceProvider="customer" portType="abc:customerPortType"
              operation="getRejection"/>
      <map ... />
   </plugLink>
   <!-- Additional plug links here -->
   ...
</globalModel>
```

Service providers (or service instances) identify a particular usage of a certain service, as opposed to the service itself. Service instances are typed according to a service type (a named set of WSDL interfaces, see "Flows as Compositions of Web Services"), and they are assigned a unique name within the global model. Plug links simply identify the source and target providers by their names, and the operations within those providers that are involved in the interaction.

Clearly, global models need not be limited to two-party interactions. Figure 18.8 shows a modification of the two-party phone order global model in which the order service has outsourced all the shipping functions to a third `shipping` service. The interaction between the customer and the phone ordering service is now limited to the initial ordering and billing. Both the phone ordering service and the customer have direct interactions with the shipping service: The phone ordering service transmits the phone shipment request to the shipper and lets it deal with all the shipping-related functions; the customer receives the delivery information directly from the shipper.

FIGURE 18.8
Global model involving three parties.

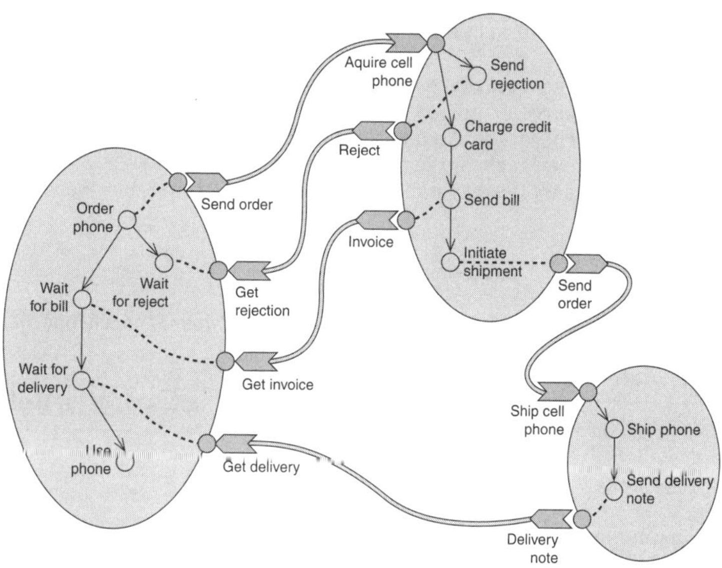

In the corresponding global model, there are three providers and three groups of plug links representing the interactions between them. You can see in the following example that the three service providers (`"customer"` on the left of the figure, `"cellPhoneOrderService"` in the middle, and `"shipper"` on the right) are declared at the top of the XML coding of the global model. In the rest of the global model, the customer to phone ordering service, phone ordering service to shipper, and shipper to customer interactions are defined in the form of sets of plug links connecting each pair of service providers. All possible pair-wise interactions between the providers are represented in the global model:

```
<globalModel name="phoneOrder">
   <serviceProvider name="customer"
                    serviceProviderType="abc:customerType"/>
   <serviceProvider name="cellPhoneOrderService"
                    serviceProviderType="cde:noShipperPhoneOrderType"/>
   <serviceProvider name="shipper"
                    serviceProviderType="cde:shipperType"/>

   <!-- customer to phone order service links -->
```

```
   <plugLink>
      <source serviceProvider="customer" portType="abc:customerPortType"
              operation="sendOrder"/>
      <target serviceProvider="cellPhoneOrderService"
              portType="cde:orderPortType" operation="receiveOrder"/>
   </plugLink>
   ...
   <!-- phone order service to shipper link -->
   <plugLink>
      <source serviceProvider="cellPhoneOrderService"
portType="cde:porderPortType"
              operation="sendOrder"/>
      <target serviceProvider="shipper"
              portType="fgh:shipperPortType" operation="receiveShippingOrder"/>
   </plugLink>

   <!-- shipper to customer link -->
   <plugLink>
      <source serviceProvider="shipper" portType="fgh:shipperPortType"
              operation="deliveryNote"/>
      <target serviceProvider="customer"
              portType="abc:customerPortType" operation="getDelivery"/>
   </plugLink>

</globalModel>
```

This example illustrates the distributed nature of the information that a global model is designed to capture. Note that in this case no single party has a complete view of the global interaction. The global transaction is a distributed composition in which two or more service providers are connected according to a certain interaction pattern to enable a level of functionality (a business goal) not provided by any service independently. Compare this form of composition with the type of compositions created when you use flows to define usage patterns of services, as described in "Flows as Compositions of Web Services."

References

For more information on the topics discussed in this chapter, see these references:

- Frank Leymann. *Web Services Flow Language (WSFL)*. IBM, April 2001. Available online at `http://www.ibm.com/software/solutions/webservices/pdf/WSFL.pdf`.
- Satish Thatte. *XLANG. Web Services for Business Process Design*. Microsoft 2001. Available online at `http://www.gotdotnet.com/team/xml_wsspecs/xlang-c/default.htm`.

Summary

This chapter reviewed the basic concepts of Web services flow languages, using WSFL as a model. Flow languages, and the fundamental notions of flows and compositions of Web services, are the basic pieces required to support complex, multiparty, and long-running service interactions, such as the ones involved in any realistic business-to-business transaction.

CHAPTER 19

Web Services Invocation Framework (WSIF)

By K. Scott Morrison

In This Chapter

Are Web services SOAP?

Sometimes it seems that way. Hardly a day passes without some vendor announcing a new SOAP-based, Web services IDE, toolkit, or even entire platform. Indeed, SOAP is the focus of much of this very book. But it is important to recognize that SOAP bound to HTTP transport is only one potential binding for accessing Web services; a Web service could similarly be involved with CORBA, Microsoft's COM+, Java RMI, or even a direct Java call within the same VM.

Arguably, expanding the scope of the definition of "Web services" in this way erodes the original intent of *Web* in the name, but consider that the service is ultimately what is important to us; the access binding is less so. In an ideal world, clients would be able to access an implementation of a service—whether a Java class, COM object, EJB, PERL script, or what have you— using a number of different protocols, serialization formats, encoding style, transports, and so on, in a functionally invariant manner, and in such a way that they could easily modify their access paradigm without necessitating significant code rewrites.

But isn't this what SOAP offers? Not really. SOAP does promise—and indeed deliver—interoperability. It builds on the now ubiquitous infrastructure of the Web, using protocols and standards that are conspicuous, well understood, and surprisingly flexible given the focus of their original intent. In SOAP there are reasonable rules describing how to serialize type systems to and from human-readable, XML-based messages that are language-neutral from the perspective of the type system. But not surprisingly, SOAP implementations, such as Apache SOAP and Microsoft's .NET, very much tie one into the SOAP protocol for messaging—that is, the SOAP packaging format, header conventions, and so on. SOAP does provide flexibility in transport, which can vary beyond HTTP (an important enhancement introduced in version 1.1 of the protocol); however, the fundamental message protocol remains SOAP-specific XML messages, contained within a greater envelope, potentially further encapsulated within a MIME multipart/related packaging.

The Web Services Invocation Framework (WSIF) is intended to overcome the tight coupling of Web services to a particular messaging protocol, and in particular to a protocol's manifestation as a concrete API. IBM has introduced WSIF under its alphaWorks program, which means that the company is not ready to release it as a product, but considers the technology mature enough for developers to experiment with—and hopefully improve by providing valuable feedback. Apache SOAP had its origins as an IBM alphaWorks release.

WSIF uses the Web Services Description Language (WSDL) discussed in Chapter 11 to inform its operations on particular Web services. WSDL is a language to document service endpoints. It is endpoint metadata, which describes a service, not simply in abstract terms of portable, language-neutral types and method calls, but also in concrete terms of transport and protocol-specific bindings. Transport, by way of example, could be HTTP or SMTP. A protocol might be Apache SOAP, which includes type encoding, communications style, and so on—essentially the algorithm driving how the service is rendered on the wire. WSDL is frequently subject to comparison with an older, but quite mature technology from CORBA: the Interface Definition Language (IDL). Like IDL, the most common positioning of WSDL is as a means to assist in the generation of client-side stub code. But WSDL, together with UDDI as an access method, will also support service browsers, something which will be of great value to developers of clients that consume Web services.

WSIF uses WSDL to dynamically (that is, at runtime) map an abstract representation of a service to a concrete means of accessing the service, such as through Apache SOAP. WSIF is a truly extensible framework. New ports that accommodate new or altered protocols and/or transports can be developed generically and independent of any client or service implementation. Registration of a new port with the framework can occur dynamically, at runtime. Clients use framework APIs that are invariant with respect to the binding to interact with services. Clients parameterize their calls to services by supplying a WSDL port identifier, which effectively names a service endpoint.

All this helps to decouple clients from a particular protocol's API, moving them instead to a model that interacts with an abstract representation of the service, as embodied in the WSDL service interface. This is quite compelling, because it shifts the focus away from the myriad of implementation details needed to realize a specific binding such as Apache SOAP, back to the service itself: that is, the service method, its associated arguments, and its return values and state—essentially the contract promulgated by the API and its functionality.

Time Server Introduction

WSIF might sound too good to be real, but it is available now, albeit in an early implementation. The best way to explore its rich capabilities is with a simple service that makes sense for both local and distributed applications to access. The explanation in this chapter breaks from the Web services tradition somewhat and does not offer a stock quote example. Instead, it builds a simple time service. This service may have only one implementation, but as you will see, it can have a number of different deployment scenarios, and thus manifest as different, but functionally congruent network service endpoints.

For example, an application that needs to access the current system time could access the time service locally within the process space of a single Java VM. Or the time service could be deployed as a network-accessible Web service, perhaps providing centralized time services so that all the systems on a LAN can synchronize their system clocks. The important thing to recognize is that either scenario accesses the same underlying Java *service* code; the access method is simply a binding to a protocol and an underlying transport method (in the remote scenario, SOAP and HTTP; in the local scenario, direct Java access using reflection and the class loader—but more on this later), something that is independent of the service implementation.

Versions and Classpaths

The examples in this chapter rely on the following core technologies:

- JDK 1.3.1_01
- Apache SOAP 2.2
- WSIF 1.0
- Tomcat 4.0
- JavaMail 1.2
- Java Activation Framework 1.0.1
- Apache Xerces 1.4.3

You can obtain the latest versions of these technologies from `http://www.javasoft.com` and `http://www.apache.org`. WSIF is available on IBM's alphaWorks site, at `http://alphaworks.ibm.com`.

Technology evolves, and software versions with it. By the time you read this, updates to this will no doubt exist. Wherever possible, I have attempted to avoid version dependencies, and to call out issues in the current builds that may affect you. Nevertheless, this is a very fast-moving technology, and it is likely that the development kits will evolve rapidly and significantly. Use reasonable circumspection as you are working through the examples.

This chapter directly uses technology from both the Apache SOAP and IBM WSIF distributions. Make sure your classpath includes the following Java archives:

- `soap.jar`
- `mail.jar`
- `activation.jar`
- A JAXP 1.1-compatible XML parser, such as Apache Xerces or Sun's Crimson parser included in the JAXP distribution (I'm using `xerces.jar`)

- `wsif-all-1.0.jar`
- `{JAVE_HOME}\lib\tools.jar` (for the code generation examples)

And finally a note on directory representation. I will consistently use Windows-style file separators when representing path names. No particular bias here—I'm actually an old Unix guy—but I did write the chapter and develop all the code on a laptop running Windows 2000.

Time Service Code

The time service should return a system time, both highly accurate and in a format that is potentially understandable by non-Java systems (after all, Web services is about interoperability). Fortunately, Java provides you with a convenient abstraction. The `java.util.Date` class, despite having had most of its functions deprecated with the introduction of `Calendar`, is still acceptable to use to return the current system time as a Java `long` type, representing milliseconds since midnight, January 1, 1970 GMT, an instant in time called the *epoch*.

Although a simple query for the current time is interesting, it doesn't demonstrate input parameters, nor does it reveal how WSIF copes with multiple associated services. So you will add a method to the time server that returns a string representation of the current time for a time zone the client supplies. The time server's actual implementation is shown in Listing 19.1.

Beware of Serializers Bearing Gifts

Do these examples imply that you are limited to using simple Java primitive types to pass arguments, even if you want to use WSIF? Absolutely not! However, custom classes may require type mappers to assist in marshalling and unmarsalling between type systems. Adding these would rapidly make this a very complicated example, but if you are interested in pursuing this, have a look at JAXB, covered in this book in Chapter 14, which is about data binding technology.

That said, some protocols provide built-in serialization services. Apache SOAP is a notable example. Given simple Java classes that follow the JavaBean specifications, Apache SOAP uses introspection to automatically marshal these into SOAP messages, and conversely unmarshal SOAP XML back into beans. This relies on the very natural and logical projection of the Java type system onto XSD. Apache also provides serializers for a number of common utility classes, including `java.util.Date` and `java.util.GregorianCalendar`.

So could you build the time server to return a serialized `Date` or `GregorianCalendar`? In theory, yes, but there are some issues to consider. First, you would still have to write a type mapper to accommodate any non-Java client. But more significant, an examination of the actual SOAP marshallings of these classes—which you can easily capture with TcpTunnel or TcpTrace—reveals some startling limitations. `GregorianCalendar` is mapped to a simple element containing a string representation of the date in the format *yyyy-mm-dd*, thus losing its time component entirely. This is always unmarshalled to a date at 12:00 am. Handling of `Date` is improved, providing the more detailed representation described in the ISO 8601 standard and recognized by the W3C in its *Date and Time Formats* note: that is, yyyy-mm-ddThh:mm:ssZ—better, but still not exactly fine enough resolution for synchronizing a system clock.

LISTING 19.1 The TimeServer Service Endpoint

```
import java.util.Date;
import java.util.TimeZone;
import java.util.GregorianCalendar;
import java.text.DateFormat;
/**
 * TimeServer
 * Provide centralized time services to distributed clients.
 */
public class TimeServer {

    public long synchronizeTime() {
        System.out.println("Call to synchronizeTime()");
        return (new Date()).getTime();
    }

    public String getTimeAtCity(String zoneName) {
        System.out.println("Call to getTimeAtCity(" + zoneName + ")");
        TimeZone timeZone = TimeZone.getTimeZone(zoneName);
        GregorianCalendar gc = new GregorianCalendar(timeZone);
        DateFormat df =
            DateFormat.getDateTimeInstance(DateFormat.FULL, DateFormat.FULL);
        df.setCalendar(gc);
        String timeAtCity = df.format(gc.getTime());
        return timeAtCity;
    }
} // class TimeServer
```

Notice that this is just a simple Java class— nothing here indicates how it might be accessed. You could call this directly from Java code, or you could install it in a SOAP application server. There is also nothing to tie this with WSIF. Indeed, WSIF is exclusively a client-side technology. As you will observe, the service side requires no modification to utilize WSIF.

Note also that you leave the `TimeServer` in the default Java package. In a real application, you would in all probability scope the class to reside within a package name space. You will leave this out here, though, to improve the readability of some of your later code.

Deployment

First, you deploy your service by using a binding to SOAP over HTTP. Specifically, you will make use of Apache SOAP, which should be familiar to most readers by now. If not, take a moment to review Chapters 7 and 8, which describe the Apache implementation.

Compile and deploy the `TimeServer.java` file into your SOAP provider. I'm using Tomcat 4.0, so I simply copied the `.class` file into my `{TOMCAT_HOME}\classes` directory and cycled the server (where `TOMCAT HOME` is the root of your Tomcat installation; if you are using Tomcat 4.0, this is the same as the `CATALINA_HOME` environment variable). In Listing 19.2, you will find the SOAP deployment descriptor for `TimeServer`.

LISTING 19.2 File `DeploymentDescriptorTimeServer.xml`, the Deployment Descriptor for the TimeServer Service Endpoint.

```
<isd:service xmlns:isd="http://xml.apache.org/xml-soap/deployment"
             id="urn:TimeServer">
    <isd:provider type="java"
                  scope="Application"
                  methods="synchronizeTime getTimeAtCity">
        <isd:java class="TimeServer" static="false"/>
    </isd:provider>
    <isd:faultListener>org.apache.soap.server.DOMFaultListener
➥</ isd:faultListener>
</isd:service>
```

You can deploy the service manually from the administration screen, or you can use the `ServiceManagerClient` included with Apache SOAP:

```
java org.apache.soap.server.ServiceManagerClient
➥http://localhost:8080/soap/servlet/rpcrouter
➥deploy DeploymentDescriptorTimeServer.xml
```

This assumes a fairly standard installation of Apache SOAP, consisting of a server listening locally on port 8080. And like all the examples demonstrating how to run a test program, it presumes that you have set your classpath to include the Java archives described earlier in the chapter.

Apache SOAP Client

First, use the classes provided by Apache SOAP to test the service. Apache provides a powerful abstraction in its `Call` class. In `Call`, you identify the service name you want to access, its location, and its arguments:

LISTING 19.3 `TimeServerClient`, an Apache SOAP Client for the TimeServer SOAP Endpoint.

```
package com.sams.jws.chapter19;
import java.util.Vector;
import java.net.URL;
import org.apache.soap.Constants;
import org.apache.soap.Fault;
import org.apache.soap.SOAPException;
import org.apache.soap.rpc.Call;
import org.apache.soap.rpc.Parameter;
import org.apache.soap.rpc.Response;

public class TimeServerClient {
    public static void main(String[] args) throws Exception {
        URL url = new URL("http://localhost:8080/soap/servlet/rpcrouter");
        String operationName = null;
        if (args.length == 0) {
            operationName = "synchronizeTime";
        } else if (args.length == 1) {
            operationName = "getTimeAtCity";
        } else {
            String className = TimeServerClient.class.getName();
            System.err.println("Usage: java " + className + " [zoneName]");
            System.err.println(
                "Eg: java "
                    + className
                    + "\t- Returns server system time as a long "
                    + "in units of millisec since epoch");
            System.err.println(
                "     java "
                    + className
                    + " America/Vancouver \t- Returns server's perspective "
                    + "on current date and time in Vancouver as a string");
            System.exit(0);
        }
```

LISTING 19.1 continued

```
        String encodingStyleURI = Constants.NS_URI_SOAP_ENC;

        // Build generic call.
        Call call = new Call();
        call.setTargetObjectURI("urn:TimeServer");
        call.setEncodingStyleURI(encodingStyleURI);

        // Set input argument for getTimeAtCity
        if (operationName.equals("getTimeAtCity")) {
            String zoneName = args[0];
            Vector parameters = new Vector();
            parameters.addElement(new Parameter("zoneName",
                                                String.class,
                                                zoneName,
                                                null));
            call.setParams(parameters);
        }
        // Build and execute call to synchronizeTime()
        call.setMethodName(operationName);

        Response response;
        try {
            response = call.invoke(url, "");
        } catch (SOAPException e) {
            System.err.println("Caught SOAPException:");
            e.printStackTrace();
            return;
        }

        // Check the response.
        if (!response.generatedFault()) {
            Parameter returnParam = response.getReturnValue();
            Object value = returnParam.getValue();
            System.out.println("Return value for "
                               + operationName + "() is: " + value);

        } else {
            Fault fault = response.getFault();

            System.err.println("Caught fault: ");
            System.err.println("Code:" + fault.getFaultCode());
            System.err.println("Fault string: " + fault.getFaultString());
        }
        System.out.println("Done.");
    } // main()
} // Class TimeServerClient
```

Running this program to get the current time in Vancouver:

```
java com.sams.jws.chapter19.TimeServerClient America/Vancouver
```

Yields the following output:

```
Return value for getTimeAtCity() is: Tuesday, December 11, 2001 6:35:29 PM PST
Done.
```

Listing 19.4 captures the HTTP request dialog. Listing 19.5 shows the corresponding response.

LISTING 19.4 HTTP Request

```
POST /soap/servlet/rpcrouter HTTP/1.0
Host: localhost
Content-Type: text/xml; charset=utf-8
Content-Length: 475
SOAPAction: ""

<?xml version='1.0' encoding='UTF-8'?>
<SOAP-ENV:Envelope xmlns:SOAP-ENV="http://schemas.xmlsoap.org/soap/envelope/"
➥xmlns:xsi="http://www.w3.org/1999/XMLSchema-instance"
➥xmlns:xsd="http://www.w3.org/1999/XMLSchema">
<SOAP-ENV:Body>
<ns1:getTimeAtCity xmlns:ns1="urn:TimeServer"
➥SOAP-ENV:encodingStyle="http://schemas.xmlsoap.org/soap/encoding/">
<zoneName xsi:type="xsd:string">America/Vancouver</zoneName>
</ns1:getTimeAtCity>
</SOAP-ENV:Body>
</SOAP-ENV:Envelope>
```

LISTING 19.5 HTTP Response

```
HTTP/1.1 200 OK
Content-Type: text/xml; charset=utf-8
Content-Length: 513
Date: Wed, 12 Dec 2001 02:35:26 GMT
Server: Apache Tomcat/4.0 (HTTP/1.1 Connector)
Set-Cookie: JSESSIONID=05D4F0B953F1C153319421C32339C4D5;Path=/soap

<?xml version='1.0' encoding='UTF-8'?>
<SOAP-ENV:Envelope xmlns:SOAP-ENV=http://schemas.xmlsoap.org/soap/envelope/
➥xmlns:xsi="http://www.w3.org/1999/XMLSchema-instance"
➥xmlns:xsd="http://www.w3.org/1999/XMLSchema">
<SOAP-ENV:Body>
<ns1:getTimeAtCityResponse xmlns:ns1="urn:TimeServer"
➥SOAP-ENV:encodingStyle="http://schemas.xmlsoap.org/soap/encoding/">
<return xsi:type="xsd:string">Tuesday, December 11, 2001 6:35:29 PM PST</return>
```

LISTING 19.5 continued

```
</ns1:getTimeAtCityResponse>

</SOAP-ENV:Body>
</SOAP-ENV:Envelope>
```

Aside from being a valuable sanity check of your installation, Listing 19.3 shows how effectively Apache SOAP insulates you from the complexity of creating SOAP messages. But in doing so, it also ties you very much into the SOAP protocol of communicating, as shown so plainly in Listings 19.4 and 19.5. You have implicitly made a number of assumptions about method signature, argument order, encoding style, communications style, and so on. To be fair, there are important abstractions here: The SOAP specification explicitly decouples itself from transport—SMTP, or message-oriented middleware can potentially be substituted—without adversely affecting code. However if you needed to substitute an entirely different, non-SOAP protocol, well, Apache SOAP probably isn't going to help you much. This issue of coupling to protocol and transport is exactly the problem that WSIF is intended to solve.

WSDL File

WSIF makes use of WSDL to describe a service as a network endpoint that both acts on and produces messages. Services are characterized abstractly (that is, independent of language, transport, or protocol) and concretely (which incorporates specific bindings to all of these). Ariba, IBM, and Microsoft introduced WSDL in late 2000, and the current version, 1.1, is quite lucidly specified in a W3C note. WSDL, a fascinating and powerful technology, is the topic of Chapter 11 in this book. It is highly recommended that you review this chapter if you are unfamiliar with WSDL.

Listing 19.6 shows the abstract definition of the Java implementation of the TimeServer. The `port` type element aggregates operations, which are groupings of functionally or logically related calls, such as the methods of a class. The `operation` element—at least in the request/response mode illustrated in this example—is composed of an input and output message. `Operation` provides you with pretty much everything you need to know to use a service: method name, argument types and order, return types and order, and faults, all in a language- and platform-independent manner. Essentially, `operation` is a method signature. It does not tell you anything about how to access the service; this is the role of the concrete binding. A single abstract service description can have multiple bindings (or endpoints), which are specified in the implementation file (covered next).

LISTING 19.6 `TimeServer-interface.wsdl`, the Service Interface Document

```
<?xml version="1.0"?>

<definitions name="TimeService"
             targetNamespace="http://localhost:8080/wsif/TimeServer-interface"
             xmlns:tns="http://localhost:8080/wsif/TimeServer-interface"
             xmlns:xsd="http://www.w3.org/1999/XMLSchema"
             xmlns="http://schemas.xmlsoap.org/wsdl/">

    <message name="synchronizeTime"/>
    <message name="synchronizeTimeResponse">
        <part name="return" type="xsd:long"/>
    </message>
    <message name="getTimeAtCity">
        <part name="zoneName" type="xsd:string"/>
    </message>
    <message name="getTimeAtCityResponse">
        <part name="return" type="xsd:string"/>
    </message>

    <portType name="TimeServicePortType">
        <operation name="synchronizeTime">
            <input message="tns:synchronizeTime"/>
            <output message="tns:synchronizeTimeResponse"/>
        </operation>
        <operation name="getTimeAtCity">
            <input message="tns:getTimeAtCity"/>
            <output message="tns:getTimeAtCityResponse"/>
        </operation>
    </portType>
</definitions>
```

Strictly speaking, this isn't the standard format for a service interface document, which typically would include the binding element as well. The standard convention is usually adopted to map the interface cleanly into a UDDI registry. In UDDI, a URL referencing the interface document is explicitly included in the tModel `<overviewURL>` element. tModels carry the restriction that they must reference a binding as well as its associated `port type`, messages, and if relevant, types. (The UDDI section of this book, Chapters 9 and 10, offers much more detail on this topic.) In the interest of maintaining clean separation between abstract and concrete definitions, you will place the binding element in the service implementation document shown in Listing 19.7.

LISTING 19.7 `TimeServer.wsdl`, the Service Implementation Document.

```
<?xml version="1.0"?>

<definitions name="TimeService"
             targetNamespace="http://localhost:8080/wsif/TimeServer"
             xmlns:tns="http://localhost:8080/wsif/TimeServer"
             xmlns:tns-inter="http://localhost:8080/wsif/TimeServer-interface"
             xmlns:xsd="http://www.w3.org/1999/XMLSchema"
             xmlns:soap="http://schemas.xmlsoap.org/wsdl/soap/"
             xmlns:java="http://schemas.xmlsoap.org/wsdl/java/"
             xmlns="http://schemas.xmlsoap.org/wsdl/">

    <import namespace="http://localhost:8080/wsif/TimeServer-interface"
            location="http://localhost:8080/wsif/TimeServer-interface.wsdl"/>

    <binding name="TimeServiceSOAPBinding"
             type="tns-inter:TimeServicePortType">
        <soap:binding style="rpc"
                      transport="http://schemas.xmlsoap.org/soap/http"/>
        <operation name="synchronizeTime">
            <soap:operation soapAction=""/>
            <input>
                <soap:body use="encoded" namespace="urn:TimeServer"
                    encodingStyle="http://schemas.xmlsoap.org/soap/encoding/"/>
            </input>
            <output>
                <soap:body use="encoded" namespace="urn:TimeServer"
                    encodingStyle="http://schemas.xmlsoap.org/soap/encoding/"/>
            </output>
        </operation>
        <operation name="getTimeAtCity">
            <soap:operation soapAction=""/>
            <input>
                <soap:body use="encoded" namespace="urn:TimeServer"
                    encodingStyle="http://schemas.xmlsoap.org/soap/encoding/"/>
            </input>
            <output>
                <soap:body use="encoded" namespace="urn:TimeServer"
                    encodingStyle="http://schemas.xmlsoap.org/soap/encoding/"/>
            </output>
        </operation>
    </binding>

    <service name="TimeService">
        <documentation>
            Central time server.
            Can provide current GMT time in milliseconds since the epoch, or
            the current time from the server's perspective for a particular
            time zone.
```

LISTING 19.7 continued

```
        </documentation>
        <port name="TimeServiceSOAPPort" binding="tns:TimeServiceSOAPBinding">
            <soap:address
                location="http://localhost:8080/soap/servlet/rpcrouter"/>
        </port>
    </service>
</definitions>
```

Because all of the arguments are primitive Java types (`long` and `String`), you can use the standard mappings defined in the W3C specification *XML Schema: Datatypes*. This is why your service interface document does not include a WSDL `Type` element.

TIP

Notice that we are referencing the XML Schema description for 1999. There have been drafts and candidate recommendations published since then; in particular, Schema has since moved to W3C Recommendation status in May 2001. WSDL files should user this later version, indicated by the URL `http://www.w3.org/2001/XMLSchema`. The earlier one is used in these examples to resolve an issue with WSIF code generation that you would otherwise encounter in an upcoming example. Note, though, that SOAP 1.1 is based on the 1999 Schema as a consequence of when the SOAP specification was released (May, 1999). Thus, if you inspect the Apache SOAP dialogs in Listings 19.4 and 19.5 you will find references to this earlier specification.

The service implementation document, shown in Listing 19.7, introduces concrete bindings to language, protocol, and transport. Here, it's SOAP over HTTP. The WSDL specification provides examples for HTTP get and post, and MIME. Later, you will expand this example to incorporate Java, and consider other providers as well.

The service implementation file is where a network endpoint definition resides; it is here that the physicality of machine location, architecture, and language manifest. Bindings declare the transport and describe how to render a message on the wire. Notice that there are two distinct `operation` elements here: one subordinate to the port type, and one subordinate to the binding. There exists a direct mapping between the abstract method signature defined in the port type operation and the concrete `operation` defined in the implementation. The concrete binding includes information on how to arrange and encode message parts into a particular message format (in this case, SOAP). This is where the extensibility of WSDL really comes into play, because bindings typically demand very implementation-specific information, such as transport, message exchange style (that is, document-oriented or RPC), specific header information, and so on. WSDL can accommodate those characteristics that are unique to a binding by introducing new elements that reside in a namespace intrinsic to the binding. For example, `<soap:binding>`, `<soap:operation>`, and `<soap:body>` are custom elements that are relevant exclusively to the SOAP protocol.

Again, this represents a break from conventional file organization. UDDI specifies a mapping of the WSDL service to the UDDI `BusinessService` element and a mapping of the ports into the `BindingTemplate` subelements. Thus, the binding should reside not here, but in the interface file.

Deploy both these WSDL files into your Web application server, as a part of the WSIF Web application. For my installation, I copied both files into `{TOMCAT_HOME}\webapps\wsif`. If you change this, don't forget to alter the import in Listing 19.7. Also make any changes appropriate to your host in the `location` attribute of the `soap:address` element under the port `TimeServiceSOAPPort`.

Configuring Web Application Servers to Serve WSDL

Because WSDL is a relatively new content type, most Web servers will not know how to set the MIME type appropriately when servicing a request for a file ending in `.wsdl`. Even in Apache 4.0, which is quite recent, this remains an issue that you will need to address. And don't be fooled if you can view a `.wsdl` file residing on your server in your browser. Some browsers are quite good at guessing what stylesheet to apply to mystery content in the absence of a proper MIME type in the HTTP `Content-Type` header. Internet Explorer, as a case in point, recognizes WSDL as XML and applies the default XML stylesheet. However, the WSDL utilities on which WSIF is built aren't quite this flexible, and will probably fail to load a WSDL file from a URL if the server cannot codify its MIME type.

Fortunately, adding new MIME types is very simple. For Apache 4.0, insert the following lines into the file `{TOMCAT_HOME}\conf\web.xml`:

```
<mime-mapping>
   <extension>wsdl</extension>
   <mime-type>text/xml</mime-type>
</mime-mapping>
```

WSIF Dynamic Client

Now it's time to investigate how WSIF can be used to access a Web service dynamically, without an explicit stub. In a sense, you can think of this as the Web services version of Java reflection and the classloader. WSIF uses the WSDL file describing the service to determine the operations published by the service, and more significantly, the concrete bindings available for the service endpoint. One of the real advantages to this arrangement is that it hides the messy details of WSDL, which can admittedly be fairly complex.

Given a WSDL document and a port named in it, WSIF can make calls to the network service endpoint that the port identifies. WSIF elicits calls on the service by making use of a *provider* specific to the binding and transport, but not specific to a particular user's service. WSIF is a flexible, pluggable framework. It provides a well-defined series of interfaces to enable developers to create new providers that a WSIF application can incorporate dynamically while running. The current distribution includes providers for SOAP over HTTP, direct Java access, and SOAP RMI; presumably as the technology evolves, providers will appear that implement other potential bindings. One example we will likely see is Java RMI, which can make use of JRMP or IIOP. Another example, a little less obvious, would be Microsoft's COM+.

Developers can realize some very tangible advantages by building applications that can delay binding until runtime. Interfaces can be changed without forcing clients to recompile and/or relink (this, of course, assumes that either the method signature does not change appreciably, or the clients are astonishingly flexible about accommodating changes). More likely, however, would be that service deployment, transport, or protocol binding might change. Because these simple configurations are named in a WSDL file, as opposed to being hard coded into a class library on which the client relies, they can easily be modified without breaking code.

This has great implications for Web services. Suppose you had a basic user profile service, such as a simplified version of Microsoft's Passport. A number of service providers may offer different implementations of a common abstract interface. A client may choose among these competing services based on functionality, quality of service, physical location (on the LAN as opposed to another continent, for example), cost, or available binding (SOAP over HTTP, SOAP over SMTP, CORBA IIOP, COM+, and so on). These factors can all change over time. Good providers get expensive; bad providers disappear. WSIF applications can choose a binding dynamically based on a name registered within a JNDI-accessible directory. This means that an application can switch to an entirely different service implementation on the fly, with no change to code.

Sound promising? Here's how WSIF does it.

The SOAP Port

WSIF must first read a WSDL service implementation file. It uses the Definition interface from the WSDL4J kit. (This is now an integral component of IBM's Web Services Toolkit on AlphaWorks, but is included in the WSIF distribution. WSDL4J has since gone on to form the basis for a new Java standard under the Java Community Process: JSR-110, Java APIs for WSDL.) Definition is an encapsulation of a WSDL document, providing method signatures to navigate to most major WSDL elements directly. An implementation of a Definition can be retrieved by using the readWSDL() method of the WSIFUtils class. The first argument is a context URL that can, in most cases, be set to null:

```
Definition definition = WSIFUtils.readWSDL(null,
➥"http://localhost:8080/wsif/TimeServer.wsdl");
```

After you have the definition, you need to select a particular service and port type from the WSDL file. Scope these to the correlated namespace in which each element resides. Both Service and PortType are Java interfaces defined in WSDL4J. Remember that WSDL defines a port type as an abstract interface definition that is distinct from a binding:

```
Service service = WSIFUtils.selectService(definition,
                    "http://localhost:8080/wsif/TimeServer",
                    "TimeService");
PortType portType = WSIFUtils.selectPortType(definition,
                    "http://localhost:8080/wsif/TimeServer-interface",
                    "TimeServicePortType");
```

Services are accessed through concrete implementations of the WSIFPort interface. A WSIFPort implementation is actually a specialization for a particular binding, such as Apache SOAP (which you will use here), Java (which you will see later), SOAP RMI, or any other bindings that the future may bring. A factory creates a WSIFPort. Initialize the factory with definition, service, and portType, but no specific binding. The getPort() method of the factory, when provided with a specific port name implemented by the service, can then determine the binding, search for a provider for this binding, and return the binding as a WSIFPort. Here wsifPort is actually a WSIFPort_ApacheSOAP instance:

```
WSIFDynamicPortFactory wsifDynPortFac = new WSIFDynamicPortFactory(definition,
                                                                   service,
                                                                   portType);
WSIFPort wsifPort = wsifDynPortFac.getPort("TimeServiceSOAPPort");
```

WSIF provides a message interface implemented as input, output, and fault messages. The input message is populated according to its abstract definition under the operation that is subordinate to the portType element. A WSIFException is thrown if in the setPart() method you attempt to set a message part that isn't part of the schema (such as changing zoneName below), or if you fail to match the expected Java type:

```
WSIFMessage inputWsifMsg = wsifPort.createInputMessage();
WSIFMessage outputWsifMsg = wsifPort.createOutputMessage();
WSIFMessage faultWsifMsg = wsifPort.createFaultMessage();

WSIFPart inputWsifPart = new WSIFJavaPart(String.class, "Europe/London");
inputWsifMsg.setPart("zoneName", inputWsifPart);
```

This exception will not be raised until you actually invoke the service, when the input message will be measured against the actual WSDL for congruency. However, this is actually a great advancement over regular Apache SOAP, because WSIF catches the error at the client side before making the call to the service. In Apache SOAP, the client doesn't note the error until the server returns a `no signature match` SOAP fault. In other words, an entire round trip between client and server is necessary to detect the problem.

The actual invocation of the service makes use of the `WSIFPort` and includes the WSDL operation name. Shown here is the RPC style, request/response paradigm; however, input-only messages (that is, send-and-forget) are also implemented, but obviously with no output or fault. WSDL also accommodates the reciprocal of these: solicit/response and notification. None of the current SOAP implementations offer this yet, but we can assume that in the future bindings will exist that do:

```
wsifPort.executeRequestResponseOperation(operationName,
                                         inputWsifMsg,
                                         outputWsifMsg,
                                         faultWsifMsg);
```

Finally, you process the return values:

```
WSIFPart outputWsifPart = outputWsifMsg.getPart("return");
System.out.println("Return value for " + operationName +
                   "() is: " + outputWsifPart.getJavaValue());
```

Attempting to retrieve a parameter that the `WSIFMessage` does not name results in a `NullPointerException`.

Consider what you have done here: Given just a WSDL file, a service name, a port, an operation, and a port type, you were able to invoke a Web service. The fact that the protocol was SOAP is a characteristic derived from this, but never explicitly named in your code. Any of these arguments could be trivially parameterized and accessed as a property—potentially using JNDI to query a central naming service—and thus could easily be changed without any code modifications. (They have not been parameterized in this example simply for clarity; obviously, this could be expanded.) To target an identical service on a different server—perhaps one with a faster response time—simply change the `location` attribute of the port you named in the WSDL file. To change from a SOAP implementation to a new protocol that has recently appeared (say, SOAP++), simply add an appropriate binding element to the WSDL file, register it as a new port, make a provider implementation available to the `WSIFDynamicPortFactory` (new providers can be registered with the factory using `Class.forName(fullyQualifiedClassName)`, identical to how new providers are registered in JDBC), and finally modify the port name parameter.

Listing 19.8 collects this code together as a standalone test client.

LISTING 19.8 `WSIFTimeServerClient.java`, Demonstration of Stubless Calls to a Service Endpoint

```
package com.sams.jws.chapter19;

import com.ibm.wsif.WSIFDynamicPortFactory;
import com.ibm.wsif.WSIFPort;
import com.ibm.wsif.WSIFPart;
import com.ibm.wsif.WSIFJavaPart;
import com.ibm.wsif.WSIFMessage;
import com.ibm.wsif.stub.WSIFUtils;
import javax.wsdl.Definition;
import javax.wsdl.Service;
import javax.wsdl.PortType;

/**
 * WsifTimeServerClient
 * Simple demonstration of the most basic WSIF functionality.
 */

public class WsifTimeServerClient {

    public static void main(String[] args) throws Exception {

        String operationName = null;
        String zoneName = null;
        if (args.length == 1) {
            operationName = "synchronizeTime";
        } else if (args.length == 2) {
            operationName = "getTimeAtCity";
            zoneName = args[1];
        } else {
            String className = WsifTimeServerClient.class.getName();
            System.err.println("Usage: java " + className +
                                   " portName [zoneName]");
            System.err.println(
                "Eg: java "
                    + className
                    + " TimeServiceSOAPPort \t- Returns server system time "
                    + "as a long in units of millisec since epoch");
            System.err.println(
```

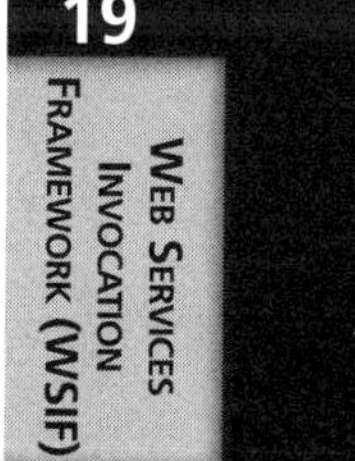

LISTING 19.8 continued

```
            "    java "
                + className
                + " TimeServiceSOAPPort America/Vancouver \t- "
                + "Returns server's perspective on current date and time "
                + "in Vancouver as a string");
        System.exit(0);
    }
    String portName = args[0];

    System.out.println("Loading WSDL document");
    Definition definition =
        WSIFUtils.readWSDL(null,
                        "http://localhost:8080/wsif/TimeServer.wsdl");

    Service service =
        WSIFUtils.selectService(
            definition,
            "http://localhost:8080/wsif/TimeServer",
            "TimeService");
    PortType portType =
        WSIFUtils.selectPortType(
            definition,
            "http://localhost:8080/wsif/TimeServer-interface",
            "TimeServicePortType");
    WSIFDynamicPortFactory wsifDynPortFac =
        new WSIFDynamicPortFactory(definition, service, portType);
    System.out.println("Retrieving WSIFPort");
    WSIFPort wsifPort = wsifDynPortFac.getPort(portName);

    WSIFMessage inputWsifMsg = wsifPort.createInputMessage();
    WSIFMessage outputWsifMsg = wsifPort.createOutputMessage();
    WSIFMessage faultWsifMsg = wsifPort.createFaultMessage();

    // Set input argument for getTimeAtCity
    if (operationName.equals("getTimeAtCity")) {
        WSIFPart inputWsifPart = new WSIFJavaPart(String.class, zoneName);
        WSIFPart inputWsifPart2 = new WSIFJavaPart(java.lang.Integer.class,
                                             new Integer(123));
        inputWsifMsg.setPart("zoneName", inputWsifPart);
    }

    // Run request
    wsifPort.executeRequestResponseOperation(
        operationName,
        inputWsifMsg,
        outputWsifMsg,
        faultWsifMsg);
```

LISTING 19.8 continued

```
        // Process return values
        WSIFPart outputWsifPart = outputWsifMsg.getPart("return");
        System.out.println(
            "Return value for "
                + operationName
                + "() is: "
                + outputWsifPart.getJavaValue());

        System.out.println("Done.");
    }
}
```

Run this using one of the following:

```
java com.sams.jws.chapter19.WsifTimeServerClient TimeServiceSOAPPort
java com.sams.jws.chapter19.WsifTimeServerClient TimeServiceSOAPPort Asia/Tokyo
```

For this example, the port `TimeServiceSOAPPort` is the only one that is available. Shortly, you will see how to implement another simple port that makes direct Java calls with only simple modifications to the service implementation document.

Java's Time Zones

Java actually recognizes a large number of world time zones in the format you see in this chapter. To get the full list, you can run the following simple program:

```
import java.util.TimeZone;

public class ListAllTimeZones {

    public static void main(String[] args) {
        System.out.println("Listing all recognized time zones:\n");
        String[] tz = TimeZone.getAvailableIDs();
        for (int i = 0; i < tz.length; i++) {
            System.out.println(tz[i]);
        }
    }

}
```

The Dynamic Invoker

The WSIF distribution includes a sample program that shows how flexible the concept of stubless, dynamic execution of services is. This program can run an astonishing number of simple Web service implementations. Unfortunately, it does have some limitations. To keep it very simple, the WSIF `DynamicInvoker` recognizes only a few simple Java primitive types. At present, this list unfortunately excludes `long`, so you can't use it to call your `synchronizeTime()` method. Nevertheless, it is still very powerful—and it can be extended very easily to accommodate more complicated types. Try this:

```
java clients.DynamicInvoker http://localhost:8080/wsif/TimeServer.wsdl
➥ getTimeAtCity Asia/Katmandu
```

Given only a WSDL definition, an operation name, and the argument this operation needs, you can use Apache SOAP to call this Web service. It's easy to imagine how this could form the basis for some powerful unit testing scripts.

Java Stub Generation

As you observed in the preceding section, using WSIF for stubless, dynamic invocation can be quite compelling; however, it does make the client code difficult to read. With so much of the software development life cycle preoccupied with maintenance, clarity in program logic and flow is critically important. Fortunately, WSIF can address this need without sacrificing functionality.

WSIF includes a code generation utility that produces (and compiles) Java stubs from a WSDL description. This in itself is not particularly new or startling: As soon as WSDL appeared, people began creating simple code generators, and now it has become a commonplace tool accompanying any Web services framework such as Microsoft's .NET. IBM's Web Services Toolkit splits its implementation into two separate tools: `proxygen`, which generates the client-side stub; and `servicegen`, which generates the server-side service skeleton. (Tools that perform the inverse function are also beginning to appear. The Web Services Toolkit offers `wsdlgen`, which can generate WSDL descriptions from objects that support some level of introspection, such as Java classes, EJBs, and COM objects. It can also generate an Apache SOAP deployment descriptor, and Apache serializers for complex compound types.)

WSIF's code generation is different from these. WSIF-generated code allows dynamic substitution of a WSDL port at run time. For example, you might develop and debug a service by using a Java port that calls a service directly within the process space of a single Java VM (more on this later). You can then deploy the service remotely, accessible to any client that can call a service using Apache SOAP. The actual client code would not undergo any adjustment to change the deployment; only the value of the port parameter would change.

Running the Generator

WSIF's tool for code generation creates both Java source and class files. It uses a package name derived from the namespace of the WSDL definition element. To run it, type the following:

```
java com.ibm.wsif.compiler.PortTypeCompiler
➥ http://localhost:8080/wsif/TimeServer.wsdl
```

The `PortTypeCompiler` can also accept the service namespace and the service name as parameters, but for this example, you can leave these out.

Generated Classes

Running the `PortTypeCompiler` generates `java` and `class` files in a subdirectory underneath the directory in which it runs. This subdirectory path, of course, is a function of the package name, which the `PortTypeCompiler` derives from the namespace of the WSDL definition element. If you need to alter these files, you should consider extending the class rather than editing these files directly, because the PortTypeCompiler overwrites them each time it's run. This is a perennial problem with most code generation.

In this example, the `PortTypeCompiler` generates the Java interface `TimeServerPortType`, which resides in the file `localhost_8080\wsif\TimeServer\TimeServicePortType.java`.This is reproduced in Listing 19.9.

LISTING 19.9 `TimeServicePortType.java`

```
package localhost_8080.wsif.TimeServer;

import java.rmi.Remote;
import java.rmi.RemoteException;

/**
 * This shows an example of a generated Java interface that
 * corresponds to a WSDL port type.
 */
public interface TimeServicePortType extends Remote
{
  public long synchronizeTime() throws RemoteException;

  public String getTimeAtCity(String zoneName) throws RemoteException;
}
```

The actual stub, a Java class shown in Listing 19.10, implements the `TimeServerPortType` interface. This interface contributes the method signatures of the services described in the WSDL file. Remember that this generated code is derived from the WSDL description and not from an inspection of the actual Java class `TimeServer`. If an error is in the WSDL description, it will not manifest until runtime—the cost of late binding is the loss of compile-time type checking. A program that validates WSDL against an actual service implementation would be valuable here.

The stub is a Java class called `TimeServerPortTypeStub`. You can find the source for this class in the file `localhost_8080\wsif\TimeServer\TimeServicePortTypeStub.java`, as well as reproduced in Listing 19.10.

LISTING 19.10 `TimeServerPortTypeStub.java`

```
package localhost_8080.wsif.TimeServer;

import java.util.*;
import javax.wsdl.*;
import com.ibm.wsdl.xml.*;
import com.ibm.wsif.*;
import com.ibm.wsif.stub.*;

/**
 * This shows an example of using the JNDI registry at runtime
 * to locate a port factory. If the JNDI lookup fails, then the
 * WSDL document is used to initialize a dynamic port factory.
 * The port factory is then consulted for a suitable port for
 * this stub to use.
 */
public class TimeServicePortTypeStub extends WSIFStub
  implements TimeServicePortType
{
  private final String DOCUMENT_BASE =
    "http://localhost:8080/wsif/TimeServer.wsdl";
  private final String PORT_TYPE_NS =
    "http://localhost:8080/wsif/TimeServer-interface";
  private final String PORT_TYPE_NAME = "TimeServicePortType";

  /**
   * Create a new stub using a port factory obtained via JNDI. If that
   * doesn't work, use the WSDL document provided at compile-time to
   * initialize a dynamic port factory. If serviceNS and serviceName
   * are not null, they will be used in selecting a service.
   */
  public TimeServicePortTypeStub(String serviceNS, String serviceName)
    throws WSIFException
  {
```

LISTING 19.10 continued

```
    locatePortFactory(
      null,
      DOCUMENT_BASE,
      WSDL_DEFINITION_STR,
      serviceNS,
      serviceName,
      PORT_TYPE_NS,
      PORT_TYPE_NAME);
  }

  /**
   * Create a new stub using a port factory obtained via JNDI. If that
   * doesn't work, use the specified WSDL document to initialize a
   * dynamic port factory. If serviceNS and serviceName are not null,
   * they will be used in selecting a service.
   */
  public TimeServicePortTypeStub(Definition def,
    String serviceNS,
    String serviceName) throws WSIFException
  {
    locatePortFactory(
      def,
      null,
      null,
      serviceNS,
      serviceName,
      PORT_TYPE_NS,
      PORT_TYPE_NAME);
  }

  public long synchronizeTime() throws WSIFException
  {
    WSIFMessage input = wp.createInputMessage();


    WSIFMessage output = wp.createOutputMessage();

    wp.executeRequestResponseOperation("synchronizeTime",
      input, output, null);

    WSIFPart part = output.getPart("return");

    return ((Long)part.getJavaValue()).longValue();
  }

  public String getTimeAtCity(String zoneName) throws WSIFException
  {
    WSIFMessage input = wp.createInputMessage();
```

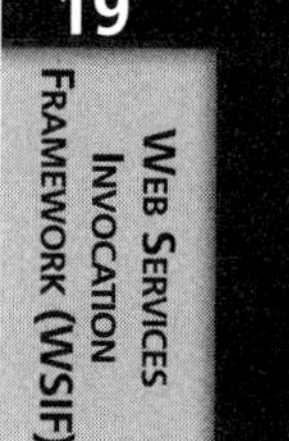

LISTING 19.10 continued

```
    input.setPart("zoneName", new WSIFJavaPart(String.class, zoneName));

    WSIFMessage output = wp.createOutputMessage();

    wp.executeRequestResponseOperation("getTimeAtCity",
      input, output, null);

    WSIFPart part = output.getPart("return");

    return (String)part.getJavaValue();
  }

  private static final String WSDL_DEFINITION_STR =
    "<?xml version=\"1.0\" encoding=\"UTF-8\"?>" + "\r\n" +
    "<definitions name=\"TimeService\" targetNamespace=\"http://localhost:8080
➥/wsif/TimeServer\" xmlns:xsd=\"http://www.w3.org/1999/XMLSchema\"
xmlns:tns=\"http://localhost:8080/wsif/TimeServer\" xmlns:java=\"
➥http://schemas.xmlsoap.org/wsdl/java/\" xmlns:tns-inter=\"
➥http://localhost:8080/wsif/TimeServer-interface\"
➥xmlns:soap=\"http://schemas.xmlsoap.org/wsdl/soap/\"
➥xmlns=\"http://schemas.xmlsoap.org/wsdl/\">" + "\r\n" +
    "  <import namespace=\"http://localhost:8080/wsif/TimeServer-interface\"
location=\"http://localhost:8080/wsif/TimeServer-interface.wsdl\"/>" + "\r\n" +
    "  <binding name=\"TimeServiceSOAPBinding\"
➥type=\"tns-inter:TimeServicePortType\">" + "\r\n" +
    "    <soap:binding style=\"rpc\" transport=\
➥"http://schemas.xmlsoap.org/soap/http\"/>" + "\r\n" +
    "    <operation name=\"synchronizeTime\">" + "\r\n" +
    "      <soap:operation soapAction=\"\"/>" + "\r\n" +
    "      <input>" + "\r\n" +
    "        <soap:body use=\"encoded\" encodingStyle=\"
➥http://schemas.xmlsoap.org/soap/encoding/\"
➥namespace=\"urn:TimeServer\"/>" + "\r\n" +
    "      </input>" + "\r\n" +
    "      <output>" + "\r\n" +
    "        <soap:body use=\"encoded\" encodingStyle=\"
➥http://schemas.xmlsoap.org/soap/encoding/\"
➥namespace=\"urn:TimeServer\"/>" + "\r\n" +
    "      </output>" + "\r\n" +
    "    </operation>" + "\r\n" +
    "    <operation name=\"getTimeAtCity\">" + "\r\n" +
    "      <soap:operation soapAction=\"\"/>" + "\r\n" +
    "      <input>" + "\r\n" +
    "        <soap:body use=\"encoded\" encodingStyle=\"
➥http://schemas.xmlsoap.org/soap/encoding/\"
➥namespace=\"urn:TimeServer\"/>" + "\r\n" +
    "      </input>" + "\r\n" +
    "      <output>" + "\r\n" +
```

LISTING 19.10 continued

```
    "         <soap:body use=\"encoded\" encodingStyle=\"
➥http://schemas.xmlsoap.org/soap/encoding/\"
➥namespace=\"urn:TimeServer\"/>" + "\r\n" +
    "       </output>" + "\r\n" +
    "     </operation>" + "\r\n" +
    "   </binding>" + "\r\n" +
    "   <service name=\"TimeService\">" + "\r\n" +
    "<documentation>" + "\r\n" +
    "    Central time server." + "\r\n" +
    "    Can provide current GMT time in milliseconds since the epoch, or"
➥ + "\r\n" +
    "    the current time from the server's perspective for a particular"
➥ + "\r\n" +
    "    time zone. " + "\r\n" +
    "    </documentation>" + "\r\n" +
    "     <port name=\"TimeServiceSOAPPort\"
➥binding=\"tns:TimeServiceSOAPBinding\">" + "\r\n" +
    "       <soap:address location=\"
➥http://localhost:8080/soap/servlet/rpcrouter\"/>" + "\r\n" +
    "     </port>" + "\r\n" +
    "   </service>" + "\r\n" +
    "</definitions>";
}
```

The stub reproduces each method in the `TimeServer` class, but with an implementation that uses a WSIF dynamic call. The stub also extends the base class `WSIFStub`, which contributes methods to set a port factory and select a particular port to work with. Your test program demonstrates this in the following section.

The constructor for `TimeServerPortTypeStub` attempts to use JNDI to get a `WSIFPortFactory` if the JNDI classes are available, and if a factory is registered against the service and default port type. Note that the version of the constructor that accepts service name without definition (that is, `TimeServicePortTypeStub(String serviceNS, String serviceName)`) uses the hard-coded document `WSDL_DEFINITION_STRING` as its WSDL source.

Tip

`PortTypeCompiler` has some problems processing WSDL files that utilize types scoped to the newer `XML Schema:Datatypes` definition. Recall that when you created the WSDL file, you backdated your xsd schema to `http://www.w3.org/1999/XMLSchema`. The purpose was to accommodate this issue. This was an issue in WSIF 1.0; however, later revisions may address this.

Testing the Service

`StubTimeServerClient`, shown in Listing 19.11, demonstrates how you can call your generated stub. Run this with the following:

```
java localhost_8080.wsif.TimeServer.StubTimeServerClient
```

`StubTimeServerClient` also optionally accepts a port name as an argument, as well as a time zone. For now, use `TimeServiceSOAPPort` as the port. This port uses the Apache SOAP binding you have identified in your WSDL file:

```
java localhost_8080.wsif.TimeServer.StubTimeServerClient TimeServiceSOAPPort
➥ Europe/London
```

To use a stub to call the service, initialize an instance of the stub class, set the port you are interested in, and then call the method directly.

LISTING 19.11 `StubTimeServerClient.java`, Test Harness for Generated Stub

```
package localhost_8080.wsif.TimeServer;
/**
 * Run test of ports for TimeServer using the generated stubs.
 */

import localhost_8080.wsif.TimeServer.*;

public class StubTimeServerClient {

    public static final String DEFAULT_PORT = "TimeServiceSOAPPort";
    public static final String DEFAULT_TIME_ZONE = "Africa/Nairobi";

    public static void main(String[] args) {

        String portName = null;
        String timeZone = null;
        if (args.length == 0) {
            // Default port
            portName = DEFAULT_PORT;
            timeZone = DEFAULT_TIME_ZONE;
        } else if (args.length == 1) {
            portName = args[0];
            timeZone = DEFAULT_TIME_ZONE;
        } else if (args.length == 2) {
            portName = args[0];
            timeZone = args[1];
        } else {
            String className = StubTimeServerClient.class.getName();
            System.err.println("Usage: java " + className +
                               " [portName] [timeZone]");
            System.err.println(
```

LISTING 19.11 continued

```
                "Eg: java "
                    + className
                    + " TimeServiceSOAPPort \t- Tests both synchronizeTime() "
                    + "and getTimeAtCity() methods using the SOAP port");
            System.err.println("Default port is " + DEFAULT_PORT);
            System.err.println("Default time zone is " + DEFAULT_TIME_ZONE);
            System.exit(0);
        }

        try {
            TimeServicePortTypeStub timeSvcPortTypeStub =
                new TimeServicePortTypeStub(null, null);
            timeSvcPortTypeStub.selectPort(portName);
            System.out.println(
                "Results of port "
                    + portName
                    + " calling synchronizeTime()="
                    + timeSvcPortTypeStub.synchronizeTime());
            System.out.println(
                "Results of port "
                    + portName
                    + " calling getTimeAtCity(\""
                    + timeZone
                    + "\")="
                    + timeSvcPortTypeStub.getTimeAtCity(timeZone));

        } catch (Exception e) {
            e.printStackTrace();
        }
    }
}
```


The Java Port

Thus far, we have used only the Apache SOAP port to explore WSIF. Although this is interesting, the real intent of this technology is to easily enable you to substitute other ports without breaking code. The next logical port to try, one for which an implementation is included in the distribution, is Java. When you use the Java port, WSIF calls the service directly in the same Java VM. As this chapter alluded to earlier, having the ability to call a service locally is ideal for development, because all testing can take place in the context of a single environment. Thus, you don't have to introduce the complexities of distributed computing early in the development process. If you are using an IDE that supports it, you can set breakpoints in the service itself and step through code line by line. This has a tremendous productivity advantage over attempting to start with distributed debugging (which more often than not degenerates into a litter of `println` statements). After the application is working, you can immediately distribute the code across the network without modifying and recompiling the source.

Changes to the Service Implementation WSDL

You will have to modify your service implementation file slightly to describe the new Java port. Note that because the abstract API is not changing—only the new binding to a protocol and transport are being added—the service interface file `TimeServer-interface.wsdl` does not have to undergo any modification.

Listing 19.12 reproduces the file `TimeServer.wsdl`, and highlights the changes in the file as boldface.

LISTING 19.12 `TimeServer.wsdl` with Additions for the Java Port in Bold

```
<?xml version="1.0"?>

<definitions name="TimeService"
             targetNamespace="http://localhost:8080/wsif/TimeServer"
             xmlns:tns="http://localhost:8080/wsif/TimeServer"
             xmlns:tns-inter="http://localhost:8080/wsif/TimeServer-interface"
             xmlns:xsd="http://www.w3.org/1999/XMLSchema"
             xmlns:soap="http://schemas.xmlsoap.org/wsdl/soap/"
             xmlns:java="http://schemas.xmlsoap.org/wsdl/java/"
             xmlns="http://schemas.xmlsoap.org/wsdl/">

    <import namespace="http://localhost:8080/wsif/TimeServer-interface"
            location="http://localhost:8080/wsif/TimeServer-interface.wsdl"/>

    <binding name="TimeServiceSOAPBinding"
             type="tns-inter:TimeServicePortType">
        <soap:binding style="rpc"
                      transport="http://schemas.xmlsoap.org/soap/http"/>
        <operation name="synchronizeTime">
            <soap:operation soapAction=""/>
            <input>
                <soap:body use="encoded" namespace="urn:TimeServer"
                    encodingStyle="http://schemas.xmlsoap.org/soap/encoding/"/>
            </input>
            <output>
                <soap:body use="encoded" namespace="urn:TimeServer"
                    encodingStyle="http://schemas.xmlsoap.org/soap/encoding/"/>
            </output>
        </operation>
        <operation name="getTimeAtCity">
            <soap:operation soapAction=""/>
            <input>
```

LISTING 19.12 continued

```
                <soap:body use="encoded" namespace="urn:TimeServer"
                    encodingStyle="http://schemas.xmlsoap.org/soap/encoding/"/>
            </input>
            <output>
                <soap:body use="encoded" namespace="urn:TimeServer"
                    encodingStyle="http://schemas.xmlsoap.org/soap/encoding/"/>
            </output>
        </operation>
    </binding>

    <binding name="TimeServiceJavaBinding"
             type="tns-inter:TimeServicePortType">
        <java:binding/>
    </binding>

    <service name="TimeService">
        <documentation>
            Central time server.
            Can provide current GMT time in milliseconds since the epoch, or
            the current time from the server's perspective for a particular
            time zone.
        </documentation>
        <port name="TimeServiceSOAPPort" binding="tns:TimeServiceSOAPBinding">
            <soap:address
                location="http://localhost:8080/soap/servlet/rpcrouter"/>
        </port>
        <port name="TimeServiceJavaPort" binding="tns:TimeServiceJavaBinding">
            <java:address class="TimeServer"/>
        </port>
    </service>
</definitions>
```

This is really a trivial change considering what it will achieve.

Accessing the Java Port in the Dynamic Client

Now that you have an updated WSDL file, you are ready to run your dynamic client. Notice that you do not have to change the client's code, nor do you have to recompile. `WsifTimeServerClient` already accepts the port name as a runtime argument. This means you can run the program immediately:

```
java com.sams.jws.chapter19.WsifTimeServerClient TimeServiceJavaPort
➥ Antarctica/Palmer
```

Notice that the output is a little more cluttered than before. You are getting the status messages from the service that were written to the standard output stream—when the service was running in the context of the servlet container, these appeared on the servlet console. Now that you are running the service in the context of a single VM, standard output for the service is standard output for your client.

Contrast the ease of this substitution with the difficulty of doing a switch manually between using Apache SOAP and calling a class directly from a client.

Accessing the Java Port in the Dynamic Invoker

Running the dynamic invoker is also easy:

```
java clients.DynamicInvoker http://localhost:8080/wsif/TimeServer.wsdl
➥ getTimeAtCity Asia/Hong_Kong
```

If this looks familiar, it should: It's exactly how you ran it before. But note also that there is nowhere to specify what port you want to use. `DynamicInvoker` is a deliberately simple example program that invokes the first port it finds in a service. In this case, it worked as you wanted and activated the local Java binding. However, this comes at the cost of the SOAP port, which is no longer accessible. Have a look at the `DynamicInvoker` class, though. You will find that it is not difficult to enhance it to accept a parameterized port name.

Using Generated Stubs to Access the Java Port

Because you have introduced a brand new service endpoint in your WSDL file, you have to regenerate your stubs. Rerun `PortTypeCompiler`, as you did earlier, using the modified WSDL file. A new `TimeServicePortType.java/.class` file is generated, although this interface will not change as a result of your modification to the WSDL. `TimeServicePortTypeStub` changes trivially. The new `Port` and `Binding` elements introduced in your modified service implementation file will obviously appear in the hard-coded version of the document referenced by string `WSDL_DEFINITION_STR`. Because this change is so minor, it will not be reproduced here.

And that's it. You can now run `StubTimeServerClient` immediately, without modification or recompilation:

```
java localhost_8080.wsif.TimeServer.StubTimeServerClient TimeServiceJavaPort
➥ America/Buenos_Aires
```

Note that the console receives the service messages sent to the standard output stream.

Summary

Although WSIF is a new technology, it holds enormous promise. One of the critical issues in Web services is going to be, ironically, interoperability. Even today, if you look at the publicly accessible test Web services published on the xMethods site (`http://www.xmethods.com`), most are dependent on a particular SOAP server and its specific implementation: Some use Apache, others use Microsoft .NET, still others Delphi, and so on. Too often, the particular SOAP wire protocol, serialization, and encoding schemes are dissimilar, not to mention the fundamental incompatibilities of their client APIs. This is typical of the problems that WSIF can help to solve. By decoupling distributed computing from implementation, returning the focus to APIs, and allowing dynamic substitution of different concrete implementations, WSIF will help to make good the promise of Web services.

Implementing Web Services

Part V

In This Part

Inventory Management Application

by Benoît Marchal

IN THIS CHAPTER

In this chapter, you'll see how to build a solution to provide timely information to retailers with the Simple Object Access Protocol (SOAP). For the purpose of this chapter, imagine that you are in the wholesale business. Your company buys goods from different suppliers, stores them in one or more warehouses, and resells them to retailers. Although you ship most products to the retailers, increasingly, you ship directly to the end buyer.

At the heart of this business is a strong commitment to managing logistics: A wholesaler is a buffer between manufacturing and retailing. Obviously, this business is highly computerized. Wholesalers typically accept orders electronically.

Note

This chapter is inspired by Chapter 9 of *Applied XML Solutions* (ISBN 0-672-32054-1). In that book, I wrote the first version of this SOAP application (called StockQ). At the time, the libraries were too primitive for practical use so I wrote my own implementation of SOAP.

You might want to compare both chapters for more insights on how SOAP works. More details on *Applied XML Solutions* are at `http://www.marchal.com`.

Furthermore, imagine that your company decides to improve services to its retailers. You participate in a brainstorming session and conclude that you want to provide more timely information—for example, up-to-the-minute inventory information over the Internet. You are tasked with the implementation.

The availability of products in your warehouse is precious information for your retailers, particularly the online ones. It enables them to better inform their customers, as in, "This product is available, you'll have it tomorrow morning" or "Looks like this item is very popular. I'm afraid it might take a few days for delivery." In exchange for the improved service, they might have to sign an exclusive agreement with your company.

Note

Some companies do just the opposite: They ask their suppliers (not customers) to check their stock and proactively supply goods when their warehouse is empty. In effect, the supplier manages the stock on behalf of the customer.

As you learned in Chapter 7, "Understanding SOAP," SOAP supports Web-based remote procedure calls (RPC). Obviously, SOAP is not specific to wholesalers. Many businesses would benefit from opening their information system to some or all of their customers.

For example, a manufacturer in a competitive industry might publish regular price updates; an airline can make flight information available online; a hotel can report free rooms; and an auction site can publish bids.

Architecture

As you review your options, after the brainstorming, you conclude that you need to investigate three possible ways to provide up-to-the minute inventory information to retailers: a Web site, distributed objects, or a Web service.

A Web Site

The first option is to build a private Web site for retailers. After logging in to the site, retailers could check the availability of products.

The main argument in favor of this approach is that it is likely to be familiar to your developers. It would require connecting your Web server to the warehouse management application. You can find tools on the market (known as *application servers*) to help you build this solution. In many cases, a simple JSP application will do.

The main issue with this solution is that it involves yet another Web site: To access stock data, retailers must start their browsers, log in to your site, and look up the data. Your Web site is completely independent from the retailer's own inventory management.

However, chances are that the retailer employees need to first search for the product in the local warehouses. It's only when the product is not available locally that they will order from you.

Figure 20.1 illustrates this. Notice the two applications: the retailer's own stock manager and yours, which is Web-accessible.

In practice, companies are increasingly reluctant to train their clerical staff to access third-party Web sites. For the retailer's IT people, it's yet another application to learn and support. For the clerk, it's an annoyance to have to enter a search twice: once in the retailer stock manager and, if the first search fails, a second time on your Web site.

Finally, you should consider online retailers. An online retailer wants to publish as much information as possible on its own Web site. This setup forces them to redirect their customers to the wholesaler's Web site, which is seldom a good idea.

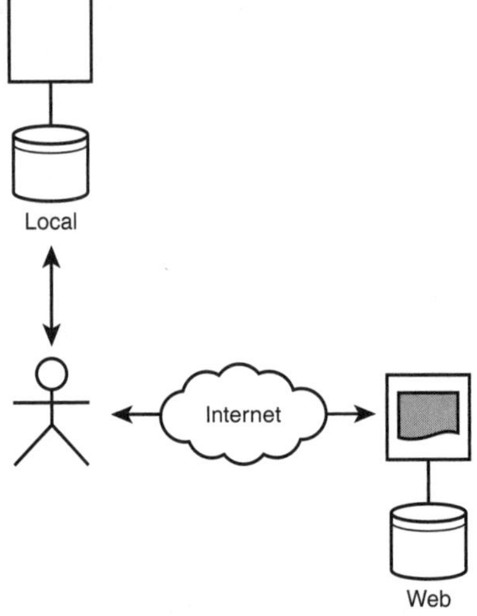

FIGURE 20.1
The wholesaler Web site is independent from the retailer's stock manager.

Distributed Objects

Having established that a Web site does not properly serve your customers' needs, you'll strive to offer a more integrated solution. Traditionally, to integrate applications running on different computers, you would use a distributed object architecture (middleware), such as OMG's CORBA, Microsoft's DCOM, or Java's RMI.

Essentially, the middleware wraps objects, such as Java or C++ objects, with a network layer. In this case, it would wrap the objects in your warehouse management application on a server.

This setup is illustrated in Figure 20.2. For retailers, this is more attractive because they can integrate your data into their application. They have only one application to support.

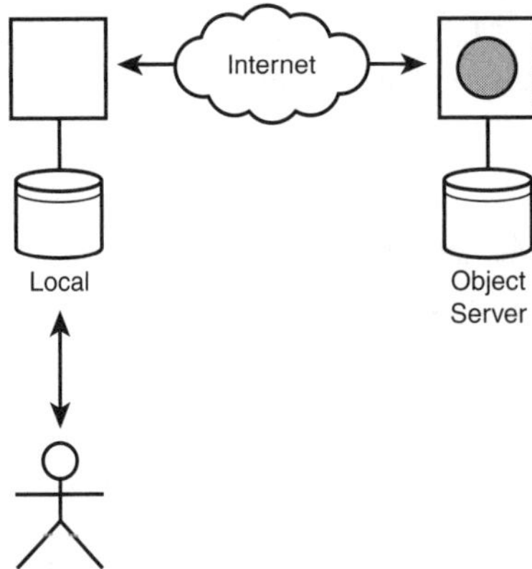

FIGURE 20.2
Because objects are available on a server, the retailer can integrate them in his application.

However, this solution suffers from the following problems:

- CORBA, DCOM, and RMI have a reputation of being complex. I believe that if you give them the benefit of doubt, you'll find that most horror stories are unjustified but, still, it may be a tough sell.
- Distributed object architectures were designed primarily to work over local networks and are not optimized for the wider Internet.

One of the first practical problems is the use of firewalls. Most corporate firewalls accept only HTTP and SMTP traffic and will block CORBA and DCOM.

Furthermore, because it's an object server, you literally expose the guts of your application. The retailer can grab one of your application's objects and call its methods. This creates a very tight coupling between the two applications.

Who really wants to share live application objects with outsiders? What happens if they inadvertently issue the wrong calls and crash your server? The security risk, as well, is enormous.

Likewise, who wants to be responsible if problems occur with the retailer's application? Whoever publishes an object is responsible for its support. Do you really want to take over such a burden?

Warning

To be fair to CORBA, DCOM, and RMI, I must mention that they provide mechanisms to alleviate these problems. For example, HTTP gateways are available to work around firewalls. Also, completely isolating your application from the objects on the server is possible.

Yet, it is when you have to deploy these advanced features that you find distributed object architectures can deserve their reputation for complexity!

Web Service

Back to square one. At this point, you re-examine the Web site idea. Its main advantages are as follows:

- It is easy to set up because it uses technology with which you are already familiar.
- It is cheap to operate for the same reason.
- It has a proven track record for being deployed over the Internet.

The only problem is the integration issue. The reseller clerks have to work with two different applications: their inventory management and your Web site.

However, you recall reading an excellent book on Web services from Sams. A Web service proposes to replace HTML with XML, a format that can efficiently transport structured information and that enables integration.

As you saw in Chapter 7 "Understanding SOAP", SOAP is a protocol that formalizes how a Web client and Web server can integrate using HTTP and XML. The most popular application of SOAP is XML-based remote procedure calls.

The Web service approach is illustrated in Figure 20.3. As you can see, it combines the best of Figure 20.1 (reliance on Web protocols) with the best of Figure 20.2 (enabling integration). In particular, note that the clerks see the reseller inventory management only. However, the reseller application may issue remote requests to your inventory management when it needs your data.

You will notice that Figure 20.3 is very close to Figure 20.2. The most visible difference is that a Web server replaces the object server. This illustrates again that Web services draw from both object middleware (the high-level architecture is very similar) and Web sites (the technical standards are the same).

Specifically, Web services:

- Work across firewalls because they run over HTTP and other Web protocols
- Are as easy to set up and manage as Web sites
- Are based on well-known technologies
- Are not limited to a local network but are designed for the Internet

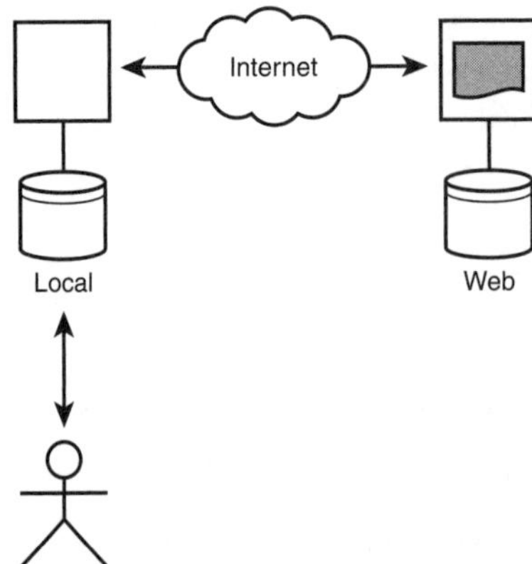

FIGURE 20.3
A Web service offers the same use of benefits as an object server but over the Web.

However, there is no such thing as a free lunch. The price you pay for the flexibility is efficiency. Web services may be slightly slower than distributed object architectures for the following reasons:

- SOAP is a text-based protocol that must be parsed on the receiving end and tends to create larger requests than binary protocols.
- SOAP relies on HTTP for communication, and HTTP is not the fastest protocol around.

A Web Inventory

For the sake of comparison, I'll start by writing a Web version of the inventory application. (I almost wrote "classic Web version.") I'll use JSP for this version.

Database

Because the focus is on Web services, not stock management, I've kept the database simple. It contains a single table, `product`, which lists products and their availability. (Negative numbers indicate back orders.) Products are identified by their manufacturer name and a product number (SKU).

Listing 20.1 is a SQL script that creates the database table and fills it with a few products.

LISTING 20.1 `wholesaler.sql`

```
CREATE TABLE inventory (manufacturer VARCHAR,sku VARCHAR,
➥    level INTEGER);
INSERT INTO inventory (manufacturer,sku,level) VALUES
➥    ('XMLi','100',1000);
INSERT INTO inventory (manufacturer,sku,level) VALUES
➥    ('XMLi','200',-500);
INSERT INTO inventory (manufacturer,sku,level) VALUES
➥    ('Playfield','101',30);
INSERT INTO inventory (manufacturer,sku,level) VALUES
➥    ('Playfield','202',100);
```

Caution

This chapter does not include a tool to update inventory levels. In practice they would be updated by the inventory management, probably with order and warehouse information. If you want to test with different inventory levels, you will need to edit them through the database user interface.

Note that it is probably not a good idea to let retailers remotely manipulate product availability! You want the database to reflect actual levels in the warehouse.

Web Access to the Inventory

Listing 20.2 is a JSP page providing online access to inventory data. The page opens a connection to the database (for increased efficiency, you would want to share the database connection between requests), selects the list of products, and displays them in a table.

If you are familiar with JSP, the code is pretty straightforward. The bulk of the page loops over a JDBC result set and prints the data in an HMTL table. Figure 20.4 shows the page in a browser.

LISTING 20.2 warehouse/index.jsp

```
<%@page import="java.sql.*"%>
<html>
<head><title>Warehouse Extranet</title></head>
<body>
<h1>Warehouse Extranet</h1>
<p>Welcome to our Web site. Here you can obtain product
availability information in real time.<br>
Note that some products are selling fast, so you might want to
order right now if your product of choice is available.</p>
<table>
<tr><td bgcolor="#000000"><b><font
    color="#ffffff">Manufacturer</font></b></td>
    <td bgcolor="#000000"><b><font
    color="#ffffff">SKU</font></b></td>
    <td bgcolor="#000000"><b><font
    color="#ffffff">In stock</font></b></td></tr>
<%
// registers the JDBC driver
new org.hsqldb.jdbcDriver();
Connection connection =
    DriverManager.getConnection("jdbc:hsqldb:db/wholesaler",
                                "sa",
                                null);
try {
    Statement stmt = connection.createStatement();
    try {
        ResultSet rs = stmt.executeQuery("select manufacturer, " +
                                         "sku, level from " +
                                         "inventory");
```

LISTING 20.1 continued

```
        int line = 1;
        try {
            while(rs.next()) {
               String bgcolor = line++ % 2 == 0 ? "#dddddd" :
                                                   "#ffffff";
%>
<tr><td valign="top"
     bgcolor="<%= bgcolor %>"><%= rs.getString(1) %></td>
    <td valign="top"
    bgcolor="<%= bgcolor %>"><%= rs.getString(2) %></td>
    <td valign="top"
    bgcolor="<%= bgcolor %>"><%= rs.getInt(3) > 0 ? "true" :
                                             "false" %></td></tr>
<%
            }
        }
        finally {
            rs.close();
        }
    }
    finally {
        stmt.close();
    }
}
finally {
    connection.close();
}
%>
</table>
</body>
</html>
```

Listing 20.2 illustrates how easily you can publish information on the Web if the information is in a database (or another data store that makes it available to a JSP page). As you will see in a moment, although it uses different tools, writing the Web service is not much more work.

Caution

Admittedly, the above example is too simple. In a real system, you would probably use JavaBeans or custom actions to make the application more maintainable.

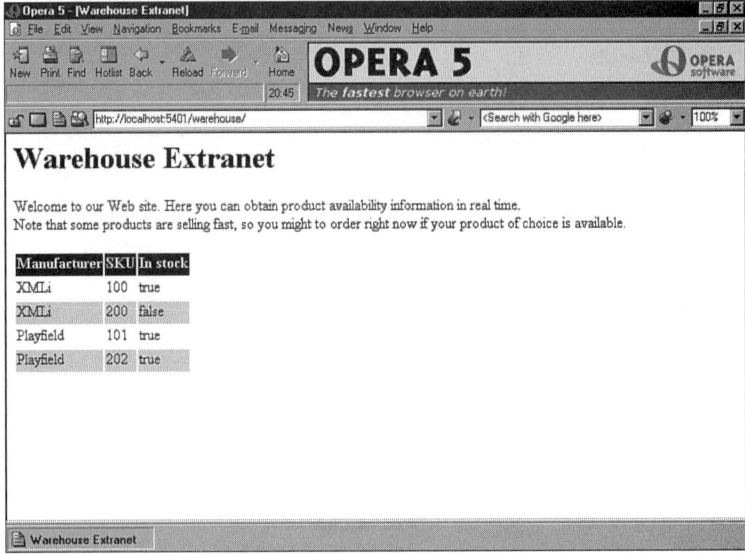

FIGURE 20.4
A simple Web page gives instant access to the inventory.

At the Wholesaler Site

Given that this is a Web service, many parties collaborate in this development:

- The wholesaler builds the service. It connects the service to its inventory management and exposes some or all of it as a Web service.
- The resellers build the clients. They add remote request capabilities to their existing inventory management system.

Obviously, in this chapter, you'll play both roles, but it is important to keep in mind that there are at least two parties involved in this development. This impacts several aspects of the project, including—perhaps most importantly—debugging.

Also note that there is no universal client. Most likely each reseller will implement his or her version of the client. Individual implementations may differ significantly depending on the specifics of each reseller's in-house inventory solution.

This multiplicity of clients has a profound impact on the Web service programmer. Ideally, the Web service should be as open as possible so as not to preclude some clients from accessing the service. I liken this to the support of Web browsers: The most successful sites are compatible with the largest variety of browsers. Likewise, the most successful Web services are compatible with many clients.

Tip

Fortunately, it is not difficult to ensure compatibility with as many clients as possible. The easiest strategy is to stick to open standards. Refrain from using vendor-specific features and you will do fine.

Again, as a simplification, in this chapter you'll write one client only.

A Few Design Considerations

From a technical standpoint, building a Web service is not difficult, but it's not something that you should do lightly. You should carefully design the system to balance your own needs (the wholesaler) and the needs of your partners (the resellers).

Consider a few issues:

- The wholesaler interest is to strengthen its relationship with resellers. Therefore, the wholesaler might be tempted to build an arcane system that forces resellers to invest heavily in integrating with the wholesaler service. It would do so in the hope that the resellers would want to stay loyal to a company with whom they have invested so much.

  This is a business decision, not a technical one, but experience shows that this strategy always backfires. Resellers choose the wholesaler that improves the profitability, not the one that locks them by technical means.
- Likewise, the wholesaler might be tempted to build locks into the system that makes it tougher for resellers to do comparison shopping. For example, by using proprietary product identification, the wholesaler may make it tougher for resellers to send the same request to several wholesalers until it finds the best one.

  Again this is a business decision. Note, however, that Web services are designed for automation, so they are doomed to enable comparison shopping.
- Optimizing access to information by providing the information that is needed in the most effective course to follow.

  When designing the service, it is important to take into account network latency (in practice, minimize the number of requests required to perform the task) and responsiveness (make sure that the whole system, as perceived by the end user, is responsive).
- It is essential that you provide a secure service. What level of security do you need? There are several aspects to consider, such as controlling access to information and making sure the new system does not weaken the security of the existing system.

Unfortunately, the need for security may contradict efforts to optimize access. For example, it might be desirable to share extremely detailed stock information and even let the resellers manipulate the information (to tentatively order products). From a security standpoint, however, this is a nightmare.

- It is important to maintain the independence of the wholesaler and reseller's systems. The Web service is an interface between two disparate systems. To allow them to evolve independently and to minimize the connection difficulties, the Web service should stick to concepts and information that are universally understood.

  For example, it is best to use a product identification scheme that is common to the wholesaler and the reseller. Contrast this with the discussion on using arcane systems.

Balancing these constraints results in the following design. The inventory Web service will offer only one operation:

```
boolean canShipToday(String manufacturer,
                     String sku,
                     int quantity)
```

This operation will return `true` if the wholesaler can ship immediately a given quantity of a product identified by the combination of its SKU and manufacturer name.

Why limit to one function? Mostly for security reasons. Recall that security is not only cryptography. The level of security needed depends on the sensitivity of the data.

This operation returns enough data to the reseller. It answers its most common question—that is, "Can you ship this product, in this quantity, right now?"—but it does not provide critical information (such as stock level or prices). Because no critical information is provided, it is easier to control access to the service.

In fact, the warehouse may very well decide not to secure access at all: Even if a non-reseller accesses the Web service, he or she cannot access privileged information. Also, the method is read-only and, because the reseller does not modify the inventory database, there is no need to control access, either.

Caution

This application makes some decisions based on a hypothetical situation. Your mileage may vary depending on the specifics of your circumstances. Use this material as guidance for the questions you should ask and the reasoning you should follow, not necessarily for the answers.

The downside to offering only one function is that less information and less service is being made available to resellers. You could imagine offering additional services, such as providing more detailed information on stock levels.

The upside is that connecting clients is dramatically easier. The resellers are more likely to successfully connect to the Web service than they would if they had to install cryptography. Note again that there is no loss in security: adding sophisticated cryptography would not increase security dramatically.

Tip

Do not underestimate the benefits of making life easy for client developers. Unlike a traditional client/server application, which typically has one server and one client built by the same team, Web services involve one server and, often, several clients built by different teams.

The logistical challenge to coordinate the development efforts is huge. Anything that reduces this work will pay off tremendously.

Note that the operation is also designed to maximize independence between the parties. For example, it identifies a product through its manufacturer's reference, which is common to both the reseller and wholesaler, rather than a wholesaler-specific identifier. The latter would have increased the workload on resellers.

The Inventory Service

Now it's time to look at the server. The server is connected to the warehouse database. This is not unlike the JSP page in Listing 20.2. The server accepts a `canShipToday` RPC, and returns the latest status on product availability.

Listing 20.3 is the inventory service. As is typical with Apache SOAP, this is a regular Java class. In addition to the constructor that registers the JDBC driver, it offers one method—`canShipToday()`—for the RPC.

LISTING 20.3 `InventoryService.java`

```
package com.psol.inventory;

import java.sql.*;

public class InventoryService
{
```

LISTING 20.3 continued

```
    public InventoryService()
    {
        try {
            Class.forName("org.hsqldb.jdbcDriver");
        }
        catch(ClassNotFoundException e) {
            e.printStackTrace();
        }
    }

    public boolean canShipToday(String manufacturer,
                                String sku,
                                int quantity)
        throws SQLException
    {
        boolean result = false;
        Connection connection =
            DriverManager.getConnection("jdbc:hsqldb:db/wholesaler",
                                        "sa",
                                        null);
        try {
            PreparedStatement stmt =
                connection.prepareStatement("select level from" +
                    " inventory where manufacturer=? and sku=?");
            try {
                stmt.setString(1,manufacturer);
                stmt.setString(2,sku);
                ResultSet rs = stmt.executeQuery();
                try {
                    if(rs.next())
                        result = rs.getInt(1) > quantity;
                }
                finally {
                    rs.close();
                }
            }
            finally {
                stmt.close();
            }
        }
        finally {
            connection.close();
        }
        return result;
    }
}
```

The method connects to the database (again for increased efficiency you might want to share connection between requests), and queries the database for a given product's inventory level. If enough products are in stock, it returns a positive (`true`) reply. Otherwise, it returns `false`.

Deployment Descriptor

Apache SOAP requires you attach an XML deployment descriptor to the Java implementation (see Listing 20.4).

LISTING 20.4 DeploymentDescriptor.xml

```
<isd:service
    xmlns:isd="http://xml.apache.org/xml-soap/deployment"
    id="http://www.psol.com/2001/inventory"
    checkMustUnderstands="true">
    <isd:provider scope="Application"
                  type="java"
                  methods="canShipToday">
        <isd:java class="com.psol.inventory.InventoryService"
                  static="false"/>
    </isd:provider>
    <isd:faultListener>org.apache.soap.server.DOMFaultListener
➥        </isd:faultListener>
</isd:service>
```

For details on the deployment descriptor, turn to Chapter 8 "SOAP Basics". Essentially it declares one service with one method (`canShipToday`). Incidentally remember that the URIs are identifiers only (much like XML namespaces). Specifically they do not point to Web sites.

There is no SOAP mapping in this deployment descriptor because the RPC uses only simple types. Incidentally, reliance on simple types further simplifies the work of client developers.

At the Reseller Site

Let's now turn to the reseller. Remember that the reseller also has an inventory management system to manage its own stock. By default, the reseller looks into its warehouse and consults with the wholesaler only if items are missing.

It is essential to understand that Web services have less value if they are not integrated in local applications. Although initially it might be appropriate to provide a simple client that enables quick access to a Web service, in the middle to long term, Web services are attractive only when they are integrated.

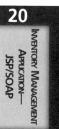

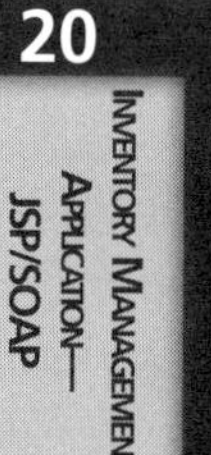

Tip

We choose to build a Web service specifically to offer integration with local applications. Indeed, if it was not for the integration with local applications, a regular Web site would have been appropriate.

Introducing the Store Inventory

Figure 20.5 illustrates the inventory client running on the store intranet. As always, to make the Web service more visible, little effort has gone into the user interface. The beauty of this client, however, is that it integrates the local (reseller) and remote (wholesaler) databases. Why don't you see two databases when looking at Figure 20.5? That's the sign of a successful integration: Although many things happen under the hood, to the end user it looks like a regular order form.

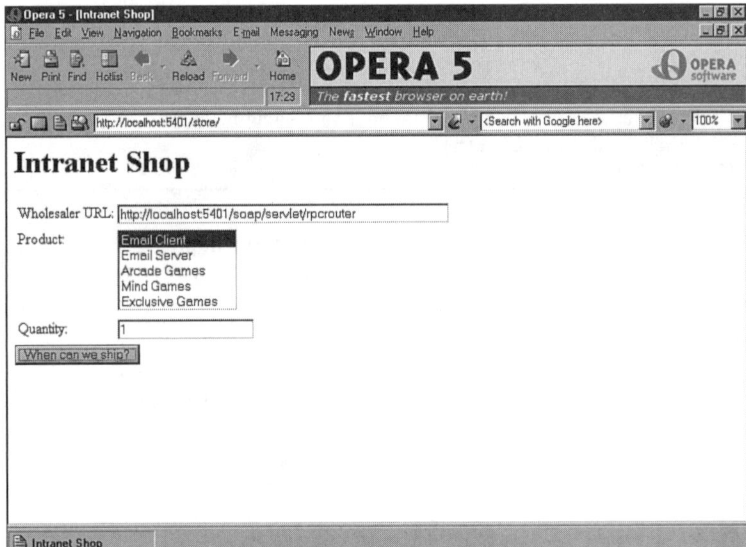

FIGURE 20.5
The client provides an integrated view of the retailer and wholesaler databases.

Indeed the client application starts by looking for the product in the local database. It is only if the product is not available locally that it connects to the wholesaler site and inquires about remote availability. The client interprets the results as follows:

- If the product is in stock locally, the client announces shipment within 24 hours.
- If the product is not available locally but is available from the wholesaler, the client reports shipment within 2–4 days.

- Finally, if the product is back-ordered both locally and at the wholesaler, the client announces a special order.

Figure 20.6 shows what happen when checking on a product that is not available locally but that can ordered through the wholesaler.

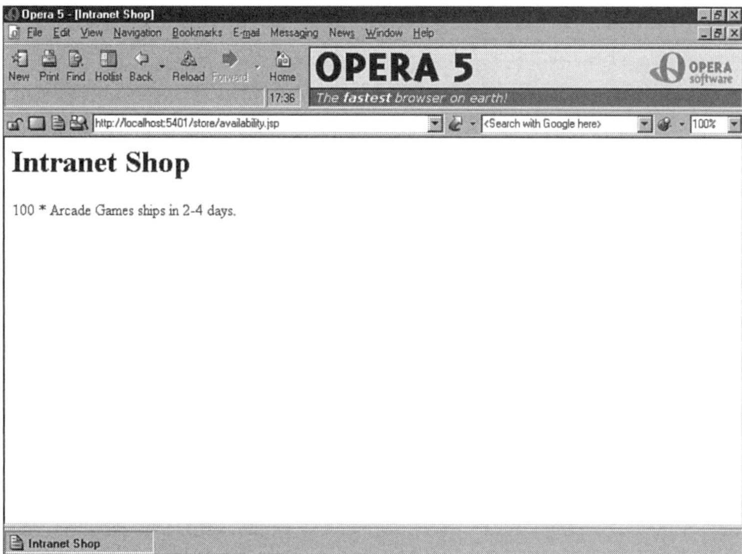

FIGURE 20.6
The store application integrates both databases.

I want to stress that Figure 20.6 integrates data from two applications. The Wholesaler URL is used to query the remote database whenever the product is not available locally.

From the user standpoint, it appears as though he is interacting with one application and one database. You know better, of course: the user is really interacting with two applications (one locally, one in the background) and as many databases.

The beauty of the Web service is that it enables the store to integrate everything under its familiar inventory application.

Local Database

The local (meaning reseller's) inventory management has a database. It is likely that the reseller and wholesaler databases will differ greatly. Again, the goal in this chapter is not to develop a full-blown inventory application but, for the sake of discussion, I made sure the databases would be somewhat different.

Listing 20.5 is a SQL script to construct the reseller's database. It has one table, `product`, with a product identifier, manufacturer name, product number (equivalent to SKU in the wholesaler database), and the inventory level in the reseller's warehouse, of course.

The script also pre-populates the database with a few records for testing.

LISTING 20.5 `reseller.sql`

```
CREATE TABLE product (id INTEGER,description VARCHAR,
➥    manufacturer VARCHAR,product_number VARCHAR,
➥    stock_level INTEGER);
INSERT INTO product (id,description,manufacturer,
➥    product_number,stock_level) VALUES
➥    (1,'Email Client','XMLi','100',10);
INSERT INTO product (id,description,manufacturer,
➥    product_number,stock_level) VALUES
➥    (2,'Email Server','XMLi','200',-1);
INSERT INTO product (id,description,manufacturer,
➥    product_number,stock_level) VALUES
➥    (3,'Arcade Games','Playfield','101',1);
INSERT INTO product (id,description,manufacturer,
➥    product_number,stock_level) VALUES
➥    (4,'Mind Games','Playfield','202',0);
INSERT INTO product (id,description,manufacturer,
➥    product_number,stock_level) VALUES
➥    (5,'Exclusive Games','Playfield','303',-1);
```

Store Application

Listing 20.6 is the first JSP page in the reseller application. Essentially it's an HTML form that lists the products from the local database. The user can enter the URL to the warehouse inventory Web service, select a product from the list, and enter the quantity he needs delivered.

Keep in mind that you would not normally write such an application: that's the reseller's job. View these JSP pages as a prototype, not a real application. Indeed, as has already been noted, you would normally move most of this code from the JSP page to a set of beans.

LISTING 20.6 `store/index.jsp`

```
<%@page import="java.sql.*"%>
<html>
<head><title>Intranet Shop</title></head>
<body>
<h1>Intranet Shop</h1>
<form action="availability.jsp" method="post">
```

LISTING 20.6 continued

```
<table>
<%
String rpcRouter = request.getParameter("rpcrouter");
if(rpcRouter == null)
    rpcRouter = "http://localhost:5401/soap/servlet/rpcrouter";
%>
<tr><td valign="top">Wholesaler URL:</td>
    <td valign="top"><input type="text" name="rpcrouter"
        size="50" value="<%= rpcRouter %>"></td></tr>
<tr><td valign="top">Product:</td>
    <td valign="top"><select name="productid" size="5">
<%
new org.hsqldb.jdbcDriver();
Connection connection =
    DriverManager.getConnection("jdbc:hsqldb:db/reseller",
                                "sa",
                                null);
try {
    Statement stmt = connection.createStatement();
    try {
        ResultSet rs = stmt.executeQuery("select id," +
                                     "description from product");
        while(rs.next()) {
%>
    <option
      value="<%= rs.getInt(1) %>"><%= rs.getString(2) %></option>
<%
        }
    }
    finally {
        stmt.close();
    }
}
finally {
    connection.close();
}
%>
</select></td></tr>
<tr><td valign="top">Quantity:</b></td>
    <td valign="top"><input type="text" name="qty"
     value="1"></td></tr>
</table>
<input type="submit" value="When can we ship?">
</form>
</body>
</html>
```

In reality, the reseller and wholesaler applications would run on different computers. For simplicity, you'll run everything through the same Web server. Note, however, that they each have their databases.

Listing 20.7 packs all the fun. When the user hits the button on `store/index.jsp`, it queries the local database for the local stock level. If it finds that the product is in back order locally, it sends a SOAP request to the wholesaler.

LISTING 20.7 `store/availability.jsp`

```
<%@page import="java.sql.*,java.net.*"%>
<%@page import="org.apache.soap.transport.*"%>
<%@page import="org.apache.soap.messaging.*"%>
<%@page import="org.apache.soap.*,org.apache.soap.encoding.*"%>
<%@page import="org.apache.soap.rpc.*,org.apache.soap.util.xml.*"%>
<%@page import="org.apache.soap.encoding.soapenc.*"%>
<%!
private String manufacturer = null,
               productNumber = null,
               description = null;
private int stockLevel = 0;
private boolean getLocalStockLevel(String productid)
   throws SQLException
{
    boolean result = false;
    new org.hsqldb.jdbcDriver();
    Connection connection =
        DriverManager.getConnection("jdbc:hsqldb:db/reseller",
                                    "sa",
                                    null);
    try {
        PreparedStatement stmt = connection.prepareStatement(
            "select description, manufacturer, product_number, " +
            "stock_level from product where id = ?");
        try {
            stmt.setString(1,productid);
            ResultSet rs = stmt.executeQuery();
            try {
                if(rs.next()) {
                    description = rs.getString(1);
                    manufacturer = rs.getString(2);
                    productNumber = rs.getString(3);
                    stockLevel = rs.getInt(4);
                    result = true;
                }
            }
            finally {
                rs.close();
            }
        }
```

LISTING 20.7 continued

```
        finally {
            stmt.close();
        }
    }
    finally {
        connection.close();
    }
    return result;
}
%>
<%
String productId = request.getParameter("productid"),
       availability = "on special order",
       stRpcRouter = request.getParameter("rpcrouter"),
       stQty = request.getParameter("qty");
URL rpcRouter = new URL(stRpcRouter);
int qty = Integer.parseInt(stQty);
if(getLocalStockLevel(productId)) {
    int missing = qty - stockLevel;
    if(missing > 0) {
        Vector params = new Vector();
        Parameter p = new Parameter("manufacturer",
                                    String.class,
                                    manufacturer,
                                    null);
        params.addElement(p);
        p = new Parameter("sku",
                          String.class,
                          productNumber,
                          null);
        params.addElement(p);
        p = new Parameter("quantity",
                          Integer.class,
                          new Integer(missing),
                          null);
        params.addElement(p);
        Call call = new Call();
        call.setTargetObjectURI("http://www.psol.com/2001/inventory");
        call.setEncodingStyleURI(Constants.NS_URI_SOAP_ENC);
        call.setMethodName("canShipToday");
        call.setParams(params);
        Response rsp = call.invoke(rpcRouter,
                                   "http://www.psol.com/2001/soapaction");
        if(!rsp.generatedFault()) {
            Boolean b =
                (Boolean)rsp.getReturnValue().getValue();
            if(b.booleanValue())
                availability = "within 2-4 days";
        }
    }
```

LISTING 20.7 continued

```
    else
       availability = "immediately";
}
%>
<html>
<head><title>Intranet Shop</title></head>
<body>
<h1>Intranet Shop</h1>
<%
if(availability != null) {
%>
<p><%= qty %> * <%= description %> ships <%= availability %>.</p>
<%
}
else {
%>
<p>Error: cannot determine the availability.</p>
<%
}
%>
<form action="index.jsp" method="post">
<input type="hidden" name="rpcrouter"
   value="<%= rpcRouter.toExternalForm() %>">
<input type="submit" value="Return to main page">
</form>
</body>
</html>
```

Listing 20.7 is more complex, so take the time to review it. First, the `getLocalStockLevel()` function runs a query on the reseller's database for the product the user chose:

```
private boolean getLocalStockLevel(String productid)
   throws SQLException
{
    boolean result = false;
    new org.hsqldb.jdbcDriver();
    Connection connection =
        DriverManager.getConnection("jdbc:hsqldb:db/reseller",
                                    "sa",
                                    null);
    try {
        PreparedStatement stmt = connection.prepareStatement(
            "select description, manufacturer, product_number, " +
            "stock_level from product where id = ?");
        try {
            stmt.setString(1,productid);
            ResultSet rs = stmt.executeQuery();
```

```
            try {
                if(rs.next()) {
                    description = rs.getString(1);
                    manufacturer = rs.getString(2);
                    productNumber = rs.getString(3);
                    stockLevel = rs.getInt(4);
                    result = true;
                }
            }
            finally {
                rs.close();
            }
        }
        finally {
            stmt.close();
        }
    }
    finally {
        connection.close();
    }
    return result;
}
```

Next, it tests to see whether the local stock level is sufficient to satisfy the request. If so, it marks it for immediate availability.

```
int missing = qty - stockLevel;
if(missing > 0) {
    // ...
}
else
    availability = "immediately";
```

Otherwise it issues a SOAP request to the Web service and marks the availability according to the response:

```
Vector params = new Vector();
Parameter p = new Parameter("manufacturer",
                            String.class,
                            manufacturer,
                            null);
params.addElement(p);
p = new Parameter("sku",
                  String.class,
                  productNumber,
                  null);
params.addElement(p);
p = new Parameter("quantity",
                  Integer.class,
                  new Integer(missing),
                  null);
```

```
params.addElement(p);
Call call = new Call();
call.setTargetObjectURI("http://www.psol.com/2001/inventory");
call.setEncodingStyleURI(Constants.NS_URI_SOAP_ENC);
call.setMethodName("canShipToday");
call.setParams(params);
Response rsp = call.invoke(rpcRouter,
                       "http://www.psol.com/2001/soapaction");
if(!rsp.generatedFault()) {
    Boolean b =
        (Boolean)rsp.getReturnValue().getValue();
    if(b.booleanValue())
        availability = "within 2-4 days";
}
```

The remainder of the page just displays the result in HTML:

```
<h1>Intranet Shop</h1>
<%
if(availability != null) {
%>
<p><%= qty %> * <%= description %> ships <%= availability %>.</p>
<%
}
else {
%>
<p>Error: cannot determine the availability.</p>
<%
}
%>
```

Building and Running the Project

You essentially have two options: the easiest (and recommended) option is to download a ready-to-run package with the inventory project. If you modify the project, however, you have to recompile it.

Ready-to-Run Package

The easiest option is to download a ready-to-run package from either `www.samspublishing.com` or `www.marchal.com`. Follow the links to this book's page and download the listings from there.

The ready-to-run package comes in a Zip file or self-installing archive. Uncompress it and install it in the directory of your choice. This package is complete with a Web server and a database so you have nothing else to install.

Under Windows, go to the directory where you uncompressed the archive and first edit the launch.bat file:

```
@echo off
set JAVA_HOME=c:\jdk1.3
call jetty
```

Change the JAVA_HOME variable to point to the JDK on your system. Save your changes and double-click launch.bat. The Web server starts.

With other operating systems, you start the Web server by changing to the directory where you uncompressed the archive and issuing the following command:

```
java -classpath lib/inventory.jar;lib/hsqldb.jar;lib/xalan.jar;
➥%JAVA_HOME%/lib/tools.jar;lib/javax.servlet.jar;
➥lib/org.mortbay.jetty.jar;lib/activation.jar;lib/mail.jar;
➥lib/org.apache.jasper.jar;lib/xerces.jar;lib/soap.jar
➥-Dorg.xml.sax.parser=org.apache.xerces.parsers.SAXParser
➥org.mortbay.jetty.Server etc/jetty.xml
```

where %JAVA_HOME% is bound to the directory where the JDK is installed on your system.

Caution

To run this application, you need to install a JDK 1.3 or above. Specifically, a JRE will not suffice because JSP needs a compiler.

Next point your Web browser to:

```
http://localhost:5401/store/
```

to get started. You should see a screen similar to Figure 20.4.

If you see an error message, the following are a few things to check:

- Check the readme file included in the Zip file. It contains last-minute updates and might point to a solution.
- Under Windows, make sure you edited the launch.bat file as explained previously.
- By default, the Web server runs on port 5401. Make sure you do not have another service running on port 5401.

Recompiling the Project

This section contains useful information if you would like to recompile the project. If you use the ready-to-run package, you do not have to recompile the project, so you may skip this section. If you would like to modify the project, you need the following information.

> **Caution**
>
> The project has been tested with the version of the libraries listed below. A more recent version should work fine, but ensuring backward compatibility is not always a priority for developers.

This Web service uses the following libraries:

- Jetty 3.1.4. Jetty is an efficient open-source Web server that supports JSP and servlets. Porting the project to another JSP-compliant Web server should not be too much work. Jetty is available from `jetty.mortbay.com`.
- hsql Database Engine 1.6.1 RC1, a lightweight open-source database that implements JDBC. I tried to stick to standard SQL as much as possible, so porting to another database should not be too much work. The hsql Database Engine is available from `www.hsqldb.org`.
- Apache SOAP 2.2, an open-source SOAP toolkit. At the time of writing, this is the closest thing to a reference implementation of SOAP for Java. Apache SOAP is available from `xml.apache.org`.

Be warned that Jetty and SOAP have dependencies on other libraries. If you update one of the libraries, make sure you read the documentation and download all the JARs.

Listing 20.8 is the configuration file for Jetty. It creates a minimal Web server with just enough options to run this application.

The line you are most likely to edit in Listing 20.8 is:

```
<Set name="Port">5401</Set>
```

This line sets the Web server port. If port 5401 is already in use on your computer (or if you'd rather use another port), change this line and restart the server.

LISTING 20.8 jetty.xml

```
<?xml version="1.0" encoding="ISO-8859-1"?>

<!DOCTYPE Configure PUBLIC
   "-//Mort Bay Consulting//DTD Configure 1.0//EN"
   "http://jetty.mortbay.com/configure_1_0.dtd">

<Configure class="org.mortbay.jetty.Server">

<!-- starts the Web server -->
<Call name="addListener">
    <Arg>
        <New class="org.mortbay.http.SocketListener">
            <!-- change port here -->
            <Set name="Port">5401</Set>
            <Set name="MinThreads">5</Set>
            <Set name="MaxThreads">255</Set>
            <Set name="MaxIdleTimeMs">60000</Set>
            <Set name="MaxReadTimeMs">60000</Set>
        </New>
    </Arg>
</Call>

<Set name="RequestLogSink">
    <New class="org.mortbay.util.OutputStreamLogSink">
        <Arg>etc/logs/yyyy_mm_dd.request.log</Arg>
        <Set name="RetainDays">90</Set>
        <Set name="Append">true</Set>
    </New>
</Set>

<Call name="addContext">
    <Arg>/jetty/*</Arg>
    <Call name="addServlet">
        <Arg>admin</Arg>
        <Arg>/</Arg>
        <Arg>org.mortbay.servlet.AdminServlet</Arg>
    </Call>
</Call>

<!-- enables SOAP -->
<Call name="addWebApplication">
    <Arg>/soap/*</Arg>
    <Arg>./webapps/soap</Arg>
    <Arg>./webapps/soap/WEB-INF/web.xml</Arg>
    <Arg type="boolean">false</Arg>
    <Call name="addServlet">
        <Arg>JSP</Arg>
        <Arg>*.jsp</Arg>
        <Arg>org.apache.jasper.servlet.JspServlet</Arg>
```

Listing 20.8 continued

```
    </Call>
</Call>

<Call name="addContext">
    <Arg>/soap/*</Arg>
    <Set name="ResourceBase">./soap/</Set>
    <Set name="ServingResources">true</Set>
    <Set name="HttpServerAccess">true</Set>
</Call>

<Call name="addContext">
    <Arg>/soap/admin/*</Arg>
    <Set name="ResourceBase">./soap/admin/</Set>
    <Set name="ClassPath">./soap/admin/</Set>
    <Set name="ServingResources">true</Set>
    <Call name="addServlet">
        <Arg>JSP</Arg>
        <Arg>/soap/admin/*.jsp</Arg>
        <Arg>org.apache.jasper.servlet.JspServlet</Arg>
    </Call>
    <Set name="HttpServerAccess">true</Set>
</Call>

<!-- enable JSP -->
<Call name="addContext">
    <Arg>/store/*</Arg>
    <Call name="addHandler">
      <Arg type="int">0</Arg>
      <Arg>
        <New class="org.mortbay.http.handler.ForwardHandler">
          <Arg>index.jsp</Arg>
        </New>
      </Arg>
    </Call>
    <Call name="addServlet">
        <Arg>JSP</Arg>
        <Arg>*.jsp</Arg>
        <Arg>org.apache.jasper.servlet.JspServlet</Arg>
    </Call>
    <Set name="ResourceBase">./store/</Set>
    <Set name="ServingResources">true</Set>
</Call>

<Call name="addContext">
    <Arg>/warehouse/*</Arg>
    <Call name="addHandler">
      <Arg type="int">0</Arg>
      <Arg>
        <New class="org.mortbay.http.handler.ForwardHandler">
```

LISTING 20.8 continued

```
            <Arg>index.jsp</Arg>
          </New>
        </Arg>
      </Call>
      <Call name="addServlet">
          <Arg>JSP</Arg>
          <Arg>*.jsp</Arg>
          <Arg>org.apache.jasper.servlet.JspServlet</Arg>
      </Call>
      <Set name="ResourceBase">./warehouse/</Set>
      <Set name="ServingResources">true</Set>
</Call>

</Configure>
```

Listing 20.9 is the Ant 1.2 build file for this project. It recompiles the SOAP node only. Because the client is written in JSP, the server recompiles it when appropriate.

If you are not familiar with Ant, I urge you to visit `http://jakarta.apache.org`. Ant is a handy tool to make Java applications.

LISTING 20.9 build.xml

```
<?xml version="1.0"?>

<!-- Ant 1.2 build file: jakarta.apache.org -->

<project name="inventory" default="jar" basedir=".">
    <property name="classpath"
              value="lib/xerces.jar;lib/soap.jar;lib/mail.jar"/>

    <target name="jar" depends="compile">
        <jar jarfile="lib/inventory.jar"
             basedir="classes"/>
    </target>
    <target name="compile" depends="prepare">
        <javac srcdir="src"
               destdir="classes"
               classpath="${classpath}"/>
    </target>
    <target name="prepare">
        <mkdir dir="classes"/>
        <mkdir dir="lib"/>
    </target>
</project>
```

Caution

Do not forget to re-deploy the service, as discussed in Chapter 8, if you change the interface to the service.

The ready-to-run package you can download includes databases for the client and the server, but if you need to re-create them, you can use Listings 20.1 and 20.5. Use HSQL database manager to execute the script. Under Windows, you launch the database manager by double-clicking the `hsqldb.bat` from the downloadable package.

Under another operating system, use the following command:

```
java -classpath lib\hsqldb.jar org.hsqldb.util.DatabaseManager
```

To connect to the database, do the following:

1. Select HSQL Database Engine Standalone from the pull-down list.
2. Enter the URLs to the database. The URLs are `jdbc:hsqldb:db/reseller` and `jdbc:hsqldb:db/wholesaler`.

Figure 20.7 is the database manager login screen. Use the File|Open Script…command to load the script. Hit Execute to create the tables.

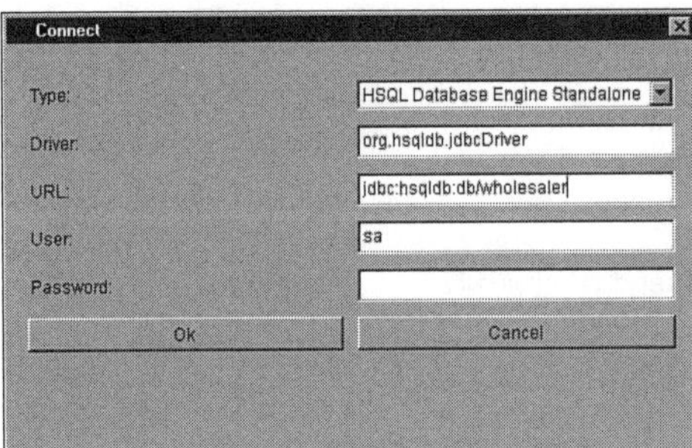

FIGURE 20.7
Log in to the database manager.

Summary

A Web service is an interface between disparate systems. Unlike traditional distributed applications where the client and server are developed in-house, the development of a Web service is a joint effort between several organizations. It will help immensely if you keep these parameters in mind as you write the service.

In the next chapter, you'll study an application for tracking stocks.

CHAPTER 21

Stock Trading Application—EJB

By Mark Wutka

In This Chapter

Although you often see example applications that retrieve stock quotes, you don't often see examples that trade stocks. In a trading application, users may submit "put" orders, which mean that the user wants to sell stock. Users can also submit "buy" orders, which mean they want to buy stock. The trading system matches put and buy requests and registers them as successful trades. This chapter presents an example of such an application.

Like many Web services, the trading application consists mostly of components that have nothing to do with the Web. The framework for receiving Web requests is simple, so you spend most of your time writing the back-end work that completes the requests. You must tackle a few Web-related issues up front, however.

User Authentication

A stock trading application can have a wide variety of schemes for authenticating users. For a sessionless application, you might have users send a username and password along with each request, or you might require users to digitally sign their requests. For a session-oriented application, users can supply a username and password up front, or use a digitally signed login request. After the initial login, the system provides the user with a session token that identifies that user's unique session. You may recall that the UDDI publishing API uses a token scheme for identifying users.

For large-scale applications, you should avoid sessions if possible. If you have the potential of tens of thousands of users, you probably can't afford to keep track of all those sessions because of resource constraints. It isn't always possible to avoid sessions, of course. You can't very well do a shopping cart application without some kind of session, for example.

Sessions are still useful in many instances. If the authentication process is lengthy, as it can be for digital signatures, you may want to use sessions to avoid repeated authentication. Sometimes you must do so much extra work to create a sessionless application that it just makes sense to use sessions, even if it means that the application consumes more system resources.

The stock trading example authenticates a user with a username and password, and then uses a session token to keep track of the user. Although the application could easily do authentication with each request, the use of a token makes the example a little more instructive. Although digital signatures are a reasonable alternative for authenticating users, using SOAP can complicate the signatures. Because SOAP doesn't have built-in support for XML digital signatures (XML-DSIG), you must either process the body of the SOAP request yourself, or use something such as Java's `SignedObject` class, which requires a custom SOAP serializer. In the end, it makes sense to keep the interface as simple as possible.

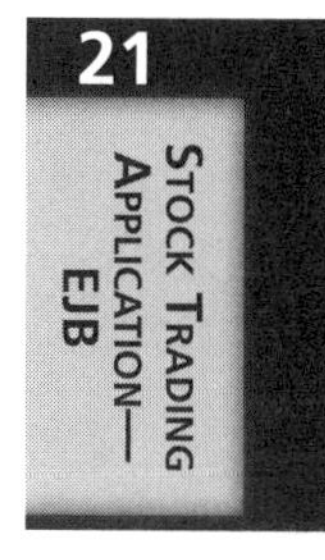

Application Architecture

The stock trading application accepts SOAP requests and then uses Enterprise JavaBeans (EJB) to store the various orders and completed trades. The EJB back-end consists of a stateful session bean and a number of entity beans. The `StockTrading` SOAP object sits between the users and the session bean, providing the transition between SOAP and EJB, as well as keeping track of the session tokens. Figure 21.1 shows the major components of the system.

FIGURE 21.1
The stock trading application uses SOAP and Enterprise JavaBeans.

SOAP and Enterprise Java Beans

The combination of SOAP with Enterprise Java Beans (EJB) is particularly potent. EJBs make it easy to create business objects that perform database operations for you. You no longer spend your time creating SQL requests, but instead focus on implementing your business logic. Although you can use CORBA to access EJBs from languages other than Java, it's pretty cumbersome. Putting a SOAP front-end on your EJB applications enables any program that can create a SOAP request to access your EJBs.

Software Packages

The wide variety of EJB servers and Web servers is both a blessing and a curse. It's wonderful to have so many choices, but each server has its own peculiar behavior that you must learn. This is especially true in the case of EJB servers, where most servers have their own format for configuration files. Although the EJB specification defines an XML structure for configuring EJBs, the specification is intentionally vague on the configuration of certain items, giving vendors freedom in their implementation, but causing headaches for the users.

The example in this chapter uses the J2EE Reference Implementation from Sun. The Reference Implementation is slower than many J2EE servers, but it is free and comes with a nice graphical deployment tool. You can download the Reference Implementation from `http://java.sun.com/ejb`.

You also need a server for handling SOAP requests, which you should already have from Chapter 8, “Soap Basics.” Finally, you need a SQL database. I used Oracle for this example, but you should be able to use other databases such as Informix, PostgreSQL, or DB2. You must configure a data source in the J2EE Reference Implementation named jdbc/webserve. My database, which runs on a machine named flamingo, is configured this way:

```
jdbcDataSource.5.name=jdbc/webserve
jdbcDataSource.5.url=jdbc:oracle:thin:@flamingo:1521:ORA1
```

The `StockTrading` SOAP Object

The `StockTrading` object is a SOAP object that doesn’t really use SOAP at all. It uses a `Hashtable` to associate randomly-generated user session tokens with their corresponding EJB session objects. The Trading EJB does most of the actual work; the `StockTrading` object just passes most of the calls through to the EJB.

The three methods that don’t rely on the `Trading` object are `login`, `logout`, and `getTradingSession`. When a user logs in, the `StockTrading` object creates a new instance of a `Trading` session. If the user supplies an incorrect userid or password, the `create` method in the `TradingHome` interface throws an exception. Otherwise, the `StockTrading` object creates a random 128-bit session key and associates it with the `Trading` session. This is a fairly common technique for creating session keys and is reasonably secure—the odds of a hacker being able to generate a valid session key are fairly low. The `login` method then returns the session key to the user, who uses the key in other method calls.

The `logout` method removes the association between a `Trading` session and a unique session key. You might also consider adding a timestamp to the session so you can automatically remove sessions after some period of time. The `getTradingSession` method returns the `Trading` session associated with a session key, which enables the other methods to quickly locate a user’s session.

Listing 21.1 shows the source for the `StockTrading` class.

LISTING 21.1 Source Code for `StockTrading.java`

```
package jwsunleashed.trading;

import java.util.*;
import javax.naming.*;
import java.rmi.*;
import javax.rmi.*;
import javax.ejb.*;
```

LISTING 21.1 continued

```
import java.security.*;
import java.math.*;
import jwsunleashed.trading.ejb.*;

public class StockTrading
{
// The table of user sessions
    protected static Hashtable users = new Hashtable();
    protected SecureRandom random;

    public StockTrading()
    {
        try
        {
// Create the object for creating random session IDs
            random = SecureRandom.getInstance("SHA1PRNG");
        }
        catch (NoSuchAlgorithmException exc)
        {
            exc.printStackTrace();
        }
    }

    public String login(String userID, String password)
        throws TradingException
    {
        try
        {
            Context context = new InitialContext();

// Locate the Trading session home interface
            TradingHome home = (TradingHome) PortableRemoteObject.narrow(
                context.lookup("ejb/TradingHome"), TradingHome.class);

// Create a new trading session
            Trading trading = home.create(userID, password);

            byte[] uniqueID = new byte[16];

// Generate a random 128-bit (16-byte) session key
            random.nextBytes(uniqueID);

// Use BigInteger to create a string of hex digits
            String uniqueIDKey = (new BigInteger(uniqueID)).toString(16);

// Associate the key with the trading session
            users.put(uniqueIDKey, trading);

// Return the key to the user
```

LISTING 21.1 continued

```
            return uniqueIDKey;
        }
        catch (NamingException exc)
        {
            exc.printStackTrace();
            throw new TradingException(exc.toString());
        }
        catch (CreateException exc)
        {
            exc.printStackTrace();
            throw new TradingException(exc.toString());
        }
        catch (RemoteException exc)
        {
            exc.printStackTrace();
            throw new TradingException(exc.toString());
        }
        catch (Exception exc)
        {
            exc.printStackTrace();
            throw new TradingException(exc.toString());
        }
    }

    public TradeResult put(String uniqueID, String stock, int shares,
        int price)
        throws TradingException
    {
// Locate the user's session
        Trading trading = getTradingSession(uniqueID);

        try
        {
// Let the trading session handle the put request
            return trading.put(stock, shares, price);
        }
        catch (RemoteException exc)
        {
            exc.printStackTrace();
            throw new TradingException(exc.toString());
        }
    }

    public TradeResult buy(String uniqueID, String stock, int shares,
        int price)
        throws TradingException
    {
// Locate the user's session
        Trading trading = getTradingSession(uniqueID);
```

LISTING 21.1 continued

```
        try
        {
// Let the trading session handle the buy request
            return trading.buy(stock, shares, price);
        }
        catch (RemoteException exc)
        {
            exc.printStackTrace();
            throw new TradingException(exc.toString());
        }
    }

    public TradeResult retractPut(String uniqueID, int putID)
        throws TradingException
    {
// Locate the user's session
        Trading trading = getTradingSession(uniqueID);

        try
        {
// Let the trading session retract the put request
            return trading.retractPut(putID);
        }
        catch (RemoteException exc)
        {
            exc.printStackTrace();
            throw new TradingException(exc.toString());
        }
    }

    public TradeResult retractBuy(String uniqueID, int buyID)
        throws TradingException
    {
// Locate the user's session
        Trading trading = getTradingSession(uniqueID);

        try
        {
// Let the trading session retract the buy request
            return trading.retractBuy(buyID);
        }
        catch (RemoteException exc)
        {
            exc.printStackTrace();
            throw new TradingException(exc.toString());
        }
    }
```

LISTING 21.1 continued

```
    public TradeResult getPutStatus(String uniqueID, int putID)
        throws TradingException
    {
// Locate the user's session
        Trading trading = getTradingSession(uniqueID);

        try
        {
// Fetch the put status from the session bean
            return trading.getPutStatus(putID);
        }
        catch (RemoteException exc)
        {
            exc.printStackTrace();
            throw new TradingException(exc.toString());
        }
    }

    public TradeResult getBuyStatus(String uniqueID, int buyID)
        throws TradingException
    {
// Locate the user's session
        Trading trading = getTradingSession(uniqueID);

        try
        {
// Fetch the buy status from the session bean
            return trading.getBuyStatus(buyID);
        }
        catch (RemoteException exc)
        {
            exc.printStackTrace();
            throw new TradingException(exc.toString());
        }
    }

    public TradeResult[] getOutstandingPuts(String uniqueID)
        throws TradingException
    {
// Locate the user's session
        Trading trading = getTradingSession(uniqueID);

        try
        {
// Fetch the outstanding puts from the session bean
            return trading.getOutstandingPuts();
        }
        catch (RemoteException exc)
        {
```

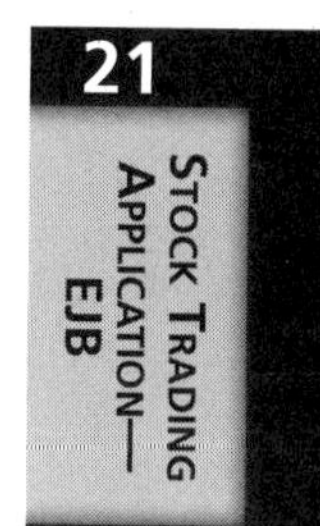

LISTING 21.1 continued

```
            exc.printStackTrace();
            throw new TradingException(exc.toString());
        }
    }

    public TradeResult[] getOutstandingBuys(String uniqueID)
        throws TradingException
    {
// Locate the user's session
        Trading trading = getTradingSession(uniqueID);

        try
        {
// Fetch the outstanding buys from the session bean
            return trading.getOutstandingBuys();
        }
        catch (RemoteException exc)
        {
            exc.printStackTrace();
            throw new TradingException(exc.toString());
        }
    }

    public void logout(String uniqueID)
        throws TradingException
    {
// Log the user out (remove the session)
        Trading trading = (Trading) users.get(uniqueID);
        if (trading != null)
        {
// Remove the session from the table
            users.remove(uniqueID);
            try
            {
// Remove the EJB session
                trading.remove();
            }
            catch (RemoveException exc)
            {
                exc.printStackTrace();
            }
            catch (RemoteException exc)
            {
                exc.printStackTrace();
            }

            return;
        }
        throw new TradingException("ID "+uniqueID+" is not logged in");
    }
```

LISTING 21.1 continued

```
    protected Trading getTradingSession(String uniqueID)
        throws TradingException
    {
        Trading trading = (Trading) users.get(uniqueID);

        if (trading != null) return trading;

        throw new TradingException("ID "+uniqueID+" is not logged in");
    }
}
```

As you can see, the `Trading` session bean handles most of the work; the `StockTrading` object just provides the glue between SOAP and EJB. Listing 21.2 shows the Apache SOAP deployment descriptor for the object.

LISTING 21.2 Source Code for `stockdeploy.xml`

```
<isd:service xmlns:isd="http://xml.apache.org/xml-soap/deployment"
    id="urn:Trading">
    <isd:provider type="java" scope="Application"
        methods="login put buy retractPut retractBuy getPutStatus
➥getBuyStatus getOutstandingPuts getOutstandingBuys logout">
        <isd:java class="jwsunleashed.trading.StockTrading" static="false"/>
    </isd:provider>
    <isd:mappings>
        <isd:map encodingStyle="http://schemas.xmlsoap.org/soap/encoding/"
            xmlns:x="urn:stocktrading" qname="x:traderesult"
            javaType="jwsunleashed.trading.ejb.TradeResult"
            java2XMLClassName="org.apache.soap.encoding.soapenc.BeanSerializer"
            xml2JavaClassName="org.apache.soap.encoding.soapenc.BeanSerializer"
        />
    </isd:mappings>
</isd:service>
```

The Trading Session Bean

The `Trading` session bean performs most of the back-end work for storing buy and put orders and registering completed trades. Listing 21.3 shows the remote interface for the bean.

LISTING 21.3 Source Code for `Trading.java`

```
package jwsunleashed.trading.ejb;

import java.rmi.*;
import javax.ejb.*;

public interface Trading extends EJBObject
{
    public TradeResult put(String stock, int shares, int price)
        throws RemoteException;
    public TradeResult buy(String stock, int shares, int price)
        throws RemoteException;

    public TradeResult retractPut(int putID)
        throws RemoteException;
    public TradeResult retractBuy(int buyID)
        throws RemoteException;

    public TradeResult getPutStatus(int putID)
        throws RemoteException;
    public TradeResult getBuyStatus(int buyID)
        throws RemoteException;

    public TradeResult[] getOutstandingPuts()
        throws RemoteException;
    public TradeResult[] getOutstandingBuys()
        throws RemoteException;
}
```

The `TradingHome` interface provides a single `create` method that requires a valid username and password. In other words, you can't create a valid `Trading` object without a username and password. Listing 21.4 shows the `TradingHome` interface.

LISTING 21.4 Source Code for `TradingHome.java`

```
package jwsunleashed.trading.ejb;

import java.rmi.*;
import javax.ejb.*;

public interface TradingHome extends EJBHome
{
    public Trading create(String userID, String password)
        throws RemoteException, CreateException;
}
```

As with all EJBs, the bulk of the code is in the implementation, not in the interfaces. The `TradingImpl` class implements all the remote methods in the `Trading` interface. It uses a variety of entity beans to store and retrieve the buy and put orders, and also to register the trades.

When you place a put order, the `TradingImpl` class uses a special finder method in the `BuyOrderHome` interface to locate all buy orders that match your put order. It then picks the earliest buy order from the list of matches. You want to match the earliest buy because the trading is on a first-come, first-served basis, so the first person to submit a particular kind of buy order should be the person who gets it.

When you place a buy order, the `TradingImpl` class uses a special finder method in the `PutOrderHome` interface to locate all matching puts and again searches for the earliest put.

The other methods in `TradingImpl` let you locate or cancel outstanding put and buy orders, and also check the status of pending orders to see whether they have been completed.

Listing 21.5 shows the `TradingImpl` class.

LISTING 21.5 Source Code for `TradingImpl.java`

```
package jwsunleashed.trading.ejb;

import java.rmi.*;
import javax.rmi.*;
import javax.ejb.*;
import javax.naming.*;
import java.util.*;

public class TradingImpl implements SessionBean
{
// References to other EJBs used by this class
    protected TradeHome tradeHome;
    protected TraderHome traderHome;
    protected BuyOrderHome buyOrderHome;
    protected PutOrderHome putOrderHome;

// The TraderID for this session's user
    protected int currTraderID;

    private SessionContext context;

    public TradingImpl()
    {
    }
```

LISTING 21.5 continued

```
/** Creates a new instance of the Trading session */
    public void ejbCreate(String userID, String password)
        throws CreateException
    {
        try
        {
            Context ctx = new InitialContext();

/** Locate the Home interfaces for the other objects this session uses */
            tradeHome = (TradeHome) PortableRemoteObject.narrow(
                ctx.lookup("java:comp/env/ejb/TradeHome"),
                TradeHome.class);

            traderHome = (TraderHome) PortableRemoteObject.narrow(
                ctx.lookup("java:comp/env/ejb/TraderHome"),
                TraderHome.class);

            putOrderHome = (PutOrderHome) PortableRemoteObject.narrow(
                ctx.lookup("java:comp/env/ejb/PutOrderHome"),
                PutOrderHome.class);

            buyOrderHome = (BuyOrderHome) PortableRemoteObject.narrow(
                ctx.lookup("java:comp/env/ejb/BuyOrderHome"),
                BuyOrderHome.class);

// Look for a Trader with the specified user ID
            Trader thisTrader = traderHome.findByUserID(userID);

            if (thisTrader == null)
            {
                throw new CreateException("Invalid User ID");
            }

            String traderPassword = thisTrader.getPassword();

// Make sure the passwords match
            if ((password == null) || (traderPassword == null) ||
                !password.equals(traderPassword))
            {
                throw new CreateException("Invalid password");
            }

// Keep track of this user's trader ID
            Integer traderKey = (Integer) thisTrader.getPrimaryKey();
            currTraderID = traderKey.intValue();
        }
        catch (NamingException exc)
        {
```

LISTING 21.5 continued

```
            throw new CreateException("Unable to create trading session: "+
                exc.toString());
        }
        catch (FinderException exc)
        {
            throw new CreateException("Invalid User ID");
        }
        catch (EJBException exc)
        {
            throw new CreateException("Unable to create trading session: "+
                exc.toString());
        }
        catch (RemoteException exc)
        {
            throw new CreateException("Unable to create trading session: "+
                exc.toString());
        }
    }

    public void setSessionContext(SessionContext aContext)
    {
        context = aContext;
    }

    public void ejbActivate()
    {
    }

    public void ejbPassivate()
    {
    }

    public void ejbRemove()
    {
    }

    public TradeResult put(String stock, int shares, int price)
        throws EJBException
    {
        try
        {
// Find a buy order that matches this put
            Collection matchedBuys = buyOrderHome.findMatches(
                stock, shares, price);

            if (matchedBuys.size() >= 1)
            {
                Iterator iter = matchedBuys.iterator();
```

LISTING 21.5 continued

```
                BuyOrder bestMatch = null;

// Find the earliest buy order that matches
                while (iter.hasNext())
                {
                    BuyOrder currMatch = (BuyOrder) PortableRemoteObject.
                        narrow(iter.next(), BuyOrder.class);

                    if ((bestMatch == null) ||
                        (currMatch.getBuyTime().before(
                            bestMatch.getBuyTime())))
                    {
                        bestMatch = currMatch;
                    }
                }

// Register this trade
                Trade newTrade = tradeHome.create();

                newTrade.setSellerID(currTraderID);
                newTrade.setBuyerID(bestMatch.getBuyerID());
                newTrade.setStock(stock);
                newTrade.setShares(shares);
                newTrade.setPrice(price);
                newTrade.setTransTime(new Date());
                newTrade.setBuyID(((Integer) bestMatch.getPrimaryKey()).
                    intValue());

// Remove the buy order from the database
                bestMatch.remove();

// Create the return result
                TradeResult result = new TradeResult();
                result.status = TradeResult.TRADE_COMPLETED;
                result.tradeID = ((Integer) newTrade.getPrimaryKey()).
                    intValue();
                result.sellerID = currTraderID;
                result.buyerID = newTrade.getBuyerID();
                result.buyID = newTrade.getBuyID();
                result.tradeType = TradeResult.PUT;
                result.stock = stock;
                result.price = price;
                result.shares = shares;

                return result;
            }
        }
        catch (FinderException exc)
        {
```

LISTING 21.5 continued

```
        }
        catch (CreateException exc)
        {
            exc.printStackTrace();
        }
        catch (RemoveException exc)
        {
            exc.printStackTrace();
        }
        catch (RemoteException exc)
        {
            exc.printStackTrace();
            throw new EJBException(exc.toString());
        }

        try
        {
// If there were no matching buy orders, create a new put order
            PutOrder newPut = putOrderHome.create();

            newPut.setSellerID(currTraderID);
            newPut.setStock(stock);
            newPut.setShares(shares);
            newPut.setPrice(price);
            newPut.setPutTime(new Date());

// Create the result
            TradeResult result = new TradeResult();
            result.status = TradeResult.TRADE_PENDING;
            result.sellerID = currTraderID;
            result.putID = ((Integer) newPut.getPrimaryKey()).intValue();
            result.tradeType = TradeResult.PUT;
            result.stock = stock;
            result.price = price;
            result.shares = shares;

            return result;
        }
        catch (CreateException exc)
        {
            exc.printStackTrace();
            throw new EJBException("Unable to create new put order");
        }
        catch (RemoteException exc)
        {
            exc.printStackTrace();
            throw new EJBException(exc.toString());
        }
    }
```

LISTING 21.5 continued

```
    public TradeResult buy(String stock, int shares, int price)
        throws EJBException
    {
        try
        {
// Find a put order that matches this buy
            Collection matchedPuts = putOrderHome.findMatches(
                stock, shares, price);

            if (matchedPuts.size() >= 1)
            {
                Iterator iter = matchedPuts.iterator();

                PutOrder bestMatch = null;

// Find the earliest put order that matches
                while (iter.hasNext())
                {
                    PutOrder currMatch = (PutOrder) PortableRemoteObject.
                        narrow(iter.next(), PutOrder.class);

                    if ((bestMatch == null) ||
                        (currMatch.getPutTime().before(
                            bestMatch.getPutTime())))
                    {
                        bestMatch = currMatch;
                    }
                }

// Register the trade
                Trade newTrade = tradeHome.create();

                newTrade.setBuyerID(currTraderID);
                newTrade.setSellerID(bestMatch.getSellerID());
                newTrade.setStock(stock);
                newTrade.setShares(shares);
                newTrade.setPrice(price);
                newTrade.setTransTime(new Date());
                newTrade.setPutID(((Integer) bestMatch.getPrimaryKey()).
                    intValue());

// Remove the buy order
                bestMatch.remove();

                TradeResult result = new TradeResult();
                result.status = TradeResult.TRADE_COMPLETED;
                result.tradeID = ((Integer) newTrade.getPrimaryKey()).
                    intValue();
                result.buyerID = currTraderID;
```

LISTING 21.5 continued

```
                result.sellerID = newTrade.getSellerID();
                result.putID = newTrade.getPutID();
                result.tradeType = TradeResult.BUY;
                result.stock = stock;
                result.price = price;
                result.shares = shares;

                return result;
            }
        }
        catch (FinderException exc)
        {
        }
        catch (CreateException exc)
        {
            exc.printStackTrace();
        }
        catch (RemoveException exc)
        {
            exc.printStackTrace();
        }
        catch (RemoteException exc)
        {
            exc.printStackTrace();
            throw new EJBException(exc.toString());
        }

        try
        {
// If there was no matching put, store this buy order in the database
            BuyOrder newBuy = buyOrderHome.create();

            newBuy.setBuyerID(currTraderID);
            newBuy.setStock(stock);
            newBuy.setShares(shares);
            newBuy.setPrice(price);
            newBuy.setBuyTime(new Date());

// Create the result to return to the client
            TradeResult result = new TradeResult();
            result.status = TradeResult.TRADE_PENDING;
            result.buyerID = currTraderID;
            result.buyID = ((Integer) newBuy.getPrimaryKey()).intValue();
            result.tradeType = TradeResult.BUY;
            result.stock = stock;
            result.price = price;
            result.shares = shares;
```

LISTING 21.5 continued

```
            return result;
        }
        catch (CreateException exc)
        {
            exc.printStackTrace();
            throw new EJBException("Unable to create new buy order");
        }
        catch (RemoteException exc)
        {
            exc.printStackTrace();
            throw new EJBException(exc.toString());
        }
    }

    public TradeResult getPutStatus(int putID)
        throws EJBException
    {
        PutOrder putOrder = null;

        try
        {
// Locate the put order with the specified ID
            putOrder = putOrderHome.findByPrimaryKey(new Integer(putID));
        }
        catch (FinderException exc)
        {
        }
        catch (RemoteException exc)
        {
            exc.printStackTrace();
            throw new EJBException(exc.toString());
        }

        try
        {
// If there was no put order found, see whether it has already been
// accepted for a trade
            if (putOrder == null)
            {
                Trade trade = null;

                try
                {
                    trade = tradeHome.findByPutID(putID);
                }
                catch (FinderException exc)
                {
                }
```

LISTING 21.5 continued

```
// If the put was accepted for a trade, return a result describing the trade
                if ((trade != null) &&
                    (trade.getSellerID() == currTraderID))
                {
                    TradeResult result = new TradeResult();
                    result.status = TradeResult.TRADE_COMPLETED;
                    result.tradeID = ((Integer) trade.getPrimaryKey()).
                        intValue();
                    result.sellerID = currTraderID;
                    result.buyerID = trade.getBuyerID();
                    result.tradeType = TradeResult.PUT;
                    result.stock = trade.getStock();
                    result.price = trade.getPrice();
                    result.shares = trade.getShares();

                    return result;
                }
            }

// If there was no put found, tell the user
            if ((putOrder == null) ||
                (putOrder.getSellerID() != currTraderID))
            {
                TradeResult result = new TradeResult();
                result.status = TradeResult.NO_PUT_FOUND;
                result.putID = putID;

                return result;
            }

// Return a result describing the put
            TradeResult result = new TradeResult();

            result.status = TradeResult.TRADE_PENDING;
            result.sellerID = putOrder.getSellerID();
            result.putID = ((Integer) putOrder.getPrimaryKey()).intValue();
            result.tradeType = TradeResult.PUT;
            result.stock = putOrder.getStock();
            result.price = putOrder.getPrice();
            result.shares = putOrder.getShares();

            return result;
        }
        catch (RemoteException exc)
        {
            exc.printStackTrace();
            throw new EJBException(exc.toString());
        }
    }
```

LISTING 21.5 continued

```
    public TradeResult getBuyStatus(int buyID)
        throws EJBException
    {
        BuyOrder buyOrder = null;

        try
        {
// See whether there is a buy order matching the specified ID
            buyOrder = buyOrderHome.findByPrimaryKey(
                new Integer(buyID));
        }
        catch (FinderException exc)
        {
        }
        catch (RemoteException exc)
        {
            exc.printStackTrace();
            throw new EJBException(exc.toString());
        }

        try
        {
// If there was no matching buy order, see whether it has been
// converted to a trade
            if (buyOrder == null)
            {
                Trade trade = null;

                try
                {
                    trade = tradeHome.findByBuyID(buyID);
                }
                catch (FinderException exc)
                {
                }

// If the buy has been converted to a trade, describe the trade
                if ((trade != null) &&
                    (trade.getBuyerID() == currTraderID))
                {
                    TradeResult result = new TradeResult();
                    result.status = TradeResult.TRADE_COMPLETED;
                    result.tradeID = ((Integer) trade.getPrimaryKey()).
                        intValue();
                    result.sellerID = trade.getSellerID();
                    result.buyerID = currTraderID;
                    result.tradeType = TradeResult.BUY;
                    result.stock = trade.getStock();
                    result.price = trade.getPrice();
                    result.shares = trade.getShares();
```

LISTING 21.5 continued

```
                    return result;
                }
            }

// If there was no buy order found, tell the user
            if ((buyOrder == null) ||
                (buyOrder.getBuyerID() != currTraderID))
            {
                TradeResult result = new TradeResult();
                result.status = TradeResult.NO_BUY_FOUND;
                result.buyID = buyID;

                return result;
            }

// Otherwise, decribe the buy order
            TradeResult result = new TradeResult();

            result.status = TradeResult.TRADE_PENDING;
            result.buyerID = buyOrder.getBuyerID();
            result.buyID = ((Integer) buyOrder.getPrimaryKey()).intValue();
            result.tradeType = TradeResult.BUY;
            result.stock = buyOrder.getStock();
            result.price = buyOrder.getPrice();
            result.shares = buyOrder.getShares();

            return result;
        }
        catch (RemoteException exc)
        {
            exc.printStackTrace();
            throw new EJBException(exc.toString());
        }
    }

    public TradeResult retractPut(int putID)
        throws EJBException
    {
        try
        {
// Locate the put order to retract
            PutOrder putOrder = putOrderHome.findByPrimaryKey(
                new Integer(putID));

            if ((putOrder == null) ||
                (putOrder.getSellerID() != currTraderID))
            {
```

LISTING 21.5 continued

```
                TradeResult result = new TradeResult();
                result.status = TradeResult.NO_PUT_FOUND;
                result.putID = putID;

                return result;
            }

// Create the result before removing the put
            TradeResult result = new TradeResult();

            result.status = TradeResult.TRADE_RETRACTED;
            result.sellerID = putOrder.getSellerID();
            result.putID = ((Integer) putOrder.getPrimaryKey()).intValue();
            result.tradeType = TradeResult.PUT;
            result.stock = putOrder.getStock();
            result.price = putOrder.getPrice();
            result.shares = putOrder.getShares();

// Delete the put from the database
            putOrder.remove();

            return result;
        }
        catch (FinderException exc)
        {
            TradeResult result = new TradeResult();
            result.status = TradeResult.NO_PUT_FOUND;
            result.putID = putID;

            return result;
        }
        catch (RemoveException exc)
        {
            exc.printStackTrace();
            throw new EJBException("Unable to remove put order");
        }
        catch (RemoteException exc)
        {
            exc.printStackTrace();
            throw new EJBException(exc.toString());
        }
    }

    public TradeResult retractBuy(int buyID)
        throws EJBException
    {
        try
        {
```

LISTING 21.5 continued

```
// Locate the buy order
            BuyOrder buyOrder = buyOrderHome.findByPrimaryKey(
                new Integer(buyID));

            if ((buyOrder == null) ||
                (buyOrder.getBuyerID() != currTraderID))
            {
                TradeResult result = new TradeResult();
                result.status = TradeResult.NO_BUY_FOUND;
                result.buyID = buyID;

                return result;
            }

// Create the result before deleting
            TradeResult result = new TradeResult();

            result.status = TradeResult.TRADE_RETRACTED;
            result.sellerID = buyOrder.getBuyerID();
            result.buyID = ((Integer) buyOrder.getPrimaryKey()).intValue();
            result.tradeType = TradeResult.BUY;
            result.stock = buyOrder.getStock();
            result.price = buyOrder.getPrice();
            result.shares = buyOrder.getShares();

// Remove the buy order
            buyOrder.remove();

            return result;
        }
        catch (FinderException exc)
        {
            TradeResult result = new TradeResult();
            result.status = TradeResult.NO_BUY_FOUND;
            result.buyID = buyID;

            return result;
        }
        catch (RemoveException exc)
        {
            exc.printStackTrace();
            throw new EJBException("Unable to remove buy order");
        }
        catch (RemoteException exc)
        {
            exc.printStackTrace();
            throw new EJBException(exc.toString());
        }
    }
```

LISTING 21.5 continued

```
    public TradeResult[] getOutstandingPuts()
        throws EJBException
    {
        try
        {
// Locate all puts for this trader
            Collection puts = putOrderHome.findBySellerID(currTraderID);

            Iterator iter = puts.iterator();

            ArrayList results = new ArrayList();

            while (iter.hasNext())
            {
                PutOrder putOrder = (PutOrder) PortableRemoteObject.narrow(
                    iter.next(), PutOrder.class);

// Create a TradeResult for each outstanding put
                TradeResult result = new TradeResult();
                result.status = TradeResult.TRADE_PENDING;
                result.sellerID = putOrder.getSellerID();
                result.putID = ((Integer) putOrder.getPrimaryKey()).intValue();
                result.tradeType = TradeResult.PUT;
                result.stock = putOrder.getStock();
                result.price = putOrder.getPrice();
                result.shares = putOrder.getShares();

                results.add(result);
            }

// Return the list of results as an array
            return (TradeResult[]) results.toArray(
                new TradeResult[results.size()]);
        }
        catch (FinderException exc)
        {
            exc.printStackTrace();
            return new TradeResult[0];
        }
        catch (RemoteException exc)
        {
            exc.printStackTrace();
            throw new EJBException(exc.toString());
        }
    }

    public TradeResult[] getOutstandingBuys()
        throws EJBException
    {
```

LISTING 21.5 continued

```
        try
        {
// Locate all the outstanding buys for this trader
            Collection buys = buyOrderHome.findByBuyerID(currTraderID);

            Iterator iter = buys.iterator();

            ArrayList results = new ArrayList();

            while (iter.hasNext())
            {
                BuyOrder buyOrder = (BuyOrder) PortableRemoteObject.narrow(
                    iter.next(), BuyOrder.class);

// Create a result for each buy
                TradeResult result = new TradeResult();
                result.status = TradeResult.TRADE_PENDING;
                result.buyerID = buyOrder.getBuyerID();
                result.buyID = ((Integer) buyOrder.getPrimaryKey()).intValue();
                result.tradeType = TradeResult.BUY;
                result.stock = buyOrder.getStock();
                result.price = buyOrder.getPrice();
                result.shares = buyOrder.getShares();

                results.add(result);
            }

// Return the list as an array
            return (TradeResult[]) results.toArray(
                new TradeResult[results.size()]);
        }
        catch (FinderException exc)
        {
            exc.printStackTrace();
            return new TradeResult[0];
        }
        catch (RemoteException exc)
        {
            exc.printStackTrace();
            throw new EJBException(exc.toString());
        }
    }
}
```

Entity Beans

Although the stock trading application uses a number of entity beans, the entity bean code is very simple. All the beans use container-managed persistence (CMP), so they don't worry about persisting themselves in the database. The one difficulty you often find with CMP is that it doesn't handle automatically-generated keys (sequenced keys) very well. You usually must generate the sequenced key yourself. Listing 21.6 shows a simple base class that generates a sequenced key automatically. If you subclass this class, you don't have to write any special code to generate your keys.

LISTING 21.6 Source Code for `AutoKeyEJB.java`

```
package jwsunleashed.trading.ejb;

import java.rmi.*;
import java.util.*;
import javax.ejb.*;
import java.sql.*;
import javax.sql.*;
import javax.naming.*;

public abstract class AutoKeyEJB implements EntityBean
{
/** The entity context provided by the EJB container. An entity bean must
    hold on to the context it is given. */

    private EntityContext context;

/** The database connection used by this entity bean */

    private Connection conn;

/** An EJB must have a public, parameterless constructor */

    public AutoKeyEJB()
    {
    }

/** Called by the EJB container to set this entity's context */

    public void setEntityContext(EntityContext aContext)
    {
        context = aContext;
    }

/** Called by the EJB container to clear this entity's context */
```

LISTING 21.6 continued

```
    public void unsetEntityContext()
    {
        context = null;
    }

/** Returns the name of the database to use for retrieving the new key */
    public abstract String getKeyDatabaseName();

/** Returns the name of the table to use for retrieving the new key.
    Use this method if your database doesn't support sequences */
    public abstract String getKeyTableName();

/** Returns the name of the key column in the key table or sequence */
    public abstract String getKeyColumnName();

/** Called by the EJB container when a client calls the create() method in
    the home interface */

    public abstract Integer ejbCreate()
        throws CreateException;

/** Called by the EJB container after ejbCreate to enable the bean to do
    any additional setup that may be required. */
    public void ejbPostCreate()
        throws CreateException
    {
    }

/** Called by the EJB container to tell put the bean into active mode */

    public void ejbActivate()
        throws EJBException
    {
    }

/** Called by the EJB container to tell this bean that it is being
    deactivated and placed back into the pool */

    public void ejbPassivate()
        throws EJBException
    {
    }

/** Called by the container to tell the entity bean to read its data from
    the database */

    public void ejbLoad()
        throws EJBException
    {
    }
```

LISTING 21.6 continued

```
/** Called by the EJB container to tell the entity bean to
    write its data out to the database */
    public void ejbStore()
        throws EJBException
    {
    }

/** Called by the EJB container to tell this bean that it has been
    removed. */

    public void ejbRemove()
        throws EJBException
    {
    }

/** Although this class uses CMP, you still need to locate a connection
 * to generate the primary key (Person generates its own unique
 *  id automatically.
 */
    protected Connection getConnection()
        throws SQLException, NamingException
    {
// Get a reference to the naming service
        InitialContext context = new InitialContext();

// Get the data source for the database
        DataSource ds = (DataSource) context.lookup(
            "java:comp/env/jdbc/"+getKeyDatabaseName());

// Ask the data source to allocate a database connection
        return ds.getConnection();
    }

/** Uses a separate database table to generate a unique ID number.
    You should perform the update before you read the value
    to make sure you don't have any locking problems.
    */
    protected int getNextId()
        throws SQLException
    {
        Connection conn = null;

        try
        {
            conn = getConnection();

// Increment the next ID number
            PreparedStatement ps = conn.prepareStatement(
                "update "+getKeyTableName()+" set "+
                getKeyColumnName()+" = "+getKeyColumnName()+" + 1");
```

LISTING 21.6 continued

```
            if (ps.executeUpdate() != 1)
            {
                throw new SQLException("Unable to generate"+
                    getKeyColumnName());
            }

            ps.close();

// Read the next ID number
            ps = conn.prepareStatement(
                "select "+getKeyColumnName()+" from "+getKeyTableName());

            ResultSet rs = ps.executeQuery();

            if (rs.next())
            {
                return rs.getInt(getKeyColumnName());
            }
            else
            {
                throw new SQLException("Unable to generate id"+
                    getKeyColumnName());
            }
        }
        catch (NamingException exc)
        {
            exc.printStackTrace();
            throw new SQLException("Unable to generate id", exc.toString());
        }
        finally
        {
            try
            {
                conn.close();
            }
            catch (Exception ignore) {}
        }
    }
}
```

Listing 21.7 shows the remote interface to the `BuyOrder` entity bean, which represents an outstanding buy.

LISTING 21.7 Source Code for `BuyOrder.java`

```
package jwsunleashed.trading.ejb;

import java.rmi.*;
import javax.ejb.*;
import java.util.Date;

public interface BuyOrder extends EJBObject
{
    public int getBuyerID() throws RemoteException;
    public void setBuyerID(int aBuyerID) throws RemoteException;

    public String getStock() throws RemoteException;
    public void setStock(String aStock) throws RemoteException;

    public int getShares() throws RemoteException;
    public void setShares(int numShares) throws RemoteException;

    public int getPrice() throws RemoteException;
    public void setPrice(int thePrice) throws RemoteException;

    public Date getBuyTime() throws RemoteException;
    public void setBuyTime(Date aBuyTime) throws RemoteException;
}
```

Listing 21.8 shows the source code for the `BuyOrderHome` interface. The `findMatches` finder method locates buys that match a particular put request. You can actually change the matching algorithm at deployment time by modifying the EJBQL query used to perform the find.

LISTING 21.8 Source Code for `BuyOrderHome.java`

```
package jwsunleashed.trading.ejb;

import java.rmi.*;
import javax.ejb.*;
import java.util.*;

public interface BuyOrderHome extends EJBHome
{
    public BuyOrder create() throws RemoteException, CreateException;

    public BuyOrder findByPrimaryKey(Integer putOrderID)
        throws RemoteException, FinderException;

    public Collection findByBuyerID(int buyerID)
        throws RemoteException, FinderException;
```

LISTING 21.8 continued

```
    public Collection findMatches(String stock, int shares,
        int price) throws RemoteException, FinderException;
}
```

Listing 21.9 shows the implementation of the `BuyOrder` entity bean. Because the `AutoKeyEJB` base class implements many of the required-but-unused methods, the `BuyOrderImpl` class is actually quite short for an entity bean.

LISTING 21.9 Source Code for `BuyOrderImpl.java`

```
package jwsunleashed.trading.ejb;

import java.rmi.*;
import java.util.*;
import javax.ejb.*;
import java.sql.*;
import javax.sql.*;
import javax.naming.*;
import java.util.Date;

public abstract class BuyOrderImpl extends AutoKeyEJB
{
/** An EJB must have a public, parameterless constructor */

    public BuyOrderImpl()
    {
    }

    public String getKeyDatabaseName() { return "TradingDB"; }
    public String getKeyTableName() { return "BUY_ORDER_ID_SEQ"; }
    public String getKeyColumnName() { return "BUY_ORDER_ID"; }

/** Called by the EJB container when a client calls the create() method in
    the home interface */

    public Integer ejbCreate()
        throws CreateException
    {
        try
        {
// compute the new primary key for this object
            setBuyOrderId(getNextId());

            return null;
        }
        catch (SQLException exc)
        {
```

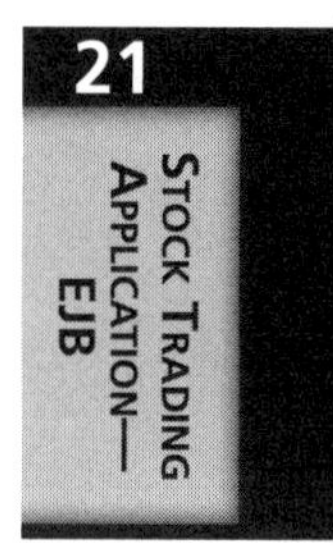

LISTING 21.9 continued

```
            throw new CreateException(
                "Unable to access database: "+exc.toString());
        }
    }

// Implement the get/set methods for all the data elements

    public abstract int getBuyOrderId();
    public abstract void setBuyOrderId(int aBuyOrderId);

    public abstract int getBuyerID();
    public abstract void setBuyerID(int aBuyerID);

    public abstract String getStock();
    public abstract void setStock(String aStock);

    public abstract int getShares();
    public abstract void setShares(int numShares);

    public abstract int getPrice();
    public abstract void setPrice(int thePrice);

    public abstract Date getBuyTime();
    public abstract void setBuyTime(Date aTransTime);
}
```

The other entity beans are so similar to `BuyOrder` that there is little point in listing them here. You can download them from `http://www.samspublishing.com`, however, along with the completed deployment EAR file for use with the J2EE Reference Implementation.

When you deploy the beans, make sure you generate a client JAR file (the `deploytool` lets you specify a location for the client JAR), containing the classes used to access the beans. You need the JAR file for your SOAP object. Even if you deploy the SOAP object in the same server, you need to add the client JAR file to the SOAP server's class path.

A Test Client

Because the `StockTrading` class is available as a SOAP object, you have many ways to call it. Listing 21.10 shows an example client that logs in, issues a buy and a put, and then logs out.

LISTING 21.10 Source Code for `StockClient.java`

```
import java.util.*;
import java.io.*;
import java.net.*;
import jwsunleashed.trading.ejb.TradeResult;
import jwsunleashed.trading.TradingException;

import org.apache.soap.*;
import org.apache.soap.encoding.*;
import org.apache.soap.encoding.soapenc.*;
import org.apache.soap.rpc.*;
import org.apache.soap.util.xml.*;

public class StockClient
{
    public static void main(String[] args)
    {
        try
        {
            URL url = new URL("http://localhost:8000/soap/servlet/rpcrouter");

// Create a new call for logging in
            Call call = new Call();
            call.setTargetObjectURI("urn:Trading");
            call.setMethodName("login");
            call.setEncodingStyleURI(Constants.NS_URI_SOAP_ENC);

// Create the list of parameters
            Vector params = new Vector();

            params.addElement(new Parameter("userID", String.class,
                "mark", null));
            params.addElement(new Parameter("password", String.class,
                "secret", null));

            call.setParams(params);

// Invoke the call
            Response resp = call.invoke(url, "");

            String uniqueID = null;

            if (!resp.generatedFault())
            {
                Parameter ret = resp.getReturnValue();

                uniqueID = (String) ret.getValue();

                System.out.println("Your login ID is: "+uniqueID);
            }
```

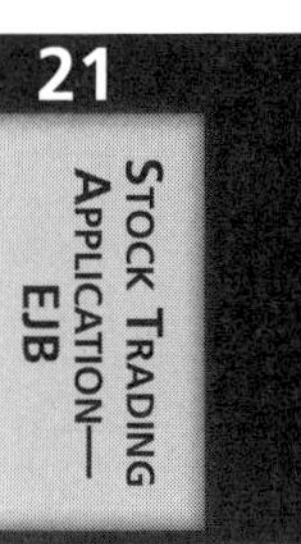

LISTING 21.10 continued

```
            else
            {
                Fault fault = resp.getFault();
                System.err.println("Generated fault:");
                System.err.println("  Fault code    = " + fault.getFaultCode());
                System.err.println("  Fault string  = " +
                    fault.getFaultString());
                System.exit(0);
            }

// For the other calls, you need a BeanSerializer to process the
// TradeResult objects
            BeanSerializer ser = new BeanSerializer();

            SOAPMappingRegistry reg = new SOAPMappingRegistry();

            reg.mapTypes(Constants.NS_URI_SOAP_ENC,
                new QName("urn:stocktrading", "traderesult"),
                    TradeResult.class, ser, ser);

// Create another call for issuing a put order
            call = new Call();

            call.setTargetObjectURI("urn:Trading");
            call.setMethodName("put");
            call.setEncodingStyleURI(Constants.NS_URI_SOAP_ENC);

// Tell the call how to deserialize a TradeResult
            call.setSOAPMappingRegistry(reg);

// Create the parameter list
            params = new Vector();

            params.addElement(new Parameter("uniqueID", String.class,
                uniqueID, null));
            params.addElement(new Parameter("stock", String.class,
                "SUNW", null));
            params.addElement(new Parameter("shares", Integer.class,
                new Integer(1000), null));
            params.addElement(new Parameter("price", Integer.class,
                new Integer(2000), null));

            call.setParams(params);

// Invoke the call
            resp = call.invoke(url, "");

            if (!resp.generatedFault())
            {
                Parameter ret = resp.getReturnValue();
```

LISTING 21.10 continued

```
                    TradeResult result = (TradeResult) ret.getValue();

                    System.out.println(result);
                }
                else
                {
                    Fault fault = resp.getFault();
                    System.err.println("Generated fault:");
                    System.err.println("  Fault code   = " + fault.getFaultCode());
                    System.err.println("  Fault string  = " +
                        fault.getFaultString());
                    System.exit(0);
                }

// Create a call for issuing a buy order
                call = new Call();
                call.setTargetObjectURI("urn:Trading");
                call.setMethodName("buy");
                call.setEncodingStyleURI(Constants.NS_URI_SOAP_ENC);

// Tell the call how to deserialize a TradeResult
                call.setSOAPMappingRegistry(reg);

// Create the parameter list
                params = new Vector();

                params.addElement(new Parameter("uniqueID", String.class,
                    uniqueID, null));
                params.addElement(new Parameter("stock", String.class,
                    "SUNW", null));
                params.addElement(new Parameter("shares", Integer.class,
                    new Integer(1000), null));
                params.addElement(new Parameter("price", Integer.class,
                    new Integer(2200), null));

                call.setParams(params);

// Invoke the call
                resp = call.invoke(url, "");

                if (!resp.generatedFault())
                {
                    Parameter ret = resp.getReturnValue();

                    TradeResult result = (TradeResult) ret.getValue();

                    System.out.println(result);
                }
```

LISTING 21.10 continued

```
            else
            {
                Fault fault = resp.getFault();
                System.err.println("Generated fault:");
                System.err.println("  Fault code    = " + fault.getFaultCode());
                System.err.println("  Fault string  = " +
                    fault.getFaultString());
                System.exit(0);
            }

// Create a call for logging out
            call = new Call();
            call.setTargetObjectURI("urn:Trading");
            call.setMethodName("logout");
            call.setEncodingStyleURI(Constants.NS_URI_SOAP_ENC);

// Create the parameter list
            params = new Vector();

            params.addElement(new Parameter("uniqueID", String.class,
                uniqueID, null));

            call.setParams(params);

// Invoke the call
            resp = call.invoke(url, "");

            if (!resp.generatedFault())
            {
                System.out.println("You have logged out successfully.");
            }
            else
            {
                Fault fault = resp.getFault();
                System.err.println("Generated fault:");
                System.err.println("  Fault code    = " + fault.getFaultCode());
                System.err.println("  Fault string  = " +
                    fault.getFaultString());
                System.exit(0);
            }
        }
        catch (Exception exc)
        {
            exc.printStackTrace();
        }
    }
}
```

Summary

Enterprise JavaBeans are easy to write, although they can be difficult to deploy. When you combine them with SOAP, however, you have an excellent platform for implementing Web services quickly and easily. After you create a Web service, you still need to make sure it works properly, and possibly improve the performance. In the next chapter, you'll learn more about testing and optimizing Web services.

Testing Web Services

By Frank Cohen

In This Chapter

We are living through the biggest expansion of software development projects ever. As software developers, we find upper management has new expectations for how fast we can integrate and deliver scalable and reliable systems. Customers have new expectations for functionality and ease-of-use. And every project in an IT group now has a requirement for interoperability and connectivity. What an exciting time it is to be a software developer!

The projects we are building look easy from the outside, but are incredibly complex on the server side. For example, browse a Web site today and you will likely be using many server software application packages—this is especially true for dynamic Web sites offering personalized content. A sign-in to the manufacturing Web pages of a company internal portal is expected to also sign the user in to check the fulfillment team's reports, even if different servers are providing the service.

Behind the scenes, scores of engineers are doing their best to keep the backend systems interoperating. New hardware (routers, servers, storage) and server software (J2EE, Oracle Server, SunONE) appear with alarming frequency. Software engineers constantly write expensive and difficult-to-maintain custom software to keep the systems sharing data.

What we need is a single self-describing API to write interoperable software! Thank you IBM, Sun, Microsoft, BEA, and everyone who chose SOAP, WSDL, and UDDI to deliver the next generation of Java, Windows, WebSphere, and WebLogic. Web services are the biggest move forward toward interoperability yet, because every part of the operating system is now expected to use these standard protocols and API definitions to integrate with our code.

The benefits of being able to write server applications that freely communicate with other servers, platforms, and hardware are many. Less time is spent on maintaining the code and the programmer gets to concentrate on solving bigger problems. The operations manager has a wider choice of platforms and hardware, and users benefit by having more advanced applications available.

Tools that use SOAP to enable interoperable software are inexpensive, freely available, and widely supported. However, considerations for tools, hardware, and network equipment will greatly determine performance and scalability potentials for deployed SOAP-based Web services. With that in mind, this chapter discusses a scalable framework for developing Web services, strategies for avoiding performance problems, and offers an open-source set of test objects and a scripting language called TestMaker that can help with performance and scalability testing.

Framework for Developing Web services

Web services protocols (SOAP, WSDL, UDDI) were designed to be implemented within an existing Web environment, including using existing routers, Web servers, firewalls, load balancers, and databases. An emerging framework for developing scalable SOAP-based Web services favors a Web architecture with many small servers that are accessed through a load balancer, providing a front-end to a powerful database server.

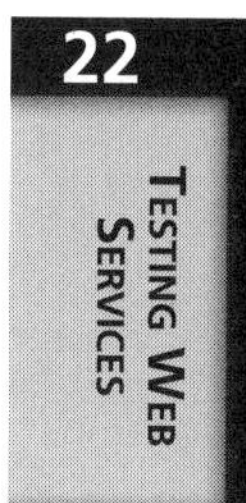

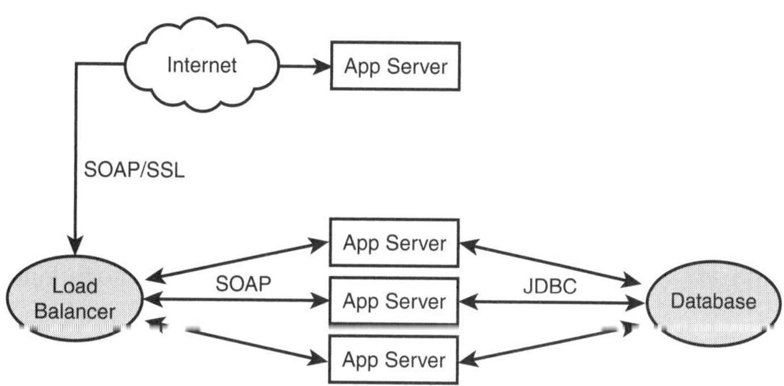

FIGURE 22.1
Web Service Datacenter

The framework described in Figure 22.1 for building SOAP-based Web services in Java uses these components:

- Apache SOAP, found at `http://xml.apache.org/soap/index.html`. Based largely on IBM's SOAP contribution to the Apache Jakarta project group, Apache SOAP is an open-source project delivering a full-featured SOAP implementation for Java. Although Apache SOAP was the first stable, widely distributed SOAP implementation, Apache SOAP suffers from mediocre performance and will likely be eclipsed by other SOAP implementations. Apache SOAP delivers the right mix of features and support, including implementing most of the SOAP v1.1 specification. Additional Apache SOAP supports SOAP messages and comes with both server and client implementations. Apache SOAP comes with full source code under an Apache-style license (which means you can change the code and even deploy proprietary software products with your changes.) Later in this chapter we delve into the interoperability problems that come SOAP implementations, including mixing Apache SOAP with Microsoft SOAP.
- JDOM. Apache SOAP comes with the Xerces XML parser; however, any SAX-compliant XML parser can be used instead. Java developers will find JDOM to be an easier, friendlier API to manipulate SOAP's XML request and response

documents. JDOM also enables you to change the underlying XML parser without recoding the SOAP application. This flexibility gives you many choices when you're trying to solve scalability and performance problems in a particular XML parser. JDOM is also distributed under an Apache-style open-source license. JDOM may become part of Java. Sun accepted JDOM as JSR102; see `http://jcp.org/jsr/detail/102.jsp`.

- Load balancer with SSL support. The SOAP 1.1 protocol does not define encryption and authentication methods. Until SOAP defines an authentication method, the framework recommends you write your business logic into a servlet, then use the underlying Web server's SSL support to make an HTTPS request to the Web service. The Load balancer's SSL support unecrypts the request and passes it along to the Web service as an unencrypted SOAP call. This frees up your Web service server from the computing overhead of SSL.
- Load balancer with cookie-based session tracking. The SOAP 1.1 specification does not define a session management mechanism, yet many Web services will need to handle stateful user requests. Application servers such as BEA WebLogic and Microsoft .NET provide an application- and session-tracking mechanism to store state information for a Web service. In the framework, though, the real goal of cookies is to make certain the application server that started a user session handles the next request from the same user. Failover to another machine can be handled nicely if the session information is stored in the database, rather than in the local object store of the application server. In a load-balanced environment, some of your SOAP requests are bound to carry stateful information. For example, communication with a Web service may require multiple requests and responses in series. The load balancer must have the option to bring your request to the same Web service server during a session. Most load balancers support cookie-based session tracking.

The framework in Figure 22.2 has many benefits. Java developers find debugging less complex because fewer threads are typically running at any time and problems are more easily isolated when a single Web service server may be monitored. Company financial managers like the framework because they can buy many small, inexpensive servers and avoid giant system purchases. Network managers like the flexibility all those small servers give.

This leaves one question: Are Web services ready for production environments?

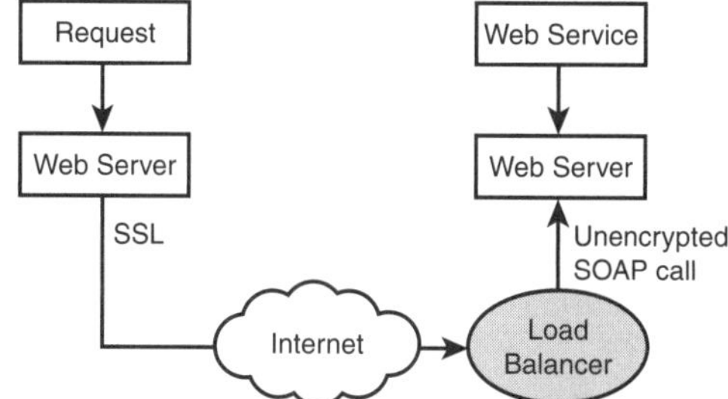

FIGURE 22.2
Load balancer with SSL support.

Design for Performance and Scalability

Web services are a very new and untested technology. Inside SOAP, for example, are many places to harbor performance and scalability problems. Determining production worthiness requires both unit and system-level testing. An understanding of the process a Web service uses to handle a request is a good starting point to avoiding scalability and performance problems (see Figure 22.3).

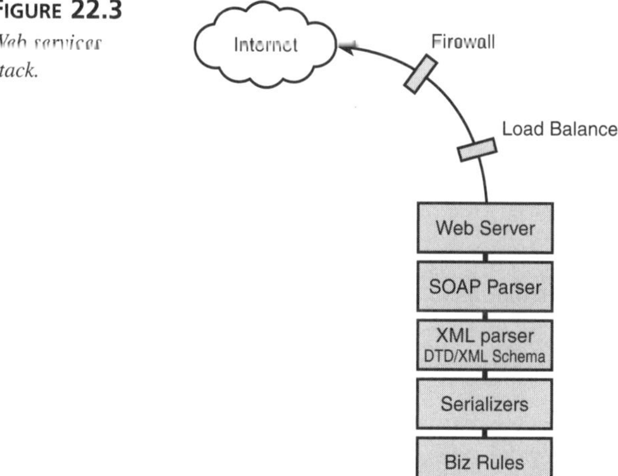

FIGURE 22.3
Web services stack.

The SOAP protocol uses a multistep process to complete a request. The SOAP request begins with business logic of your application learning the method and parameter to call from a Web Services Description Language (WSDL) document.

As an example, here is part of the WSDL for a publicly available Web service that returns the current weather for a U.S. postal zip code.

```
<message name = "getTempRequest">
 <part name = "zipcode" type = "xsd:string"/>
</message>
<message name = "getTempResponse">
 <part name = "return" type = "xsd:float"/>
</message>
```

The weather service requires you to call the `getTempRequest` method by passing in a `zipcode` value as a string. The service responds with a floating-point value for the temperature.

Because the WSDL rarely changes, many developers embed the WSDL definition into their code to avoid the overhead of getting the WSDL every time. Although this will improve performance, it also becomes a maintenance headache when the WSDL changes over time.

The better way to avoid maintenance problems is to cache the WSDL in the centralized database and then periodically check the timestamp/version number of the WSDL to see if a newer one is available. The WSDL includes references to the DTD that defines the WSDL document contents. If possible, storing the DTD in the database and periodically checking for updates is a more scalable solution than reading the DTD every time.

Another way to improve performance is to turn XML validation off. In this case, your application should validate the response results. For example, this WSDL defines the schema for the response:

```
<element name="zipcode" type="int"/>
<element name="temperature" type="float"/>
<element name="remarks" type="string"/>
```

The result of a call to this service looks like this:

```
<zipcode>95008</zipcode>
<temperature>65 F</temperature>
<remarks>Storm warning</remarks>
```

This response should throw an exception because the `temperature` value is not a float type. It is actually a string. Validating the response in an application will normally be much faster than depending on the DTD or XML schema code to validate the response.

Parameter types in SOAP present a possible scalability problem. The SOAP 1.1 specification defines only a few simple data types: `String`, `Int`, `Float`, and `NegativeInteger`. The WSDL may include non-trivial new data types. For example, imagine that the temperature Web service also retrieved maps. The schema for the call might look like this:

```
<message name = "getTempRequest">
 <part name = "zipcode" type = "xsd:string"/>
</message>
```

```
<message name = "getTempResponse">
 <part name = "return" type = "xsd:float"/>
 <part name = "map" type = "xsd: http://www.pushtotest.com/wsdl/mapformat"/>
</message>
```

While reading the response, a validating XML parser will contact the `pushtotest.com` host to get the XML schema definition for the `mapformat`. The overhead to complete the request can be a huge. A cascade-style failure is possible, too, when two schemas refer to each other. Caching schema definitions in the database is one solution. Defining parameters for external documents is another way to go.

Custom data types are probably the biggest problem for SOAP's platform-independent interoperability. When a SOAP request is made, the request document may include custom data types. Each custom data type requires the SOAP library to have access to a serializer to read the data type into the local language (C++, VB, C#, Java, and others). A general performance rule is to stay with the simple SOAP data types unless there is a compelling need to use another data type. Each new data type introduces a serializer to convert from the XML value into a platform-specific value and back again. The serializer may cause performance problems, interoperability problems, or just be buggy. For example, the Apache and Microsoft SOAP implementations both include a BigDecimal data type. However, they are not compatible.

A choice of SOAP implementation may also stall an application's interoperability. For example, Microsoft SOAP has data serializers it needs to interoperate with Windows-based Web services not provided in other SOAP implementations, including Hailstorm and Passport.

SOAP is unique among interoperability standards in that it does not require both ends of a request and response to be implemented with SOAP. For example, SOAP may interoperate with Java RMI or CORBA. SOAP transports XML data, which is self-describing through the DTD mechanism. That means products such as Cape Clear's CapeStudio can visually map SOAP requests and do transformations on the data as it moves from one system to another. CapeStudio even outputs Java or Visual Basic code to handle the SOAP communication and transformations.

Although SOAP was designed to work within existing Web application environments, the protocol may introduce firewall and routing problems. Unlike the normal Web server that uses HTTP and HTML, all SOAP messages are the equivalent of HTTP Form Submits. The calls move much more data than the average HTTP get or post. Although it would be almost trivial to use data compression on a SOAP request and response document, the SOAP v1.1 specification does not cover compression. Consequently, SOAP's impact on network performance is bound to be significant. Special testing of the firewall and routing equipment should be undertaken. For example, check the firewall's security policy to make certain it does not monitor SOAP requests as Web traffic. If it does, you may find the firewall shunting away traffic that looks like a Denial of Service (DOS) attack.

The early Web services were very straightforward: Make a SOAP call and get a response. More advanced SOAP applications make series of get and response calls until a transaction is finished. Transactional SOAP calls need to identify sessions and cache the state of the sessions. Caching mechanisms for SOAP transactions are potential problem spots for scalability. Just imagine an Akamai caching proxy server handling SOAP requests and responses over the Internet.

Although the places for scalability and performance problems are many, SOAP makes good on its promise of easier and more maintainable interoperability. The next section looks at actually testing SOAP-based Web services for scalability and performance.

Test Strategies

Moving a SOAP-based Web service into a production environment requires assurances of high availability and predictably good performance. Imagine an e-commerce Web service that was not available or did not perform well! Here is a checklist Java developers should keep in mind when planning to test a Web service:

- **Stateful testing.** When you use SOAP to put a product in a shopping basket, is the product in the shopping basket later on?
- **Privilege testing.** What happens when one user tries to put a product into another user's shopping basket?
- **Speed testing.** Has it taken more than five seconds to put the product into the shopping basket?
- **Boundary timing testing.** What happens when a Web services request times out, or takes a really long time to respond?
- **Regression testing.** Did a new build break an existing Web service function?

These are fairly common tests for any software application. Because this is a Web Service, though, the test list expands into a matrix, as the following table of a Web service test agent describes:

Web Service Test Agent	*1*	*50*	*500*
Stateful testing	ok	ok	
Privilege testing	ok		
Speed testing			
Boundary timing testing			
Regression			

Java developers testing Web applications used to be able to ask their friends and family to grab a keyboard or mouse and test a new piece of software. Web services exchange XML documents. Although some network technicians have learned to read live TCP/IP data streams, reading XML streams is probably not a skill that will further your career. Manually reading the XML documents emitted during a SOAP transaction becomes time consuming very rapidly. Developing and using automated test agents is a must.

Testing Web Services Using TestMaker

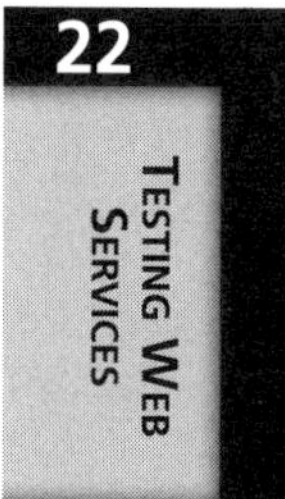

A free open-source utility, TestMaker, is available from the PushToTest Web site. It writes test automation agents for performance and scalability testing of SOAP-based Web services. TestMaker offers a script-language to operate a library of test objects. The combination enables you to develop intelligent test agents that drive a Web Service. Multiple concurrent running copies of the script show how the Web Service performs under simulated production situations.

Look at how TestMaker would be used to call the weather temperature service discussed previously. Here is the script in its entirety:

```
# Web service test agent

# Create a new SOAP protocol handler object

protocol = SOAPProtocol()
body = SOAPBody()

# Tell it what to send to the Web service host

body.addParameter("zipcode","95008")
body.setTarget("urn:xmethods-Temperature ")
body.setMethod("getTemp ")

# Tells where to find the wether service
protocol.setHost("services.xmethods.net ")
protocol.setPath("/soap/servlet/rpcrouter ")
protocol.setPort(80)
protocol.setBody(body)

response = protocol.connect()
params = response.getParameterKeys()

# Shows returned temperature
print response.toString()
```

```
# Report how long it took to make the SOAP call
print("")
print("Timing statistics to find temperature (milliseconds)")
print("Total: " + Long(response.getTotalTime()).toString())
print("Setup: " + Long(response.getSetupTime()).toString())
print("")
```

The script begins with a `SOAPProtocol` object that is assigned to a simple variable for later reference. The `SOAPProtocol` object handles all communication, timeouts, data translation, and request document set-up for you:

```
protocol = SOAPProtocol()
```

Whereas `SOAPProtocol` handles SOAP specifically, TestMaker also implements protocol handlers for generic HTTP transactions, and TestMaker may be extended to handle FTP, SMTP, and IMAP protocols with little effort. Many times you will just need to change an existing TestMaker agent, rather than write an agent from scratch.

The `SOAPBody` object builds the XML request document that will be sent to the SOAP host. The request document is fairly simple this time around. The SOAP object needs to know the zip code for the desired area. The WSDL definition for the weather service tells which target and method to use on the SOAP host to get the weather reading:

```
body = SOAPBody()
body.addParameter("zipcode","95008")
body.setTarget("urn:xmethods-Temperature ")
body.setMethod("getTemp ")
```

Unfortunately, this weather service works for only valid U.S. Post Office zip codes. The zip code 95008 in the example agent is for Campbell, California, in the heart of the Silicon Valley. Try using different zip codes here.

The last step before actually calling the SOAP host is to tell the `SOAPProtocol` object the URI to the host, including the host domain name and the path to the SOAP host object running on the server. The path usually triggers a servlet, script, or CGI on the host:

```
# Tells where to find the weather service
protocol.setHost("services.xmethods.net ")
protocol.setPath("/soap/servlet/rpcrouter ")
protocol.setPort(80)
```

In a bit of object-oriented magic, the body object is paired with the `SOAPProtocol` object. An unlimited number of body objects may be created and individually used with a `SOAPProtocol` object. This is really handy when the Web service offers many options:

```
protocol.setBody(body)
```

The `connect()` method of the `SOAPProtocol` object assembles the request document from the body object, makes the HTTP call to the host, creates a response object, and returns the response document from the host to the response object:

```
response = protocol.connect()
```

The agent displays the actual response document in a logging window in TestMaker and also saves the response to a log file for later analysis:

```
# Shows returned temperature
print("")
print("Response document received:")
print response.toString()
```


The `SOAPProtocol` object implements a set of timers so the agent may understand and act on the time it takes to set up and call the host. Both times are given in milliseconds (1000 milliseconds is 1 second; for example, 1458 milliseconds is 1.458 seconds):

```
# Report how long it took to make the SOAP call
print("")
print("Timing statistics to find temperature (milliseconds):")
print("Total: " + Long(response.getTotalTime()).toString())
print("Setup: " + Long(response.getSetupTime()).toString())
print("")
```

The TestMaker object library is fully threaded. Therefore, multiple requests may be made at the same time, thus simulating real-world use of the Web service. This simple agent could be run in 100 threads concurrently. To the Web service it would appear that 100 users have requested the weather. TestMaker also includes commands for looping, random values, posting dummy text, and access to 20 other test objects. A more complex example comes later in this chapter.

TestMaker is licensed under terms similar to those of the Apache Web server. You download the TestMaker program and all its source code. You can change TestMaker to fix bugs and add new features. The license even lets you build commercially exploitable new products based on the code.

Before you go any further in depth on building test agents with TestMaker, you need to understand the methodologies needed to construct Web services tests so the tests will provide meaningful data. Without a good test methodology the results may be meaningless—or worse, misleading.

New Web Services Technology, New Test Methodology

As we live through the biggest expansion of software development projects ever, the way we test and monitor these projects has dramatically changed. Test methodologies used in the mainframe and desktop computing era have mostly fallen aside. New methodologies have arisen, including extreme programming and unit testing.

Software testing is as new as the computer industry—less than 40 years old altogether. So it is no surprise that new software testing methods appear every year. In the age of Internet software development, testing methods fall into these categories:

- Click-stream testing
- Unit testing (state, boundary, error, privilege)
- System testing
- Scalability and performance testing

These categories are linked by the software developers' common goal to deliver highly usable, productive, and quality applications.

Click-Stream Testing

Early Internet software development projects were primarily concerned with content delivery: Are the users seeing the pages we're creating? In 1996 a Web search engine company—Excite—won praise from the computer magazines by adding a personalization feature. Excite users could log in and set their preference to see weather information for their city. And so began the age of the portal. Prior to Excite's innovation, Web pages were only updated by the Web site editors—the Web functioned more like network television where viewers changed channels. Today everyone expects Web applications to offer personalization; Web sites that do not operate like desktop applications appear to be inconsequential.

In the early days, testing Web sites meant checking that the personalization worked and then checking the infrastructure to make sure the site continued to work. The infrastructure was everything between the user's browser and the database driving the Web application, including network routers, switches, load balancers, server hardware, Web server software and CGI programs.

The early Web application developers were very interested in *click-stream* testing statistics. In a click-stream the user clicks from one page to another on a Web site. The more clicks, the more money a Web site publisher earned in advertising or sponsorship of pages. The click-stream tools showed which URLs the user clicked, the Web site activity by time period during the day, and other data otherwise found in the Web server logs. Popular choices for click-stream testing statistics include KeyNote systems Internet weather report, WebTrends log analysis utility, and the NetMechanic monitoring service.

Click-stream testing statistics tell one almost nothing about the user's ability to achieve their goals with the Web site. A Web site may show a million page views, but 2/3 of the page views may be of an Error page.

Team Development Meets Team Testing

As developers, when we sit down in front of a computer in the 2000s, we have more development tool choices than ever before. Source code editors, compilers, version control systems, code libraries, and powerful operating systems and languages. And most of these are free.

The choice of development tools is becoming less important, and this is encouraging team-based software development. By the 1990s, every computer programming language and operating system platform had an object-oriented programming strategy. Consequently, the languages and platforms now look almost identical, with any differences being only superficial. Teams of developers now work on software projects together while each individual uses his or her own tools to produce object-oriented code.

In a team, individual engineers work on code modules and guarantee the module's functions. The team is bound together through a series of contracts that define a module's functions and interfaces. The internal workings of the module are the responsibility of the engineer. It is common sense, then, to expect an engineer's primary concern will be making certain a module is giving good and valid data when called, but the engineer doesn't care how the module is constructed internally. Assuring the module's responses are valid is called *unit testing*.

Unit Testing

Unit testing is accomplished by adding a small amount of the code to the module that validates the module's responses. For example, a module may check the temperature of an air conditioner. The module may look like this:

```
class public checktemperature
{
  public integer gettemp()
  {
         return temperature;
  }

  public boolean validate( int temperature )
  {
         if ( temperature > 40 && temperature < 110 )
         return true;
         else
         return false;
  }
}
```

The `checktemperature` module implements an object. The `gettemp` method returns the temperature found in the air conditioner. The developer of `checktemperature` also included the `validate` method. The air conditioner temperature sensor is able to operate only within a range of 40° to 110° Fahrenheit. If the temperature is actually 20°, then the returned value is invalid.

Validation methods can be built into all modules in a project. Imagine having modules check themselves when the software modules are being compiled into a Web application. This is accomplished by using a Make utility (a program that tells the compiler which source files to work with and in what order) that performs unit tests during compilation:

```
Compiling bigproject.
Compiling checktemperature.
Running unit test on checktemperature, input value is 55.
Unit test successful.
Building bigproject file.
```

Unit testing finds problems and errors at the module level before the software leaves the development team.

Although unit testing is a huge win for developers, some developers are lulled into a false sense of security. "It passed the unit tests, so the software quality should be high," thinks the developer. Unfortunately, unit tests can be meaningless if used by themselves to determine the health of Web applications. The unit test on the Galileo space probe succeeded, but the probe crashed into Mars when two units failed to work as one system.

A thorough test of a Web application must include intelligent end-to-end system tests. A system test checks the whole Web application, from the user operating a keyboard and mouse, to the Web application logic, to the database and communication systems underneath. If everything is not working, the user will not have the ability to accomplish his or her goals.

System Testing

Although unit testing is a fine technique for developers to use, users will never operate an individual module. Instead, the user access collections of modules that make up the overall system. As Figure 22.4 shows, system tests check the software from end to end.

FIGURE 22.4
Components of a Web application.

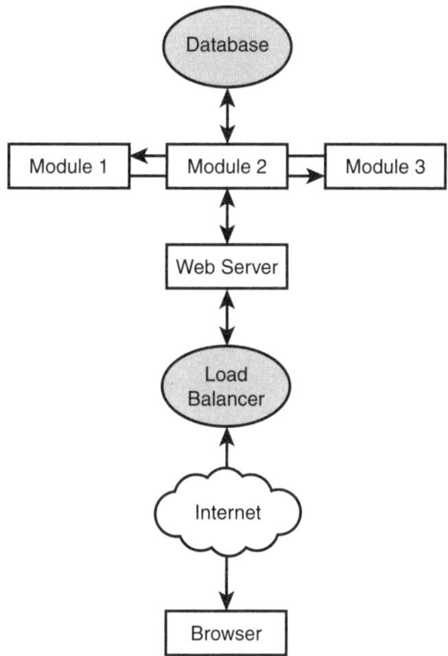

System tests check the entire application, from Web browser to database and everything between. Web application frameworks deploy Web browser software, TCP/IP networking routers, bridges and switches, load balancing routers, Web servers, Web application software modules, and a database. Additional systems may be deployed to provide directory service, media servers to stream audio and video, and messaging services for e-mail.

A mistake test professionals frequently make is to believe they are conducting system tests while they are actually testing a single component of the system. For example, checking that the Web server returns a page is not a system test if the page contains only a static HTML page. Such a test checks the Web server and not all the system components.

System tests are the most difficult of all tests because they require the test to know something of the user goals. Translating user goals into a test agent can be very challenging.

A Web application increases in value as the software enables users to achieve their goals. The goal will be different for each user. Although it may be possible to identify groups of users by their goals, experience shows that understanding a single user's goals and determining how well the Web application got that one user to his or her goals is the best way to determine a Web application's capability to perform and to scale. The test professional is challenged to translate the user goals into a test agent.

Test Agents

The formal way to perform system tests is to define a test agent. A test agent models an individual user's operation of the Web application to achieve an individual goal. A test agent is composed of a checklist, a test process, and a reporting method:

Test agent Component	*Description*
Checklist	Defines conditions and states
Process	Defines transactions needed to perform the checklist
Reports	Notes results after the process and checklist are completed

Suppose a Web application provides travel agents with an on-line order entry service in which they can receive travel brochures from tour operators. The order entry service adds new brochures every spring and removes the prior season's brochures. A test agent for the order entry service simulates a travel agent ordering a current brochure and an outdated brochure. The test agent's job is to guarantee that an operation succeeds or fails.

Building a test agent requires a checklist, a process, and a reporting method. The checklist defines the conditions and states the Web application will achieve. For example, the checklist for a shopping basket application looks like this:

- Brochure order entry service check-list.
- View list of current brochures—how many brochures appear?
- Order a current brochure—does the service provide a confirmation number?
- Order an out-of-date brochure—does the service indicate an error?

Checklists determine the desired Web application state. For example, while testing the Web application to order a current brochure, the Web application state is set to hold the current brochure. Otherwise, the application is in an error state when an out-of-date brochure order is processed.

A test agent process defines the steps needed to initialize the Web application, then to run the Web application through its paces, including going through the checklist. The test agent process deals with transactions. In the travel agent brochure order entry system, these transactions are needed to complete a system test:

1. Initialize the order entry service.
2. Look up a brochure number.
3. Order a brochure.

The transactions require a number of individual steps. For example, transaction 2 requires the test agent to sign in to the order entry service, post a request to show the desired brochure number, confirm that the brochure exists, post a request to order the brochure, and then sign out.

Finally, a test agent must include a reporting method that defines where and in what format the results of the process will be saved for later analysis. The brochure order entry system test agent reports the number of brochures successfully ordered and the number of outdated brochures ordered.

Test agents can be represented in a number of forms. A test agent may be defined on paper and run by a person. A test agent may be a program that drives a Web application. The form is not important. The test agent must define a repeatable means to have a Web application produce a result. The more automated a test agent becomes, the better position a development manager will be in to certify that a Web service ready for users.

With a test agent defined, regression tests are simple. For each new update or maintenance change to the Web application software, the test agent shows the functions that still work and the functions that now fail. Regression tests indicate how close a Web application is to being ready for users. The lower the regression, the sooner the launch.

Developing test agents also provides a faster path to scalability and performance testing. Because a test agent models an individual user's use of a Web service, running multiple copies of the same test agent concurrently makes scalability and performance testing much more simple.

Scalability and Performance Testing

Web services are very different to test than desktop software. At any time a Web service handles 1 to 5000 requests. Learning the performance and scalability characteristics of a Web application under the load of hundreds of users is important for managing software development projects, to build sufficient data centers, and to guarantee a good user experience. The interoperating modules of a Web service often do not show their interdependent nature until loaded with user activity.

There are two ways to analyze a Web application: scalability and performance. By now, common sense tells you that learning one without the other can give you meaningless answers. What good would it be to learn a Web application's ability to serve 1000 users quickly if 100 users receive error pages?

Scalability describes a Web application's capability to serve users under varying levels of load. To measure scalability, run a test agent and measure its time. Then run the same test agent with 5, 50, and 100 concurrent users. Scalability is the function of the measurements.

Scalability measures a Web application's ability to complete a test agent under conditions of load. The test agent is run over and over again. Summarizing the measurements enables a development manager to predict the Web service's capability to serve users under load conditions.

Figure 22.5 shows an example of a scalability test. A single test agent is run on a Web application over and over again. Depending on the cost of running a test agent, experience shows a test agent should be run at least ten times for it to give meaningful results. In Figure 22.5, the top line shows the results of running a test agent. 85% of the time the Web application completed the test agent in less than one second. 10% of the time the test agent completed in less than 6 seconds, and 5% of the time the test agent took 6 or more seconds to finish.

FIGURE 22.5
Scalability of a Web application.

Scalability	<1 second	2-5 seconds	6> seconds
1	85%	10%	5%
50	75%	15%	10%
500	70%	20%	10%
5000	60%	25%	15%

Notice what happens when the Web service is put under load. When 50 users concurrently run the same test agent, the Web service does not perform as well. With 50 users, the same test agent is completed in less than 1 second only 75% of the time. The Web application begins to really suffer when 5000 users begin running the test agent. At 5000 users only 60% will complete the test agent in less than 1 second.

You can extrapolate the scalability results for a Web application after a minimum of data points exist. If the scalability results contained tests at 1 and 50 users, the scalability extrapolation for 5000 users would be meaningless. Running the scalability tests with at least 4 levels of load provides meaningful data points from which extrapolations will be valid.

Performance is a Siamese twin to scalability. Scalability measures a Web application's capability to serve users under conditions of increasing load. Scalability testing assumes that valid test agents completed correctly. Scalability can be blind to the user experience. On the other hand, performance testing measures failures.

Performance testing evaluates a Web application's ability to accurately deliver functions. A performance test agent looks at the results of a test agent to see whether the Web application produced an exceptional result. For example, in the scalability test example shown in Figure 22.5, a performance test shows the percentage of error pages returned under the various conditions of load.

Figure 22.6 shows the performance results of the example Web application whose scalability was profiled in Figure 22.5. The performance results show a different picture of the same Web application. At the 500 and 5000 concurrent user levels, a development manager may still decide to release a Web application to users even though 10% to 15% of users will encounter very slow response times—test agents take 6 or more seconds to complete. Would the development manager still release the Web application looking at the performance test results?

FIGURE 22.6
Performance test agent results.

Performance	<1 second	2-5 seconds	6> seconds
1	1%	5%	7%
50	2%	4%	10%
500	4%	9%	14%
5000	15%	25%	40%

The Web application cannot complete the test agent due to errors 15% of the time when a test agent completes in less than 1 second at the 5000 concurrent user level. Add the 25% value for test agents that complete in 2-5 seconds and the development manager has a good basis for expecting that 40% of the users will encounter errors when 5000 users concurrently load the Web application.

Scalability and performance are measures needed to determine how well a Web service will serve users in production environments. Taken individually, the results may not show the true nature of the Web application. Or even worse, they may show misleading results. Taken together, scalability and performance testing show the true nature of a Web service.

Testing for the Single User

Web applications are very different to test than desktop software. At any time, 1 or 500 users may be accessing a Web application. Each user may have an entirely unique goal. With so many diverse user goals, which test agent should be developed first?

Many developers think testing is not complete until the test agents cover a general cross-section of the user community. Other developers believe high-quality software should be tested against the original design goals of a Web application as defined by a product manager, project marketer, or lead developer. These approaches are all wrong because they test toward the middle.

Testing toward the middle makes large assumptions of how the aggregate group of users will use the Web application and the steps they will take as a group to accomplish their common goal. Web applications are simply not used this way. In reality, each user has an individual goal and method of using a Web application.

Intuit, publishers of the popular Quicken personal finance management software, recognized the distinctiveness of each user early on. Intuit developed the "Follow me home" software testing method. Intuit developers and product managers visited local software retail stores. They waited in the aisles near the Intuit products and watched for a customer to pick up a copy of Quicken. When the customer appeared ready to buy Quicken, the Intuit manager introduced him or herself and asked for permission to follow the customer home to learn the user experience installing and using the Quicken software.

Intuit representatives could have stayed in their offices and made grand speculations about the general types of Quicken users. Instead, they developed user archetypes—prototypical Web application users—based on the real people they met and the experience these users had. The same power can be applied to developing test agents.

The best way to build a test agent is to start with a single user. Choose just one user, watch her use the Web application and learn what steps she expects to use. Then model a test agent against the single user.

The better understood an individual user's needs, the more valuable will be your test agent. Some developers have taken the archetypal user method to heart. They name their archetypes, describe their backgrounds and habits. They give depth to the archetype so the rest of the development team can understand the test agent better.

As an example, consider the archetypal users defined for the Inclusion.net Web application software. In 1997, Inclusion.net developed a Web application to provide collaborative messaging services to geographically disbursed teams in global corporations. Companies such as BP (formerly British Petroleum) used the Web application to build a secure private extranet where BP employees and contractors in the financial auditing groups would exchange ideas and best practices while doing their normal work. Test agents for the BPextranet were designed around these archetypal users:

- Jack—field auditor, 22 years old, just joined BP from Northwestern University, unmarried but has a steady girlfriend, has been using spreadsheet software since high school, open to using new technology if it gets his job done faster, loves motocross and snow skiing.
- Madeline—central office manager, 42 years old, married 15 years with 2 children, came up through the ranks at BP, worked in IT group for 3 years before moving into management, respects established processes but will work the system to bring in technology that improves team productivity.
- Lorette—IT support, 27 years old, wears 2 pagers and 1 mobile phone, works very long hours maintaining systems, does system training for new employees, loves to go on training seminars in exotic locations.

The test agents developed for Jack concentrate on accessing and manipulating data. Jack often needs to find previously stored spreadsheets, so the first test agent developed signed in to the Web application and used the search functions to locate a document. The test agent modified the document and checked to make sure the modifications were stored correctly.

The test agent developed for Madeline concentrated on usage data. The first test agent signed in to the Web application using Madeline's high-level security clearance. This gives permission to run usage reports to see which of her team members is making most use of the Web application. That will be important to Madeline when performance reviews are needed. The test agent also tried to sign in as Jack and access the same reports. If the Web application performed correctly, only Madeline would have access to the reports.

Lorette's test agents concentrated on accessing data. When Lorette is away from the office on a training seminar, she still needs access to the Web application as though she were in the office. The test agent uses a remote login capability to access the needed data.

Understanding the archetypes is the key to making the test agents intelligent. For example, a test agent for Lorette may behave more persistently than a test agent for Madeline. If a test agent tries to make a remote connection that fails, the test agent for Lorette would try again and then switch to a different access number. Archetype behavior makes a test agent intelligent.

Using archetypes to describe a user is more efficient and more accurate than making broad generalizations about the nature of a Web application's users. Archetypes make it easier to develop test agents modeled after each user's individual goals and methods of using a Web application.

Building Maintainable Test Agents with TestMaker

Many developers are skeptical when evaluating commercial test tools. "Why should my company pay all this money for a tool," they think, "with a new set of instructions or a language to learn, when I could just write the test agent myself?"

The problem with writing a test agent comes down to one word: maintenance. Just like every other software application, the test agent needs to be maintained. Master developers ask themselves, "Who will maintain the code when I am no longer here?"

A brief, unscientific survey of Silicon Valley developers who write their own test agents finds that maintaining test agents grows from a minor irritation to a huge problem. The typical developer's first attempt at writing test agents usually results in a fairly robust set of Java classes or Visual Basic methods that issues SOAP requests to a SOAP-enabled Web server and does some simple analysis of the results. Writing a test agent consists of writing Java code that sequentially calls the correct test object.

For example, an agent that reads through an online discussion forum message-base looks like this:

1. Ask for the catalog of messages (which includes URLs to the discussion messages).
2. Randomly read a discussion message.
3. If the message has a reply, then read the reply message.
4. Repeat step 3 until there are no more reply messages.

The resulting test agent is a small Java application. At one point, though, the format for the URL format for the first page of the site changed. The test agent needed maintenance.

As a matter of fact, every new change to the Web service required some subtle change in the test agent. Each and every change brought the developer back to the test agent code. Although the test objects—getting Web pages, signing in, testing for the correct return values—stayed the same from test agent to test agent, the calling sequence was always different.

Neither Java nor Visual Basic defines a common way to define the calling sequence of Java objects. Every programmer has to invent a way to call objects in a particular sequence. As a result, many programmers invent a simple scripting language inside their code. Some of the more advanced applications even expose a scripting language to users.

In the whole of computing there are literally thousands of applications with their own scripting languages.

Looking at the test agent code, does it make sense to add a scripting language to assemble test agents from a library of test objects? The test objects perform the individual test routines—routines that rarely need to change. And a scripting language is used to assemble and control the parameters of the objects—a scripting language that is easier to alter for different levels and types of Web application testing.

The benefit to all developers, QA managers, and IT managers is that a programmer writes the more labor-intensive test objects *only once* and adapts the scripting language as needed. The scripting language enables engineers more comfortable with scripts than hard-core test object code to write their own test agents. The scripts are readable by mere human beings and can easily be shared and swapped with others.

The key to making Web application test agents in this form lies with the ability of scripting languages to provide a common reference for the way notations, variables, and program flow are stated.

Script Languages and Test Agents

A script language enables developers to rapidly develop and easily maintain test agents. A script language also permits regular expression evaluation, program flow control, and code reuse. As an example, consider a test agent written with TestMaker that monitors weather conditions at a major airport and signals an alert when the temperature becomes too cold for certain equipment to function properly.

The Airport Weather Alert Agent in Listing 22.1 learns the weather from a weather service specific to airports. A second Web service handles signaling the alert by sending an email message to a manager.

LISTING 22.1 Airport Weather Alert Agent

```
# Airport Weather Alert Agent
#
# Demonstration of an intelligent test agent
# This agent checks the temperature at San Jose International Airport
# by communicating with a SOAP-based Web service.
# If the temperature is below 50 degrees, the agent signals an
# alert by using a Web service to send an email message.
#
# by Frank Cohen (fcohen@pushtotest.com)
# (c) 2001 All rights reserved.
#
```

LISTING 22.1 continued

```
# This script was written for Java Web services by SAMS Publishing.
# Details on this agent are at: http://www.pushtotest.com

from com.pushtotest.tool.protocolhandler import Header
from com.pushtotest.tool.protocolhandler import Body
from com.pushtotest.tool.protocolhandler import SOAPProtocol
from com.pushtotest.tool.protocolhandler import SOAPBody
from com.pushtotest.tool.protocolhandler import SOAPHeader
from com.pushtotest.tool.response import Response
from java.lang import Long

# Find the <return> element, which will hold the
# temperature for the defined airport.
# Define XML elements we're looking for, in this
# case we are looking for a single <return> value

# getReturnElement: Returns the contents of an XML element
# response_doc = xml document
# rval = Element tag
# rvalend = Element tag terminator

def getReturnElement( response_doc, rval, rvalend ):
    s1 = response_doc.find( rval )          # find the start of the element
    if s1>0:
        s1 = s1 + len( rval )               # skip the element tag
        s2 = response_doc.find( rvalend )   # find the end of the element
        return response_doc[s1:s2]          # return the <return> value
    else:
        return 999;
        print( "Response was not valid: Count not find " + rval )

# Use a Send-an-email Web service to send an alert message

def sendAlert( ts, toaddress, fromaddress ):

    # Construct the body of the message
    msg = "Airport Weather Alert Agent noticed the temperature\r\n"
    msg = msg + "is too cold for safe conditions.\r\n"
    msg = msg + "\r\n"
    msg = msg + ts + "\r\n"
    msg = msg + "\r\n"
    msg = msg + "[Note] This message was generated from an intelligent\r\n"
    msg = msg + "agent described in the book Java Web services, published\r\n"
    msg = msg + "by SAMS Publishing Inc. For details see:\r\n"
    msg = msg + "http://www.pushtotest.com"

    protocol2 = SOAPProtocol()
    body2 = SOAPBody()
    body2.addParameter("ToAddress", toaddress )
```

LISTING 22.1 continued

```
    body2.addParameter("FromAddress", fromaddress )
    body2.addParameter("ASubject", "Alert: Temperature too cold [TestMaker
Agent]" )
    body2.addParameter("MsgBody", "Hi" )
    body2.setTarget("urn:EmailIPortTypeInft-IEmailService#SendMail")
    body2.setMethod("SendMail")

    protocol2.setHost("webservices.matlus.com")
    protocol2.setPath("/scripts/emailwebservice.dll/soap/IEmailservice")
    protocol2.setPort(80)
    protocol2.setBody(body)

    response2 = protocol2.connect()

    print ("Email alert sent.")

# Main routine for Airport Weather Alert Agent

print("Airport Weather Alert Agent")
print("")

# Make a SOAP call to a temperature service hosted by
# Cape Clear (http://www.capeclear.com)

protocol = SOAPProtocol()
body = SOAPBody()
body.addParameter("getTemperature","KSJC")
body.setTarget("capeconnect:AirportWeather:com.capeclear.weatherstation.Station"
)
body.setMethod("getTemperature")

protocol.setHost("www.capescience.com")
protocol.setPath("/ccgw/GWXmlServlet")
protocol.setPort(80)
protocol.setBody(body)

response = protocol.connect()

# Report how long it took to make the SOAP call

print("")
print("Timing statistics to find temperature")
print("Total: " + Long(response.getTotalTime()).toString())
print("Data : " + Long(response.getDataTime()).toString())
print("Setup: " + Long(response.getSetupTime()).toString())
print("")

# Get the response from the call and determine the temperature value
```

LISTING 22.1 continued

```
r = response.toString()
ts = getReturnElement( r, '<return  xsi:type="xsd:string">', '</return>' )

print "The temperature is: " + ts[ ts.find('is '), ts.find(' F') ]

# now isolate just the temperature reading
u0 = 'is '
u1 = ts.find( 'is ' ) + len( u0 )
u2 = ts.find( ' F' )
u3 = ts[ u1:u2 ]
temperature = float( u3 )

if temperature < 50:
    # Temperatures less than 50 degrees are considered too cold to operate
    # so send an alert message to a system operator

    print "Warning: Sending alert message (temperature < 50)"
    sendAlert( "this is the body", "info@pushtotest.com", "info@pushtotest.net"
)

    print "Warning send."
    print "Agent ending."

else:
    # Temperature is fine.

    print "Temperature satisfactory."
    print "Agent ending."
```

The Airport Weather Alert Agent breaks down into several components. First, the agent uses a special airport weather Web service. The agent parses the response document to find the temperature reading. If the temperature falls below 50° Fahrenheit the agent uses a second Web service to send an e-mail alert message.

The agent uses TestMaker's `SOAPProtocol` object to communicate with the weather Web service. Cape Clear (`http://www.capeclear.com`) provides the Web service. Details on the weather Web service are found on the Cape Clear Web site at: `http://www.capescience.com/webservices/airportweather/index.html`. Cape Clear publishes the WSDL definition for this call, which gives the URI to the Web service and the request and response parameters to use:

```
protocol = SOAPProtocol()
protocol.setHost("www.capescience.com")
protocol.setPath("/ccgw/GWXmlServlet")
protocol.setPort(80)
```

Although the `SOAPProtocol` object handles SOAP specifically, TestMaker also implements protocol handlers for generic HTTP transactions and TestMaker may be extended to handle FTP, SMTP, and IMAP protocols with little effort. This has great benefits for code reuse.

The `SOAPBody` object builds the XML request document that will be sent to the SOAP host. The request document is fairly simple. The request sends an airport code and receives the temperature:

```
body = SOAPBody()
body.addParameter("getTemperature","KSJC")
body.setTarget("capeconnect:AirportWeather:com.capeclear.weatherstation.Station"
)
body.setMethod("getTemperature")
```

Actually, the Web service reports on weather at all airports and airfields that have a registered ICAO (International Civil Aviation Organization) number. The agent sends the ICAO designation—for example, KSJC identifies San Jose International airport in California—and receives one of several items.

The weather service has methods for retrieving various weather items, including `getWind()` and `getTemperature()`, which both return a string. There is also a method, `getSummary()`, which returns a complex object, the fields of which an agent can inspect. The Airport Weather Alert Agent is solely concerned with temperature, so it uses the `getTemperature()` method.

The U.S. government's National Weather Service provides the weather service data. The data is freely available and reusable, but may not become proprietary in its raw form. Although the test agent is set to find San Jose weather, a publicly available Web site finds any local airport designation: `http://www.ar-group.com/icaoiata.htm`.

Next the script pairs the body object with the `SOAPProtocol` object. An unlimited number of body objects may be created and individually used with a `SOAPProtocol` object. This is really handy when the Web service offers many options. You could create several body objects and use each as appropriate:

```
protocol.setBody(body)
```

The `connect()` method of the `SOAPProtocol` object assembles the request document from the body object, makes the HTTP call to the host, creates a response object, and returns the response document from the host to the response object:

```
response = protocol.connect()
```

The TestMaker object library is fully threaded. So multiple requests may be made at the same time, simulating real-world use of the Web service. This simple agent could be run in 100 threads concurrently. To the Web service it would appear that 100 users have requested the weather.

The `SOAPProtocol` object implements a set of timers so the agent may understand and act on the time it takes to set up and call the host. Both times are given in milliseconds) For this agent, the time is not important; the temperature concerns the agent greatly:

```
# Report how long it took to make the SOAP call

print("")
print("Timing statistics to find temperature")
print("Total: " + Long(response.getTotalTime()).toString())
print("Data : " + Long(response.getDataTime()).toString())
print("Setup: " + Long(response.getSetupTime()).toString())
print("")
```

The agent uses the `getReturnElement` function to find the temperature value returned from the Web service call:

```
ts = getReturnElement( r, '<return  xsi:type="xsd:string">', '</return>' )
```

The WSDL for the weather service indicates that the return value will appear in the XML response document in the `<return>` element and the value will be a `String` data type. The `getReturnElement` function returns a string for the found element. For example, the `ts` value after `getReturnElement` is called may be set to:

```
The Temperature at San Jose, San Jose International Airport, CA, United States
is 48.9 F (9.4 C)
```

The scripting language uses indentation and the `def` keyword to define the `getReturnElement`. Think of the indentation as `{ }` markers in Java:

```
# Find the <return> element, which will hold the
# temperature for the defined airport.
# Define XML elements we're looking for, in this
# case we are looking for a single <return> value

# getReturnElement: Returns the contents of an XML element
# response_doc = xml document
# rval = Element tag
# rvalend = Element tag terminator

def getReturnElement( response_doc, rval, rvalend ):
    s1 = response_doc.find( rval )          # find the start of the element
    if s1>0:
        s1 = s1 + len( rval )               # skip the element tag
        s2 = response_doc.find( rvalend )   # find the end of the element
```

```
        return response_doc[s1:s2]          # return the <return> value
    else:
        return 999;
        print( "Response was not valid: Count not find " + rval )
```

Note

Experienced developers may notice similarities between the TestMaker scripting language and Python. TestMaker uses Jython—a version of Python implemented in Java—to implement its scripting language. Details on Jython are at `http://www.jython.org`.

With the `ts` variable holding the weather service temperature for San Jose airport, the agent may now parse the actual temperature value. The temperature variable is a float value of the actual temperature at the airport:

```
print "The temperature is: " + ts[ ts.find('is '), ts.find(' F') ]

# now isolate just the temperature reading
u0 = 'is '
u1 = ts.find( 'is ' ) + len( u0 )
u2 = ts.find( ' F' )
u3 = ts[ u1:u2 ]
temperature = float( u3 )
```

When the temperature falls below 50° Fahrenheit, the agent sends an alert message. The `sendAlert` function uses a second Web service to handle sending the alert:

```
if temperature < 50:
    # Temperatures less than 50 degrees are considered too cold to operate
    # so send an alert message to a system operator

    print "Warning: Sending alert message (temperature < 50)"
    sendAlert( "this is the body", "info@pushtotest.com", "info@pushtotest.net"
)

    print "Warning send."
    print "Agent ending."

else:
    # Temperature is fine.

    print "Temperature satisfactory."
    print "Agent ending."
```

First the sendAlert function constructs the body of the message to send:

```
def sendAlert( ts, toaddress, fromaddress ):

    # Construct the body of the message
    msg = "Airport Weather Alert Agent noticed the temperature\r\n"
    msg = msg + "is too cold for safe conditions.\r\n"
    msg = msg + "\r\n"
    msg = msg + ts + "\r\n"
    msg = msg + "\r\n"
    msg = msg + "[Note] This message was generated from an intelligent\r\n"
    msg = msg + "agent described in the book Java Web services, published\r\n"
    msg = msg + "by SAMS Publishing Inc. For details see:\r\n"
    msg = msg + "http://www.pushtotest.com"
```

Then the sendAlert function constructs a second `SOAPProtocol` object to communicate with the e-mail-sending Web service:

```
    protocol2 = SOAPProtocol()
    body2 = SOAPBody()
    body2.addParameter("ToAddress", toaddress )
    body2.addParameter("FromAddress", fromaddress )
    body2.addParameter("ASubject", "Alert: Temperature too cold [TestMaker
Agent]" )
    body2.addParameter("MsgBody", "Hi" )
    body2.setTarget("urn:EmailIPortTypeInft-IEmailService#SendMail")
    body2.setMethod("SendMail")
```

The WSDL definition for the e-mail-sending Web service is found at `http://www.xmethods.org/detail.html?id=97`:

```
    protocol2.setHost("webservices.matlus.com")
    protocol2.setPath("/scripts/emailwebservice.dll/soap/IEmailservice")
    protocol2.setPort(80)
    protocol2.setBody(body)
```

Simply sending the request document is all that is needed to initiate the e-mail message:

```
    response2 = protocol2.connect()

    print ("Email alert sent.")
```

A more prudent test agent may test the `response2` object to make sure the Web service responds with an e-mail-completed status.

The Airport Weather Alert Agent shows how a script language enables developers to rapidly develop and easily maintain test agents. The TestMaker script language also permits regular expression evaluation, program flow control, and code reuse.

Monitoring Web Services for Service Level Guarantees

So far this chapter has discussed test issues. In reality, an intelligent test agent is useful for testing and monitoring. After a Web service goes into a production environment the test agent continues to run. When the Web service is "live" the same test agents monitor a Web service for problems and availability. The test agent may send email messages, pager messages, or otherwise sound an alarm when a Web service fails. Intermittent problems are also ideal for the scrutiny of a Web services test agent. The logging from a Web services test agent becomes the ideal proof of meeting a Service Level Agreement (SLA.)

Resources

The following resources are related to topics discussed in this chapter:

- TestMaker, a free open-source utility for testing SOAP-based Web services for scalability and performance, `http://www.pushtotest.com`
- SoapClient maintains a concise list of Web services resources, `http://www.soapclient.com/Resources.html`
- Cape Clear CapeStudio is a graphical tool for working with SOAP and WSDL resources, `http://www.capeclear.com`
- Web Services Definition Language (WSDL) specification, `http://www.w3.org/TR/wsdl`
- List of publicly available Web services, `http://www.xmethods.org/`
- SOAP v1.1 specification, `http://www.w3.org/TR/SOAP/`
- Microsoft SOAP resource, `http://msdn.microsoft.com/nhp/Default.asp?contentid=28000523`

Summary

Programming and delivering production-quality Web services is made easier and faster when you test quality under the stress of multiple concurrent requests. The scripting language and test objects in the open-source TestMaker utility can offer you a way to make your work more productive when you test SOAP-based Web services.

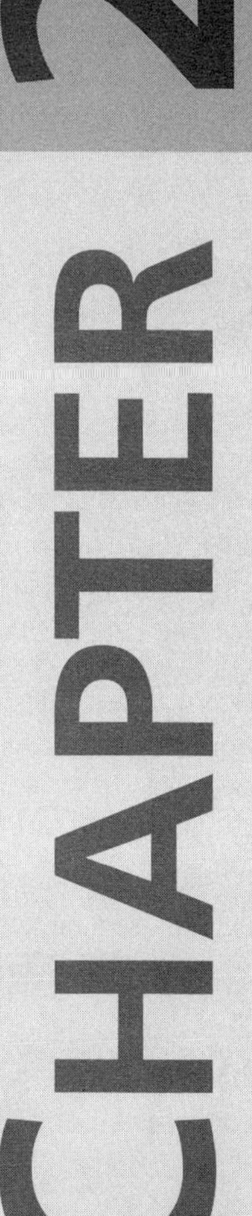

Tools for Building Web Services

by Arthur Ryman

IN THIS CHAPTER

By now you might be starting to feel overwhelmed by all the new XML specifications and Java APIs involved in Web services. The good news is that you can reap the benefits of Web services without becoming an expert in all the Web services plumbing. Web services tools that take care of the plumbing for you and let you focus on solving your business problems are now available. Of course you'll still need some understanding of the principles behind Web services to design a solution that satisfies your performance, scalability, security, and other requirements, but you won't need to be concerned with the bytes and angle brackets. I hope this chapter will prove to you that Web services development is easy, provided that you have the right tools.

This chapter examines the new development tasks that are associated with Web services and discusses the tools required for each of these tasks. For purposes of illustration, I have drawn examples from IBM's new WebSphere Studio Application Developer (see `http://www.ibm.com/software/ad/studioappdev/`) tool suite, which is based on the Eclipse project (see `http://www.eclipse.org`), a Java Open Source tool integration framework.

My selection of WebSphere Studio Application Developer is based on my role in its development as the architect for Web services tools. However, this chapter is neither a tutorial on WebSphere Studio Application Developer nor is it a comparison of tools from different vendors, because that would be inappropriate. Only a neutral party can give you an unbiased comparison. Rather, my goal is to discuss where tools can help in Web services development and to illustrate their use with some real examples taken from WebSphere Studio Application Developer. This discussion should provide you with a framework for evaluating Web services development tools and environments from other vendors.

I have limited the discussion in this chapter to tools that support the specifications that are of greatest relevance at present, namely XML Schema (XSD), Simple Object Access Protocol (SOAP), Web services Description Language (WSDL), Universal Description, Discovery, and Integration (UDDI), and Web Services Inspection Language (WS-Inspection). XML schema is the standard way to describe data in XML and is used in WSDL. SOAP, WSDL, UDDI, and WS-Inspection were jointly developed by several key vendors, including IBM and Microsoft, and are becoming both de facto and de jure standards.

Finally, I have limited coverage of Web services runtimes to Apache SOAP (see `http://xml.apache.org/soap`), because it is Java Open Source, runs on both Apache Tomcat and IBM WebSphere, and is supported by WebSphere Studio Application Developer.

Overview of Web Services Development Tasks

Web services technology adds some new tasks to Java development. It is useful to organize these tasks accordingly to a life cycle, and to examine the tools required for each stage in the life cycle. This section is a brief overview of the new tasks. This will be followed by a detailed discussion of the tools.

In this chapter, I'll use the following classification of Web services development life cycle tasks:

- Provide
    - Create
    - Deploy
    - Test
    - Publish
- Consume
    - Discover
    - Access

The two major tasks are Provide and Consume. The Provide task produces new Web services, and the Consume task assembles them into new applications. These two tasks do form a cycle because Web services can be assembled into new Web services. Indeed, Web services may become the dominant component model in distributed computing. In the future it may be commonplace to include Web services interfaces in new applications. The end of the Consume task, therefore, naturally leads into the beginning of the Provide task.

Provide

The purpose of the Provide task is to produce a new Web Service. To accomplish this, the developer must create a component that implements the Web service, deploy it on an application server, test it, and publish it.

Create

The Create task consists of developing the Web Service implementation component—for example, a Java class or Enterprise JavaBean (EJB)—its WSDL, and any helper classes required to perform mapping between XML and Java types. The sequence in which these artifacts are created depends on the project requirements and the development process used. The Create task can be further classified as Bottom-Up, Top-Down, and Meet-In-The-Middle to take into account the development sequence. This terminology refers to the level of abstraction of the development artifacts. The WSDL is at a higher level of abstraction than the component that implements it. The WSDL is therefore regarded as being at the Top of the Web service, and its implementation is at the Bottom.

Bottom-Up development starts with the implementation component, such as a Java class, and proceeds to the development of its WSDL. In many cases, tools can automatically generate the WSDL from the implementation component. Bottom-Up development is therefore very important because it provides a simple path to rapidly turn existing components into Web services. This ease of creating Web services from existing components will help drive the widespread adoption of Web services technology.

In Top-Down development, work starts from the WSDL interface and proceeds towards its implementation. There are two reasons why Top-Down development might be used. The first reason is that the WSDL may already exist and the developer's job is to implement it. This is a very important scenario because standard interfaces are likely to be defined for key Web services. A good example of this is the UDDI interface itself. Industry associations are likely to define standard WSDL interfaces for vertical applications. For example, a travel industry association might define a standard WSDL interface for requesting flight schedules. Each airline would then implement this interface. The second reason for using Top-Down development is that it is a good software engineering practice. The resulting Web service is likely to be easier to use if it has a cleanly designed interface. In either case, Top-Down development requires new interface design skills and tools to support them. After the interface has been developed, tools can automatically generate a skeleton for the implementation component.

Meet-in-the-Middle development is used when the WSDL interface and its implementation component have been developed independently. The task here is to map the interface to the implementation. Mapping is required both at the operation and datatype level. Tools that allow the mapping to be specified and that can automatically generate mapping code are likely to appear in the near future.

Deploy

The Deploy task installs the Web service on an application server where it can be invoked by clients. Deployment may involve the creation of descriptors or other configuration artifacts for the Web service, and the installation and configuration of supporting runtime components. Ideally, tools should automate deployment as much as possible because a Web service may have to be redeployed many times in the course of its development.

The point at which the Create task ends and the Deploy task begins may depend on the runtime. For example, consider the problem of mapping between Java and XML types. Code to perform the mapping might be developed in the Create task or it might be automatically generated as part of the Deploy task. Also, WSDL might be developed in the Create task or be automatically generated at runtime.

Test

The Test task consists of exercising the operations of the Web service. In principle, it is possible to test a Web service by dynamically interpreting its WSDL. The Test task is related to the Access task since another way to test a Web service is to access it via a proxy. Tools can dynamically test the proxy or can generate a sample application that uses the proxy. Testing can also be aided by tools that monitor and validate message traffic.

Publish

After a Web service is functioning correctly, its WSDL must be made available to potential consumers. The Publish task consists of publishing the WSDL in various formats. Publishing may involve creating entries in a UDDI business registry. However, UDDI does not typically store the complete WSDL, but instead stores references to WSDL stored in other locations such as XML repositories or application servers. Publishing therefore may also involve storing artifacts in repositories.

In addition to UDDI registries, application servers themselves may contain information about the Web services they host by listing the Web services in WS-Inspection documents. Publishing may involve generating and updating this information, or the runtime may automatically generate this information. Tools that automate the Publish task are available and are evolving with the standards.

Consume

The Consume task consists of assembling available Web services into new applications and Web services. This task includes discovering Web services and accessing them.

Discover

The Discover task consists of locating published information about Web services. The two main sources of published Web service information are registries such as UDDI, and applications servers that use specifications such as WS-Inspection to describe their hosted Web services. Tools for exploring and querying these sources are available. Powerful search engines are likely to emerge in the future.

Access

The Access task consists of developing code that can invoke the operations of the Web service. Tools that generate client proxies from WSDL are available. Accessing a Web service through a client proxy reduces the application development task to standard programming techniques; the main difference is that the client proxy can throw exceptions that arise as a consequence of distributed computing.

As already mentioned, the Test task is closely related to the Access task. It is often desirable to test a Web Service before incorporating it into your application. Testing helps you to validate a Web service's operation and to understand its semantics. The same test tools that are used when creating Web services can be applied to accessing Web services.

A Quick Tour of Web Services Tools

The preceding discussion is fine in theory, but how do these tools work in practice? To answer that question, I use WebSphere Studio Application Developer to show you how to develop a Web service. In the rest of this chapter I'll illustrate the tools by developing a simple Web application that gives Canadian travelers weather information about their U.S. destinations. Because Canada uses the Celsius temperature scale and the U.S. uses the Fahrenheit scale, our first task is to develop a Web service that performs temperature conversion.

I have used this temperature conversion example in other contexts and am sometimes criticized by those who claim this is not a convincing Web service. Temperature conversion is a simple mathematical function that does not require access to remote data as does, for example, currency conversion. Currency conversion is a much more convincing Web service because it requires access to a remote database of changing currency conversion rates. Critics point out that it is much more efficient to make the temperature conversion function a reusable library so the Web application can call it directly. That is certainly true, and my initial motivation for using it as an example was simply that I was getting tired of using Hello World. However, on further reflection, I think that there is a deeper issue that is worth discussing.

Making even simple functions into Web services does have some merits. For example, a Web service can be invoked from any programming language, whereas a library is usually restricted to a single language or a tightly coupled set of languages that share a common runtime. A Web service can be hosted on a single machine, so maintenance is easier, whereas you have to distribute updates of a library to each machine that uses it.

On balance, I do agree that temperature conversion is too simple to be a convincing Web service, but it may make sense for more complex functions. After all, network and processor performance continue to improve, so the efficiency issue is becoming less of a concern and the benefits of Web services may begin to make them a viable alternative to traditional software libraries. Nevertheless, here I am using temperature conversion just to keep the example simple.

Creating the `TemperatureConverter` Web Service

You start by developing the Java class `TemperatureConverter`, which has public methods for each of the operations in your planned service. The operations convert between the temperature scales and also report absolute zero. WebSphere Studio Application Developer has a modern, integrated Java development environment that includes a Java editor, a class browser, a debugger, and many of the advanced capabilities that Java programmers have come to expect. Figure 23.1 shows `TemperatureConverter` open in an editor.

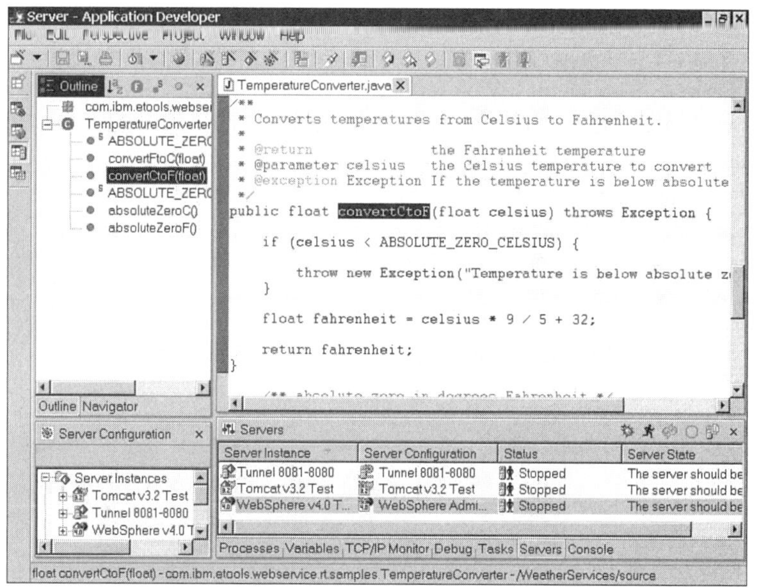

FIGURE 23.1
`TemperatureConverter.java` open in an editor.

Note the Outline in Figure 23.1, which shows the structure of the `TemperatureConverter` class which is being edited. The user interface of WebSphere Studio Application Developer is based on *editors* and *views*, which are grouped into *perspectives*. There are many predefined perspectives, for example, for Java, Debug, Web, XML, Database, and so on, and the user can modify these or create new ones. Each perspective contains several views which can each be freely moved or removed, and new views can be added. Multiple editors can be open at the same time. There are many built-in views and editors, and users can develop their own using the built-in Plug-in Development Environment. The most common views are Outline, which shows a content tree for the currently active editor; Navigator, which shows a file tree for all the projects; and Tasks, which lists error messages, bookmarks, and other file annotations.

Java classes can be developed in several types of projects. Here I've created a Web project named `WeatherServices` to contain the Web services. I've also created a second Web project named `WeatherApp` to contain the Web application that uses the services. WebSphere Studio Application Developer enables you to manage multiple application servers and add Web projects to them. There is a built-in instance of WebSphere, and you can also use externally installed instances of WebSphere and Tomcat. To illustrate this flexibility, I'll run the `WeatherServices` project in the built-in instance of WebSphere on port 8080, and the `WeatherApp` project in an external instance of Tomcat on port 8082.

Deploying the Class as a Web Service

Your next step is to deploy the class as a Web service. WebSphere Studio Application Developer handles most Web services development tasks through easy-to-use wizards. Simply select the implementation class and launch the Web Service wizard. Here you use the wizard to deploy, test, and publish the temperature conversion service. Figure 23.2 shows the Start page of the wizard with the selected tasks checked.

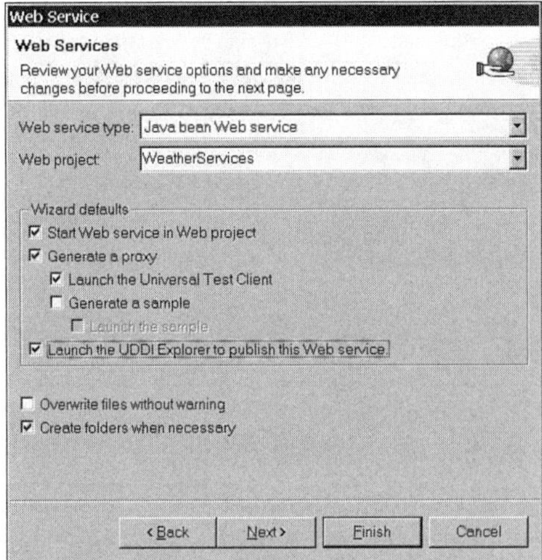

FIGURE 23.2
Web Service Wizard Start page.

WebSphere Studio Application Developer offers several ways to test a service. Here you'll generate a client proxy and test it with the Universal Test Client. The wizard has many options which can be modified in the pages that are presented by clicking the Next button, but here just accept the defaults and click Finish. The wizard performs the following steps:

- Deploy task:
    1. Adds the `WeatherServices` project to an application server configuration if it is not already part of one. By default, when you created the Web project it was added to the built-in instance of WebSphere.
    2. Installs the Apache SOAP runtime in the application server if it has not already been installed.
    3. Configures the Apache SOAP servlets in the `WeatherServices` project if this has not already been done.
    4. Generates Java classes for mapping between the XML types and the Java types in the service. In this example, no classes are generated because the service uses only primitive types, which the runtime already knows how to handle.
    5. Generates an Apache SOAP deployment descriptor (ISD file) for the service and adds it to the configuration.
    6. Generates the WSDL for the service. The WSDL is split into two files (service and binding) that conform to the UDDI Best Practices recommendation.
    7. Starts the application server to make the service available for use.

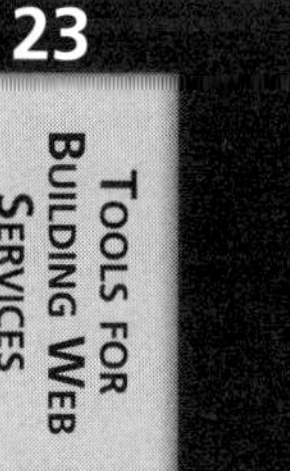

- Test task:
    1. Generates a Java client proxy.
    2. Launches a Web browser to run the Universal Test Client against the proxy. You can now start testing the service.
- Publish task:
    1. Launches the UDDI Explorer. You can now access a UDDI registry and publish the service.

Figure 23.3 shows the Universal Test Client for testing the service. Note that WebSphere Studio Application Developer includes an embedded Web browser, but the test client can run from any Web browser. The Universal Test Client is a Web application that runs on the application server where the proxy is installed and can be used to test any Java class or EJB. You select operations on the proxy and enter input values to test the service. Here, the operation `convertCtoF`, which converts a Celsius temperature (for example, 20) to Fahrenheit (for example, 68), has just been tested.

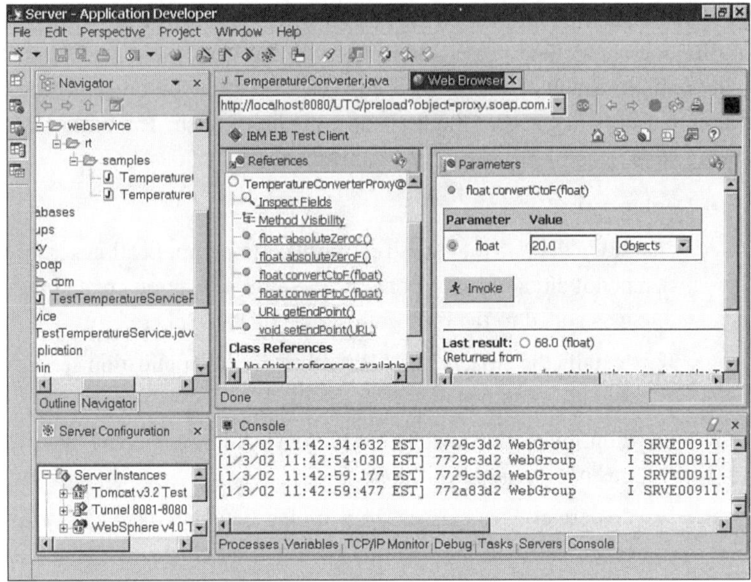

FIGURE 23.3
Universal Test Client testing the `Temperature-Converter` *Service.*

Figure 23.4 shows the UDDI Explorer, which is also a Web application. However, the UDDI Explorer is hosted in a built-in servlet engine which, in this example, is running on port 1078. The UDDI Explorer is being accessed here with an external Web browser, but the embedded Web browser could also be used. You enter some additional information, such as service description and classification, to publish the service in the UDDI registry.

As you can see, the wizard automated many of the tasks. Additional user input was required to test the service and to publish it.

Creating the Web Application

The preceding example illustrated the Provide task, which results in a running, published Web service. Now it's time to consider the Consume task. Continuing with the application, you next need to start working on the Web application that accesses the service. Your first task is to find the WSDL and import it into the `WeatherApp` project. Of course, you could cheat and simply copy the WSDL from the `WeatherServices` project, but in general you'll be using services that are hosted elsewhere. Therefore, you'll use the UDDI Explorer again to search for the service you just published and import its WSDL into the `WeatherApp` project. Figure 23.5 shows the UDDI Explorer, this time importing the WSDL.

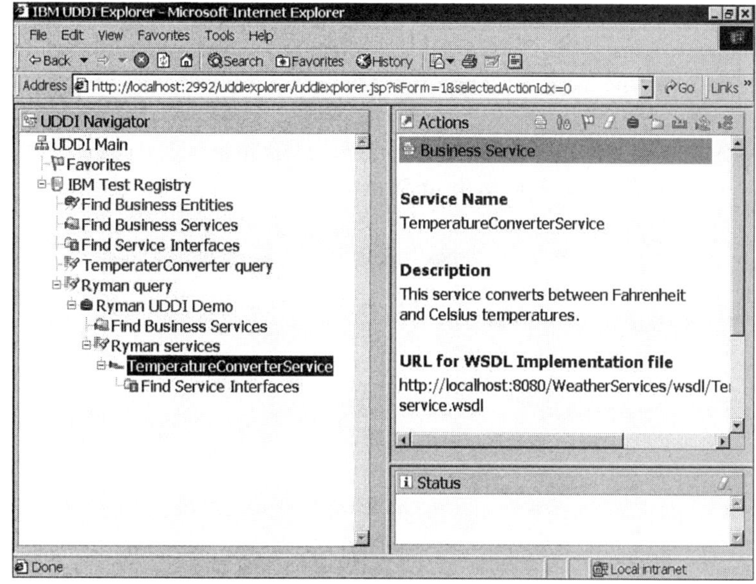

FIGURE 23.4
The UDDI Explorer publishing the `Temperature-Converter` *Web service.*

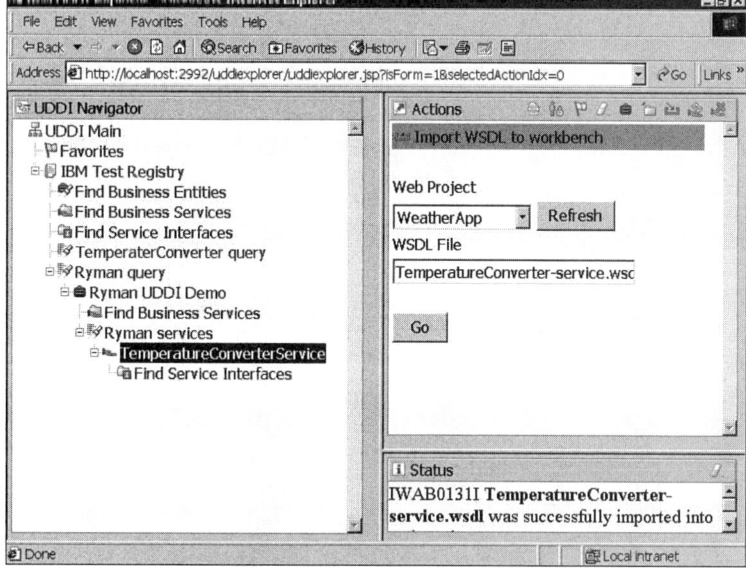

FIGURE 23.5
UDDI Explorer importing the `Temperature-Converter` *WSDL.*

Now that you have the WSDL, you can access the service. Select the WSDL and launch the Web Service Client wizard. Figure 23.6 shows the wizard Start page. Here you choose to generate a client proxy and to test it by generating a sample application instead of using the Universal Test Client. The sample application is more useful in this context because it gives you a head start on developing your own application. You can copy the code that invokes the proxy from it.

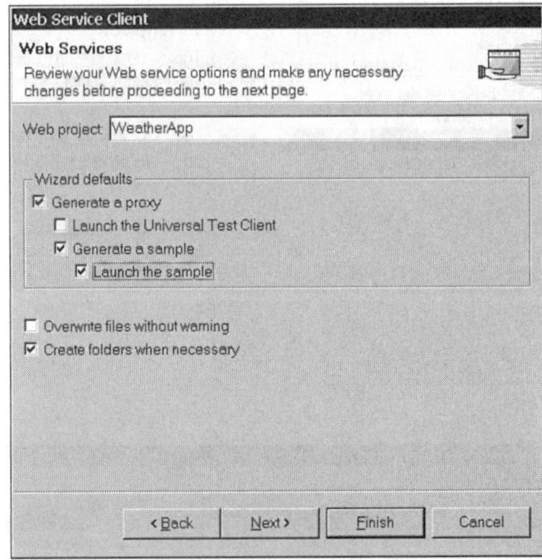

FIGURE 23.6
Web service client wizard Start page.

Again, you can simply click Finish. The wizard performs the following actions:

1. Adds the WeatherApp project to an application server configuration if it is not in one yet. As mentioned above, you previously added this project to the Tomcat configuration.
2. Installs the SOAP client runtime in the Web application if it has not been previously installed.
3. Generates the proxy.
4. Generates any required XML-to-Java mapping code. In this case you are using simple types, so no mapping code is generated.
5. Generates the JSP sample application.
6. Starts the application server.
7. Launches the sample application. You can now start testing.

Figure 23.7 shows the sample application running in the embedded Web browser. The `convertFtoC` operation has just been tested

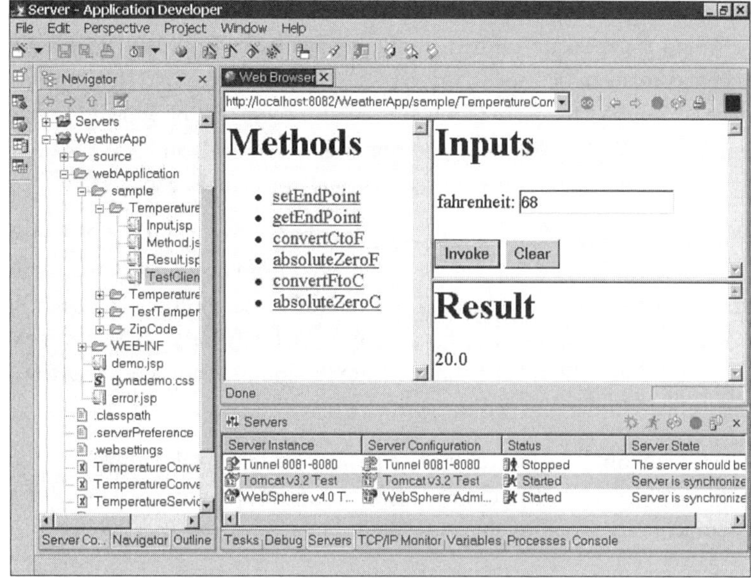

FIGURE 23.7
The Universal Test Client testing the `TemperatureConverter` service proxy.

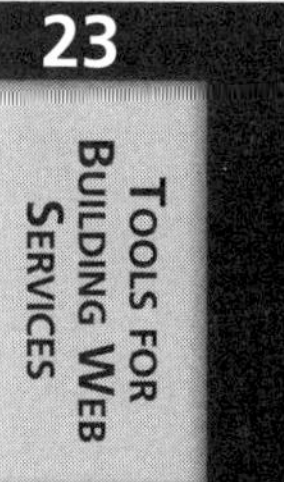

This concludes the quick tour. You have now seen a brief glimpse of Web services tools for the Create, Deploy, Test, Publish, Discover, and Access tasks. These will be discussed in greater detail in the following sections.

Tools for Creating Web Services

This section continues the discussion of tools for creating Web services by exploring the Top-Down, Bottom-Up, and Meet-in-the-Middle approaches, as well as examining how to create simple data-oriented Web services directly from SQL statements.

Top-Down Development

Top-Down development starts by developing the WSDL. As mentioned earlier, Top-Down development normally occurs when standard interfaces are required. For example, an industry association might define a standard interface—for example, to request flight schedules—and publish it. Service providers, such as airlines, would then implement the standard interface so that applications, such as travel agents, would need to handle only one interface as opposed to one from each provider.

A WSDL description of a Web service includes XSD descriptions of the data that is transmitted in requests and responses. It is therefore useful to discuss tools for authoring both WSDL and XSD. Because WSDL and XSD are XML vocabularies, standard XML editors can be used. Many XML editors can provide additional user assistance if the schema for the document being edited is available. Both WSDL and XSD have XSD schemas that can be used to drive such editors. But beyond treating WSDL and XSD like generic valid XML, there is much scope for tools that provide additional user assistance based on an understanding of the semantics of WSDL and XSD. Examples include creation wizards, builders, style checkers, and correctness checkers.

WebSphere Studio Application Developer has a strong suite of XSD tools that include an XSD editor, a wizard that can generate XSD from a sample XML instance document, and a wizard that can convert a DTD to XSD. The ability to generate XSD from sample XML is especially attractive because it is relatively easy to create an example based on some test data. The wizard can generate the initial version of the XSD, which can be further refined in the XSD editor.

WebSphere Studio Application Developer also has a validating XML editor that can be used to edit WSDL documents. Tools that provide more assistance for authoring WSDL documents are likely to appear in the future.

After the WSDL is available, the next step is to create a component that implements it. Here tools can help by generating a server skeleton from the WSDL. WebSphere Studio Application Developer includes a wizard that can generate a Java class skeleton from WSDL. Wizards that generate other types of implementation components, such as EJBs, are likely to appear.

Now it's time to continue with the weather application. The application needs to obtain the temperature for a U.S. location. An Internet search reveals that XMethods (see `http://xmethods.com`) hosts such a service. Figure 23.8 shows the description of the `Weather-Temperature` service that contains a link to its WSDL. I could have also obtained this information with the UDDI Explorer because XMethods also hosts a UDDI registry.

Creating the `TestTemperatureService` Web Service

You plan to use this service, but for local testing purposes, it would be useful to have an instance of it running on your development machine. That way you could work during airplane trips or demo it where there was no Internet access. You therefore save the WSDL in the `WeatherServices` project as `TemperatureService.wsdl`, select it, and launch the Web service wizard. Figure 23.9 shows the Web service wizard Start page where you can choose to also deploy the skeleton and generate a proxy so you can test the service later. You'll fill in the Java skeleton method body to generate sensible-looking data before you begin testing. Call the new service `TestTemperatureService`.

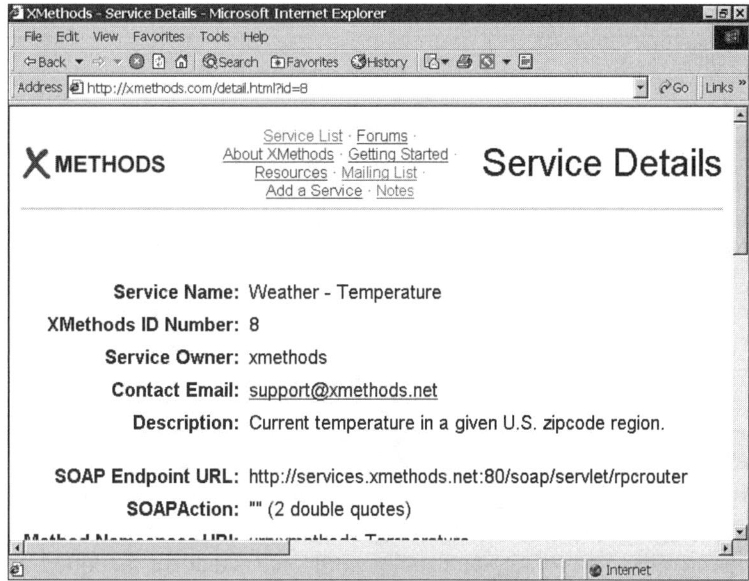

FIGURE 23.8
XMethods `Weather-Temperature` *service details.*

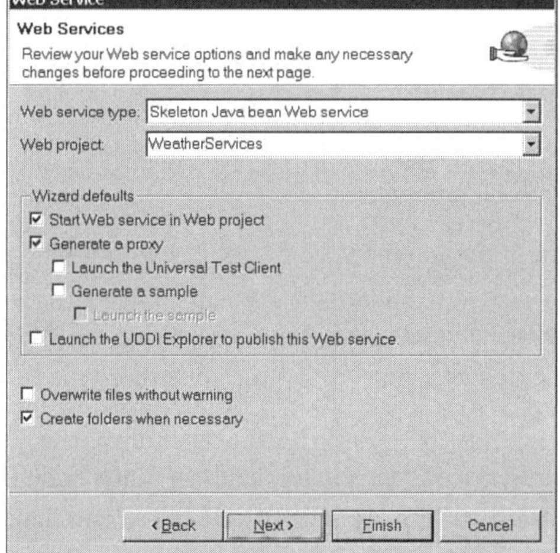

FIGURE 23.9
Generating a Java server skeleton from WSDL.

Listing 23.1 shows the generated skeleton with the method body filled in. As you can see, it is extremely simple. It contains a single operation, `getTemp`, that takes a `String` zip code as input and produces a float Fahrenheit temperature as output.

LISTING 23.1 TestTemperatureService.java

```
package service;
import org.w3c.dom.*;
public class TestTemperatureService
{
  public float getTemp(java.lang.String zipcode)
  {
    // generate a plausible random temperature
    float temp = (float) (60 + 10 * Math.random());
    temp = (float) (Math.round(10 * temp) * 0.1);
    return temp;
  }
}
```

Bottom-Up Development

Bottom-Up development starts by developing the implementation component and then creating the Web service from it. When evaluating Web services tools it is important to consider the types of implementation components that are supported. WebSphere Studio Application Developer supports Bottom-Up development for the following implementation component types:

- Servlets and JSPs
- Java classes
- Stateless session beans
- SQL statements and stored procedures

Servlets and JSPs can be used to implement Web services without the need for any supporting runtime components, aside from perhaps an XML parser. WebSphere Studio Application Developer includes a wizard that helps you create the WSDL to describe a Web service that is implemented as a servlet, JSP, or any other type of URL-addressable server program.

However, developing a Web Service from scratch leads to much code duplication; therefore, common runtime libraries, such as Apache SOAP, have been developed. Apache SOAP contains standard servlets that you can configure to route Web service requests to Java classes, stateless session beans, and other types of components. You configure the Apache SOAP servlets by creating deployment descriptors that map the Web service ID to either the Java implementation class or to a pluggable provider. Apache SOAP includes pluggable providers for some standard components, such as stateless session beans, and you can extend the runtime by developing your own pluggable providers. For example, WebSphere Studio Application Developer includes a pluggable provider for SQL statements.

Java classes are an attractive way to implement Web services because they are familiar to programmers and can access a wide variety of enterprise resources. This allows existing enterprise applications and transactions to be wrapped in a Java class and then deployed as a Web service. In Apache SOAP, Java classes that implement services run in the same Web container as the routing servlet. As illustrated earlier, WebSphere Studio Application Developer has a wizard that can deploy a Java class as a Web service. The wizard generates WSDL by introspecting the Java class.

Stateless session beans offer an alternate to Java classes when you require the scalability, security, and transactional support of an EJB. Although it is technically possible to expose stateful session beans and entity beans as Web services, they are less suitable. Stateful session beans would not scale as well as stateless session beans because a new instance of the bean would have to be created for each session, whereas stateless session beans can be pooled and reused. Entity beans would not perform well because they are primarily intended for persistence and do not normally contain methods that perform useful services. However, stateless session beans are an excellent candidate for Web services because they perform complex business logic and can handle requests from many sessions. WebSphere Studio Application Developer has a wizard that can deploy stateless session beans as Web services. Its operation is similar to the Java class case, but the wizard also understands the J2EE EJB programming model (for example, Home and Remote interfaces) and provides suitable additional assistance.

Databases provide an easy way to implement simple Web services. Many Web services will handle simple information requests. These can be implemented as queries against a database. More complex processing can be implemented as stored procedure invocations or database triggers that invoke Java business logic. In this architecture, the SOAP router servlet invokes a pluggable provider that uses JDBC to send SQL statements to the database. The query or stored procedure executes in the database and returns the resultset to the servlet. WebSphere Studio Application Developer includes tools and a pluggable provider for using SQL statements to implement Web services. In this approach, the implementation component is an XML Document Access Definition Extension (DADX) file, which contains operations that you implement with SQL statements.

Creating the `ZipCode` Web Service

Proceeding with the weather application example, you now have services that can get the Fahrenheit temperature for a zip code, and that can convert a Fahrenheit temperature to Celsius. The next service to build is one that can look up the zip codes in a city. Because this is an information-oriented service, it is natural to use a database to implement it. For simplicity, you'll use a database, `TRAVEL`, that has a single table, `CITY_TAB`, with columns for `ZIPCODE` and `CITY`. WebSphere Studio Application Developer has several tools that can help you create a Web service to access this database.

First you use the DADX Configuration wizard to add a Web service group to the `WeatherServices` application. The Web services group is a directory that contains any DADX files that access the database. The wizard also configures an instance of an invoker servlet that handles requests for DADX services. The invoker servlet extends the Apache SOAP router servlet with additional functions, such as HTTP GET and POST bindings, test page generation, and WSDL generation. These extensions to Apache SOAP are part of the IBM Web Services Object Runtime Framework (WORF) component, which supports both DADX and Java classes.

To create the DADX file, use the Relational Schema Centre to connect to the database and import its table definitions into the `WeatherServices` project. Then use the SQL Builder to create the SQL statements that will become the Web service's operations. The SQL Builder enables you to use a point-and-click user interface to create SQL statements. Here you create operations to find all the zip codes in the database, find all the zip codes for a given city, insert a new zip code, update the city for a given zip code, and delete a given zip code. Figure 23.10 shows the SQL Builder open on the `findZipCodes` operation, which takes a city as input and returns a list of zip codes as output.

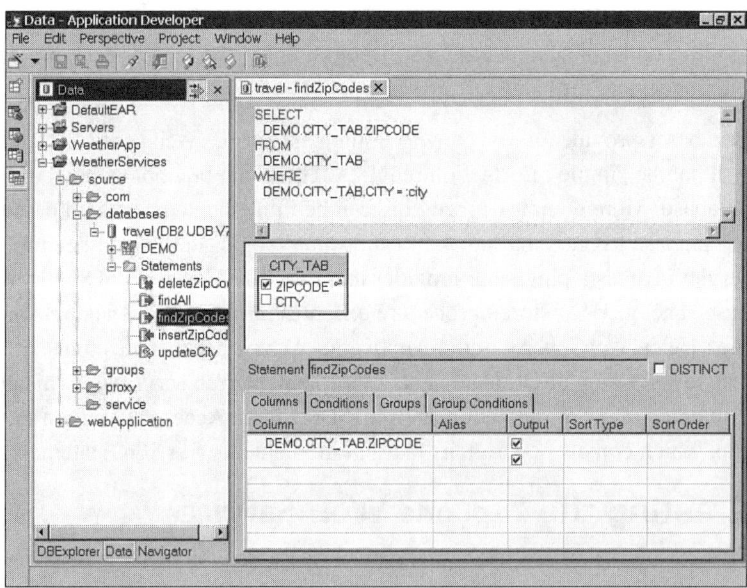

FIGURE 23.10
The SQL Builder creating the `findZipCodes` operation.

Next you use the XML From SQL Wizard to generate the DADX file, `ZipCode.dadx`. This wizard enables you to select the set of SQL statements that you want to become a Web service's operations. The wizard combines the selected SQL statements into a single DADX file that becomes the implementation component for the Web service. Listing 23.2 shows the generated DADX file.

LISTING 23.2 ZipCode.dadx

```
<?xml version="1.0" encoding="UTF-8"?>
<dadx:DADX xmlns:dadx="http://schemas.ibm.com/db2/dxx/dadx"
      xmlns:xsi="http://www.w3.org/2001/XMLSchema-instance"
      xmlns:xsd="http://www.w3.org/2001/XMLSchema"
      xmlns:wsdl="http://schemas.xmlsoap.org/wsdl/"
      xsi:schemaLocation="http://schemas.ibm.com/db2/dxx/dadx dadx.xsd
                          http://schemas.xmlsoap.org/wsdl/ wsdl.xsd">
    <wsdl:documentation xmlns="http://www.w3.org/1999/xhtml">
        Access the database of zipcodes and cities.
    </wsdl:documentation>
    <dadx:operation name="findAll">
        <wsdl:documentation xmlns="http://www.w3.org/1999/xhtml">
            Finds all the zip codes and cities.
        </wsdl:documentation>
        <dadx:query>
            <dadx:SQL_query>
<![CDATA[
                SELECT DEMO.CITY_TAB.ZIPCODE, DEMO.CITY_TAB.CITY
                FROM DEMO.CITY_TAB
]]>
            </dadx:SQL_query>
        </dadx:query>
    </dadx:operation>
    <dadx:operation name="findZipCodes">
        <wsdl:documentation xmlns="http://www.w3.org/1999/xhtml">
            Finds the zip codes for a city.
        </wsdl:documentation>
        <dadx:query>
            <dadx:SQL_query>
<![CDATA[
                SELECT DEMO.CITY_TAB.ZIPCODE
                FROM DEMO.CITY_TAB
                WHERE DEMO.CITY_TAB.CITY = :city
]]>
            </dadx:SQL_query>
            <dadx:parameter name="city" type="xsd:string"/>
        </dadx:query>
    </dadx:operation>
    <dadx:operation name="insertZipCode">
        <wsdl:documentation xmlns="http://www.w3.org/1999/xhtml">
            Inserts a new zip code.
        </wsdl:documentation>
        <dadx:update>
            <dadx:SQL_update>
<![CDATA[
                INSERT INTO DEMO.CITY_TAB ( ZIPCODE, CITY )
                VALUES ( :zipCode, :city )
]]>
            </dadx:SQL_update>
```

LISTING 23.2 continued

```
            <dadx:parameter name="zipCode" type="xsd:string"/>
            <dadx:parameter name="city" type="xsd:string"/>
        </dadx:update>
    </dadx:operation>
    <dadx:operation name="updateCity">
        <wsdl:documentation xmlns="http://www.w3.org/1999/xhtml">
            Updates the city for a zip code.
        </wsdl:documentation>
        <dadx:update>
            <dadx:SQL_update>
<![CDATA[
                UPDATE DEMO.CITY_TAB
                SET CITY = :city
                WHERE DEMO.CITY_TAB.ZIPCODE = :zipCode
]]>
            </dadx:SQL_update>
            <dadx:parameter name="zipCode" type="xsd:string"/>
            <dadx:parameter name="city" type="xsd:string"/>
        </dadx:update>
    </dadx:operation>
    <dadx:operation name="deleteZipCode">
        <wsdl:documentation xmlns="http://www.w3.org/1999/xhtml">
            Deletes a zip code.
        </wsdl:documentation>
        <dadx:update>
            <dadx:SQL_update>
<![CDATA[
                DELETE FROM DEMO.CITY_TAB
                WHERE DEMO.CITY_TAB.ZIPCODE = :zipCode
]]>
            </dadx:SQL_update>
            <dadx:parameter name="zipCode" type="xsd:string"/>
        </dadx:update>
    </dadx:operation>
</dadx:DADX>
```

The `ZipCode` Web service is now complete. To deploy it, select the `ZipCode.dadx` file and launch the Web service wizard as usual.

Meet-in-the-Middle Development

In Meet-in-the-Middle development, your task is to use an existing component to implement a Web service that satisfies a given WSDL interface. This scenario is likely to occur more frequently as industry associations define standard WSDL interfaces for common services. One approach to this task is to generate a Java server skeleton from the WSDL and then manually code operation method bodies that delegate to the existing component. This task can be aided by mapping tools that generate code to deserialize the XML types in the request message into Java types that form the input arguments to operation methods, and that serialize the Java return types into the XML types in the response message.

WebSphere Studio Application Developer can generate Java beans from XSD, but currently does not have tools that can map between XSD and given Java beans. However, it does have tools for mapping between both XSD and relational data. The XML Mapper can map between two XSD files. The result of the mapping is an Extensible Stylesheet Language Transformation (XSLT) file that can be applied to an input XML document to create the desired output XML. One use of this technology is to generate an HTML document from XML data. However, it can also be used to transform between XML message formats. The RDB Mapper can map between XSD and relational data. The mapping is represented by a Document Access Definition (DAD) file that the DB2 XML Extender supports. The DAD file describes how XML data is shredded into relational tables, and how a query result is formatted into an XML document. A DADX Web service can use operations a DAD defines to retrieve and store XML documents into a DB2 database; however, this support requires the DB2 XML Extender.

Tools for Deploying Web Services

Deploying a Web service involves installing and configuring the implementation components on an application server. Therefore, the first task is to install and configure an application server to host the Web services, and to install the SOAP runtime and any components that it requires. In Apache SOAP, Web services are deployed as part of a Web application. A Web application must therefore be created and configured with SOAP runtime components, which for Apache SOAP are router servlets. In addition to the implementation components, a deployment descriptor must be created and added to the configuration. The deployment descriptor forms the link between the SOAP request message and the implementation component. The implementation component may also make use of helper classes for mapping between XML and Java types.

Deploying the Web Service goes beyond simply installing the service in the application server. In addition to having a running service, you must also make its WSDL and XSD accessible to potential users of the service. Recall that UDDI is a registry, not a repository, so simply publishing the service description is not enough. A UDDI registry stores URLs to the complete WSDL for the Web service. The WSDL itself may contain URLs for additional WSDL and XSD documents. All the WSDL and XSD documents must therefore be stored on servers that are accessible to the Web service's users. One solution is to store the WSDL and XSD in the same Web application as the Web service; however, this might lead to replication of common documents. XML repositories are specialized databases for storing documents such as WSDL and XSD, and using them may be a preferred solution. If you use an XML repository, deployment also includes storing the WSDL and XSD files in the XML repository.

A final consideration in deploying Web services is related to the Publish task. Although Web service descriptions can be registered in UDDI, another approach is to include descriptive information in a format that Web Service browsers and crawlers can access. This type of information can be complementary to UDDI if the crawlers are used to populate UDDI registries. Microsoft implemented an early version of the technology based on the DISCO specification, but this will be superceded by WS-Inspection, which was developed jointly with IBM. Deploying a Web service may therefore also involve generating WS-Inspection documents, or the Web Service runtime may generate these automatically.

WebSphere Studio Application Developer automates all aspects of Web Service deployment to the application server. WebSphere Studio Application Developer includes a copy of WebSphere Application Server, which is used as the default. The developer is therefore completely freed of the tasks of acquiring, installing, and configuring an application server. However, WebSphere Studio Application Developer also supports externally installed copies of both WebSphere and Tomcat because the developer may prefer to use those. The Web service wizards automatically install the SOAP runtime and configure the Web application with the required servlets. The wizards also generate the deployment descriptor, WSDL, and XSD, and add the service to the configuration. At present, there is no tool support for XML repositories or WS-Inspection because they are not yet part of the WebSphere runtime.

Tools for Testing Web Services

Testing is of interest both when creating a new Web service and when accessing an existing one. Because WSDL describes Web service interfaces, it is possible to automatically generate user interfaces that let the developer unit test the service. There are several approaches to generating a test user interface. The most direct approach is to dynamically generate a user interface by interpreting the WSDL. This approach would be very useful in conjunction with a UDDI browser. Imagine browsing to any interesting Web service and then being able to instantly test it without writing or generating any code. The next level of testing would be to generate a proxy for the service and then dynamically test that. This would give you information about both the Web Service and the proxy, but would not actually help you write your own application to use the proxy. Finally, it would be useful to generate a complete test application based on the proxy. Then you could extract useful code snippets and copy them into your own application.

In addition to exercising the interface, it is often useful to monitor the actual SOAP message traffic. In fact, it is feasible to automatically validate the message traffic against the WSDL because XSD describes all the data. A tool that automatically monitored the SOAP message traffic and validated it against WSDL and XSD would help you verify that you were generating XML that conformed to the service definition.

WebSphere Studio Application Developer supports interface testing in three ways, and includes a TCP/IP monitor for examining the message traffic. The three testing tools are the Universal Test Client, generated sample application, and dynamic server test pages. Dynamic interpretation of WSDL is not currently supported. You have already seen the Universal Test Client in Figure 23.3. To use it for testing Web services, apply it to the proxy. The Universal Test Client generates a user interface for the Web service by using the Java reflection API to analyze the proxy at runtime. You have also already seen the generated sample application in Figure 23.7. The sample application is a JSP user interface that the Web Service Client Wizard generates for a proxy. It is simpler to use than the Universal Test Client and can act as a source of useful code snippets. A dynamic server test page is an automatically generated HTML page that can be used to test the Web service. Dynamic server test pages are generated by the WORF component. Figure 23.11 shows the test page generated for the `ZipCodes` Web service.

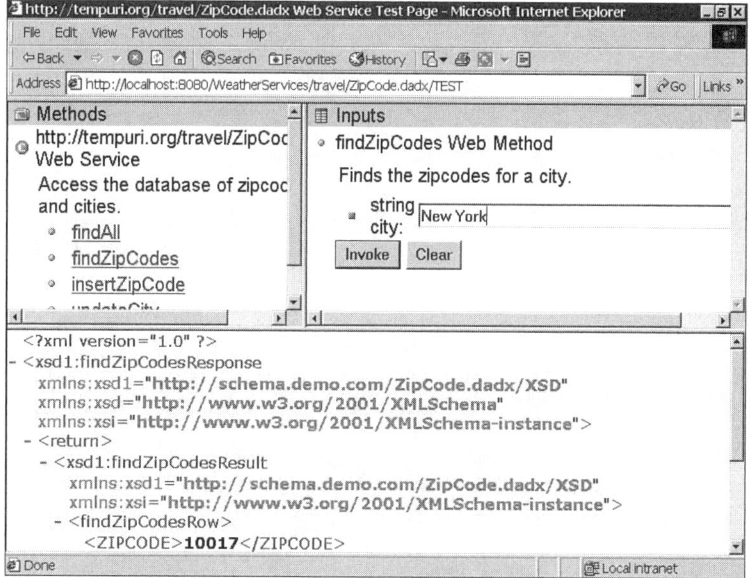

FIGURE 23.11
Server test page for `ZipCode` Web service.

The `findCodes` operation is being tested, with the input city New York giving the result zip code 11017. The test page is an HTML client and uses the HTTP `POST` binding of the Web service. As already described, WORF extends the Apache SOAP runtime by adding support for the HTTP `GET` and `POST` bindings. The advantage of a dynamically generated server test page is that it does not require WebSphere Studio Application Developer or any other development environment. Any potential user of your service can instantly try it out. Of course, for this to work you must use the WORF extension to deploy your Web service. Dynamic test page generation is likely to become a standard feature of the SOAP runtime in the future.

WebSphere Studio Application Developer includes a TCP/IP Monitor Server for examining message traffic. You can create multiple instances of this server and can configure each instance to listen on a specified port and forward the request to a specified host and port. To illustrate this, create the TCP/IP monitor to listen on port 8081 and forward to port 8080, which is where the `WeatherServices` application is deployed. Next, you monitor the message traffic. Figure 23.12 shows the TCP/monitor with the request and response messages.

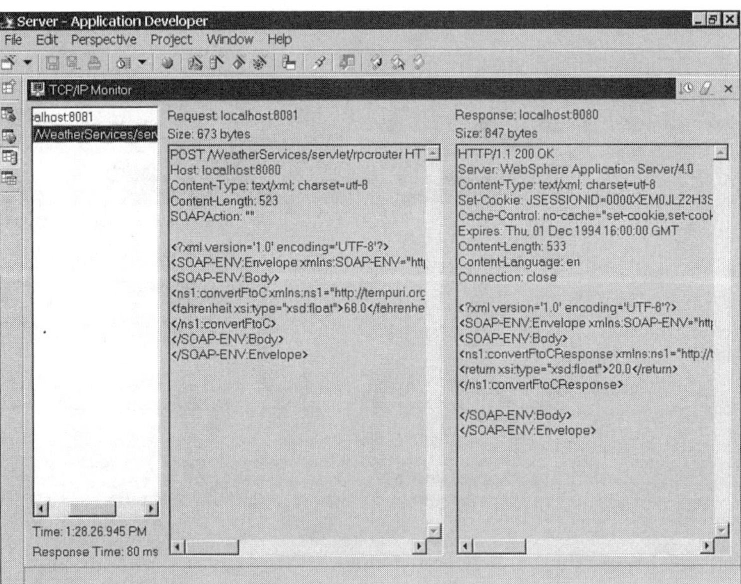

FIGURE 23.12
TCP/IP Monitor displaying message traffic for `Temperature-Converter` *Web service.*

You can examine the HTTP headers and bodies of request and response. For example, there is no cookie in the request because this is the first request of the session. The response therefore includes a `Set=Cookie` header. The request contains a `SOAPAction` header that is part of the SOAP binding for HTTP. Both the request and response bodies are XML messages that conform to the SOAP envelope format. The request message invokes the convertFtoC operation with the temperature of 68.0 degrees Fahrenheit and the response message returns the result of 20.0 degrees Celsius. The TCP/IP monitor does not perform any validation on the message traffic.

Tools for Publishing Web Services

The Publish task involves making information about your Web Service available to potential users of it. At present, the primary way to publish a Web service is to register it in a UDDI registry and to deploy its WSDL and XSD files on a Web server. Publishing in UDDI requires more than simply describing the Web service, because every Web Service is owned by some business entity. You must therefore first register your business entity. In addition, you may be registering a standard Web service interface for use within some industry rather than registering an implementation. Tools that simplify the publishing task are clearly desirable.

UDDI registries support SOAP access to all their publishing functions. It is therefore possible to write your own applications to publish Web Service information; however, this would require a detailed understanding of the UDDI service interface. Most UDDI registry implementations also include a Web user interface that enables you to publish your Web service information without understanding the details of the UDDI service interface. However, each implementation has a different user interface, so if you are working with multiple implementations, you'll have to learn multiple user interfaces. Also, because the user interface is simply a Web application hosted on the UDDI registry server, it will not be integrated with your development environment.

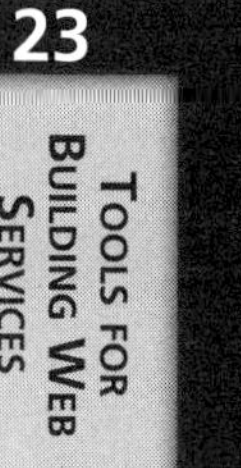

A further consideration is how UDDI and WSDL work together. The UDDI model of a Web service is very general and allows you to use any language to describe a service. There is some overlap in the information modeled by UDDI and that modeled by WSDL, but the two specifications are largely independent. So that you can use WSDL smoothly with UDDI, certain guidelines have been established in a Best Practices document. The guidelines recommend that the WSDL be split into two parts: one that describes the service instance and another that describes the binding. The binding information can be reused by many service instances. Clearly it is highly desirable for tools to understand this split and to enable WSDL to flow easily into and out of UDDI registries.

Before publishing information for use in production, it is useful to publish to a test server. Both IBM and Microsoft have public test registries, but these place some restrictions on what you can do, and they require network access. It is sometimes desirable to use UDDI when there is no network access—to do work while traveling, for example, or to demonstrate an application in a meeting room. Ideally, your development environment should include a lightweight local UDDI registry that you can use for testing.

UDDI is a registry, not a repository. This means that UDDI does not store WSDL or XSD documents. Instead, UDDI stores URLs that reference WSDL. The WSDL, and any XSD that it references, must be stored on some other server. Although WSDL and XSD can be stored on any Web server, specialized XML repositories may become popular. An XML repository is a database that helps you manage and share XML documents. Publishing a Web service description to UDDI may therefore also involve publishing WSDL and XSD to an XML repository.

The WS-Inspection specification provides a standard way to provide Web service information on application servers. This information could be browsed directly or it could be harvested by crawlers and used to populate a UDDI or other registry. Imagine a Google for Web services. Publishing may therefore also involve generating WS-Inspection documents.

WebSphere Studio Application Developer includes the UDDI Explorer for publishing Web service information. The UDDI Explorer, as you saw earlier in Figure 23.4, provides an easy-to-use Web user interface that can access any compliant UDDI registry. In addition, the UDDI Explorer can directly access your development project, and it supports the UDDI Best Practices recommendation for WSDL. WebSphere Studio Application Developer currently does not include a local test UDDI registry, nor does it support either XML repositories or WS-Inspection.

Tools for Discovering Web Services

The considerations for using UDDI registries for discovering Web services are similar to those for publishing them. Your development environment should provide an easy-to-use user interface for searching UDDI registries. When a promising Web service is found, your tools should make it easy to import the WSDL into your development project and to test the service. As WS-Inspection becomes more widely adopted, your discovery tool should also support browsing application servers for the Web services they host.

WebSphere Studio Application Developer includes the UDDI Explorer for discovering Web services. As was shown in Figure 23.5, the UDDI Explorer is integrated with the development environment and can download the WSDL directly into your project, where you can use it for testing, access, creation, and so on. WebSphere Studio Application Developer currently cannot browse application servers for WS-Inspection information, nor can it dynamically test WSDL.

Tools for Accessing Web Services

After you have found the Web services you need for your application, your next task is to access them. Tools can greatly simplify this task by generating a proxy from the WSDL. The proxy lets you invoke the service's operations as if you were invoking a local class's methods. The main difference is that the proxy can throw exceptions that occur in distributed computing.

In WSDL, XSD describes the data types used in the service interface. The proxy can use generic XML objects to represent these types—for example, as W3C DOM Elements—or it can represent them as Java beans. Tools can generate Java beans from XSD. In the case of Meet-in-the-Middle development, tools can help by generating mapping code to transform between the XSD and existing Java beans.

Because Web services involve network access, it is often useful to use threading to improve performance and responsiveness. It is possible to manually use the Java threading library for this purpose, but a better alternative is to have tools do this for you by generating proxies that can make asynchronous calls. In this approach, the application registers a listener on the proxy, and then makes a call that returns immediately but does not include the response. Instead, the proxy raises an event when the response is received.

Access from Java is useful when complex processing must be performed on the response. However, for simple applications, direct access from Web browsers may be preferable. A Web browser can use HTML forms or hyperlinks to directly invoke Web services that support the HTTP `GET` and `POST` bindings. Microsoft provides an HTML component called the WebService Behavior that runs in Internet Explorer. The WebService Behavior can dynamically interpret WSDL and make asynchronous SOAP calls, but this requires scripting—for example, with JavaScript. Processing the response also involves scripting.

WebSphere Studio Application Developer can generate synchronous Java proxies from WSDL and can generate Java beans from XSD. It also includes a JavaScript editor that can be used for browser-based access. To illustrate the use of Java proxies, the next thing to try is creating a proxy for the `ZipCode` service in the weather application. Select the `ZipCode` service WSDL and launch the Web Service Client Wizard again, but this time examine the data type mappings. Figure 23.13 shows the mappings page where you can choose to map the response from the `findZipCodes` operation to a Java bean.

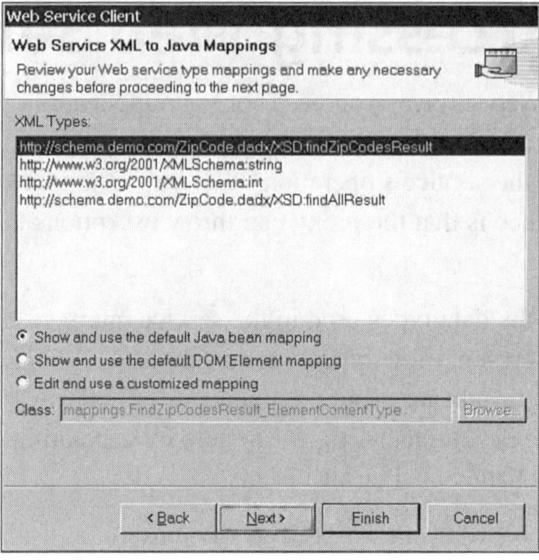

FIGURE 23.13 *Web Service Client Wizard XML-to-Java Mappings page.*

Listing 23.3 shows the XSD definition for `findZipCodesResult`.

LISTING 23.3 XSD Definition of `findZipCodesResult`

```
<element name="findZipCodesResult">
  <complexType>
    <sequence>
      <element maxOccurs="unbounded" minOccurs="0" name="findZipCodesRow">
        <complexType>
          <sequence>
            <element name="ZIPCODE" type="string"/>
          </sequence>
        </complexType>
      </element>
    </sequence>
  </complexType>
</element>
```

The result of the `findZipCodes` operation is a sequence of 0 or more `findZipCodesRow` elements, each of which contains a single `ZIPCODE` element. Listing 23.4 shows the Java bean generated for the XML element `findZipCodesResult`.

LISTING 23.4 Java Bean for XML `findZipCodesResult` Element

```
package mappings;
import com.ibm.etools.xsd.bean.runtime.AnyType;
import java.math.BigDecimal;
import java.math.BigInteger;
import java.util.Arrays;
import java.util.Date;
import java.util.GregorianCalendar;
```

LISTING 23.4 continued

```
import java.util.Hashtable;
import java.util.List;
import java.util.Vector;
import org.w3c.dom.Element;

public class FindZipCodesResult_ElementContentType extends AnyType
{
  public FindZipCodesResult_ElementContentType()
  {
    addElement("findZipCodesRow",
    FindZipCodesRow_ElementLocalContentType.class);
  }
  public static class FindZipCodesRow_ElementLocalContentType extends AnyType
  {
    public FindZipCodesRow_ElementLocalContentType()
    {
      addElement("ZIPCODE", String.class);
    }
    public String getZIPCODE()
    {
      return (String)this.basicGet("ZIPCODE", 0);
    }
    public void setZIPCODE(String zIPCODE)
    {
      this.basicSet("ZIPCODE", 0, zIPCODE);
    }
  }

  public FindZipCodesRow_ElementLocalContentType getFindZipCodesRow(int index)
  {
    return (FindZipCodesRow_ElementLocalContentType)this.basicGet(
    "findZipCodesRow", index);
  }
  public void setFindZipCodesRow(int index,
  FindZipCodesRow_ElementLocalContentType findZipCodesRow)
  {
    this.basicSet("findZipCodesRow", index, findZipCodesRow);
  }
  public FindZipCodesRow_ElementLocalContentType[] getFindZipCodesRow()
  {
    List result = this.basicGet("findZipCodesRow");
    return (FindZipCodesRow_ElementLocalContentType[])basicToArray(result, new
    FindZipCodesRow_ElementLocalContentType[result.size()]);
  }
  public void setFindZipCodesRow(FindZipCodesRow_ElementLocalContentType[]
  findZipCodesRow)
  {
    this.basicSet("findZipCodesRow", basicToList(findZipCodesRow
  }
}
```

The generated Java bean contains two classes because there are two complex types: `findZipCodesResult` and `findZipCodesRow`. The row class is nested in the result class because it is a local element. Each class has accessors for its contents.

You can now complete the weather application by writing a Java bean, `TemperatureLister`, to invoke the Web services and collect the results so that the user interface can display them. The user interface is implemented by a JSP, `demo.jsp`. Figure 23.14 shows the finished application.

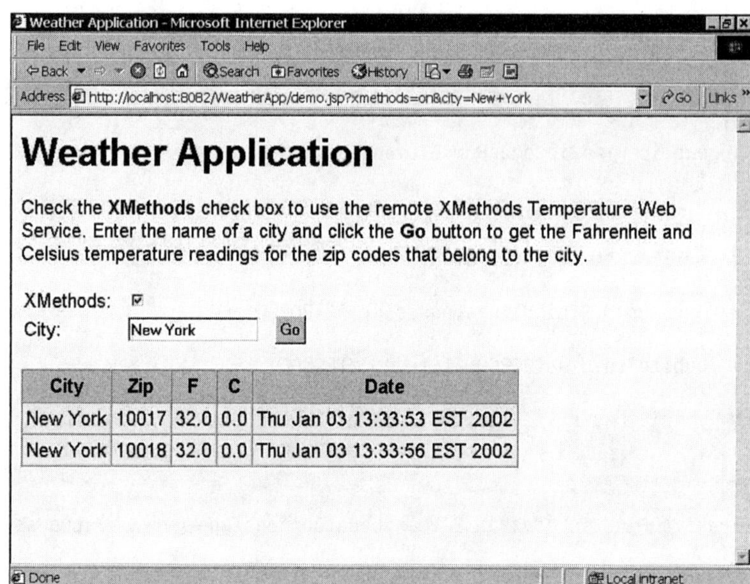

FIGURE 23.14 *The weather application.*

Here the zip code database has two entries for New York City to illustrate the handling of multiple rows in the resultset of the `findZipCodes` operation. Listing 23.5 shows the `TemperatureLister` class, which invokes the Web services.

LISTING 23.5 The `TemperatureLister` Class

```
package com.ibm.dynademo;
import proxy.soap.*;
import mappings.*;
/**
 * <codeTemperatureLister</code lists temperature readings.
 * It uses three Web Services:
 * 1. ZipCode Service lists zip codes and cities.
 * 2. Temperature Service gives the Fahrenheit temperature at a zip code.
 *    TestTemperatureService is a local version for use when disconnected.
 * 3. TemperatureConverter Service converts from Fahrenheit to Celsius.
```

LISTING 23.5 continued

```
 *
 * @author Arthur Ryman
 * @version 1.0
 */
public class TemperatureLister {
 /** use the TestTemperatureService when local is true */
 private boolean local;
 public void setLocal(boolean local) {
  this.local = local;
 }
 public boolean isLocal() {
  return local;
 }
 /**
  * Lists the temperature readings for a city.
  *
  * @return the temperature listing
  * @param city the string city name
  */
 public TemperatureListing forCity(String city) {
  // get the array of zip codes
  try {
   ZipCodeProxy proxy = new ZipCodeProxy();
   TemperatureServiceProxy temperatureProxy = new TemperatureServiceProxy();
   TestTemperatureServiceProxy testProxy = new TestTemperatureServiceProxy();
   TemperatureConverterProxy converterProxy = new TemperatureConverterProxy();
   FindZipCodesResult_ElementContentType result = proxy.findZipCodes(city);
   FindZipCodesResult_ElementContentType
    .FindZipCodesRow_ElementLocalContentType[] rows =
    result.getFindZipCodesRow();
   TemperatureReading[] readings = new TemperatureReading[rows.length];
   for (int i = 0; i < readings.length; i++) {
    String zipCode = rows[i].getZIPCODE();
    // get the temperature
    float fahrenheit =
     isLocal() ? testProxy.getTemp(zipCode) :
     temperatureProxy.getTemp(zipCode);
    // convert the temperature
    float celsius = converterProxy.convertFtoC(fahrenheit);
    // round to one decimal place
    celsius = (float) (Math.round(celsius * 10) * 0.1);
    TemperatureReading reading = readings[i] = new TemperatureReading();
    reading.setCity(city);
    reading.setZipCode(zipCode);
    reading.setFahrenheit(fahrenheit);
    reading.setCelsius(celsius);
   }
   return new TemperatureListing(readings);
  } catch (Exception e) {
```

LISTING 23.5 continued

```
    return new TemperatureListing(e.getMessage());
   }
  }
}
```

Using the generated Java bean for the `findZipCodes` operation's result eliminates the need for accessing the XML DOM. Listing 23.6 shows the JSP user interface, `demo.jsp`.

LISTING 23.6 The Weather Application User Interface `demo.jsp`

```
<%@ page errorPage="error.jsp" import="com.ibm.dynademo.*" %>
<jsp:useBean id="lister" scope="request"
  class="com.ibm.dynademo.TemperatureLister" />

<%

String xmethods = request.getParameter("xmethods");
boolean local = xmethods == null;
String CHECKED = local ? "" : "CHECKED";

String city = request.getParameter("city");
if (city == null) {
        city = "New York";
}

lister.setLocal(local);
TemperatureListing listing = lister.forCity(city);

%>

<!doctype html public "-//w3c//dtd html 4.0 transitional//en">
<html>
<head>
<meta http-equiv="Content-Type"
  content="text/html; charset=iso-8859-1">
<meta name="GENERATOR"
  content="Mozilla/4.73   (Windows NT 5.0; U) [Netscape]">
<meta name="Author" content="Arthur Ryman">
<LINK REL="STYLESHEET" HREF="dynademo.css" TYPE="text/css">
<TITLE>Weather Application</TITLE>
</HEAD>
<BODY>
<h1>Weather Application</h1>
Check the <b>XMethods</b> check box to use the remote
XMethods Temperature Web Service.
Enter the name of a city and click the <b>Go</b>
button to get the Fahrenheit
and Celsius temperature
```

LISTING 23.6 continued

```
readings for the zip codes that belong to the city.
<FORM>
<TABLE>
<TR>
<TD>XMethods:</TD>
<TD WIDTH="10"></TD>
<TD><INPUT TYPE="CHECKBOX"
  NAME="xmethods" VALUE="on" <%=CHECKED%>></TD>
</TR>
<TR>
<TD>City:</TD>
<TD WIDTH="10"></TD>
<TD><INPUT TYPE="TEXT"
  NAME="city" VALUE="<%=city%>" SIZE=16></TD>
<TD WIDTH="10"></TD>
<TD><INPUT TYPE="SUBMIT" VALUE="Go"></TD>
</TR>
</TABLE>
</FORM>

<% if (listing.isError()) { %>
<P>The following error occurred:
<%=listing.getErrorMessage()%>.
Try another city.</P>
<% } else {

       TemperatureReading[] readings = listing.getReadings();
       if (readings.length == 0) { %>

<P>No readings where found for <%=city%>.
Try another city.</P>

<%     } else { %>

<TABLE BORDER="1"
  CELLSPACING="0" CELLPADDING="4" BGCOLOR="#FFFF00">

<TR BGCOLOR="#CCCCCC">
<TH>City</TH>
<TH>Zip</TH>
<TH>F</TH>
<TH>C</TH>
<TH>Date</TH>
</TR>

<% for (int i = 0; i < readings.length; i++) {

  TemperatureReading reading = readings[i]; %>
```

LISTING 23.6 continued

```
<TR>
<TD><%=reading.getCity()%></TD>
<TD><%=reading.getZipCode()%></TD>
<TD><%=reading.getFahrenheit()%></TD>
<TD><%=reading.getCelsius()%></TD>
<TD><%=reading.getDate()%></TD>
</TR>

<% } %>

</TABLE>

<% }
} %>
</BODY>
</HTML>
```

The complete source for this application is provided on this book's Web site and can be downloaded from `http://www.samspublishing.com`.

Summary

In this chapter I introduced a task-oriented framework for evaluating Web services tools. The main tasks for providing services are Create, Deploy, Test, and Publish, and those for consuming services are Discover and Access. The boundaries between these tasks are not absolute, but instead depend on the facilities that the runtime provides. Within the Create task, I further discussed the main approaches, which are Top-Down, Bottom-Up and Meet-in-the-Middle. The Bottom-Up approach will be the most important one in the immediate future because it provides a way to quickly turn existing business functions into Web services. As the industry matures, standard Web service interfaces will emerge and the Top-Down approach will become more important. I then discussed the tools that were applicable to each of these tasks and approaches, and illustrated them with WebSphere Studio Application Developer by developing a simple weather application that combines several Web services.

Web services technology is still in its early stages, but already tools have emerged to automate many development tasks. These tools handle the details of the Web services specifications and runtimes, thereby allowing you, the developer, to focus on solving your business problems.

CHAPTER 24

Building Web Services with WebLogic

By Frank Cohen

In This Chapter

Next generation Web services development toolkits make Web services easy to build and deploy. Early tools provided build and deployment mechanisms for applications to provide UDDI, WSDL, and SOAP interfaces. Now we find tools that provide developer assistance with these protocols, including graphical tools and code generators. In BEA's product WebLogic and its codenamed WebLogic Workshop technology Web services, developers have ease-of-use and scalable strength to quickly deploy powerful Web services.

BEA WebLogic is server software meant to run server-based applications. At its core, WebLogic is a framework of software components to run Java servlets, Enterprise Java Beans, Java Server Pages, directory services, and Web services. BEA's promise with developers is to continually add new technologies as they appear. WebLogic provides a substantial and stable platform to develop applications that require interoperability and connectivity.

This chapter describes how WebLogic implements the Web services protocols and offers a detailed example that shows how to use WebLogic to build and deploy a Web service.

Web Services in WebLogic

BEA introduced the world of Web services to WebLogic developers with WebLogic Server version 6.1 in the very early days of Web services. WebLogic implements WSDL and SOAP 1.1, both SOAP-based RPC and message-based SOAP. BEA wrote its own Web services implementation and provides ongoing support and updates.

WebLogic implements UDDI services to interact with the UDDI.org business directory. WebLogic also enables businesses to deploy their own private UDDI registries behind a corporate firewall to publish services that are private to the company.

WebLogic implements SOAP With Attachments. SOAP messages may need to reference an attached file, often in binary format, such as an image or spreadsheet file. The SOAP Messages With Attachments specification describes a standard way to associate a SOAP message with one or more attachments. The attachments are transported in a multipart MIME structure.

WebLogic Web services use standard J2EE components, including Enterprise JavaBeans and Java Message Services (JMS). They are packaged and deployed as standard J2EE Enterprise Applications. As you will see later in this chapter, BEA introduced a new approach to Web service authoring with code-named WebLogic Workshop technology that lets developers build Web services from scratch with very little prior Java or J2EE experience.

The programming model for a Web service implemented with WebLogic describes how to implement, assemble, deploy, and invoke Web services. Apart from writing the Enterprise JavaBeans code that performs the actual work of the Web service, you develop most of the Web service itself by using an `Ant`, which is a Java-based open-source build/make utility, and `wsgen`, which is an `Ant` script that generates and installs the Web service's components.

WebLogic Server supports two types of Web services: remote procedure call (RPC)-style and message-style.

Remote Procedure Calls

You use a stateless session EJB to implement a remote procedure call (RPC)-style Web service. It appears as a remote object to the client application.

The interaction between a client and an RPC-style Web service centers around a service-specific interface. Clients call the Web service, sending parameters, and then receive return values. The back-and-forth conversation means RPC-style Web services are tightly coupled and resemble traditional distributed systems protocols, including RMI, CORBA, and DCOM. RPC-style Web services are synchronous: The client sends a request and waits around for a response.

Message-Based Calls

SOAP 1.1 defines an asynchronous message-based Web service protocol. Message-based Web services package the request parameters into a MIME attachment and use a transfer agent—such as the JMS message listener or message-driven bean—to transport the request to a Web service system.

Message-style Web services are loosely coupled and document-driven, rather than being associated with a service-specific interface. When a client invokes a message-style Web service, the client sends the request in a document, such as a purchase order, rather than a discrete set of parameters. The Web service accepts the entire document, processes it, and may or may not return a result message. Because no tightly coupled request-response communication between the client and Web service occurs, message-style Web services promotes a looser coupling between client and server.

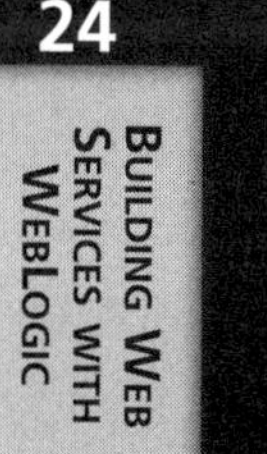

How It Works

WebLogic Web services run-time component comes as a bundled set of servlets and the associated infrastructure needed to create a Web service. Developers implement custom business logic for a Web service in an Enterprise JavaBean and use the WebLogic Web service deployment infrastructure to make the bean's methods available as SOAP requests.

WebLogic Server includes its own implementation of both the SOAP 1.1 and SOAP 1.1 With Attachments specifications for responding to Web service requests. WebLogic handles RPC-style Web services with the SOAP 1.1 message format, and message-style Web services use the SOAP 1. message format.

Web services developers use an `Ant` task, named `wsgen`, and the Administration Console to assemble and deploy Web services as standard J2EE Enterprise applications in an Enterprise Archive Files (EAR) file. The EAR file contains all the components of the Web service: the EJBs, references to the SOAP servlets, the `web.xml` file, the `weblogic.xml` file, and so on.

The WebLogic Server automatically generates the WSDL-compliant definition of the Web service and publishes the WSDL document through a special URL. Developers writing a SOAP system's client part use the WSDL to correctly identify the location and request parameters for the Web service.

WebLogic Server optionally generates a thin Java client that acts as sample code a developer uses to build requests that invoke the Web service. The thin Java client includes all the classes needed to invoke a Web service, including the Java client API classes and interfaces, a parser to handle the SOAP requests and responses, and a Java interface to the EJB.

WebLogic Web Services Architecture

Developing a WebLogic Web service is fairly straightforward and yet very powerful. You use standard J2EE components to implement Web services in WebLogic, including stateless session EJBs, message-driven beans, and JMS destinations. WebLogic Web services inherit from the J2EE platform, so WebLogic Web services come with a simple and familiar component-based development model, easy scalability, unified security model, and easy access to other enterprise APIs such as JDBC, JTA, and eventually JAX.

WebLogic Server Web services come as standard J2EE Enterprise applications that consist of the following:

- A Web application that contains a servlet that sends and receives SOAP messages to and from a requesting application or other server. Developers do not write this servlet themselves, because it comes as part of the WebLogic Web services system.
- A stateless session EJB implementing an RPC-style Web service or a JMS listener for a message-style Web service.

For RPC-style Web services, the stateless session EJBs may do all the actual work of the Web service, or they may parcel out the work to other EJBs. The Web service implementor decides which EJBs do the real work. In message-style Web services, a J2EE object is typically a message-driven bean that gets a message from the JMS destination and processes it.

WebLogic packages and deploys Web services as Enterprise Archive Files (EAR) that contain the Web Archive (WAR) files of the Web application and EJB Archive (JAR) files. The next section shows how the RPC-style and message-style Web service requests are actually handled.

RPC-Style SOAP Requests

Figure 24.1 illustrates the architecture of RPC-style WebLogic Web services.

FIGURE 24.1
Handling an RPC-style request.

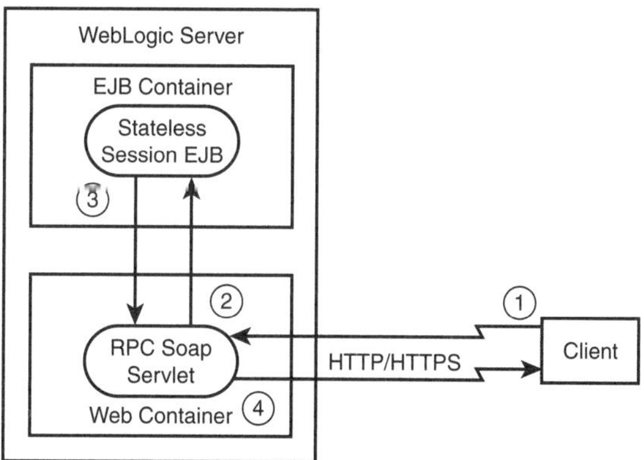

When a client application or server uses WebLogic to invoke an RPC-style Web service request, the WebLogic system marshals several resources to handle the request. The WebLogic Server receives the SOAP request over HTTP or a secure HTTPS protocol connection. The SOAP message contains instructions, conforming to the WSDL of the Web service, to invoke an RPC-style Web service.

The WebLogic SOAP servlet handles RPC SOAP requests as though it were part of any other Web application. The servlet sees the request as an HTTP form submit containing the SOAP message envelope. The SOAP message identifies the stateless session EJB target. The servlet then unmarshals the parameters, binds them to the appropriate Java objects, invokes the target stateless session EJB, and passes the parameters to the bean.

The stateless session EJB acts like a program dispatcher by handling the Web service logic itself or calling other EJBs to form a response. The invoked stateless session EJB uses SOAP to construct a response XML document, which the RPC SOAP servlet uses to respond to the request over the open HTTP or HTTPS connection.

The RPC SOAP servlet catches exceptional states caused by errors, and returnes them to the requestor. The exception information is put into a response XML document. SOAP also uses the HTTP response value to indicate errors—including 404 for service not found and 500 for SOAP errors.

Message-Style SOAP Requests

Message-style Web services sends a request document through JMS or some other transport. In WebLogic, the developer specifies whether a message-style Web service will send or receive messages to or from the Web service. Of course, WebLogic enables developers to combine two message-style Web services: one for sending and the second for receiving.

Figure 24.2 shows how WebLogic handles sending and receiving message-style Web service calls. Figure 24.2 illustrates using JMS to move SOAP messages. Other message protocols may be applied, however, including IBM MQ-Series, IONA Messenger, and Microsoft Exchange.

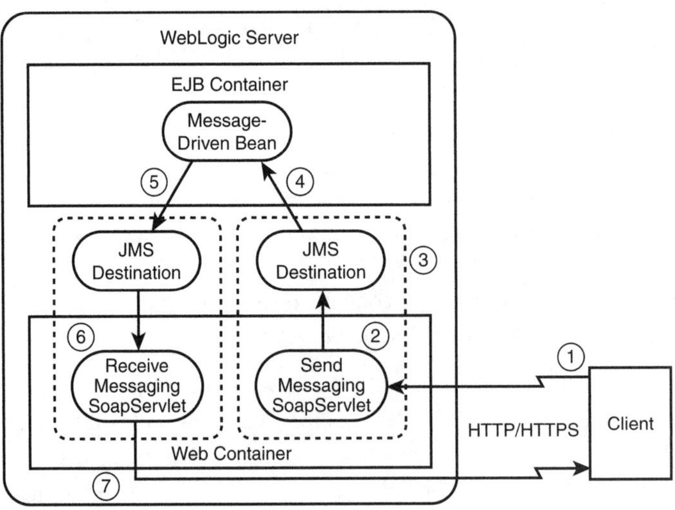

FIGURE 24.2
Handling message-style SOAP requests.

When the client sends a message-style SOAP request to a Web service, the WebLogic Server receives the request as a normal HTTP or HTTPS request. The SOAP message invokes the Web service by sending a WSDL-compliant request message.

The messaging SOAP servlet in the Web application invoked by the client unwraps the SOAP envelope, decodes the body of the message, and puts the resulting object on the appropriate JMS destination. The message sits in the JMS destination until the appropriate JMS listener bean picks it up.

The message-driven bean picks up the message from the JMS destination and either handles all the work itself or calls other EJBs. The message-driven bean packages up a SOAP response document and sends it to a JMS destination that is associated with the response message-style Web service that is configured to allow clients to receive messages.

The messaging SOAP servlet on the receiving end picks up the message from the JMS destination. The messaging SOAP servlet sends the document back to the client when the client invokes the second receive Web service.

Development Lifecycle and Environment

Working with WebLogic to develop and deploy new Web services is made easy when you use the included developer tools. The tools establish a development lifecycle where new source code is edited, built, and tested.

The WebLogic Web service lifecycle begins by setting up the correct environment for you to build EJBs, servlets, and installation documents. Here are the steps we recommend to develop an RPC-style WebLogic Web service:

1. Set up your environment. WebLogic uses EJBs, Web applications, JNDI, `Ant`, and Java to build Web services. It should be common sense, then, that these technologies need the correct environment settings to operate. WebLogic includes shell scripts for Windows and the Unix Bourne shell to make certain the environment settings are established. The environment setup script is found in `BEA_home\config\domain-name\setEnv.cmd`. Please note that domain-name refers to the name of the domain where WebLogic is installed.

   Here is a portion of the `senEnv.cmd` shell script for Windows that shows which environment variables are set. The script expects the system parameters `WL_HOME` to point to WebLogic's root directory and for `JAVA_HOME` to point to the root directory of a complete Java Runtime installation:

   ```
   @rem Set user-defined variables.
   set WL_HOME=I:\bea\wlserver6.1
   set JAVA_HOME=I:\bea\jdk131
   :setEnv
   ```

```
set APPLICATIONS=%WL_HOME%\config\examples\applications
set CLIENT_CLASSES=%WL_HOME%\config\examples\clientclasses
set SERVER_CLASSES=%WL_HOME%\config\examples\serverclasses
set
EX_WEBAPP_CLASSES=%WL_HOME%\config\examples\applications\examplesWebApp\
➥WEB-INF\classes



set CLASSPATH=%JAVA_HOME%\lib\tools.jar;%WL_HOME%\lib\weblogic_sp.jar;
➥%WL_HOME%\lib\weblogic.jar;%WL_HOME%\lib\xmlx.jar;
➥%WL_HOME%\samples\eval\cloudscape\lib\cloudscape.jar;%CLIENT_CLASSES%;
➥%SERVER_CLASSES%;%EX_WEBAPP_CLASSES%;I:\\bea
set PATH=%WL_HOME%\bin;%JAVA_HOME%\bin;%PATH%
```

2. Write the Java interfaces and classes for the Web service as a stateless session EJB.
3. Compile the EJB Java code into class files.
4. Create the EJB deployment descriptors.
5. Assemble the EJB class files and deployment descriptors into a JAR file.
6. Create the `build.xml` Java `Ant` build file used to assemble the WebLogic Web service.
7. Create a staging directory.
8. Copy the EJB JAR file and the `build.xml` file into the staging directory.
9. Execute the Java `Ant` utility to assemble the Curmudgeon Web service into an ear archive file.
10. Auto-deploy the Web service for testing purposes by copying the EAR archive file to the `BEA_HOME/config/domain/applications` directory, where `BEA_HOME` refers to the main WebLogic Server installation directory, and `domain` refers to the name of the domain where WebLogic is installed.
11. To test the Web service, use a SOAP-enabled test environment such as TestMaker (described in Chapter 22, "Testing Web Services," and discussed later in this chapter.)

WebLogic includes additional instructions for building and deploying Web services. This file may be opened using any browser:

```
BEA_HOME/samples/examples/webservices/rpc/package-summary.html file
```

The Curmudgeon

WebLogic comes with all the necessary ingredients to build and deploy a Web service, including Enterprise Java Beans, directory services that use JNDI, and deployment descriptors. The Curmudgeon is an example Web service that shows how to build and deploy a Web service on WebLogic.

The Curmudgeon is a Web service that takes a question as input and states an opinion. Don't expect kind answers from the Curmudgeon. As a matter of fact, it seems the only thing the Curmudgeon likes are things containing chocolate.

WSDL for the Curmudgeon

Listing 24.1 provides a description of the interface that makes it possible to speak with the Curmudgeon.

LISTING 24.1 Curmudgeon Web Service

```
<definitions targetNamespace="java:examples.webservices.rpc.curmudgeonEJB"
➥ xmlns="http://schemas.xmlsoap.org/wsdl/" xmlns:xsi="http://www.w3.org/1999/
➥XMLSchema-instance" xmlns:xsd="http://www.w3.org/1999/XMLSchema"
➥xmlns:soap="http://schemas.xmlsoap.org/wsdl/soap/"
➥ xmlns:tns="java:examples.webservices.rpc.curmudgeonEJB">
<types>
  <schema targetNamespace="java:examples.webservices.rpc.curmudgeonEJB"
➥ xmlns="http://www.w3.org/1999/XMLSchema" />
</types>
<message name="getCurmudgeonOpinionRequest">
  <message name="getCurmudgeonOpinionResponse">
    <part name="return" type="xsd:string" />
  </message>
  <portType name="CurmudgeonPortType">
    <operation name="getCurmudgeonOpinion">
      <input message="tns:getCurmudgeonOpinionRequest" />
      <output message="tns:getCurmudgeonOpinionResponse" />
    </operation>
  </portType>
  <binding name="CurmudgeonBinding" type="tns:CurmudgeonPortType">
    <soap:binding style="rpc" transport="http://schemas.xmlsoap.org/
➥soap/http" />
    <operation name="getCurmudgeonOpinion">
      <soap:operation soapAction="urn:getCurmudgeonOpinion" />
        <input>
          <soap:body use="encoded" namespace="urn:Curmudgeon"
➥ encodingStyle="http://schemas.xmlsoap.org/soap/encoding/" />
        </input>
```

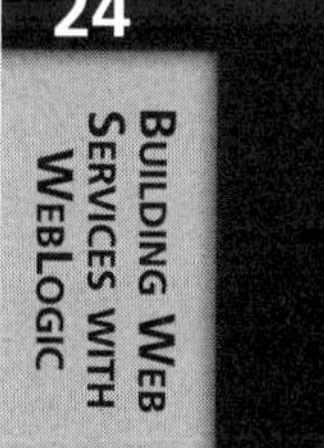

LISTING 24.1 continued

```
      <output>
        <soap:body use="encoded" namespace="urn:Curmudgeon"
➥ encodingStyle="http://schemas.xmlsoap.org/soap/encoding/" />
      </output>
    </operation>
  </binding>
<service name="Curmudgeon">
  <documentation>todo</documentation>
<port name="CurmudgeonPort" binding="tns:CurmudgeonBinding">
  <soap:address location="http://localhost:7001/curmudgeon/curmudgeonuri" />
  </port>
  </service>
  </definitions>
```

The important part of the `Curmudgeon`'s WSDL definition describes the input value expected. The `Curmudgeon` Web service simply wants to be passed a `String` containing a question:

```
<message name="getCurmudgeonOpinionRequest">
<message name="getCurmudgeonOpinionResponse">
  <part name="return" type="xsd:string" />
  </message>
```

In return, the `Curmudgeon` replies with a `String` containing an opinion:

```
<output>
  <soap:body use="encoded" namespace="urn:Curmudgeon"
➥encodingStyle="http://schemas.xmlsoap.org/soap/encoding/" />
</output>
```

Writing the `Curmudgeon` Bean Code

The WSDL defines a single public method for the `Curmudgeon` Web service. A stateless session EJB is used to implement the method. The method takes a single argument—your question—checks to see whether the term "chocolate" exists within the question, and then returns a random answer from an array of 10 possible answers. If the term "chocolate" exists, a special answer is returned.

The Java code in Listing 24.2 defines the `Curmudgeon` EJB's public interface.

LISTING 24.2 Curmudgeon interface

```
package examples.webservices.rpc.curmudgeonEJB;
import java.rmi.RemoteException;
import javax.ejb.EJBObject;
```

LISTING 24.2 continued

```
/**
 * Note: This is largely taken from an example EJB found in the
 * BEA WebLogic examples distribution.
 *
 * @author Frank Cohen 2002 for Java Web services Unleashed, published by SAMS
 */
public interface Curmudgeon extends EJBObject {
  /**
*
   * @param quandry           String quandry is the question to ask
➥ the Curmudgeon
   * @return                 String answer
   * @exception              RemoteException if there is
   *                         a communications or systems failure
   */
  public String getCurmudgeonOpinion( String quandry ) throws RemoteException;
}
```

The methods in the interface are the public face of CurmudgeonBean. The methods' signatures are identical to those of the Enterprise JavaBean object, except that these methods throw a java.rmi.RemoteException. The EJBean object does not actually implement this interface. The corresponding code-generated EJBObject, CurmudgeonBean, which you can see in Listing 24.3, implements this interface and delegates to the bean.

The Java code in Listing 24.3 is the actual stateless session EJB class.

LISTING 24.3 The EJB Class

```
package examples.webservices.rpc.curmudgeonEJB;
import javax.ejb.CreateException;
import javax.ejb.SessionBean;
import javax.ejb.SessionContext;
import javax.naming.InitialContext;
import javax.naming.NamingException;
import java.lang.Math;
import java.util.Random;
/**
 * Note: This is largely taken from an example EJB found in the
 * BEA WebLogic examples distribution.
 *
* @author Frank Cohen 2002 for Java Web services Unleashed, published by SAMS
 */
public class CurmudgeonBean implements SessionBean {
  private static final boolean VERBOSE = true;
  private SessionContext ctx;
  private int tradeLimit;
  private Random randy = new Random();
```

LISTING 24.3 continued

```
  private String opinions [] = {
      "Your quandry makes me think of the time I realized that I was
➥a genius chucked into a world filled with idiots.",
      "And when did you come to this quandry?",
      "Just how hard could it be to accomplish your goal?",
      "Why bother with a quandry like that?",
      "If you had only listened to me the first time.",
      "I am strongly in favor of your ideas, with a few of my refinements.",
      "That has to be the dumbest thing I have heard today.",
      "Your quandry is just like something I experienced before,
➥please buy my book.",
      "I knew a great lady named Betsy who would have been able to
➥answer your quandry in no time.",
      "Yes, you know the answer to this yourself, now go and do it.",
      };

  // You might also consider using WebLogic's log service
  private void log(String s) {
    if (VERBOSE) System.out.println(s);
  }
  /**
   * This method is required by the EJB Specification,
   * but is not used by this example.
   *
   */
  public void ejbActivate() {
    log("ejbActivate called");
  }
  /**
   * This method is required by the EJB Specification,
   * but is not used by this example.
   *
   */
  public void ejbRemove() {
    log("ejbRemove called");
  }
  /**
   * This method is required by the EJB Specification,
   * but is not used by this example.
   *
   */
  public void ejbPassivate() {
    log("ejbPassivate called");
  }
  /**
   * Sets the session context.
   *
   * @param ctx               SessionContext Context for session
```

LISTING 24.3 continued

```
    */
   public void setSessionContext(SessionContext ctx) {
     log("setSessionContext called");
     this.ctx = ctx;
   }
   /**
    * This method corresponds to the create method in the home interface.
    * "CurmudgeonHome.java".
    * The parameter sets of the two methods are identical. When the client calls
    * <code>CurmudgeonHome.create()</code>, the container allocates an instance
of
    * the EJBean and calls <code>ejbCreate()</code>.
    *
    * @exception               javax.ejb.CreateException if there is
    *                          a communications or systems failure
    * @see                     examples.ejb.basic.statelessSession.Weather
    */
   public void ejbCreate () throws CreateException {
     log("ejbCreate called");
     try {
       InitialContext ic = new InitialContext();
     } catch (NamingException ne) {
       throw new CreateException("Failed to find environment value "+ne);
     }
   }
   /**
    * Asks the curmudgeon for an opinion on the quandry provided.
    *
    * @param quandry           String quandry can be anything at all; the
➥ curmudgeon will have an opinion.
    * @return                  String opinion
    * @exception               RemoteException if there is
    *                          a communications or systems failure
    */
   public String getCurmudgeonOpinion(String quandry) {
     log("getCurmudgeonOpinion called");
     if ( quandry.toLowerCase().indexOf( "chocolate" ) >1 )
     {
         return "Anything with chocolate can't be entirely bad.";
     }

     return opinions[ randy.nextInt() % 9 ];

   }
}
```

`CurmudgeonBean` is a stateless session bean. As such, the bean has no persistence of state between calls to the session bean and it looks up values from the environment objects.

One last bit of code is left to enable the bean. `CubmudgeonHome.java` defines the home interface for `CurmudgeonBean.java`, which in WebLogic is implemented by the code-generated container class `CurmudgeonBeanC`. This is the WebLogic way to create the methods that correspond to methods named `ejbCreate` in the `EJBean` object.

The Java code in Listing 24.4 is the `Home` interface of the Curmudgeon EJB.

LISTING 24.4 Curmudgeon EJB Interface

```
package examples.webservices.rpc.curmudgeonEJB;
import java.rmi.RemoteException;
import javax.ejb.CreateException;
import javax.ejb.EJBHome;
/**
 * Note: This is largely taken from an example EJB found in the
 * BEA WebLogic examples distribution.
 *
* @author Frank Cohen 2002 for Java Web services Unleashed, published by SAMS
 */
public interface CurmudgeonHome extends EJBHome {
Curmudgeon create() throws CreateException, RemoteException;
}
```

That is it for the code needed to implement the `Curmudgeon` Web service in WebLogic. The next step is to see how WebLogic helps to compile and deploy a Web service.

EJB Deployment in WebLogic

WebLogic uses the standard EJB deployment mechanism to install the `Curmudgeon` bean. The deployment descriptor in Listing 24.5 is an XML-formatted document that instructs WebLogic on the installation parameters.

LISTING 24.5 Deployment Descriptor

```
<?xml version="1.0"?>
<!DOCTYPE ejb-jar PUBLIC '-//Sun Microsystems, Inc.//
➥DTD Enterprise JavaBeans 1.1//EN'
➥'http://java.sun.com/j2ee/dtds/ejb-jar_1_1.dtd'>
<ejb-jar>
        <enterprise-beans>
                <session>
                        <ejb-name>statelessSession</ejb-name>
                        <home>examples.webservices.rpc.curmudgeonEJB.
➥CurmudgeonHome</home>
                        <remote>examples.webservices.rpc.curmudgeonEJB.
➥Curmudgeon</remote>
```

LISTING 24.5 continued

```
                    <ejb-class>examples.webservices.rpc.curmudgeonEJB.
➥CurmudgeonBean</ejb-class>
                    <session-type>Stateless</session-type>
                    <transaction-type>Container</transaction-type>
            </session>
      </enterprise-beans>
      <assembly-descriptor>
            <container-transaction>
                    <method>
                      <ejb-name>statelessSession</ejb-name>
                            <method-intf>Remote</method-intf>
                            <method-name>*</method-name>
                    </method>
                    <trans-attribute>Required</trans-attribute>
            </container-transaction>
      </assembly-descriptor>
</ejb-jar>
```

In addition to the standard EJB deployment descriptor, a special deployment descriptor in Listing 24.6 tells WebLogic to install the `Curmudgeon` bean in the proper place. The descriptor identifies the stateless bean and defines the object name to install in the WebLogic namespace.

LISTING 24.6 Stateless Bean Definition

```
<?xml version="1.0"?>
<!DOCTYPE weblogic-ejb-jar PUBLIC
➥'-//BEA Systems, Inc.//DTD WebLogic 5.1.0 EJB//EN'
➥'http://www.bea.com/servers/wls510/dtd/weblogic-ejb-jar.dtd'>
<weblogic-ejb-jar>
      <weblogic-enterprise-bean>
        <ejb-name>statelessSession</ejb-name>
            <caching-descriptor>
                    <max-beans-in-free-pool>100</max-beans-in-free-pool>
            </caching-descriptor>
            <jndi-name>statelessSession.CurmudgeonHome</jndi-name>
      </weblogic-enterprise-bean>
</weblogic-ejb-jar>
```


Building the EJB

So far you have been working with individual files that now need to be built into an archive file for deployment into WebLogic. The manual steps for building the archive are fairly straightforward:

1. Create a temporary staging directory.
2. Copy the compiled Java EJB class files into the staging directory.
3. Create a META-INF subdirectory in the staging directory.
4. Copy the ejb-jar.xml and weblogic-ejb-jar.xml deployment descriptors into the META-INF subdirectory.
5. Create the curmudgeon.jar archive file using the jar utility:

   ```
   jar cvf weather.jar -C staging_dir .
   ```

Automating the Build Process with Ant

Of course there is a much easier way to build and deploy Web services in WebLogic: by using Ant. Ant is an open-source Java-based software build tool. Ant's inventors see it as a more flexible tool than existing build tools, including make, gnumake, make, jam, and others. Ant has become very popular and many open-source Java projects ship with Ant build scripts.

Ant is written in Java and uses XML-based scripts, so it is highly portable. Ant is distributed under an Apache-style open source license. The portable and flexible nature of Ant makes Ant a good choice for automating the development lifecycle of a Web service that will be deployed on WebLogic. The version of Ant bundled into WebLogic comes with special extensions for easy deployment of Web services.

The following build.xml file references the wsgen Java ant task that assembles the curmudgeon.jar archive file into a WebLogic Web service and curmudgeon.ear enterprise application archive file:

```
<project name="curmudgeon-webservice" default="wsgen">
    <target name="wsgen">
      <wsgen
         destpath="curmudgeon.ear"
         context="/curmudgeon ">
        <rpcservices path="curmudgeon.jar">
                <rpcservice bean="statelessSession" uri="/curmudgeonuri"/>
        </rpcservices>
      </wsgen>
    </target>
</project>
```

To actually build and run the curmudgeon Web service, run the following Ant build script:

```
<project name="curmudgeon" default="webservice">
  <target name="webservice">
    <ant dir="." antfile="build-ejb.xml"/>
    <ant dir="." antfile="build-ws.xml"/>
  </target>
</project>
```

This runs two other Ant build scripts. The first is build-ejb.xml (see Listing 24.7) which creates the EJB.

LISTING 24.7 Build Script

```
<project name="ejb-basic-statelessSession" default="all" basedir=".">
  <!-- set global properties for this build -->
  <property name="WL_HOME" value="I:\bea\wlserver6.1"/>
  <property file="${WL_HOME}/samples/examples.properties"/>
  <property name="src" value="."/>
  <property name="build" value="${src}/build"/>
  <property name="dist" value="."/>
  <target name="all" depends="clean, init, compile_ejb, jar_ejb, ejbc"/>
  <target name="init">
    <!-- Create the time stamp -->
    <tstamp/>
    <!-- Create the build directory structure tocompile
    and copy the deployment descriptors into it-->
    <mkdir dir="${build}"/>
    <mkdir dir="${build}/META-INF"/>
    <copy todir="${build}/META-INF">
      <fileset dir="${src}">
        <include name="*.xml"/>
      </fileset>
    </copy>
  </target>
  <!-- Compile ejb classes into the build directory (jar preparation) -->
  <target name="compile_ejb">
    <javac srcdir="${src}" destdir="${build}"
       includes="Curmudgeon.java, CurmudgeonHome.java, CurmudgeonBean.java"/>
  </target>
  <!-- Make a standard ejb jar file, including XML deployment descriptors -->
  <target name="jar_ejb" depends="compile_ejb">
    <jar jarfile="${dist}/a_statelessSession.jar"
      basedir="${build}">
    </jar>
  </target>
  <!-- Run ejbc to create the deployable jar file -->
  <target name="ejbc" depends="jar_ejb">
    <java classname="weblogic.ejbc" fork="yes">
      <sysproperty key="weblogic.home" value="${WL_HOME}"/>
      <arg line="-compiler javac ${dist}/a_statelessSession.jar
➥./curmudgeon.jar"/>
      <classpath>
        <pathelement path=
➥"${WL_HOME}/lib/weblogic_sp.jar;${WL_HOME}/lib/weblogic.jar"/>
      </classpath>
    </java>
  </target>
  <target name="clean">
```

LISTING 24.7 continued

```
    <delete dir="${build}"/>
  </target>
</project>
```

The second build script installs the EJB into WebLogic (see Listing 24.8).

LISTING 24.8 Installation Script

```
<project name="curmudgeon-webservice" default="copy">
  <!-- set global properties for this build -->
  <property file="${WL_HOME}/samples/examples.properties"/>
    <property name="module" value="curmudgeon"/>
    <property name="jar.path" value="${module}.jar"/>
    <property name="ear.path" value="${module}.ear"/>
    <target name="wsgen">
      <wsgen
         destpath="${ear.path}"
         context="/curmudgeon">
        <rpcservices path="${jar.path}">
            <rpcservice bean="statelessSession" uri="/curmudgeonuri"/>
        </rpcservices>
      </wsgen>
    </target>
    <target name="copy" depends="wsgen">
        <copy file="${ear.path}" todir="I:\bea\wlserver6.1\
➥config\examples\applications"/>
    </target>
</project>
```

With the `Curmudgeon` Web service built and deployed, it's time to test the Web service.

Testing the `Curmudgeon`

A free open-source utility, `TestMaker`, is available from the PushToTest Web site. It writes test automation agents for performance and scalability testing of SOAP-based Web services. Chapter 22 gives detailed explanations of `TestMaker`, including sample code to build intelligent test agents to test Web services. `TestMaker` offers a script language to operate a library of test objects. The combination enables you to develop intelligent test agents that drive a Web service. Multiple concurrent running copies of the script show how the Web service performs under simulated production situations.

Look at how `TestMaker` would be used to call the `Curmudgeon` service already discussed. Listing 24.9 presents the script in its entirety.

LISTING 24.9 Test Agent Script

```
from com.pushtotest.tool.protocolhandler import Header
from com.pushtotest.tool.protocolhandler import Body
from com.pushtotest.tool.protocolhandler import SOAPProtocol
from com.pushtotest.tool.protocolhandler import SOAPBody
from com.pushtotest.tool.protocolhandler import SOAPHeader
from com.pushtotest.tool.response import Response
from java.lang import Long
# Ask the Curmudgeon a question
ask =  "What do you think about Web services?"
protocol = SOAPProtocol()
body = SOAPBody()
body.addParameter( "arg0", ask )
body.setTarget( "" )
body.setMethod( "getCurmudgeonOpinion" )

protocol.setHost("localhost")
protocol.setPath("/curmudgeon/curmudgeonuri")
protocol.setPort(7001)
protocol.setBody(body)

response = protocol.connect()
# Show the results
print( response.toString() )
# Report how long it took to make the SOAP call
print("")
print("Timing statistics to find temperature (milliseconds):")
print("Total: " + Long(response.getTotalTime()).toString())
print("Setup: " + Long(response.getSetupTime()).toString())
print("")
```

Now look at how the individual functions work.

First, you create a `SOAPProtocol` object that is assigned to a simple variable for later reference. The `SOAPProtocol` object handles all communication, timeouts, data translation, and request document setup for you:

```
protocol = SOAPProtocol()
```

Although `SOAPProtocol` handles SOAP specifically, `TestMaker` also implements protocol handlers for generic HTTP transactions, and `TestMaker` may be extended to handle FTP, SMTP, and IMAP protocols with little effort. Many times you just need to change an existing `TestMaker` agent, rather than write an agent from scratch.

The `SOAPBody` object builds the XML request document that is sent to the SOAP host. The request document is fairly simple this time around. The SOAP object needs to know the `String` containing the question for the `Curmudgeon`. The WSDL definition for the

`Curmudgeon` tells which target and method to use on the SOAP host to get the Curmudgeon's opinion:

```
body = SOAPBody()
body.addParameter( "arg0", ask )
body.setTarget( "" )
body.setMethod( "getCurmudgeonOpinion" )
```

The last step before actually calling the SOAP host is to tell the `SOAPProtocol` object the URI to the host, including the host domain name and the path to the SOAP host object running on the server. The path usually triggers a servlet, script, or CGI on the host:

```
protocol.setHost("localhost")
protocol.setPath("/curmudgeon/curmudgeonuri")
protocol.setPort(7001)
protocol.setBody(body)
```

In a bit of object-oriented magic, you pair the `body` object with the `SOAPProtocol` object. An unlimited number of `body` objects may be created and individually used with a `SOAPProtocol` object. This is really handy when the Web service offers many options:

```
protocol.setBody(body)
```

The `SOAPProtocol` object's `connect()` method assembles the request document from the `body` object, makes the HTTP call to the host, creates a `response` object, and returns the response document from the host to the `response` object:

```
response = protocol.connect()
```

The agent displays the actual response document in a logging window in `TestMaker` and also saves the response to a log file for later analysis:

```
# Show the results
print( response.toString() )
```

The `SOAPProtocol` object implements a set of timers so the agent may understand and act on the time it takes to set up and call the host. Both times are given in milliseconds (1000 milliseconds is 1 second; for example, 1458 milliseconds is 1.458 seconds):

```
# Report how long it took to make the SOAP call
print("")
print("Timing statistics to find temperature (milliseconds):")
print("Total: " + Long(response.getTotalTime()).toString())
print("Setup: " + Long(response.getSetupTime()).toString())
print("")
```

The `TestMaker` object library is fully threaded. So multiple requests may be made at the same time, thus simulating real-world use of the Web service. This simple agent could be run in 100 threads concurrently. To the Web service it would appear that 100 users have requested the Curmudgeon's opinion. `TestMaker` also includes commands for looping, random values, posting dummy text, and access to 20 other test objects.

`TestMaker` is licensed under terms similar to those of the Apache Web server. You download the `TestMaker` program and all its source code from `http://www.pushtotest.com`. You can change `TestMaker` to fix bugs and add new features. The license even lets you build commercially exploitable new products based on the code.

Next Generation Web services

As mentioned at the beginning of this chapter, the first generation of Web services tools provided build and deployment mechanisms for applications to provide UDDI, WSDL, and SOAP interfaces. Next generation tools, such as BEA WebLogic with code-named WebLogic Workshop technology, provide developer assistance with these protocols, including graphical tools and code generators.

Just as HTTP, browsers, and the Web are ubiquitous today, so are UDDI, WSDL, and SOAP becoming. Something is needed to bridge the span from the way Web services are developed today to the future, where every software application will be a Web service. Nevertheless, Web service applications need to be deployed on trusted and reliable enterprise platforms. To make this process easier for all developers and possible for developers who are not familiar with J2EE technologies, BEA introduced a new product code-named WebLogic Workshop. WebLogic Workshop makes it easier to build powerful, enterprise-class Web services.

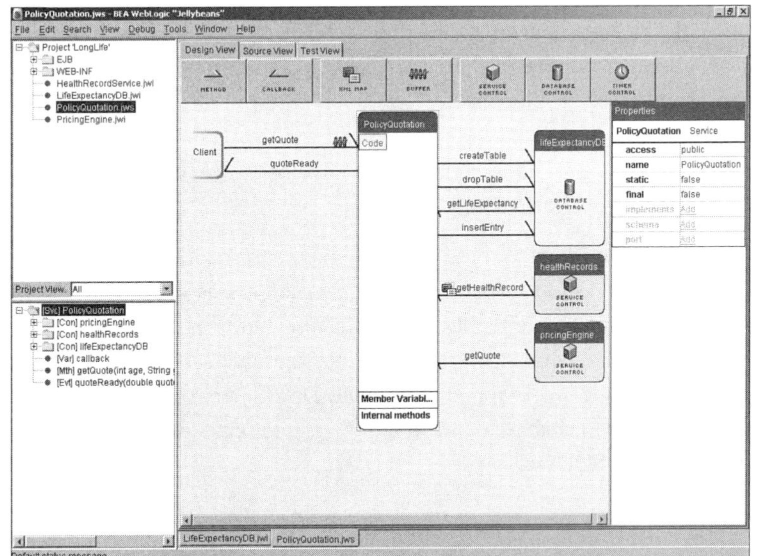

FIGURE 24.3
Visual SOAP Toolkit.

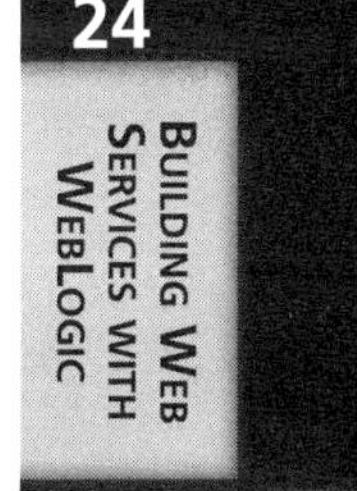

WebLogic Workshop includes two major components: A design-time tool shown in Figure 24.3 that lets developers write Java code to implement Web services and a run-time framework that provides the Web services infrastructure, testing, debugging, and deployment environment for WebLogic Workshop applications.

The WebLogic Workshop Tool

The WebLogic Workshop tool is a Java application that provides all the functions of an Integrated Development Environment; however, you are most likely to use it in combination with your existing developer tools rather than as a replacement for an IDE. Standard features such as project management, syntax highlighting, code completion, and integrated debugging, are found in WebLogic Workshop.

WebLogic Workshop moves beyond standard IDEs with specific support for Web services. The WebLogic Workshop design view lets users graphically create new Web services and illustrates how they interact with the outside world. It also provides a visual metaphor to hang business logic code and set properties on methods and controls. The goal is to enable developers to focus on writing business logic—the code that is executed in response to each incoming method—not the machinery of typical Java programming. The WebLogic Workshop design view supports two-way editing—developers may make changes directly to the Java code and the changes are reflected in the graphical editing tools immediately.

WebLogic Workshop Controls

Although J2EE provides a powerful and flexible platform for building enterprise applications, the richness and sophistication of J2EE APIs sometimes keep non-Java experts from taking advantage of these technologies. To mitigate this problem, WebLogic Workshop gives developers easy access to enterprise resources, Web services, and J2EE APIs through a new set of controls. WebLogic Workshop controls simplify the construction process by providing controls that developers use to call functions on local classes and set properties to control operation.

WebLogic Workshop controls are defined by standard Java interfaces with special WebLogic Workshop Javadoc annotations used to encode properties and special functionality. For example, one WebLogic Workshop control provides access to the JDBC API SQL statements, which are embedded into reusable Java objects that appear as controls in the WebLogic Workshop environment. Developers make a single function call to use the SQL query. Database controls can be further customized or extended simply by adding a new SQL statement:

```
/**
 * @sql statement="SELECT SCORE FROM CUSTOMERS WHERE SSN = {ssn}"
 */
int getScore(String ssn) throws SQLException, ControlException;
```

This method, which is in a database control that executes a simple `select` statement, embeds the SQL statement in the method's JavaDoc-style comments. After a method has been defined on a control in this way, WebLogic Workshop users of the control simply call the function to execute the SQL command. This frees developers from the usual steps of programming with the JDBC API—5 or 6 function calls are reduced to 1, and developers need only know SQL, not a new API.

WebLogic Workshop provides controls to access databases, Web services, EJBs, JMS queues, and applications exposed through the J2EE Connector Architecture. WebLogic Workshop also provides a timer control to help manage asynchronous events.

Java Web Service Files (.JWS)

WebLogic Workshop moves code generation out of the tool and into the framework so developers can concentrate on the business logic of their Web services and avoid the overhead of the Web services' build and deployment lifecycles. WebLogic Workshop manages the connection between the design-time tool and the runtime framework in Java Web service files. JWS files are standard Java source files with JavaDoc-style annotations that describe how methods in the Web service should operate. Developers write standard Java classes and WebLogic Workshop automatically compiles the code into the required EJBs and deploys them to WebLogic Service directly.

WebLogic Workshop uses annotations in a JWS file to encode everything, from what SOAP style a Web service uses to how XML messages are converted into Java objects. This annotated Java code approach is also a simple but powerful way to smooth the ramp between developer skill sets. WebLogic Workshop developers work in a simplified programming environment, but still write standard Java code so Java experts can always add value over time.

The WebLogic Workshop Framework

With a JWS file, the WebLogic Workshop framework has all it needs to generate the standard EJB code needed to implement a Web service. WebLogic Workshop supports building sophisticated enterprise-class Web services with specific support at the JWS annotation for more advanced usage scenarios. In particular, WebLogic Workshop provides specific Web service infrastructure such as:

- **Conversations**. WebLogic Workshop uses a conversational metaphor to enable asynchronous communication with a Web service, including message correlation and state management across messages in a conversation. Users mark methods as starting, finishing, or continuing a conversation, and the WebLogic Workshop framework takes care of the details. WebLogic Workshop generates a unique ID to identify the conversation and persistently manages any state (stored in class member variables) across methods in a conversation using entity Java beans. WebLogic Workshop supports two-way conversations where the client sends SOAP messages to the WebLogic Workshop Web service and the WebLogic Workshop Web service executes an asynchronous callback to the client.
- **Loose Coupling**. WebLogic Workshop enables loose coupling between systems with an easy system for mapping XML to Java and Java to XML. This cleanly separates internal implementation details from the public contract of the Web service so any changes over time can be accommodated without breaking existing integrations. The WebLogic Workshop XML map technology lets developers declaratively map variables.portions of an XML message to Java fields and visa versa.
- **High Availability**. WebLogic Workshop enables availability with JMS queues. One strategy for Web service scalability is to buffer SOAP requests in a JMS message queue. Writing this code by hand however would normally require 70-80 lines of code and detailed knowledge of the JNDI and JMS APIs. In WebLogic Workshop, developers can select that a Web service uses a message buffer just by setting a property on a control.

When working with Web service code, WebLogic Workshop may compile and deploy a Web service instantly by using the equivalent to a Publish button. WebLogic deploys a Web service when the JWS files are placed into the Applications directory similar to the JSP deployment model. The WebLogic Workshop framework handles creating the necessary EJB and J2EE components, including session beans to host application logic, entity beans to manage state, and message queues to enable scalability. The deployment process takes care of all the lower level details of working with deployment descriptors and WLS configuration but still lets developers take advantage of the features of the J2EE platform. This ensures WebLogic Workshop Web services are enterprise class in nature and supports the major performance and scalability capabilities in WebLogic of connection pooling, caching, security, and transaction management.

The WebLogic Workshop framework creates a Web page for each service to provide all the information necessary to call the service from another application, including a WSDL file that describes the Web service and a Java proxy that makes it easy to invoke the Web service from another Java application. You use the Web interface as a test and monitoring system as you receive messages from the Web service.

The WebLogic Workshop framework exposes a complete debugging environment that is accessible through the IDE. This enables you to execute a Web service and step through the Web service code as it executes, watch variable values, and test expressions. The debugger even enables debugging of Web services running on remote WebLogic servers.

BEA introduced WebLogic Workshop technology with WebLogic Server 7.0. WebLogic Workshop is a toolkit to rapidly build Web services. With the JWS format, control architecture, and "write and run" approach to deployment, Canjun enables a new generation of sophistication and ease of use for Web services.

Resources

The following resources are related to topics discussed in this chapter:

- BEA WebLogic details are on the BEA Web site at `http://www.bea.com`. The site offers many resources, including free trial versions of WebLogic that you can use to run the Curmudgeon example described in this chapter.
- `TestMaker`, a free open-source utility for testing SOAP-based Web services for scalability and performance, `http://www.pushtotest.com`.
- SoapClient maintains a concise list of Web services resources, `http://www.soapclient.com/Resources.html`.
- Web Services Definition Language (WSDL) specification, `http://www.w3.org/TR/wsdl`.
- List of publicly available Web services, `http://www.xmethods.org/`.
- SOAP v1.1 specification, `http://www.w3.org/TR/SOAP/`.
- Microsoft SOAP resource, `http://msdn.microsoft.com/nhp/Default.asp?contentid=28000523`.

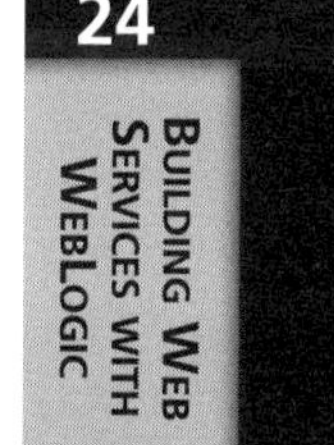

Summary

BEA WebLogic is a stable and rich platform to develop Web services. WebLogic provides Web services technology to work with UDDI, SOAP, and WSDL protocols. WebLogic code-named WebLogic Workshop technology delivers next-generation Web services tools in a set of graphical tools and runtime framework. Building and deploying Web services with WebLogic is efficient and productive.

INDEX

A

B

C

D

E

F

I

J - K

L - M

N - O

P

Q - R

S

T

U - V

W

X - Y - Z